MOOSEWOOD RESTAURANT
LOW-FAT FAVORITES

Other books from Moosewood Restaurant

New Recipes from Moosewood Restaurant

Sundays at Moosewood Restaurant

The Moosewood Restaurant Kitchen Garden

Moosewood Restaurant Cooks at Home: Fast and Easy Recipes for Any Day

Moosewood Restaurant Cooks for a Crowd

Contributors to this book include
Joan Adler, Ned Asta, Penny Condon, Tony Del Plato,
Linda Dickinson, Susan Harville, David Hirsch,
Nancy Lazarus, Eliana Parra, Maggie Pitkin, Sara Wade Robbins,
Maureen Vivino, Lisa Wichman, and Kip Wilcox

MOOSEWOOD RESTAURANT LOW-FAT FAVORITES

FLAVORFUL RECIPES FOR HEALTHFUL MEALS

THE MOOSEWOOD COLLECTIVE

CLARKSON POTTER/PUBLISHERS

NEW YORK

Published by Clarkson N. Potter, Inc.,
201 East 50th Street, New York, New York 10022.
Member of the Crown Publishing Group.
Random House, Inc.
New York, Toronto, London, Sydney, Auckland

http://www.randomhouse.com/

CLARKSON N. POTTER, POTTER, and colophon
are trademarks of Clarkson N. Potter, Inc.

Printed in the United States of America

BOOK DESIGN BY SHERI G. LEE / JOYFUNSTUDIO
ILLUSTRATIONS BY THORINA ROSE

Library of Congress Cataloging-in-Publication Data
Moosewood Restaurant low-fat favorites: flavorful recipes
for healthful meals / by the Moosewood Collective.
Includes index.
1. Vegetarian cookery. 2. Low-fat diet—Recipes.
3. Moosewood Restaurant. I. Moosewood Collective.
TX837.M6744 1996
641.5′636—dc21   96-49430

ISBN 0-517-70210-X (hardcover)
ISBN 0-517-88494-1 (paper)

10 9 8 7

THIS BOOK IS DEDICATED TO
OUR ROLE MODELS AND FAVORITE TEACHERS,
WHO TAUGHT US THAT WE SHOULD
BE GRATEFUL AND RESPECT ONE ANOTHER,
AND WHO URGED US TO EXPRESS
OURSELVES CREATIVELY, TO DISCOVER HEALTH
AND THE MEANING OF ENOUGH, AND TO
MEASURE OUR SUCCESS
BY THE HAPPINESS IN OUR HEARTS

ACKNOWLEDGMENTS

Creating a cookbook such as this one requires the efforts of a large cast of characters and a set of unusually supportive circumstances. At Moosewood, this web of interconnectedness is especially obvious; with so many of us participating in the developing, testing, research, writing, and other literary particulars, the roster of backstage helpers becomes enormous.

Without the enthusiastic cooperation of our friends, neighbors, fellow workers, and families, whose kitchens we used and whose valuable feedback guided us in the right direction, we couldn't have managed to complete this cookbook—we most heartily thank each and every one of you. Even if you only pretended to want to try our third attempt at the same dish in two weeks, your encouragement and appetites were invaluable.

For astute advice, impeccable discretion, humor, insight, and love of good food, we most fondly thank our literary agents, Arnold and Elise Goodman. They have given us unwavering support for ten years and, like good wine, have only improved with age. Quite frankly, we can't imagine Moosewood without them. They are a vital part of our network and simply irreplaceable.

Pam Krauss has been everything anyone could want in an editor: thorough, precise, flexible, witty, prompt, attentive, and organized. We especially loved when she got excited by reading a recipe, went home and made it, and would write amidst the flurry of editing marks on the manuscript, "This was really delicious." Knowing she cared about how the food tasted and not just how the recipes were written made us feel incredibly secure. We dub her our editor deluxe.

Thanks are also in order to the CBORD Group, Inc., of Ithaca, New York, for providing the nutritional analyses for the recipes in this cookbook and more specifically to Laura Winter Falk and Laura Ryan for coordinating the effort.

We would also like to thank the following companies for allowing us to try their high-quality nonstick cookware during the course of our work on this book: All Clad, Berndes, Calphalon, Circulon, and Farberware.

Most of all, those of us who worked directly on this book want to thank the entire Moosewood staff—both employees and other Moosewood Collective members—for their loyalty, patience, hard work, discerning palates, and endless quips. We love you.

CONTENTS

recipes by chapter x

introduction 1

going lower: tips for low-fat cooking and eating 9

ABOUT THE RECIPES 16

appetizers 19

breakfast or brunch 45

SOUPS 69

breads & sandwiches 107

salads 127

BEANS 153

grains 175

pasta 199

OTHER MAIN DISHES
(INCLUDING STUFFED VEGETABLES) 223

stews 259

fish 281

SIDE DISHES 307

dressings, sauces & seasonings 339

desserts 369

NUTRITION FACTS 396

glossary of cooking techniques and terms 414

guide to ingredients 420

SPECIAL RECIPE LISTS AND MENUS 442

common foods analyzed 448

selected bibliography and further reading 452

ABOUT THE AUTHORS 453

index 454

RECIPES BY CHAPTER

APPETIZERS

garlic basil cheese spread 22
greek lima bean dip 23
asian eggplant spread 24
guacamole with asparagus 25
guacamole with cottage cheese 26
guacamole with roasted corn 27
one step bean guacamole 28
indian chickpea spread 29
spinach artichoke heart dip 30
herbed cottage cheese chèvre spread 31
eggplant strata 32
broiled eggplant thai style 34
greek spinach rice balls 35
nori vegetable rolls 36
tofu vegetable dumplings 38
tunisian potato turnovers 40
savory stuffed mushrooms 42
roasted garlic 43

BREAKFAST OR BRUNCH

black bean and hominy frittata 49
swiss chard and tomato frittata 50
spanish potato pepper frittata 51
spinach mushroom frittata 52
watercress omelet 53
indian potato pancakes 54
ful 55
cinnamon apple crêpes 56
sticky buns 58
irish soda bread 59
aafke's spicy quick bread 60
applesauce cranberry muffins 61
banana muffins 62
cornmeal spice muffins 63
pumpkin oat muffins 64
mango-banana shake 65
peach-berry shake 66
sesame citrus delight 67

SOUPS

basic vegetable stock 73
garlic broth 74
konbu dashi 75
shiitake dashi 76
southeast asian vegetable stock 77
tropical gazpacho 78
chilled beet and buttermilk soup 79
essential miso soup with tofu 80
asian noodle soup 81
cream of green vegetable soup 82
spring soup 84
harira 85
minestrone genoa 86
vietnamese hot and sour soup 87
japanese soba and vegetable soup 88
korean vegetable noodle soup 89
cream of cauliflower soup 90
creamy potato kale soup 91
golden split pea soup 92
orzo and pea soup 93
dried mushroom soup with barley 94
new england squash soup 96
spanish potato garlic soup 97
carbonada 98
catalan potato lima soup 99
curried carrot parsnip soup 100
tomato bulgur soup 101
southwestern corn and potato soup 102
basque white bean soup 103
savannah beans and greens soup 104
callaloo 105

BREADS & SANDWICHES

almost fat-free cornbread 110
brown bread 111
herb and cheese muffins 112
herbed cottage cheese bread 113
homemade biscuits 114

buttermilk rolls 115
asian tofu salad 116
egg salad 117
ira's lunch 118
middle eastern cannellini patties 119
mexican seitan pita 120
mushroom pâté almondine 121
smoky eggplant and pepper spread 122
tempeh salad sandwich filling 123
tuscan sandwich 124
white bean and red pepper spread 125

SALADS
vegetables à la grecque 130
caesar salad 131
cabbage salad 132
cucumbers vinaigrette 133
carrot orange salad 134
spinach avocado grapefruit salad 135
mango coconut cucumber salad 136
baked sweet potato salad 137
potato bean salad 138
potato beet salad 139
sesame beets 140
quinoa black bean salad 141
caribbean pigeon pea salad 142
mediterranean couscous salad 144
tabouli salad 145
sushi rice salad 146
wild rice waldorf salad 147
mexican pasta salad 148
chinese orzo vegetable salad 149
creamy macaroni salad 150
lentil salad 151

BEANS
barbecue beans 156
bean and bean gumbo 157
vegetarian feijoada 158

cassoulet 160
festive black bean chili 161
tamale pie 162
black bean chilaquile 164
fat tuesday's skinny red beans 165
lentil sambar 166
tuscan beans with sage 168
middle eastern chickpeas with spinach 169
garlicky black-eyed peas 'n' greens 170
sweet-and-sour lentils 171
sweet potato and black bean burrito 172
chili burgers 173

GRAINS
bulgur with savory greens 178
couscous with peas and onions 179
curried couscous pilaf 180
kasha pilaf 181
millet pilaf 182
orzo and green herbs 183
quinoa pine nut pilaf 184
golden basmati rice 185
five-spice rice 186
brazilian rice 187
bulgur rice pilaf 188
fragrant jasmine rice 189
thai fried rice 190
midsummer risotto 191
squash and kale risotto 192
onion and feta risotto 194
mushroom wheatberry pilaf 195
spring vegetable paella 196

PASTA
macaroni and cheese 203
vegetable udon sauté 204
pasta with eggplant 205
pasta primavera 206
zucchini saffron pasta 207

pasta and sun-dried tomatoes 208
pasta, lentils, and artichoke hearts 209
pasta with beans and greens 210
pasta with chickpeas 211
pasta with salsa cruda 212
penne with creamy walnut sauce 213
penne with puttanesca sauce 214
spaghetti with onions 215
vegetable lasagne béchamel 216
lighter lasagne 218
stuffed manicotti verde 219
curried rice noodles 220

OTHER MAIN DISHES

roasted vegetables three ways 226
luscious basil and feta pizza 228
curried sweet potato roti 230
seitan fajitas 232
vegetable-filled pancakes 233
mushroom spinach crêpes 234
sun-dried tomato polenta cutlets 236
another shepherd's pie 238
mushroom polenta pie 240
eggplant parmesan 241
vegetable filo roll extravaganza 242
mexican stuffed peppers and tomatoes 244
middle eastern tofu-stuffed peppers 246
mushroom- and spinach-stuffed zucchini 247
savory indian sweet potatoes 248
stuffed baked potatoes 249
potato cheese gnocchi 250
curried potato cabbage roll-ups 251
swiss chard rolls two ways 252
fresh spring rolls 254
cabbage rolls 256

STEWS

giambotta 263
french vegetable bean stew 264
caribbean stew 265
greek stew 266

mediterranean stew 267
thai vegetable curry 268
ukrainian beet and bean stew 269
armenian stew with pilaf 270
three sisters stew 272
creole stew 273
persian split pea and barley stew 274
quinoa vegetable stew 276
mushroom sesame tofu stew 277
wild mushroom stew trieste 278
southwestern hominy stew 279

FISH

baltic fish 287
baked fish with mustard marinade 288
fish with herbs and lime 289
fish steaks with fennel 290
fish tagine with chermoulla 291
fish with pineapple chutney 292
savory hoisin fish 293
southeast asian fish rolls 294
baked flounder rolls 295
herbed fish in a packet 296
breaded garlic dill fish 297
honey mustard fish 298
italian fish stew 299
poached fish with russian mushroom sauce 300
poached fish with vegetables 301
thai fish cakes 302
gingered shrimp and soba 303
sicilian scallop salad 304
thai seafood yum 305

SIDE DISHES

seasoned steamed artichokes 311
roasted asparagus 312
citrus-dressed asparagus 313
baked beets and shallots 314
gingered broccoli 315
broccoli rabe and garlic 315
morrocan carrots 316

mustard carrots 317
cauliflower agrodolce 318
cauliflower with curry sauce 319
gingered fennel with garlic 320
carolina kale 321
broiled portabella mushrooms 322
sweet sweet potatoes 323
spanish potatoes 324
scalloped potatoes and carrots 325
oven "fries" 326
potato cakes 327
garlic mashed potatoes 328
snap peas with mushrooms 329
japanese sesame spinach 330
holiday cranberry squash 331
curried squash 332
broiled zucchini with herbs 333
southeast asian coconut zucchini 334
zucchini with cilantro sauce 335
thai baked tofu 336
jerk tofu 337

DRESSINGS, SAUCES & SEASONINGS

creamy dill dressing 342
honey mustard garlic dressing 342
creamy ginger miso dressing 343
southeast asian pineapple sesame dressing 343
green mayonnaise 344
minted dill yogurt dressing 345
cilantro lime yogurt dressing 345
yogurt tahini dressing 346
japanese carrot dressing 346
italian tomato basil dressing 347
orange tarragon dressing 348
spicy peanut dressing 349
tomato wine sauce 350
chunky tomato sauce 351
mushroom sauce 352
salsa verde liguria 353
skordalia thessalonike 354

creamy roasted red pepper sauce 355
barbecue sauce 355
hot tamarind and guava sauce
for fish or vegetables 356
hungarian lesco 357
blender hot sauce 358
brazilian hot pepper and lemon sauce 359
fresh tomato salsa 360
corn relish 361
mango peach chutney 362
savory onion marmalade 363
susan's pesto 364
cilantro pesto 364
thai curry paste 365
tomato corn salsa 366
asian cucumber condiment 367

DESSERTS

red berry kissel 372
creamy dairyless rice pudding 373
dark chocolate pudding 374
tapioca fruit parfaits 375
pumpkin custard 376
lemon pudding cake 377
coffee angelfood cake 378
chocolate cocoa cake 380
applesauce spice cake 381
banana bundt cake 382
blueberry peach cobbler 383
apple apricot strudel 384
apple cherry crisp 385
ginger peach crumble 386
our best no-butter brownies 387
fruit-filled meringue shells 388
maple walnut biscotti 390
anise lemon biscotti 391
chocolate hazelnut biscotti 392
cardamom oatmeal cookies 393
pineapple buttermilk sherbet 394
vanilla cream 395

At **MOOSEWOOD**, we like to cook and we *love* to eat. All of our senses are engaged. We love the perfect, vivid beauty of a basket of oranges, the intricate design of a cabbage, the swirls of color revealed when you slice into a beet. We delight in the firm smooth skin of an eggplant and in the pleasingly rough texture of wild greens. We enjoy the slippery feel of wet pasta in our mouths and the crumbly flakiness of filo pastry. Feeling the airy froth that tops a cappuccino against our lips is a large part of that beverage's appeal.

The scent of freshly baked bread draws us irresistibly to its source, and the heady perfume released when olive oil is drizzled on toasty warm bread is intoxicating. We want to inhale more deeply the compelling aromas of lemon, cinnamon, chocolate, fresh basil, garlic. The satisfying sound of biting into a crisp apple, the thwack of cutting open a watermelon—each is an unmistakable signal of pleasures to come. Our tongues can recognize an incredible variety of flavors—savory, pungent, briny, tart, sweet, bitter—and we appreciate most of them, from the vibrant bite of mustard or pickles to the sweet silky succulence of fresh peaches and cream.

When, after a fine meal, our hunger for these sensations is temporarily satisfied, we often linger at the table and feel that the world is various and good. Our outlook is broader and more benevolent.

And yet, intruding on these warm, comforting feelings is a growing concern about how food choices affect our health. We feel a nagging uneasiness that we ought to try to keep up with the latest clinical studies. We contemplate making sweeping changes in our diets in order to increase our chances of living disease-free. At times, we're left wondering whether we're well informed enough to make dinner.

Unfortunately, living to eat and eating to live have become difficult to reconcile; it seems you must give up something on one side to gain on the other.

Moosewood Restaurant Low-Fat Favorites is for people who share these health concerns but who insist that their daily diet be rewarding. The food should be healthful, and it *must* be delicious. We want to make it easier to make smart choices *and* to enjoy the results.

Although large-scale nutritional studies have been conducted in this country for more than forty years, in the last decade, nutrition has become headline news. The media devotes a lot of attention to nutrition because people *are* interested. Nonetheless, too much of what we learn comes from food advertising. The result has been widespread confusion and some wholesale skepticism about the validity of *any* of the current nutritional claims. Meanwhile, most Americans aren't eating as well as they could.

We've received so much nutritional advice—and some of it apparently contradictory—that each new piece of the puzzle can seem to be just another food fad. Remember the basic four food groups, instituted in 1956, that we were taught in grammar school? Dairy products and meat represented two of the four groups, and the illustrated examples of healthy meals were along the lines of eggs and bacon for breakfast, a bologna and cheese sandwich at lunch, and fried chicken for dinner along with a fruit, a vegetable (with a big pat of butter on it), and bread. This seems like a bad joke now, but at that time it was a proud celebration of prosperity and abundance.

In the seventies, sugar and salt were all-around villains. And over the last decade, we've read or heard a lot about grapefruit diets, polyunsaturated oils, tropical oils, margarine versus butter, calcium, cholesterol, oat bran, omega-3 fatty acids from fish, how many eggs to consume in a week, red wine, antioxidants, and phytonutrients. And, of course, low-fat diets.

Some of these nutritional "breakthroughs" have turned out to be based on misinformation. For instance, it now looks like sugar is *not* the underlying cause of hyperactive behavior in children. Large doses of calcium will not necessarily ensure strong bones and teeth; the body's ability to absorb calcium is equally important. Margarine has plenty wrong with it and is *not* a healthful substitute for butter.

Nutrition is an evolving science, research is restrictively funded, and sometimes studies are poorly interpreted in the media. Many reputable health newsletters moved quickly to correct the misconception that pasta makes you fat, after the *New York Times* gave that pronouncement a front-page headline. But sometimes confusion lasts for years. Think of all the "cholesterol-free" labeling that appeared on foods such as olive oil and breakfast cereals, which never contained cholesterol in the first place (dietary cholesterol is found only in foods from animal sources). While the labels are not technically untrue, they are clearly an attempt to cash in on people's confusion about the difference between blood cholesterol and dietary cholesterol.

Nutritional information can also be blown out of proportion, taken out of context, or viewed in isolation while ignoring the interactions of the body system. Oat bran is still a very healthful food, and wine may have some effect against heart disease, but neither is a magical medicine.

Many segments of the food industry have powerful lobbies in Washington, D.C. Lobbyists may pressure government agencies and ultimately influence nutritional guidelines. The United States Department of Agriculture (USDA) is in the potentially compromising position of promoting public health while simultaneously promoting U.S. agriculture. Government agencies can move notoriously slowly, far more slowly than advertisers. It can take a long time before well-documented, much-needed changes are implemented in official regulations or recommendations.

In the absence of definitive guidelines for eating healthfully, we believe concerned consumers must decide what is optimal for themselves. We think that more information is better than less. We think that every piece of the puzzle adds to the big picture, and we are grateful that nutritional science is advancing apace despite the roadblocks. And we think that one important part of the picture is coming through very clearly—for many of us, a high-fat diet may be a serious health risk.

There is a long-standing, overwhelming body of evidence to support this hypothesis. A diet high in fat, especially saturated fat, contributes to the risk of heart disease, stroke, hypertension, various cancers, diabetes mellitus, osteoporosis, and obesity. Of course, genetics, environment, and activity level are all important components in the health equation also, but cutting fat in our diets seems to be one step everyone can take to enhance long-term well-being. We're betting that this won't be a passing fad. However, simply substituting lower-fat versions of our usual high-fat foods isn't enough. Despite their conflicting views on types and percentages of fat in our diets, all of the experts agree that we should be eating more fruits, vegetables, and grains—nourishing foods that help protect against disease and provide a delicious base for a low-fat diet. Nonfat cheesecake just can't do the same thing.

Research indicates that in 1995, about 37 percent of the average American's total caloric intake was from fat. Since about 1977, the U.S. government (Congress, in fact) and many mainstream health organizations have backed dietary models that suggest the calories from fat be limited to 30 percent of the total calories a person consumes. Other more recent research supports claims for lower fat intake, such as 20 percent or even as low as 10 percent. None of the evidence is, or perhaps ever will be, conclusive.

In this cookbook, we have tried to keep the fat numbers as low as we can while sidestepping any sense of deprivation. We want a sensible diet that will establish a satisfying pattern for a lifetime. It wouldn't be healthy, nor even possible, to cut *all* of the fat from our diet. A strict 10 percent diet seems a bit drastic to us and is probably unpalatable to most people. Fat provides both substance and a creamy texture, and is a flavor carrier. We think that small amounts of fat, used judiciously, go a long way toward creating a diet that can be sustained. By using all added fats with discretion, it's often not difficult to get below the 30 percent of calories from fat guideline set by the U.S. Food and Drug Administration (FDA). In fact, the recipes in *Moosewood Restaurant Low-Fat Favorites* average 16 percent to 17 percent of calories derived from fat. Although a recipe's percentage of calories from fat is one guideline, we think it is more useful on a day-to-day basis to count total grams of fat than to figure percentages. Applying a percent-of-fat standard to each food or each recipe can be misleading and very limiting. Many healthful dishes would be eliminated for no good reason.

For example, our recipe for Japanese Sesame Spinach derives 40 percent of its calories from fat, although it has only 2.6 grams of fat per serving. It works out this way because spinach, which is the bulk of the recipe, has very few calories, so the small amount of sesame seeds, which are high in both calories and fat, contribute disproportionately to the overall calorie count of the dish as a whole. Meanwhile, it's a very tasty preparation for spinach that even children love, plus it's nutrient-rich and low in actual grams of fat consumed.

We have provided a simple rule of thumb in the "Nutrition Facts" section of this book to help you decide how many grams of fat you want to aim for in a daily diet. It can be very interesting and quite revealing to analyze your diet in this way. We suggest that you make the computations for only a couple of weeks or so, until you are familiar with where your fats come from, which foods to eat in moderation, and which foods you can eat without a second thought. Once you know this, you can forget the math and just enjoy yourself.

In our busy, work-oriented lives, it can be difficult to sustain a low-fat lifestyle. When we're getting hungry at six o'clock and giving our first thought to what to cook for dinner, it's easy to forego all good intentions and fall back on old habits. Low-fat cooking can seem inconvenient, expensive, and a distant goal we have no hope of accomplishing this evening. Most of us find it difficult to restructure our kitchens or our lives.

We think this cookbook can help. Our primary inspiration all along at Moosewood Restaurant has been ethnic grain-based cuisines that are low in saturated fats and high in plant foods. We have drawn from Southeast Asian, Indian, Japanese, West African, and Caribbean cuisines, to name just a few, and we expect an increase in nutritionists' interest in Asian diets in the coming years. We have plenty of practice in converting traditional dishes to vegetarian ones, and it's just one more step to lower the fat content. So we did a lot of nuts-and-bolts tinkering, testing and retesting dishes, to eliminate as much fat as possible while maintaining our standards of taste.

While developing recipes for this book, we sifted through nutritional information as well as more inspirational guides like travel books and cookbooks. We visited other people's kitchens and continued to learn about other cultural backgrounds. We went to restaurants. When we finally began to write recipes, we worked to impress each other, the most discriminating and hard-to-please audience we know. We often worked together to improve a dish. We chose some dishes that are already low-fat, such as miso soup. With other dishes, we adjusted the proportions of ingredients. For example, our guacamoles are a bit scant on high-fat avocados but are rounded out with other ingredients like beans or roasted corn. Sometimes we were able to eliminate a high-fat ingredient altogether, as in our oil-free pesto sauces. Sometimes we replaced fats with something else, the way sweet potatoes replace the usual cheese in our black bean burrito. And we made some ingredients optional to allow a wider range of personal choice.

In many cases, switching to a lower-fat cooking technique can make a big difference in the finished dish's fat content. Our updated eggplant parmesan with baked rather than fried eggplant slices is a great improvement over the higher-fat original. Nonstick pans can be a big help but are only required by a handful of our recipes. When cooking in a nonstick pan, we usually use a lower heat and take a little more time to allow vegetables to release their own juices. In some dishes the barest minimum of oil is used to brown vegetables or bring out flavor. We think the added flavor justifies this little bit of added fat. When fashioning low-fat recipes, taking a nip here, a tuck there, we sometimes need to add a little embroidery, an embellishment such as extra herbs, spices, fruit or vegetable purée, vinegar, sun-dried tomatoes, dried mushrooms, miso, soy sauce, or garlic. Our no-butter brownies get extra flavor and moisture from applesauce rather than from butter and egg yolks. Two small calamata olives enliven the Caesar Salad Dressing. A little sauerkraut adds interest to an Italian mushroom stew.

You'll find a few unusual foodstuffs here, but, for the most part, all of the ingredients used in these recipes are very accessible. The recipes range from new versions of old standards, like macaroni and cheese, egg salad, and banana cake, to some new-to-us discoveries, such as Vietnamese hot and sour soup and berry kissel, to our new inventions, like Fish with Pineapple Chutney, Chinese Orzo Vegetable Salad, and Hot Tamarind and Guava Sauce for Fish or Vegetables. We have avoided synthetic, highly processsed, artificial foods that have had the fats tortured out of them—they don't taste as good, and that sort of compromise isn't necessary. We do, however, find some low-fat and fat-free dairy products very useful on occasion. We prefer 1% milk, nonfat yogurt, and low-fat cottage cheese to their full-fat counterparts for reasons of taste as well as health, and we've made good use of skim milk and naturally low-fat buttermilk.

Cheese appears in some recipes, usually a very flavorful cheese, such as feta, so that a small amount will suffice. The few egg yolks that appear were considered essential. Tofu, which is high-fat itself, can still have a place in an overall low-fat diet. It has no saturated fat and is rich in protein, vitamins, phytoestrogens, and minerals, including calcium.

We offer variations and shopping suggestions here and there, and a list of tips for lightening your own old favorite recipes begins on page 9. We recommend a well-stocked pantry as an invaluable aid when cooking low-fat.

Many of our dishes are perfect for entertaining, but our emphasis is on everyday meals. The menu-planning suggestions should give you plenty of ideas for all occasions (don't miss our Special Recipe Lists, pages 442–447). The total times listed at the top of each recipe give you a general notion of how long it may take but, remember, it's likely that you can work on two or sometimes three dishes simultaneously. Our portions are generous, not shaved to make the numbers look better. Every recipe has a nutritional analysis and we've included a nutritional breakdown of many ingredients in the chart at the back entitled "Common Foods Analyzed."

The nutritional, glossary, and guide sections are crammed with useful and interesting information especially concerning low-fat nutrition. Check out the definitions of nutritional terms, how to figure the percentage of calories from fat, how to calculate grams of fat, and how to read labels. Find useful, invaluable tips in the Glossary of Cooking Techniques and Terms and in the Guide to Ingredients. We've included a selected bibliography to help you find further information in case you'd like to know more.

Even if you find it difficult at first to begin the process of healthier cooking and eating, keep in mind how great are the rewards. The surest source of nutritious and delicious food is your own kitchen. Home cooking is a key to daily enjoyment and well-being as well as future wellness.

One possible reward that may become evident to you in time is a loss of body fat as a result of a low-fat diet. Because fat is a concentrated source of calories, when fat is limited it can be easier to lose weight. A low-fat dish is automatically lower in calories than its higher-fat counterpart. Even if you do consume excess calories from grains, legumes, fruits, and vegetables, they don't carry the same health risks as excess fat.

At the beginning of this project, we felt some trepidation about writing a low-fat cookbook. We've really been interested in gourmet cuisine at Moosewood, not deprivation diet food. We're concerned about healthy diets for ourselves, but at the restaurant, many of our customers have come to expect an indulgent, special-occasion dining experience. For instance, our customers almost always choose roasted vegetables over steamed vegetables. A cheese dish on the menu usually outsells a beans and rice dish. Our fudge brownie with ice cream, a paragon of sensual overindulgence, is the ultimate goal of many diners. We realize that people tend to splurge when they go out to eat, so we still offer a full spectrum of choices at Mooscwood Restaurant.

Nevertheless, we *have* lightened up our entire cuisine over the years, and many of our customers are happily choosing from among our lighter offerings. In fact, when we cook and serve a lower-fat dish from this cookbook at the restaurant, what we discover is that an unsuspecting diner probably won't notice a difference, or certainly not a lack of anything. They enjoy the mango-peach chutney or the honey-mustard-garlic salad dressing just as much as if it were fat-laden. They rave about the Brazilian feijoada and the lemon pudding cake, never considering that these are healthful, low-fat dishes.

So it's a happy surprise that the dishes we created for this cookbook don't come off as merely healthful diet foods. This food is exciting, ethnically diverse, and satisfyingly delicious. *Moosewood Restaurant Low-Fat Favorites* is as much a celebration of the pleasures of eating as it is about low-fat cooking.

In Moosewood's early days (when yogurt was a counterculture food and many people couldn't pronounce "quiche"), eating a meatless diet was considered weird. Most of us hadn't been vegetarians for very long and we were trying to make the food appealing to skeptics. Today, not only have the health benefits of a meatless diet been validated but, oddly enough, it's become glamorous. Buttoned-up businessmen collect recipes. College students surf computer networks for recipe exchanges. Our customers at Moosewood Restaurant ask very serious and informed questions. Even nihilistic rock stars make it known that they take care of their health.

It's a great time to be interested in food and there's more good food around. The convenience foods at the health food store are coming in from the fringe and looking quite attractive. Our supermarkets and farmers' markets are spilling over with colorful new fruits and beautiful fresh vegetables. There's more attention and pride given to local and organic produce and even an interest in heritage varieties. We're finding more space devoted to an array of healthful greens. Just a few years ago it was hard to find kale, collards, and turnip greens, let alone mizuna, arugula, and mesclun. We see choices of wild mushrooms, many varieties of potatoes, and a bounty of fresh herbs. You'll probably find quinoa, Middle Eastern beans, Asian condiments, and good Italian pastas at your grocery store. There are more artisan bakeries, producing wonderful whole grain breads.

We think we may be entering a culinary golden age. We make a prediction: More and more natural foods and wholesome products will become available, and they will be better and better, especially as educated consumers demand more. All of this interest in food and personal health, extending from farm to market to home, will surely encourage further concern for the well-being of our environment and our planet.

Here's wishing you the best of health and good appetite.

GOING LOWER: TIPS FOR LOW-FAT COOKING AND EATING

As you develop an awareness of the fats you consume, you may recognize that a few simple changes in your everyday eating patterns can make a significant difference and improve your health in the long run. The dilemma is always how to satisfy a desire for rich flavor, creamy texture, and a sense of fulfillment without the excess fat—and how to avoid hidden fat in packaged foods or restaurant fare. While you may not wish to banish fats from your diet altogether, you may want to "go lower" than your present fat intake.

General good eating habits are a good place to start. We think it's important to eat what you like and to experiment with new foods. Set aside enough time to sit down and enjoy your meal (rather than eating while standing in front of the open refrigerator, driving the car, or rushing down the street). Eat slowly enough that the body's natural enzymatic mechanism for telling us when we've had enough has a chance to work. And exercise regularly— it's one of the most tried-and-true appetite suppressants available to us.

Experiment with your favorite recipes and make adjustments to reduce the fat. Following are some specific ideas that may help you lower the fat in your diet without sacrificing flavor and enjoyment:

1 **CHOOSE MORE HEALTHY STYLES OF PREPARATION.** In general, pass up anything fried, breaded, or creamed. Lightly blanch or steam vegetables and top them with lemon juice and garlic or with an herbed vinaigrette made with very little olive or canola oil. Refrain from topping vegetables with butter.

Poach fish or bake it. Good poaching or baking liquids are vegetable stock, tomato juice, diluted wine or sherry, and fresh lemon or lime juice. When roasting, broiling, or grilling vegetables or fish, use condiments like pesto, onion marmalade, mustard, horseradish, preserves, or chutneys for a glaze instead of oil.

Lighten up pasta sauces by reserving some of the water the pasta was cooked in and add about ½ cup of the reserved cooking liquid instead of oil to the drained, cooked pasta to moisten the noodles.

2 **SAUTÉ USING LESS OIL.** For soups, stews, sautés, and side dishes, use only 1 teaspoon of oil to sauté the vegetables rather than the usual 2 or 3 tablespoons. Use lower heat and cover the pan; the moisture from the vegetables will escape and provide enough liquid to prevent sticking and burning. Sprinkling the vegetables with a little salt will also encourage them to release their juices. Increase the amount of aromatic herbs and vegetables, such as onions and mushrooms, to boost the flavor.

In many cases, especially with soups and stews, you can get away with no oil at all, even if you are not using nonstick cookware. Just add a little water, vegetable stock, or bouillon broth and stir constantly until the vegetables begin to soften. Once you add the main body of liquid, sticking is no longer an issue.

Invest in some nonstick cookware (see page 13) or use a well-seasoned cast-iron or other heavy skillet. Use very light coatings of cooking spray or oil on pans or casserole dishes. Be sparing with butter—1 teaspoon of butter carefully melted and spread with a brush will adequately coat a 10-inch saucepan or skillet. Paper liners, pleated paper muffin cups, and wax paper can reduce the need for oil when using the oven.

3 **DON'T ADD HIGH-FAT LIQUID OR THICKENERS TO FOODS.** If you need to add liquid to dishes, use fruit or vegetable juice, low-fat dairy products, vegetable stock, wine, or beer instead of regular milk, cream, or sour cream. Use vegetables, fruits, or beans puréed with stock or water instead of a creamy roux to thicken soups, stews, and sauces.

Raw oats will also thicken puréed soups without adding any milk or cheese. Use about ½ cup of oats for every 3 cups of vegetables, varying the amount slightly according to the density of the vegetables being used. Stir the oats into the soup for the final 15 minutes of simmering, then purée as usual. The puréed oats lend body and a silken smooth creaminess to the soup—very similar to the texture that results from adding cream cheese. The blended oats are unobtrusive, and no one is likely to be able to identify them. However, they do add a slightly sweet flavor to the soup, which will enhance many soups but may not be desirable in all cases. We especially recommend using oats as a thickener in soups that feature mild or slightly sweet vegetables such as carrots, zucchini, squash, celery, onions, or leeks.

4 **USE FEWER WHOLE EGGS.** Lightly beaten egg whites can replace some or all of the eggs in most recipes. Omitting the yolks reduces the fat considerably. In baking, there is no foolproof rule of thumb for substitutions, but you will almost always be able to find a workable alternative that uses fewer eggs with experimentation. In general, you can replace 1 large egg with 2 egg whites and 2 medium eggs with 3 egg whites.

5 **SUBSTITUTE FRUIT PURÉES FOR FAT IN BAKED GOODS.** Applesauce can replace much of the oil in some baked flour products. It gives a similar loft and moistness while adding only a negligible amount of fat. Other good substitutions are pumpkin, squash, apricot, or prune purées, plum sauce, or cooked grated beets. You'll be amazed at how these just disappear into the dough or batter and inconspicuously do their job.

6 **USE LOW-FAT DAIRY PRODUCTS.** Almost all of the common cheeses and spreads now come in low-fat or nonfat versions. Not all of them taste good, but many of them do. Eating a plain slice of these lower-fat cheeses may not be very satisfying, since there is an easily discernible loss of both flavor and consistency. However, when we combined them in a spread, stuffing, or casserole or used them as a topping on a flavorful soup, stew, or main dish, we found many of the lower-fat brands worked fine. Be sure to read the labels of products marked "light" or "lite." Some contain additives or preservatives you would want to avoid, and "lite" may not always refer to the fat content of the product.

We have found quite a few brands of low-fat and nonfat products that are delicious. Lifetime brand makes an additive-free nonfat Cheddar cheese and Cabot Creamery produces a good reduced-fat (50%) Cheddar. Shop around and stock your favorites. Here's a checklist of good low-fat dairy products: buttermilk or nonfat buttermilk, 1% cottage cheese, 2% milk, 1% milk, skim milk, low-fat Cheddar cheese, Neufchâtel (low-fat cream cheese), reduced-fat mozzarella, nonfat ricotta cheese, nonfat sour cream, and nonfat yogurt. When incorporated into recipes, most of these are indistinguishable from their higher-fat originals.

Evaporated skimmed milk, which is produced by evaporating about half of the water from fresh nonfat milk and sterilizing it, is thick and can often replace cream in a recipe for a savings of 800 fat calories per cup. The sterilizing process does brown the milk sugars to produce a somewhat sweeter milk, however, so it works best in an already sweet sauce or one with a robust flavor that will not be affected by the hint of sweetness.

7 TRY SUBSTITUTES FOR DAIRY MILK IN YOUR DIET. Soy milk, with an overall fat content similar to low-fat milk but with the advantage that the fat is unsaturated, can be used in sauces, in baking, or even on morning cereal. In general, regular soy milk has quite a creamy texture and may be slightly sweet from the addition of rice or maple syrup. Many "light" soy milks have a milder soybean flavor and a texture closer to that of dairy milk. The taste varies a lot from brand to brand, so shop around for one you like. Children often like it better than milk, especially if they're not alerted that this is a "healthy" choice.

Rice beverages are quite sweet (sweeteners are often added), and while they may be too sweet for your cereal, they are perfect in custards, flans, puddings, sweet sauces, or icings.

Anasake is an organic naturally sweet rice drink with a thick, somewhat granular, but not at all unpleasant texture. Like rice beverages, it can be used in baked goods and other desserts, but you may need to reduce the amount of sweetening in the original recipe.

Try fruit juice on your cereal or granola instead of milk. Enjoy the rich creaminess of oatmeal made with water or apple juice. Oatmeal has depth, an almost nutty flavor, and a soothing texture that can be enjoyed plain or with chopped fresh fruit or berries, natural fruit preserves, or a little maple syrup and cinnamon or nutmeg.

8 CUT DOWN ON OIL-BASED DRESSINGS. For salads, depend on herbs and spices for flavor instead of heavy oil dressings. For raw salads, add interest by using a variety of greens and sprouts.

When making dressings, opt for canola or olive oil, which are high in monounsaturated fats—but use them in moderation or sparingly. Combine the oil with fruit juice, flavorful herb vinegars, balsamic vinegar, cider vinegar, or rice vinegar. Orange juice, apple juice, rice vinegar, or balsamic vinegar will require less oil than wine vinegar to offset their acidity. Add a dash of soy sauce for saltiness or mirin for sweetness. Grated ginger, minced scallions, herbs, citrus zests, or garlic can provide an additional accent.

9 **AVOID FAT-LADEN SPREADS, SAUCES, AND TOPPINGS.** Instead of using butter or cream cheese as your usual spreads, use fresh fruit preserves, applesauce, bean purées, miso spread, fresh salsas or high-quality bottled salsas such as the Guiltless Gourmet brand, vegetable pâtés, or one of our lower-fat guacamoles (pages 25–28).

As a rule, avoid heavy sauces. Beurre blanc, béarnaise, hollandaise, gravies, and most white sauces contain a lot of milk, cream, cheese, and/or butterfat. Instead choose stock-based sauces and create a velvety texture by using flour, cornstarch, arrowroot, or potato starch as thickeners. See "thickening" on page 419 for details. Use cocoa powder (or carob powder, if you like its flavor) in place of chocolate in dessert sauces.

Be aware of high-fat garnishes and toppings and use them judiciously or find good substitutes. For example, finely shred cheeses and mince or grind nuts to make a little go a long way. Sharp cheeses, rather than mild, and toasted nuts, rather than raw, will provide more richness per gram of fat. Use nonfat yogurt in place of sour cream to garnish hot, savory dishes. On desserts, replace whipped cream with our Vanilla Cream (page 395).

10 **STOCK UP ON LOW-FAT STAPLES.** Quick-cooking grains and beans, dried fruits, and pastas are all good pantry items. So are bagels, whole wheat English muffins, pita, breadsticks, low-fat cereal, gingersnaps, and graham crackers—all of which make good snacks too. Limit the use of processed foods that list fat or oil as their first ingredient; try to avoid foods with highly saturated oils such as palm oil, coconut oil, and palm kernel oil, and also those with hydrogenated oils. Keep fresh fruit and vegetables, nonfat yogurt, and low-fat spreads on hand. Training yourself to spend the 15 minutes it may take to make a delicious broccoli-couscous salad, rather than downing a bag of potato chips, is more than half the battle.

11 **BE ESPECIALLY CAREFUL ABOUT SNACK FOODS.** There really is quite a selection of lower-fat snacks, but not all "munchies" are created equal, so read the label to be sure a product meets your low-fat standard. Good snack choices include nonfat and baked tortilla chips, baked potato chips, various types of rice cakes, rice puffs, potato puffs, rye crisps, and sourdough pretzels. Many snack foods that were previously available only cooked in oil are now available baked.

Eat air-blown popcorn. If you want to add flavor, spray it with a little cooking spray or add 1 teaspoon of oil or melted butter, toss it well to coat, and add sea salt or other seasonings such as paprika, cayenne, gomashio (toasted sesame seeds and sea salt), or Parmesan cheese in moderation. Sesmark Foods, Inc., makes an unusually delicious cracker called "Original Sesame Thins" with no preservatives, no artificial flavorings or colorings, and less than 1 gram of fat per cracker—with most of the fat unsaturated.

Keep frozen berries for making quick sauces, sorbets, toppings, and additions to nonfat yogurt and other desserts. Eat frozen nonfat yogurt rather than ice cream. Make your own frozen fruit juice bars to have on hand for yourself and friends and family.

12 MAKE SMART CHOICES WHEN EATING AWAY FROM HOME. Eating out is meant to be pleasurable and, at times, even indulgent. But in a culture in which growing numbers of us eat out regularly, it's important to pay attention.

When eating out, try starting with a brothy soup, unbuttered bread, or a light seafood appetizer to take the edge off your hunger. Choose fresh salads that are not already dressed with mayonnaise or other creamy dressings. Even better, request your dressing on the side so you can decide how much to use, and ask for a wedge of lemon or lime. A squeeze or two can add just the right amount of zip.

Choose steamed, poached, blanched, broiled, roasted, or baked dishes without heavy sauces or breading. Try not to stuff yourself, since expanding your stomach increases your capacity and therefore your appetite. Share a dessert, or ask to take part of it home. Be satisfied sometimes to enjoy just an after-dinner beverage, good conversation, or the ambience.

THE NEW NONSTICK COOKWARE

Using nonstick cookware is one of the most painless ways to reduce the fat in your diet. We were excited by and pleased with many of our findings about the nonstick cookware presently available in the marketplace. At Moosewood Restaurant, we always use stainless steel cookware and after being disenchanted with the first generation of Teflon-coated pans—which really weren't nonstick and often began to shed their potentially toxic coatings in short order—few of us had tried any of the new nonstick cookware at home. We all had our seasoned cast-iron skillets, woks, and a variety of medium-sized stainless steel pans, and that was that.

When we decided to launch this low-fat cookbook project, however, we thought it would be interesting to try some leading high-quality, nonstick pans. Twelve cooks tried a variety of pans from five different companies over a period of several months, and overall our verdict is unanimously positive. Some of these products are expensive, but we think that someone who is serious about cooking

with less oil and adopting a lower-fat way of eating will view the purchase of one or two good nonstick pans as a worthwhile investment.

All of the nonstick cookware we tested was truly nonstick. Very little or no oil was necessary for sautéing as long as we stirred frequently and added a bit of liquid when needed. Reheating a cheesy pasta or making a risotto was completely without risk, and cleanup was easier and speedier, too. Many of the pans were quite good-looking and could be used as serving dishes at informal meals. None of the coatings chipped or peeled, although most require the use of nonmetallic utensils, such as wooden spoons or plastic spatulas.

Many cookware companies offer a large line of nonstick products, from saucepans and frying pans to Dutch ovens and baking pans. When asked to choose a single piece of nonstick cookware for home use, most of us selected either a 2- or 3-quart saucepan or a 10-inch skillet. If you follow the simple directions that accompany high-quality nonstick pans, most will hold up quite well. Many companies offer lifetime guarantees to demonstrate their faith in their product.

When selecting a good nonstick pan, look for one that is well designed and well balanced. Pick it up, move it around, tip it from side to side. Most of this cookware is relatively heavy, so imagine it full of food as you pick it up. Some companies have developed sturdy lines that are significantly lighter than the others, so if you need lightweight cookware, look around—it's available.

Choose saucepans that have hollow, stay-cool handles. But be careful—some of the handles that were advertised as heat resistant really weren't. The hollow ones seemed best for temperature control. On the other hand, metal handles—which do get hot—permit oven use, which plastic handles cannot withstand. We also like handles that are not too narrow and are easy to grip. The metal handles with rubber grips can be extremely helpful, since many plain metal handles were slippery, especially when lifted with a pot holder. If the rubber grips are not removable, however, it reduces the pan's versatility, since it won't be ovenproof. Handles on each side of the pan make lifting and transferring much easier. Some saucepans and skillets have one regular long handle and a C-shaped handle you can grip on the other side. This is a great innovation, especially for the larger, heavier pans. Check that protruding handles are amply long and angled for easy manipulation. We found that the handles attached at 30° to 45° angles remained cooler longer, especially when several pots and pans were being used at once on the stove top.

All of the cookware we tried had well-fitting covers—a must for keeping released liquid or steam in the pot where it will do the most good. Some of the cookware had glass lids, a feature we love, because it allows you to watch the transformation of the food without prematurely releasing all of the steam. All of the glass lids we tried were durable and shatterproof. We think the extra care in handling that they require is worth the benefits they provide. If you are buying a pan mainly for sautéing, choose one with sloped sides.

Also on the market is heavy cookware that combines a 3-ply bonded construction with a stainless steel interior, providing even cooking with very minimal sticking. They are not technically nonstick cookware, but they work very well, are not any heavier than most of the nonstick cookware available, and are comparably priced.

Investing in nonstick pans will bring you many years of cooking—and cleaning—pleasure. All of us at Moosewood now want at least one nonstick pan in our home cupboards.

After all of this lauding of nonstick cookware, we do need to include one word of warning that recently came to our attention. In the "Notes from Readers" section of the July/August 1995 issue of *Cook's Illustrated* magazine, we read that the manufacturing process used for nonstick pans released more airborne toxins than the process for making conventional cast-iron pans. There always seems to be a trade-off.

COOKING SPRAY

Using cooking spray may reduce the amount of oil you use, but don't assume that you will add no fat whatsoever to your diet—the stuff is still oil. It takes about 15 seconds to spray the equivalent of 1 tablespoon of oil or 14 grams of fat, about 5 seconds to get a teaspoon of oil or 4.33 grams of fat.

The amount necessary to very lightly cover a 10-inch skillet can be sprayed in about 1¼ seconds, according to the can's Nutrition Facts label. To successfully coat the skillet this quickly takes some practice. Use a deft circular motion of the wrist with a good aim a couple of inches away from the skillet. Most people will probably take at least 2 to 3 seconds to complete the task. If you manage to do it in 1¼ seconds, however, you will have added only 1 gram of fat to your dish. Of course, the longer you spray, the more fat you've added.

Select a monounsaturated spray oil, such as canola or olive oil, since they are generally healthier and less prone to becoming rancid.

ABOUT THE RECIPES

In most of our recipes, the ingredients list gives the quantity of prepared vegetables and fruits in cups. Occasionally this is followed parenthetically by the number of whole vegetables you will need to yield this amount—particularly for less common or more expensive vegetables. In some cases, when the exact amount of each vegetable is not crucial, such as in soup and stew recipes, we simply call for "1 onion," and we mean a middle-of-the-road, medium-sized one.

To peel or not to peel is largely a matter of the eventual function of the fruit or vegetable in a dish and your aesthetic judgment. We always peel sweet potatoes, parsnips, beets, and carrots. Fruit, potatoes, eggplant, and cucumbers are peeled or not on a case-by-case basis.

When we give the amount of a fresh herb followed by its dried equivalent in parentheses in the ingredient list, this indicates that either is fine, although we prefer the fresh herb if it's available. When only the fresh herb is listed, we do not recommend using its dried counterpart instead. If you prefer to use a fresh herb where we have used dried, use about 3 to 4 times the dried amount and add the fresh herbs near the end of the cooking process.

The recipes in this book have been nutritionally analyzed by CBORD Group, Inc., of Ithaca, New York, who prepared and provided the data for the nutritional bars that follow each recipe. Each bar lists the number of calories and the amounts of protein, fat, carbohydrates, saturated fat, polyunsaturated fat, monounsaturated fat, cholesterol, sodium, and total dietary fiber in one serving. For definitions and descriptions of the nutritional terms, turn to page 400 in our "Nutrition Facts" section. Read about the fact that some recipes with relatively high percentages of calories from fat may be low in actual grams of fat because all or most of the calories in the dish come from fat.

When a recipe suggests a range of servings, the analysis applies to the largest number of servings listed. Our serving sizes at Moosewood, which are reflected in this cookbook, are considered generous (in some cases, very generous) when compared with the usual industry standards.

When several choices appear in the original ingredient list, the nutritional calculations are based on the first choice that appears. Any time oil is not listed as an ingredient (such as when the procedure simply says, "lightly spray or oil a baking pan"), it is not figured into the analysis. In almost all cases, this will be a negligible amount of oil and will make little, if any, practical difference. In most cases we did not think a separate nutritional analysis was necessary for variations, as they did not differ significantly from the original. Whenever there was a substantial difference, however, you will find an additional nutritional bar, which immediately follows the main recipe bar.

In some recipes, we have suggested optional ingredients or toppings. Using just a tablespoon per serving of grated cheese, toasted nuts, seeds, yogurt, or sour cream can enhance the texture, flavor, and visual appeal of a dish without adding a lot of fat. The nutritional analysis does not include optional ingredients or garnishes for which no quantity is specified. So here is a list of our most frequently suggested garnishes and the total amount of fat in grams contained in 1 tablespoon of each item:

ITEM	FAT IN GRAMS
CHEESES—1 tablespoon, grated	
Cheddar	2.3
Feta	2.0
Monterey jack	2.1
Parmesan	1.5
Romano (Pecorino)	1.4
NUTS AND SEEDS—1 tablespoon, chopped raw	
Almonds	3.8
Peanuts	5.5
Pine nuts	5.1
Sesame seeds	3.8
Walnuts	4.0
¼ AVOCADO	7.7
SOUR CREAM, 1 tablespoon	
regular	2.5
nonfat	0
YOGURT, 1 tablespoon	
regular (plain, whole milk)	0.5
low-fat (with fruit)	0.2

garlic basil cheese spread 22

greek lima bean dip 23

ASIAN EGGPLANT SPREAD 24

guacamole with asparagus 25

guacamole with cottage cheese 26

GUACAMOLE WITH ROASTED CORN 27

one step bean guacamole 28

indian chickpea spread 29

SPINACH ARTICHOKE HEART DIP 30

herbed cottage cheese chèvre spread 31

eggplant strata 32

BROILED EGGPLANT THAI STYLE 34

greek spinach rice balls 35

nori vegetable rolls 36

TOFU VEGETABLE DUMPLINGS 38

tunisian potato turnovers 40

savory stuffed mushrooms 42

ROASTED GARLIC 43

APPETIZERS

When guests are arriving, we can think of no better way to set a convivial mood and put people at ease than with a beautiful tray of **APPETIZERS**. It creates a sense of good fellowship and provides a focus until people settle into their places for the main meal.

Many of the popular snack foods served as appetizers are very high in fat. We've tried to steer a middle course and to create luscious, yet more healthful hors d'oeuvres that can all be enjoyed without ruining the resolve to eat low-fat foods. You'll find unusual dishes such as Eggplant Strata and Tunisian Potato Turnovers as well as new versions of old standards, like Guacamole with Roasted Corn, Herbed Cottage Cheese Chèvre Spread, and Savory Stuffed Mushrooms. Vegetable crudités, low-fat crackers, baked or nonfat chips, hearty breads, or lightly toasted pita wedges are some excellent choices to accompany any of the dips and spreads in this chapter.

Don't feel obliged to serve our appetizers only as appetizers. Asian Eggplant Spread, the four guacamoles, Greek Lima Bean Dip, Garlic Basil Cheese Spread, and Indian Chickpea Spread also make great sandwich spreads. Dishes that are visually impressive, such as Savory Stuffed Mushrooms, Roasted Garlic, and Nori Vegetable Rolls, can bring an otherwise modest meal to life. Eggplant Strata, Broiled Eggplant Thai Style, Greek Spinach Rice Balls, Tofu Vegetable Dumplings, and Tunisian Potato Turnovers need not be limited to starter courses. See the serving suggestions given with each recipe for ways to serve these dishes as larger meals.

Perhaps best of all, most of the recipes in this chapter can be prepared well in advance of serving—a real bonus for a busy cook.

Other recipes in this book that can be pressed into duty as appetizers include:

Asian Tofu Salad (page 116)
Ira's Lunch (page 118)
Middle Eastern Cannellini Patties (page 119)
Mushroom Pâté Almondine (page 121)
Smoky Eggplant and Pepper Spread (page 122)
Tempeh Salad Sandwich Filling (page 123)
White Bean and Red Pepper Spread (page 125)
Luscious Basil and Feta Pizza (page 228)
Vegetable Filo Roll Extravaganza (page 242)
Fresh Spring Rolls (page 254)

GARLIC BASIL CHEESE SPREAD

This creamy cheese spread is greatly enhanced by the combination of aromatic basil and the savory mellowness of roasted garlic. One clove of fresh garlic can be used in place of the roasted garlic, which will result in a sharper flavor. Adding the optional roasted red pepper gives the spread a rosy hue.

If you roast the garlic in advance while the yogurt drains, the spread can be assembled in only minutes.

¾ cup plain nonfat yogurt
⅔ cup 1% cottage cheese
1 tablespoon Roasted Garlic (page 43)*
2 tablespoons chopped fresh basil
salt and ground black pepper to taste
¼ cup diced roasted red peppers (optional, page 436)

*About 6 medium garlic cloves will yield
1 tablespoon of roasted garlic paste.

Makes 1½ cups

**Yogurt straining time:
1 hour**

**Preparation time:
10 minutes, using
preroasted garlic**

Sitting time: 30 minutes

Place the yogurt in a yogurt drainer or in a strainer lined with a coffee filter. Set aside to drain for about an hour. This should yield about ½ cup of drained yogurt.

Combine the drained yogurt, cottage cheese, garlic, and basil in a food processor and blend until smooth. Add salt and pepper to taste. Stir in the roasted red peppers, if using. Cover and refrigerate, allowing to sit for at least 30 minutes so the flavors will marry.

PER 1-OZ SERVING: 21 CALORIES, 2.6 G PROTEIN, .3 G FAT, 1.9 G CARBOHYDRATES, .2 G SATURATED FATTY ACIDS, 0 G POLYUNSATURATED FATTY ACIDS, .1 G MONOUNSATURATED FATTY ACIDS, 1 MG CHOLESTEROL, 77 MG SODIUM, 0 G TOTAL DIETARY FIBER

MENU SUGGESTIONS Serve with a crusty French or sourdough bread along with **Cassoulet** (page 160), **Giambotta** (page 263), or **Mexican Stuffed Peppers and Tomatoes** (page 244). Or serve with **Watercress Omelet** (page 53) for breakfast or brunch.

GREEK LIMA BEAN DIP

Mint, dill, garlic, and lemon give smooth puréed lima beans a classic Greek accent.

If you'd like to cook your own lima beans for this recipe, soak them, drain, and then simmer them in plenty of water, with the pot lid slightly ajar, for about an hour, or until tender. While you're at it, you may want to cook extra beans to have on hand for later, but if you want just enough for this recipe, start with 1 cup of dried beans.

Makes 2½ cups

Total time: 20 minutes

> **NOTE:**
> Canned lima beans may be labeled "butter beans" in the supermarket. If you choose to cook your own beans rather than using canned beans, 1 generous cup of dried beans will yield about 3 cups of cooked beans.

3 cups cooked lima beans (two 15-ounce cans, drained and liquid reserved) (see Note)
2 garlic cloves, minced or pressed
¼ cup fresh lemon juice
2 tablespoons minced fresh dill
1 tablespoon chopped fresh mint
1 teaspoon olive oil
⅓ cup minced red onions
salt and ground black pepper to taste

In a blender or food processor, purée the limas, garlic, lemon juice, dill, and mint. If needed, add about ¼ cup of the reserved bean liquid to aid in puréeing. Add the olive oil and process until smooth and creamy. Fold in the red onions by hand and add salt and pepper to taste. Serve at room temperature, or chill for at least an hour and serve cold.

PER 2-OZ SERVING: 56 CALORIES, 3.1 G PROTEIN, .6 G FAT, 9.8 G CARBOHYDRATES, .1 G SATURATED FATTY ACIDS, .1 G POLYUNSATURATED FATTY ACIDS, .4 G MONOUN-SATURATED FATTY ACIDS, 0 MG CHOLESTEROL, 31 MG SODIUM, .1 G TOTAL DIETARY FIBER

MENU SUGGESTIONS Serve this as a dip for crackers, pita, crudités, or steamed artichokes. Or try it as a spread for French, sourdough, or marbled rye bread accompanied by **Italian Roasted Vegetables** (page 226), or make a pita sandwich with lettuce and tomato paired with **Tomato Bulgur Soup** (page 101) or **Greek Stew** (page 266).

ASIAN EGGPLANT SPREAD

Here is a chunky spread with the traditional flavors of China.

1 medium eggplant
1 teaspoon grated fresh ginger root
½ teaspoon ground anise
2 scallions, minced
1½ tablespoons soy sauce
½ teaspoon dark sesame oil
1 tablespoon rice vinegar

Makes 1½ cups

**Preparation time:
15 minutes**

**Baking time:
45 to 60 minutes**

Preheat the oven to 350°.

Pierce the eggplant with a fork in several spots, place it directly on the oven rack with a baking sheet on the rack below to catch drips, and bake it for 45 to 60 minutes, until very soft and somewhat collapsed. Remove the eggplant from the oven.

When it is cool enough to handle, cut the eggplant in half, scoop out the flesh, and discard the skin. Thoroughly chop through the flesh crosswise and lengthwise; you should have about 1½ cups. In a bowl, combine the eggplant with the ginger, anise, scallions, soy sauce, sesame oil, and rice vinegar and mix well. Add more soy sauce to taste as needed.

PER 2.50-OZ SERVING: 27 CALORIES, .9 G PROTEIN, .6 G FAT, 5.5 G CARBOHYDRATES, .1 G SATURATED FATTY ACIDS, .2 G POLYUNSATURATED FATTY ACIDS, .2 G MONOUNSATURATED FATTY ACIDS, 0 MG CHOLESTEROL, 205 MG SODIUM, 1.9 G TOTAL DIETARY FIBER

MENU SUGGESTIONS Serve with pita, rice cakes, or crackers, or as a garnish with **Chinese Orzo Vegetable Salad** (page 149), **Vietnamese Hot and Sour Soup** (page 87), **Korean Vegetable Noodle Soup** (page 89), **Essential Miso Soup with Tofu** (page 80), or **Vegetable Udon Sauté** (page 204).

GUACAMOLE WITH ASPARAGUS

Make this version of guacamole in the spring when fresh asparagus is abundant. Green and creamy, it has just a hint of asparagus flavor. Serve with baked tortilla chips, crackers, pita bread, or vegetable sticks.

½ pound asparagus
1 ripe Hass avocado
2 tablespoons fresh lemon juice
1 very small fresh chile, seeded and minced,
    or a pinch of cayenne
1 tablespoon minced red onions
½ teaspoon salt
1 tomato, diced

a few sprigs of fresh cilantro (optional)

Makes 1½ to 2 cups

Total time: 20 minutes

> **NOTE:**
> When exposed to the air for more than an hour or two, the surface of the guacamole may darken. If this occurs, stir well before serving. Or, to prevent discoloration, before storing in the refrigerator lightly press plastic wrap directly on the surface to make an airtight seal.

Snap off and discard the tough stem ends of the asparagus. Cut the stalks into 1-inch pieces and cook in about a cup of water for 10 minutes, or until soft. Drain well.

Meanwhile, slice the avocado lengthwise and twist to separate the halves. Remove the pit and scoop the avocado flesh into the bowl of a food processor. Add the lemon juice, chile or cayenne, red onions, and salt. Add the cooked asparagus to the food processor and purée until smooth. Stir in the tomatoes. Serve immediately or chill (see Note). If desired, serve topped with a few sprigs of cilantro.

PER 2-OZ SERVING: 41 CALORIES, 1.1 G PROTEIN, 3.1 G FAT, 3.5 G CARBOHYDRATES, .5 G SATURATED FATTY ACIDS, .4 G POLYUNSATURATED FATTY ACIDS, 1.9 G MONOUNSATURATED FATTY ACIDS, 0 MG CHOLESTEROL, 113 MG SODIUM, 1.3 G TOTAL DIETARY FIBER

MENU SUGGESTIONS This is perfect before **Mexican Pasta Salad** (page 148), **Festive Black Bean Chili** (page 161), or **Tamale Pie** (page 162).

GUACAMOLE WITH COTTAGE CHEESE

Before you even taste this guacamole, you will be impressed by its lovely light green shade. We've never seen anything quite like it before, and the bonus is that it doesn't darken *a bit* as it sits, the way most other guacamoles do. Collective member Ned Asta's seven-year-old son Tazio devoured most of this recipe in one sitting and asked if he could have it every time he went to Moosewood.

1 ripe avocado, preferably Hass
⅔ cup low-fat cottage cheese
2 tablespoons fresh lime juice
1 tablespoon chopped scallions
¾ teaspoon minced fresh chile
2 garlic cloves, pressed
salt and ground black pepper to taste

Makes 1½ cups

Total time: 10 minutes

Slice the avocado in half lengthwise and separate the halves by gently twisting. Remove the pit. With a tablespoon or soup spoon, scoop out the flesh of each half. In a food processor, combine the avocado, cottage cheese, lime juice, scallions, chile, and garlic and purée until smooth. Add salt and pepper to taste and serve immediately or chill.

The flavor of the guacamole will increase in intensity as it sits.

PER 2-OZ SERVING: 63 CALORIES, 4.0 G PROTEIN, 4.1 G FAT, 3.4 G CARBOHYDRATES, .9 G SATURATED FATTY ACIDS, .5 G POLYUNSATURATED FATTY ACIDS, 2.4 G MONOUNSATURATED FATTY ACIDS, 2 MG CHOLESTEROL, 135 MG SODIUM, 1.5 G TOTAL DIETARY FIBER

MENU SUGGESTIONS Serve it spread on rice cakes, as a dip with low-fat tortilla chips or crackers, or alongside a platter of colorful crudités. Guacamole with Cottage Cheese is also a delicious filling for pita sandwiches or served beside **Black Bean Chilaquile** (page 164) or **Southwestern Hominy Stew** (page 279).

GUACAMOLE WITH ROASTED CORN

In this lavish guacamole, the sweet aromatic flavor of roasted corn contrasts with the sharp and savory red onion. Be sure to use a fragrant, ripe avocado, preferably the Hass variety.

You can tell that an avocado is just right when it yields slightly to pressure, has no extremely soft spots, and is still shapely. When you cut it open, the flesh should not be discolored (if so, it is overripe or bruised) and the skin should peel away from the flesh easily (if not, it is underripe). To hasten ripening of an avocado, place it in a paper bag at room temperature.

1 cup fresh or frozen corn kernels
3 tablespoons minced red onions
½ teaspoon ground cumin
1 teaspoon minced fresh chile
2 garlic cloves, pressed or minced
2 teaspoons canola or other vegetable oil
1 avocado, halved, pitted, peeled, and cubed
1 tomato, chopped
3 tablespoons fresh lime juice
2 teaspoons cider vinegar
1 to 2 tablespoons chopped fresh cilantro
salt and ground black pepper to taste

Makes 2½ cups

Total time: 25 minutes

Preheat the broiler.

In a bowl, mix together the corn, red onions, cumin, chile, garlic, and oil. Spread the vegetable mixture onto a baking pan and roast about 3 inches from the flame or heat source for about 10 minutes, stirring often—at least three times or more. When the corn is tender and golden brown, remove the pan from the broiler and set aside to cool.

Combine the avocado, tomato, lime juice, vinegar, and cilantro in a serving bowl. Stir in the roasted corn mixture and add salt and pepper to taste. Serve immediately or chill and serve later.

PER 2-OZ SERVING: 67 CALORIES, 1.2 G PROTEIN, 4.2 G FAT, 7.8 G CARBOHYDRATES, .6 G SATURATED FATTY ACIDS, 1.2 G POLYUNSATURATED FATTY ACIDS, 2.1 G MONOUNSATURATED FATTY ACIDS, 0 MG CHOLESTEROL, 29 MG SODIUM, 1.9 G TOTAL DIETARY FIBER

MENU SUGGESTIONS This guacamole is delicious served alongside **Quinoa Pine Nut Pilaf** (page 184), **Spanish Potato Pepper Frittata** (page 51), or **Bean and Bean Gumbo** (page 157). Serve it as an appetizer with tortilla chips or fresh raw vegetables.

ONE STEP BEAN GUACAMOLE

A recipe quicker and easier than this would be almost impossible to find. But your guests will never guess it took you only minutes to make this robust guacamole. For an excellent filling for a pita sandwich, just mash half of the kidney beans before mixing them into the guacamole.

1 avocado, preferably Hass
1½ cups cooked kidney beans (15-ounce can, drained)
½ cup prepared Mexican-style red salsa
1 to 2 tablespoons chopped fresh cilantro
salt and ground black pepper to taste (optional)

Makes 2 cups

Total time: 10 minutes

Halve the avocado lengthwise and gently twist the halves to separate from the pit. Make lengthwise and crosswise cuts about ½ inch apart in the flesh of each half. Scoop the avocado cubes out of the skins and into a serving bowl. Stir in the kidney beans, salsa, and cilantro. Add salt and pepper, if desired, and serve.

PER 2-OZ SERVING: 69 CALORIES, 3.3 G PROTEIN, 2.9 G FAT, 8.5 G CARBOHYDRATES, .4 G SATURATED FATTY ACIDS, .4 G POLYUNSATURATED FATTY ACIDS, 1.7 G MONOUNSATURATED FATTY ACIDS, 0 MG CHOLESTEROL, 166 MG SODIUM, 1.1 G TOTAL DIETARY FIBER

MENU SUGGESTIONS Serve with baked tortilla chips to accompany **Mexican Seitan Pita** (page 120) and **Southwestern Corn and Potato Soup** (page 102) or as a dip before **Seitan Fajitas** (page 232).

INDIAN CHICKPEA SPREAD

This spicy and aromatic variation of hummus is also called *neeta's chole*. It can be used as an appetizer, side dish, dip, or sandwich spread. Try it in pita bread with fresh greens and grated carrots, on crackers or poppadums, or with vegetable crudités.

½ cup minced onions
1 teaspoon canola or other vegetable oil
2 garlic cloves, minced or pressed
1 teaspoon ground coriander
½ teaspoon ground cumin
½ teaspoon garam masala (page 428)
⅛ to ¼ teaspoon cayenne
1 cup diced tomatoes
1½ cups cooked chickpeas (16-ounce can)
2 teaspoons fresh lime juice
1 tablespoon chopped fresh cilantro
salt to taste

Makes 2 cups

Total time: 20 minutes

In a heavy or nonstick skillet, sauté the onions in the oil on low heat for about 5 minutes, until softened. Add the garlic, coriander, cumin, garam masala, and cayenne and sauté for another minute, stirring constantly to prevent sticking. Stir in the tomatoes, cover, and gently simmer for about 5 minutes.

Meanwhile, drain the chickpeas, reserving the liquid. In a food processor, grind the chickpeas with just enough reserved liquid (or water) to make a smooth purée. Stir the purée into the simmering tomato mixture, add the lime juice and cilantro, and cook on low heat for about 5 minutes. Add salt to taste.

Serve hot or cold.

PER 1-OZ SERVING: 34 CALORIES, 1.3 G PROTEIN, .6 G FAT, 6.1 G CARBOHYDRATES, .1 G SATURATED FATTY ACIDS, .3 G POLYUNSATURATED FATTY ACIDS, .1 G MONOUNSATURATED FATTY ACIDS, 0 MG CHOLESTEROL, 78 MG SODIUM, 1.2 G TOTAL DIETARY FIBER

MENU SUGGESTIONS Serve this spread with **Mango Coconut Cucumber Salad** (page 136) paired with **Tropical Gazpacho** (page 78), **Thai Vegetable Curry** (page 268), or **Savory Indian Sweet Potatoes** (page 248).

SPINACH ARTICHOKE HEART DIP

This dip, with its bits of artichoke in a spinach and herb purée, is delicious with crudités or crackers as an appetizer or snack. It's also snazzy enough to be part of a combo plate that features a contrasting crisp or crunchy item such as falafels or a stuffed filo package.

5 ounces fresh spinach, rinsed and stemmed

2 garlic cloves, pressed or minced

1½ cups cooked butter beans or cannellini
(15-ounce can, drained and rinsed)

1 cup chopped scallions

2 tablespoons chopped fresh basil

2 to 3 tablespoons fresh lemon juice, to taste

5 to 6 artichoke hearts or bottoms, minced
(15-ounce can)

salt and ground black pepper to taste

Makes 3 cups

Total time: 15 minutes

Using just the water clinging to the leaves after rinsing, steam the spinach until just wilted, 2 or 3 minutes. Drain.

In a food processor, purée the spinach, garlic, beans, scallions, basil, and 2 tablespoons of the lemon juice until very smooth. Fold in the minced artichoke hearts and add more lemon juice and salt and pepper to taste. Serve chilled or at room temperature.

PER 1.50-OZ SERVING: 26 CALORIES, 1.8 G PROTEIN, .1 G FAT, 5.3 G CARBOHYDRATES, 0 G SATURATED FATTY ACIDS, .1 G POLYUNSATURATED FATTY ACIDS, .0 G MONOUNSATURATED FATTY ACIDS, 0 MG CHOLESTEROL, 88 MG SODIUM, 2.3 G TOTAL DIETARY FIBER

MENU SUGGESTIONS This dip is perfect on a combo plate with **Roasted Garlic** (page 43), pita bread, crisp fresh crudités, and **Tunisian Potato Turnovers** (page 40). Or serve it as a prelude to **Spanish Potato Pepper Frittata** (page 51), **Italian Fish Stew** (page 299), or **Fish Tagine with Chermoulla** (page 291).

HERBED COTTAGE CHEESE CHÈVRE SPREAD

This creamy spread is perfect for a party dip with crudités, for between-meal snacks on crackers or crostini, or as a sandwich served with soup.

1 tablespoon minced fresh parsley
1 minced scallion or 1 tablespoon minced chives
1 teaspoon dried dill
½ teaspoon dried tarragon
1 cup low-fat cottage cheese
2 ounces chèvre or other mild fresh goat cheese

pimiento strips

Makes about 1 cup

Total time: 15 minutes

In a blender or food processor, whirl the parsley, scallions or chives, dill, tarragon, cottage cheese, and chèvre until smooth and creamy. Transfer to a serving bowl and garnish with the pimiento strips.

VARIATION For a leaner version, omit the chèvre from the spread.

PER 1.25-OZ SERVING: 28 CALORIES, 4.0 G PROTEIN, .6 G FAT, 1.6 G CARBOHYDRATES, .3 G SATURATED FATTY ACIDS, 0 G POLYUNSATURATED FATTY ACIDS, .2 G MONOUNSATURATED FATTY ACIDS, 2 MG CHOLESTEROL, 117 MG SODIUM, .1 G TOTAL DIETARY FIBER

MENU SUGGESTIONS Serve on a good crusty bread or crackers along with **French Vegetable Bean Stew** (page 264) or **Giambotta** (page 263) or as a sandwich with lettuce and sliced tomato to accompany **Cream of Green Vegetable Soup** (page 82), **Dried Mushroom Soup with Barley** (page 94), or **Orzo and Pea Soup** (page 93).

EGGPLANT STRATA

Beautiful layers of vivid red, green, and white offer a multiplicity of tastes and textures in this elegant chilled salad, which makes impressive company fare. The preparation is a bit involved, but it can all be done well in advance or even in increments: Roast the eggplant one day, assemble and chill the next.

Serves 8

Total time: 1 hour

Chilling time: 2 hours

1 medium to large eggplant
1 tablespoon extra-virgin olive oil
¼ teaspoon salt
1½ to 2 cups cooked Great Northern, cannellini,
   or white kidney beans (15-ounce can, drained)
1 tablespoon fresh lemon juice
¼ teaspoon ground cumin
½ cup nonfat ricotta cheese
2 tablespoons grated feta cheese
2 tablespoons chopped fresh dill
   (2 teaspoons dried)
1 cup loosely packed stemmed parsley
2 garlic cloves, minced or pressed
½ cup chopped tomatoes
⅔ cup roasted red peppers, cut into narrow strips
   (drained canned, or see page 436)

Turn on the broiler.

Stem the eggplant and cut it lengthwise into ½-inch-thick slices. Peel the curved outer surface of the top and bottom slices. Place the eggplant slices on the broiler tray or in a baking dish, drizzle with 2 teaspoons of the olive oil, and sprinkle with the salt. Broil about 5 inches from the heat for 5 to 10 minutes on each side, until browned and tender. Cool slightly, then slice the eggplant pieces crosswise into ½-inch strips and set aside.

Combine the beans, 2 teaspoons of lemon juice, the remaining teaspoon of olive oil, and the cumin in a blender, food processor, or large bowl. Blend or mash the beans well and set them aside. In a separate bowl, combine the ricotta, feta cheese, and dill and set aside. In a blender or food processor, whirl the parsley, garlic, and tomatoes until the mixture reaches a consistency similar to pesto and set aside.

Fully line a 9 × 5-inch nonreactive loaf pan with clear plastic wrap. Arrange ⅓ of the eggplant strips on the bottom of the pan, placing them parallel to the short sides of the pan (don't worry about the gaps). Spread all of the bean mixture over the eggplant, then layer all of the pepper strips parallel to the short sides of the pan. Follow with another ⅓ of the eggplant strips as before and all of the cheese mixture. Sprinkle all of the parsley mixture over the cheese and top with the final ⅓ of the eggplant strips arranged as before.

To compress the salad in its mold, spread a sheet of plastic wrap directly onto the top layer of the salad. Place an empty loaf pan on top of the plastic wrap and weight it with one or two cans or jars borrowed from the pantry. Refrigerate for at least 2 hours or overnight.

To unmold, remove the weighted pan and the top sheet of plastic wrap. Cover the pan of molded salad with a serving plate and quickly invert. Peel off the rest of the plastic wrap and *voila!* Use a sharp knife to cut the molded salad into 2-inch slices.

PER 5-OZ SERVING: 101 CALORIES, 6.0 G PROTEIN, 2.6 G FAT, 14.1 G CARBOHYDRATES, .6 G SATURATED FATTY ACIDS, .3 G POLYUNSATURATED FATTY ACIDS, 1.4 G MONOUNSATURATED FATTY ACIDS, 2 MG CHOLESTEROL, 149 MG SODIUM, 4.5 G TOTAL DIETARY FIBER

MENU SUGGESTIONS Serve after a bowl of **Tomato Bulgur Soup** (page 101) or **Savory Stuffed Mushrooms** (page 42), or as a combo plate with **Seasoned Steamed Artichokes** (page 311) and **Tabouli Salad** (page 145). Eggplant Strata is a delicious appetizer before **Fish Tagine with Chermoulla** (page 291), **Sicilian Scallop Salad** (page 304), **Italian Fish Stew** (page 299), **Bulgur Rice Pilaf** (page 188), or **Swiss Chard Rolls Two Ways** (page 252).

BROILED EGGPLANT THAI STYLE

Broiling with a glaze of soy sauce and garlic creates a succulent eggplant that is further enhanced with this refreshing sauce. Serve the eggplant with brown rice or coconut rice (page 425), with the juices from the pan spooned on top. Put the rice on to cook a few minutes before starting this recipe.

EGGPLANT

1 large eggplant (about 1¼ pounds)
2 garlic cloves, minced or pressed
1½ tablespoons soy sauce

SAUCE

2 tablespoons chopped fresh cilantro
1 tablespoon fresh lime juice
¼ cup reduced-fat coconut milk (page 425)
1 teaspoon brown sugar
½ teaspoon seeded minced fresh chile
1 teaspoon grated fresh ginger root
1 teaspoon peanut butter (optional)

**Serves 2 as a main dish with rice,
4 to 6 as an appetizer or part of a larger meal**

**Preparation time:
15 minutes**

**Broiling time:
8 to 10 minutes**

Preheat the broiler.

Cut the eggplant lengthwise into ½-inch-thick slices. Peel the end slices to remove the excess tough skin. Using a sharp paring knife, score the top side of each slice in a 1-inch-square diamond pattern, cutting about ¼ inch into the flesh. Place the eggplant slices in a single layer on the largest baking pan that your broiler can accommodate. Combine the garlic and soy sauce and pour over the eggplant, coaxing it into the scored diamonds with the back of a spoon.

Broil the eggplant about 6 inches from the heat until browned and tender, about 4 minutes on each side. Remove from the oven and set aside.

Meanwhile, combine the cilantro, lime juice, coconut milk, brown sugar, chile, ginger, and peanut butter, if using. Serve the eggplant warm or at room temperature. Drizzle with the pan juices and top with some of the sauce just before serving.

PER 4-OZ SERVING: 40 CALORIES, 1.0 G PROTEIN, 1.1 G FAT, 7.6 G CARBOHYDRATES, .5 G SATURATED FATTY ACIDS, .1 G POLYUNSATURATED FATTY ACIDS, 0 G MONOUNSATURATED FATTY ACIDS, 0 MG CHOLESTEROL, 207 MG SODIUM, 2.3 G TOTAL DIETARY FIBER

MENU SUGGESTIONS Serve as an appetizer to accompany **Curried Rice Noodles** (page 220), **Thai Fried Rice** (page 190), or **Thai Fish Cakes** (page 302) with **Carrot Orange Salad** (page 134) or a green salad with **Southeast Asian Pineapple Sesame Dressing** (page 343).

GREEK SPINACH RICE BALLS

These tasty rice balls are fun to make with the kids for an everyday meal or a snack. They also make good finger food at parties and are a welcome contribution to dish-to-pass suppers.

2 pounds fresh spinach, washed and large stems removed
1 cup chopped scallions (about 6 scallions)
2 teaspoons olive oil
2 cups cooked brown rice
2 tablespoons finely chopped fresh dill (2 teaspoons dried)
1½ tablespoons fresh lemon juice
salt and ground black pepper to taste
1 cup plain or herbed bread crumbs

Makes about 24 Ping-Pong–sized rice balls

Total time: 40 minutes

In a large covered pot, steam the spinach in the water that clings to the leaves until just wilted, 2 or 3 minutes. Drain and chop the spinach and set it aside. In another pan, lightly sauté the scallions in the oil for about 5 minutes, or until softened and slightly browned.

Preheat the oven to 350°.

In a large mixing bowl, combine the spinach, scallions, rice, dill, and lemon juice. Add salt and pepper to taste. Stir well, mashing the rice mixture against the sides of the bowl with the back of a large spoon until the mixture holds together.

Prepare a baking sheet or large baking dish with cooking spray or a very light coating of vegetable oil. With dampened hands, pack a heaping ¼ cup of the rice mixture into a firm, round ball (like making a snowball). Roll the ball in the bread crumbs and place it on the baking sheet. Continue making balls until all of the rice mixture is used, arranging the balls on the baking sheet about an inch apart. Bake for 20 to 25 minutes, until the balls are heated through and crisp on the outside.

VARIATION Add 1 cup of grated feta cheese to the rice mixture.

PER 2-OZ SERVING: 48 CALORIES, 1.9 G PROTEIN, .9 G FAT, 8.6 G CARBOHYDRATES, .2 G SATURATED FATTY ACIDS, .2 G POLYUNSATURATED FATTY ACIDS, .4 G MONOUNSATURATED FATTY ACIDS, 0 MG CHOLESTEROL, 72 MG SODIUM, 1.2 G TOTAL DIETARY FIBER

MENU SUGGESTIONS This is the perfect appetizer for **Fish Steaks with Fennel** (page 290), **Baked Flounder Rolls** (page 295), **Herbed Fish in a Packet** (page 296), or **Tuscan Beans with Sage** (page 168). Accompany with a tossed salad with **Minted Dill Yogurt Dressing** (page 345) or **Orange Tarragon Dressing** (page 348).

NORI VEGETABLE ROLLS

Many people immediately associate sushi rolls with traditional fillings of crab, eel, tuna, or mackerel. However, sushi chefs also turn out intriguing vegetarian rolls filled with burdock, squash, cucumber, avocado, or shiso leaf and plum paste. When you use vegetables of different bright colors in the centers of the rolls, it's a gorgeous sight to behold.

Be sure to have a *sudore* (bamboo rolling mat) on hand and prepare the rice and vegetables ahead, since cold rice won't work. We've tried to describe how to use a *sudore*, but seeing it once is worth a thousand words. If you can find someone to show you how to do it the first time, then it's a cinch and, like riding a bike, you'll never forget how.

RICE MIXTURE

1½ cups sushi rice or brown rice (page 435)
2 or 3 cups water, depending on the rice used
4 teaspoons rice vinegar (page 440)
4 teaspoons mirin (page 431)
1 teaspoon toasted sesame seeds (page 67)

1 to 2 tablespoons wasabi powder (page 440)
1 to 2 tablespoons water
½ carrot, peeled
¼ red bell pepper, seeded
¼ cucumber, peeled and seeded
2 scallions
2 to 3 ounces tofu-kan or other seasoned tofu (page 439)
6 sheets of nori (page 432)

DIPPING SAUCE

2 teaspoons wasabi powder, more or less to taste
2 teaspoons water
1 tablespoon fresh lemon juice
4 teaspoons soy sauce

Makes 36 pieces

Total time: 45 to 60 minutes—not as long as you might think

> **NOTE:**
> We think that buying a *sudore* is money well spent. Available in Asian food stores, they are relatively inexpensive and clean easily with a stiff brush.
>
> It is harder to make nori rolls using a smooth dish towel. You'll need to pull the towel free of the roll as you shape it.
>
> Rolling by hand is also possible, but the rolls will not be as firm or well-shaped.

Combine either the sushi rice and 2 cups of water or the brown rice and 3 cups of water in a soup pot. Cover and bring to a boil, then lower to a simmer and cook for about 15 minutes for the sushi rice or 30 minutes for brown rice, until the rice is quite soft and has absorbed the water. Meanwhile, stir together the rice vinegar, mirin, and sesame seeds and set aside.

While the rice cooks, combine equal amounts of the wasabi powder and water to form a smooth paste and set it aside to allow the flavor to develop. Julienne the carrot, bell pepper, cucumber, scallions, and tofu-kan. Lightly steam the julienned carrots and bell peppers until crisp-tender. If your nori is not pretoasted, lightly toast it for about ½ minute over a very low open flame or bake it in a 300° oven for 2 to 3 minutes.

When the rice is ready, stir in the vinegar-mirin mixture and transfer it to a bowl to cool somewhat. In a separate bowl, mix together the dipping sauce ingredients.

Place a nori sheet on the *sudore* and align the bottom edges—the ones nearest to you. Moisten your hands and evenly spread about ¾ cup of the seasoned rice on the nori, beginning 1½ inches from its top edge and ending ½ inch from its bottom edge. One-third of the way up from the bottom, make a horizontal ½-inch-wide depression in the rice and spread a small amount of the wasabi paste in it. Artfully arrange a few of the julienned vegetables and/or tofu slices side by side in a single layer on top of the wasabi paste to fill in the ½-inch depression. Be careful not to overdo the vegetables in the center or you'll create a bulging, hard-to-eat roll—a little Zen-like aesthetic comes in handy here.

Now you're ready to roll. Take the bottom edge of the *sudore* and lift it up and over, as if beginning to form a jelly roll. Use the *sudore* to guide the nori wrapper until it contacts the rice (forming a circle). Lift the *sudore* out of the way and tuck in the bottom edge of the nori with your fingers to begin the roll. Once again, bring the *sudore* up and over the roll, but don't tuck it in. Allow the bottom edge of the *sudore* to move gradually away from you toward its top edge as you continue rolling. Press evenly and steadily on the *sudore* with the palms of both hands while rolling to produce a well-shaped roll. Don't worry if a bit of rice squeezes out the sides. Continue rolling until the *sudore* is completely turned over—its original top edge is now at the bottom and closest to you and a firmly packed nori roll emerges from beneath it. If it hasn't already sealed itself, seal the roll by spreading a little water along the uncovered top edge.

When you finish making all six rolls, use a sharp wet knife to trim the ends of the rolls and cut them into 1¼-inch slices. Arrange the pieces, cut side up, on a platter and serve with chopsticks and a shallow bowl of the dipping sauce.

VARIATIONS Julienned (page 416) and steamed green beans, parsnips, beets, daikon and spinach are other possible vegetable fillings. Commercial umeboshi plum paste or homemade miso–rice vinegar paste can replace the wasabi in the rolls, or you can omit it altogether and use the wasabi only in the dipping sauce. Pickled ginger is another traditional condiment available in Asian markets and makes a lovely addition to the dipping sauce, as does finely grated raw daikon.

PER 1.20-OZ SERVING: 33 CALORIES, 1.0 G PROTEIN, .4 G FAT, 6.5 G CARBOHYDRATES, .1 G SATURATED FATTY ACIDS, .2 G POLYUNSATURATED FATTY ACIDS, .1 G MONOUNSATURATED FATTY ACIDS, 0 MG CHOLESTEROL, 33 MG SODIUM, .2 G TOTAL DIETARY FIBER

TOFU VEGETABLE DUMPLINGS

Although time-consuming to prepare, vegetarian dumplings are a rare and welcome treat.

Try them as appetizers with a Japanese-style dipping sauce: Whisk together 2 tablespoons of soy sauce, 2 teaspoons of rice wine vinegar, and 1 minced scallion. Or simmer them in Garlic Broth (page 74) for a delicious vegan wonton soup.

Serves 8 to 12

Makes 48 dumplings

**Total time:
1 to 1¼ hours**

1 ounce dried shiitake mushrooms (page 437)
2 cups boiling water
6 garlic cloves, minced or pressed
1 tablespoon grated fresh ginger root
1 teaspoon ground anise
1 cup peeled and grated carrots
2 cups minced fresh mushrooms (about 6 ounces)
1 cup minced Chinese cabbage (page 424)
1 teaspoon canola or other vegetable oil
4 ounces pressed tofu, crumbled (page 419)
3 tablespoons soy sauce
2 scallions, minced
1 tablespoon hoisin sauce (optional)
1 teaspoon chili paste (optional)

1 package wonton or dumpling wrappers (page 441)

Place the shiitake in a heatproof bowl, cover with the boiling water, and set aside for at least 20 minutes (see Note). When the shiitake have softened, drain them; you can strain and reserve the liquid to use as dashi (page 427) another time. Cut off and discard the tough stems. Mince the caps.

In a saucepan on medium-low heat, combine the shiitake, garlic, ginger, anise, carrots, fresh mushrooms, cabbage, and oil. Cover and cook for 5 minutes, stirring frequently. Add the tofu, soy sauce, scallions, and optional hoisin sauce and chili paste and cook for 3 minutes, mixing everything well.

Place a rounded teaspoon of the tofu-vegetable mixture on the center of a wrapper. Moisten the outer edges of the wrapper, fold one corner over to the diagonally opposite corner to form a triangle, then press the edges together to seal the dumpling. Use a little more water if the wrapper opens at the joint. Place the filled dumplings on a large platter or several plates, cover with clear plastic wrap, and refrigerate them or package and freeze them until ready for use (see Note).

Cook dumplings in one of the following three ways: 1) Gently simmer the dumplings in water or broth for 5 minutes. 2) Sauté them in a skillet prepared with ½ teaspoon of oil or nonstick spray for 2 minutes on each side. Pour in ¼ cup of water, cover, and steam for 4 minutes. 3) Steam the dumplings in a steamer basket or sieve over boiling water for 7 to 10 minutes.

PER 3-OZ SERVING: 111 CALORIES, 4.4 G PROTEIN, 1.4 G FAT, 20.4 G CARBOHYDRATES, .2 G SATURATED FATTY ACIDS, .7 G POLYUNSATURATED FATTY ACIDS, .3 G MONOUNSATURATED FATTY ACIDS, 3 MG CHOLESTEROL, 376 MG SODIUM, 1.1 G TOTAL DIETARY FIBER

NOTES:
It is also possible to place the shiitake and enough water to cover in a small bowl and microwave until softened, about 5 minutes.

To freeze uncooked dumplings, arrange them in a single layer on a dish (don't let them overlap), place a sheet of wax paper between layers, and continue to stack them, finally covering everything with a freezer bag. Or you can freeze them on a plate and then transfer the frozen dumplings to either a freezer bag or a doubled plastic bag sealed with a twist tie. Remove as much air as possible before sealing the storage bag. Frozen dumplings will keep for at least 4 months.

MENU SUGGESTIONS Serve alongside a little bowl of Chinese-style rice with **Asian Cucumber Condiment** (page 367) or as an accompaniment to **Savory Hoisin Fish** (page 293), **Cantonese Roasted Vegetables** (page 226) on greens, **Gingered Broccoli** (page 315), or **Broiled Portabella Mushrooms** (page 322).

TUNISIAN POTATO TURNOVERS

These attractive filo triangles are layered with a spicy potato filling. When new cooks first learn the technique for making them, their eyes light up as though they have just understood a basic theorem. After that, there's no stopping them. The kitchen soon looks like a geometry workshop: lots of perfect triangles, and every one of them delicious.

Makes 16 pastries

Preparation time: 1 hour

Baking time: 15 to 20 minutes

2 cups peeled and cubed potatoes
2 cups peeled and cubed sweet potatoes
4 garlic cloves, minced or pressed
3 tablespoons plain nonfat yogurt
2 tablespoons minced scallions
1 teaspoon ground caraway
1 teaspoon ground coriander
½ teaspoon ground cumin
⅛ to ¼ teaspoon cayenne
1 to 2 tablespoons fresh lemon juice
½ teaspoon salt, or more to taste
12 sheets filo pastry, each about 12 × 17 inches
   (page 428)
3 tablespoons olive oil
whole caraway seeds (optional)

Preheat the oven to 400° (see Note).

Cook the potatoes, sweet potatoes, and garlic in water to cover until tender, 15 to 20 minutes. Drain the potatoes and thoroughly mash them by hand with the yogurt, scallions, caraway, coriander, cumin, cayenne, lemon juice, and salt until very smooth. Add more salt to taste.

Prepare a baking sheet with a light coating of oil or cooking spray or use one with a nonstick coating. Set it aside near your work area.

Place the filling, filo, oil, a pastry brush, and a clean damp towel on the counter within easy reach. Unfold the stack of filo and in one smooth motion, remove a sheet and place it flat on the counter top with one of the short sides nearest you. Brush it lightly with olive oil. Working quickly, add a second and then a third sheet, oiling each lightly. Cover the remaining stack of filo with the damp towel as you work to prevent it from drying out and becoming brittle.

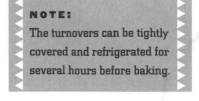

Cut lengthwise through the three oiled sheets to make four strips. Place 2 rounded tablespoons of filling on each strip, one near the bottom and one about a third of the way up. With a table knife or the back of a spoon, spread the filling to thinly cover the bottom half of each strip. Fold the lower left corner up and over diagonally so that the bottom edge is aligned with the right side. Fold straight up and then to the left. Continue to fold as you would a flag to make a small triangular pastry. Place each triangle on the baking sheet.

Repeat 3 more times until all of the filo and filling has been used and you have 16 turnovers. Brush the tops with any remaining oil and sprinkle them with whole caraway seeds, if desired (see Note).

Bake for 15 to 20 minutes, until puffed and golden. The turnovers should be served soon after removing them from the oven because the pastry loses its crispness as it sits.

PER 3.50-OZ SERVING: 97 CALORIES, 1.7 G PROTEIN, 2.9 G FAT, 15.9 G CARBOHY-DRATES, .4 G SATURATED FATTY ACIDS, .3 G POLYUNSATURATED FATTY ACIDS, 2.0 G MONOUNSATURATED FATTY ACIDS, 0 MG CHOLESTEROL, 118 MG SODIUM, 1.3 G TOTAL DIETARY FIBER

> **NOTE:**
> The turnovers can be tightly covered and refrigerated for several hours before baking.

MENU SUGGESTIONS Serve as part of a combo plate with **Spinach Artichoke Heart Dip** (page 30), crudités, and fresh tomatoes on crisp ruby lettuce or try the turnovers paired with **Golden Split Pea Soup** (page 92) or **Curried Carrot Parsnip Soup** (page 100).

SAVORY STUFFED MUSHROOMS

These seasoned bite-sized treats are perfect to serve to hungry guests when they arrive at your house for dinner. While your company enjoys instant gratification, you can finish the last-minute details of the main course. These mushrooms are satisfying and rich-flavored, yet so light everyone will have plenty of appetite for the rest of the meal. They also make excellent hors d'oeuvres for fancy parties or casual get-togethers.

1 pound mushrooms (larger ones are best for stuffing)
1 cup finely chopped onions
2 garlic cloves, minced or pressed
2 teaspoons olive oil
3 tablespoons chopped fresh basil
½ cup chopped fresh parsley
¾ cup fresh bread crumbs (page 422)
salt and ground black pepper to taste
3 tablespoons dry sherry
1 tablespoon soy sauce

Makes 16 to 20 stuffed mushrooms

Preparation time: 25 minutes

Baking time: 15 to 20 minutes

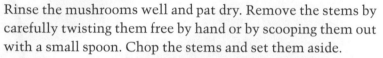

Rinse the mushrooms well and pat dry. Remove the stems by carefully twisting them free by hand or by scooping them out with a small spoon. Chop the stems and set them aside.

Preheat the oven to 450°.

In a large skillet, sauté the onions and garlic in the oil on medium heat for about 8 minutes, until golden. Stir in the chopped mushroom stems and continue to sauté for another 2 minutes. Add the basil, parsley, bread crumbs, and salt and pepper. Cook for another 2 or 3 minutes, stirring constantly, and set aside.

In a mixing bowl, combine the sherry and soy sauce. Tumble the mushroom caps in the sauce to thoroughly coat them. Fill each mushroom with the sautéed bread crumb mixture. Arrange the stuffed mushrooms in a nonstick or very lightly oiled or sprayed baking pan and bake, uncovered, for 15 to 20 minutes, until the mushrooms begin to release their juices and the filling is browned and crunchy. Serve hot.

VARIATIONS When you add the bread crumbs, herbs, and seasonings to the filling, you may also stir in ¼ cup of grated Parmesan cheese. Or try adding 3 tablespoons of finely chopped reconstituted sun-dried tomatoes for a more sophisticated, tart-sweet filling.

PER 1.40-OZ SERVING: 31 CALORIES, 1.1 G PROTEIN, .9 G FAT, 4.7 G CARBOHYDRATES, .1 G SATURATED FATTY ACIDS, .1 G POLYUNSATURATED FATTY ACIDS, .5 G MONOUNSATURATED FATTY ACIDS, 0 MG CHOLESTEROL, 92 MG SODIUM, .7 G TOTAL DIETARY FIBER

MENU SUGGESTIONS Serve with **Onion and Feta Risotto** (page 194), **Sicilian Scallop Salad** (page 304), **Italian Fish Stew** (page 299), or **Fish Steaks with Fennel** (page 290).

ROASTED GARLIC

Although traditionally served in rich French cuisine, roasted garlic is actually quite useful in low-fat cooking. We use it as a fat-free spread for bread, to thicken salad dressings, and to impart a mellow garlic flavor to almost any savory dish.

Roasted garlic is great to have on hand, so make a point of roasting some whenever you bake another dish. Don't worry if the oven temperature is lower than 375°—it will just take a little longer for the heads to soften.

2 to 4 heads garlic

Preheat the oven to 375°.

Remove some of the papery skin from the heads of garlic, but be careful not to break the cloves apart. Cut off the top ½ inch of each head. Place the heads of garlic in a small, unoiled baking dish or on a sheet of aluminum foil. Add a tablespoon of water and either cover the baking dish tightly with foil or fold the sheet of aluminum foil to form a sealed package.

Bake for 45 to 60 minutes, until the cloves are very soft to the touch. Baking time will vary depending upon the size of the heads of garlic. Let cool. Squeeze the garlic paste from the heads as needed. Sealed and refrigerated, roasted garlic will keep for at least a week.

Makes ¼ to ½ cup paste

Preparation time: 5 minutes

Baking time: 45 to 60 minutes

PER 0.90-OZ SERVING: 37 CALORIES, 1.6 G PROTEIN, .1 G FAT, 8.2 G CARBOHYDRATES, 0 G SATURATED FATTY ACIDS, .1 G POLYUNSATURATED FATTY ACIDS, 0 G MONOUNSATURATED FATTY ACIDS, 0 MG CHOLESTEROL, 4 MG SODIUM, .5 G TOTAL DIETARY FIBER

black bean and hominy frittata 49

swiss chard and tomato frittata 50

SPANISH POTATO PEPPER FRITTATA 51

spinach mushroom frittata 52

watercress omelet 53

INDIAN POTATO PANCAKES 54

ful 55

cinnamon apple crêpes 56

STICKY BUNS 58

irish soda bread 59

aafke's spicy quick bread 60

APPLESAUCE CRANBERRY MUFFINS 61

banana muffins 62

cornmeal spice muffins 63

PUMPKIN OAT MUFFINS 64

mango-banana shake 65

peach-berry shake 66

SESAME CITRUS DELIGHT 67

BREAKFAST OR BRUNCH

In most households we know of, **BREAKFAST** tends to be a rushed affair. Morning meals are eaten in shifts timed to each person's departure, and the kitchen activity bears little resemblance to the (possibly mythical) morning gatherings of a bygone era. There are days, however, when time permits some creativity in the morning and there is a chance to share the pleasures of a homemade breakfast or brunch that goes beyond toast or cold cereal. When we give benefit brunches at Moosewood, we try to create a more leisurely and home-like atmosphere in the restaurant.

Freshly baked muffins and quick breads give us double satisfaction, first when their aroma fills the kitchen and later when we enjoy these as lightly sweet treats. Aafke's Spicy Quick Bread is a sweet, Scandinavian-inspired loaf that is quite moist and keeps well. Irish Soda Bread is a naturally low-fat bread that is perfect served warm from the oven with jam and tea. And no one would ever guess that delectably rich Sticky Buns are low in fat. Commercially baked muffins, including many labeled "light" or containing "healthy" ingredients such as bran and oats, can be quite high in fat. Our low-fat muffins are made with nonfat or low-fat dairy products, and we often reduce the amount of oil and eggs generally called for in muffin recipes by adding mashed fruit or fruit purées. These purées have the additional advantage of contributing sweetness and flavor as well as moistness to baked goods.

Eggs have gotten a bum rap in recent years, but we think they may have a place in nonvegan, low-fat menus. The American Dietetic Association's current guidelines suggest that people without cholesterol problems can eat four or more egg yolks a week without ill effect, depending on what other fats are consumed. Each egg contains 15 percent of the daily requirement for protein, plus high amounts of vitamins and minerals. Egg whites contain no fat, but have the same "setting" properties as whole eggs in omelets, frittatas, and baked goods. A standard substitution is 2 egg whites for each whole egg. The frittatas that follow make generous use of egg whites and are lighter than their higher-fat counterparts, but just as flavorful, because they're crammed with other good things. Nonstick cookware (page 13) is the best bet for cooking egg dishes; you need only a little oil and the pan is easy to wash.

Of course, none of our breakfast/brunch recipes need be limited to the first meal of the day. Muffins and the other quick breads can be a snack, luncheon treat, or simple dessert and are also compatible with sandwich fillings in our breads and sandwiches chapter and with spreads in the appetizers chapter. Try Pumpkin Oat Muffins with Herbed Cottage Cheese Chèvre Spread, Irish Soda Bread with Egg Salad, or Cornmeal Spice Muffins with One Step Bean Guacamole. Ful, while perhaps an unconventional choice for breakfast in this part of the world, is a savory bean dish for any meal.

The fruit shakes can serve as appetizer soups and can also be nutritious and pleasing desserts. Indian Potato Pancakes and the frittatas make wonderful dinners. Frittatas reheat nicely in a microwave oven, and leftover plain crêpes will keep for several days in the refrigerator, to be stuffed and enjoyed for a second round.

Don't let all this talk of leisurely brunches leave you with the impression that these recipes are complicated and time-consuming. Fruit shakes and Sesame Citrus Delight can be whipped together in only 5 minutes. Ful and Watercress Omelet don't take much time either.

Other foods in this book that make good breakfast items are:

Oven "Fries" (page 326)
Herbed Cottage Cheese Chèvre Spread (page 31)
Essential Miso Soup with Tofu (page 80)
Sun-Dried Tomato Polenta Cutlets (page 236)
Apple Apricot Strudel (page 384)
Blueberry Peach Cobbler (page 383)
Pumpkin Custard (page 376)
Creamy Dairyless Rice Pudding (page 373)
breads in the Breads and Sandwiches chapter (pages 110–125)

BLACK BEAN AND HOMINY FRITTATA

This unusual frittata is interesting enough to serve to company, yet hearty enough to be everyday supper fare. Because the ingredients are mostly staples and pantry items that can be kept on hand, this is a fabulous meal to whip up on the spur of the moment.

2 cups chopped onions
2 teaspoons canola or other vegetable oil
1 green or red bell pepper, seeded and julienned
1 jalapeño or other fresh chile, seeded and minced (optional)
1½ cups canned white hominy or corn kernels
    (15-ounce can, drained)
1½ cups cooked black beans
    (16-ounce can, drained and rinsed)
2 tablespoons chopped fresh cilantro
3 whole eggs
5 egg whites
½ teaspoon salt

Fresh Tomato Salsa (page 360) or prepared salsa
nonfat sour cream or nonfat yogurt (optional)

Serves 4 to 6

Preparation time: 10 to 15 minutes

Stove-top cooking time: 30 minutes

NOTE:
The frittata-flipping technique we describe won't work well in a regular skillet without using a lot of oil. Instead, brown the bottom of the frittata on the stove top, then place under the broiler until the eggs are firm and golden on top.

Read our discussion of nonstick cookware and low-fat cooking on page 13.

Place the onions and 1 teaspoon of the oil in a 10- to 12-inch nonstick skillet (see Note). Cover and cook on medium heat, stirring occasionally, for about 5 minutes, until the onions are soft and golden. Add the bell peppers and chile and sauté on medium heat for 5 minutes. Stir in the hominy, black beans, and cilantro, cover, lower the heat, and cook for about 5 minutes, until hot. Remove the skillet from the heat.

In a large mixing bowl, beat the eggs, egg whites, and salt until fluffy. Stir the bean and hominy mixture into the eggs.

Coat the bottom of the same skillet with the remaining teaspoon of oil and return it to medium heat. When the skillet is hot, pour in the egg mixture and distribute the hominy and beans evenly. Cover and cook for 5 to 7 minutes, until the edges are firm and the bottom has browned. Place a large, flat plate or pizza pan over the skillet and flip the skillet over so that the frittata falls onto the plate. Slide the frittata back into the skillet and cook for about 5 minutes more, until the eggs are fully cooked.

Cut the frittata into wedges and serve hot or at room temperature, topped with salsa and a dollop of sour cream or yogurt.

PER 8-OZ SERVING: 187 CALORIES, 12.3 G PROTEIN, 5.3 G FAT, 22.7 G CARBOHYDRATES, 1.3 G SATURATED FATTY ACIDS, 1.5 G POLYUNSATURATED FATTY ACIDS, 1.7 G MONOUNSATURATED FATTY ACIDS, 132 MG CHOLESTEROL, 515 MG SODIUM, .9 G TOTAL DIETARY FIBER

SWISS CHARD AND TOMATO FRITTATA

Filled with vitamin-rich greens and juicy tomato slices, this flavorful frittata is a satisfying light meal for any time at all.

1 pound Swiss chard
4 garlic cloves, minced or pressed
1 cup chopped onions
2 teaspoons olive oil
6 egg whites
2 whole eggs
3 tablespoons chopped fresh basil
¼ teaspoon salt
¼ teaspoon ground black pepper
1 medium tomato, sliced
grated Parmesan cheese (optional)

Serves 4

Preparation time: 15 minutes

Cooking time: 15 to 20 minutes

NOTES: To bake, preheat the oven to 375°. Prepare a 9 × 13-inch or 10 × 12-inch baking pan with a light coating of cooking spray or oil. Pour in the Swiss chard-egg mixture, arrange the tomato slices on top, and bake for about 30 minutes, until the eggs are solid and the top is golden. Serve immediately or at room temperature.

Please see the note on page 49 for another frittata-flipping technique.

Wash the Swiss chard, remove and discard the large stems, and finely chop the leaves. In a 10- to 12-inch nonstick skillet (see Note), sauté the garlic and onions in 1 teaspoon of the oil for 3 minutes on medium heat. Add the Swiss chard, stir, cover, lower the heat, and cook for about 10 minutes. Remove the skillet from the heat and drain the Swiss chard if juicy.

In a large bowl, beat the egg whites, eggs, basil, salt, and pepper until blended. Stir in the sautéed Swiss chard.

Coat the bottom of the skillet with the remaining teaspoon of oil and return it to medium heat. When the skillet is hot, pour in the Swiss chard-egg mixture and arrange the tomato slices on top. Cover and cook for 5 to 8 minutes, until the edges are firm and the bottom is golden and beginning to brown. Place a large, flat plate or pizza pan over the skillet and flip the skillet over so that the frittata falls onto the plate. Slide the frittata back into the skillet and cook for about 5 minutes, until the eggs are fully cooked. Serve immediately or at room temperature, topped with grated Parmesan if you wish.

PER 9-OZ SERVING: 140 CALORIES, 12.6 G PROTEIN, 6.0 G FAT, 10.0 G CARBOHYDRATES, 1.4 G SATURATED FATTY ACIDS, .7 G POLYUNSATURATED FATTY ACIDS, 3.0 G MONOUNSATURATED FATTY ACIDS, 132 MG CHOLESTEROL, 445 MG SODIUM, 2.8 G TOTAL DIETARY FIBER

MENU SUGGESTIONS Serve with **Pumpkin Oat Muffins** (page 64) at breakfast or with **Oven "Fries"** (page 326), **Broiled Zucchini with Herbs** (page 333), or toasted bread with **Mushroom Pâté Almondine** (page 121) at dinner. Or serve after **New England Squash Soup** (page 96), **Giambotta** (page 263), or **Savory Stuffed Mushrooms** (page 42).

SPANISH POTATO PEPPER FRITTATA

The eggs are just able to hold together all the delicious vegetables crammed into this Spanish-style frittata, which makes a fortifying breakfast, brunch, lunch, or supper. Dress it up with toppings of salsa, low-fat sour cream, and capers and/or a few black olives.

1 large onion (about 2 cups sliced)
2 bell peppers, 1 red and 1 green
1 cubanelle or other mild fresh chile
1 pound potatoes (about 3 medium), scrubbed
2 teaspoons olive oil
½ teaspoon dried thyme
½ teaspoon salt
2 whole eggs
6 egg whites
2 tablespoons water
¼ teaspoon ground black pepper

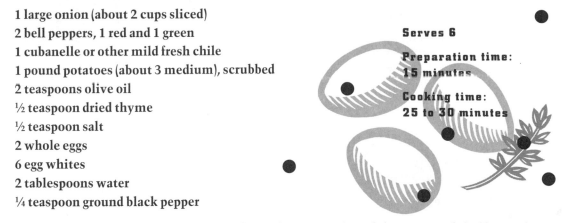

Serves 6

Preparation time:
15 minutes

Cooking time:
25 to 30 minutes

Cut off the ends of the onion. Cut it in half lengthwise, peel, and then cut each half into thin strips. Stem and seed the bell peppers and the cubanelle. Cut them into thin strips. Cut the potatoes into ⅛-inch slices.

In an 11- or 12-inch nonstick skillet, heat 1 teaspoon of the olive oil. Add the onions and potatoes and cook for 5 minutes. Add the bell peppers, cubanelle, thyme, and ¼ teaspoon of the salt. Cover and cook on medium heat, stirring occasionally, for about 15 minutes, until the potatoes are tender. Remove the skillet from the heat.

In a large bowl, whisk together the eggs, egg whites, water, remaining ¼ teaspoon of salt, and black pepper until blended. Stir the potatoes, onions, and peppers into the eggs.

Coat the bottom of the skillet with the remaining teaspoon of oil and return it to medium heat. When the skillet is hot, pour in the potato-egg mixture and distribute the vegetables evenly. Cover and cook for 5 to 8 minutes, until the edges are firm and the bottom has browned. Place a large, flat plate or pizza pan over the skillet and flip the skillet over so that the frittata falls onto the plate. Slide the frittata back into the skillet and cook for about 5 minutes more, until the eggs are fully cooked. To bake, see Note, opposite. Serve immediately or at room temperature.

PER 6-OZ SERVING: 135 CALORIES, 8.3 G PROTEIN, 3.9 G FAT, 16.7 G CARBOHYDRATES, .9 G SATURATED FATTY ACIDS, .5 G POLYUNSATURATED FATTY ACIDS, 2.0 G MONOUNSATURATED FATTY ACIDS, 88 MG CHOLESTEROL, 293 MG SODIUM, 1.8 G TOTAL DIETARY FIBER

MENU SUGGESTIONS Serve this hearty frittata with a lettuce and tomato salad dressed with **Apple Basil Dressing** (page 348) or beside **Spinach Avocado Grapefruit Salad** (page135), **Broccoli Rabe and Garlic** (page 315), or **Guacamole with Roasted Corn** (page 27).

SPINACH MUSHROOM FRITTATA

This nicely textured, very tasty frittata, featuring classic Greek flavorings, is an appetizing brunch dish that is hearty enough for supper also.

2 to 3 garlic cloves, minced or pressed
1 large onion, chopped
2 teaspoons olive oil
10 ounces mushrooms, sliced (about 4 cups)
½ teaspoon dried thyme
10 ounces spinach, stemmed and rinsed
2 whole eggs
6 egg whites
1 tablespoon fresh dill (1 teaspoon dried)
¼ teaspoon salt
¼ teaspoon ground black pepper
½ cup grated feta cheese (optional)

Serves 4

Preparation time: 15 to 20 minutes

Cooking time: 15 to 20 minutes

> **NOTE:**
> To bake, preheat the oven to 375°. Oil a 9 × 13-inch baking pan. Pour in the spinach-egg mixture and bake for about 30 minutes, until the eggs are solid and the top is golden.

In a 10- to 12-inch nonstick skillet, sauté the garlic and onions in 1 teaspoon of the olive oil on low heat for about 5 minutes. Add the mushrooms and thyme, cook for 5 minutes, and remove the skillet from the heat. Meanwhile, in a separate pot, cover and cook the spinach on low heat with just the water that clings to it from rinsing, until the spinach is just wilted. Let cool in a colander, press to remove some liquid, and chop.

In a large bowl, beat the eggs, egg whites, dill, salt, and pepper until evenly colored. Stir the spinach, mushrooms, and feta, if using, into the eggs.

Coat the bottom of the skillet with the remaining teaspoon of oil and return it to medium heat. When the skillet is hot, pour in the egg mixture. Cover and cook for 5 to 8 minutes, until the edges are firm and the bottom is golden and just beginning to brown. Place a large, flat plate or pizza pan over the skillet and flip the skillet over so that the frittata falls onto the plate. Slide the frittata back into the skillet and cook about 5 minutes more, until the eggs are fully cooked. Serve immediately or at room temperature.

PER 8-OZ SERVING: 134 CALORIES, 13.1 G PROTEIN, 6.2 G FAT, 7.9 G CARBOHYDRATES, 1.4 G SATURATED FATTY ACIDS, .8 G POLYUNSATURATED FATTY ACIDS, 3.0 G MONOUNSATURATED FATTY ACIDS, 132 MG CHOLESTEROL, 329 MG SODIUM, 2.9 G TOTAL DIETARY FIBER

MENU SUGGESTIONS Serve this frittata with **Tomato Bulgur Soup** (page 101) and **Herbed Cottage Cheese Bread** (page 31), or with **Citrus-dressed Asparagus** (page 313), **Cauliflower Agrodolce** (page 318), or **Seasoned Steamed Artichokes** (page 311), **Cucumbers Vinaigrette** (page 133), **Carrot Orange Salad** (page 134), or **Vegetables à la Grecque** (page 130).

WATERCRESS OMELET

We made a good, old-fashioned omelet that is lower in fat by using fewer egg yolks and low-fat cottage cheese instead of a richer cheese. You'll find it will satisfy omelet lovers just the same. The fresh-tasting bite of watercress is quite delicious in combination with the creamy eggs.

Serves 2

Total time: 30 to 35 minutes

2 eggs
4 egg whites
⅓ cup chopped chives or scallions
⅛ cup chopped fresh dill
¼ teaspoon salt
½ cup low-fat cottage cheese
½ cup chopped watercress
1 tablespoon freshly grated Parmesan cheese
1 tablespoon fresh lemon juice (optional)
1 teaspoon canola or other vegetable oil

Whisk together the eggs, egg whites, chives or scallions, dill, and salt until evenly colored and foamy. In a separate bowl, combine the cottage cheese, watercress, Parmesan, and lemon juice, if using, and set aside.

Heat an 8- or 9-inch nonstick skillet or a well-seasoned cast-iron skillet or omelet pan on medium heat. Add the oil and swirl to cover the bottom of the skillet. Pour in the eggs, cover, and cook for about 10 minutes. When the edges of the omelet are firm, the bottom golden, and the center solid, immediately spoon the watercress mixture onto the middle of the omelet. Using a spatula, fold half of the omelet up and over the filling, cover, and reduce the heat. After about 2 minutes, turn the omelet to brown the other side. When both sides are browned and the filling is hot, serve immediately.

PER 8-OZ SERVING: 231 CALORIES, 26.2 G PROTEIN, 11.4 G FAT, 4.4 G CARBOHY-DRATES, 3.9 G SATURATED FATTY ACIDS, 2.3 G POLYUNSATURATED FATTY ACIDS, 3.8 G MONOUNSATURATED FATTY ACIDS, 273 MG CHOLESTEROL, 823 MG SODIUM, .6 G TOTAL DIETARY FIBER

MENU SUGGESTIONS Serve to follow **Curried Carrot Parsnip Soup** (page 100) or **Spanish Potato Garlic Soup** (page 97) with **Cornmeal Spice Muffins** (page 63). Other good side dishes are **Mustard Carrots** (page 317), **Roasted Asparagus** (page 312), **Millet Pilaf** (page 182), or **Spanish Potatoes** (page 324).

INDIAN POTATO PANCAKES

Although we had already realized some of the virtues of nonstick cookware, many of us at Moosewood were sold on it when we found that we could make potato pancakes that weren't drenched in oil.

These awesome little pancakes make a nice brunch item or an appetizer, or they can serve as one part of a more complex meal. Serve them topped with a dollop of nonfat yogurt, Sesame Citrus Delight (page 67), or Mango Peach Chutney (page 362), if desired.

1½ cups grated white potatoes, well packed
1½ teaspoons garam masala (page 428) or curry powder
½ teaspoon salt
¼ cup finely chopped scallions
1 egg white, lightly beaten

**Makes eight
3-inch pancakes**

Total time: 25 minutes

Combine the potatoes, garam masala or curry, salt, scallions, and egg white. Warm a large, nonstick skillet. Drop the potato batter by a scant ¼-cup measure onto the skillet and gently flatten into a circle with a spatula. Make as many pancakes as will fit in your skillet, but leave enough room to flip them (see Note).

Cook on medium heat for about 5 minutes, or until browned. Flip the pancakes over, cover, and cook for 3 minutes on the second side. Then uncover and cook until browned, about 3 minutes.

VARIATION Replace the white potatoes with sweet potatoes and use 2 egg whites.

PER 1.80-OZ SERVING: 42 CALORIES, 1.4 G PROTEIN, .1 G FAT, 9.1 G CARBOHYDRATES, 0 G SATURATED FATTY ACIDS, 0 G POLYUNSATURATED FATTY ACIDS, 0 G MONOUNSATURATED FATTY ACIDS, 0 MG CHOLESTEROL, 161 MG SODIUM, 1.0 G TOTAL DIETARY FIBER

MENU SUGGESTIONS Begin with **Mango-Banana Shake** (page 65) and then serve the pancakes beside **Mango Coconut Cucumber Salad** (page 136), **Lentil Salad** (page 151), or a tossed salad with **Curried Mango Yogurt Dressing** (page 151).

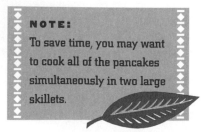

NOTE:
To save time, you may want to cook all of the pancakes simultaneously in two large skillets.

FUL

Ful, a fava bean dish simmered with garlic, olive oil, and lemon juice and traditional throughout the Middle East, North Africa, and parts of the Horn of Africa, must have as many variations as there are cooks. In Egypt, where it is considered the national dish, *ful* is eaten at all times of the day, but it is most popular for breakfast.

We often serve *Ful* with *berbere* paste, pita bread, and a side dish of yogurt or Sesame Citrus Delight (page 67). *Berbere* is a complex spice mixture available in groceries that stock Eritrean and Ethiopian foods. *Harissa* could be used as a substitute. Or, to make your own *berbere*, see page 421 or follow the recipe on page 509 of *Sundays at Moosewood Restaurant*, then mix the *berbere* with enough water to make a paste and serve it on the side of the *Ful*. It is delicious and very spicy hot.

We strongly recommend using fava beans imported from the Middle East, sometimes called *ful medamas*, which are smaller and are more appropriate for this recipe.

2 teaspoons olive oil
1 cup finely chopped onions
5 garlic cloves, minced or pressed
¼ teaspoon salt
½ teaspoon dried mint
1 teaspoon ground cumin
1 tomato, chopped (about 1 cup)
1¾ cups fava beans (15½-ounce can, drained and rinsed)
1 tablespoon fresh lemon juice, or more to taste
5 tablespoons chopped fresh parsley

Serves 2 to 4

Total time: 35 minutes

Warm the oil in a saucepan. Add the onions, garlic, and salt, cover, and cook on low heat, stirring occasionally, until the onions are soft, about 7 minutes. Add the mint and cumin and sauté for another 2 minutes, stirring constantly. Stir in the tomatoes, cover, and cook for 5 minutes. Add the beans and simmer, uncovered, for 5 minutes, stirring occasionally. Stir in the lemon juice and parsley. Serve hot or at room temperature.

PER 6.50-OZ SERVING: 122 CALORIES, 6.6 G PROTEIN, 3.0 G FAT, 18.9 G CARBOHYDRATES, .4 G SATURATED FATTY ACIDS,
.4 G POLYUNSATURATED FATTY ACIDS, 1.8 G MONOUNSATURATED FATTY ACIDS, 0 MG CHOLESTEROL, 608 MG SODIUM,
1.2 G TOTAL DIETARY FIBER

MENU SUGGESTIONS Use as part of a Middle Eastern combination plate with **Tunisian Potato Turnovers** (page 40) or **Greek Spinach Rice Balls** (page 35) and with **Seasoned Steamed Artichokes** (page 311) or **Carrot Orange Salad** (page 134). For a flavorful luncheon, serve with **Tomato Bulgur Soup** (page 101). Or offer as an appetizer before **Bulgur with Savory Greens** (page 178), **Swiss Chard Rolls with mushroom filling** (page 252), or **Mediterranean Couscous Salad** (page 144).

CINNAMON APPLE CRÊPES

These versatile, fluffy crêpes, with their warm, not-too-sweet apple and cheese filling, can make a very special centerpiece for a breakfast, brunch, dessert, or lunch. The filling takes only minutes to make, and if the crêpes are prepared ahead, the assembly and baking can take less than 30 minutes.

Crêpes can be frozen for a month or more, but remember to place a piece of wax paper between every crêpe so that you can easily separate them later. With the crêpes ready and waiting, you can make different fillings for several meals. Try one of our favorite savory fillings, Mushroom Spinach Crêpes (page 234), or create fillings of your own.

Serves 5 or 6

Makes fourteen to sixteen 7-inch crêpes

Total time: 45 minutes

CRÊPES
¾ cup unbleached white flour
½ teaspoon salt
½ teaspoon baking powder
1 whole egg
2 egg whites
1 cup evaporated skimmed milk
¼ teaspoon pure vanilla extract

FILLING
1½ cups low-fat cottage cheese*
1 to 2 tablespoons sugar
1 teaspoon freshly grated lemon peel
¼ teaspoon salt
1½ cups peeled and grated apple,
    firmly packed (1 large apple)
½ teaspoon ground cinnamon

If you prefer, you can omit the cottage cheese and increase the amount of grated apple to 3 cups.

Sift together the flour, salt, and baking powder. In a blender or food processor, whirl the dry ingredients with the egg, egg whites, evaporated skimmed milk, and vanilla for about 30 seconds until well blended. If necessary, stop once and scrape the sides of the blender or processor with a rubber spatula.

Heat a nonstick 8-inch skillet or crêpe pan on medium-high heat (see Note). Ladle about ⅛ cup of the batter into the skillet—use just enough to thinly coat the bottom of the pan. Tilt the pan in all directions to spread the batter evenly. Cook each crêpe until the underside is slightly browned and the top looks dry, ½ to 1 minute. Lift the edge of the crêpe with a spatula, take hold of it with the fingertips of both hands (being careful not to burn yourself), flip it over in one fluid motion, and cook the other side for 15 to 20 seconds, or until just light brown. Remove the crêpe to a platter.

Continue making crêpes and stacking them on the platter until no batter is left. The cooked crêpes won't stick together! If, however, the crêpe batter begins to stick to the cooking pan, try using a light coating of cooking spray. Fill and bake immediately, or freeze for future use.

Preheat the oven to 350°.

In a food processor or blender, purée the cottage cheese, sugar, lemon peel, and salt until very smooth. Transfer the purée to a bowl and thoroughly mix in the grated apple and cinnamon.

Place about 3 tablespoons of the filling on the lower half of each crêpe, roll it up, and lay it, seam side down, on a baking dish prepared with cooking spray. Cover and bake for about 15 minutes, until hot.

PER 6-OZ SERVING: 184 CALORIES, 14.9 G PROTEIN, 2.5 G FAT, 25.2 G CARBOHYDRATES, 1.1 G SATURATED FATTY ACIDS, .3 G POLYUNSATURATED FATTY ACIDS, .8 G MONOUNSATURATED FATTY ACIDS, 50 MG CHOLESTEROL, 634 MG SODIUM, 1.3 G TOTAL DIETARY FIBER

NOTE:
If you have two crêpe pans or skillets, using both pans simultaneously to cook the crêpes will significantly reduce your preparation time for this dish.

STICKY BUNS

Glazed sticky buns in a low-fat cookbook—even *we* never dreamed of such a thing. But that's what happens when a cook has a little leftover dough and doesn't want to waste it! Moosewood's Sara Robbins spontaneously made a tiny cinnamon-sugar bun with some extra dough scraps and popped it into the oven with the Buttermilk Rolls she was testing. The rolls passed the test, but the cinnamon-sugar bun was just as much of a hit. So she whipped up a little clear glaze, and there you have it—a variation that was so good we had to honor it with its own page.

BUNS
1 recipe Buttermilk Rolls (page 115)
1 cup packed brown sugar
2 teaspoons ground cinnamon

CLEAR GLAZE
1 cup confectioners' sugar
1 tablespoon pure vanilla extract
2 tablespoons skim or 1% milk

Makes twenty-four 3-inch sticky buns

Preparation time: 15 minutes, once the dough is formed

Rising time: 45 minutes

Baking time: 15 to 20 minutes

Prepare two 9-inch round cake pans or two 10-inch pie pans with a light coating of oil or cooking spray. Set aside.

Divide the dough into two equal parts. On a lightly floured surface, use a rolling pin to flatten each portion into a 9 × 12-inch rectangle. Evenly spread ½ cup brown sugar on each rectangle and sprinkle with 1 teaspoon of cinnamon. Beginning at one long edge, use both hands and firm steady pressure to roll up each rectangle jelly roll fashion to form two logs. Slice each log into 12 equal pieces.

Arrange 12 of the buns, cut side down, in each round cake or pie pan. Don't worry if the buns don't quite fill the pans or if some of the buns are touching one another. Cover the sticky buns with a damp towel and allow to rise in a warm, draft-free place for 45 minutes.

When the buns have almost finished rising, preheat the oven to 350°. When completely risen, bake for 15 to 20 minutes, until golden brown. Remove from the oven and set aside.

While the buns bake, whisk together the glaze ingredients in a small bowl. Pour the glaze over the hot sticky buns—it will bubble up and soften the dough slightly as it glazes. Serve the sticky buns right from the pan or transfer to a serving platter. Cover tightly with aluminum foil or plastic wrap to store for later.

PER 2-OZ SERVING: 154 CALORIES, 2.9 G PROTEIN, 2.2 G FAT, 30.8 G CARBOHYDRATES, .4 G SATURATED FATTY ACIDS, 1.1 G POLYUNSATURATED FATTY ACIDS, .5 G MONOUNSATURATED FATTY ACIDS, 1 MG CHOLESTEROL, 202 MG SODIUM, 1.3 G TOTAL DIETARY FIBER

IRISH SODA BREAD

Irish hospitality just wouldn't be the same without fresh bread and strong, delicious tea. In many homes in Ireland, breadmaking is still an everyday affair. Almost every town's grocery store has fresh loaves of local bread for sale each day—if you arrive early, they're often unwrapped and still warm!

Always ready to be sociable at the drop of a hat, the Irish have perfected a number of quick breads. Here's our low-fat Irish soda bread, a rustic, hearty loaf that is sweet with currants. Serve it warm for brunch or afternoon tea—it's best eaten the same day.

1½ cups unbleached white flour
1½ cups whole wheat pastry flour
1 teaspoon salt
1 teaspoon baking soda
½ teaspoon baking powder
2 tablespoons packed brown sugar
2 tablespoons cold butter, cut into pieces
1 egg white
1 cup buttermilk
1 cup currants

Makes one 9-inch round loaf

Preparation time: 10 minutes

Baking time: 45 minutes

Preheat the oven to 375°.

Prepare a baking sheet with cooking spray or a light coating of oil.

In a large mixing bowl, sift together the white flour, whole wheat flour, salt, baking soda, and baking powder. Thoroughly mix in the brown sugar. Using a pastry cutter, two knives, or a food processor, cut the butter pieces into the flour until the mixture is crumbly and resembles coarse meal.

In a separate bowl, beat the egg white until frothy. Add the buttermilk and currants. Pour the buttermilk mixture into the dry ingredients, stirring just until the dough is evenly moistened; the dough will be very soft. Turn it out onto a lightly floured board and, with floured hands, gently knead for just 30 to 45 seconds—overkneading will toughen the bread.

Mound the dough into a dome about 9 inches across on the baking sheet. With a sharp knife, cut an X about ½ inch deep in the center of the loaf. Bake for 45 minutes, or until the crust is firm to the touch and golden brown. Serve immediately.

VARIATION Replace the butter with 2 tablespoons of canola or other vegetable oil. Stir the oil into the buttermilk mixture just before you combine the wet and dry ingredients. It's hard to taste any difference between the oil and butter versions of the bread, although the loaf made with oil is a wee bit more dense.

PER 2-OZ SERVING: 146 CALORIES, 4.2 G PROTEIN, 2.2 G FAT, 29.0 G CARBOHYDRATES, 1.2 G SATURATED FATTY ACIDS, .2 G POLYUNSATURATED FATTY ACIDS, .6 G MONOUNSATURATED FATTY ACIDS, 5 MG CHOLESTEROL, 254 MG SODIUM, 2.6 G TOTAL DIETARY FIBER

AAFKE'S SPICY QUICK BREAD

Aafke Steenhuis, a friend of ours who comes from the Netherlands, now lives in Ithaca and cooks "fusion" food with the best of them. This recipe is adapted from one of Aafke's favorites, which is probably Finnish in origin. We've replaced the butter in the original recipe with prune butter and the result is a moist, dark, sweet, and spicy bread that is very low in fat. Is the bread better with the optional oil? We're about equally divided yea or nay, so we're leaving that decision to you.

Aafke's Spicy Quick Bread is a good snack or even a dessert. We like to serve thin slices spread with Neufchâtel.

DRY INGREDIENTS

2½ cups unbleached white flour
½ cup brown sugar
1½ teaspoons baking soda, sifted
1 teaspoon baking powder
1 teaspoon ground cinnamon
½ teaspoon ground cloves
½ teaspoon ground cardamom
½ teaspoon ground coriander
¼ teaspoon salt

Makes 1 loaf

Preparation time: 10 minutes

Baking time: 50 to 60 minutes

WET INGREDIENTS

1½ cups buttermilk
½ cup prune butter or prune purée (see instructions, page 63)
2 tablespoons canola or other vegetable oil (optional)

Preheat the oven to 350°.

Prepare a 9 × 5 × 3-inch loaf pan with a light coating of cooking spray or oil.

Stir together the dry ingredients in a large bowl. In a separate bowl, combine the wet ingredients. Add the wet ingredients to the dry ingredients and stir until well mixed.

Spoon the batter into the loaf pan and bake for about 1 hour, until the top is firm to the touch and a knife inserted in the center comes out clean. Tip out onto a wire rack to cool.

PER 2-OZ SERVING: 113 CALORIES, 2.8 G PROTEIN, .4 G FAT, 24.7 G CARBOHYDRATES, .2 G SATURATED FATTY ACIDS, .1 G POLYUNSATURATED FATTY ACIDS, .1 G MONOUNSATURATED FATTY ACIDS, 1 MG CHOLESTEROL, 134 MG SODIUM, 1.0 G TOTAL DIETARY FIBER

APPLESAUCE CRANBERRY MUFFINS

Unsweetened applesauce gives these muffins a hint of sweetness and a sumptuous, moist texture that makes them especially popular in lunchboxes or picnic baskets as well as on the breakfast table.

Makes 12 muffins

**Preparation time:
20 minutes**

**Baking time:
20 to 25 minutes**

2 cups unbleached white flour
1 tablespoon baking powder
½ teaspoon salt
½ teaspoon ground cinnamon
¼ teaspoon nutmeg
1 egg
1 egg white
½ cup evaporated skimmed milk
2 tablespoons canola or other vegetable oil
⅓ cup packed brown sugar
¾ cup applesauce
½ cup dried cranberries

Preheat the oven to 400°.

Prepare a standard muffin tin with paper liners, cooking spray, or a light coating of oil.

In a large bowl, sift together the flour, baking powder, salt, cinnamon, and nutmeg. In another bowl, lightly beat the whole egg with the egg white. Stir in the evaporated skimmed milk, oil, brown sugar, and applesauce. Fold the wet ingredients into the flour mixture just until combined. Gently fold in the dried cranberries.

Spoon the batter into the prepared muffin tin and bake for 20 to 25 minutes, or until a toothpick inserted in the center of a muffin comes out clean and dry. Cool in the tin for 5 minutes and run a knife around the edge of each muffin before tipping it out of the tin.

PER 2.30-OZ SERVING: 139 CALORIES, 3.7 G PROTEIN, 3.1 G FAT, 24.2 G CARBOHY-DRATES, .5 G SATURATED FATTY ACIDS, 1.5 G POLYUNSATURATED FATTY ACIDS, .8 G MONOUNSATURATED FATTY ACIDS, 22 MG CHOLESTEROL, 214 MG SODIUM, 1.1 G TOTAL DIETARY FIBER

BANANA MUFFINS

Bananas lend moistness to this fragrant, delicious, low-fat muffin. If you would like a completely fat-free muffin, try the variation, which is quite tasty for a muffin without oil or eggs but not as rich or light in texture as the original recipe.

Makes 12 muffins

**Preparation time:
10 to 15 minutes**

**Baking time:
20 to 25 minutes**

1 cup unbleached white flour
¼ cup packed brown sugar
½ teaspoon baking soda
1 teaspoon baking powder
½ teaspoon ground cinnamon
¼ teaspoon nutmeg
1 cup rolled oats
1 egg white
1 egg
2 tablespoons canola or other vegetable oil
1 cup mashed ripe bananas (about 2 bananas)
½ cup plain nonfat yogurt
½ cup raisins or currants

Preheat the oven to 400°.

Prepare a muffin tin with paper liners, cooking spray, or a very light coating of oil.

In a large bowl, sift together the flour, brown sugar, baking soda, baking powder, cinnamon, and nutmeg. Whirl the oats in a blender until they reach the consistency of cornmeal; you should have about ¾ cup of processed oats. Stir them into the dry ingredients. In another bowl, beat the egg white for 3 minutes until foamy and increased in volume but not stiff. Stir in the egg, oil, mashed bananas, yogurt, and raisins or currants. Fold the wet ingredients into the flour mixture just until combined.

Spoon the batter into the muffin tin and bake for 20 to 25 minutes, until a toothpick inserted in the center of a muffin comes out clean and dry. Cool in the tin for 5 minutes, loosen each muffin by running a knife around the edge, and then tip out onto a rack to cool completely.

VARIATION For a nonfat banana muffin, use 2 well-beaten egg whites in place of the whole egg and egg white and omit the oil.

PER 2.50-OZ SERVING: 171 CALORIES, 4.8 G PROTEIN, 3.9 G FAT, 30.2 G CARBOHY-
DRATES, .7 G SATURATED FATTY ACIDS, 1.8 G POLYUNSATURATED FATTY ACIDS,
1.0 G MONOUNSATURATED FATTY ACIDS, 22 MG CHOLESTEROL, 68 MG SODIUM,
2.3 G TOTAL DIETARY FIBER

CORNMEAL SPICE MUFFINS

Prunes are the "mystery" ingredient in these dark, spicy-sweet muffins.

1 cup unbleached white flour
½ teaspoon baking soda
1 teaspoon baking powder
½ teaspoon salt
½ teaspoon ground ginger
¼ teaspoon ground allspice
½ teaspoon ground cinnamon
1 cup cornmeal
1 egg
1 egg white
¾ cup prune purée *
½ cup plain nonfat yogurt
¼ cup skim milk
¼ cup pure maple syrup
2 tablespoons canola or other vegetable oil

Makes 12 muffins

Preparation time: 15 to 20 minutes, using prepared prune purée

Baking time: 20 to 25 minutes

Use a commercial prune purée (often available in the baby food section of the supermarket) or make your own by simmering 1 cup of pitted prunes in ½ cup of orange juice on very low heat for 10 minutes, stirring occasionally, until soft. Purée in a blender or food processor.

Preheat the oven to 400°.

Prepare a standard muffin tin with paper liners, cooking spray, or light coating of oil.

In a large bowl, sift together the flour, baking soda, baking powder, salt, ginger, allspice, and cinnamon. Stir in the cornmeal. In another bowl, lightly beat the whole egg with the egg white. Stir in the prune purée, yogurt, skim milk, maple syrup, and oil. Fold the wet ingredients into the dry ingredients until just combined.

Spoon the batter into the prepared muffin tin and bake for 20 to 25 minutes, or until a toothpick inserted in the center of a muffin comes out clean and dry. Cool in the tins for 5 minutes, loosen each muffin by running a knife around the edge, and then tip out onto a rack to cool completely.

PER 2.40-OZ SERVING: 141 CALORIES, 3.8 G PROTEIN, 3.3 G FAT, 24.1 G CARBOHYDRATES, .5 G SATURATED FATTY ACIDS, 1.6 G POLYUNSATURATED FATTY ACIDS, .9 G MONOUNSATURATED FATTY ACIDS, 22 MG CHOLESTEROL, 168 MG SODIUM, 1.7 G TOTAL DIETARY FIBER

PUMPKIN OAT MUFFINS

Who would have imagined the marriage of apricots and pumpkin could be so good? These muffins are wonderfully chewy thanks to the oats. If you decide to make your own pumpkin, squash, or sweet potato purée, just boil the peeled ½-inch cubes in water until tender, drain, and purée in a food processor or blender. Making your own purée will add about 20 minutes to the preparation time.

1¼ cups unbleached white flour
1 tablespoon baking powder
½ teaspoon salt
¼ teaspoon ground cinnamon
1 cup rolled oats
1 egg
1 egg white
¾ cup pumpkin, winter squash, or sweet potato purée*
¾ cup evaporated skimmed milk
½ cup unsweetened pineapple juice
2 tablespoons canola or other vegetable oil
¼ cup packed brown sugar
4 to 5 tablespoons apricot preserves

Makes 12 muffins

Preparation time: 15 to 20 minutes

Baking time: 20 to 25 minutes

Small jars of pure squash or sweet potato purée can often be found in the baby food section of the supermarket. We have only been able to find large cans of pure cooked pumpkin, so if you use canned pumpkin, you may just have to save the rest for a pumpkin pie!

Preheat the oven to 400°.

Prepare a standard muffin tin with paper liners, cooking spray, or a light coating of oil.

In a large bowl, sift together the flour, baking powder, salt, and cinnamon. Whirl the oats in a blender until they reach the consistency of cornmeal and add them to the flour mixture. In another bowl, lightly beat the whole egg with the egg white. Stir in the pumpkin purée, evaporated skimmed milk, pineapple juice, oil, and brown sugar. Fold the wet ingredients into the dry ingredients just until combined.

Spoon the batter into the prepared muffin tin and dot the center of each muffin with a scant teaspoon of apricot preserves. Bake for 20 to 25 minutes, or until a toothpick inserted in the center of a muffin comes out clean and dry. Cool in the tins for 5 minutes, loosen each muffin by running a knife around the edge, and then tip out onto a rack to cool completely.

PER 3-OZ SERVING: 170 CALORIES, 5.4 G PROTEIN, 3.9 G FAT, 28.9 G CARBOHYDRATES, .7 G SATURATED FATTY ACIDS, 1.8 G POLYUNSATURATED FATTY ACIDS, 1.1 G MONOUNSATURATED FATTY ACIDS, 23 MG CHOLESTEROL, 200 MG SODIUM, 1.8 G TOTAL DIETARY FIBER

MANGO-BANANA SHAKE

Enjoyable any time of the day, this shake could be a quick breakfast, a brunch appetizer, a refreshing reward after a workout at the gym, or a summertime after-theater indulgence. As a cold soup, it also makes a delectable first course for a luncheon or a quick light dessert. Kids love it. In fact, it can be frozen in Popsicle forms and enjoyed weeks later.

1 large ripe mango, peeled and cut
   into chunks (page 431)

2 ripe bananas

2 cups orange juice

½ cup plain nonfat yogurt

⅛ teaspoon ground cardamom

¼ cup pure maple syrup (optional)

Serves 4

Total time: 15 minutes

In a blender or food processor, purée the mango, bananas, orange juice, yogurt, and cardamom until smooth. Taste the shake and if you would like it a bit sweeter, add a little of the maple syrup at a time until it's right for you; how much you use will depend upon the ripeness of the fruits and your personal preference.

PER 9-OZ SERVING: 188 CALORIES, 3.3 G PROTEIN, .7 G FAT, 44.9 G CARBOHYDRATES, .2 G SATURATED FATTY ACIDS, .1 G POLYUNSATURATED FATTY ACIDS, .1 G MONOUNSATURATED FATTY ACIDS, 1 MG CHOLESTEROL, 26 MG SODIUM, 2.1 G TOTAL DIETARY FIBER

MENU SUGGESTIONS Serve as a breakfast drink with toasted **Brown Bread** (page 111) or **Cornmeal Spice Muffins** (page 63). Or serve before or after **Sweet Potato and Black Bean Burrito** (page 172), **Seitan Fajitas** (page 232), or **Lentil Sambar** (page 166).

PEACH-BERRY SHAKE

This is a luxuriously smooth breakfast drink that can be quickly prepared. We have known Moosewood's own David Hirsch to serve this in tall glasses garnished with paper parasols, elegant twists of lime peel, and vibrant edible flowers (or plastic palm fronds in a pinch).

Serves 4

**Total time:
10 to 15 minutes**

2½ cups frozen peach slices or 1½ cups
   fresh slices
1 cup ripe fresh or frozen strawberries, stemmed
1 cup plain nonfat yogurt
¼ cup pure maple syrup or honey
⅛ teaspoon nutmeg
1 tablespoon fresh lime juice (optional)

Combine the peaches, strawberries, yogurt, maple syrup or honey, nutmeg, and lime juice, if using, in a blender or food processor and purée until smooth and creamy. Serve at once or chill until serving time.

PER 9-OZ SERVING: 131 CALORIES, 4.2 G PROTEIN, .3 G FAT, 30.0 G CARBOHY-DRATES, .1 G SATURATED FATTY ACIDS, .1 G POLYUNSATURATED FATTY ACIDS, .1 G MONOUNSATURATED FATTY ACIDS, 1 MG CHOLESTEROL, 45 MG SODIUM, 3.1 G TOTAL DIETARY FIBER

MENU SUGGESTIONS Serve with **Banana Muffins** (page 62) and **Watercress Omelet** (page 53) for brunch. Or offer as an appetizer or dessert for **Curried Sweet Potato Roti** (page 230), **Thai Fried Rice** (page 190), or **Caribbean Pigeon Pea Salad** (page 142).

SESAME CITRUS DELIGHT

Moosewood's Maureen Vivino remembers eating this treat with her friends Jim Oden and Arlene Nies on many a hot summer afternoon on their front porch. At the time, both Maureen and Jim were trying to reduce their ice cream intake from a habitual three dishes a day to something a tad more moderate and healthy.

In the beginning, it was a hardship to give up years of contented attachment to ice cream, but Sesame Citrus Delight ladled on freshly-picked berries helped ease the transition. Covered and refrigerated, it will keep until several days after the expiration date stamped on the yogurt container.

1 cup plain yogurt
1 tablespoon toasted sesame seeds*
2 tablespoons honey
1 teaspoon freshly grated orange peel
1 teaspoon freshly grated lemon peel
⅛ teaspoon salt

Makes 1½ cups

Total time: 5 minutes

*Toast sesame seeds on an unoiled baking tray in a conventional or toaster oven at 350° for 2 to 3 minutes, until fragrant and golden brown.

Combine the yogurt, sesame seeds, honey, orange and lemon peels, and salt in a bowl and mix thoroughly.

PER 1-OZ SERVING: 31 CALORIES, 1.5 G PROTEIN, .5 G FAT, 5.6 G CARBOHYDRATES, .1 G SATURATED FATTY ACIDS, .2 G POLYUNSATURATED FATTY ACIDS, .2 G MONOUNSATURATED FATTY ACIDS, 0 MG CHOLESTEROL, 48 MG SODIUM, .1 G TOTAL DIETARY FIBER

MENU SUGGESTIONS Serve on fresh strawberries, raspberries, peaches, or cherries, or any combination of your favorite fruits, or cover and chill for at least 30 minutes and then serve in small glass custard cups alone or topped with fruit. Sesame Citrus Delight is also good mixed with granola for a quick breakfast.

basic vegetable stock 73

garlic broth 74

KONBU DASHI 75

shiitake dashi 76

southeast asian vegetable stock 77

TROPICAL GAZPACHO 78

chilled beet and buttermilk soup 79

essential miso soup with tofu 80

ASIAN NOODLE SOUP 81

cream of green vegetable soup 82

spring soup 84

HARIRA 85

minestrone genoa 86

vietnamese hot and sour soup 87

JAPANESE SOBA AND VEGETABLE SOUP 88

korean vegetable noodle soup 89

cream of cauliflower soup 90

CREAMY POTATO KALE SOUP 91

golden split pea soup 92

orzo and pea soup 93

DRIED MUSHROOM SOUP WITH BARLEY 94

new england squash soup 96

spanish potato garlic soup 97

CARBONADA 98

catalan potato lima soup 99

curried carrot parsnip soup 100

TOMATO BULGUR SOUP 101

southwestern corn and potato soup 102

basque white bean soup 103

SAVANNAH BEANS AND GREENS SOUP 104

callaloo 105

Homemade **SOUP** is probably the oldest, most traditional, and most universal one-pot meal, one that has unfortunately become a rare offering. Requiring no more than a few ingredients on hand, a large heavy pot, and very little time, preparing soup is a satisfying and creative way to spend time in the kitchen. At Moosewood, we make soups from adaptations of classic recipes, from leftovers, from impulse and whim. Whether it is served as a quickly prepared, nutritious, low-fat meal in a bowl or as the first course of a special dinner, there is no reason why soup made from scratch should remain an endangered species. A beautiful soup, one that looks fresh and colorful with a savory, sweet, or spicy aroma, will entice the appetite and enhance the enjoyment of any meal.

Because many low-fat soups, especially brothy ones, begin with a good stock, we've included several different stock recipes in this book. Stock adds nutritious water-soluble vitamins and deepens and enriches your soups. With full-flavored stock, you don't need to sauté in oil to have a tasty soup, an important consideration in low-fat cooking. Although an almost instant stock can be made from vegetable bouillon cubes, an easy, basic, all-purpose homemade stock can be quickly made from a few chopped vegetables such as carrots, onions, garlic, potatoes, parsley, summer squash, and other kitchen snippings. Avoid strong-flavored vegetables from the brassica family such as cauliflower, broccoli, cabbage, Brussels sprouts, bok choy, and mustard greens. Simmer the vegetables in water and then strain; store the stock in the refrigerator or freeze it in one-quart containers for convenient later use. Specialty stocks, such as Konbu Dashi, Shiitake Dashi, and Southeast Asian Vegetable Stock, are helpful in creating the authentic flavor of certain ethnic cuisines. We've found dried shiitake and konbu to be valuable in creating low-fat soups in general. Try these dashis and you'll be pleasantly surprised how quickly and easily you can prepare a rich, flavorful broth for soup made with whatever vegetables you have on hand.

In our general soup-making method, we begin by sweating the onions, garlic, and spices and then add the root vegetables, which cook slowly and hold their shape well. Next we add watery vegetables like squash and tomatoes, along with more stock or liquid. Greens, peas, and fresh beans and herbs are added at the end to retain their color and texture. Delicate, leafy basil, cilantro, dill, parsley, and chives should be tossed into the pot just before serving. Pesto, miso, lemon juice, and yogurt are good last-minute flavor enhancers that can add just the right finishing touch.

Quick, low-fat soups can be made by puréeing smooth-textured vegetables such as potatoes, sweet potatoes, yams, squash, or beans and blending with a little stock or other liquid and spices or herbs. Buttermilk or evaporated skimmed milk adds richness to Cream of Cauliflower Soup, Cream of Green Vegetable Soup, and Creamy

Potato Kale Soup. As this book goes to press, we've begun to experiment with a new technique for creating "creamy" low-fat vegan soups that uses dry rolled oats. See page 10 in the Going Lower section for details.

Try using fruit juices in puréed root vegetable soups, such as Curried Carrot Parsnip Soup, as well as in chilled fruit soups. For an interesting smooth-chunky texture, purée just a portion of a bean soup, such as Basque White Bean Soup, and recombine with the remainder of the soup. Give your soup extra texture and color with garnishes—a sprig of cilantro in Catalan Potato Lima Soup, basil in Creamy Potato Kale Soup, or chewy soaked dried mushrooms in New England Squash Soup.

To round out a pot-of-soup meal, be sure to include a good, crusty bread or fresh, hot muffins and a salad or side dish. Serve the steaming soup in bowls warmed in the oven. Be sure to make enough soup to enjoy leftovers a few days later when the flavors have melded and mellowed. A meal of good, homemade, richly flavored, yet low-fat soup is a tradition to revive and savor any day of the week, any season of the year.

BASIC VEGETABLE STOCK

While it's true that decent vegetable stock is now readily available in the supermarket, there is nothing quite like a homemade stock for enhancing the flavor of soups and stews. It only takes minutes to prepare and can cook while you make your meal, visit with family or friends, or just relax.

Here is a basic recipe that you can vary according to the vegetables available in your garden or refrigerator. The only vegetables to avoid are tomatoes, eggplants, bell peppers, asparagus, and all of those in the cabbage family, such as broccoli, cauliflower, and Brussels sprouts. If you scrub the vegetables, there is no need to peel them.

Makes 2 quarts

Preparation time: 15 minutes

Cooking time: 45 to 60 minutes

2 medium onions, peeled and quartered
2 medium sweet potatoes, thickly sliced
3 garlic cloves
2 large white potatoes, thickly sliced
2 celery stalks, coarsely chopped
2 fresh parsley sprigs
1 bay leaf
6 peppercorns
4 allspice berries
10 cups water

Combine all of the ingredients in a large soup pot, bring to a boil, then lower the heat, cover, and simmer for 45 minutes to an hour. Strain the stock through a colander, pressing out as much liquid as possible; discard or compost the solids. Covered and refrigerated, this vegetable stock will keep for 3 or 4 days.

PER 8-OZ SERVING: 78 CALORIES, 1.5 G PROTEIN, .2 G FAT, 18.1 G CARBOHYDRATES, 0 G SATURATED FATTY ACIDS, .1 G POLYUNSATURATED FATTY ACIDS, 0 G MONO-UNSATURATED FATTY ACIDS, 0 MG CHOLESTEROL, 12 MG SODIUM, 1.9 G TOTAL DIETARY FIBER

GARLIC BROTH

Whether or not garlic actually delivers all of the health benefits attributed to it, it does satisfy powerful cravings. Here garlic, its rough edges made smooth by roasting, becomes a seductive elixir with a pervasive, intoxicating aroma and flavor.

Although Spanish or French cuisines, in which garlic soups abound, would never add Japanese miso to the broth, we think that garlic and miso are a perfect partnership: Miso has its own wide reputation as a health tonic and it makes the broth taste even better. Any type of miso works, but we usually favor a combination of full-flavored dark miso and a mellow light miso.

The basic Garlic Broth is easily prepared. If you're making Roasted Garlic (page 43), put an extra garlic head in the oven to use for this recipe. While the garlic roasts, prepare the ingredients for Orzo and Pea Soup (page 93), Spanish Potato Garlic Soup (page 97), or Asian Noodle Soup (page 81), and in less than a half hour, you'll have a big pot of soup that's *much* better than any you can buy in a can or a box. Stale bread is the traditional addition to garlic broth, but you could easily cook some Tofu Vegetable Dumplings (page 38) in it. The broth is also a delicious cooking liquid for rice or other grains.

1 large whole head garlic (about 20 cloves)
¼ cup miso (see Note)
3 cups water
3 cups Basic Vegetable Stock (page 73) or
    canned vegetable broth (see Note)

Makes 6 cups

Total time: 45 minutes

Preheat a toaster oven or, if you don't have one, a conventional oven to 400°. The toaster oven works fine and saves energy.

Cut off the stem end of the garlic head, break it into cloves, and peel. Bake the garlic on an unoiled pie plate for 15 to 20 minutes, until golden but not browned. In a blender on high speed, purée the roasted garlic, miso, and water until smooth. Combine with the stock or broth and gently heat.

PER 8-OZ SERVING: 48 CALORIES, 1.8 G PROTEIN, .7 G FAT, 9.4 G CARBOHYDRATES, .1 G SATURATED FATTY ACIDS, .4 G POLYUNSATURATED FATTY ACIDS, .1 G MONOUNSATURATED FATTY ACIDS, 0 MG CHOLESTEROL, 358 MG SODIUM, 1.7 G TOTAL DIETARY FIBER

NOTES:

The color of the broth will vary depending upon the miso you use. For a light, golden broth—good for a risotto—use a light, beige-colored miso. For a dark broth that mimics the color of beef broth—good for stews —use red barley or dark soy miso.

We recommend Pritikin low-sodium, nonfat vegetable broth.

KONBU DASHI

"Dashi" means stock or broth in Japanese and is the ingredient that gives many of that country's dishes their subtle but distinctive flavor. Dashi is commonly made from *konbu*, dried kelp, often with the addition of flakes of dried bonito, a fish in the mackerel family. Dried shiitake mushrooms also make a flavorful dashi (page 76).

Makes about 3½ cups

Total time: 10 minutes

2 six-inch pieces konbu (¼ ounce) (page 430)
4 cups cold water

Combine the konbu and water in a saucepan. Slowly bring the konbu and water to a boil, uncovered, on medium-low heat. Lower the heat, cover, and simmer for 10 minutes. Remove the konbu and either discard it or save it for use in another dish. The dashi is ready to use immediately or can be refrigerated for up to 1 week.

VARIATION For a richer dashi, after the konbu has simmered for 10 minutes, add ½ cup of dried bonito flakes to the pot. Simmer for 1 minute. Place a sieve or colander inside a large pot and strain the dashi to remove the konbu and bonito flakes. Konbu-Bonito Dashi is especially delicious in a simple miso soup.

PER 12-OZ SERVING: 1 CALORIE, 0 G PROTEIN, 0 G FAT, .2 G CARBOHYDRATES, 0 G SATURATED FATTY ACIDS, 0 G POLYUNSATURATED FATTY ACIDS, 0 G MONOUN-SATURATED FATTY ACIDS, 0 MG CHOLESTEROL, 5 MG SODIUM, 0 G TOTAL DIETARY FIBER

SHIITAKE DASHI

This is an earthier, richer version of the essential Japanese stock. The seasonings in this dashi not only make the stock delicious, but also enhance the flavor of the mushrooms, which can be used later in soups or stews, on pasta, or marinated as a side dish. However, you may wish to reduce the amount of salt, soy sauce, or miso called for in a recipe if you will be substituting Shiitake Dashi for a conventional unsalted stock.

8 dried shiitake mushrooms (page 437)

4 cups cold water

4 quarter-sized slices fresh ginger root

2 tablespoons soy sauce

2 tablespoons sake or dry sherry (optional)

Makes about 3 cups

Total time: 30 minutes

Combine all of the ingredients in a medium pot and bring them to a boil. Lower the heat and simmer, covered, for 15 minutes. Turn off the heat and allow the mushrooms to soak for an additional 15 minutes. Remove the ginger slices from the dashi and discard them. Store the shiitake and the dashi separately if not using immediately.

PER 8-OZ SERVING: 101 CALORIES, 3.3 G PROTEIN, .4 G FAT, 23.4 G CARBOHYDRATES, .1 G SATURATED FATTY ACIDS, .1 G POLYUNSATURATED FATTY ACIDS, .1 G MONOUNSATURATED FATTY ACIDS, 0 MG CHOLESTEROL, 545 MG SODIUM, 3.4 G TOTAL DIETARY FIBER

SOUTHEAST ASIAN VEGETABLE STOCK

This basic Asian vegetable stock can make the difference between a good soup and a great one. It will keep for up to 4 days refrigerated and indefinitely frozen.

1 onion, peeled and sliced
6 garlic cloves, peeled
2 celery stalks, chopped
2 medium carrots, peeled and sliced
3-inch piece fresh ginger root, sliced
1 fresh lemongrass stalk, chopped
   (2 tablespoons dried) (page 430)
2 tablespoons coriander seeds
1 teaspoon black peppercorns
1 bay leaf
1 star anise (or ½ teaspoon anise seed)
9 cups water

Makes 7 cups

**Preparation time:
15 minutes**

**Cooking time:
45 minutes**

Combine all of the ingredients in a large stockpot and bring them to a rapid boil. Reduce the heat and simmer, covered, for 45 minutes. Strain the stock through a colander or sieve, pressing as much liquid as possible out of the vegetables. Discard the vegetables and spices.

PER 8-OZ SERVING: 31 CALORIES, 1.2 G PROTEIN, .3 G FAT, 6.8 G CARBOHYDRATES, 0 G SATURATED FATTY ACIDS, .1 G POLYUNSATURATED FATTY ACIDS, 0 G MONOUNSATURATED FATTY ACIDS, 0 MG CHOLESTEROL, 35 MG SODIUM, 1.7 G TOTAL DIETARY FIBER

TROPICAL GAZPACHO

Pineapple's tangy sweetness adds an unusual twist to this Spanish chilled soup. The result is certainly a departure from the traditional gazpacho, but we think you'll like it. The addition of bread adds a surprising creamy smoothness, which complements the crispness of the raw vegetables, but the soup is excellent without the bread too, if you prefer to omit it.

4 garlic cloves, minced or pressed
1½ cups peeled, seeded, and diced cucumbers
1½ cups diced red bell peppers
½ cup diced red onions
1 cup diced tomatoes
1 cup canned unsweetened pineapple chunks in juice
2 tablespoons red wine vinegar
generous pinch of cayenne, or more to taste
1 teaspoon ground cumin
1½ cups French or Italian bread,
    crusts removed, torn into chunks
3 cups tomato juice
salt and ground black pepper to taste

thin slices of lemon and/or lime

Serves 4 to 6

Preparation time: 45 minutes

Chilling time: 1 to 2 hours

In a blender or food processor, combine the garlic, ¾ cup of the diced cucumbers, ¾ cup of the diced bell peppers, the red onions, ½ cup of the tomatoes, the pineapple and its juice, vinegar, cayenne, cumin, bread chunks, and tomato juice and purée until smooth. Transfer to a bowl, then stir in the remaining diced cucumbers, bell peppers, and tomatoes for texture and visual appeal. Add salt and black pepper to taste. Refrigerate for 1 to 2 hours until cold. Serve garnished with lemon and/or lime slices.

PER 10-OZ SERVING: 111 CALORIES, 3.4 G PROTEIN, .9 G FAT, 24.9 G CARBOHYDRATES, .1 G SATURATED FATTY ACIDS, .3 G POLYUNSATURATED FATTY ACIDS, .2 G MONOUNSATURATED FATTY ACIDS, 0 MG CHOLESTEROL, 531 MG SODIUM, 3.0 G TOTAL DIETARY FIBER

MENU SUGGESTIONS Tropical Gazpacho works well with many cuisines from warm latitudes. Try it as an appetizer for **Savory Indian Sweet Potatoes** (page 248), **Tempeh Salad Sandwich** (page 123), **Quinoa Black Bean Salad** (page 141), or **Caribbean Roasted Vegetables** (page 226) with **Jerk Tofu** (page 337).

CHILLED BEET AND BUTTERMILK SOUP

A refreshing hot weather soup that's also simple to prepare, this ravishingly colored soup will keep refrigerated for 4 or 5 days.

Serves 4 to 6

Preparation time: 15 minutes with canned beets, 50 minutes with fresh

Chilling time: 2 hours

4 cups chopped cooked beets*
1 cup unsweetened apple juice
2 cups buttermilk
1 tablespoon minced fresh dill
¼ cup minced scallions or chives
salt to taste

finely chopped cucumber

*Two 15-ounce cans of whole beets, drained and coarsely chopped, are fine in this recipe. If you're using fresh beets, 4 or 5 medium beets (about 1½ pounds) is the right amount. Trim the leaf stems to about an inch and simmer the beets in water to cover for about 40 minutes, until they are easily pierced with a knife. Drain the beets and rinse them with cold water. When the beets have cooled enough to handle, squeeze them with your hands and the skins will slide off easily. Cut off the stem ends and chop.

In a blender or food processor, combine the beets, apple juice, and buttermilk and purée until smooth. Transfer to a bowl or storage container and stir in the dill and scallions or chives. Refrigerate for at least 2 hours.

Add salt to taste and serve topped with finely chopped cucumber.

PER 9-OZ SERVING: 118 CALORIES, 5.2 G PROTEIN, 1.0 G FAT, 23.8 G CARBO-HYDRATES, .5 G SATURATED FATTY ACIDS, .1 G POLYUNSATURATED FATTY ACIDS, .3 G MONOUNSATURATED FATTY ACIDS, 3 MG CHOLESTEROL, 198 MG SODIUM, 2.8 G TOTAL DIETARY FIBER

MENU SUGGESTIONS Serve with **Brown Bread** (page 111) or pumpernickel and salad or fruit for a light summer lunch or supper. Or serve it with **Mushroom Pâté Almondine** (page 121) on rye bread along with **Wild Rice Waldorf Salad** (page 147).

ESSENTIAL MISO SOUP WITH TOFU

Miso, a traditional Japanese fermented soybean-and-grain product, is a thick purée used for flavoring many kinds of dishes including stews, dressings, spreads, sauces, and soups. Many varieties are available from light rice miso, to red barley miso, to dark soy miso.

Lately, many health benefits have been attributed to including miso regularly in your diet. Pair this with the fact that a leading nutritional journal recently reported a study showing a high correlation between eating soup regularly and maintaining good health, and this becomes one powerful little soup. Either way, we find it's a great replacement for chicken soup if you're a little under the weather.

Our miso-tofu soup is an easily prepared basic broth with tiny cubes of tofu. Although more elaborate miso soups are certainly possible, we like the simplicity of this version. Any dashi will make a delicious soup and each will add its own characteristic touch. Konbu-Bonito Dashi will give you that distinctive "Japanese restaurant" flavor, and Shiitake Dashi will be a bit more salty. If you do use the saltier Shiitake Dashi, you will need only 2 tablespoons of miso for the soup.

Serves 4

Dashi preparation: 10 to 30 minutes depending on the dashi

Total time: 10 minutes, once the dashi is ready

NOTE:
While any tofu may be used, silken tofu is especially good in this soup.

1 recipe Konbu, Konbu-Bonito, or Shiitake Dashi (pages 75–76)
3 ounces tofu, cut into ¼-inch cubes
2 to 3 tablespoons light miso
2 scallions, thinly sliced

a few blanched snow peas (optional)
a bit of crumbled nori seaweed (optional, page 432)

Heat the dashi in a saucepan and add the diced tofu. In a small bowl, mash the miso with about 3 tablespoons of the warm dashi until it forms a smooth sauce, then stir the miso sauce back into the soup. Heat the miso broth until it is very hot but not boiling. Sprinkle in the scallions and serve at once. Add 1 or 2 lightly blanched snow peas and a pinch of nori to each bowl of soup, if desired.

PER 8-OZ SERVING: 114 CALORIES, 5.5 G PROTEIN, 1.8 G FAT, 21.3 G CARBOHYDRATES, .3 G SATURATED FATTY ACIDS, .9 G POLYUNSATURATED FATTY ACIDS, .4 G MONOUNSATURATED FATTY ACIDS, 0 MG CHOLESTEROL, 736 MG SODIUM, 3.6 G TOTAL DIETARY FIBER

MENU SUGGESTIONS Serve with **Vegetable Udon Sauté** (page 204), **Sushi Rice Salad** (page 146), or **Savory Hoisin Fish** (page 293), or make a combo plate with **Fresh Spring Rolls** (page 254) and **Broiled Eggplant Thai Style** (page 34). Serve **Tapioca Fruit Parfait** (page 375) for dessert.

Asian Noodle Soup

This soup is so much better than the freeze-dried ramen noodle soups in the supermarket, there is *no* comparison. And you'll feel good that your soup is filled with fresh wholesome ingredients instead of who knows what.

6 cups Garlic Broth (page 74)
½ cup peeled and thinly sliced carrots
**4 cups shredded bok choy or other Chinese cabbage
    (page 424)**
1 cake tofu, cut into small cubes (about 12 ounces)
¼ pound buckwheat, soba, or ramen noodles

mung sprouts (optional)

Serves 4 to 6

Total time: 20 minutes

Gently heat the garlic broth. Add the carrots and simmer for about 3 minutes. Add the cabbage and tofu and return to a simmer. Add the noodles and cook until al dente.

Serve hot, topped with mung sprouts, if you wish.

PER 10-OZ SERVING: 167 CALORIES, 10.1 G PROTEIN, 3.6 G FAT, 26.7 G CARBOHYDRATES, .5 G SATURATED FATTY ACIDS, 2.0 G POLYUNSATURATED FATTY ACIDS, .8 G MONOUNSATURATED FATTY ACIDS, 0 MG CHOLESTEROL, 538 MG SODIUM, 3.6 G TOTAL DIETARY FIBER

MENU SUGGESTIONS Serve with **Asian Eggplant Spread** (page 24) or **Broiled Portabella Mushrooms** (page 322), or as a first course for **Savory Hoisin Fish** (page 293).

CREAM OF GREEN VEGETABLE SOUP

Think of this recipe as the basic template for making a low-fat creamy soup. We've given specific ingredients for making broccoli, spinach, or asparagus soup. The soup base is also good for carrot, celery, and zucchini soups.

Serves 6

Total time: 45 minutes

SOUP BASE

2½ cups chopped onions

1 garlic clove, minced or pressed

3 cups diced potatoes

1 cup chopped celery

3 cups water

vegetables and herbs of your choice (see below)

CHOOSE ONE OF THE FOLLOWING:

BROCCOLI

5 cups chopped broccoli
   (florets and peeled stems)

½ teaspoon minced fresh thyme
   (¼ teaspoon dried)

2 tablespoons chopped fresh basil
   (1 teaspoon dried)

1 tablespoon fresh marjoram
   (½ teaspoon dried)

SPINACH

10 ounces fresh spinach, rinsed, tough stems removed

¼ teaspoon nutmeg

2 tablespoons chopped fresh basil (1 teaspoon dried)

½ teaspoon minced fresh thyme (¼ teaspoon dried)

ASPARAGUS

5 cups chopped asparagus
   (about 3 pounds in the store)

2 tablespoons minced fresh dill
   (2 teaspoons dried)

½ teaspoon ground white or black pepper

2 cups buttermilk

salt to taste

In a soup pot, combine the onions, garlic, potatoes, celery, and water. Bring to a boil, then cover, lower the heat, and simmer for 20 minutes. Add your chosen combination of green vegetable and herbs and simmer for 10 to 15 minutes more, until the vegetables are tender. Working in batches in a blender or food processor, purée the soup with the buttermilk. Return it to the soup pot. Add salt to taste, reheat, and serve.

CREAM OF GREEN VEGETABLE SOUP WITH BROCCOLI PER 10-OZ SERVING: 126 CALORIES, 5.8 G PROTEIN, 1.0 G FAT, 25.1 G CARBOHYDRATES, .5 G SATURATED FATTY ACIDS, .2 G POLYUNSATURATED FATTY ACIDS, .2 G MONOUNSATURATED FATTY ACIDS, 3 MG CHOLESTEROL, 141 MG SODIUM, 3.5 G TOTAL DIETARY FIBER

CREAM OF GREEN VEGETABLE SOUP WITH SPINACH PER 10-OZ SERVING: 122 CALORIES, 5.5 G PROTEIN, 1.0 G FAT, 24.1 G CARBOHYDRATES, .5 G SATURATED FATTY ACIDS, .2 G POLYUNSATURATED FATTY ACIDS, .2 G MONOUNSATURATED FATTY ACIDS, 3 MG CHOLESTEROL, 158 MG SODIUM, 3.2 G TOTAL DIETARY FIBER

CREAM OF GREEN VEGETABLE SOUP WITH ASPARAGUS PER 10-OZ SERVING: 132 CALORIES, 6.4 G PROTEIN, 1.1 G FAT, 26.0 G CARBOHYDRATES, .5 G SATURATED FATTY ACIDS, .2 G POLYUNSATURATED FATTY ACIDS, .2 G MONOUNSATURATED FATTY ACIDS, 3 MG CHOLESTEROL, 138 MG SODIUM, 3.7 G TOTAL DIETARY FIBER

MENU SUGGESTIONS Serve with **Roasted Vegetables** (page 226) or with the sandwich versions of **Ira's Lunch** (page 118) or **Egg Salad** (page 117).

SPRING SOUP

Unlike the more familiar minestrones, dense with long stewing, this version has a light, delicate broth with tender, sweet-tasting vegetables.

2 garlic cloves, minced or pressed
1 cup chopped onions
1 small carrot, peeled and minced
1 celery stalk, minced
1 teaspoon dried thyme (1 tablespoon fresh)
1 teaspoon dried basil (1 tablespoon fresh)
¼ cup water
6 cups Basic Vegetable Stock (page 73) or
    canned vegetable broth
3 fresh or canned plum tomatoes, chopped
1½ cups fresh or frozen lima beans
1 pound fresh asparagus, cut into 1-inch lengths,
    or an 8-ounce package frozen asparagus
¼ pound spaghetti, broken into 2-inch lengths
1 teaspoon salt
1 tablespoon fresh lemon juice
1½ cups fresh or frozen green peas

Serves 4 to 6 as a main dish, 8 to 10 as a first course

Total time: 45 to 60 minutes

In a covered soup pot on low heat, cook the garlic, onions, carrots, celery, thyme, and basil in the water until the vegetables have softened, about 10 minutes. Add the vegetable stock or broth and the tomatoes and bring to a boil. Add the lima beans and asparagus and return to a boil. Stir in the spaghetti and cook until al dente. Add the salt, lemon juice, and peas and cook for about 5 minutes. Serve hot.

PER 8-OZ SERVING: 140 CALORIES, 6.3 G PROTEIN, .7 G FAT, 28.9 G CARBOHYDRATES, .1 G SATURATED FATTY ACIDS, .3 G POLYUNSATURATED FATTY ACIDS, .1 G MONOUNSATURATED FATTY ACIDS, 0 MG CHOLESTEROL, 296 MG SODIUM, 3.9 G TOTAL DIETARY FIBER

MENU SUGGESTIONS For a lovely spring evening meal, serve this soup with toast and **Spinach Artichoke Heart Dip** (page 30). It is an appetizing first course before **Baked Flounder Rolls** (page 295), **Watercress Omelet** (page 53), or **Broiled Portabella Mushrooms** (page 322). **Fruit-filled Meringue Shells** (page 388) with fresh strawberries is our choice for dessert.

HARIRA

Harira is traditionally served in North Africa at the evening meal during Ramadan, the Muslim month of daytime fasting. This healthful, hearty soup is wonderfully fragrant and satisfying.

1 cup chopped onions
4 cups Basic Vegetable Stock (page 73)
1 teaspoon ground cinnamon
1 teaspoon turmeric
1 tablespoon grated fresh ginger root
⅛ teaspoon cayenne
1 cup peeled and diced carrots
½ cup diced celery
1 cup undrained canned tomatoes, chopped
1½ cups diced potatoes
pinch of saffron
1 cup cooked lentils (about ⅓ to ½ cup dried, page 414)
1 cup drained cooked chickpeas
1 to 2 tablespoons chopped fresh cilantro
1 tablespoon fresh lemon juice
salt and ground black pepper to taste

lemon wedges

Serves 4 to 6

Total time: 1 hour

In a covered soup pot, simmer the onions in 1 cup of the stock for 10 minutes. Combine the cinnamon, turmeric, ginger, and cayenne in a small bowl and add 2 to 3 tablespoons of the hot liquid to form a paste. Stir this paste into the pot along with the carrots, celery, and the remaining stock. Bring to a boil, then lower the heat, cover, and simmer for 5 minutes. Add the tomatoes and potatoes and continue to cook, covered, for 15 to 20 minutes, until the potatoes are tender. Crumble in the saffron. Stir in the lentils, chickpeas, cilantro, lemon juice, and salt and pepper to taste. Reheat.

Serve immediately with lemon wedges.

PER 9-OZ SERVING: 186 CALORIES, 9.0 G PROTEIN, 1.6 G FAT, 36.5 G CARBOHYDRATES, .2 G SATURATED FATTY ACIDS, .6 G POLYUNSATURATED FATTY ACIDS, .3 G MONOUNSATURATED FATTY ACIDS, 0 MG CHOLESTEROL, 130 MG SODIUM, 8.0 G TOTAL DIETARY FIBER

MENU SUGGESTIONS Accompany with **Carrot Orange Salad** (page 134), **Greek Spinach Rice Balls** (page 35), or **Spinach Artichoke Heart Dip** (page 30) on toasted pita bread wedges. Cups of Harira may serve as a first course to **Onion and Feta Risotto** (page 194).

MINESTRONE GENOA

The variations on minestrone are almost infinite. The hills around Genoa are covered with fragrant herbs, and minestrone there is usually spiked with pesto, a trick we have adopted for this quick-cooking rendition. You could add to or replace some of the vegetables listed here—zucchini, turnips, and spinach or other greens are all fine additions or substitutions.

Serves 4 to 6

**Preparation time:
15 to 20 minutes**

**Simmering time:
20 to 25 minutes**

6 cups **Basic Vegetable Stock (page 73)**
2 cups **chopped onions**
1 cup **chopped celery**
1 cup **peeled and chopped carrots**
2 cups **cubed peeled potatoes**
2 cups **chopped cabbage**
1 cup **cut green beans, in 2-inch pieces (about 6 ounces)**
3 cups **cooked cannellini or white kidney beans
    (two 15-ounce cans, rinsed and drained)**
1 cup **Susan's Pesto, prepared without pine nuts (page 364)**
salt and ground black pepper to taste

In a soup pot, bring the stock to a boil. Add the onions, celery, and carrots, lower the heat, and simmer for 10 minutes. Add the potatoes, cabbage, and green beans and simmer for 10 to 12 minutes more, until the potatoes are tender. Stir in the cannellini and pesto and heat thoroughly. Add salt and pepper to taste. Serve hot or at room temperature.

VARIATION Add 2 or 3 bay leaves to the simmering vegetables and remove them before serving the soup.

PER 10-OZ SERVING: 225 CALORIES,
11.1 G PROTEIN, 1.2 G FAT, 46.1 G CARBOHY-
DRATES, .2 G SATURATED FATTY ACIDS,
.5 G POLYUNSATURATED FATTY ACIDS,
.1 G MONOUNSATURATED FATTY ACIDS,
0 MG CHOLESTEROL, 305 MG SODIUM,
11.0 G TOTAL DIETARY FIBER

MENU SUGGESTION This minestrone is a hearty, one-dish meal, served with warm, crisp garlic toast, a green salad, and a glass of Chianti.

NOTE:
If you have leftover mine-strone, consider serving it the Italian way, called *ribollita,* "reboiled." Soak thick slices of stale bread in the soup until the bread nearly dissolves. The soup should be almost thick enough to hold up a spoon. Gently reheat it on the stove or bake it in a baking dish, sprinkled with a little grated cheese.

VIETNAMESE HOT AND SOUR SOUP

Traditional Southeast Asian hot and sour soups are almost always made with shrimp or firm white-fleshed fish. At Moosewood, however, we like to use tofu instead. The soup's dark, rich, clear broth is the perfect backdrop for the small, white cubes of tofu that enrich our version. Pineapple and mint provide the refreshing hint of sweetness common to traditional Asian soups. This recipe yields a generous amount of soup, so plan a party or store some for later. Tightly covered and refrigerated, it will keep for up to 4 days.

2 cups thinly sliced onions
2 teaspoons canola or other vegetable oil
5 garlic cloves, minced or pressed
1 or 2 fresh chiles, seeded and minced, or to taste
7 cups Southeast Asian Vegetable Stock (page 77)
1½ cups canned straw mushrooms (15-ounce can, drained)
¾ cup canned pineapple chunks (8-ounce can, undrained)
    or 1 cup diced fresh pineapple
1 cup chopped fresh tomatoes
2 tablespoons chopped fresh basil
1 tablespoon chopped fresh mint or cilantro
2 tablespoons fresh lime juice
¼ cup soy sauce or Asian fish sauce (page 420)
1½ cups diced tofu, cut into ½-inch cubes (about 8 ounces)

mung sprouts, basil leaves, lime wedges

Serves 6 to 8

**Preparation time:
25 to 30 minutes**

**Cooking time:
20 minutes**

In a large soup pot, sauté the onions in the oil on low heat for about 5 minutes, until softened. Add the garlic and chiles and sauté for another minute, stirring to prevent sticking. Stir in the stock, straw mushrooms, pineapple, and tomatoes and bring to a boil. Reduce the heat and simmer for 5 minutes. Add the basil, mint or cilantro, lime juice, soy sauce or fish sauce, and tofu. Simmer for 5 to 10 minutes, until the flavors are well blended.

Sprinkle with mung sprouts and basil leaves and accompany each serving with a wedge of lime.

VARIATION Replace the tofu in the recipe with 1 pound of shelled deveined shrimp or cubes of firm, white-fleshed fish. You may need to simmer the soup a little longer to ensure that the fish is thoroughly cooked.

PER 10-OZ SERVING: 125 CALORIES, 7.0 G PROTEIN, 4.1 G FAT, 18.4 G CARBOHYDRATES, .6 G SATURATED FATTY ACIDS, 2.2 G POLYUNSATURATED FATTY ACIDS, .9 G MONOUNSATURATED FATTY ACIDS, 0 MG CHOLESTEROL, 472 MG SODIUM, 3.4 G TOTAL DIETARY FIBER

MENU SUGGESTIONS Serve with brown rice and either **Asian Cucumber Condiment** (page 367) or **Gingered Broccoli** (page 315). Finish with frozen yogurt topped with plum sauce.

JAPANESE SOBA AND VEGETABLE SOUP

Eat this soup as soon as it is ready, while the spinach is still bright green and the noodles have not yet expanded. This fragrant soothing soup is light and brothy enough to serve as the first course of a larger meal but satisfying enough to savor alone—especially on a chilly evening while sipping hot sake.

We have made the mirin and miso optional, but you should really include at least one of them for a more flavorful broth. For a heartier version of this soup, add 4 ounces of tofu cut into ½-inch cubes when you add the spinach.

1 recipe Shiitake Dashi (page 76)
8 shiitake mushrooms, reserved from
    making the dashi and thinly sliced
1 cup finely chopped leeks, white parts only
2 teaspoons grated fresh ginger root
2 teaspoons rice vinegar or cider vinegar
2 teaspoons soy sauce
1 tablespoon mirin (optional)
3 ounces soba noodles
2 cups washed, stemmed, and chopped spinach
1 to 2 tablespoons light miso (optional)

thinly sliced scallions
toasted sesame seeds (see Note)

Serves 4

Total time: 25 minutes

NOTE:
Toast a single layer of sesame seeds on an unoiled baking tray in a conventional or toaster oven at 350° for 2 to 3 minutes, until fragrant and golden brown.

In a soup pot, bring the dashi to a boil. Add the shiitake, leeks, ginger, vinegar, soy sauce, and mirin, if using. Cover and simmer until the leeks are tender, about 10 minutes.

Meanwhile, in a separate pot, cook the soba noodles in boiling water to cover for about 5 minutes, until al dente.

When the leeks are tender, add the spinach and simmer for another minute, until the spinach has wilted but is still bright green. In a small bowl, combine the miso with a few tablespoons of the hot broth to make a smooth sauce, then stir it back into the soup.

Drain the soba noodles and evenly divide them among four individual serving bowls. Ladle on the soup and top with sliced scallions and a sprinkling of toasted sesame seeds.

PER 10-OZ SERVING: 152 CALORIES, 6.1 G PROTEIN, .5 G FAT, 34.1 G CARBOHYDRATES, .1 G SATURATED FATTY ACIDS, .1 G POLYUNSATURATED FATTY ACIDS, .1 G MONOUNSATURATED FATTY ACIDS, 0 MG CHOLESTEROL, 590 MG SODIUM, 3.3 G TOTAL DIETARY FIBER

MENU SUGGESTIONS Serve with **Nori Vegetable Rolls** (page 36), **Sesame Beets** (page 140), or **Sushi Rice Salad** (page 146). Try an exotic fresh fruit for dessert, perhaps Asian pear apples.

KOREAN VEGETABLE NOODLE SOUP

This brothy soup features cellophane noodles, a delicate translucent noodle made from mung bean starch. They are available in Asian markets and in the ethnic section or pasta aisle of many supermarkets. Their other names are "bean thread noodles" or "bean sticks."

2 ounces cellophane noodles (page 423),
  soaked in hot water for 10 to 15 minutes
1 recipe Konbu Dashi (page 75)
1 small carrot, peeled and thinly sliced on the diagonal
4 garlic cloves, minced or pressed
3 tablespoons soy sauce, or to taste
1 tablespoon rice vinegar
2 teaspoons grated fresh ginger root
1 quart water
1 small zucchini, thinly sliced on the diagonal
2 cups thinly sliced bok choy or Chinese cabbage
1 tablespoon light miso
1 teaspoon dark sesame oil

sesame seeds
sliced scallions

Serves 4 to 6

Total time: 15 to 20 minutes, once the dashi is made

> **NOTE:**
> If you want to serve the soup later, refrigerate the noodles and soup in separate containers and combine them when you reheat the soup. Cellophane noodles disintegrate if stored in liquid.

Drain the cellophane noodles and cut them into 3- to 4-inch lengths and set aside.

Add water to the dashi to make a total of 4 cups of liquid. In a soup pot, bring the slightly diluted dashi to a boil and add the carrots, garlic, soy sauce, rice vinegar, and ginger. Lower the heat and simmer, uncovered, for about 5 minutes.

In a separate pot, bring about a quart of water to a boil.

Meanwhile, stir the zucchini and the bok choy into the simmering dashi and cook for 4 minutes, until the vegetables are just tender. In a bowl, mash the miso with 3 tablespoons of the hot soup broth to make a thick sauce and return it to the soup. Add the sesame oil.

When the water is boiling, ease the soaked cellophane noodles into the pot and cook for 2 or 3 minutes, until just tender, and drain. To serve, evenly divide the noodles among the soup bowls, ladle the soup over the noodles, and garnish with sesame seeds and scallions.

PER 9-OZ SERVING: 43 CALORIES, 2.1 G PROTEIN, 1.1 G FAT, 7.1 G CARBOHYDRATES, .2 G SATURATED FATTY ACIDS, .5 G POLYUNSATURATED FATTY ACIDS, .4 G MONOUNSATURATED FATTY ACIDS, 0 MG CHOLESTEROL, 521 MG SODIUM, 1.6 G TOTAL DIETARY FIBER

MENU SUGGESTIONS Serve with **Asian Tofu Salad** (page 116), **Nori Vegetable Rolls** (page 36), or **Cabbage Rolls** (page 256) on **Fragrant Jasmine Rice** (page 189).

CREAM OF CAULIFLOWER SOUP

For a creamy smooth soup, this is very low in fat. Buttermilk enhances the other flavors, and caraway is the perfect foil for the cauliflower.

Serves 6

**Preparation time:
35 minutes**

**Simmering time:
35 to 40 minutes**

2 cups chopped onions
1 garlic clove, minced
3 cups diced potatoes
1 cup chopped celery
5 cups water
1 cup peeled and chopped carrots
1 medium head cauliflower, chopped (about 5 cups)
1 heaping tablespoon chopped fresh dill (2 teaspoons dried)
1 tablespoon fresh lemon juice
1 teaspoon ground dried mustard
¼ teaspoon caraway seeds
2 cups buttermilk
salt to taste

chopped scallions

In a soup pot, combine the onions, garlic, potatoes, celery, and water. Bring to a boil, reduce the heat, and then simmer for 10 minutes. Add the carrots and continue to simmer for 10 more minutes. Add the cauliflower, dill, lemon juice, mustard, and caraway seeds and simmer for 15 to 20 minutes longer, until the carrots are tender. In a blender or food processor, purée the soup with the buttermilk, working in batches. Add salt to taste. Gently reheat.

Serve topped with chopped scallions.

PER 10-OZ SERVING: 143 CALORIES, 6.5 G PROTEIN, 1.4 G FAT, 28.3 G CARBOHYDRATES, .5 G SATURATED FATTY ACIDS, .4 G POLYUNSATURATED FATTY ACIDS, .3 G MONOUNSATURATED FATTY ACIDS, 3 MG CHOLESTEROL, 158 MG SODIUM, 5.5 G TOTAL DIETARY FIBER

MENU SUGGESTIONS This soup is nice paired with **Watercress Omelet** (page 53), **Mushroom Wheatberry Pilaf** (page 195), or **Herbed Cottage Cheese Bread** (page 113) topped with **Mushroom Pâté Almondine** (page 121).

CREAMY POTATO KALE SOUP

This is a delightful, creamy white soup, jeweled with bits of green, full of complex flavors, and pleasing to the eye. Kale is a very nutritious vegetable that brings necessary iron and calcium to the vegetarian diet, and the evaporated skimmed milk has the richness lacking in ordinary skim milk.

1 cup finely chopped onions
⅔ cup finely chopped leeks
½ teaspoon salt
1 tablespoon canola or other vegetable oil
4 cups Basic Vegetable Stock (page 73)
4 cups coarsely chopped potatoes
¼ teaspoon ground fennel
½ cup finely chopped celery
2 tablespoons white wine
½ teaspoon dried dill
2 teaspoons Dijon mustard
2 tablespoons minced scallions
1½ tablespoons minced fresh basil
½ cup evaporated skimmed milk
4 cups loosely packed shredded kale
salt and ground black pepper to taste
squeeze of fresh lemon juice (optional)

Serves 4 to 6

Total time: 45 minutes

In a 3- or 4-quart covered soup pot, sauté the onions, leeks, and salt in the oil on very low heat for about 7 minutes, until tender. Add the stock and bring it to a boil. Add the potatoes, fennel, celery, wine, and dill. Simmer for about 20 minutes, covered, until the potatoes are tender. In a blender or food processor, purée the soup in batches until smooth. Return the soup to the pot and stir in the mustard, scallions, basil, and evaporated skimmed milk.

In a separate pot, gently boil the kale in just enough water to cover. When the kale is just tender, drain it and stir it into the soup. Add salt and pepper to taste and lemon juice, if desired. Carefully reheat the soup until it is very hot but not boiling.

PER 9-OZ SERVING: 168 CALORIES, 4.6 G PROTEIN, 4.3 G FAT, 28.8 G CARBOHYDRATES, 1.2 G SATURATED FATTY ACIDS, 1.6 G POLYUNSATURATED FATTY ACIDS, 1.1 G MONOUNSATURATED FATTY ACIDS, 6 MG CHOLESTEROL, 311 MG SODIUM, 3.9 G TOTAL DIETARY FIBER

MENU SUGGESTIONS Serve with **Savory Stuffed Mushrooms** (page 42), **Lentil Salad** (page 151), or **Wild Rice Waldorf Salad** (page 147), and finish with **Chocolate Hazelnut Biscotti** (page 392).

GOLDEN SPLIT PEA SOUP

This is one of our favorite split pea soups—it's so delicious. The recipe calls for puréeing all of the mixture, but if you like a chunkier soup, remove about 3 cups of the vegetables from the soup with a slotted spoon, purée the rest, and then stir the reserved vegetables back into the soup when you reheat it.

3 cups chopped onions
1 teaspoon vegetable oil
1½ teaspoons ground cumin
½ teaspoon turmeric
1 teaspoon ground coriander
1 tablespoon grated fresh ginger root
1 cup dried yellow split peas
7 cups water
2 cups peeled and cubed sweet potatoes
1 cup peeled, cored, and cubed apples
3-inch cinnamon stick
2 teaspoons chili powder
¾ cup chopped tomatoes
2 tablespoons fresh lime juice
1 tablespoon soy sauce

nonfat yogurt
minced cilantro (optional)

Serves 6 to 8

Preparation time: 20 minutes

Cooking time: 1 hour

In a soup pot, sauté the onions in the oil for about 8 minutes, until golden, stirring frequently. Add the cumin, turmeric, coriander, and ginger and cook for another minute. Add the split peas, water, sweet potatoes, apples, cinnamon, and chili powder, cover, and bring to a boil. Lower the heat and simmer for 40 minutes, or until the split peas are tender.

In a bowl, combine the tomatoes, lime juice, and soy sauce. When the split peas are tender, add the tomato mixture. Purée the soup in a blender or food processor, working in batches and adding more water, if needed. Return the soup to the pot and gently reheat. Serve topped with nonfat yogurt and minced cilantro, if you like.

PER 9-OZ SERVING: 138 CALORIES, 4.4 G PROTEIN, 1.3 G FAT, 28.9 G CARBOHYDRATES, .2 G SATURATED FATTY ACIDS, .5 G POLYUNSATURATED FATTY ACIDS, .2 G MONOUNSATURATED FATTY ACIDS, 0 MG CHOLESTEROL, 125 MG SODIUM, 5.2 G TOTAL DIETARY FIBER

MENU SUGGESTIONS Serve with **Mango Coconut Cucumber Salad** (page 136), **Fragrant Jasmine Rice** (page 189), and **Banana Bundt Cake** (page 382).

ORZO AND PEA SOUP

This Italian-style soup is very simple and appetizing, with sweet peas and slippery little noodle bits in a savory broth.

1 teaspoon dried thyme
6 cups Garlic Broth (page 74)
½ pound orzo (about 1⅓ cups) (page 433)
2 cups fresh or frozen green peas

grated Pecorino cheese (optional)

Serves 4 to 6

Total time: 15 minutes

Add the thyme to the garlic broth and gently heat.

Meanwhile, in a separate pot of boiling water, cook the orzo until al dente, about 5 minutes. Drain. Add the orzo and peas to the broth. Simmer until the peas are tender but still bright green, about 1 minute for frozen peas, longer for fresh.

Serve hot, topped with grated Pecorino, if you wish.

PER 12-OZ SERVING: 236 CALORIES, 9.7 G PROTEIN, 1.5 G FAT, 46.3 G CARBOHYDRATES, .2 G SATURATED FATTY ACIDS, .7 G POLYUNSATURATED FATTY ACIDS, .2 G MONOUNSATURATED FATTY ACIDS, 0 MG CHOLESTEROL, 412 MG SODIUM, 6.3 G TOTAL DIETARY FIBER

MENU SUGGESTIONS Serve this brothy light soup for lunch with crusty bread and a tomato salad or with a sandwich of **Ira's Lunch** (page 118). Serve it as a prelude to **Luscious Basil and Feta Pizza** (page 228), **Eggplant Strata** (page 32), or **Spinach Mushroom Frittata** (page 52).

DRIED MUSHROOM SOUP WITH BARLEY

Dried mushrooms give this very low-fat soup an impressive flavor boost and make the broth rich and hearty. This is a great soup to serve nonvegetarians—it won't even occur to them to ask, "Where's the beef?"

Dried mushrooms seem expensive when you're in the produce section surrounded by piles of lush vegetables and fruit. But remember, that little cardboard box of almost weightless shriveled mushrooms goes a long way, and the ones you don't use in this recipe will keep until you need them. Each variety of dried mushrooms has a distinct flavor, and just about any kind will work fine in this recipe, but we favor a combination of porcini and shiitake mushrooms.

Dried Mushroom Soup with Barley is good for an everyday supper or for serving to your most discerning guest. It tastes even better the next day and it freezes well, so consider making a big batch. If you plan to freeze it, reduce the amount of black pepper by about half since the flavor will intensify as it sits; then add pepper to taste when you serve it.

Serves 4 to 8

Preparation time: 30 minutes

Cooking time: 45 minutes

½ ounce dried mushrooms, such as porcini, shiitake, chanterelle, and/or morel (about ⅔ cup)
6 cups boiling water
1 teaspoon canola or other vegetable oil
2 cups chopped onions
2 garlic cloves, pressed or minced
1 cup finely chopped celery
1 cup peeled and finely chopped carrots
3 cups sliced fresh mushrooms (about 10 ounces)
¼ cup soy sauce
pinch of dried thyme
¼ teaspoon ground black pepper
½ cup raw pearl barley
¼ cup dry sherry or 2 teaspoons honey (optional)
salt and ground black pepper to taste

In a saucepan, cover the dried mushrooms with 6 cups of boiling water. Simmer for 15 minutes. Remove from the heat and set aside for at least 15 minutes.

Meanwhile, warm the oil in a soup pot on low heat. Add the onions and garlic, cover, and cook for 5 minutes, stirring occasionally. Add the celery and carrots and cook for 5 minutes, stirring occasionally. Add the fresh mushrooms, increase the heat to medium, and cook, stirring continuously, for about 3 minutes, until the mushrooms begin to release their juices. Remove from the heat and set aside.

Drain the dried mushrooms, reserving the mushroom stock. Cut off and discard any tough stems, then rinse and chop the mushrooms. Strain the stock through a sieve or, if dirt or sand is evident, through a paper coffee filter. Add enough water to the stock to make 7 cups of liquid. Add the chopped dried mushrooms, mushroom stock, soy sauce, thyme, pepper, barley, and optional sherry or honey to the pot of sautéed vegetables. Bring to a boil and then cover, reduce the heat, and simmer for 45 minutes.

When ready to serve, add salt and pepper to taste. This soup should be brothy, so if it has cooked down and become thick, add a bit more water.

PER 8-OZ SERVING: 94 CALORIES, 3.5 G PROTEIN, 1.2 G FAT, 19.0 G CARBOHYDRATES, .2 G SATURATED FATTY ACIDS, .6 G POLYUNSATURATED FATTY ACIDS, .2 G MONOUNSATURATED FATTY ACIDS, 0 MG CHOLESTEROL, 453 MG SODIUM, 4.3 G TOTAL DIETARY FIBER

MENU SUGGESTIONS Serve a satisfying lunch with a sandwich of **Ira's Lunch** (page 118), **Egg Salad** (page 117), or **Herbed Cottage Cheese Chèvre Spread** (page 31). On chilly evenings, serve before **Swiss Chard Rolls Two Ways** (page 252) accompanied by **Baked Beets and Shallots** (page 314), or before **Holiday Cranberry Squash** (page 331) with **Cucumbers Vinaigrette** (page 133), or along with **Honey Mustard Fish** (page 298) and a salad with **Creamy Dill Dressing** (page 342). A wonderful dessert for any of these menus is **Apple Apricot Strudel** (page 384).

NEW ENGLAND SQUASH SOUP

For a creamy, soothing soup to warm you on a chilly day, this is the ticket. Yet for all its apparent richness, it's essentially fat-free! This is an excellent recipe to make ahead of time and its flavor is even better the next day. This soup is the perfect light first course for Thanksgiving dinner.

1 cup diced onions
1 celery stalk, chopped
1 garlic clove, minced or pressed
1 cup unsweetened apple juice
1 butternut squash (about 1 pound), peeled, seeded, and cubed
1 potato, diced
3 cups water or vegetable stock
1 bay leaf
½ teaspoon dried thyme
½ teaspoon salt
¼ teaspoon nutmeg
2 cups sliced mushrooms (about 6 ounces)
3 tablespoons dry sherry
1 tablespoon soy sauce
pinch of dried marjoram
⅔ cup evaporated skimmed milk
salt and ground black pepper to taste

Serves 4 to 6

Total time: 1 hour

Combine the onions, celery, garlic, and apple juice in a large soup pot. Cover and simmer for about 10 minutes, until the vegetables soften. Add the squash, potato, water or stock, bay leaf, thyme, salt, and nutmeg. Bring to a boil, cover, lower the heat, and simmer until the vegetables are very soft, about 20 to 25 minutes.

While the soup simmers, sauté the mushrooms in an uncovered skillet with the sherry, soy sauce, and marjoram until the mushrooms are tender and most of the liquid has evaporated, about 5 minutes. Set aside.

When the squash and potatoes are very soft, remove the soup pot from the heat and, working in batches, purée the soup with the evaporated skimmed milk in a blender or food processor. Reheat gently. Add salt and pepper. Serve topped with the sautéed mushrooms.

PER 9-OZ SERVING: 131 CALORIES, 4.4 G PROTEIN, .5 G FAT, 28.2 G CARBOHYDRATES, .1 G SATURATED FATTY ACIDS, .1 G POLYUNSATURATED FATTY ACIDS, 0 G MONOUNSATURATED FATTY ACIDS, 1 MG CHOLESTEROL, 418 MG SODIUM, 2.5 G TOTAL DIETARY FIBER

MENU SUGGESTIONS Serve with **Wild Rice Waldorf Salad** (page 147) or with **Swiss Chard Rolls Two Ways** (page 252) on **Bulgur Rice Pilaf** (page 188). This soup is the perfect light first course for Thanksgiving dinner.

SPANISH POTATO GARLIC SOUP

What could be better than potatoes and onions in a steaming hot, garlicky red broth? Serve it in earthenware bowls. Let there be classical guitar music. Discuss passion and death.

1 large onion, thinly sliced (about 2 cups)
2 large potatoes, cut into thin slices
1 teaspoon paprika
2 teaspoons olive oil
1 cup chopped tomatoes
1 teaspoon dried thyme
6 cups Garlic Broth (page 74)

Serves 4 to 6

Total time: 35 minutes

Sauté the onions, potatoes, and paprika in the oil, stirring constantly, for about 5 minutes, until the onions have softened. Add the tomatoes and thyme and simmer for 3 or 4 minutes. Add the garlic broth and simmer gently for about 10 minutes, until the potatoes are tender.

PER 11.50-OZ SERVING: 141 CALORIES, 3.8 G PROTEIN, 2.6 G FAT, 27.6 G CARBOHYDRATES, .4 G SATURATED FATTY ACIDS, .6 G POLYUNSATURATED FATTY ACIDS, 1.3 G MONOUNSATURATED FATTY ACIDS, 0 MG CHOLESTEROL, 365 MG SODIUM, 3.8 G TOTAL DIETARY FIBER

MENU SUGGESTIONS Serve as a satisfying lunch with **Caesar Salad** (page 131) or **Mexican Seitan Pita** (page 120). Or offer as a first course before **Fish Steaks with Fennel** (page 290) or **Chili Burgers** (page 173) along with **Citrus-dressed Asparagus** (page 313).

CARBONADA

Here is a robust meatless version of a traditional Chilean vegetable soup adapted from a recipe of Eliana Parra's family. We all remember when Eliana first began to work in the Moosewood kitchen. Celeste Materi, who was fluent in Spanish, was appointed to train her, since Eliana had just come to this country and was still learning English. Now Eliana, or Nana as we call her, has been a cook at the restaurant for more than ten years and also teaches Spanish in the Ithaca schools.

1 medium onion, chopped
2 celery stalks, chopped
3 garlic cloves, minced or pressed
2 teaspoons olive oil
1 teaspoon paprika
1 teaspoon dried dill
½ teaspoon dried oregano
1 bay leaf
4 cups water or vegetable stock
½ cup dry white wine
1 medium potato, diced
1 carrot, peeled and diced
1 green or red bell pepper, seeded and diced
¾ cup cubed seitan (page 437) (see Note)
½ cup cooked brown rice
1 medium tomato, chopped
1 tablespoon fresh lemon juice
salt and ground black pepper to taste

Serves 4 to 6

Total time: 45 minutes

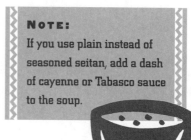

NOTE:

If you use plain instead of seasoned seitan, add a dash of cayenne or Tabasco sauce to the soup.

Combine the onions, celery, garlic, and oil in a heavy soup pot, cover, and sauté for about 10 minutes, until the onions become translucent, stirring often to prevent sticking. Add the paprika, dill, oregano, and bay leaf and sauté for about a minute. Stir in the water or stock, wine, potatoes, carrots, and bell peppers. Bring to a boil, cover, and lower the heat to simmer the vegetables and broth for 10 minutes.

Add the seitan, rice, and tomatoes and simmer until all of the vegetables are tender, 5 to 10 minutes. Add the lemon juice and salt and pepper to taste.

PER 10-OZ SERVING: 139 CALORIES, 3.7 G PROTEIN, 2.8 G FAT, 23.7 G CARBOHYDRATES, .4 G SATURATED FATTY ACIDS, .7 G POLYUNSATURATED FATTY ACIDS, 1.4 G MONOUNSATURATED FATTY ACIDS, 0 MG CHOLESTEROL, 73 MG SODIUM, 3.5 G TOTAL DIETARY FIBER

MENU SUGGESTIONS Serve with a green salad, **Guacamole with Roasted Corn** (page 27), and **Herb and Cheese Muffins** (page 112), **Buttermilk Rolls** (page 115), or **Almost Fat-Free Cornbread** (page 110).

CATALAN POTATO LIMA SOUP

This thick, puréed soup, hearty and full flavored, is a longtime favorite at Moosewood. For this recipe, you should use only fresh or frozen lima beans; dried limas would give a very different result.

2 cups chopped onions
2 teaspoons olive oil
4 cups sliced or cubed potatoes
2 cups cooked fresh or frozen green lima beans
4 cups water or vegetable stock
¼ cup chopped fresh cilantro
salt and ground black pepper to taste
1 cup skim milk or buttermilk (optional)

roasted red pepper or pimiento strips

Serves 4 to 6

Total time: 25 minutes

Sauté the onions in the oil for about 5 minutes, until translucent. Add the potatoes, lima beans, and water or stock and bring to a boil. Add the cilantro and salt and pepper to taste, lower the heat, and simmer for 10 minutes. Purée in batches in a blender or food processor, return to the soup pot, and gently reheat, if necessary. If you prefer a creamy soup, stir the skim milk or buttermilk into the soup and gently reheat.

Serve garnished with roasted red pepper or pimiento strips.

PER 9-OZ SERVING: 217 CALORIES, 6.7 G PROTEIN, 2.1 G FAT, 44.7 G CARBOHYDRATES, .3 G SATURATED FATTY ACIDS, .3 G POLYUNSATURATED FATTY ACIDS, 1.2 G MONOUNSATURATED FATTY ACIDS, 0 MG CHOLESTEROL, 69 MG SODIUM, 4.2 G TOTAL DIETARY FIBER

MENU SUGGESTIONS Serve with **Quinoa Pine Nut Pilaf** (page 184), **Guacamole with Roasted Corn** (page 27), or **Seitan Fajitas** (page 232) along with a crisp green salad and **Dark Chocolate Pudding** (page 374).

CURRIED CARROT PARSNIP SOUP

This colorful, zesty soup is loaded with beta-carotene and vitamin C! Served hot or cold, it makes a lively first course that is especially attractive served in cobalt blue bowls.

1½ cups chopped onions
3 garlic cloves, minced or pressed
1 tablespoon grated fresh ginger root
¼ teaspoon salt
1 teaspoon canola or other vegetable oil
½ teaspoon ground cinnamon
½ teaspoon turmeric
1 teaspoon ground coriander
1 teaspoon ground cumin
pinch of cayenne
1 cup unsweetened apple or pear juice
4 cups water or vegetable stock
2 cups peeled and sliced carrots
2 cups sliced parsnips
1 cup orange juice
1 tablespoon fresh lemon juice
salt and ground black pepper to taste

plain nonfat yogurt
chopped fresh cilantro, finely chopped scallions

Serves 4 to 6

Total time: 40 minutes

In a small, covered nonstick pan or seasoned cast-iron frying pan, sauté the onions, garlic, ginger, and salt in the oil for 5 minutes, stirring once or twice. Add the cinnamon, turmeric, coriander, cumin, and cayenne and cook, stirring, for another minute or two. Pour in the apple or pear juice, stir to deglaze the pan, and transfer the onion mixture to a large soup pot. Add the water or stock, carrots, and parsnips. Cover and simmer for 20 minutes, or until the vegetables are soft.

In a blender or food processor, purée the vegetable mixture with the orange juice, working in batches. Stir in the lemon juice, and salt and pepper to taste. Gently reheat to serve hot or chill for at least 3 hours and serve cold. This soup is especially delicious with a dollop of yogurt, a sprinkling of cilantro or scallions, or all three.

PER 9-OZ SERVING: 139 CALORIES, 3.1 G PROTEIN, 1.5 G FAT, 30.7 G CARBOHYDRATES, .2 G SATURATED FATTY ACIDS, .6 G POLYUNSATURATED FATTY ACIDS, .3 G MONOUNSATURATED FATTY ACIDS, 0 MG CHOLESTEROL, 193 MG SODIUM, 5.1 G TOTAL DIETARY FIBER

MENU SUGGESTIONS Serve with **Broiled Eggplant Thai Style** (page 34), **Spinach Mushroom Frittata** (page 52), or **Egg Salad** (page 117) as a sandwich.

Tomato Bulgur Soup

This is a very easy-to-make, quick-cooking soup with readily available ingredients that are found in almost every pantry. Here a light tomato broth is made hearty with the addition of bulgur. The soup tends to thicken as it sits, so if you aren't serving it immediately, you may want to add a bit of water or stock.

3 cups Basic Vegetable Stock (page 73)
1 cup finely chopped onions
1 cup peeled and diced carrots
¾ cup diced celery (2 medium stalks)
2 large garlic cloves, minced or pressed
1 teaspoon salt
1 teaspoon dried dill
½ teaspoon ground fennel
2 cups undrained canned tomatoes, chopped (16-ounce can)
¼ cup bulgur
ground black pepper to taste

Serves 4 to 6

Total time. 30 minutes

In a large soup pot, combine the vegetable stock, onions, carrots, celery, garlic, salt, dill, and fennel. Bring to a boil, then reduce the heat, cover, and simmer gently for about 5 minutes. Stir in the tomatoes and their juice. Add the bulgur and mix well. Return to a boil and simmer, covered, for another 15 minutes, or until the bulgur is tender, stirring occasionally. Add pepper to taste.

PER 9-OZ SERVING: 78 CALORIES, 2.9 G PROTEIN, .5 G FAT, 17.2 G CARBOHYDRATES, .1 G SATURATED FATTY ACIDS, .1 G POLYUNSATURATED FATTY ACIDS, .1 G MONOUNSATURATED FATTY ACIDS, 0 MG CHOLESTEROL, 538 MG SODIUM, 3.4 G TOTAL DIETARY FIBER

MENU SUGGESTIONS Serve with **Cabbage Rolls** (page 256), **Ful** (page 55), **Middle Eastern Cannellini Patties** (page 119), or **Garlicky Black-Eyed Peas 'n' Greens** (page 170).

SOUTHWESTERN CORN AND POTATO SOUP

Everyone who has tried this soup absolutely loves it. It was one of the very first low-fat recipes we ever created, and some of us were still a bit dubious about cooking without first sautéing everything in a little oil. To quiet the skeptics, Lisa Wichman made two batches of soup, one with and one without oil. When in a blind taste test her co-cooks preferred the oil-free batch, we knew we were on our way to even more healthful cooking techniques!

Serves 4 to 6

Total time: 50 minutes

1 cup finely chopped onions
2 garlic cloves, minced or pressed
1 small fresh chile, seeded and minced
¼ teaspoon salt
3 cups Basic Vegetable Stock (page 73)
2 teaspoons ground cumin
1 medium sweet potato, diced (about 2 cups)
½ red bell pepper, finely chopped
3 cups fresh or frozen corn kernels
salt to taste

lime wedges
finely chopped cilantro leaves

In a covered soup pot, simmer the onions, garlic, chile, and salt in 1 cup of the vegetable stock for about 10 minutes, or until the onions are soft. In a small bowl, make a paste with the cumin and a tablespoonful of the stock, stir it into the pot, and simmer for another 1 to 2 minutes. Add the sweet potatoes and the remaining stock and simmer for about 10 minutes, until the sweet potatoes soften. Add the bell pepper and corn and simmer, covered, for another 10 minutes, or until all of the vegetables are tender.

Purée about half of the soup in a blender or food processor and return it to the pot. The soup will be creamy and thick. Add salt to taste and gently reheat on low heat. If desired, serve with lime wedges and top with cilantro.

PER 9-OZ SERVING: 186 CALORIES, 4.8 G PROTEIN, 1.5 G FAT, 42.7 G CARBOHYDRATES, .2 G SATURATED FATTY ACIDS, .6 G POLYUNSATURATED FATTY ACIDS, .3 G MONOUNSAT-URATED FATTY ACIDS, 0 MG CHOLESTEROL, 207 MG SODIUM, 5.3 G TOTAL DIETARY FIBER

MENU SUGGESTIONS Serve with **Mexican Seitan Pita** (page 120), **One Step Bean Guacamole** (page 28), or **Caesar Salad** (page 131).

BASQUE WHITE BEAN SOUP

We at Moosewood have learned a little about the Basque region of Spain through William Foote Whyte, Professor Emeritus at Cornell University, coauthor of *Making Mondragon*. Exploring how Mondragon's network of cooperative businesses operates gave us our initial taste of Basque culture.

We were tickled to discover that these unique people, much like us, have a strong appreciation for—in fact, a downright preoccupation with—food. They wholeheartedly support food clubs where culinary talents are honed, demonstrated, and applauded. A toast to creative cuisine and cooperative effort!

This is a good soup to make ahead of time. The flavors blend and deepen as it sits.

2 cups chopped onions
2 garlic cloves, minced or pressed
1 tablespoon olive oil
1 tablespoon ground fennel
1 teaspoon dried thyme
1 cup thinly sliced cabbage
4 celery stalks with leaves, sliced (about 2 cups)
1 butternut squash, peeled, seeded, and cubed (about 3 cups)
¾ cup minced red bell peppers
6 cups Basic Vegetable Stock (page 73)
2 cups cooked or canned white beans, such as cannellini, navy, or kidney beans (15-ounce can, well rinsed)
generous pinch of saffron, or more to taste
salt and ground black pepper to taste

Serves 4 to 6

Total time: 35 minutes

In a soup pot, sauté the onions and garlic in the oil for about 10 minutes, until deeply browned and caramelized. Stir in the fennel and thyme. Add the cabbage and celery, cover, and sweat the vegetables until they are nearly tender, about 5 minutes. Add the squash and bell peppers, pour in the stock, bring to a boil, and cook for 5 to 10 minutes more, until the squash softens. Stir in the white beans and crumble in the saffron. When the soup is hot, add salt and pepper to taste.

PER 10-OZ SERVING: 215 CALORIES, 9.0 G PROTEIN, 3.4 G FAT, 40.9 G CARBOHYDRATES, .5 G SATURATED FATTY ACIDS, 1.8 G POLYUNSATURATED FATTY ACIDS, .8 G MONOUNSATURATED FATTY ACIDS, 0 MG CHOLESTEROL, 96 MG SODIUM, 7.9 G TOTAL DIETARY FIBER

MENU SUGGESTIONS Serve with a simple green salad and **Caesar Salad Dressing** (page 131) accompanied by **Spanish Potatoes** (page 324), or with crusty bread and **Roasted Garlic** (page 43). Finish with **Fruit-filled Meringue Shells** (page 388).

SAVANNAH BEANS AND GREENS SOUP

Thick and substantial, this soup is a quickly prepared meal in itself. It thickens significantly as it sits, so if you serve it left over or if you prefer a brothy soup, add more water before serving.

2 cups finely chopped onions
2 garlic cloves, pressed or minced
3 cups water or vegetable stock
½ pound fresh collard greens or kale
2 cups undrained canned tomatoes, chopped
   (16-ounce can)
3 to 4 cups cooked black-eyed peas*
1 tablespoon white or cider vinegar
1 tablespoon brown sugar
pinch of dried thyme
¼ teaspoon ground allspice
couple splashes of Tabasco or
   other hot pepper sauce, or to taste
2 cups cooked rice
salt to taste

Serves 4

Preparation time: 30 minutes

Simmering time: 20 minutes

Use two 10-ounce packages of frozen black-eyed peas or two 16-ounce cans, drained and rinsed. If you prefer to cook your own, use ½ pound dried.

In a soup pot, combine the onions and garlic in 2 cups of the water or stock. Bring to a boil, then reduce the heat and simmer for 15 minutes. Meanwhile, prepare the collards or kale by rinsing well and removing the coarse stems. Stack the leaves and slice them thinly cross-wise and then slice through the stack lengthwise once or twice. Add the greens, tomatoes and their juice, black-eyed peas, the additional cup of water, vinegar, brown sugar, thyme, allspice, and Tabasco to the pot. Simmer for 15 minutes. Stir in the rice and cook for 5 minutes more. Add salt to taste.

PER 10-OZ SERVING: 255 CALORIES, 12.2 G PROTEIN, 1.2 G FAT, 50.4 G CARBOHYDRATES, .2 G SATURATED FATTY ACIDS, .4 G POLYUNSATURATED FATTY ACIDS, .1 G MONOUNSATURATED FATTY ACIDS, 0 MG CHOLESTEROL, 144 MG SODIUM, 9.0 G TOTAL DIETARY FIBER

MENU SUGGESTIONS Serve with **Almost Fat-Free Cornbread** (page 110) and a citrus salad such as **Spinach Avocado Grapefruit Salad** (page 135). Or serve with **Baked Sweet Potato Salad** (page 137) and **Home-made Biscuits** (page 114).

CALLALOO

Callaloo (page 422) is the name given to the leaves of several different plants with edible tubers that grow in the Caribbean. If you can find fresh callaloo, seize the opportunity, but if it's unavailable, kale or spinach are reasonably good substitutes.

1½ cups finely chopped onions
3 garlic cloves, minced or pressed
2 teaspoons canola or other vegetable oil
2 teaspoons grated fresh ginger root
1 teaspoon turmeric
2 teaspoons ground coriander
½ teaspoon dried thyme
¼ teaspoon ground allspice
5 cups water or vegetable stock
2 cups diced sweet potatoes (about 1 large potato)
2 cups chopped callaloo or kale or 3 cups chopped spinach,
    rinsed and stems removed
1 cup fresh or frozen sliced okra
1 cup diced tomatoes (about 1 large tomato)
2 tablespoons fresh lime juice
½ teaspoon salt
1 cup reduced-fat coconut milk (optional, see Note)

Serves 4

Total time: 40 minutes

NOTE:
Several brands of reduced-fat coconut milk are now available in supermarkets and natural food stores. At Moosewood, we often use the Thai Kitchen brand. Although it is not as rich and creamy as regular coconut milk, the reduced-fat product still conjures up that coconut flavor reminiscent of the Tropics and it is significantly lower in fat.

In a covered soup pot, sauté the onions and garlic in the oil on low heat for about 5 minutes, until softened. Add the ginger, turmeric, coriander, thyme, and allspice and sauté for another minute, stirring to prevent sticking.

Stir in the water or stock, add the sweet potatoes, and bring to a boil. Simmer for 5 minutes, then stir in the callaloo or kale. (If you are using spinach, do not add it yet.) Add the okra and simmer for another 5 minutes. Stir in the tomatoes, lime juice, salt, and spinach, if you are using it, and cook for another 3 or 4 minutes, until all of the vegetables are tender. Add more salt or lime juice to taste and stir in the coconut milk, if you like.

PER 10-OZ SERVING: 188 CALORIES, 3.7 G PROTEIN, 5.7 G FAT, 32.2 G CARBOHYDRATES, 2.3 G SATURATED FATTY ACIDS, 1.2 G POLYUNSATURATED FATTY ACIDS, .5 G MONOUNSATURATED FATTY ACIDS, 0 MG CHOLESTEROL, 254 MG SODIUM, 4.9 G TOTAL DIETARY FIBER

MENU SUGGESTIONS Serve with **One Step Bean Guacamole** (page 28) and **Almost Fat-Free Cornbread** (page 110) and finish with **Lemon Pudding Cake** (page 377) or **Banana Bundt Cake** (page 382).

almost fat-free cornbread 110

brown bread 111

HERB AND CHEESE MUFFINS 112

herbed cottage cheese bread 113

homemade biscuits 114

BUTTERMILK ROLLS 115

asian tofu salad 116

egg salad 117

IRA'S LUNCH 118

middle eastern cannellini patties 119

mexican seitan pita 120

MUSHROOM PÂTÉ ALMONDINE 121

smoky eggplant and pepper spread 122

tempeh salad sandwich filling 123

TUSCAN SANDWICH 124

white bean and red pepper spread 125

BREADS & SANDWICHES

Homemade **BREADS** are incomparably appealing and expressive of home as a place of warmth, care, and comfort. They can transform a simple meal into a special one.

In many traditional breads, especially quick breads, it is the fat that produces a smooth, moist, soft texture and rich flavor. Our aim was to develop breads with these same qualities, but without high fat contents. We've done this by replacing all or some of the usual fat, butter, or oil with nonfat buttermilk or yogurt or with fruit or vegetable purées. We've discovered that egg whites alone, instead of whole eggs, often make tasty, good-textured breads.

Almost Fat-Free Cornbread uses all of these tricks and this new version of our old standard is still delicious, moist, and satisfying . . . and only 3 percent fat! We've included both yeasted and quicker baked goods in this chapter, but there are also recipes for muffins and other quick breads in the Breakfast and Brunch chapter.

It can be tricky to find the perfect place for bread to rise. The best conditions are warm and draft-free. Some of us preheat the oven to 200° for about 5 minutes, place pots of very hot water in it to maintain the warmth and moisture, turn off the oven, and let the bread rise in there. Because it is well insulated, a microwave is another good place to let bread rise.

As easy, portable fare for picnics, lunches, and potlucks, **SANDWICHES** can't be beat. Many of the recipes from our appetizer chapter combine nicely with sandwich fillings for salad plates or sandwiches. Leftover dips, spreads, and vegetable dishes can be readily incorporated into sandwiches. Try filling a pita pocket with Middle Eastern Cannellini Patties, Roasted Garlic, cucumbers, and tomatoes. Other appetizers (pages 18 to 43) that are likely candidates for sandwiches are Greek Lima Bean Dip, all of the guacamoles and cheese spreads, and Indian Chickpea Spread.

When we think of low-fat condiments on sandwiches, we tend to include mustard, lettuce, and tomato and to exclude mayonnaise, but a little splurge of a flavorful low-fat dressing provides extra flavor and richness. A sandwich filled with vegetables will not accumulate many grams of fat when dressed with Spicy Peanut Dressing (page 349) or with Yogurt Tahini Dressing (page 346).

Although we've grouped sandwich fillings together with breads, we don't want to give the impression that these fillings are limited to sandwiches. Most of the sandwich fillings, especially Smoky Eggplant and Pepper Spread and Mushroom Pâté Almondine, may be served as starter courses with low-fat crackers or wedges of lightly toasted pita bread. Asian Tofu Salad can serve as the main attraction on a salad plate along with greens and bread for lunch or supper.

ALMOST FAT-FREE CORNBREAD

Pumpkin, this recipe's secret ingredient, lends both a deep golden color and welcome moistness to an already exceptional bread. The corn and pumpkin combination makes it a perfect choice with most foods from the Americas, especially soups, stews, and bean dishes.

2 tablespoons brown sugar
2 egg whites
¾ cup nonfat yogurt or buttermilk
½ cup puréed cooked pumpkin, sweet potato,
   or winter squash*
1 cup cornmeal
1 cup unbleached white flour
½ teaspoon salt
1 tablespoon baking powder

Makes one 8-inch square or 9-inch round cornbread

Preparation time: 20 minutes

Baking time: 20 to 25 minutes

Small cans or jars of pure squash or sweet potato purée can often be found in the baby food section of the supermarket. A 4- or 4 ½-ounce can will work fine in this recipe. If you use canned pumpkin purée, which usually comes in 16-ounce cans, you can freeze the leftover purée in a tightly sealed container for at least a month.

Preheat the oven to 350°.

Prepare an 8-inch square or 9-inch round baking pan with cooking spray or very lightly coat it with oil. Set it aside.

In a large bowl, beat the brown sugar, egg whites, yogurt or buttermilk, and pumpkin (or sweet potato or squash) until frothy. Sift the cornmeal, flour, salt, and baking powder into the mixing bowl. Gently fold the dry ingredients into the wet ingredients until just mixed.

Pour the batter into the oiled pan and bake, uncovered, for 20 to 25 minutes, until a knife inserted in the center comes out clean. Serve hot or at room temperature.

VARIATION For a low-fat cornbread with a lighter texture than this nonfat version, add ¼ cup of canola oil and 1 egg yolk to the wet ingredients and follow the rest of the recipe as before.

PER 3-OZ SERVING: 156 CALORIES, 5.5 G PROTEIN, .5 G FAT, 32.1 G CARBOHYDRATES, .1 G SATURATED FATTY ACIDS, .2 G POLYUNSATURATED FATTY ACIDS, .1 G MONOUNSATURATED FATTY ACIDS, 0 MG CHOLESTEROL, 341 MG SODIUM, 1.4 G TOTAL DIETARY FIBER

MENU SUGGESTIONS Try the cornbread with **Mushroom Sesame Tofu Stew** (page 277) for dinner or with peach jam or apple butter for brunch.

BROWN BREAD

Heavy, coarse-textured, and slightly sweet, these baked loaves are reminiscent of classic American steamed brown bread but are much quicker and easier to make. Serve with Barbecue Beans (page 156) and applesauce, of course. Brown Bread is also wonderful toasted for breakfast.

1 cup whole wheat or rye flour
1 cup cornmeal
1 cup unbleached white flour
1 cup raisins
¼ cup packed brown sugar
½ teaspoon salt
2 teaspoons baking soda
1 teaspoon ground cinnamon
¼ teaspoon ground ginger
½ teaspoon ground allspice
2 cups buttermilk
½ cup molasses

Makes two 8-inch loaves

Preparation time: 25 minutes

Baking time: 40 to 45 minutes

Cooling time: 15 minutes

Preheat the oven to 350°. Prepare two 8-inch loaf pans by lightly buttering or coating with cooking spray.

In a large bowl, stir together the whole wheat or rye flour, cornmeal, white flour, raisins, brown sugar, salt, baking soda, cinnamon, ginger, and allspice. Add the buttermilk and molasses and stir just until a batter forms. Pour the batter into the prepared loaf pans. Bake for 40 to 45 minutes, until the loaves are firm and pull away from the sides of the pans. Cool the bread in the pans for 15 minutes. Remove the loaves from the pans and serve warm. Cool the bread completely before wrapping for storage.

PER 2-OZ SERVING: 130 CALORIES, 3.0 G PROTEIN, .5 G FAT, 29.4 G CARBOHYDRATES, .2 G SATURATED FATTY ACIDS, .1 G POLYUNSATURATED FATTY ACIDS, .1 G MONOUNSATURATED FATTY ACIDS, 1 MG CHOLESTEROL, 134 MG SODIUM, 1.6 G TOTAL DIETARY FIBER

HERB AND CHEESE MUFFINS

A savory muffin nicely rounds out a simple meal of soup and salad and adds a special touch to any brunch. We think this one is especially satisfying and flavorful.

1 cup unbleached white flour
1½ teaspoons baking powder
½ teaspoon baking soda
½ teaspoon salt
1 cup cornmeal
1 tablespoon brown sugar
1 whole egg
1 egg white
1 cup buttermilk
3 tablespoons minced scallions
½ teaspoon Dijon mustard
1 teaspoon dried dill
½ teaspoon dried thyme
¼ teaspoon ground black pepper
1 tablespoon canola or other vegetable oil (optional)
1 cup grated low-fat Cheddar cheese (4 ounces)

Makes 12 muffins

Preparation time: 15 minutes

Baking time: 20 minutes

Preheat the oven to 400°.

Prepare a 12-cup muffin tin with cooking spray or a very light coating of oil.

Sift together the flour, baking powder, baking soda, and salt in a large mixing bowl. Thoroughly mix in the cornmeal and brown sugar. In a separate bowl, beat the egg and egg white until frothy. Add the buttermilk, scallions, mustard, dill, thyme, pepper, and optional oil to the beaten eggs. Reserve 2 tablespoons of the grated cheese and stir the rest into the egg mixture. Add the egg mixture to the dry ingredients, stirring just enough to make a uniformly moist batter.

Spoon the batter into the prepared muffin tins and sprinkle the muffin tops with the reserved cheese. Bake for about 20 minutes, until a knife inserted into the center of a muffin comes out clean. Cool in the tins for 5 minutes, loosen each muffin by running a knife around the edge, and then tip out onto a rack to cool completely.

PER 2.25-OZ SERVING: 130 CALORIES, 6.1 G PROTEIN, 2.7 G FAT, 19.7 G CARBOHYDRATES, 1.3 G SATURATED FATTY ACIDS, .2 G POLYUNSATURATED FATTY ACIDS, .3 G MONOUNSATURATED FATTY ACIDS, 23 MG CHOLESTEROL, 186 MG SODIUM, 1.3 G TOTAL DIETARY FIBER

HERBED COTTAGE CHEESE BREAD

Moist and lightly accented with aromatic herbs, this savory yeasted bread has the added richness and body of low-fat cottage cheese.

Makes 1 loaf

**Preparation time:
35 minutes**

**Rising time:
1¼ to 1½ hours**

**Baking time:
about 40 minutes**

1 tablespoon yeast
1 teaspoon sugar
½ cup warm water (105° to 115°)
1 cup low-fat cottage cheese
1 tablespoon canola or other vegetable oil
¼ cup honey
1 teaspoon salt
1 teaspoon minced fresh thyme leaves
1 teaspoon minced fresh rosemary
3 tablespoons minced scallions
1 cup whole wheat bread flour
1½ to 2 cups unbleached white flour
1 teaspoon baking powder

Prepare a 2-quart casserole dish with a light coating of cooking spray or oil. In a small bowl, combine the yeast with the sugar and warm water. Set aside to proof until bubbles rise to the surface, 5 to 10 minutes.

In a small saucepan on low heat, gently warm the cottage cheese, oil, honey, salt, thyme, rosemary, and scallions. Transfer the cheese mixture to a large bowl. When the yeast is bubbly, add it to the bowl. Stir in the whole wheat flour and beat by hand 100 strokes. Combine a cup of the white flour with the baking powder and mix into the batter, then stir in enough additional white flour to make a stiff dough. Turn out onto a floured surface and knead until smooth and elastic, about 5 to 10 minutes.

Shape the dough into a ball, place it in a lightly oiled bowl, and turn it once to coat with oil. Cover with a damp towel and set aside in a warm spot for about 45 minutes, until doubled in size (page 108). After the dough has risen, punch it down, turn it onto a lightly floured surface, and knead for about 2 minutes. Shape it into a ball and place in an oiled 2-quart casserole dish. Return the dough to its warm place and let it rise again until doubled, about 30 to 45 minutes.

Preheat the oven to 350° near the end of the second rising time.

When the dough has doubled in size, bake for 30 to 40 minutes, until the bread is golden brown and sounds hollow when thumped on the bottom. Cool on a rack for about 10 minutes (if you can bear to wait that long) and it will be easier to slice.

PER 2.25-OZ SERVING: 137 CALORIES, 5.7 G PROTEIN, 1.9 G FAT, 25.2 G CARBOHYDRATES, .4 G SATURATED FATTY ACIDS, .8 G POLYUNSATURATED FATTY ACIDS, .4 G MONOUNSATURATED FATTY ACIDS, 2 MG CHOLESTEROL, 303 MG SODIUM, 1.9 G TOTAL DIETARY FIBER

HOMEMADE BISCUITS

There may be nothing more enticing than a warm batch of fresh biscuits. So if it's the weekend, a holiday, or a special personal day and you have an extra half hour, take the opportunity to make this lovely treat. We like biscuits for breakfast, lunch, or supper—they can dress up a meal of soup, stew, or salad any time of day. For dessert, try our shortbread variation piled with fresh fruit.

Makes 4 large or 6 smaller biscuits

Preparation time: 10 minutes

Baking time: 15 to 20 minutes

1½ cups unbleached white flour
½ teaspoon salt
1 teaspoon baking powder
1 to 2 tablespoons sugar (optional, to taste)
2 tablespoons canola or other vegetable oil
5 tablespoons nonfat or regular buttermilk

Preheat the oven to 350°.

Lightly oil or spray a baking sheet or pie pan.

In a large bowl, sift together the flour, salt, baking powder, and sugar, if you are using it. Combine the oil and buttermilk. Blend the buttermilk mixture into the dry ingredients, adding it in a thin, steady stream while making swift short strokes from the sides of the bowl toward the center. Avoid overstirring, which will make the biscuits tough.

When a dough begins to form, turn it onto a floured surface and, with floured hands, press the dough into a ball. Instead of kneading, which would overwork this dough, cut the dough in half, place one half on top of the other, and press down. Repeat this sequence three more times, then mold the dough into an oblong shape and slice it into four or six equal pieces. Shape each piece into a biscuit and arrange on the baking sheet.

Bake for 15 to 20 minutes, until slightly puffed and golden brown.

VARIATION To make shortbread, include the optional sugar in the recipe and add 1 teaspoon of pure vanilla extract to the wet ingredients. Cut and press the dough as above, then spread the dough out in a pie pan or pat it into a circle and place on a baking sheet, bake, and cut into wedges.

PER 1.50-OZ SERVING: 150 CALORIES, 3.3 G PROTEIN, 5.1 G FAT, 22.4 G CARBOHY-DRATES, .7 G SATURATED FATTY ACIDS, 2.9 G POLYUNSATURATED FATTY ACIDS, 1.2 G MONOUNSATURATED FATTY ACIDS, 0 MG CHOLESTEROL, 265 MG SODIUM, .9 G TOTAL DIETARY FIBER

BUTTERMILK ROLLS

The love of bread making has passed down to Moosewood's Lisa Wichman through the generations. For many years she baked all of the bread for her family; now she makes time to "indulge" in baking whenever she can.

Lisa has wonderful childhood memories of the fantastic aroma of the rolls her mom baked for holidays and special occasions. With her mother's input and blessing, Lisa developed this low-fat version of the original rolls. Try these once and we're sure you too will find the time to squeeze them into even the busiest schedule.

1 tablespoon dry yeast
¼ cup warm water (105° to 115°)
1½ teaspoons sugar
2 cups nonfat or regular buttermilk
3 tablespoons canola or other vegetable oil
1½ teaspoons salt
1 cup whole wheat flour
1½ teaspoons baking soda
2½ to 3 ½ cups unbleached white flour

Makes 20 to 22 rolls

Preparation time: 25 minutes

Rising time: 1 to 1¼ hours

Baking time: 15 to 20 minutes

In a small bowl, combine the yeast, water, and sugar and set aside until bubbles begin to rise to the surface, about 5 minutes.

Warm the buttermilk, oil, and salt in a saucepan to about 115°. Transfer to a large bowl. In a separate bowl, sift together the whole wheat flour, baking soda, and 2 cups of the white flour. When the yeast is bubbly and dissolved, add it to the buttermilk mixture. Stir in the flour mixture and beat vigorously 100 strokes. Add enough additional white flour to make a stiff dough. Turn out onto a lightly floured surface and cover with the bowl for 15 minutes. Uncover and knead well for 5 to 10 minutes, until the dough is smooth and elastic.

Prepare two muffin tins with cooking spray. Pinch off pieces of dough about the size of large walnuts, roll each piece into a ball, and place 2 dough balls in each muffin tin. You will have about 21 "double" rolls. Cover the rolls with a damp towel and place them in a warm spot until doubled in size, about 45 minutes to an hour. (See page 108 for information on rising.)

When the rolls have almost finished rising, preheat the oven to 350°.

When completely risen, uncover the rolls and bake for 15 to 20 minutes, until golden brown. Remove from the pans immediately and enjoy.

PER 1.65-OZ SERVING: 102 CALORIES, 3.1 G PROTEIN, 2.4 G FAT, 17.0 G CARBOHYDRATES, .4 G SATURATED FATTY ACIDS, 1.2 G POLYUNSATURATED FATTY ACIDS, .6 G MONOUNSATURATED FATTY ACIDS, 1 MG CHOLESTEROL, 215 MG SODIUM, 1.2 G TOTAL DIETARY FIBER

ASIAN TOFU SALAD

We've made lots of tofu salads at Moosewood, but this snappy version is one of our favorites. Normally modest tofu is given a kick in the pants by the spirited combination of garlic, chili paste, and scallions. Asian Tofu Salad keeps well for up to 2 or 3 days, so you can make it ahead and use it in place of the wasabi in Nori Vegetable Rolls (page 36) for a delicious luncheon presentation.

DRESSING
2 garlic cloves, minced or pressed
2 teaspoons grated fresh ginger root
½ teaspoon chili paste, or more to taste
2 tablespoons soy sauce
1 tablespoon rice vinegar
1 teaspoon dark sesame oil

Serves 4

Total time: 20 minutes

SALAD
1 cake firm tofu (about 12 ounces)
⅓ cup chopped red bell peppers
⅓ cup chopped scallions
1 tablespoon chopped fresh parsley

Whisk together all of the dressing ingredients in a bowl and set aside.

Using a wooden spoon, a fork, or your hands, crumble the tofu into a separate bowl. Add the peppers, scallions, parsley, and dressing and mix well. Serve at room temperature or chilled.

PER 4.50-OZ SERVING: 90 CALORIES, 7.7 G PROTEIN, 5.3 G FAT, 4.7 G CARBOHYDRATES, .8 G SATURATED FATTY ACIDS, 2.8 G POLYUNSATURATED FATTY ACIDS, 1.4 G MONOUNSATURATED FATTY ACIDS, 0 MG CHOLESTEROL, 422 MG SODIUM, 1.8 G TOTAL DIETARY FIBER

MENU SUGGESTIONS Tuck Asian Tofu Salad into a pita with watercress, baby mizuna, or arugula or serve it with rice crackers and **Korean Vegetable Noodle Soup** (page 89). Try it on a combo plate with **Cantonese Roasted Vegetables** (page 226) and **Japanese Sesame Spinach** (page 330) or with **Five-Spice Rice** (page 186) and **Fresh Spring Rolls** (page 254).

Soybeans and soy products are the subject of much research for a variety of health-related reasons. They contain seven components that may have anti-cancer properties, they may have cholesterol-lowering properties, they contain soluble fiber and have very little saturated fat, and they boast all of the essential amino acids as well as calcium, iron, zinc, and B vitamins.

EGG SALAD

If egg salad is an old favorite that you've relegated to your diet's "out" list these days, try this spirited rendition. Most of the egg yolks are missing, along with most of the fat and cholesterol, while other strongly flavored ingredients more than make up for the banished yolks.

Egg Salad is excellent on crackers, as a side salad, as a dip for julienned carrots or celery sticks, stuffed into blanched red and green bell pepper halves, or as a sandwich with ruby lettuce and a few alfalfa sprouts.

6 eggs
1 celery stalk
½ red bell pepper, seeded
1 to 2 tablespoons minced dill pickle
¼ cup minced red onion
2 tablespoons minced fresh dill
2 tablespoons reduced-fat mayonnaise
2 teaspoons prepared horseradish
1 teaspoon Dijon mustard

Makes 2 cups

Total time: 30 minutes

NOTE:
Peeling eggs is sometimes easy and sometimes hard. We find that rapidly cooling the hot eggs can make them easier to peel. Another helpful technique is to crack each egg lightly all around and gently roll it between the palms of your hands or on the counter with one hand to loosen the shell.

Some of us at Moosewood add a tablespoon of vinegar to the cooking water before boiling our eggs because we've heard it makes them easier to peel. Although we have never scientifically verified whether this really works every time, it often seems to and it certainly can't hurt.

Place the eggs in a pot with cold water to cover. Bring to a boil, lower the heat, and simmer for about 10 minutes.

While the eggs cook, dice the celery and bell pepper and set aside in a large bowl. Add the dill pickle, red onion, and dill to the bowl.

When the eggs are cooked, drain them and immediately submerge them in very cold water to cool. Peel the eggs (see Note). Chop 2 of the eggs and add them to the bowl. Remove and discard the yolks from the remaining 4 eggs, chop the whites, and add to the bowl. Stir in the mayonnaise, horseradish, and mustard and mix well. Serve chilled.

PER 4.50-OZ SERVING: 166 CALORIES, 12.3 G PROTEIN, 11.0 G FAT, 3.8 G CARBOHYDRATES, 3.2 G SATURATED FATTY ACIDS, 1.4 G POLYUNSATURATED FATTY ACIDS, 3.8 G MONOUNSATURATED FATTY ACIDS, 400 MG CHOLESTEROL, 145 MG SODIUM, .5 G TOTAL DIETARY FIBER

MENU SUGGESTIONS Serve with **Cream of Green Vegetable Soup** (page 82), **Curried Carrot Parsnip Soup** (page 100), **Barbecue Beans** (page 156), or **Potato Bean Salad** (page 138).

IRA'S LUNCH

Ira Rabois was a Moosewood collective member during the first decade of our history. When he started his teaching career, Linda Dickinson (we call her LD) invented this dish for his take-to-school lunch. When we decided to offer it on our lunch menu, we had no idea how popular it would become.

LD's sandwich spread uses tofu-kan, a pressed seasoned tofu that is produced locally by Ithaca Soy and distributed throughout the Northeast. It is similar to Chinese five-spice bean curd, which you can use if tofu-kan is not available.

1 cake tofu-kan (7 ounces), grated
½ cup diced red or green bell peppers
½ cup chopped celery (optional)
2 tablespoons minced scallions or red onions
2 tablespoons minced fresh parsley
1 tablespoon chopped fresh dill (1 teaspoon dried)
1 teaspoon Dijon mustard
1 teaspoon fresh lemon juice
⅓ cup reduced-fat mayonnaise
dash of ground black pepper, or more to taste

greens, such as ruby or buttercrunch lettuce or spinach
tomato slices

Serves 4

Total time: 10 minutes

Mix together the tofu, bell peppers, celery, if using, scallions or red onions, parsley, dill, mustard, lemon juice, mayonnaise, and black pepper in a bowl until well combined. Serve immediately on greens with fresh tomato slices or chill to serve later.

PER 3.25-OZ SERVING: 71 CALORIES, 4.5 G PROTEIN, 4.8 G FAT, 3.7 G CARBOHYDRATES, .8 G SATURATED FATTY ACIDS, 1.4 G POLYUNSATURATED FATTY ACIDS, .5 G MONOUNSATURATED FATTY ACIDS, 9 MG CHOLESTEROL, 11 MG SODIUM, 1.1 G TOTAL DIETARY FIBER

MENU SUGGESTIONS Ira's Lunch is wonderful spread on toast or stuffed into pita pockets with some leafy greens and chopped tomatoes. It is also fine as a buffet or party dip with crackers or crudités. For a complete luncheon, serve it as a salad with **Chilled Beet and Buttermilk Soup** (page 79) or **Tomato Bulgur Soup** (page 101) and some crusty sourdough bread.

MIDDLE EASTERN CANNELLINI PATTIES

These versatile patties are the perfect alternative to fat-laden falafels. They can elevate an ordinary salad into a protein-rich meal or they can be stuffed into pita pockets with cucumber slices, grated carrots, and Yogurt Tahini Dressing (page 346). Any way you serve them, they are sure to hit the spot.

2 teaspoons olive oil
2 cups minced onions
2 large garlic cloves, minced or pressed
1 teaspoon salt
1 cup minced bell peppers
2 teaspoons ground cumin
4 cups cooked cannellini or other white beans
   (two 20-ounce cans, drained)
1 cup minced fresh parsley
2 cups cooked brown rice (page 435)
1 tablespoon fresh lemon juice
ground black pepper to taste

Serves 6

Makes 18 patties

Preparation time: 30 minutes, if using already cooked rice and beans

Total time: 1 hour, if frying three batches, less if using two skillets

Warm the olive oil in a medium nonstick skillet. Add the onions, garlic, and salt and cook on medium-low heat, stirring often, for 5 to 10 minutes, until the onions are tender. Add the bell peppers and cumin and cook for 5 minutes more, until the peppers are soft, stirring frequently. Remove from the heat and set aside.

Thoroughly mash the beans by hand in a large mixing bowl. Combine the parsley, rice, and lemon juice with the mashed beans. Add the cooked vegetables and mix well. Add black pepper to taste.

Shape the mixture into 18 small patties, about 2½ inches across. Prepare a large nonstick skillet with cooking spray. Heat the skillet and cook the patties on medium heat until golden brown on the underside, about 5 to 10 minutes. Gently turn them and lightly brown the other side, about 5 minutes longer. Serve hot or at room temperature.

PER 10-OZ SERVING: 239 CALORIES, 10.6 G PROTEIN, 2.9 G FAT, 44.2 G CARBOHYDRATES, .4 G SATURATED FATTY ACIDS, .6 G POLYUNSATURATED FATTY ACIDS, 1.4 G MONOUNSATURATED FATTY ACIDS, 0 MG CHOLESTEROL, 941 MG SODIUM, 10.8 G TOTAL DIETARY FIBER

MENU SUGGESTIONS For a summer supper, arrange the patties on a platter with **Vegetables à la Grecque** (page 130) and **Tabouli Salad** (page 145) and drizzle them with **Yogurt Tahini Dressing** (page 346). Or serve them as an appetizer for main dishes such as **Greek Stew** (page 266) or **Potato Beet Salad** (page 139).

MEXICAN SEITAN PITA

Seasoned seitan comes in a variety of flavors, colors, and textures and we suggest you try several of those available in your area to discover your favorite ones. We add a spicy, refreshing salsa and stuff both in a pita pocket with lettuce and grated cheese for a zesty south-of-the-border sandwich. The salsa tastes best when made a bit in advance.

**Makes 4 filled
pita halves**

Total time: 15 minutes

NOTE:

Pitas are best toasted on a medium setting in a toaster oven, but you can also use a regular toaster or the broiler of a standard oven. If you use a regular toaster, use the lightest setting. If you use the broiler, toast the pita for about 2 or 3 minutes on each side. It should be hot but still soft and pliable. Remove the toasted pita from the toaster or oven as soon as it's ready; otherwise it can harden to a cracker-like texture within minutes.

SALSA

1 tomato, diced
1 tablespoon minced red onions
1 teaspoon fresh lime or lemon juice
¼ cup peeled, seeded, and diced cucumber
¼ teaspoon ground cumin
a splash of Tabasco, or to taste
salt and ground black pepper to taste
1 tablespoon minced fresh cilantro (optional)

SANDWICH

2 pitas, cut in half
shredded lettuce
4 ounces seasoned seitan, sliced or chopped
¼ to ½ cup grated fat-free or low-fat Cheddar cheese

Combine all of the salsa ingredients and set aside for at least 15 minutes or up to 2 hours. Toast the pitas (see Note). Assemble the sandwiches by placing some lettuce, about an ounce of seitan, 1 or 2 tablespoons of grated Cheddar, and about ¼ cup of salsa in each pita half. Serve immediately.

PER 4.50-OZ SERVING: 128 CALORIES, 6.8 G PROTEIN, 1.7 G FAT, 23.6 G CARBOHYDRATES, .1 G SATURATED FATTY ACIDS, .3 G POLYUNSATURATED FATTY ACIDS, .1 G MONOUNSATURATED FATTY ACIDS, 5 MG CHOLESTEROL, 365 MG SODIUM, .7 G TOTAL DIETARY FIBER

MENU SUGGESTIONS Serve with **Catalan Potato Lima Soup** (page 99), with **Southwestern Corn and Potato Soup** (page 102), or with a side dish of **One Step Bean Guacamole** (page 28). **Pineapple Buttermilk Sherbet** (page 394) is a refreshing dessert.

MUSHROOM PÂTÉ ALMONDINE

The heyday of mock chopped liver may have come and gone, but whether you remember it or not, this low-fat pâté is an updated version that is savory and delicious.

2 cups chopped onions
2 teaspoons olive or canola oil
4 garlic cloves, minced or pressed
1½ cups chopped green beans
4 cups sliced mushrooms (about 14 ounces)
2 tablespoons dry white wine or sherry
1 tablespoon soy sauce
½ teaspoon dried thyme
2 tablespoons toasted almonds*
1 hard-boiled egg white, chopped

Serves 6

Total time: 40 minutes

Toast a single layer of raw almonds on an unoiled baking sheet at 350° for about 5 minutes, until fragrant and lightly browned.

Sauté the onions in the oil for about 10 minutes, until translucent. Add the garlic, green beans, mushrooms, wine or sherry, soy sauce, and thyme. Cover and cook for 10 minutes and then uncover and cook for another 10 to 15 minutes, until the vegetables are soft and most of the liquid has evaporated.

In a food processor or by hand, chop the almonds. Combine the chopped nuts, cooked vegetables, and egg white in a blender or food processor and purée until well mixed. Spread on bread or spoon into your favorite pita pocket.

PER 5-OZ SERVING: 84 CALORIES, 4.1 G PROTEIN, 3.4 G FAT, 10.7 G CARBOHYDRATES, .4 G SATURATED FATTY ACIDS, .6 G POLYUNSATURATED FATTY ACIDS, 2.1 G MONOUNSATURATED FATTY ACIDS, 0 MG CHOLESTEROL, 156 MG SODIUM, 3.1 G TOTAL DIETARY FIBER

MENU SUGGESTIONS Make a savory pita sandwich with lettuce, tomato, shredded carrots, and sprouts and serve with **Chilled Beet and Buttermilk Soup** (page 79) or **Cream of Cauliflower Soup** (page 90). Use as an appetizer spread on crackers, **Herbed Cottage Cheese Bread** (page 113), or thinly sliced rye bread and serve before **Ukrainian Beet and Bean Stew** (page 269), **Potato Beet Salad** (page 139), or **Swiss Chard and Tomato Frittata** (page 50).

SMOKY EGGPLANT AND PEPPER SPREAD

During inclement weather when grilling outdoors is inconvenient, try this stove-top technique for charring vegetables to infuse them with a rich, smoky flavor. It works best on a gas stove, but if you use high heat on your electric stove, you'll have good results as well.

The flavors of this spread intensify over time, so if you prepare it a day in advance, you'll be rewarded with an enhanced, full-bodied taste. In fact, after several days, it's at its best. Try it as a pizza topping on your favorite homemade crust—we think you'll like it.

1 large eggplant (about 1¼ pounds)
1 or 2 garlic cloves
2 lemons
1 large red bell pepper
1 tablespoon olive oil
salt and ground black pepper to taste

Serves 8 as a side dish

Makes 2 cups

**Total time:
30 to 45 minutes**

> **NOTE:**
> This recipe makes a chunky spread. For a creamy version, purée everything in a blender or food processor.

With a fork, prick the eggplant in several places and wrap it in three thicknesses of aluminum foil. Place directly on the stove burner and cook on medium heat. Using long tongs or an oven mitt to avoid burning yourself, turn the eggplant every 3 or 4 minutes so that it chars evenly all around. When the eggplant is soft and collapsed, about 15 to 20 minutes, remove it from the heat. Being careful to avoid escaping steam, peel back the foil, slice the eggplant in half lengthwise, and put it in a colander to cool and drain.

While the eggplant roasts, peel and press (or mince) the garlic cloves and squeeze 4 teaspoons of lemon juice. Set aside.

Place the bell pepper directly on a second stove burner and center it to maximize contact with the flame. Adjust the flame to medium-high heat and, using long tongs, turn the pepper every 1 to 2 minutes to char the skin evenly, roasting it for 5 to 10 minutes in all. Place the roasted pepper in a covered bowl or paper bag to cool.

When the pepper is cool enough to handle, use a paring knife or your fingers to peel and discard the skin, then cut it in half and remove the seeds. Scoop the eggplant flesh from its shell. Finely chop the eggplant and bell pepper (see Note). Combine them with the garlic, lemon juice, olive oil, and salt and pepper to taste. Serve at room temperature or chilled.

PER 3-OZ SERVING: 39 CALORIES, .7 G PROTEIN, 2.0 G FAT, 5.6 G CARBOHYDRATES, .3 G SATURATED FATTY ACIDS, .2 G POLYUNSATURATED FATTY ACIDS, 1.3 G MONOUNSATURATED FATTY ACIDS, 0 MG CHOLESTEROL, 24 MG SODIUM, 1.9 G TOTAL DIETARY FIBER

MENU SUGGESTIONS Serve as a combo plate with **Cucumbers Vinaigrette** (page 133) and either **Greek Spinach Rice Balls** (page 35) or **Middle Eastern Cannellini Patties** (page 119), or with **Vegetables à la Grecque** (page 130) and **Ful** (page 55).

TEMPEH SALAD SANDWICH FILLING

Tempeh is a traditional Indonesian food made from cultured whole soybeans that are pressed into thin cakes. This high-protein product can be found in the frozen foods section of most natural food stores.

This hearty sandwich filling can also be served buffet style with crackers or crudités.

SALAD
8-ounce package tempeh
½ cup diced celery
½ cup diced bell peppers
¼ cup minced red onions
2 tablespoons chopped fresh parsley
1 tablespoon soy sauce

Serves 4

Total time: 30 minutes

DRESSING
¼ cup plain nonfat yogurt
2 tablespoons reduced-fat mayonnaise
1 tablespoon Dijon mustard
ground black pepper to taste

Cut the tempeh into ½-inch cubes. Place them in a steamer over boiling water and steam for 20 minutes.

Meanwhile, in a medium bowl, mix together the celery, bell peppers, red onions, and parsley. When the tempeh is soft and thoroughly cooked, sprinkle the soy sauce over it and add it to the vegetables. In a small bowl, whisk together the dressing ingredients and stir into the salad. Toss everything well. Serve at once or chill for later.

PER 4.50-OZ SERVING: 146 CALORIES, 12.4 G PROTEIN, 5.5 G FAT, 14.2 G CARBOHYDRATES, .8 G SATURATED FATTY ACIDS, 2.5 G POLYUNSATURATED FATTY ACIDS, 1.0 G MONOUNSATURATED FATTY ACIDS, 4 MG CHOLESTEROL, 277 MG SODIUM, .8 G TOTAL DIETARY FIBER

MENU SUGGESTIONS Serve on toast or in a whole wheat pita pocket with lettuce and tomato slices. Serve it with **Curried Carrot Parsnip Soup** (page 100), **Spanish Potato Garlic Soup** (page 97), **Tropical Gazpacho** (page 78), or **Caesar Salad** (page 131).

TUSCAN SANDWICH

This is a hearty, rustic sandwich of tomatoes, greens, red onions, and seitan sparked by roasted red peppers, basil, garlic, and mild balsamic vinegar and served in a baguette. If available, an Italian-seasoned seitan works best in this sandwich.

4 garlic cloves, minced or pressed
1 head of greens, such as escarole, kale, or broccoli rabe, chopped
1 teaspoon olive oil
16-inch baguette, halved lengthwise
1 tomato, sliced
balsamic vinegar or Italian Tomato Basil Dressing (page 347)
½ cup sliced canned pimientos or roasted red peppers (page 436)
½ cup sliced red onions
4 ounces Italian-seasoned seitan, sliced
¼ cup grated Parmesan cheese (optional)
4 fresh basil leaves, whole or chopped (optional)

**Serves 4 for lunch
2 for dinner**

Total time: 20 minutes

NOTE:
To give the baguette a little extra flavor, slice a large garlic clove in half and rub juices from the cut side of the garlic on the cut side of the bread before toasting. This works best with a crusty bread. Or spread some soft Roasted Garlic (page 43) on the baguette after toasting it.

Preheat the oven or toaster oven to 375°.

Combine the minced garlic, greens, and oil in a saucepan. Cover and sauté on medium heat for about 5 minutes, stirring to prevent sticking, until just wilted. Drain, transfer to a serving bowl or platter, and set aside.

Lightly toast the baguette directly on the oven rack until golden, about 5 minutes (see Note). Slice it crosswise into quarters.

Arrange everything on a platter or in bowls and assemble the sandwiches at the table.

PER 10-OZ SERVING: 303 CALORIES, 10.5 G PROTEIN, 4.6 G FAT, 55.7 G CARBOHYDRATES, .8 G SATURATED FATTY ACIDS, 1.1 G POLYUNSATURATED FATTY ACIDS, 2.0 G MONOUNSATURATED FATTY ACIDS, 0 MG CHOLESTEROL, 677 MG SODIUM, 5.9 G TOTAL DIETARY FIBER

MENU SUGGESTIONS Serve with **Cream of Green Vegetable Soup** (page 82), **Minestrone Genoa** (page 86), or **Orzo and Pea Soup** (page 93). For the full ethnic effect, serve with a glass of Chianti and a platter of **Tuscan Beans with Sage** (page 168) and offer clusters of dark grapes or luscious fresh pears with **Chocolate Hazelnut Biscotti** (page 392) for dessert.

WHITE BEAN AND RED PEPPER SPREAD

This simply prepared, rosy-colored spread has no added fat and plenty of zip. In fact, the garlic will become more pronounced as the spread sits. Use it to top crostini, fill a sandwich, or accompany chips, crackers, or a vegetable platter. The basic recipe can be multiplied without revision to feed a crowd. If you want to cook your own white beans, use about ⅔ cup of dried beans, soak and drain them, and then cook them in plenty of fresh water for about an hour, until tender.

1½ cups cooked white beans (16-ounce can, drained)
⅓ cup roasted red peppers *
1 garlic clove, pressed or minced
2 to 3 tablespoons fresh lemon juice, to taste
2 tablespoons chopped fresh parsley
salt and ground black pepper to taste

*If you prefer to roast a fresh bell pepper, 1 medium red pepper will work fine. See page 418 for technique.

Makes about 2 cups

**Preparation time:
15 minutes, with already cooked beans and roasted red peppers**

Chilling time: 30 minutes

Combine the beans, roasted peppers, garlic, and 2 tablespoons of the lemon juice in a food processor and purée until smooth. Stir in the parsley and add salt and pepper to taste. Add more lemon juice, if you like, and whirl for a few moments until just combined. Chill for at least 30 minutes to allow the flavors to meld.

VARIATIONS Replace the fresh garlic with a tablespoon of Roasted Garlic (page 43). Try adding 1 to 2 tablespoons of chopped fresh dill or basil to the finished spread.

PER 2-OZ SERVING: 65 CALORIES, 4.0 G PROTEIN, .3 G FAT, 12.1 G CARBOHYDRATES, .1 G SATURATED FATTY ACIDS, .1 G POLYUNSATURATED FATTY ACIDS, 0 G MONOUNSATURATED FATTY ACIDS, 0 MG CHOLESTEROL, 23 MG SODIUM, .1 G TOTAL DIETARY FIBER

MENU SUGGESTIONS Serve as a sandwich filling with sliced tomatoes, chopped black olives, and fresh leafy greens. Pair the sandwich with a cup of **Cream of Green Vegetable Soup** (page 82) or **Orzo and Pea Soup** (page 93). Or serve it spread on thinly sliced, toasted baguette rounds as a crostini before **Mushroom- and Spinach-stuffed Zucchini** (page 247), **Midsummer Risotto** (page 191), or **Pasta with Eggplant** (page 205).

Offer as a dip with crudités before **Luscious Basil and Feta Pizza** (page 228), or as part of a combination plate with **Vegetables à la Grecque** (page 130) and **Tabouli Salad** (page 145) or **Greek Spinach Rice Balls** (page 35).

vegetables à la grecque 130

caesar salad 131

CABBAGE SALAD 132

cucumbers vinaigrette 133

carrot orange salad 134

SPINACH AVOCADO GRAPEFRUIT SALAD 135

mango coconut cucumber salad 136

baked sweet potato salad 137

POTATO BEAN SALAD 138

potato beet salad 139

sesame beets 140

QUINOA BLACK BEAN SALAD 141

caribbean pigeon pea salad 142

mediterranean couscous salad 144

TABOULI SALAD 145

sushi rice salad 146

wild rice waldorf salad 147

MEXICAN PASTA SALAD 148

chinese orzo vegetable salad 149

creamy macaroni salad 150

LENTIL SALAD 151

SALADS

Time was, **SALAD** was synonymous with lettuce. And while we love fresh, leafy greens and raw vegetables tossed with tasty dressings—you'll find an outstanding Caesar Salad and a spinach salad in this chapter—the bulk of these salads are made up of vegetables, grains, and beans and can be served as main dishes, side dishes, and even snacks. Most of our salads will keep in the refrigerator for a few days, and that's part of their appeal—once made, they're ready to be enjoyed anytime.

Mango Coconut Cucumber Salad and Spinach Avocado Grapefruit Salad are colorful salads with flavor combinations that surprise and delight the palate. Over and over again, we find ourselves serving Carrot Orange Salad and Cucumbers Vinaigrette as side salads with a wide variety of main dishes. One-dish meals include Quinoa Black Bean Salad, Caribbean Pigeon Pea Salad, and Lentil Salad.

All too often salads, and especially salad dressings, harbor unhealthy amounts of fat. We've cut down on the fat usually found in oily dressings in several ways. Sometimes it's merely a matter of changing the proportions. In our new tabouli, there is no oil, but more moist, fresh tomatoes and a lot of tangy parsley. Chickpeas are added for their contrasting texture and taste. Adding bits of assertive flavor is another way to satisfy with less fat, as in our Sushi Rice Salad with its crumbled, briny nori seaweed and the sharp bite of wasabi. In our lower-fat Caesar Salad, just two little calamata olives boost the flavor usually provided by anchovies and oil, and we use buttermilk and low-fat cottage cheese rather than the usual oil and egg yolks for creaminess. In some of our creamy dressings, cottage cheese and yogurt substitute for mayonnaise and sour cream. In Vegetables à la Grecque, the vegetables are cooked directly in a spirited dressing so that they fully absorb plenty of flavor and don't need to be coated further with dressing.

At Moosewood, we often serve salad plates for lunches and warm weather dinners. Our salad plates are usually accompanied by a cup of soup and are composed of one or two salads on greens, bread or crackers, an accent such as a bean dip or guacamole, and a simple fruit or vegetable garnish. Some salads that we suggest pairing include:

Potato Beet Salad and *Cucumbers Vinaigrette*

Tabouli Salad and *Vegetables à la Grecque*

Lentil Salad and *Carrot Orange Salad*

Sushi Rice Salad and *Sesame Beets*

Baked Sweet Potato Salad and *Mango Coconut Cucumber Salad*

Caribbean Pigeon Pea Salad
and *Mango Coconut Cucumber Salad*

Mexican Pasta Salad and
Spinach Avocado Grapefruit Salad

VEGETABLES À LA GRECQUE

This is a great dish for buffets or picnics—colorful vegetables cooked in a wine and herb marinade with no oil. We leave the choice of vegetables to you, but do include at least four vegetables of varied colors. Potatoes, sweet potatoes, carrots, and parsnips should be peeled and julienned or thinly sliced. Green beans and sugar snaps should be stemmed. Bell peppers are best cut into strips. Slice onions and zucchini into rounds. Mushrooms and cauliflower or broccoli florets should be bite-sized.

The vegetables can be prepared up to 2 days in advance and then tossed with the marinade shortly before serving.

MARINADE

½ teaspoon black peppercorns

2 bay leaves

1 large fresh rosemary sprig (½ teaspoon crumbled dried)

2 large fresh tarragon sprigs (1 teaspoon dried)

2 large fresh thyme sprigs (½ teaspoon dried)

2 cups dry white wine

2 cups water

4 garlic cloves, pressed or minced

¼ cup cider vinegar

1 teaspoon salt

vegetables of your choice (8 to 10 cups, sliced or chopped)

Serves 6 to 8

Preparation time: 25 minutes

Cooking time: 15 to 40 minutes for the vegetables

> **NOTE:**
> Try garnished with several several cherry tomatoes and/or calamata olives.

Place the peppercorns and bay leaves in a tea ball. Tie all of the fresh herb sprigs together with kitchen string or, if using dried herbs, add them to the tea ball. In a nonreactive saucepan, bring all of the marinade ingredients to a boil, then reduce the heat, cover, and simmer for 15 minutes.

While the marinade simmers, slice or chop the vegetables you've chosen. Then blanch each vegetable in succession in the marinade until just tender and remove it to a platter with a slotted spoon or strainer. Begin with the blander vegetables and end with the strongest flavored ones, such as cauliflower. Potatoes and carrots take about 10 minutes to cook, while bell peppers, onions, and mushrooms take only 2 or 3 minutes. Pour any remaining marinade over the cooked vegetables and serve or chill for later.

PER 9-OZ SERVING: 94 CALORIES, 3.1 G PROTEIN, .3 G FAT, 12.1 G CARBOHYDRATES, .1 G SATURATED FATTY ACIDS, .1 G POLYUNSATURATED FATTY ACIDS, 0 G MONOUNSATURATED FATTY ACIDS, 0 MG CHOLESTEROL, 332 MG SODIUM, 3.5 G TOTAL DIETARY FIBER

MENU SUGGESTIONS Serve with **Mushroom Spinach Crêpes** (page 234), **Luscious Basil and Feta Pizza** (page 228), **Mediterranean Couscous Salad** (page 144), or **Middle Eastern Tofu-stuffed Peppers** (page 246).

CAESAR SALAD

We did a lot of experimenting to create a Caesar Salad dressing with the characteristic smooth, eggy flavor without the traditional surplus of egg yolks and oil. Our secret: two little calamata olives, which add just the right briny note. Try it on steamed asparagus or cauliflower, or as a dip for artichokes.

Covered and refrigerated, it will keep for several days.

DRESSING

2 hard-boiled eggs, whites only
1 teaspoon Dijon mustard
1 garlic clove, pressed or minced
¼ cup nonfat or low-fat cottage cheese
¼ cup nonfat or regular buttermilk
3 tablespoons fresh lemon juice
2 calamata olives, pitted and minced
2 teaspoons Pickapeppa sauce (see Note), soy sauce,
    or Worcestershire sauce (optional)
salt and ground black pepper to taste

CROUTONS

4 slices bread, each ½ inch thick
1 large garlic clove

SALAD

2 hearts of romaine or 1 whole head of romaine lettuce
1 ounce freshly grated Pecorino Romano cheese (about ⅓ cup)

Serves 4

Makes 1 cup of dressing

Total time:
25 to 30 minutes

NOTE:
Pickapeppa sauce, a fruity, mild hot sauce from Jamaica, contains tomatoes, onions, sugar, cane vinegar, mangoes, raisins, tamarind, and spices.

In a blender, combine all of the dressing ingredients, except the salt and pepper. Purée until smooth. Add salt and pepper to taste. Cover and refrigerate.

Toast the bread slices. Peel the garlic clove, slice it in half, and rub the cut surfaces on both sides of the toast. Cut into ½-inch cubes, and lightly toast again on an unoiled tray at 350°.

Rinse and dry the lettuce. Tear it into 2-inch pieces and combine it with the croutons in a serving bowl. Gently toss with about ¼ cup of dressing to lightly coat the lettuce and croutons. Sprinkle with the grated cheese and serve immediately.

PER 6.50-OZ SERVING: 157 CALORIES, 10.7 G PROTEIN, 4.3 G FAT, 19.1 G CARBOHYDRATES, 1.8 G SATURATED FATTY ACIDS, .4 G POLYUNSATURATED FATTY ACIDS, 1.1 G MONOUNSATURATED FATTY ACIDS, 9 MG CHOLESTEROL, 472 MG SODIUM, 2.9 G TOTAL DIETARY FIBER

MENU SUGGESTIONS Serve alone as a luncheon dish, or with **Creamy Potato Kale Soup** (page 91) or **New England Squash Soup** (page 96), or as a green salad before a larger meal.

CABBAGE SALAD

This crunchy, tart, distinctive coleslaw is most appropriate with Indian, Mexican, Middle Eastern, Spanish, or American food. Prepare the Cumin Yogurt Dressing before chopping the vegetables so the dressing has time to develop some depth.

Serves 4 to 6

Total time: 20 to 25 minutes

NOTE:
Freshly ground cumin seeds are more intensely flavored than preground cumin, so use more or less to taste. If you have the time and inclination, toast the whole cumin seeds and then grind them for a "sweeter" cumin flavor.

CUMIN YOGURT DRESSING
½ cup nonfat or low-fat yogurt
1 small garlic clove, pressed
1 teaspoon fresh lime or lemon juice
½ teaspoon ground cumin (see Note)
¼ teaspoon grated red onions
pinch of ground cinnamon
½ to 1 teaspoon minced fresh cilantro or mint (optional)
salt to taste

VEGETABLES
2 cups finely shredded savoy or green cabbage
½ cup finely chopped red or green bell peppers
½ cup finely chopped celery
¼ cup finely chopped red onions

Whisk together all of the dressing ingredients and set aside.

Combine the cabbage, bell peppers, celery, and onions in a large bowl. Add the dressing and toss well. Chill for at least 15 minutes before serving.

CABBAGE SALAD WITH DRESSING PER 3.50-OZ SERVING: 33 CALORIES, 2.2 G PROTEIN, .3 G FAT, 6.2 G CARBOHYDRATES, 0 G SATURATED FATTY ACIDS, .1 G POLYUNSATURATED FATTY ACIDS, 0 G MONOUNSATURATED FATTY ACIDS, 0 MG CHOLESTEROL, 53 MG SODIUM, 1.6 G TOTAL DIETARY FIBER

CUMIN YOGURT DRESSING PER 1-OZ SERVING: 18 CALORIES, 1.7 G PROTEIN, .1 G FAT, 2.5 G CARBOHYDRATES, 0 G SATURATED FATTY ACIDS, 0 G POLYUNSATU-RATED FATTY ACIDS, 0 G MONOUNSATURATED FATTY ACIDS, 1 MG CHOLESTEROL, 44 MG SODIUM, .1 G TOTAL DIETARY FIBER

MENU SUGGESTIONS Serve with **Barbecue Beans** (page 156), **Millet Pilaf** (page 182), **Bean and Bean Gumbo** (page 157), **Fat Tuesday's Skinny Red Beans** (page 165), or **Fish with Herbs and Lime** (page 289).

CUCUMBERS VINAIGRETTE

Those of us at Moosewood who either grew up on farms or regularly visited relatives who lived in the country have fond memories of this very simple dish. Best in the summertime when cucumbers are at their freshest, this crisp sweet-and-sour side salad complements almost any main course or makes a satisfying light lunch with a hearty whole grain bread and cup of soup.

2 medium cucumbers, peeled (see Note)
¼ cup cider vinegar
2 tablespoons sugar
½ teaspoon salt
½ teaspoon ground dried mustard
ground black pepper to taste

Serves 4

Total time: 15 minutes

Slice the cucumbers crosswise into ⅛- to ¼-inch rounds.

Combine the vinegar, sugar, salt, and mustard in a serving bowl. Toss with the sliced cucumbers and add pepper to taste. Serve immediately or refrigerate until ready to use.

PER 3-OZ SERVING: 36 CALORIES, .5 G PROTEIN, .2 G FAT, 9.1 G CARBOHYDRATES, 0 G SATURATED FATTY ACIDS, 0 G POLYUNSATURATED FATTY ACIDS, 0 G MONO-UNSATURATED FATTY ACIDS, 0 MG CHOLESTEROL, 300 MG SODIUM, .6 G TOTAL DIETARY FIBER

NOTE:
Always completely peel waxed cucumbers. If they're not waxed, peel them or not as you like. With unwaxed cucumbers, we often make a striped pattern by alternately peeling a ½-inch-wide strip lengthwise, then leaving a strip of the skin intact. With this method, the cucumber slices have some decorative dark green accents and a little bit of extra crunchiness.

CARROT ORANGE SALAD

Here is a dramatically bright and zesty salad that simply *must* be good for you. If blood oranges are available, use them in place of navel oranges for an attractive variation. It's fine to make the salad in advance. Well chilled, it keeps nicely, and after 3 or 4 hours the flavor is even better.

2 or 3 large carrots, peeled and grated (about 4 cups)
2 navel oranges
2 tablespoons fresh lemon juice
1 tablespoon honey
½ teaspoon ground cinnamon

Serves 4 to 6

Total time: 15 minutes

Place the grated carrots in a bowl large enough to hold the completed salad and set it aside.

Slice off the ends of the oranges, place each one, cut side down, on the working surface, and slice down the curved sides with broad strokes all of the way around, positioning the knife just deep enough to remove the peel and all of the white pith. Holding each peeled orange over the serving bowl, slip a paring knife between the membrane and one of the sides of each orange section, cut in toward the center of the orange, and then cut back out the other side with a motion resembling a V. The orange section will fall into the bowl. Repeat this process around the entire orange and then squeeze the juice from the membrane into the bowl. Combine the lemon juice, honey, and cinnamon in a small bowl and pour over the carrot-orange mixture. Before serving, allow the salad to sit for at least 10 minutes so the flavors will mingle.

PER 3.50-OZ SERVING: 61 CALORIES, .9 G PROTEIN, .2 G FAT, 15.4 G CARBOHYDRATES, 0 G SATURATED FATTY ACIDS, .1 G POLYUNSATURATED FATTY ACIDS, 0 G MONOUNSATURATED FATTY ACIDS, 0 MG CHOLESTEROL, 16 MG SODIUM, 3.0 G TOTAL DIETARY FIBER

MENU SUGGESTIONS Serve with **Fish Tagine with Chermoulla** (page 291), **Greek Stew** (page 266), **Middle Eastern Chickpeas with Spinach** (page 169), **Mushroom Wheatberry Pilaf** (page 195), or **Stuffed Baked Potatoes** (page 249).

SPINACH AVOCADO GRAPEFRUIT SALAD

Bob Love, a good friend of Moosewood and a cook here for many years, made this refreshing salad for one of our benefit brunches. We think the bright tart grapefruit and the creamy smooth avocado are an unusual and surprisingly complementary combination.

Serves 4

Total time: 15 minutes

5 ounces fresh spinach
1 teaspoon olive oil
1 garlic clove, pressed
1 grapefruit
1 avocado (preferably Hass)
salt and ground black pepper to taste

Stem and rinse the spinach. Spin or gently pat it dry. Tear the large leaves into smaller pieces but keep the small leaves whole. In a large bowl, mix together the oil and garlic, add the spinach, and toss well. Set aside.

Peel, seed, and section the grapefruit. Halve the avocado, remove the pit, peel, and cut it into 1-inch slices. In a small bowl, gently mix together the grapefruit and avocado. Add them to the bowl of spinach. Sprinkle with salt and pepper, toss lightly, and serve immediately.

PER 5-OZ SERVING: 123 CALORIES, 2.5 G PROTEIN, 9.5 G FAT, 10.0 G CARBOHY-DRATES, 1.5 G SATURATED FATTY ACIDS, 1.2 G POLYUNSATURATED FATTY ACIDS, 6.0 G MONOUNSATURATED FATTY ACIDS, 0 MG CHOLESTEROL, 77 MG SODIUM, 4.8 G TOTAL DIETARY FIBER

MENU SUGGESTIONS Serve with **Southwestern Corn and Potato Soup** (page 102), **Bean and Bean Gumbo** (page 157), **Fat Tuesday's Skinny Red Beans** (page 165), **Corn and Bean Stuffed Baked Potatoes** (page 249), **Breaded Garlic Dill Fish** (page 297), **Southwestern Hominy Stew** (page 279), or **Quinoa Black Bean Salad** (page 141).

Mango Coconut Cucumber Salad

Refreshing and *versatile* are the best words to describe this tropical mélange. It can be a side dish or a salsa, and it pairs beautifully with Caribbean, Mexican, Brazilian, African, Thai, or Indian cuisine.

Serves 2 to 4

Total time: 15 minutes

1 cucumber, peeled, seeded, and diced
½ teaspoon minced fresh chile
1 tablespoon fresh lemon juice
1 tablespoon fresh lime juice
2 teaspoons brown sugar
2 tablespoons unsweetened dried shredded coconut
1 mango, peeled and diced (page 431)
1 small red bell pepper, minced

chopped fresh cilantro or spearmint leaves

In a large bowl, combine the cucumber, chile, lemon and lime juice, brown sugar, coconut, mango, and bell pepper. Toss well. Cover and chill for at least 15 to 20 minutes and serve cold or at room temperature. Just before serving, top with cilantro or spearmint.

PER 4-OZ SERVING: 59 CALORIES, .9 G PROTEIN, 1.1 G FAT, 13.1 G CARBOHYDRATES, .8 G SATURATED FATTY ACIDS, .1 G POLYUNSATURATED FATTY ACIDS, .1 G MONOUN-SATURATED FATTY ACIDS, 0 MG CHOLESTEROL, 10 MG SODIUM, 1.9 G TOTAL DIETARY FIBER

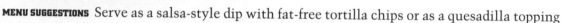

MENU SUGGESTIONS Serve as a salsa-style dip with fat-free tortilla chips or as a quesadilla topping on a tortilla with shredded lettuce and beans or cheese. Try it with **Caribbean Pigeon Pea Salad** (page 142), **Lentil Sambar** (page 166), **Festive Black Bean Chili** (page 161), or **Curried Sweet Potato Roti** (page 230). End with **Pineapple Buttermilk Sherbet** (page 394) or **Banana Bundt Cake** (page 382).

BAKED SWEET POTATO SALAD

This unusual salad has a tropical bent, making it a perfect accompaniment to Southeast Asian and Caribbean dishes. We highly recommend baking the sweet potatoes to bring out the sweet flavor and produce the most pleasant texture, but this salad would still be great made with steamed or boiled sweet potatoes, which will cook in half the time.

2½ pounds sweet potatoes
1 cup Cilantro Lime Yogurt Dressing (page 345) or
    Curried Mango Yogurt Dressing (page 151)
1 red bell pepper
3 celery stalks (about 1 cup chopped)
¼ red onion
1 fresh or preserved chile (optional)

Serves 6

**Baking time:
40 to 60 minutes**

**Preparation time:
25 minutes**

Preheat the oven to 400°.

Wash the sweet potatoes, pierce them in several places with a fork or paring knife, and bake them until soft, 40 to 60 minutes, depending on their size. Meanwhile, prepare the Cilantro Lime Yogurt Dressing and store it in the refrigerator.

While the dressing chills, seed and chop the bell pepper, chop the celery, thinly slice the red onion, and mince the chile, if desired. Place all of the prepared ingredients in a large bowl and set aside.

Remove the baked sweet potatoes from the oven, and when they are cool enough to handle, peel and cube them. Add them to the bowl and gently toss with the other ingredients. Carefully stir in the dressing. Serve warm, at room temperature, or chilled.

PER 8-OZ SERVING: 200 CALORIES, 5.2 G PROTEIN, .6 G FAT, 44.2 G CARBOHYDRATES, .2 G SATURATED FATTY ACIDS, .3 G POLYUNSATURATED FATTY ACIDS, 0 G MONOUNSATURATED FATTY ACIDS, 1 MG CHOLESTEROL, 97 MG SODIUM, 4.9 G TOTAL DIETARY FIBER

MENU SUGGESTIONS Serve beside **Garlicky Black-Eyed Peas 'n' Greens** (page 170), **Fish with Pineapple Chutney** (page 292), or **Carolina Kale** (page 321). Or, for a lighter meal, try with **Tropical Gazpacho** (page 78), **Almost Fat-Free Cornbread** (page 110), and a finale of **Tapioca Fruit Parfaits** (page 375).

POTATO BEAN SALAD

This attractive and filling salad is a perfect match for either our Curried Mango Yogurt Dressing or our Cumin Yogurt Dressing. Because these dressings are quite distinctive, you should really consider this two recipes in one.

Serves 4 to 6

Total time: 40 minutes

3 cups cubed potatoes
¼ red onion, thinly sliced (about ½ cup)
3 cups cut green beans (2-inch pieces)
2 cups cooked chickpeas (16-ounce can, drained)
1 cup Curried Mango Yogurt Dressing (page 151) or
    Cumin Yogurt Dressing (page 132)
salt and ground black pepper to taste

In a saucepan, bring the potatoes and enough cool, salted water to cover to a boil on high heat. Lower the heat and simmer for about 15 minutes, until the potatoes are tender.

When the potatoes are cooked, remove them to a large bowl with a sieve or a slotted spoon and immediately stir in the red onions. Add the green beans to the saucepan of hot water and simmer until tender, 5 to 10 minutes. Drain and add to the bowl. Stir in the chickpeas and set aside to cool. When the vegetables are cool, stir in the yogurt dressing of your choice. Add salt and pepper to taste. Serve immediately or store, covered, in the refrigerator.

PER 8-OZ SERVING: 161 CALORIES, 6.8 G PROTEIN, .9 G FAT, 33.0 G CARBOHYDRATES, .1 G SATURATED FATTY ACIDS, .3 G POLYUNSATURATED FATTY ACIDS, .2 G MONOUNSATURATED FATTY ACIDS, 1 MG CHOLESTEROL, 245 MG SODIUM, 5.9 G TOTAL DIETARY FIBER

MENU SUGGESTIONS Serve as a main dish with **Cucumbers Vinaigrette** (page 133) or **Broiled Portabella Mushrooms** (page 322) alongside **Tomato Bulgur Soup** (page 101). Or use as a side dish for **Breaded Garlic Dill Fish** (page 297) or **Honey Mustard Fish** (page 298).

NOTE:
If you don't have either of the yogurt dressings on hand, there is time to prepare one while the potatoes are cooking and cooling. To preserve the creamy texture of the dressing, make sure the potatoes have cooled at least to room temperature before combining them with the dressing.

POTATO BEET SALAD

Add a splash of color to your meal with this gorgeous fuschia salad.

The beets take about 40 minutes to cook, so there's plenty of time to prepare the rest of the vegetables and the dill while the beets simmer.

4 medium beets, scrubbed and leaf stems trimmed to 1 inch
5 potatoes, peeled and cubed
½ cup minced red onions or scallions
1 cup nonfat yogurt
¼ cup chopped fresh dill
2 teaspoons cider vinegar
2 small dill pickles, chopped (about ½ cup)
2 teaspoons prepared horseradish (optional)
1 teaspoon sugar (optional)
salt and ground black pepper to taste

Serves 6

**Preparation time:
40 to 60 minutes
(small beets cook faster)**

**Chilling time:
30 minutes**

> **NOTE:**
> Peeling cooked beets is far more efficient than peeling raw beets. After the cooked beets have cooled, the skins will slide off easily just by squeezing the beets in your hand.

In a covered pot, boil the beets in plenty of water until tender, 40 to 60 minutes. Meanwhile, in a separate pot, boil the potatoes in lightly salted water for about 20 minutes, just until soft. Drain the potatoes and set aside to cool.

When the beets are easily pierced with a sharp knife, drain them and plunge them in cold water. When they have cooled enough to handle, peel (see Note) and chop them into bite-sized pieces. In a serving bowl, mix together the beets, potatoes, red onions or scallions, yogurt, dill, vinegar, pickles, and, if using, the horseradish and sugar. Add salt and pepper to taste and chill for at least 30 minutes.

PER 8-OZ SERVING: 157 CALORIES, 5.3 G PROTEIN, .3 G FAT, 34.4 G CARBOHYDRATES, .1 G SATURATED FATTY ACIDS, .1 G POLYUNSATURATED FATTY ACIDS, 0 G MONOUNSATURATED FATTY ACIDS, 1 MG CHOLESTEROL, 339 MG SODIUM, 3.4 G TOTAL DIETARY FIBER

MENU SUGGESTIONS Serve with **Mushroom Pâté Almondine** (page 121), **Egg Salad** (page 117) on pumpernickel bread, **Broiled Portabella Mushrooms** (page 322), or **Snap Peas with Mushrooms** (page 329). As a side dish, this salad pairs well with **Baked Fish with Mustard Marinade** (page 288).

SESAME BEETS

Beets add such a gorgeous color to any meal, they're worth making just for their visual appeal. Luckily, they are delicious and nutritious too, although, depending upon the time of year and soil conditions, their sweetness varies. If your beets are not very sweet, we suggest you add an extra bit of sugar to this zesty recipe.

1 pound beets
2 tablespoons fresh lemon juice
1 to 2 teaspoons cider vinegar
1 tablespoon toasted sesame seeds*
2 tablespoons minced onions or scallions
1 teaspoon sugar
salt and ground black pepper to taste

Serves 4 as a side dish

Preparation time: 10 minutes

Cooking time: 30 to 40 minutes

Chilling time: 30 minutes

Toast sesame seeds on an unoiled baking tray in a conventional or toaster oven at 350° for 2 to 3 minutes, until fragrant and golden brown.

Trim the leaf stems of the beets to about an inch (see Note), scrub the beets, and place them in a pot with water to cover. Bring to a boil, then lower the heat, cover, and simmer for about 30 to 40 minutes, until tender and easily pierced with a sharp knife. Drain and rinse with cold water until cool enough to handle. Remove and discard the skins, which should slip off easily, and slice the beets into a bowl. Toss with the lemon juice, vinegar, sesame seeds, onions or scallions, and sugar. Add salt and pepper to taste. Chill thoroughly for about 30 minutes and serve.

> **NOTE:**
> Beet greens are delicious, so save them and use them later—raw in a salad or lightly steamed as a side dish.
>
> Be forewarned that beet juice will stain your cutting board, your hands, and your clothing. If you aren't crazy about fuschia, you may wish to cover your cutting surface with wax paper and wear latex or plastic gloves.

PER 4-0Z SERVING: 67 CALORIES, 2.2 G PROTEIN, 1.3 G FAT,
13.1 G CARBOHYDRATES, .2 G SATURATED FATTY ACIDS,
.6 G POLYUNSATURATED FATTY ACIDS,
.5 G MONOUNSATURATED FATTY ACIDS,
0 MG CHOLESTEROL, 124 MG SODIUM, 2.2 G TOTAL DIETARY FIBER

MENU SUGGESTIONS Serve with **Poached Fish with Russian Mushroom Sauce** (page 300), with **Baltic Fish** (page 287), or with **Cabbage Rolls** (page 256) and **Potato Cakes** (page 327).

QUINOA BLACK BEAN SALAD

Higher in protein than any other grain, quinoa is chewy with a delicious, almost nutlike flavor. Bolstered with the nutritional power of black beans, this salad is hearty, healthy eating at its best.

⅓ cup quinoa (see page 435)
1 cup water
1 teaspoon olive oil
4 teaspoons fresh lime juice, or more to taste
¼ teaspoon ground cumin
¼ teaspoon ground coriander
1 tablespoon finely chopped fresh cilantro
2 tablespoons minced scallions
1½ cups cooked black beans (15-ounce can, drained)
2 cups diced tomatoes
1 cup diced bell peppers (red, green, yellow, or a mixture)
2 teaspoons minced fresh green chiles
salt and ground black pepper to taste

lemon or lime wedges

Serves 4 as a side dish

Total time: 30 minutes

Rinse the quinoa well in a sieve under cool running water. In a saucepan, bring the water to a boil, add the quinoa, cover, and simmer on low heat, until all of the water is absorbed and the quinoa is tender, about 10 to 15 minutes. Allow to cool for 15 minutes.

In a large bowl, combine the oil, lime juice, cumin, coriander, cilantro, and scallions. Stir in the beans, tomatoes, bell peppers, and chiles. Add the cooled quinoa, and salt and pepper to taste, and combine thoroughly. Refrigerate until ready to serve. Garnish with lemon or lime wedges.

PER 11-OZ SERVING: 197 CALORIES, 8.9 G PROTEIN, 2.8 G FAT, 35.1 G CARBOHYDRATES, .3 G SATURATED FATTY ACIDS, .4 G POLYUNSATURATED FATTY ACIDS, 1.0 G MONOUNSATURATED FATTY ACIDS, 0 MG CHOLESTEROL, 389 MG SODIUM, 3.4 G TOTAL DIETARY FIBER

MENU SUGGESTIONS Serve this unusual salad as a side dish with **Seitan Fajitas** (page 232), or as a main dish with **Zucchini with Cilantro Sauce** (page 335) or **Southwestern Corn and Potato Soup** (page 102).

CARIBBEAN PIGEON PEA SALAD

Dress up any meal with this nutritious and filling main-dish salad, which boasts a lively combination of zesty tropical flavors and festive good looks besides.

Annatto, also known as achiote seed, is a small red seed that releases a vibrant yellow-orange color and subtle flavor when sautéed in a small amount of oil. Annatto is available in Latin American grocery stores and often in the Mexican or ethnic sections of supermarkets.

The rice will take about 40 minutes to cook, so there is time to blend the salsa dressing and chop the vegetables while it simmers. The salad is at its best when served slightly chilled, but not icy cold.

Serves 4 to 6

**Total time:
45 to 50 minutes**

**Chilling time:
30 minutes**

RICE
1 teaspoon annatto (achiote seed)
2 teaspoons canola or other vegetable oil
1¼ cups brown rice
½ teaspoon dried thyme
3 garlic cloves, pressed or minced
2 cups water

DRESSING
2 medium tomatoes, chopped
3 garlic cloves, minced or pressed
3 tablespoons fresh lime juice
2 tablespoons cider vinegar*
1 tablespoon olive oil
½ teaspoon dried thyme, or more to taste
¼ teaspoon ground allspice
salt and ground black pepper to taste

VEGETABLES
½ cup chopped red onions
1½ cups diced bell peppers, preferably
    a combination of 2 or more colors
½ cup chopped celery
1½ cups pigeon peas (page 434)
⅓ cup chopped Spanish olives (optional)

*If you prefer a less tangy salad, reduce the amount
 of cider vinegar to 1 tablespoon.

In a very small pan on low heat, sauté the annatto in the oil for about a minute, until the oil begins to sizzle and the seeds start to darken. Stir often to avoid scorching the seeds. When the oil turns bright yellowish-orange, drain it through a strainer into the rice cooking pot. Discard the seeds. Add the rice, thyme, and garlic to the pot and sauté for a minute or two, stirring to coat the rice with the annatto oil. Pour in the water, bring to a boil, and then reduce to a simmer and cook for about 40 minutes, until the rice is tender.

While the rice cooks, combine all of the dressing ingredients in a blender, purée until smooth, and set aside. In a large bowl, combine the red onions, bell peppers, celery, pigeon peas, and olives, if using.

When the rice is ready, mix it into the chopped vegetables and pigeon peas. Pour the dressing over the salad, toss to combine thoroughly, and chill for about 30 minutes.

PER 10-OZ SERVING: 253 CALORIES, 7.8 G PROTEIN, 5.4 G FAT, 45.0 G CARBOHYDRATES, .8 G SATURATED FATTY ACIDS, 1.7 G POLYUNSATURATED FATTY ACIDS, 2.6 G MONOUNSATURATED FATTY ACIDS, 0 MG CHOLESTEROL, 46 MG SODIUM, 5.8 G TOTAL DIETARY FIBER

MENU SUGGESTIONS Serve with **Tropical Gazpacho** (page 78), **Carolina Kale** (page 321), and **Sweet Potato Oven "Fries"** (page 326). Or offer as a side dish for **Curried Sweet Potato Roti** (page 230) or **Caribbean Stew** (page 265).

Mediterranean Couscous Salad

This assortment of colorful diced vegetables with a fluffy grain is enlivened by a garlic vinaigrette. Grated chèvre or feta cheese makes an excellent garnish. Avoid overcooking the vegetables in this dish—they should be tender but still brightly colored.

1½ cups whole wheat couscous (see Note)
2½ cups boiling water
⅓ cup (about 10) sun-dried tomatoes (not packed in oil)

Serves 4 to 6

Preparation time: 45 minutes

Chilling time: 1 hour

Dressing

2 garlic cloves, pressed or minced
1 tablespoon olive oil
2 tablespoons chopped fresh dill
3 tablespoons fresh lemon juice
3 tablespoons balsamic vinegar

Vegetables

1 cup peeled and diced carrots
1 cup diced zucchini
½ cup diced red bell peppers
½ cup diced red onions
½ cup diced celery
salt and ground black pepper to taste
1 tomato, diced

a few fresh parsley or dill sprigs

> **NOTE:**
> We prefer the heartier flavor of whole wheat couscous for this dish. If you use regular couscous, cook it in only 1¼ cups of water.
>
> ❋ ❋ ❋
>
> Blanching times: carrots, 8 minutes; zucchini, 3 minutes; bell peppers, 2 minutes.

Place the couscous in a pot, pour 1¾ cups of the boiling water over it, cover, and set aside. Place the sun-dried tomatoes and ¾ cup of boiling water in a covered heatproof bowl. While the tomatoes soften, whisk together the dressing ingredients and set aside. Uncover the couscous and fluff it with fork.

Blanch the carrots, zucchini, and bell peppers in boiling water until just tender (see Note). Drain well. Drain and chop the sun-dried tomatoes. In a large bowl, combine the couscous, sun-dried tomatoes, blanched vegetables, red onions, celery, and dressing. Add salt and pepper. Chill for at least an hour. Add the diced tomatoes just before serving. Top with parsley or dill sprigs.

PER 9.50-OZ SERVING: 238 CALORIES, 8.7 G PROTEIN, .9 G FAT, 50.1 G CARBOHYDRATES, .1 G SATURATED FATTY ACIDS, .3 G POLYUNSATURATED FATTY ACIDS, .1 G MONOUNSATURATED FATTY ACIDS, 0 MG CHOLESTEROL, 323 MG SODIUM, 5.7 G TOTAL DIETARY FIBER

MENU SUGGESTIONS Try with **Herbed Fish in a Packet** (page 296), **Eggplant Strata** (page 32), or **Seasoned Steamed Artichokes** (page 311) topped with **Caesar Salad Dressing** (page 131).

TABOULI SALAD

The assertive and clear flavors of garlic, lemon, parsley, and mint carry this traditional Middle Eastern salad without any added oil. The amount of parsley in tabouli can vary greatly. Traditionally, tabouli is mostly parsley with just a smattering of bulgur for texture and color. Although a generous amount of parsley is a must, we have given a wide range in this recipe so you can adjust it to your taste.

Serves 6 to 8

Total time: 30 minutes

1½ cups boiling water
1 cup bulgur
⅓ to ½ cup fresh lemon juice
1 garlic clove, minced or pressed
1 to 3 cups chopped fresh parsley
4 scallions, chopped
3 tomatoes, diced
1 cup drained cooked chickpeas
salt and ground black pepper to taste
chopped fresh mint to taste (optional)

In a large bowl, pour the boiling water over the bulgur. Cover tightly and set aside for 20 to 30 minutes.

Meanwhile, in a separate bowl, stir together ⅓ cup of lemon juice and the garlic, parsley, scallions, tomatoes, and chickpeas. When the bulgur has absorbed the water and softened, stir it with a fork to fluff the grains. Toss the lemon-vegetable mixture with the bulgur, and add salt and pepper and mint, if you like, to taste. Tabouli tastes best after sitting refrigerated or at room temperature for ½ hour to 2 hours so the flavors blend thoroughly. Add more lemon juice to taste before serving.

PER 6.50-OZ SERVING: 130 CALORIES, 5.1 G PROTEIN, .9 G FAT, 27.8 G CARBOHYDRATES, .1 G SATURATED FATTY ACIDS, .4 G POLYUNSATURATED FATTY ACIDS, .2 G MONOUNSATURATED FATTY ACIDS, 0 MG CHOLESTEROL, 125 MG SODIUM, 6.5 G TOTAL DIETARY FIBER

MENU SUGGESTIONS Make a great combo plate with **Middle Eastern Cannellini Patties** (page 119), **Greek Lima Bean Dip** (page 23), **Seasoned Steamed Artichokes** (page 311), black olives, fresh tomato wedges, and pita bread. Or start with **Cream of Green Vegetable Soup** (page 82) or **Curried Carrot Parsnip Soup** (page 100) and pair with **Carrot Orange Salad** (page 134).

SUSHI RICE SALAD

This festive, light, briny salad is like a nori roll turned inside out. Other garnishes could be avocado slices, shrimp, surimi, pickled ginger, soy sauce, and additional wasabi. The "bite" of wasabi powders varies, so start with less and add more to taste.

1 cup brown rice, preferably short-grain
1¾ cups water

Serves 4 to 6

Total time: 45 minutes

SAUCE
⅓ cup rice vinegar
2 tablespoons sugar
1 teaspoon salt
2 teaspoons grated fresh ginger root

2 small carrots, peeled and diced
1 red bell pepper, seeded and diced
1 cucumber, peeled, seeded, and diced
1 to 2 teaspoons wasabi powder dissolved
   in an equal amount cold water
1 sheet nori seaweed
1 tablespoon black or brown sesame seeds
fresh rinsed greens

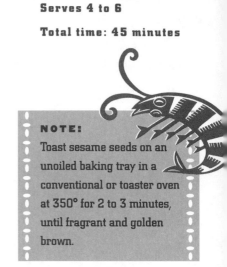

NOTE:
Toast sesame seeds on an unoiled baking tray in a conventional or toaster oven at 350° for 2 to 3 minutes, until fragrant and golden brown.

Combine the rice and water in a small, heavy saucepan and bring to a boil. Stir, cover, reduce the heat to low, and cook until the rice is tender, 40 to 45 minutes. Bring a separate covered pot of water to a boil for blanching the vegetables.

Meanwhile, in a small nonreactive pan, combine the sauce ingredients, simmer for 5 minutes, and set aside. When the water boils, blanch the carrots and then the peppers just until tender. In a serving bowl, combine the cucumbers, blanched vegetables, and sauce.

When the rice is done, toss the wasabi paste with the sauce and vegetables. Add the rice and toss to mix well. Serve the salad at room temperature or chilled. Just before serving, toast the sheet of nori by briefly passing it over a low flame or baking it for a minute or so in a 300° toaster oven, until it deepens in color. Crumble it into a small bowl. Toast the sesame seeds (see Note). Spoon the rice salad onto individual beds of greens, sprinkle with sesame seeds and nori, and serve.

PER 8-OZ SERVING: 163 CALORIES, 3.9 G PROTEIN, 1.8 G FAT, 33.1 G CARBOHYDRATES, .3 G SATURATED FATTY ACIDS, .7 G POLYUNSATURATED FATTY ACIDS, .6 G MONOUNSATURATED FATTY ACIDS, 0 MG CHOLESTEROL, 426 MG SODIUM, 2.8 G TOTAL DIETARY FIBER

MENU SUGGESTIONS Start with **Japanese Soba and Vegetable Soup** (page 88) and end with vanilla frozen yogurt.

WILD RICE WALDORF SALAD

Perfect for holiday meals, this colorful crunchy salad combines tart apples and citrus, sweet currants and maple syrup, savory vegetables, rice, and nuts—all in one appetizing dish. If you have leftover rice or have already cooked the rice (see Note), the dish can be ready in only 20 minutes. Serve at room temperature or chilled.

SALAD

⅔ cup wild rice

2½ cups hot water

1 cup brown rice, preferably long-grain

1 large tart apple, such as Crispin or Granny Smith

3 tablespoons fresh lemon juice

1 bell pepper, seeded and diced, any color

1 cup diced celery

½ cup minced red onions

½ cup currants or raisins

¼ cup toasted almonds or walnuts, chopped or slivered*

DRESSING

½ cup orange juice

1 tablespoon pure maple syrup or honey

1 teaspoon ground coriander

½ teaspoon ground cardamom

1 tablespoon canola or other vegetable oil

Toast raw nuts on an unoiled baking sheet at 350° for about 5 minutes, until fragrant.

Serves 6

Total time: 1¼ hours, including cooking the rice

> **NOTE:**
> You need about 2 cups of cooked wild rice and 3 cups of cooked brown rice for this recipe.

In a saucepan with a tight-fitting lid, soak the wild rice in 1 cup of the hot water for 30 minutes. Add the brown rice and the remaining 1½ cups of water, bring to a boil, then lower to a simmer, cover, and cook for about 45 minutes, until the rice is tender.

When the rice has cooked for about 30 minutes, dice the apple and toss with the lemon juice in a large bowl. Add the peppers, celery, red onions, currants or raisins, and almonds or walnuts and set aside. Whisk together all of the dressing ingredients. Add the cooked rice and the dressing to the bowl and toss well to combine.

PER 9.50-OZ SERVING: 301 CALORIES, 7.0 G PROTEIN, 6.4 G FAT, 56.9 G CARBOHYDRATES, .8 G SATURATED FATTY ACIDS, 2.5 G POLYUNSATURATED FATTY ACIDS, 2.7 G MONOUNSATURATED FATTY ACIDS, 0 MG CHOLESTEROL, 22 MG SODIUM, 4.0 G TOTAL DIETARY FIBER

MENU SUGGESTIONS Serve with **Holiday Cranberry Squash** (page 331) and a bright orange, puréed carrot soup. Or try with **Three Sisters Stew** (page 272), **Curried Squash** (page 332), or **Bean and Bean Gumbo** (page 157).

MEXICAN PASTA SALAD

This substantial and colorful dish is an interesting twist on the usual pasta salad. To save time, you can prepare the rest of the ingredients while the water comes to a boil and the pasta cooks.

½ pound short, chunky pasta, such as small shells, orecchiette, or penne
1 cup fresh or frozen corn kernels
3 scallions, minced
1 cup chopped bell peppers, red, green, yellow, or a mixture
1½ cups cooked kidney beans, pinto beans, pink beans, or black beans (15-ounce can, drained and rinsed)
1 cup chopped tomatoes
¼ cup sliced Spanish olives
2 teaspoons olive oil
3 tablespoons fresh lemon juice, lime juice, or a combination
2 teaspoons ground cumin
2 tablespoons chopped fresh cilantro
½ teaspoon ground black pepper
salt to taste

grated low-fat Cheddar cheese (optional)
prepared Mexican-style red salsa (optional)

Serves 4 to 6

**Total time:
20 to 25 minutes**

Bring a large covered pot of water to a boil. Cook the pasta for about 10 minutes, until al dente. Add the corn during the final 2 minutes of cooking. Drain the pasta and corn, rinse with cold water, and set aside to drain for a few minutes.

Meanwhile, combine the scallions, bell peppers, beans, tomatoes, olives, olive oil, lemon or lime juice, cumin, cilantro, and black pepper in a large bowl. Mix in the pasta and corn and add salt to taste. If desired, top each serving with a tablespoon of grated Cheddar and a spoonful of salsa. Serve immediately or chill to serve later.

PER 10-OZ SERVING: 289 CALORIES, 12.2 G PROTEIN, 4.7 G FAT, 52.2 G CARBOHY-DRATES, .6 G SATURATED FATTY ACIDS, .7 G POLYUNSATURATED FATTY ACIDS, 1.4 G MONOUNSATURATED FATTY ACIDS, 0 MG CHOLESTEROL, 357 MG SODIUM, 4.1 G TOTAL DIETARY FIBER

NOTE:
Remember that song, "does your bubble gum lose its flavor on the bedpost overnight?" Well, here's a slight variation on the theme: "Does your tomato lose its flavor in the refrigerator overnight?" And the answer is yes. Tomato flavor is a result of the interactions of natural sugars, organic acids, and aromatic compounds, and it intensifies as the tomato ripens. Refrigeration interferes with the ripening process, which otherwise continues as long as post-harvest temperatures remain above 55° F. Even if the refrigerated tomato turns red, it will pale in flavor when compared with a tomato which ripens naturally at room temperature releasing its aromatic compounds in the process.

MENU SUGGESTIONS Serve as a main dish with **Guacamole with Cottage Cheese** (page 26) and crudités, **Tropical Gazpacho** (page 78), or **Mango-Banana Shake** (page 65). Or offer as a side dish with **Chili Burgers** (page 173).

CHINESE ORZO VEGETABLE SALAD

Sometimes we just can't help ourselves as we scamper across international culinary borders and combine ingredients that traditionally have rarely shared a plate.

Orzo is a small rice-shaped pasta. Here we use it in a salad full of vegetables common to the Mediterranean with the addition of—you guessed it—baby corn and a distinctly Chinese dressing. Another Moosewood mix-and-match dish enters the world of food.

SALAD

1½ cups orzo (page 433)

2 quarts boiling water

1 tablespoon dark sesame oil

2 cups sliced asparagus, cut on the diagonal
    into 1-inch pieces

1 cup chopped red bell peppers

1 cup canned baby corns, cut in half crosswise

½ cup chopped celery

3 scallions, thinly sliced on the diagonal

Serves 4 to 6

Total time: 30 minutes

NOTE:
To save time, you can prepare the vegetables and dressing ingredients while the water comes to a boil and the orzo cooks.

DRESSING

3 tablespoons rice vinegar

3 tablespoons soy sauce

1 teaspoon Chinese chili paste

1 tablespoon grated fresh ginger root

2 garlic cloves, pressed or minced

salt and ground black pepper to taste

Cook the orzo in a large pot of boiling water for 10 to 12 minutes, until al dente, stirring frequently (see Note). Drain the orzo in a colander with small holes or with a strainer, rinse it with cold water, and transfer it to a serving bowl. Toss the orzo with the sesame oil and set aside.

Blanch the asparagus in boiling water to cover for about 3 minutes, until just tender, then briefly submerge in cold water to help maintain their bright green color. Add the bell peppers, baby corns, celery, scallions, and asparagus to the orzo.

Whisk together all of the dressing ingredients in a separate bowl and pour it over the orzo and vegetables. Gently toss to coat everything evenly with the dressing and serve.

PER 9.50-OZ SERVING: 287 CALORIES, 9.8 G PROTEIN, 3.9 G FAT, 54.3 G CARBOHYDRATES, .6 G SATURATED FATTY ACIDS, 1.7 G POLYUNSATURATED FATTY ACIDS, 1.2 G MONOUNSATURATED FATTY ACIDS, 0 MG CHOLESTEROL, 462 MG SODIUM, 3.5 G TOTAL DIETARY FIBER

MENU SUGGESTIONS Serve with **Southeast Asian Fish Rolls** (page 294), with **Fish with Herbs and Lime** (page 289), or accompanied by broiled tofu with **Spicy Peanut Dressing** (page 349).

CREAMY MACARONI SALAD

A low-fat version of the typical picnic or deli macaroni salad, this one is generous with vegetables and a creamy light dressing. When the garden is peaking with fresh asparagus, tomatoes, and dill, the dish is at its very best. Top with fresh basil and tomato wedges.

PASTA
½ pound penne or other tubular pasta

CHEESE MIXTURE
½ cup low-fat cottage cheese
¼ cup reduced-fat mayonnaise
1 tablespoon cider vinegar
1 tablespoon olive oil (optional)
1 garlic clove, pressed or minced

SALAD
1 cup broccoli florets
1 cup cut asparagus spears (1-inch pieces)
1 cup chopped tomatoes
½ cup peeled, seeded, and diced cucumbers
¼ cup chopped celery
2 scallions, thinly sliced on the diagonal
1 dill pickle, diced
1 tablespoon minced fresh dill
salt and ground black pepper to taste

Serves 4 to 6

Preparation time:
30 to 35 minutes

Chilling time:
20 minutes

NOTES:
To save time, you can prepare the vegetables and herbs while the water heats and the pasta cooks.
If using a blender, add 1 tablespoon of water if necessary to help purée the cheese mixture.

Bring a large pot of water to a boil and cook the penne until al dente (see Note). Drain the pasta, rinse it with cold water, and set aside.

Combine the cheese mixture ingredients in a blender or food processor, purée until smooth, and set aside (see Note).

Steam the broccoli for about 5 minutes, until crisp-tender and still bright green. Remove the broccoli, briefly submerge it in cold water, and set aside to drain. Likewise, steam the asparagus until just tender, submerge for about 30 seconds in cold water, and drain.

Mix together the pasta, the puréed cheese mixture, and all of the salad ingredients in a serving bowl. Chill for 20 minutes, until the flavors marry.

PER 9-OZ SERVING: 204 CALORIES, 9.4 G PROTEIN, 2.6 G FAT, 36.4 G CARBOHYDRATES, .6 G SATURATED FATTY ACIDS, .4 G POLYUNSATURATED FATTY ACIDS, .2 G MONOUNSATURATED FATTY ACIDS, 6 MG CHOLESTEROL, 242 MG SODIUM, 3.0 G TOTAL DIETARY FIBER

MENU SUGGESTIONS Serve as a natural companion to **Barbecue Beans** (page 156), **Corn Relish** (page 361), and **Cabbage Salad** (page 132). For dessert, serve **Our Best No-Butter Brownies** (page 387) or **Cardamom Oatmeal Cookies** (page 393).

LENTIL SALAD

This sweet and spicy lentil dish has an unusual flavor that is especially refreshing on a hot summer day. You can prepare the lentils and dressing ahead of time and assemble the salad just before serving.

Because prepared mango chutneys vary, the amount we call for is a recommendation only. Experiment with store-bought mango chutneys until you find the chutney that suits your taste. If your chutney has large pieces of mango chop them for this recipe.

SALAD

1½ cups lentils
1 cup chopped onions
2 garlic cloves, chopped
4 cups water
1 cup finely chopped red and/or green bell peppers
1 cup finely chopped celery
1 cup finely chopped red onions

CURRIED MANGO YOGURT DRESSING

1 cup plain nonfat or low-fat yogurt
3 tablespoons prepared mango chutney
1½ teaspoons curry powder
2 teaspoons finely minced red onions
1 tablespoon fresh lime juice

Serves 4 to 6

Total time: 1 hour

> **NOTE:**
> This spicy, sweet-tart dressing can also be used on baked potatoes, baked fish, spinach salad, green salad, or cucumber salad. It transforms plain boiled potatoes, green peas, and thinly sliced red onions into an elegant side dish.

In a saucepan, combine the lentils, onions, garlic, and water. Cover, bring to a boil, then reduce the heat and simmer for 30 to 40 minutes, until the lentils are tender but not mushy. Meanwhile, combine the bell peppers, celery, and red onions in a nonreactive bowl. When the lentils are cooked, drain and add them, while hot, to the bowl. Stir and set aside at room temperature for 15 minutes.

In a separate bowl, combine all of the yogurt dressing ingredients. Stir the dressing into the lentils and serve. If you'll be serving the lentil salad later, store it in the refrigerator, then let it return to room temperature before serving.

PER 10-OZ SERVING: 113 CALORIES, 7.4 G PROTEIN, .5 G FAT, 21.2 G CARBOHYDRATES, .1 G SATURATED FATTY ACIDS, .2 G POLYUNSATURATED FATTY ACIDS, .1 G MONOUNSATURATED FATTY ACIDS, 1 MG CHOLESTEROL, 84 MG SODIUM, 5.6 G TOTAL DIETARY FIBER

MENU SUGGESTIONS Serve with our crunchy, tart **Cabbage Salad** (page 132), **Sweet Potato Oven "Fries"** (page 326), **Zucchini with Cilantro Sauce** (page 335), or **Broiled Eggplant Thai Style** (page 34), or simply on a bed of fresh spinach leaves. Try eating it in a crisp lettuce leaf "boat." **Callaloo** (page 105), **Tropical Gazpacho** (page 78), and **Roasted Garlic** (page 43) spread on crusty bread are other good complements.

barbecue beans 156

bean and bean gumbo 157

VEGETARIAN FEIJOADA 158

cassoulet 160

festive black bean chili 161

TAMALE PIE 162

black bean chilaquile 164

fat tuesday's skinny red beans 165

LENTIL SAMBAR 166

tuscan beans with sage 168

middle eastern chickpeas with spinach 169

GARLICKY BLACK-EYED PEAS 'N' GREENS 170

sweet-and-sour lentils 171

sweet potato and black bean burrito 172

CHILI BURGERS 173

BEANS

A shelf of glass jars filled with colorful dried **BEANS** is a beautiful sight, one that gives us a comfortable feeling of abundance and well-being. Rich in protein, vitamins, minerals, fiber, and complex carbohydrates, beans are also a naturally low-fat food containing both insoluble and soluble fiber. Insoluble fiber is beneficial to the health of the lower digestive tract and soluble fiber has been shown to reduce cholesterol and triglyceride levels. Beans are also one of the world's most economical foods.

Every day, the Moosewood menu includes a bean dish from our continually developing repertoire. Many of our bean dishes, such as Lentil Sambar and Tuscan Beans with Sage, come out of cuisines with a strong tradition of meatless meals. Others, such as Vegetarian Feijoada, Fat Tuesday's Skinny Red Beans, and Cassoulet, are our low-fat vegetarian versions of dishes traditionally made with meat.

We combine beans and grain-based foods both for nutrition and to create varied, tasty meals. Whole grains, bread, pasta, tortillas, and pilafs are good foods to serve with beans. Another of our considerations is the pairing of contrasting colors (Lentil Sambar with Golden Basmati Rice) or textures (creamy Tuscan Beans with Sage and a crusty Italian bread or focaccia). On each of our bean recipes, we recommend accompaniments.

Cooked beans are versatile and easy to store. Keep cooked beans in a tightly covered container in the refrigerator for up to 5 days or in the freezer for up to 6 months. You'll find techniques and tips for cooking different kinds of beans on page 414. One generous batch may be used in many different ways. A pot of chickpeas could be made into Middle Eastern Chickpeas with Spinach, puréed to make Indian Chickpea Spread, added to soups, and/or marinated for garnishing tossed salads. A batch of black beans could be served as Vegetarian Feijoada and later be made into Black Bean Chilaquile. And leftovers of many of our bean dishes make an excellent beginning for a delicious soup. Create a black bean soup by thinning Festive Black Bean Chili with stock and orange or tomato juice. Thin Lentil Sambar with tomato or apple juice for a curried lentil soup.

TAMING THE WILD BEAN

Some people have trouble digesting beans because of an inability to break down specific sugars contained in legumes. Try the following suggestions if you've had this problem:

- After soaking dried beans, drain them. Cook them in fresh water. Adding a pinch of baking soda to the soaking water may also help.
- Be sure beans are well cooked.
- Drain and gently rinse canned beans. This is also helpful in reducing the saltiness of some brands of canned beans.
- People who eat beans regularly have few or no problems digesting them, so start with small servings eaten often and work up to a larger amount of beans as a regular part of your diet.
- Try one of the commercial enzyme products, most notably Beano, which helps people digest complex carbohydrates. A few drops of Beano added to cooked foods right before eating will not change the taste and may aid digestion. Beano is available in natural food stores and well-stocked supermarkets.

BARBECUE BEANS

These robust, sweet, and savory beans are reminiscent of New England Saturday night suppers and backyard picnics.

If you plan ahead to cook the beans, the rest of this recipe is a snap, and it has the added bonus of being almost fat-free. Sometimes, though, there's simply no time to plan ahead. So for a much quicker alternative to cooking the beans from scratch, use a good brand of well-rinsed canned beans and sauté the garlic and onions in a small amount of oil before combining and simmering all of the ingredients.

2 cups dried navy beans, soaked at least
    8 hours in water to cover by 2 inches
2 to 4 garlic cloves, chopped
1 cup chopped onions
½ cup prepared nonfat barbecue sauce*
¼ cup prepared mustard
¼ cup molasses or pure maple syrup
1 tablespoon cider vinegar
Tabasco or other hot pepper sauce to taste
salt and ground black pepper to taste

Low-fat and nonfat barbecue sauce is commercially available. To make your own, see page 355.

Serves 6 to 8 as a side dish

Preparation time: 5 minutes

Bean cooking time: 1½ hours

Baking or simmering time: 20 to 30 minutes

NOTE:
You may need to add a little water during the final simmering or baking process, but be careful not to make the consistency too thin. The finished beans should be thick and saucy.

Drain the soaked beans and combine with the garlic and onions in a large soup pot. Cover with water by at least an inch and bring to a rapid boil. Lower the heat, cover, and simmer for about 1½ hours, until tender. Add water to the pot as necessary to maintain the water level throughout cooking.

When the beans are ready, drain them and stir in the barbecue sauce, mustard, molasses or maple syrup, and vinegar. Add Tabasco, salt, and pepper to taste. To cook the beans on the stove top, gently simmer on low heat with a heat diffuser for 20 to 30 minutes, stirring often. To bake them, transfer the beans to a baking dish and bake, uncovered, at 350° for 20 to 30 minutes, stirring once or twice during baking.

PER 6-OZ SERVING: 121 CALORIES, 5.4 G PROTEIN, .7 G FAT, 23.8 G CARBOHYDRATES, .1 G SATURATED FATTY ACIDS, .2 G POLYUNSATURATED FATTY ACIDS, 0 G MONOUNSATURATED FATTY ACIDS, 0 MG CHOLESTEROL, 231 MG SODIUM, .2 G TOTAL DIETARY FIBER

MENU SUGGESTIONS For supper, try with **Brown Bread** (page 111) and **Wild Rice Waldorf Salad** (page 147). Complete a picnic with **Creamy Macaroni Salad** (page 150) or **Potato Beet Salad** (page 139) and **Corn Relish** (page 361). Try **Blueberry Peach Cobbler** (page 383) for dessert.

BEAN AND BEAN GUMBO

Don't let the long list of ingredients scare you off—making this spicy dish is much simpler than it looks. Serve on rice or with freshly baked Almost Fat-Free Cornbread (page 110).

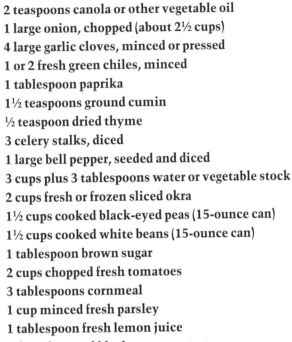

2 teaspoons canola or other vegetable oil
1 large onion, chopped (about 2½ cups)
4 large garlic cloves, minced or pressed
1 or 2 fresh green chiles, minced
1 tablespoon paprika
1½ teaspoons ground cumin
½ teaspoon dried thyme
3 celery stalks, diced
1 large bell pepper, seeded and diced
3 cups plus 3 tablespoons water or vegetable stock
2 cups fresh or frozen sliced okra
1½ cups cooked black-eyed peas (15-ounce can)
1½ cups cooked white beans (15-ounce can)
1 tablespoon brown sugar
2 cups chopped fresh tomatoes
3 tablespoons cornmeal
1 cup minced fresh parsley
1 tablespoon fresh lemon juice
salt and ground black pepper to taste

Serves 6

Makes 8½ cups

Total time: 1 hour

> **NOTE:**
> If you prefer not to use a lot of bottled sauces, this gumbo is especially for you!

In a saucepan, warm the oil. Stir in the onions, garlic, and chiles. Cover and cook on low heat, stirring frequently, until the onions are tender, about 8 minutes. Add the paprika, cumin, thyme, celery, bell peppers, and 3 cups of the water or stock. Bring to a simmer, cover, and cook for about 5 minutes. Add the okra, black-eyed peas, white beans, brown sugar, and tomatoes and simmer for another 5 minutes, or until the vegetables are tender.

In a small bowl, whisk together the cornmeal and the remaining 3 tablespoons of water or stock and stir into the gumbo. Simmer for 5 to 10 minutes, until the cornmeal is cooked and the gumbo thickens slightly. Add the parsley, lemon juice, and salt and pepper.

PER 12-OZ SERVING: 266 CALORIES, 11.9 G PROTEIN, 3.2 G FAT, 51.6 G CARBOHYDRATES, .5 G SATURATED FATTY ACIDS, 1.5 G POLYUNSATURATED FATTY ACIDS, .6 G MONOUNSATURATED FATTY ACIDS, 0 MG CHOLESTEROL, 300 MG SODIUM, 10.6 G TOTAL DIETARY FIBER

MENU SUGGESTIONS For a bayou feast, serve with **Mango Coconut Cucumber Salad** (page 136), corn on the cob, **Sweet Sweet Potatoes** (page 323), **Carolina Kale** (page 321), and **Fruit-filled Meringue Shells** (page 388).

VEGETARIAN FEIJOADA

Feijoada (fay-ZHWA-dah) originated among Brazilian slaves, who prepared flavorful dishes from the leftover foods they were given. Today, feijoada is the festive national dish of Brazil. It is eaten in a leisurely fashion by friends and family as they sit around socializing and chatting, taking a little of this and a little of that from the feijoada groaning board.

There are a multitude of regional, family, and personal variations of feijoada, which traditionally would include several different smoked meats. The elements that transform black beans into feijoada are Brazilian rice, greens, fresh orange sections, hot pepper-lemon sauce, and toasted cassava meal, which is called *farinha* in Brazil.

Our Brazilian Hot Pepper and Lemon Sauce should be made several hours or more in advance. However, you can make the beans while the Brazilian Rice simmers. The rice will be ready just a few minutes before the feijoada is finished cooking.

Present the feijoada in the center of the table on a large platter: black beans on a bed of the rice with the greens piled to one side and the oranges arranged around the edges. Serve the hot pepper-lemon sauce and any other condiments and side dishes in separate bowls.

Serves 6

Total time: 45 minutes

> **NOTE:**
> If you plan to use dried beans, make cooking the beans your first step and be sure to allow enough time for whatever cooking method you decide to use. 1¾ cups dried beans will yield about 5 cups.

Brazilian Hot Pepper and Lemon Sauce (page 359)
Brazilian Rice (page 187)

2 cups chopped onions
2 garlic cloves, pressed or minced
1 cup minced celery
2 red, yellow, and/or green bell peppers, chopped
½ cup water
2 cups canned tomatoes (18-ounce can, undrained)
¼ cup chopped fresh cilantro
¼ teaspoon dried thyme
½ teaspoon ground fennel
1 teaspoon ground coriander
5 cups cooked black beans
    (four 15-ounce cans, drained) (see Note)
salt to taste

1½ pounds collard greens or kale
1 cup water

4 oranges
2 tablespoons soy sauce
toasted cassava meal (optional, page 423)

Place the onions, garlic, celery, bell peppers, and water in a large saucepan. Drain the juice from the tomatoes into the pan, squeeze the juice from each tomato into the pan, and then chop the tomatoes and set them aside. Place the pan on high heat and boil the vegetables, stirring often, for about 15 minutes, until the onions are translucent. Lower the heat and stir in the cilantro, thyme, fennel, and coriander. Add the black beans and chopped tomatoes, cover, and simmer on low heat for about 15 to 20 minutes. Add salt to taste.

While the black beans simmer, remove and discard the collard or kale stems and rinse the leaves well. Stack the leaves and slice them crosswise into ¼-inch strips. In a saucepan, bring the greens and water to a boil. Cover and simmer, stirring frequently as the greens wilt, for about 15 minutes, until the greens are tender.

Meanwhile, peel and section the oranges (page 418) and set aside. When the black beans and the rice are ready, drain the greens and toss with the soy sauce. Serve the feijoada on a large platter as described above or on individual plates. Pass the toasted cassava meal at the table, if desired.

PER 18-OZ SERVING: 301 CALORIES, 16.2 G PROTEIN, 1.5 G FAT, 59.6 G CARBOHYDRATES, .2 G SATURATED FATTY ACIDS, .5 G POLYUNSATURATED FATTY ACIDS, .2 G MONOUNSATURATED FATTY ACIDS, 0 MG CHOLESTEROL, 1189 MG SODIUM, 5.4 G TOTAL DIETARY FIBER

MENU SUGGESTIONS Very little is needed to complete this dish. You might like crudités with **Guacamole with Cottage Cheese** (page 26), **Sweet Potato Oven "Fries"** (page 326), **Corn Relish** (page 361), **Cornmeal Spice Muffins** (page 63), or a crisp tossed salad. For dessert, we recommend **Pumpkin Custard** (page 376), or **Coffee Angelfood Cake** (page 378).

LEFTOVERS? Heat leftover black beans and greens, stirred together, and serve on mashed sweet potatoes. Or make a delicious soup: In a blender or food processor, purée the leftover black beans, greens, and oranges with tomato juice, reheat gently, and serve with leftover pepper and lemon sauce and low-fat sour cream.

CASSOULET

Cassoulet is the name for the classic baked bean dish that is popular bistro fare throughout France. Although baking is the traditional method, you can gently simmer our vegetarian version for 20 minutes on the stove top instead.

1 teaspoon olive oil
6 garlic cloves, minced or pressed
1½ cups chopped onions
½ teaspoon dried thyme
3 bay leaves
½ teaspoon dried marjoram
1 teaspoon minced fresh or dried rosemary
½ cup dry red wine
1 cup peeled and diced carrots
¾ cup diced celery
1 cup diced potatoes
1 cup diced tomatoes
¾ cup diced pepperoni seitan (see Note and page 437)
1 tablespoon molasses
1 tablespoon Dijon mustard
1½ cups cooked kidney beans (15-ounce can, drained)
1½ cups cooked cannellini beans (15-ounce can, drained)
salt and ground black pepper to taste

Serves 4 to 6

Preparation time: 30 minutes, if using already cooked or canned beans

Baking time: 45 minutes

> **NOTE:**
> Almost any highly flavored seitan will work in this dish, but if only plain seitan is available, we suggest adding more herbs, garlic, and mustard to taste.

Preheat the oven to 350°.

In a medium saucepan, warm the olive oil. Add the garlic, onions, thyme, bay leaves, marjoram, and rosemary and sauté for 2 minutes. Add the wine, cover, and simmer until the onions are soft, about 5 minutes. Stir in the carrots, celery, potatoes, and tomatoes, cover, and simmer 10 more minutes, stirring occasionally. Add the seitan, molasses, mustard, and both kinds of beans. Return to a simmer, stirring gently, just until the seitan and beans are heated through. Add salt and pepper to taste. Transfer to a casserole dish that has been prepared with cooking spray, cover, and bake for 45 minutes.

PER 8-OZ SERVING: 237 CALORIES, 11.9 G PROTEIN, 1.7 G FAT, 42.7 G CARBOHYDRATES, .2 G SATURATED FATTY ACIDS, .4 G POLYUNSATURATED FATTY ACIDS, .7 G MONOUNSATURATED FATTY ACIDS, 0 MG CHOLESTEROL, 164 MG SODIUM, 5.1 G TOTAL DIETARY FIBER

MENU SUGGESTIONS Serve with a baguette topped with **Roasted Garlic** (page 43) or **Mushroom Pâté Almondine** (page 121). Accompany with **Roasted Asparagus** (page 312), **Snap Peas with Mushrooms** (page 329), **Seasoned Steamed Artichokes** (page 311), or **Caesar Salad** (page 131).

FESTIVE BLACK BEAN CHILI

This is a colorful black bean dish that requires little effort to make and is attractive enough to serve on a special occasion. Serve plain or on rice or polenta. If you have leftover chili, you could use it to make a variation of Black Bean Chilaquile (page 164). Just use leftover chili, tortillas, greens, and Cheddar cheese. The chili can replace the beans-and-corn layer in the chilaquile—and the salsa layer, too, since this chili is already spicy.

2 cups chopped onions
2 garlic cloves, minced or pressed
½ cup water
1 tablespoon ground cumin
1 tablespoon ground coriander
1 cup prepared Mexican-style red salsa*
2 red and/or green bell peppers, chopped
3 cups cooked black beans (two 15-ounce cans, drained and rinsed)
3 cups canned whole tomatoes, with juice (28-ounce can)
2 cups fresh or frozen corn kernels (11-ounce package)
salt to taste
Tabasco or other hot pepper sauce to taste
¼ cup chopped fresh cilantro, or to taste (optional)

Serves 4 to 6

Total time: 35 minutes

*Prepared salsa gives this chili a "finished" flavor without a lot of cooking. We recommend a clean-, crisp-flavored salsa, such as La Victoria brand Casera Salsa or Pace brand Picante Sauce.

In a covered soup pot, cook the onions and garlic in the water on high heat, stirring frequently, for about 5 minutes. Add the cumin and coriander and stir on high heat for a minute. Stir in the salsa and bell peppers, lower the heat, cover, and simmer for about 5 minutes, stirring occasionally. Add the black beans and tomatoes; simmer for 10 minutes. Add the corn and continue to cook for 10 minutes. Add salt and Tabasco to taste. Stir in the cilantro, if desired.

PER 11-OZ SERVING: 222 CALORIES, 10.7 G PROTEIN, 2.0 G FAT, 45.7 G CARBOHYDRATES, .3 G SATURATED FATTY ACIDS, .7 G POLYUNSATURATED FATTY ACIDS, .3 G MONOUNSATURATED FATTY ACIDS, 0 MG CHOLESTEROL, 618 MG SODIUM, 3.8 G TOTAL DIETARY FIBER

MENU SUGGESTIONS Smooth, sweet, baked winter squash is the perfect complement for this sparky chili. Add a crisp green salad with **Cumin Yogurt Dressing** (page 132), and you have a wonderful meal. Or serve with **Almost Fat-Free Cornbread** (page 110) and **Guacamole with Cottage Cheese** (page 26) with **Sweet Potato Oven "Fries"** (page 326) on the side. **Coffee Angelfood Cake** (page 378) or **Chocolate Cocoa Cake** (page 380) will complete a festive meal.

TAMALE PIE

This colorful, hearty casserole is our lighter version of the traditional Mexican dish. It makes an impressive centerpiece when company's coming or when you want to take a crowd-pleaser to a dish-to-pass supper.

Serves 6

**Baking time:
30 to 35 minutes**

2 teaspoons olive oil
1 cup chopped onions
3 tablespoons minced garlic
1 tablespoon ground cumin
2 teaspoons ground coriander
1 teaspoon dried oregano
1 to 2 tablespoons water
1 cup peeled and diced carrots
1 cup diced red and/or green bell peppers
1 cup diced zucchini
1 small fresh green chile, minced, seeds removed
   for a milder "hot"
2 cups canned crushed tomatoes (15-ounce can, undrained)
1½ cups cooked pinto, kidney, or black beans
   (15-ounce can, drained)
salt and ground black pepper to taste
4 ounces grated low-fat Cheddar cheese (optional)
¾ cup cornmeal
1 tablespoon unbleached white flour
½ teaspoon salt
1 teaspoon baking powder
¼ teaspoon baking soda
2 egg whites, beaten
½ cup nonfat or regular buttermilk
2 teaspoons canola or other vegetable oil

minced scallions
chopped fresh cilantro
nonfat sour cream (optional)

Warm the olive oil in a heavy or nonstick saucepan. Add the onions and garlic, cover, and cook on medium heat for about 10 minutes. Add the cumin, coriander, oregano, enough water to prevent sticking, and the carrots, cover, and cook for 5 minutes. Add the bell peppers, zucchini, and chile, cover, and cook for another 5 minutes. Stir in the tomatoes and beans, cover, and simmer for 5 to 10 minutes. Remove from the heat. Add salt and black pepper to taste.

Preheat the oven to 400°.

Prepare a 2-quart nonreactive casserole dish with cooking spray or a very light coating of oil. Spread the vegetable-bean mixture in the bottom of the dish. If you are using the Cheddar cheese, sprinkle it evenly on top. Set aside.

In a mixing bowl, thoroughly combine the cornmeal, flour, salt, baking powder, and baking soda. In a separate bowl, mix together the beaten egg whites, buttermilk, and oil. Gently fold the wet ingredients into the dry, stirring just until mixed. Pour the batter directly on top of the vegetable-bean mixture, pressing it down a little with a spatula. Bake for 30 to 35 minutes, until the top is golden and a knife inserted into the topping comes out clean.

Garnish with minced scallions, chopped cilantro, and, if you like, nonfat sour cream.

PER 10-OZ SERVING: 251 CALORIES, 11.8 G PROTEIN, 4.4 G FAT, 43.2 G CARBOHYDRATES, .6 G SATURATED FATTY ACIDS, 1.3 G POLYUNSATURATED FATTY ACIDS, 1.7 G MONOUNSATURATED FATTY ACIDS, 1 MG CHOLESTEROL, 462 MG SODIUM, 3.4 G TOTAL DIETARY FIBER

MENU SUGGESTIONS Begin with **Southwestern Corn and Potato Soup** (page 102) or **Guacamole with Asparagus** (page 25) as a dip. Serve with **Carolina Kale** (page 321) and **Corn Relish** (page 361) or with **Spinach Avocado Grapefruit Salad** (page 135). Finish with fresh fruit, **Our Best No-Butter Brownies** (page 387), or **Dark Chocolate Pudding** (page 374).

BLACK BEAN CHILAQUILE

Here is one of our favorite casseroles. The cooks at Moosewood always try to make more Chilaquile than the customers can possibly order so the staff won't be disappointed at the end of the shift. Chilaquile is colorful, jumping with flavor, and filling to boot.

1 cup chopped onions
1 tablespoon olive oil
1 cup chopped tomatoes
1½ cups fresh or frozen corn kernels
1½ cups cooked black beans (15-ounce can, drained)
2 tablespoons fresh lime juice
1 teaspoon salt
½ teaspoon ground black pepper
2 cups rinsed, stemmed, and chopped Swiss chard or spinach
2 cups crushed baked tortilla chips
8 ounces grated fat-free sharp Cheddar cheese
2 cups prepared Mexican-style red salsa or
    Blender Hot Sauce (page 358)

Serves 4 to 6

Preparation time: 35 minutes

Baking time: 35 to 40 minutes

Preheat the oven to 350°. Sauté the onions in the oil for about 8 minutes, until translucent. Stir in the tomatoes, corn, black beans, lime juice, salt, and pepper and continue to sauté for another 5 to 10 minutes, until just heated through.

Meanwhile, in another saucepan, blanch the greens in boiling water to cover for 1 to 3 minutes, until just wilted but still bright green. Drain immediately and set aside.

Prepare an 8 × 8-inch casserole dish or baking pan with a very light coating of oil or cooking spray. Spread half of the crushed tortilla chips on the bottom. Spoon the sautéed vegetables over the tortilla chips and sprinkle on about two-thirds of the grated Cheddar. Arrange the greens evenly over the cheese and spoon on half of the salsa. Finish with the rest of the tortilla chips and top with the remaining salsa and Cheddar. Bake for about 35 to 40 minutes, until the cheese is bubbling and beginning to brown.

PER 8-OZ SERVING: 245 CALORIES, 16.4 G PROTEIN, 4.0 G FAT, 40.0 G CARBOHYDRATES, .4 G SATURATED FATTY ACIDS, .5 G POLYUNSATURATED FATTY ACIDS, 1.9 G MONOUNSATURATED FATTY ACIDS, 20 MG CHOLESTEROL, 1725 MG SODIUM, 2.2 G TOTAL DIETARY FIBER

MENU SUGGESTIONS Because this is a substantial main course, we suggest a light fruit soup such as **Mango-Banana Shake** (page 65) or chilled **Tropical Gazpacho** (page 78) and a simple tossed salad of baby greens vinaigrette or refreshing **Spinach Avocado Grapefruit Salad** (page 135). Try **Pineapple Buttermilk Sherbet** (page 394) or **Lemon Pudding Cake** (page 377) for dessert.

FAT TUESDAY'S SKINNY RED BEANS

There are several ways to present this dish, but we can assure you that no matter how it's served, it's as snazzy and popular as a Mardi Gras parade.

Fresh herbs add a nice touch. Multiply the dried herb quantity by two or three, depending on your preference, and add the fresh herbs with the tomatoes and beans.

2 cups chopped onions
1 tablespoon minced garlic
2 teaspoons olive oil
1 cup chopped carrots
1 cup chopped celery
1 cup chopped bell peppers (red, green, yellow,
   or orange, or a combination)
1 teaspoon dried oregano
¼ teaspoon dried thyme
1 teaspoon dried basil
1 teaspoon dried marjoram
pinch of cayenne, or more to taste
3 cups chopped fresh or canned tomatoes (28-ounce can)
1½ cups cooked or canned kidney beans (15-ounce can, drained)
1 tablespoon Dijon mustard
1 tablespoon brown sugar
1 cup fresh or frozen sliced okra (optional)
salt and ground black pepper to taste
chopped fresh parsley or minced scallions

Serves 4 to 6

Total time: 35 minutes

Combine the onions, garlic, and olive oil in a soup pot. Cover and sauté on medium heat for about 8 minutes, stirring occasionally, until the onions are softened. Add the carrots, celery, bell peppers, oregano, thyme, basil, marjoram, and cayenne. Cover and cook for another 5 to 10 minutes, stirring to prevent sticking. When the vegetables are just tender, stir in the tomatoes, kidney beans, mustard, brown sugar, and okra, if desired. Simmer gently for 5 to 10 minutes. Add salt and pepper to taste and serve topped with parsley or scallions.

PER 8-OZ SERVING: 139 CALORIES, 6.2 G PROTEIN, 2.4 G FAT, 26.0 G CARBOHYDRATES, .3 G SATURATED FATTY ACIDS, .4 G POLYUNSATURATED FATTY ACIDS, 1.2 G MONOUNSATURATED FATTY ACIDS, 0 MG CHOLESTEROL, 104 MG SODIUM, 3.2 G TOTAL DIETARY FIBER

MENU SUGGESTIONS Serve these beans on rice topped with salsa or in bowls as a stew with **Almost Fat-Free Cornbread** (page 110) and a side of **Carolina Kale** (page 321). For dessert, have **Banana Bundt Cake** (page 382) or **Ginger Peach Crumble** (page 386).

LENTIL SAMBAR

One of the great pleasures of cooking is experimenting with new spices or new combinations of old favorites. At Moosewood we are always looking for new flavor blends and adapting them to suit our needs and tastes.

Sambar powder or *masala* is used in southern Indian cooking and is traditionally fiery hot. Here is our version of sambar, a colorful dish that pleases the eye and the palate. Make it as spicy as you dare, and don't forget to make the Mango Peach Chutney to go with it!

Serves 4 to 6

Total time:
45 to 60 minutes

1 cup dried lentils
3 cups water
1 onion
1 small head of cauliflower
2 sweet potatoes
1 red bell pepper
2 teaspoons canola or other vegetable oil
1 teaspoon mustard seeds
½ teaspoon fenugreek seeds
1 teaspoon cumin seeds
1 teaspoon turmeric
1 teaspoon ground coriander
1 teaspoon ground cinnamon
¼ teaspoon cayenne
1 fresh green chile, minced, seeds removed for a milder "hot"
1 tablespoon tamarind concentrate, dissolved in 1 cup hot water
1 teaspoon salt
2 to 3 tablespoons minced fresh cilantro

cooked brown basmati rice
Mango Peach Chutney (page 362)
nonfat yogurt (optional)

Rinse the lentils, place them in a small saucepan with the 3 cups of water, and bring them to a boil. Reduce the heat, cover, and simmer for 45 to 60 minutes, until tender. Stir occasionally, adding more water if necessary.

While the lentils are cooking, chop the onion, cauliflower, sweet potatoes, and bell pepper into bite-sized pieces and set aside. Warm the oil in a pot and sauté the mustard, fenugreek, and cumin seeds on medium heat, covering the pot and shaking it occasionally to prevent burning. When the mustard seeds begin to pop, stir in the turmeric, coriander, cinnamon, cayenne, and chopped chile and sauté for another 2 minutes, stirring constantly.

Stir in the tamarind liquid, then add the onions, cauliflower, sweet potatoes, and salt and combine. Cover and simmer for 10 minutes. Add the bell peppers, cover, and continue to cook until all of the vegetables are tender, about 5 minutes.

Drain the cooked lentils and stir them into the vegetable mixture. Reheat if necessary, then stir in the cilantro. Ladle over basmati rice and serve with Mango Peach Chutney and a generous dollop of yogurt, if desired.

PER 14-OZ SERVING: 320 CALORIES, 11.1 G PROTEIN, 4.0 G FAT, 64.1 G CARBOHYDRATES, .6 G SATURATED FATTY ACIDS, 1.8 G POLYUNSATURATED FATTY ACIDS, .9 G MONOUNSATURATED FATTY ACIDS, 0 MG CHOLESTEROL, 478 MG SODIUM, 10.3 G TOTAL DIETARY FIBER

MENU SUGGESTIONS Serve with a light crisp side dish such as **Carrot Orange Salad** (page 134), **Cabbage Salad** (page 132), or **Asian Cucumber Condiment** (page 367). Chilled **Mango-Banana Shake** (page 65) makes a good appetizer or dessert. Other dessert ideas are **Tapioca Fruit Parfaits** (page 375) and **Pineapple Buttermilk Sherbet** (page 394).

TUSCAN BEANS WITH SAGE

Sage grows wild in Tuscany and many of the bean dishes there are seasoned with this distinctive herb. Don't try to substitute dried sage for fresh in this dish; the flavor just isn't the same. Fragrant and full of gusto, these beans can be a meal in themselves, accompanied by a green salad and Italian breadsticks.

Serves 4 to 6

Total time: 20 minutes

> **NOTE:**
> If you cook your own beans, 1⅓ cups of dried cannellini will yield 3 cups of cooked beans, and if you soak the dried beans overnight with a sprig of sage in the water, it enhances the flavor of the dish.

1 to 2 tablespoons chopped fresh sage
6 garlic cloves, minced or pressed
1 tablespoon olive oil
2½ cups chopped fresh or canned tomatoes
   (28-ounce can, drained)
1½ tablespoons fresh lemon juice
3 cups cooked cannellini (two 15-ounce cans, drained)
salt and ground black pepper to taste

Combine the sage, garlic, and oil in a saucepan and sauté on medium-low heat for several minutes, until the garlic is golden. Add the tomatoes, lemon juice, and cannellini and continue to cook for about 10 minutes, until everything is hot. Add salt and pepper to taste. Serve immediately or chill to serve later.

PER 8-OZ SERVING: 147 CALORIES, 7.6 G PROTEIN, 3.1 G FAT, 24.0 G CARBOHY-DRATES, .4 G SATURATED FATTY ACIDS, .5 G POLYUNSATURATED FATTY ACIDS, 1.8 G MONOUNSATURATED FATTY ACIDS, 0 MG CHOLESTEROL, 492 MG SODIUM, 9.1 G TOTAL DIETARY FIBER

MENU SUGGESTIONS Serve with **Broccoli Rabe and Garlic** (page 315) and dark bread spread with either **Roasted Garlic** (page 43), **Savory Onion Marmalade** (page 363), or **Mushroom Pâté Almondine** (page 121). Try beside **Sun-Dried Tomato Polenta Cutlets** (page 236), **Spicy Broccoli Stuffed Baked Potatoes** (page 249), or **Broiled Portabella Mushrooms** (page 322), or serve as a thick sauce for a short chunky pasta, such as ditalini.

MIDDLE EASTERN CHICKPEAS WITH SPINACH

Aromatic and tangy, this handsome dish goes well with pita, couscous, or rice. Our first choice, though, is to serve it on a bed of orzo and garnished with mint sprigs.

SAUCE
⅔ cup plain nonfat yogurt
1 small garlic clove, minced or pressed
1 teaspoon chopped fresh mint (½ teaspoon dried)
dash of salt

Serves 4

**Total time:
30 to 35 minutes**

BEANS
1 medium onion, chopped
2 teaspoons olive oil
1 red bell pepper, seeded and cubed
2 teaspoons ground coriander
1 teaspoon ground cumin
pinch of saffron
1½ cups canned chickpeas, with liquid reserved
   (16-ounce can)
10 ounces spinach, rinsed, stemmed, and coarsely chopped
2 tablespoons fresh lemon juice
salt and ground black pepper to taste

PASTA
cooked orzo (page 433)

Combine the yogurt, garlic, mint, and salt in a bowl and set aside to blend the flavors.

In a skillet, sauté the onions in the oil on medium heat until softened, about 6 to 8 minutes. Add the bell pepper, coriander, cumin, and saffron and continue to sauté for another 2 or 3 minutes, stirring often. Stir in the chickpeas and ¼ cup of their liquid and simmer for about 5 minutes, until the peppers are just tender, adding more of the reserved chickpea liquid if necessary. Add the spinach and cook, stirring often, for 2 or 3 minutes, until the spinach is bright and wilted. Stir in the lemon juice and add salt and pepper.

Serve immediately on orzo topped with the yogurt sauce.

VARIATION Replace the chickpeas with cannellini or butter beans.

PER 10-OZ SERVING: 342 CALORIES, 14.3 G PROTEIN, 4.7 G FAT, 62.2 G CARBOHYDRATES, .6 G SATURATED FATTY ACIDS, 1.1 G POLYUNSATURATED FATTY ACIDS, 2.1 G MONOUNSATURATED FATTY ACIDS, 1 MG CHOLESTEROL, 425 MG SODIUM, 7.6 G TOTAL DIETARY FIBER

MENU SUGGESTIONS For a complete meal, serve with **Cucumbers Vinaigrette** (page 133), **Vegetables à la Grecque** (page 130), **Moroccan Carrots** (page 316), or **Seasoned Steamed Artichokes** (page 311).

GARLICKY BLACK-EYED PEAS 'N' GREENS

Inspired by foods of the South, where black-eyed peas and collard greens are an everyday affair, this dish, which combines them, is both easy to make and satisfying to eat.

We usually serve this dish on rice; a pot of brown rice conveniently takes almost exactly the same amount of time to cook as the black-eyed peas. On the other hand, you may enjoy a plain bowl of beans and greens all by itself.

2 cups dried black-eyed peas
4 garlic cloves, peeled
¾ pound collard greens, kale, or mustard greens,
    rinsed and chopped (about 6 cups loosely packed)
1 tablespoon olive oil
2 to 4 tablespoons minced garlic
1 teaspoon dried thyme
salt and ground black pepper to taste

cooked rice
chopped scallions or red onions
lemon wedges or hot pepper vinegar

Serves 4 to 6

Total time: 1 hour

Rinse the black-eyed peas. Place them in a soup pot with the garlic cloves and enough water to cover. Bring to a boil, then lower the heat, cover, and cook for 45 minutes, until tender, adding water occasionally as needed. The black-eyed peas should be moist but not soupy, so it is ideal when most of the water has been absorbed at the end of cooking. When the black-eyed peas are tender, if most of the water has not been absorbed, lightly drain them. Cover and set aside.

Rinse the greens and set aside.

In a large skillet, heat the oil and sauté the minced garlic and thyme for 1 minute, stirring constantly. Add the damp greens and continue to stir until they are wilted but still bright green. Stir the greens into the black-eyed peas and mix. Add salt and pepper to taste.

Serve on rice, topped with scallions or red onions, and with lemon wedges or hot pepper vinegar on the side.

PER 10-OZ SERVING: 272 CALORIES, 15.9 G PROTEIN, 3.6 G FAT, 46.8 G CARBOHYDRATES, .6 G SATURATED FATTY ACIDS, .6 G POLYUNSATURATED FATTY ACIDS, 1.8 G MONOUNSATURATED FATTY ACIDS, 0 MG CHOLESTEROL, 53 MG SODIUM, 13.8 G TOTAL DIETARY FIBER

MENU SUGGESTIONS Other dishes that mix well with this Southern classic are **Baked Sweet Potato Salad** (page 137), **Cucumbers Vinaigrette** (page 133), and **Corn Relish** (page 361). Or serve it as a side dish for **Honey Mustard Fish** (page 298).

SWEET-AND-SOUR LENTILS

Here's a new twist on lentils that has been a hit with both the staff and customers at Moose-wood. Instead of using the curry spices found in a traditional Indian lentil dahl, we have ventured farther east and introduced ginger, soy sauce, and rice vinegar into ours. The sweetness provided by the apple juice and diced carrots will vary depending upon the brand of juice used and the quality of the produce. If you would like the dish sweeter, add a small amount of brown sugar or honey. Sweet-and-Sour Lentils are delicious chilled as well as hot.

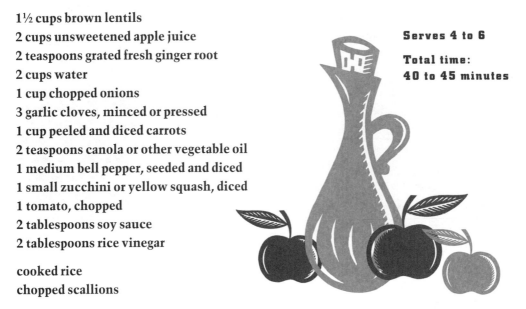

1½ cups brown lentils
2 cups unsweetened apple juice
2 teaspoons grated fresh ginger root
2 cups water
1 cup chopped onions
3 garlic cloves, minced or pressed
1 cup peeled and diced carrots
2 teaspoons canola or other vegetable oil
1 medium bell pepper, seeded and diced
1 small zucchini or yellow squash, diced
1 tomato, chopped
2 tablespoons soy sauce
2 tablespoons rice vinegar

cooked rice
chopped scallions

Serves 4 to 6

**Total time:
40 to 45 minutes**

Rinse the lentils. Combine them in a saucepan with the apple juice, ginger, and water. Bring to a boil, then lower the heat and simmer, uncovered, for 30 to 40 minutes, until the lentils are tender. Add a little water near the end of cooking if necessary to prevent sticking.

While the lentils cook, sauté the onions, garlic, and carrots in the oil for about 5 minutes, until the onions begin to soften. Add the bell peppers, zucchini or squash, and tomatoes, cover, and cook on low heat for about 10 minutes, until just tender. Stir in the soy sauce and vinegar.

When the lentils are ready, combine them with the vegetables. Serve on rice and top with chopped scallions.

PER 11.50-OZ SERVING: 141 CALORIES, 5.5 G PROTEIN, 2.1 G FAT, 26.7 G CARBOHYDRATES, .3 G SATURATED FATTY ACIDS, 1.1 G POLYUNSATURATED FATTY ACIDS, .4 G MONOUNSATURATED FATTY ACIDS, 0 MG CHOLESTEROL, 292 MG SODIUM, 5.6 G TOTAL DIETARY FIBER

MENU SUGGESTIONS Try the lentils on **Five-Spice Rice** (page 186) or **Golden Basmati Rice** (page 185), with **Japanese Sesame Spinach** (page 330) or a green salad with **Japanese Carrot Dressing** (page 346).

SWEET POTATO AND BLACK BEAN BURRITO

Sweet potatoes add an unexpected creaminess to the filling in these burritos. One young Moosewood waitperson said this was the first time she had ever *loved* a burrito without cheese. Serve the burritos on a bed of rice, if you like, with plenty of salsa.

5 cups peeled cubed sweet potatoes
½ teaspoon salt
2 teaspoons canola or other vegetable oil
3 ½ cups diced onions
4 large garlic cloves, minced or pressed
1 tablespoon minced fresh green chile
4 teaspoons ground cumin
4 teaspoons ground coriander
4 ½ cups cooked black beans (three 15-ounce cans, drained)
⅔ cup lightly packed cilantro leaves
2 tablespoons fresh lemon juice
1 teaspoon salt
8 eight-inch flour tortillas
Fresh Tomato Salsa (page 360)

Serves 4 to 6

Preparation time: 35 minutes

Baking time: 30 minutes

> **NOTE:**
> You can also mash the ingredients in a large bowl by hand using a potato masher. The result will be a less smooth but nicely textured filling.

Preheat the oven to 350°.

Place the sweet potatoes in a medium saucepan with the salt and water to cover. Cover and bring to a boil, then simmer until tender, about 10 minutes. Drain and set aside.

While the sweet potatoes are cooking, warm the oil in a medium skillet or saucepan and add the onions, garlic, and chile. Cover and cook on medium-low heat, stirring occasionally, until the onions are tender, about 7 minutes. Add the cumin and coriander and cook for 2 to 3 minutes longer, stirring frequently. Remove from the heat and set aside.

In a food processor, combine the black beans, cilantro, lemon juice, salt, and cooked sweet potatoes and purée until smooth (see Note). Transfer the sweet potato mixture to a large mixing bowl and mix in the cooked onions and spices.

Lightly oil a large baking dish. Spoon about ⅔ to ¾ cup of the filling in the center of each tortilla, roll it up, and place it, seam side down, in the baking dish. Cover tightly with foil and bake for about 30 minutes, until piping hot. Serve topped with salsa.

PER 20-OZ SERVING: 572 CALORIES, 19.6 G PROTEIN, 6.1 G FAT, 113.7 G CARBOHYDRATES, .5 G SATURATED FATTY ACIDS, 1.6 G POLYUNSATURATED FATTY ACIDS, .5 G MONOUNSATURATED FATTY ACIDS, 0 MG CHOLESTEROL, 1401 MG SODIUM, 7.5 G TOTAL DIETARY FIBER

MENU SUGGESTIONS Start with **Tropical Gazpacho** (page 78) and end with fresh fruit salad à la **Pineapple Buttermilk Sherbert** (page 394). Try topping with **Cilantro Pesto** (page 364) for a change of pace.

CHILI BURGERS

Tex-Mex seasonings add great flavor to this nicely textured burger. Beans and oats together create a perfect protein.

If you would like to cook the beans yourself, rather than use canned, you will need 1 generous cup of dried beans. For cooking instructions, see page 414.

1 cup chopped onions
4 garlic cloves, minced or pressed
2 teaspoons olive oil
½ cup peeled and grated carrots
1½ teaspoons chili powder
1 teaspoon ground cumin
3 cups cooked pinto or kidney beans
   (two 15-ounce cans, drained)
2 tablespoons Dijon mustard
2 tablespoons soy sauce
2 tablespoons ketchup or 1 tablespoon tomato paste
1½ cups rolled oats
salt and ground black pepper to taste

Serves 6

Total time: 45 minutes

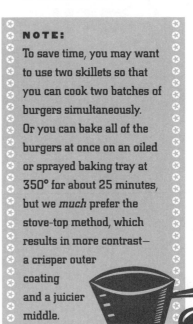

NOTE:
To save time, you may want to use two skillets so that you can cook two batches of burgers simultaneously. Or you can bake all of the burgers at once on an oiled or sprayed baking tray at 350° for about 25 minutes, but we *much* prefer the stove-top method, which results in more contrast— a crisper outer coating and a juicier middle.

Sauté the onions and garlic in the oil for about 5 minutes, until the onions begin to soften. Add the carrots, chili powder, and cumin and cook on low heat for 5 minutes. Set aside.

Mash the beans in a large bowl with a potato masher or the back of a spoon. Add the mustard, soy sauce, ketchup or tomato paste, and the sautéed vegetables. Mix in the oats. Add salt and pepper to taste.

Moisten your hands and form the burger mixture into six 3- to 4-inch patties. Lightly spray or oil a nonstick skillet and cook the burgers on medium-low heat for 5 to 8 minutes on each side (see Note).

PER 7.50-OZ SERVING: 360 CALORIES, 17.6 G PROTEIN, 5.0 G FAT, 63.5 G CARBOHYDRATES, .8 G SATURATED FATTY ACIDS, 1.2 G POLYUNSATURATED FATTY ACIDS, 2.0 G MONOUNSATURATED FATTY ACIDS, 0 MG CHOLESTEROL, 437 MG SODIUM, 16.0 G TOTAL DIETARY FIBER

MENU SUGGESTIONS We like this burger on whole wheat toast or a sesame bun topped with ketchup, **Creamy Roasted Red Pepper Sauce** (page 355), **Cilantro Pesto** (page 364), or **Barbecue Sauce** (page 355). Or serve it on a bed of fresh greens topped with **Fresh Tomato Salsa** (page 360) or **Guacamole with Cottage Cheese** (page 26), garnished with tomato wedges, red onion rings, and a few baked tortilla chips. Nice side dishes are **Brazilian Rice** (page 187), **Baked Sweet Potato Salad** (page 137), or **Oven "Fries"** (page 326).

bulgur with savory greens 178

couscous with peas and onions 179

CURRIED COUSCOUS PILAF 180

kasha pilaf 181

millet pilaf 182

ORZO AND GREEN HERBS 183

quinoa pine nut pilaf 184

golden basmati rice 185

FIVE-SPICE RICE 186

brazilian rice 187

bulgur rice pilaf 188

FRAGRANT JASMINE RICE 189

thai fried rice 190

midsummer risotto 191

SQUASH AND KALE RISOTTO 192

onion and feta risotto 194

mushroom wheatberry pilaf 195

SPRING VEGETABLE PAELLA 196

GRAINS

GRAINS, such as rice, wheat, corn, millet, oats, and buckwheat, are the foods that sustain most of the world. The crucial importance of grains historically is reflected in folklore, religion, and language. In Chinese, Japanese, and Thai the word for "rice" is the same as the word for "meal" or "food." The Iroquois called "corn" by a name meaning "our life." The Chinese called rice kernels "little buddhas" to express their respect and gratitude for the grain, and England, Scotland, and Ireland all have ballads and folk songs that laud the praises of oats and barley. Grains are traditionally given as offerings and blessings. They are the symbols of prosperity, abundance, and well-being.

Grains are certainly the background, the support, of a low-fat vegetarian cuisine. Our national shift to a healthier diet has resulted in wider interest in grain-based dishes, a change supported by the USDA's recommendation of 6 to 11 servings per day from the bread, cereal, rice, and pasta group. You might find ten or even twenty different kinds of rice in a well-stocked supermarket today. Older grains, such as kamut, spelt, and quinoa, are seeing a resurgence in popularity. When we make a variety of grains the base of our diet, we are rewarded with good nutrition and a renewed enjoyment of eating well. Still today, we are inspired to give humble thanks for the bounty of the earth.

Brown rice is the grain of choice at Moosewood, partly because it's a versatile whole grain and also because it was important in the vegetarian culture of the early 1970s, where Moosewood has its roots. We serve brown rice with something almost every day at the restaurant, although many other grains could be more quickly prepared. Bulgur, quinoa, millet, jasmine or basmati rice, couscous, and orzo also appear on our menus.

In this chapter, we offer many ways to get more grains into your diet. Most grains are mildly flavored and unassuming, making them good foils for assertively seasoned foods. The grains themselves can also be enlivened with traditional spices and herbs or more unorthodox seasonings. For example, Fragrant Jasmine Rice is seasoned with authentically Southeast Asian ingredients—lemongrass, Thai basil, and chiles—whereas in Curried Couscous Pilaf, we've mixed things up a bit by sparking this North African grain with Indian spices. Some of these hearty mixtures of grains and vegetables, including Kasha Pilaf, Spring Vegetable Paella, the risottos, and Thai Fried Rice, work as interesting and delicious main dishes.

Grains are useful in making pilafs, casseroles, and stuffed vegetables and can be easily reheated by steaming or microwaving to accompany stews, soups, or cooked vegetables for a later meal; we often prepare more than will be needed for a specific meal to ensure leftovers. Plain vegetables and grains can be jazzed up with sauces and seasonings, such as those on pages 338 to 367, for a quick yet satisfying meal.

BULGUR WITH SAVORY GREENS

Bulgur, a quick-cooking grain made from wheatberries, is most readily found in natural food stores or the Middle Eastern section of supermarkets. Here it is part of a grains-and-greens side dish that is delicious hot or at room temperature.

Serves 6

Preparation time: 30 minutes

Cooking time: 15 minutes

2½ cups chopped onions
4 garlic cloves, minced or pressed
1 tablespoon olive oil
1 pound Swiss chard or escarole,
    rinsed and chopped (about 8 cups)
2 tablespoons fresh lemon juice, or more to taste
1½ cups bulgur
1 teaspoon salt
2½ cups water
ground black pepper to taste

lemon wedges
fresh mint leaves
red wine vinegar or balsamic vinegar

In a large skillet, sauté the onions and garlic in the oil for about 8 minutes, until the onions are translucent. Add the greens and lemon juice, cover, and cook until the greens have just wilted. Stir in the bulgur and salt. Add the water, cover, and cook on medium-low heat for about 15 minutes, until the bulgur is tender and most of the water has been absorbed. Sprinkle with pepper and add more lemon juice to taste. Serve garnished with lemon wedges and mint, and offer a cruet of vinegar at the table.

VARIATION Add ½ cup cooked chickpeas just before serving.

PER 10-OZ SERVING: 366 CALORIES, 13.1 G PROTEIN, 4.0 G FAT, 81.3 G CARBOHY-DRATES, .6 G SATURATED FATTY ACIDS, .8 G POLYUNSATURATED FATTY ACIDS, 1.9 G MONOUNSATURATED FATTY ACIDS, 0 MG CHOLESTEROL, 431 MG SODIUM, 18.7 G TOTAL DIETARY FIBER

MENU SUGGESTIONS Serve with a simple baked fish, such as **Fish with Herbs and Lime** (page 289), or with **Harira** (page 85) and **Seasoned Steamed Artichokes** (page 311).

COUSCOUS WITH PEAS AND ONIONS

Fresh sage enlivens an exemplary grain dish that is terrifically easy to make. We prefer the heartier flavor of whole wheat couscous with the mellow peas and onions, but regular couscous is fine too. If you use regular couscous, reduce the amount of water in the recipe to 1 cup.

1½ cups finely chopped onions
1 tablespoon olive oil
1 cup fresh or frozen green peas
1½ teaspoons chopped fresh sage
½ teaspoon salt
1⅓ cups water
1 cup whole wheat couscous
salt to taste

a few fresh sage leaves
lemon wedges or balsamic vinegar

Serves 4

Total time: 25 minutes

Combine the onions and oil in a heavy skillet, preferably nonstick. Cover and sauté, stirring occasionally, for 10 to 15 minutes, until lightly browned. Add the peas, sage, salt, water, and couscous, cover, and cook on low heat for about 5 minutes, until the peas are tender but still bright green and all of the water is absorbed. Stir the couscous with a fork to fluff it. Add salt to taste.

Garnish with a few sage leaves and serve with fresh lemon wedges or pass a cruet of balsamic vinegar at the table.

PER 8-OZ SERVING: 265 CALORIES, 9.1 G PROTEIN, 4.2 G FAT, 48.5 G CARBOHYDRATES, .6 G SATURATED FATTY ACIDS, .5 G POLYUNSATURATED FATTY ACIDS, 2.7 G MONOUNSATURATED FATTY ACIDS, 0 MG CHOLESTEROL, 389 MG SODIUM, 5.6 G TOTAL DIETARY FIBER

MENU SUGGESTIONS Serve with **Fish Steaks with Fennel** (page 290), or with **Vegetables à la Grecque** (page 130) accompanied by either **Savory Stuffed Mushrooms** (page 42) or **Broiled Portabella Mushrooms** (page 322).

CURRIED COUSCOUS PILAF

Lentils and spinach boost the nutritional value of this couscous dish, the curry spices enliven it with a zesty vibrant flavor, and the garlic, ginger, and cayenne add just the right amount of heat. To save time, put the lentils on to simmer before preparing the rest of the ingredients for the dish.

½ cup dried lentils
1½ cups water
2 teaspoons canola or other vegetable oil
2 large garlic cloves, minced or pressed
1 tablespoon grated fresh ginger root
1 tablespoon curry powder or garam masala
pinch of cayenne
½ cup water or orange juice
1 teaspoon salt
1 cup peeled and diced carrots
2 cups stemmed chopped fresh spinach, lightly packed
½ cup chopped scallions
1½ cups quick-cooking couscous
1½ cups boiling water
salt and ground black pepper to taste

Serves 6

Total time: 45 minutes

In a small saucepan, combine the lentils and water and bring to a boil. Cover and simmer on low heat for 35 to 40 minutes, until the lentils are tender, adding more water as necessary.

When the lentils have been cooking for 10 to 15 minutes, warm the oil in a medium saucepan. Add the garlic, ginger, curry powder or garam masala, and cayenne and sauté for 1 to 2 minutes, stirring constantly. Add the water or orange juice, salt, and carrots. Cover and simmer until the carrots are tender, about 5 minutes. Add the spinach, cover, and cook until the spinach wilts, 1 to 2 minutes. Add the scallions, couscous, and boiling water and cook for 1 minute, stirring constantly. Cover, remove from the heat, let sit for 5 minutes, and then fluff the couscous with a fork.

When the lentils are tender, drain them and then stir them into the pilaf. Add salt and pepper to taste. Serve hot.

PER 8-OZ SERVING: 264 CALORIES, 11.3 G PROTEIN, 2.4 G FAT, 49.9 G CARBOHYDRATES, .3 G SATURATED FATTY ACIDS, 1.2 G POLYUNSATURATED FATTY ACIDS, .5 G MONOUNSATURATED FATTY ACIDS, 0 MG CHOLESTEROL, 465 MG SODIUM, 8.0 G TOTAL DIETARY FIBER

MENU SUGGESTIONS Serve with either **Broiled Eggplant Thai Style** (page 34), **Cabbage Salad** (page 132), or **Southeast Asian Coconut Zucchini** (page 334). Finish with chilled **Mango-Banana Shake** (page 65).

KASHA PILAF

Kasha, a high-fiber, lysine-rich grain made from buckwheat groats, is common throughout Eastern Europe. It has a distinctive earthy flavor, so some people consider it an acquired taste, but many of us at Moosewood like it a lot. Like rice, kasha can be eaten plain alongside a juicy main dish such as beans or sautéed vegetables, but it has the advantage of being quick-cooking—a mere 15 minutes and it's ready.

This savory pilaf can stand on its own as a side dish or serve as a first-class stuffing for tomatoes, bell peppers, or winter squash.

1¼ cups chopped onions
1 cup diced celery
4 garlic cloves, minced or pressed
1 tablespoon canola or other vegetable oil
1 cup kasha (buckwheat groats)
1⅓ cups water
1 cup peeled and diced carrots
2 cups sliced mushrooms
¼ cup dry red wine
2 tablespoons soy sauce
2 tablespoons chopped fresh dill (2 teaspoons dried)
ground black pepper to taste

a few fresh dill or parsley sprigs
tomato wedges

Serves 4 to 6

Total time: 45 minutes

In a large skillet, sauté the onions, celery, and garlic in the oil for about 10 minutes, until the onions are translucent. Add the kasha and sauté for another minute to lightly toast it. Pour in the water, add the carrots, cover, and simmer for 5 minutes. Add the mushrooms, red wine, soy sauce, and dill. Cover and cook on low heat until the liquid is absorbed and the kasha and vegetables are tender, about 10 minutes. Add pepper to taste. Serve garnished with dill or parsley sprigs and tomato wedges.

PER 6.50-OZ SERVING: 128 CALORIES, 4.0 G PROTEIN, 3.2 G FAT, 21.5 G CARBOHYDRATES, .5 G SATURATED FATTY ACIDS, 1.7 G POLYUNSATURATED FATTY ACIDS, .8 G MONOUNSATURATED FATTY ACIDS, 0 MG CHOLESTEROL, 306 MG SODIUM, 3.9 G TOTAL DIETARY FIBER

MENU SUGGESTIONS Serve with **Baltic Fish** (page 287) and a side dish of **Baked Beets and Shallots** (page 314), or with a bowl of **Cream of Cauliflower Soup** (page 90) and a crisp spinach and marinated mushroom salad topped with grated carrots and **Apple Basil Dressing** (page 348).

MILLET PILAF

Millet is an interesting grain that somehow has never become a staple in this country—it is still waiting in the wings for its debut as a popular American grain. At Moosewood, we like it for a change of pace and for its quick cooking time. For variety, try using brown rice, couscous, or bulgur in place of the millet in this recipe.

1 cup millet
2 cups boiling water
¼ teaspoon salt
pinch of saffron
1 teaspoon olive oil
1 cup minced onions
2 garlic cloves, minced or pressed
½ cup minced celery
½ teaspoon oregano
½ teaspoon ground cinnamon
½ cup minced red or green bell peppers
½ cup fresh or frozen green peas
¼ cup currants
1 to 2 tablespoons fresh lemon juice
salt and ground black pepper to taste

Serves 4

**Total time:
30 to 40 minutes**

In a cast-iron skillet or other heavy pan, toast the millet on medium-high heat, stirring constantly, until it is fragrant and begins to brown, about 3 to 5 minutes. Carefully pour the boiling water into the very hot skillet in a thin, steady stream. Add the salt and saffron, cover, and cook on very low heat for 15 minutes.

While the millet is cooking, warm the oil in a medium saucepan. Add the onions, garlic, celery, oregano, and cinnamon. Sauté for 2 minutes, stirring constantly, then cover and cook on low heat for 5 minutes. Add the bell peppers and peas, cover, and continue to cook until all of the vegetables are tender, about 5 minutes.

Meanwhile, fluff the millet with a fork, replace the cover, and remove it from the heat. When the vegetables are tender, stir in the currants and lemon juice and cook for another minute, until thoroughly hot. Mix the vegetables into the millet and add salt and black pepper to taste.

PER 8.50-OZ SERVING: 187 CALORIES, 5.5 G PROTEIN, 2.6 G FAT, 36.9 G CARBOHYDRATES, .4 G SATURATED FATTY ACIDS, .8 G POLYUNSATURATED FATTY ACIDS, 1.1 G MONOUNSATURATED FATTY ACIDS, 0 MG CHOLESTEROL, 185 MG SODIUM, 5.4 G TOTAL DIETARY FIBER

MENU SUGGESTIONS Serve with **Creamy Potato Kale Soup** (page 91) and **Vegetables à la Grecque** (page 130).

ORZO AND GREEN HERBS

This is a handsome, quickly prepared dish, and when the hot pasta warms the fresh herbs and extra-virgin olive oil, a lovely fragrance is released. Orzo and Green Herbs can accompany steamed or roasted vegetables, main-dish salads, or simple grilled or broiled fish. If you can't resist a larger portion than the scant cup per person offered here, the recipe can easily be doubled.

6 to 8 cups water
1 cup orzo (about 7 ounces)
1 cup finely chopped mixed fresh herbs
    (thyme, chives, garlic chives, basil, sage, oregano,
    parsley, marjoram, chervil, tarragon)
2 teaspoons extra-virgin olive oil
½ teaspoon salt
freshly ground black pepper to taste

Serves 4

Total time: 15 minutes

Bring the water to a rolling boil in a large, covered pot. Stir in the orzo and cook for about 7 minutes, until al dente.

Place the herbs, oil, salt, and pepper in a serving bowl. When the pasta is ready, drain it and add it to the bowl. Toss well and serve immediately.

PER 5.50-OZ SERVING: 235 CALORIES, 7.7 G PROTEIN, 3.6 G FAT, 43.4 G CARBOHYDRATES, .5 G SATURATED FATTY ACIDS, .7 G POLYUNSATURATED FATTY ACIDS, 1.9 G MONOUNSATURATED FATTY ACIDS, 0 MG CHOLESTEROL, 305 MG SODIUM, 2.3 G TOTAL DIETARY FIBER

MENU SUGGESTIONS Start with **Savory Stuffed Mushrooms** (page 42), follow with **Fish Steaks with Fennel** (page 290) accompanied by this orzo and **Citrus-dressed Asparagus** (page 313), and finish with **Chocolate Cocoa Cake** (page 380).

QUINOA PINE NUT PILAF

Quinoa is an Incan grain that is very high in protein, vitamins, and minerals. With its slightly crunchy texture and nutty flavor, it is enjoying a heyday of popularity in natural foods cuisine and can readily be found in health food stores and many supermarkets.

Our pilaf becomes a mosaic of colors when both red and green bell peppers are used, so if you have them on hand, include both for the visual effect. The pine nuts are a great match for quinoa's flavor and they only add about 1½ grams of fat per serving, so indulge a little.

1 large onion, chopped
3 garlic cloves, minced or pressed
1 tablespoon canola or other vegetable oil
1 red or green bell pepper or a combination
2 teaspoons ground cumin
2 teaspoons ground coriander
1 cup quinoa
1⅔ cups water
½ cup chopped fresh basil
1½ cups fresh or frozen corn kernels
salt and ground black pepper to taste
1½ tablespoons toasted pine nuts*

Serves 4 or 5

Total time: 35 minutes

To toast pine nuts, spread them in a single layer on an unoiled baking sheet and bake in a conventional or toaster oven at 350° for about 3 to 5 minutes, until just slightly deepened in color.

In a heavy saucepan, sauté the onions and garlic in the oil for 5 minutes, until softened. Add the bell peppers, cumin, and coriander and continue to sauté for 5 more minutes, stirring occasionally. While the vegetables cook, place the quinoa in a fine sieve and rinse well under cold running water for a minute or two. Add the rinsed quinoa and the water to the saucepan, cover tightly, and simmer gently for 15 minutes. Stir in the basil and corn and cook 5 to 10 minutes longer, or until the quinoa is tender.

Stir the pilaf to fluff it, add salt and pepper to taste, and serve topped with the toasted pine nuts.

PER 7.50-OZ SERVING: 280 CALORIES, 8.5 G PROTEIN, 7.4 G FAT, 45.9 G CARBOHYDRATES, .7 G SATURATED FATTY ACIDS, 2.6 G POLYUNSATURATED FATTY ACIDS, 1.4 G MONOUNSATURATED FATTY ACIDS, 0 MG CHOLESTEROL, 47 MG SODIUM, 5.3 G TOTAL DIETARY FIBER

MENU SUGGESTIONS This pilaf nicely complements Three Sisters Stew (page 272), Roasted Vegetables Three Ways (page 226), Curried Squash (page 332), or Spinach Avocado Grapefruit Salad (page 135).

GOLDEN BASMATI RICE

Usually rice is considered just a backdrop for the rest of the meal, but this fragrant pilaf flecked with orange elevates rice to noteworthy status.

1 cup white basmati rice
1 cup diced onions
2 teaspoons canola or other vegetable oil
½ teaspoon turmeric
½ teaspoon ground cinnamon
¼ teaspoon ground cardamom
2 cups water
1½ cups peeled and grated carrots
1 teaspoon freshly grated orange peel
¾ teaspoon salt

Serves 4

Soaking time for rice: 30 minutes

Total time: 45 to 50 minutes, plus 10 minutes to sit

Rinse the rice and soak it in water to cover for 30 minutes.

When the rice has soaked for about 20 minutes, sauté the onions in the oil for about 5 minutes. Add the turmeric, cinnamon, and cardamom. Cook, stirring constantly, for another minute and set aside. Bring the 2 cups of water to a boil in a medium saucepan with a tight-fitting lid. Stir in the onion mixture, carrots, orange peel, and salt. Drain the rice and add it to the saucepan. Return it to a boil, then reduce the heat to low, cover, and simmer for 15 minutes, until tender.

Remove from the heat and allow to sit for 10 minutes. Just before serving, stir the rice to fluff it.

PER 7.50-OZ SERVING: 215 CALORIES, 4.1 G PROTEIN, 2.9 G FAT, 42.7 G CARBOHYDRATES, .4 G SATURATED FATTY ACIDS, 1.6 G POLYUNSATURATED FATTY ACIDS, .7 G MONOUNSATURATED FATTY ACIDS, 0 MG CHOLESTEROL, 486 MG SODIUM, 2.9 G TOTAL DIETARY FIBER

MENU SUGGESTIONS Golden Basmati Rice is a wonderful complement to Indian curries or **Lentil Sambar** (page 166). Or serve it with **Caribbean Stew** (page 265) and **Jerk Tofu** (page 337) or with **Fish Tagine with Chermoulla** (page 291).

FIVE-SPICE RICE

This rice is tasty enough to eat all by itself. The addition of steamed broccoli florets and sliced seasoned tofu makes it a quick, nutritious lunch, and it would be a fitting side dish for almost any Southeast Asian sauté or fish dish.

Chinese five-spice powder can be found in large supermarkets and specialty groceries. Its distinctive, slightly sweet flavor comes from a combination of star anise, fennel, cloves, Szechuan peppercorns, and cumin or cinnamon. Although most five-spice powders are similar, the amounts of each spice can vary and some mixtures even include ginger, licorice, and/or white pepper.

1 cup long-grain brown rice
1 teaspoon dark sesame oil
1 teaspoon grated fresh ginger root
1 garlic clove, minced or pressed
1 teaspoon five-spice powder
¼ teaspoon salt
1½ cups water
¼ cup dry sherry or Chinese rice wine
a few splashes of soy sauce

Serves 2 to 4

Preparation time: 10 minutes

Cooking time: 45 minutes

In a colander or sieve, rinse the rice with cool water and set aside to drain.

Warm the oil in a medium saucepan and add the ginger, garlic, and five-spice powder. Sauté for 1 minute, stirring constantly. Add the rice and salt and sauté for another 2 minutes, continuing to stir. Add the water and sherry or rice wine, cover, bring to a boil, and then gently simmer for about 40 minutes, until all of the water is absorbed and the rice is tender. Add soy sauce to taste and serve.

PER 8-OZ SERVING: 180 CALORIES, 3.4 G PROTEIN, 2.4 G FAT, 33.6 G CARBOHYDRATES, .4 G SATURATED FATTY ACIDS, .9 G POLYUNSATURATED FATTY ACIDS, .9 G MONOUNSATURATED FATTY ACIDS, 0 MG CHOLESTEROL, 159 MG SODIUM, .2 G TOTAL DIETARY FIBER

MENU SUGGESTIONS Serve this rice with **Vegetable-filled Pancakes** (page 233) or **Savory Hoisin Fish** (page 293), or use it in place of the noodles called for in **Poached Fish with Vegetables** (page 301).

BRAZILIAN RICE

This is the rice to serve with Vegetarian Feijoada (page 158) and other Latin American dishes. Just a very small amount of oil creates a rich and more flavorful rice.

Serves 6 to 8

**Preparation time:
15 minutes**

**Cooking time:
40 minutes**

2 cups chopped onions
1 teaspoon vegetable oil
2 cups chopped fresh tomatoes
1 teaspoon salt
2 cups brown rice
3 cups water

In a covered saucepan, sauté the onions in the oil for 5 minutes on medium-high heat, stirring frequently. Add the tomatoes and salt and continue to cook for 5 minutes. Stir in the rice and water, cover, and bring to a boil. Reduce the heat and gently simmer on a heat diffuser or on very low heat for about 40 minutes, until the rice is tender.

PER 7-OZ SERVING: 186 CALORIES, 4.1 G PROTEIN, 2.0 G FAT, 38.4 G CARBOHY-
DRATES, .3 G SATURATED FATTY ACIDS, .9 G POLYUNSATURATED FATTY ACIDS,
.6 G MONOUNSATURATED FATTY ACIDS, 0 MG CHOLESTEROL, 304 MG SODIUM,
1.0 G TOTAL DIETARY FIBER

BULGUR RICE PILAF

This healthful side dish, refreshed by the flavors of mint and lemon, is a very pleasant way to help fulfill your recommended daily quota of grains. Here the bulgur adds a nutty flavor and firm, chewy texture to the already nutritious rice. Don't worry about the fact that rice and bulgur have such different cooking times—much to our surprise, they cook together quite compatibly in one pot.

Serves 6

Total time: 40 minutes

1 cup bulgur
1 cup brown rice, preferably long-grain
3 cups water
1 teaspoon salt
2 teaspoons extra-virgin olive oil
2 cups thinly sliced leeks, white and tender green parts
4 garlic cloves, minced or pressed
2 celery stalks, minced
¼ cup minced fresh parsley
2 tablespoons minced fresh dill (2 teaspoons dried)
1 teaspoon dried mint
1 teaspoon freshly grated lemon peel
salt and ground black pepper to taste

lemon wedges
fresh mint leaves or fresh dill sprigs

In a 2-quart saucepan with a tight-fitting lid, bring the bulgur, rice, water, and salt to a boil. Reduce the heat, cover, and simmer for about 40 minutes, or until all of the water has been absorbed and the rice is tender.

Meanwhile, warm the oil in a separate saucepan. Stir in the leeks, garlic, and celery, cover, and cook gently until the leeks are tender, about 10 minutes, stirring frequently. When both the grains and the vegetables are ready, combine them and add the parsley, dill, mint, and lemon peel. Add salt and pepper to taste. Garnish with lemon wedges and fresh mint or dill.

PER 7-OZ SERVING: 340 CALORIES, 10.0 G PROTEIN, 3.3 G FAT, 72.1 G CARBOHYDRATES, .5 G SATURATED FATTY ACIDS, .8 G POLYUNSATURATED FATTY ACIDS, 1.6 G MONOUNSATURATED FATTY ACIDS, 0 MG CHOLESTEROL, 454 MG SODIUM, 11.2 G TOTAL DIETARY FIBER

MENU SUGGESTIONS Serve with **Swiss Chard Rolls** with cheese and leek filling (page 252), **Roasted Vegetables Three Ways** (page 226), **Fish Steaks with Fennel** (page 290), or **Baked Fish with Mustard Marinade** (page 288). Finish with **Chocolate Hazelnut Biscotti** (page 392).

FRAGRANT JASMINE RICE

Although plain jasmine rice smells wonderful enough as it cooks, when we combine it with lemongrass, basil, and pineapple, it makes an aromatic sensation. You will surely want to eat it, but the scent is *almost* enough.

We wondered whether lemongrass, which many people might not have on hand, could be distinguished from commonplace lemon zest in this recipe. So we tried both. The dish is good with lemon zest, but we all prefer the authentic taste of lemongrass. Look for it in well-stocked supermarkets or specialty groceries—and if you can find Thai basil, all the better.

If you plan to serve this rice with other very spicy dishes, you may wish to omit the fresh chile or replace it with a small pinch of cayenne.

2 cups jasmine rice (page 436)
1 teaspoon canola or other vegetable oil
2 tablespoons minced lemongrass* or
   2 teaspoons freshly grated lemon peel
4 garlic cloves, minced or pressed
1 small fresh green chile, minced, seeds removed
   for a milder "hot"
½ teaspoon salt
1 cup undrained unsweetened crushed pineapple
2 tablespoons chopped fresh basil
2½ cups boiling water

Serves 4 to 6

Total time: 40 minutes

Peel off at least two layers of the tough outer leaves of the lemongrass and cut off the root ends and the tops. Mince only 3 or 4 inches of the tender lower stalk.

Place the rice in a colander or sieve, rinse with cool water, and set aside.

In a medium saucepan, preferably nonstick, warm the oil and add the lemongrass or lemon peel, garlic, chile, and salt. Cook on medium heat for 2 to 3 minutes, stirring frequently. Add the pineapple with its juice the basil, rice, and boiling water. Cover and bring to a boil, reduce the heat, and cook for 15 minutes. Remove from the heat and allow to sit for 5 minutes before serving.

PER 7-OZ SERVING: 242 CALORIES, 4.0 G PROTEIN, .8 G FAT, 53.6 G CARBOHYDRATES, .1 G SATURATED FATTY ACIDS, .5 G POLYUNSATURATED FATTY ACIDS, .2 G MONOUNSATURATED FATTY ACIDS, 0 MG CHOLESTEROL, 200 MG SODIUM, 1.6 G TOTAL DIETARY FIBER

MENU SUGGESTIONS Serve with **Thai Vegetable Curry** (page 268) or other curried dishes, or with **Cantonese Roasted Vegetables** (page 226).

THAI FRIED RICE

Fragrant herbs and a spicy curry paste enliven this colorful rice. Jasmine or white basmati rice are nice choices for this dish, although brown rice works well too. If you are pressed for time, try using a store-bought Thai curry paste.

1 cup chopped onions
3 garlic cloves, minced or pressed
3 to 4 tablespoons Thai Curry Paste (page 439)
1 tablespoon canola or other vegetable oil
1 cup peeled and diced carrots
2 cups finely chopped Chinese cabbage
1 cup diced red bell peppers
5 cups cooked rice
½ cup diced tomatoes
1 cup mung bean sprouts
3 tablespoons soy sauce
2 tablespoons chopped fresh mint
2 tablespoons chopped fresh cilantro or basil

Serves 4 to 6

Total time: 45 minutes

In a large nonstick skillet, sauté the onions, garlic, and curry paste in the oil for about 5 minutes. Add the carrots and cabbage, cover, and cook for 5 minutes, stirring occasionally. Add the peppers, cover, and cook for 3 to 4 minutes, until the vegetables are just tender. Stir in the rice, tomatoes, sprouts, and soy sauce and cook, stirring constantly, until the rice is heated through. Add the mint, cilantro or basil and, if desired, additional soy sauce or curry paste.

PER 11-OZ SERVING: 250 CALORIES, 6.6 G PROTEIN, 3.1 G FAT, 49.8 G CARBOHYDRATES, .5 G SATURATED FATTY ACIDS, 1.6 G POLYUNSATURATED FATTY ACIDS, .7 G MONOUNSATURATED FATTY ACIDS, 0 MG CHOLESTEROL, 509 MG SODIUM, 3.1 G TOTAL DIETARY FIBER

MENU SUGGESTIONS Serve with **Broiled Eggplant Thai Style** (page 34), **Gingered Fennel with Garlic** (page 320), or steamed greens lightly coated with **Spicy Peanut Dressing** (page 349). Or use as a side dish for **Thai Baked Tofu** (page 336), **Thai Fish Cakes** (page 302), **Southeast Asian Fish Rolls** (page 294), or **Thai Seafood Yum** (page 305). For dessert, choose either **Pumpkin Custard** (page 376) or fresh fruit.

MIDSUMMER RISOTTO

Arborio rice characteristically releases a great deal of starch while it cooks, giving the illusion of creaminess while the individual grains of rice remain firm. Even mock creaminess can feel satisfying in a low-fat diet.

This light and healthful risotto features several vegetables associated with midsummer. Corn purée adds sunny richness that can stand in for the cheese usually included in risottos. If you like, replace up to ½ cup of the tomato juice with an equal amount of dry white wine.

2 cups tomato juice
3 cups water or vegetable stock
1 vegetable bouillon cube
3 cups fresh or frozen corn kernels
1 cup minced onions
2 teaspoons olive oil
1½ cups arborio rice
2 cups diced zucchini
1 teaspoon salt
1 cup chopped tomatoes
2 tablespoons chopped fresh basil
ground black pepper to taste

Serves 4 to 6

Total time: 30 minutes

Combine the tomato juice, water or stock, and bouillon cube in a pot and bring to a simmer. Transfer 1 cup of the broth to a blender, add 1½ cups of the corn, and purée until smooth. Stir the puréed corn into the simmering broth. Set aside the remaining corn kernels.

In a separate, heavy saucepan, preferably nonstick, combine the onions and the oil and sauté for about 5 minutes, until softened. Reduce the heat to medium-low. Add the rice, stirring with a wooden spoon to avoid breaking the grains, until the rice is coated with oil.

Ladle about a cup of the broth into the rice and stir constantly for several minutes, until the liquid has been absorbed. Add the zucchini and another cup of broth. Continue to stir frequently, adding a cup of broth every few minutes for the next 15 minutes, until all of the broth has been added and the rice is tender but firm. Add the reserved corn, the salt, tomatoes, basil, and pepper to taste. Cook for another minute or so and serve immediately.

PER 11-OZ SERVING: 287 CALORIES, 6.9 G PROTEIN, 3.4 G FAT, 62.3 G CARBOHYDRATES, .4 G SATURATED FATTY ACIDS, .7 G POLYUNSATURATED FATTY ACIDS, 1.5 G MONOUNSATURATED FATTY ACIDS, 0 MG CHOLESTEROL, 716 MG SODIUM, 6.5 G TOTAL DIETARY FIBER

MENU SUGGESTIONS Serve as a first course for **Breaded Garlic Dill Fish** (page 297) with **Snap Peas with Mushrooms** (page 329). Or serve the risotto as a main dish with **Broiled Portabella Mushrooms** (page 322), **Cucumbers Vinaigrette** (page 133), or **Caesar Salad** (page 131). An appropriate appetizer would be crackers with either **Roasted Garlic** (page 43) or **Herbed Cottage Cheese Chèvre Spread** (page 31). For dessert, have wedges of watermelon and **Our Best No-Butter Brownies** (page 387).

SQUASH AND KALE RISOTTO

Characteristically, risottos consist of firm and flavorful grains of rice suspended in a smooth, creamlike base along with vegetables and herbs. The variations are almost endless. And when it contains low-fat, vitamin-rich additions such as kale and orange-fleshed squash, risotto is delicious, nutritious, economical, and versatile.

Risottos are often considered intimidating for the less experienced cook, and that's a shame. After you've made risotto once or twice, you'll see how easy it is to prepare. Traditionally, risotto is stirred constantly after the first addition of liquid, but we've found, especially when you use a nonstick pan, continuous stirring isn't necessary for achieving risotto's characteristic creaminess. A nonstick pan also greatly minimizes cleanup.

To save time, prepare the squash and kale while the onions sauté and the rice cooks.

Serves 4

**Total time:
1 hour or more**

4½ to 5 cups vegetable stock *
   or Garlic Broth (page 74)
1 cup minced onions
2 to 3 teaspoons olive oil
1½ cups arborio rice
½ cup dry white wine (optional)
2 cups peeled and cubed winter squash
   (¾- to 1-inch cubes)
3 cups stemmed and chopped kale, packed
   (about ½ pound before stemming)
⅛ to ¼ teaspoon nutmeg
1 teaspoon freshly grated lemon peel
salt and ground black pepper to taste
¼ cup grated Pecorino or Parmesan cheese

Use homemade Basic Vegetable Stock (page 73), canned vegetable broth (we recommend low-sodium, nonfat Pritikin brand), or 2 vegetable bouillon cubes dissolved in 5 cups water. If you use the wine in the recipe, you will only need about 4½ cups of stock or broth.

Bring the vegetable stock to a boil and then reduce it to a simmer.

Meanwhile, in a heavy saucepan, preferably nonstick, sauté the onions in 2 teaspoons of the oil for about 5 minutes, until softened but not browned. Add more oil, if necessary, to prevent sticking. Using a wooden spoon to avoid breaking the grains, add the rice and stir until it is well coated with oil. Add the wine, if using. When it is absorbed (it won't take long), ladle in 2½ cups of the simmering stock, ½ cup at a time, stirring frequently for 2 to 3 minutes between each addition, until the rice has absorbed the liquid. Add the squash and the kale and stir.

Continue adding ½ cup of broth every few minutes for about 10 minutes, stirring often, until all of the stock has been added and the rice is tender but firm. Add the nutmeg, lemon peel, and salt and pepper to taste. Remove the risotto from the heat, stir in the cheese, and serve immediately.

VARIATIONS In addition to or in place of kale, add any of the following: chopped Swiss chard, cabbage, radicchio, or fresh fennel, chopped celery, roasted red peppers, sun-dried tomatoes, green peas, green beans, or even seedless black grapes.

PER 14-OZ SERVING: 417 CALORIES, 12.0 G PROTEIN, 6.6 G FAT, 80.8 G CARBOHYDRATES, 2.1 G SATURATED FATTY ACIDS, .6 G POLYUNSATURATED FATTY ACIDS, 2.6 G MONOUNSATURATED FATTY ACIDS, 7 MG CHOLESTEROL, 243 MG SODIUM, 11.2 G TOTAL DIETARY FIBER

MENU SUGGESTIONS Serve as a first course before **Poached Fish with Russian Mushroom Sauce** (page 300) with **Cauliflower Agrodolce** (page 318). Or begin with **Savory Stuffed Mushrooms** (page 42) and serve the risotto as a main dish along with **Jerk Tofu** (page 337) and **Mango Coconut Cucumber Salad** (page 136). End with **Applesauce Spice Cake** (page 381).

ONION AND FETA RISOTTO

This simple but flavorful risotto is quite versatile and quickly made. Arborio rice is an extremely glutinous short-grained rice, known for its ability to absorb a lot of liquid quickly and still remain firm.

4 cups Basic Vegetable Stock (page 73), Garlic Broth
    (page 74), or two 14 ½-ounce cans vegetable broth plus
    enough water to make 4 cups liquid*
2 cups chopped onions
4 garlic cloves, minced or pressed
2 teaspoons olive oil
1½ cups arborio rice
½ cup grated or crumbled feta cheese (about 2 ounces)
½ cup chopped fresh parsley
1 tablespoon chopped fresh dill or thyme, or more to taste
1 teaspoon freshly grated lemon peel (optional)
salt and freshly ground black pepper to taste

Serves 4

**Total time:
30 to 40 minutes**

We recommend Pritikin low-sodium, nonfat vegetable broth.

In a small saucepan, heat the vegetable stock or broth to a simmer. Combine the onions, garlic, and oil in a large, heavy, preferably nonstick, pan and sauté on medium heat for 5 or 6 minutes, until the onions soften. Using a wooden spoon to avoid breaking the grains, add the rice, stirring until it is coated with oil.

Ladle about a cup of the stock or broth into the rice and stir constantly for several minutes, until the liquid has been absorbed. Continue to stir frequently, adding ½ cup of broth every 2 to 3 minutes for the next 20 minutes, until all of the broth has been added and absorbed and the rice is tender but firm. Remove from the heat and stir in the feta, parsley, dill or thyme, and lemon peel, if using. Add salt and pepper to taste. Serve immediately.

VARIATIONS Replace up to ½ cup of the vegetable stock with white wine. Use very sweet onions, such as Vidalia or Bermuda.

PER 11-OZ SERVING: 379 CALORIES, 8.8 G PROTEIN, 6.6 G FAT, 73.2 G CARBOHYDRATES, 2.5 G SATURATED FATTY ACIDS, .4 G POLYUNSATURATED FATTY ACIDS, 2.5 G MONOUNSATURATED FATTY ACIDS, 13 MG CHOLESTEROL, 233 MG SODIUM, 7.7 G TOTAL DIETARY FIBER

MENU SUGGESTIONS Serve with **Broiled Portabella Mushrooms** (page 322) and a plate of sliced fresh tomatoes. Or try as a side dish for **Spinach Mushroom Frittata** (page 52) or **Italian Roasted Vegetables** (page 226). This simple risotto could also be served as a first course before **Baked Flounder Rolls** (page 295) or **Giambotta** (page 263).

MUSHROOM WHEATBERRY PILAF

Wheatberries provide a welcome "chewiness" in this already hearty dish. For special occasions, splurge and replace some of the fresh mushrooms with porcini mushrooms or some other flavorful dried mushrooms of your choice.

½ cup raw dark wheatberries, soaked overnight *

1 cup brown rice (or 2½ cups cooked rice)

1 large onion, chopped (about 1½ cups)

5 garlic cloves, minced or pressed

2 teaspoons olive oil

1 pound mushrooms, sliced (about 5 cups)

1 teaspoon dried thyme

1 teaspoon minced fresh rosemary
   (½ teaspoon dried, crumbled)

3 teaspoons soy sauce

½ cup dry red wine

Soak the wheatberries in ample water to cover in a medium, covered saucepan for at least 8 hours.

Serves 6 as a side dish

Total time: about 1 hour

> **NOTE:**
> Leftover pilaf is a perfect stuffing for almost any vegetable—cabbage leaves, zucchini, peppers, tomatoes, eggplant, or squash. Refrigerated and tightly covered, it will keep for 2 or 3 days, ready to reappear in its new role as a filling or simply to be reheated for a snack.

Using a colander or a large sieve, drain the soaked wheatberries. Return them to the saucepan with fresh water to cover. Bring to a boil, lower the heat, cover, and simmer for about an hour, until tender.

In a separate pot, add 2 cups of cool water to the rice, cover tightly, and bring to a boil on high heat. When steam escapes from below the lid, turn off the heat and let stand for 5 minutes. Return to very low heat and simmer for about 35 minutes, or until all of the water has been absorbed.

While the grains cook, sauté the onions and garlic in the oil in a large, covered skillet on low heat for about 10 minutes, until golden. Stir occasionally to prevent sticking. Add the mushrooms, thyme, rosemary, and soy sauce and cook for 5 minutes. Pour in the wine and continue to simmer until the wine evaporates. Set aside.

When the wheatberries are soft, drain any excess liquid and then add to the sautéed mushrooms. Stir in the cooked rice, mix thoroughly, and serve immediately.

PER 6.50-OZ SERVING: 158 CALORIES, 4.3 G PROTEIN, 2.7 G FAT, 27.5 G CARBOHYDRATES, .4 G SATURATED FATTY ACIDS, .5 G POLYUNSATURATED FATTY ACIDS, 1.4 G MONOUNSATURATED FATTY ACIDS, 0 MG CHOLESTEROL, 142 MG SODIUM, 3.6 G TOTAL DIETARY FIBER

MENU SUGGESTIONS For a meal to warm a chilly night, serve with **Cream of Green Vegetable Soup** (page 82), **Mustard Carrots** (page 317), and **Pumpkin Custard** (page 376).

SPRING VEGETABLE PAELLA

Paella, Spain's beloved rice dish, is traditionally a lavish and celebratory meal that includes a variety of fresh, tempting vegetables and seafood. Our vegetarian spring vegetable version is flavored with saffron, thyme, and extra-virgin olive oil. While the rice is cooking, there is time to prepare all of the vegetables for the dish.

Serves 6

**Total time:
about 1 hour**

RICE
5 to 6 artichoke hearts, packed in brine (14- or 16-ounce can)
1½ cups brown rice
1 teaspoon salt
generous pinch of saffron (scant ½ teaspoon)

VEGETABLES
2 cups minced onions
1 cup finely chopped celery
2 garlic cloves, minced or pressed
1 tablespoon extra-virgin olive oil
1 teaspoon dried thyme
1 red bell pepper, seeded and chopped
1 pound asparagus, rinsed, trimmed, and cut
    into 2-inch pieces (about 2 cups)
1½ cups fresh or frozen green peas
    (10-ounce package)
1 cup chopped tomatoes
salt and ground black pepper to taste

½ cup chopped chives or scallions
steamed snow peas (optional)

Drain the artichoke hearts, reserving the brine. Quarter the artichoke hearts and set aside. Add water to the artichoke brine to make 2½ cups of liquid and combine it with the rice, salt, and saffron in a heavy saucepan with a tight-fitting lid. Cover and bring to a boil on high heat. Reduce the heat and very gently simmer until the rice is tender and the liquid has been absorbed, 45 to 60 minutes.

When the rice has simmered for about 25 minutes, sauté the onions, celery, and garlic in the olive oil on medium-high heat for about 5 minutes, until the onions soften. Add the thyme, bell peppers, and asparagus, cover, and sauté on medium heat, stirring frequently, for 5 minutes. Add the peas, tomatoes, and reserved artichoke hearts, stir well, cover, and simmer for 5 to 10 minutes, until the vegetables are tender. Add salt and pepper to taste.

To serve the paella, spread the rice on a large platter or in a large bowl. Top the rice with the vegetables and their juices. Sprinkle with chopped chives or scallions and steamed snow peas, if you like.

VARIATIONS For a seafood version, top the vegetable paella with about ½ pound of freshly steamed mussels, scallops, clams, and/or shrimp. For extra flavor, add strips or cubes of seasoned seitan to the simmering vegetables along with the peas and artichoke hearts.

PER 15-OZ SERVING: 300 CALORIES, 11.1 G PROTEIN, 4.4 G FAT, 58.2 G CARBOHYDRATES, .7 G SATURATED FATTY ACIDS, 1.0 G POLYUNSATURATED FATTY ACIDS, 2.2 G MONOUNSATURATED FATTY ACIDS, 0 MG CHOLESTEROL, 545 MG SODIUM, 7.4 G TOTAL DIETARY FIBER

MENU SUGGESTIONS Begin with crudités or thinly sliced toast spread with either **Roasted Garlic** (page 43) or **Guacamole with Asparagus** (page 25). Serve with a salad of citrus fruits or a tossed salad with **Cumin Yogurt Dressing** (page 132). Finish with **Fruit-filled Meringue Shells** (page 388).

macaroni and cheese 203

vegetable udon sauté 204

PASTA WITH EGGPLANT 205

pasta primavera 206

zucchini saffron pasta 207

PASTA AND SUN-DRIED TOMATOES 208

pasta, lentils, and artichoke hearts 209

pasta with beans and greens 210

PASTA WITH CHICKPEAS 211

pasta with salsa cruda 212

penne with creamy walnut sauce 213

PENNE WITH PUTTANESCA SAUCE 214

spaghetti with onions 215

vegetable lasagne béchamel 216

LIGHTER LASAGNE 218

stuffed manicotti verde 219

curried rice noodles 220

PASTA

PASTA, in its myriad shapes, flavors, and brands, is a staple on our shelves, a familiar and welcome meal on our tables. At Moosewood, we feature pasta dishes on the menu several times a week. With its chewy texture and mild flavor, pasta goes beautifully with fresh vegetables and sauces for a hearty, enjoyable, low-fat main dish. You need little more than a salad to round out the meal. And pasta is a snap to prepare. Many of our sauces can be made in the time it takes to heat the water and cook the pasta.

Most of these recipes use Italian-style pasta made from semolina flour, which comes from hard durum wheat. Pasta, a complex carbohydrate, is high in protein, B vitamins, and iron and low in fat, calories, and sodium. A good semolina pasta has a springy texture and doesn't clump together when cooked. In general, we believe that Italian-made pastas are superior to most domestic brands. For one thing, the Italian government imposes rigid standards for ingredients. Also, the manufacturing process results in better pasta. For instance, the pasta is extruded through bronze rather than Teflon dies, giving it a rougher, more porous texture, and the pasta is dried more slowly at lower temperatures, ensuring that the protein is not denatured and making it firmer when cooked. At Moosewood, we use De Cecco brand, a fine pasta that is widely available in this country.

Fifteen years ago, many of us tried cooking with nutritious

whole wheat pasta, but gave up in despair over its crumbly and gummy texture. Fortunately, Italian companies are now beginning to distribute whole grain pastas with pleasing, full-bodied textures and earthy flavors, and many U.S. manufacturers are following close behind. Pastas made from whole grains, such as wheat, buckwheat, kamut, quinoa, and spelt, are higher in protein, iron, and fiber and have fewer calories than refined flour pastas. The quality of whole grain pastas varies a great deal; if you find one you like, try it in recipes with robust ingredients, such as Penne with Puttanesca Sauce, Pasta and Sun-Dried Tomatoes, and Pasta with Beans and Greens.

Some of our recipes use Asian-style pastas. Traditional Japanese udon noodles are prepared with sesame, soy, and ginger in Vegetable Udon Sauté, while rice noodles are absolutely delicious with bright Indian curry spices and colorful vegetables in Curried Rice Noodles.

We also offer you here our lower-fat versions of "classic" baked pastas like Lighter Lasagne and Macaroni and Cheese. Our Pasta Primavera is a real celebration of spring vegetables. Zucchini Saffron Pasta has an unusual lemony flavor. Pasta with Chickpeas is based on a delicious, rosemary-flavored soup traditionally served with little pasta shapes in the soup; a few refinements and it makes a wonderful sauce to serve over pasta.

Other possible pasta toppings found elsewhere in this book include:

Chunky Tomato Sauce (page 351)

Susan's Pesto (page 364)

Creamy Roasted Red Pepper Sauce (page 355)

Hungarian Lesco (page 357)

Mushroom Sauce (page 352)

Tomato Wine Sauce (page 350)

Broccoli Rabe and Garlic (page 315)

Giambotta (page 263)

Wild Mushroom Stew Trieste (page 278)

Middle Eastern Chickpeas with Spinach (page 169)

MACARONI AND CHEESE

Our own absolutely perfect children are perhaps more adventurous eaters than most, but from parents of children who are less-than-perfect eaters, we've heard over and over that there is a desperately felt need for a healthful macaroni and cheese. We wanted ours to be easy to make and enough like the full-fat original that fans will eat it up. Reduced-fat cheese doesn't fool anybody in *this* dish. So we use a modest amount of extra-sharp Cheddar, tangy buttermilk, creamy cottage cheese, and savory onions and mustard.

Probably no macaroni and cheese could meet the nutritional needs of a heart patient, but this version is a vast improvement healthwise, especially for kids who eat it a lot.

Serves 4

Preparation time: 20 minutes

Baking time: 45 minutes

1½ cups 1% cottage cheese
1½ cups skim milk or buttermilk
1 teaspoon dried mustard or 1 tablespoon prepared mustard
pinch of cayenne
¼ teaspoon nutmeg
½ teaspoon salt
¼ teaspoon ground black pepper
¼ cup grated onions
1 cup grated extra-sharp Cheddar cheese (4 ounces)
½ pound uncooked elbow macaroni
2 tablespoons finely grated Pecorino or Parmesan cheese
¼ cup bread crumbs

Preheat the oven to 375°. Prepare a 9- or 10-inch square baking pan with a light coating of cooking spray or oil.

In a blender, combine the cottage cheese, skim milk or buttermilk, mustard, cayenne, nutmeg, salt, and pepper and purée until smooth. In a large bowl, combine the puréed mixture with the onions, Cheddar cheese, and uncooked macaroni. Stir well. Pour the macaroni and cheese mixture into the baking pan. Combine the grated Pecorino or Parmesan cheese and the bread crumbs and sprinkle over the top.

Bake for about 45 minutes, until the topping is browned and the center is firm.

PER 10-OZ SERVING: 471 CALORIES, 30.7 G PROTEIN, 13.2 G FAT, 55.7 G CARBOHYDRATES, 7.7 G SATURATED FATTY ACIDS, .8 G POLYUNSATURATED FATTY ACIDS, 3.7 G MONOUNSATURATED FATTY ACIDS, 38 MG CHOLESTEROL, 1008 MG SODIUM, 1.9 G TOTAL DIETARY FIBER

MENU SUGGESTIONS Serve with **Chili Burgers** (page 173) and **Corn Relish** (page 361), **Carolina Kale** (page 321), or **Vegetables à la Grecque** (page 130). Or try with **Garlicky Blackeyed Peas 'n' Greens** (page 170) and **Cucumbers Vinaigrette** (page 133). Most three-year-olds we know like macaroni and cheese with carrot sticks and apple slices for stirring it up.

VEGETABLE UDON SAUTÉ

This savory dish of noodles and vegetables is welcome any time of the year. If asparagus is not in season, substitute a green vegetable such as broccoli, snow peas, or green beans.

1 ounce dried shiitake mushrooms
2 tablespoons dry sherry or sake
2 tablespoons soy sauce
2 cups water
1 medium onion
2 red or yellow bell peppers (or 1 of each)
1 pound fresh asparagus
2 teaspoons dark sesame oil
2 teaspoons grated fresh ginger root
½ pound udon noodles or linguine
2 teaspoons cornstarch dissolved in 1 tablespoon cold water
2 or 3 scallions, sliced on the diagonal

Serves 3 or 4

**Total time:
40 to 45 minutes**

In a small saucepan, combine the shiitake mushrooms, sherry or sake, soy sauce, and water. Bring to a boil, then lower the heat, cover, and simmer for 15 minutes. Set aside to cool.

Meanwhile, bring 3 quarts of water to a boil in a large pot.

While the shiitake simmer and the water heats, peel and thinly slice the onion. Seed the peppers and slice into long, thin strips. Snap off and discard the tough ends of the asparagus; then diagonally slice the spears and tender stalks into 2-inch pieces.

Drain the shiitake and reserve the stock. Slice off and discard the shiitake stems and thinly slice the caps. In a nonstick skillet, sauté the onions in the oil for 5 minutes. Stir in the peppers, shiitake caps, and ginger and cook until the vegetables are just tender, 5 to 10 minutes. Stir occasionally, adding some of the reserved shiitake stock if needed.

When the pot of water is boiling, ease in the asparagus and cook just until tender, about 3 minutes. Remove them with a sieve or slotted spoon and set aside. Then cook the udon noodles in the boiling water for 7 to 10 minutes, until al dente. Drain and rinse the noodles with cold water to remove the excess starch. (If using linguine, rinsing is not necessary.)

Add the remaining shiitake stock and the dissolved cornstarch to the vegetables and simmer until the sauce thickens. Stir in the asparagus and the cooked noodles and gently toss to coat and heat the noodles. Sprinkle with the scallions and serve.

PER 13-OZ SERVING: 313 CALORIES, 12.3 G PROTEIN, 5.3 G FAT, 56.4 G CARBOHYDRATES, .9 G SATURATED FATTY ACIDS, 1.9 G POLYUNSATURATED FATTY ACIDS, 1.6 G MONOUNSATURATED FATTY ACIDS, 49 MG CHOLESTEROL, 424 MG SODIUM, 3.8 G TOTAL DIETARY FIBER

MENU SUGGESTIONS Serve with **Vietnamese Hot and Sour Soup** (page 87) and **Carrot Orange Salad** (page 134) or **Sesame Beets** (page 140).

PASTA WITH EGGPLANT

Rich, savory baked eggplant adds a lot of meaty substance and is superb in combination with the bright taste of tomatoes in this very traditional southern Italian dish. While the eggplant bakes, you can prepare to cook the pasta, grate the cheese, set the table for dinner, or just relax.

2 medium eggplants
sprinkling of salt
3 large garlic cloves, minced or pressed
2 cups chopped onions
2 teaspoons olive oil
4 cups undrained canned plum tomatoes (32-ounce can)
1 tablespoon dried basil
1 pound ziti, penne, or macaroni

crumbled ricotta salata or grated Pecorino
**   or Parmesan cheese**

Serves 4 to 6

Preparation time:
25 minutes

Baking time:
30 minutes

Pasta cooking time:
10 to 15 minutes

Cut the eggplant lengthwise or crosswise into 1-inch-thick slices. Lightly salt each slice, stack the slices, and set them aside for about 20 minutes.

Preheat the oven to 475°.

In a large saucepan on low heat, sauté the garlic and onions in the oil, until the onions are golden. Stir often enough to prevent sticking. Chop and add the tomatoes to the saucepan. Add the basil and continue to cook, stirring occasionally, until the sauce begins to thicken.

While the tomato sauce cooks, rinse and dry the eggplant slices. Prepare a large nonreactive baking sheet with cooking spray or a light coating of vegetable oil. Place a single layer of eggplant slices on the baking sheet and bake, uncovered, for 15 minutes. With a metal spatula, carefully flip the slices over and bake for another 15 minutes.

About 5 minutes before the eggplant finishes baking, bring a large covered pot of water to a boil.

When the eggplant slices are tender and browned, remove them from the oven, allow to cool slightly, and then cut them into $\frac{1}{2} \times$ 3-inch strips (about the size of ziti). Stir the eggplant into the tomato sauce and cook for about 10 more minutes.

When the water boils, stir in the pasta, cover, and return to a boil. Then uncover the pot and cook the pasta until al dente. Drain and serve immediately, topped with the tomato-eggplant sauce and grated cheese.

PER 14-OZ SERVING: 409 CALORIES, 13.6 G PROTEIN, 3.8 G FAT, 81.4 G CARBOHYDRATES, .5 G SATURATED FATTY ACIDS, .9 G POLYUNSATURATED FATTY ACIDS, 1.4 G MONOUNSATURATED FATTY ACIDS, 0 MG CHOLESTEROL, 231 MG SODIUM, 7.8 G TOTAL DIETARY FIBER

MENU SUGGESTIONS Serve with **Broiled Portabella Mushrooms** (page 322), **Broccoli Rabe and Garlic** (page 315), or **Caesar Salad** (page 131).

PASTA PRIMAVERA

Too often, dishes called "Pasta Primavera" are smothered in cream sauce or dripping with oil. Here, the delicate vegetables are treated with tenderness in a lightly cooked tomato-wine sauce, creating a colorful and celebratory dish to honor the season. Be sure to have all of the ingredients prepared and assembled before beginning to cook, because timing is critical to avoid overcooking any of the vegetables.

6 garlic cloves, minced or pressed
2 teaspoons olive oil
3 cups chopped tomatoes
¼ cup dry white wine
½ cup sliced fresh basil leaves (slice them crosswise)
1 small red onion, thinly sliced
2 small carrots, peeled and cut into 2-inch matchsticks
1 pound asparagus, cut into 2-inch pieces
1 red bell pepper, cut into 2-inch matchsticks
2 small zucchini, cut into 2-inch matchsticks
1 cup fresh or frozen green peas
salt and ground black pepper to taste
1 pound fettuccine or butterfly pasta (farfalle)
¼ cup grated Pecorino or Parmesan cheese

Serves 6

**Total time:
45 to 60 minutes**

NOTE:
Substitute or add other young vegetables, such as snow peas, broccoli, yellow squash, fresh fava beans, or tiny green beans. If you prefer to steam the vegetables, allow 3 minutes between each addition of vegetables.

Bring a covered pot of water large enough to accommodate a colander or steamer basket to a boil. Meanwhile, sauté the garlic and oil in a saucepan for about 2 minutes. Add the tomatoes and wine and cook on medium heat for about 5 minutes. Add the basil and red onions, cover, and remove from the heat.

When the water is boiling, blanch the vegetables (see Note). Put the carrots in first. After 1 minute, add the asparagus and bell peppers. After another minute, add the zucchini and peas. Cook for 1 minute more and then lift out the colander and all of the vegetables and set aside to drain. Reserve the pot of boiling water for cooking the pasta. Stir the vegetables into the tomato sauce. Add salt and pepper. Cover and set aside.

Cook the pasta until al dente. Drain, reserving ¼ cup of the cooking water. Toss the pasta with the reserved cooking water and 3 tablespoons of the grated cheese. Top with the tomato-vegetable sauce. Sprinkle with the remaining cheese and serve immediately.

PER 16-OZ SERVING: 414 CALORIES, 17.7 G PROTEIN, 7.1 G FAT, 71.2 G CARBOHYDRATES, 2.1 G SATURATED FATTY ACIDS, 1.4 G POLYUNSATURATED FATTY ACIDS, 2.6 G MONOUNSATURATED FATTY ACIDS, 70 MG CHOLESTEROL, 209 MG SODIUM, 7.5 G TOTAL DIETARY FIBER

MENU SUGGESTIONS Such a lavish dish needs little more. For dessert, have fresh strawberries and Anise Lemon Biscotti (page 391).

ZUCCHINI SAFFRON PASTA

With the unexpected flavor combination of delicate saffron and fresh tart lemon, this pasta is also nicely textured and has a striking golden color. Very small, dense, young zucchini without seeds are much preferred.

1 large onion, thinly sliced (about 2 cups)
4 garlic cloves, minced or pressed
2 teaspoons olive oil
2 pounds small zucchini, sliced into rounds (about 6 cups)
¼ teaspoon saffron threads
¼ cup fresh lemon juice
salt and ground black pepper to taste
1 pound chunky pasta, such as butterfly, spirulina, or rotelli
¼ cup grated Pecorino cheese

Serves 4 to 6

Total time: 45 minutes

Bring a large covered pot of water to a boil for cooking the pasta.

Meanwhile, in a large nonstick or cast-iron skillet, sauté the onions and garlic in the oil on medium heat for 3 or 4 minutes. Add the zucchini and sauté about 5 more minutes, stirring frequently, until the onions are translucent and some of the zucchini slices have lightly browned edges.

In a small cup, crush the strands of saffron with the back of a spoon to crumble them a bit. Add about ¼ cup of hot water and stir briefly, until the water is golden colored. Stir the saffron and water into the zucchini. Pour the lemon juice into the same cup to rinse out the last bits of saffron and add it to the zucchini. Add salt and pepper to taste. Lower the heat and cover the pan to keep the sauce warm until the pasta is ready.

When the pasta water boils, add the pasta, stir, and cover the pot so that it will quickly return to a boil. When it boils, uncover the pot, stir the pasta, and cook until al dente. Drain. In a large serving bowl, toss together the pasta and the zucchini mixture. Sprinkle with the cheese and serve immediately.

VARIATIONS Add ½ cup of minced red bell pepper with the onions and 1 cup of frozen tiny peas after the saffron. Or add ½ teaspoon of ground cumin with the onions and then 1 teaspoon of grated orange peel and 1 cup of cooked chickpeas after the saffron. For a colorful contrast, add 2 cups of chopped fresh tomatoes with the lemon juice.

PER 13.50-OZ SERVING: 373 CALORIES, 13.7 G PROTEIN, 4.8 G FAT, 68.7 G CARBOHYDRATES, 1.5 G SATURATED FATTY ACIDS, .8 G POLYUNSATURATED FATTY ACIDS, 1.8 G MONOUNSATURATED FATTY ACIDS, 4 MG CHOLESTEROL, 142 MG SODIUM, 5.0 G TOTAL DIETARY FIBER

MENU SUGGESTIONS Serve with **Middle Eastern Cannellini Patties** (page 119) and steamed green beans, followed by fresh cantaloupe. Or pair with **Tropical Gazpacho** (page 78), **Fish Steaks with Fennel** (page 290), **Ful** (page 55), or **Carrot Orange Salad** (page 134).

PASTA AND SUN-DRIED TOMATOES

Much of the year, when tomatoes in the market are pale, hard, unacceptable imitations of their summer selves, it is quite possible to find good cherry tomatoes. Combining them with sun-dried tomatoes and frozen French-cut green beans makes for a handsome pasta. In midsummer when fresh tomatoes are glorious, you may use fresh green beans too, in which case the rusty brown sun-dried tomatoes add a more complex sweet note.

Serves 4

**Total time:
25 minutes**

NOTE:
Try this topped with ½ cup of grated feta cheese.

¾ cup sun-dried tomatoes, not packed in oil
1 cup boiling water
2 teaspoons olive oil
2 onions, halved lengthwise and thinly sliced
    (about 2½ cups)
5 garlic cloves, minced or pressed
1½ teaspoons dried marjoram
1 pound fresh green beans, cut in half crosswise on
    the diagonal, or frozen French-cut green beans
¾ pound ziti, gemelli, or fusilli
salt and ground black pepper to taste
2 cups quartered cherry tomatoes

Bring a large covered pot of water to a boil for cooking the pasta. Meanwhile, place the sun-dried tomatoes in a small heatproof bowl with the cup of boiling water and set aside.

Heat the olive oil in a large skillet, preferably nonstick. Add the onions and cook, stirring often, for 3 to 4 minutes, until they begin to soften. Add the garlic and marjoram and cook for 3 minutes. Blanch fresh beans in the hot pasta water for 3 to 4 minutes and remove them with a sieve to the skillet. If using frozen green beans, add them to the skillet and stir to separate. Cover and cook on medium-low heat, stirring occasionally.

Stir the pasta into the boiling water, cover, and return to a boil. Uncover, stir, and cook until al dente.

While the pasta cooks, drain the sun-dried tomatoes, reserving the liquid. Cut them into thin strips and add them with their liquid to the skillet. Add salt and pepper. Drain the pasta. Stir the green bean sauce and fresh tomatoes into the pasta and serve immediately.

PER 18-OZ SERVING: 561 CALORIES, 21.2 G PROTEIN, 6.0 G FAT, 112.8 G CARBOHYDRATES, .8 G SATURATED FATTY ACIDS, 1.6 G POLYUNSATURATED FATTY ACIDS, 2.2 G MONOUNSATURATED FATTY ACIDS, 0 MG CHOLESTEROL, 964 MG SODIUM, 15.2 G TOTAL DIETARY FIBER

MENU SUGGESTIONS Serve with a salad with **Honey Mustard Garlic Dressing** (page 342) and a side of **Broiled Portabella Mushrooms** (page 322). For an elaborate meal, serve **Savory Stuffed Mushrooms** (page 42) as an appetizer, the pasta as a first course, and **Honey Mustard Fish** (page 298) for the main course. End with **Apple Apricot Strudel** (page 384).

PASTA, LENTILS, AND ARTICHOKE HEARTS

A Middle Eastern pasta with assertive spices and a lemony tang is a welcome change of pace. Red lentils are very quick to cook and require no soaking. Butterfly-shaped farfalle makes for an especially attractive dish.

1 cup dry red lentils (3 cups cooked)
1 bay leaf
3 cups water
1 teaspoon olive oil
2 cups diced onions
2 large garlic cloves, pressed or minced
2 teaspoons ground cumin
1 teaspoon ground coriander
2 tablespoons fresh lemon juice
2 cups canned tomatoes (18-ounce can), chopped and liquid reserved
1½ cups quartered artichoke hearts
   (9-ounce package frozen or 15-ounce can)
¼ teaspoon crushed red pepper flakes
1 pound farfalle, rotini, or spirali
salt and ground black pepper to taste

crumbled feta cheese (optional)

Serves 4 to 6

Total time: 40 minutes

Bring the lentils, bay leaf, and water to a boil in a saucepan. Lower the heat, cover, and simmer for 15 to 20 minutes, until the lentils are tender.

While the lentils cook, heat the olive oil in a separate pan. Add the onions and sauté on medium heat for about 5 minutes, until golden. Add the garlic, cumin, and coriander and cook for 2 minutes, stirring frequently. Add the lemon juice, tomatoes, artichoke hearts, and crushed red pepper and simmer on low heat for about 10 minutes. Drain the cooked lentils, reserving the cooking liquid, and add the lentils to the tomato and artichoke heart mixture. Simmer for 10 minutes more, adding about ½ cup of the reserved liquid if the sauce seems dry.

Meanwhile, bring a large pot of water to a boil and cook the pasta until al dente. Drain the pasta and transfer it to a serving bowl. Top it with the lentil and artichoke heart sauce, add salt and pepper to taste, sprinkle with feta cheese, if desired, and serve immediately.

PER 18-OZ SERVING: 445 CALORIES, 21.2 G PROTEIN, 4.6 G FAT, 82.6 G CARBOHYDRATES, .8 G SATURATED FATTY ACIDS, 1.1 G POLYUNSATURATED FATTY ACIDS, 1.5 G MONOUNSATURATED FATTY ACIDS, 65 MG CHOLESTEROL, 200 MG SODIUM, 13.3 G TOTAL DIETARY FIBER

MENU SUGGESTIONS Serve with a salad or a vegetable such as **Broccoli Rabe and Garlic** (page 315) or **Cucumbers Vinaigrette** (page 133), and with **Ginger Peach Crumble** (page 386) for dessert.

PASTA WITH BEANS AND GREENS

An elegant dish for a fancy company dinner it's not. However, this blend of pasta with beans and greens is a simple, satisfying, and much beloved family supper. The appeal of beans and greens together makes this an excellent choice to have in your regular repertoire.

The age-old logic of combining grains and beans to create a complete source of protein is the foundation of this dish. Cutting through this hearty base is the sharp, astringent note of bitter greens. If you use canned beans, be sure to rinse and drain them. If you want to cook the beans from scratch, start with about 1 cup of dried beans. Soak them (page 414), drain, cover with plenty of fresh water, bring to a boil, cover, and simmer for 1 to 2 hours, until tender.

1 cup chopped onions

5 or 6 garlic cloves, minced or pressed

2 teaspoons olive oil

1 pound fresh greens, such as chicory, endive,
    escarole, or mizuna, rinsed and chopped

3 cups cooked Roman, pinto, kidney, or pink beans
    (two 15-ounce cans, drained)

½ cup finely chopped fresh basil

1 pound short chunky pasta, such as ditalini,
    tubetti, or orecchiette

salt and ground black pepper to taste

juice of 1 lemon

Serves 4 to 6

**Total time:
25 to 30 minutes**

Bring a large covered pot of water to a boil for cooking the pasta.

Meanwhile, in a well-seasoned cast-iron skillet or a nonstick saucepan on low heat, sauté the onions and garlic in the olive oil until golden, about 10 minutes. Add the greens and 1 cup of water. Increase the heat to medium, cover, and cook for 5 minutes. Add the beans and basil and continue to cook for 5 minutes. Using a potato masher, mash some of the beans right in the pan; add more water if the sauce is too thick.

Meanwhile, when the water comes to a boil, add the pasta, stir, and cover the pot until the water returns to a boil. Stir the pasta and cook, uncovered, until al dente. Drain the pasta and toss it with the beans and greens. Add salt and pepper to taste and squeeze on some lemon juice. Serve immediately.

PER 15-OZ SERVING: 474 CALORIES, 22.4 G PROTEIN, 3.4 G FAT, 89.7 G CARBOHYDRATES, .5 G SATURATED FATTY ACIDS, .9 G POLYUNSATURATED FATTY ACIDS, 1.4 G MONOUNSATURATED FATTY ACIDS, 0 MG CHOLESTEROL, 55 MG SODIUM, 5.4 G TOTAL DIETARY FIBER

MENU SUGGESTION Serve with sliced tomatoes or **Cauliflower Agrodolce** (page 318), a glass of Chianti, and fruit for dessert.

PASTA WITH CHICKPEAS

Pasta with Chickpeas is considered an unusual dish in the United States, but this combination is very common in Italian cuisine. In ancient Rome, Horace wrote about it with longing and glad anticipation. Tomatoes are a relatively recent addition to the sauce.

Our tasty sauce, thick and substantial with a high protein and high fiber content, is quickly produced from economical pantry items. There is just enough rosemary to make it interesting without being overpowering; use fresh rosemary so that the whole sprigs can be removed from the sauce.

1½ cups finely chopped onions
2 large garlic cloves, minced or pressed
3 fresh rosemary sprigs, 2 inches each
2 teaspoons olive oil
4 cups chopped fresh or 3 cups canned tomatoes
    (28-ounce can, undrained)
3½ cups cooked chickpeas (two 15- or 16-ounce cans)
salt and ground black pepper to taste
1 pound short chunky pasta, such as ditalini,
    tubetti, or orecchiette

⅔ cup crumbled feta cheese
chopped fresh tomatoes (optional)

Serves 4 to 6

Total time: 20 minutes

> **NOTE:**
> For a stronger rosemary flavor, strip the leaves from one of the rosemary sprigs and add them to the blender with the tomato-chickpea mixture before puréeing.

Combine the onions, garlic, rosemary, and oil in a well-seasoned skillet or nonstick saucepan and sauté on low heat for about 10 minutes, until the onions are soft and golden. Add the tomatoes and half of the chickpeas and cook for another 10 minutes. Remove the rosemary sprigs and discard (see Note). In a blender, purée the tomato-chickpea mixture until smooth. Return it to the skillet, stir in the remaining chickpeas, and add salt and pepper to taste.

Meanwhile, bring a large covered pot of water to a boil. When the water boils, add the pasta, stir, cover the pot, and return to a boil. Stir the pasta again and cook, uncovered, until al dente. Drain the pasta. In a large serving bowl, toss the pasta with the chickpea sauce and serve immediately. Sprinkle with feta cheese or pass the feta at the table and top with tomatoes, if desired.

PER 15-OZ SERVING: 542 CALORIES, 19.9 G PROTEIN, 7.7 G FAT, 99.1 G CARBOHYDRATES, 2.5 G SATURATED FATTY ACIDS, 1.7 G POLYUNSATURATED FATTY ACIDS, 2.3 G MONOUNSATURATED FATTY ACIDS, 11 MG CHOLESTEROL, 589 MG SODIUM, 10.6 G TOTAL DIETARY FIBER

MENU SUGGESTIONS Pair with **Italian Roasted Vegetables** (page 226) on a bed of steamed spinach and serve fresh melon and grapes for dessert. Or serve after an appetizer of crostini with **Spinach Artichoke Heart Dip** (page 30). Accompany with **Broccoli Rabe and Garlic** (page 315), **Broiled Zucchini with Herbs** (page 333), or **Moroccan Carrots** (page 316).

PASTA WITH SALSA CRUDA

This is exactly the kind of light, vibrant, and speedy dish we want for reviving flagging appetites on a hot summer day when the living's supposed to be easy. The tomatoes must be the genuine, vine-ripened articles for this uncooked sauce.

Use the sauce not only on pasta but also as a lively topping for pizza, fish, grilled vegetables, toasted bread, or baked potatoes. If you like, make the sauce a few hours ahead, cover, and store at room temperature or in the refrigerator. Or wait until you've started to boil the water for the pasta to pick the ripest tomatoes in your garden.

3 or 4 large ripe tomatoes (about 2½ pounds)
2 tablespoons minced fresh basil leaves
¼ cup minced red onions
2 teaspoons extra-virgin olive oil
2 teaspoons balsamic vinegar
1 teaspoon salt, or more to taste
plenty of freshly ground black pepper
2 garlic cloves, pressed or minced
1 pound pasta, preferably farfalle (butterflies)

Serves 4 to 6

Total time: 20 minutes

Bring a large covered pot of water to a boil for cooking the pasta.

Meanwhile, chop about half of the tomatoes into bite-sized cubes and place them in a large serving bowl. Add the basil and red onions to the bowl.

Coarsely chop the rest of the tomatoes and place them in a blender. Add the oil, vinegar, salt, pepper, and garlic and purée until smooth. Transfer to the serving bowl.

When the water comes to a boil, add the pasta, stir, and cover the pot until it boils again. Uncover, stir the pasta again, and cook until al dente. Drain the pasta, add it to the serving bowl, and toss well. Serve immediately.

VARIATIONS Add a small minced chile, 1 tablespoon of sliced black olives, or about a cup of tiny cubes of fresh mozzarella, or any combination of these.

PER 14-OZ SERVING: 357 CALORIES, 11.9 G PROTEIN, 3.6 G FAT, 69.7 G CARBOHYDRATES, .5 G SATURATED FATTY ACIDS, 1.0 G POLYUNSATURATED FATTY ACIDS, 1.4 G MONOUNSATURATED FATTY ACIDS, 0 MG CHOLESTEROL, 415 MG SODIUM, 4.9 G TOTAL DIETARY FIBER

MENU SUGGESTIONS Serve with **Broiled Portabella Mushrooms** (page 322) and **Broiled Zucchini with Herbs** (page 333) or with **Caesar Salad** (page 131).

Or serve the pasta out in the backyard in August with steamed green beans, corn on the cob, and watermelon for dessert.

PENNE WITH CREAMY WALNUT SAUCE

While we worked on this cookbook, we were blessed with a battalion of eager volunteer recipe tasters. This particular recipe was an immediate hit with everyone who tried it. It has all of the attributes of a winning recipe—it's quick, simple, creamy, and delicious.

10 ounces fresh spinach
½ cup toasted walnuts, coarsely chopped *
2 cups low-fat cottage cheese
1 garlic clove, minced or pressed
¼ cup grated Parmesan cheese
¼ cup loosely packed chopped fresh basil
½ teaspoon salt
ground black pepper to taste
1 to 1½ pounds penne (tubular pasta)
1 head broccoli

grated Parmesan cheese (optional)

Toast walnuts in a single layer on an unoiled baking tray in a conventional or toaster oven at 350° for about 5 minutes, until fragrant and golden brown.

Serves 6

Total time: 20 minutes

Bring a large covered pot of water to a rapid boil.

While the water heats, wash the spinach and transfer it to a separate large pot. The water clinging to the leaves should provide enough moisture to steam it. Cover and cook the spinach on medium-high heat for about 4 minutes, until wilted but still bright green. Drain. In a food processor or blender, combine the spinach, walnuts, cottage cheese, garlic, Parmesan, basil, and salt and purée until smooth, working in batches if necessary. Add pepper to taste and set aside.

When the water boils, stir in the pasta, cover, and return to a boil. Then uncover the pot and cook until the pasta is al dente, about 7 minutes. While the pasta cooks, cut the broccoli into spears, blanch it in boiling water to cover until just tender, about 5 minutes, and set it aside. Drain the pasta and serve immediately in individual warmed bowls, topped with spinach-walnut sauce and several steamed broccoli spears. Sprinkle with grated Parmesan cheese, if you wish.

PER 14-OZ SERVING: 470 CALORIES, 28.0 G PROTEIN, 10.3 G FAT, 67.4 G CARBOHYDRATES, 2.6 G SATURATED FATTY ACIDS, 4.4 G POLYUNSATURATED FATTY ACIDS, 2.3 G MONOUNSATURATED FATTY ACIDS, 11 MG CHOLESTEROL, 660 MG SODIUM, 6.1 G TOTAL DIETARY FIBER

MENU SUGGESTIONS Serve with **Broiled Zucchini with Herbs** (page 333) and/or sliced tomatoes with balsamic vinegar.

PENNE WITH PUTTANESCA SAUCE

Seductively spicy and piquant, puttanesca sauce is said to have invigorative powers, supposedly making it a favorite with the streetwalkers of the title. Try baking fresh scrod fillets with puttanesca sauce and then serve on a bed of orzo.

1 cup diced onions
1 tablespoon minced garlic
1 tablespoon olive oil
5½ to 6 cups chopped fresh or undrained canned tomatoes
½ teaspoon dried oregano
½ teaspoon red pepper flakes
1½ tablespoons capers, rinsed and drained
10 large calamata olives, pitted and chopped (about 3 tablespoons)
2 tablespoons minced fresh parsley
1 pound penne (tubular pasta)

a few fresh parsley sprigs (optional)
grated Parmesan cheese (optional)

Serves 4 to 6

**Total time:
30 to 40 minutes**

Combine the onions, garlic, and oil in a saucepan, cover, and sauté for about 10 minutes, until the onions are translucent, stirring occasionally. While the onions cook, chop the tomatoes—you can chop or crush canned tomatoes right in the can. Add the tomatoes to the saucepan. Stir in the oregano, red pepper flakes, capers, olives, and parsley. Simmer, uncovered, until the sauce thickens, about 20 minutes, or a little longer.

When the sauce has cooked for 10 to 15 minutes, bring a large covered pot of water to a boil. Add the penne and cook for about 7 minutes, until al dente. Drain and serve immediately with the sauce. If you wish, top with parsley sprigs and sprinkle with grated Parmesan.

PER 14-OZ SERVING: 385 CALORIES, 12.2 G PROTEIN, 6.3 G FAT, 71.4 G CARBOHYDRATES, .8 G SATURATED FATTY ACIDS, 1.1 G POLYUNSATURATED FATTY ACIDS, 2.0 G MONOUNSATURATED FATTY ACIDS, 0 MG CHOLESTEROL, 225 MG SODIUM, 5.3 G TOTAL DIETARY FIBER

MENU SUGGESTIONS Use the pasta as a sassy first course for a milder main dish, such as **Swiss Chard Rolls** with cheese and leek filling (page 252). Or begin with another assertive appetizer, such as **Mushroom Pâté Almondine** (page 121) or **Smoky Eggplant and Pepper Spread** (page 122) with crudités, or **Eggplant Strata** (page 32) or **Broiled Portabella Mushrooms** (page 322) and crusty bread. After the pasta, serve a salad and end with fruit for dessert.

SPAGHETTI WITH ONIONS

We modified this recipe from Ed Giobbi, who found it in a very old Italian cookbook. Just as he says, it's a winner.

The pasta is only partially cooked when you add it to the sauce, so as it finishes cooking, it releases the rest of its starch, creating a sauce so thick and unctuous you'd swear it had cheese in it—a bit of kitchen wizardry at work!

4 large onions
2 teaspoons olive oil
2 teaspoons ground fennel (optional)
1 pound spaghetti
1 cup skim milk
1 cup canned tomatoes, crushed or
    coarsely chopped (8-ounce can)
1 teaspoon salt
ground black pepper to taste

Serves 4

**Total time:
40 minutes**

Slice off the ends of the onions. Cut each onion in half lengthwise and remove the peel. Slice each half lengthwise into strips.

Bring a large pot of water to a boil.

While the water heats, pour the oil into a large skillet or wide soup pot and add the onions and fennel, if using. Sauté, stirring occasionally to prevent sticking, until the onions are translucent, about 10 minutes.

Ease the spaghetti into the boiling water, stir, and cover. Cook the spaghetti for just 5 minutes.

Meanwhile, add the milk and tomatoes to the onions. The milk will curdle, but don't worry. Cover and gently simmer.

When the spaghetti has cooked exactly 5 minutes, drain it and add it immediately to the onion mixture. Simmer the spaghetti in the sauce for about 5 minutes, stirring constantly, until the pasta is al dente and the sauce is smooth. Drizzle in a little more milk if the sauce becomes too stiff. Add the salt and pepper to taste. Serve immediately.

PER 10-OZ SERVING: 322 CALORIES, 11.3 G PROTEIN, 3.9 G FAT, 60.9 G CARBOHYDRATES, .6 G SATURATED FATTY ACIDS, .8 G POLYUNSATURATED FATTY ACIDS, 2.0 G MONOUNSATURATED FATTY ACIDS, 1 MG CHOLESTEROL, 753 MG SODIUM, 3.9 G TOTAL DIETARY FIBER

MENU SUGGESTIONS Serve with a piquant or savory side dish, such as **Vegetables à la Grecque** (page 130), **Roasted Asparagus** (page 312), or **Snap Peas with Mushrooms** (page 329).

VEGETABLE LASAGNE BÉCHAMEL

Graced with two sauces, one a creamy low-fat béchamel, the other a tomato-basil, this dish features vegetables simmered with wine and herbs, which replace much of the cheese traditionally used in lasagne.

Serves 6 to 8

**Preparation time:
1 hour**

Baking time: 1 hour, **plus 10 minutes to rest**

NOTE:

Here is a real time-saver we've learned over the years of cooking at the restaurant: Don't precook the noodles! If you use a generous amount of sauce as you layer the noodles and cover your baking dish tightly with aluminum foil, they will be perfectly cooked when the lasagne is done. Now our trick can work for you. Trust us, it's a lot easier.

1 tablespoon canola or other vegetable oil
2 tablespoons unbleached white flour
2½ cups 1% milk
¼ teaspoon nutmeg
½ teaspoon Dijon mustard
salt and ground black pepper to taste
1 teaspoon olive oil
4 garlic cloves, minced or pressed
2 cups chopped leeks, white and tender green parts
½ teaspoon dried thyme
1 cup dry white wine
1½ cups peeled and diced carrots
½ cup peeled and diced broccoli stalks
2½ cups broccoli florets
3 cups undrained canned tomatoes (28-ounce can)
⅓ cup chopped fresh basil
¾ pound uncooked lasagna noodles
   (see Note)
½ cup grated Parmesan cheese
¼ cup grated low-fat mozzarella cheese

Warm the oil in a small saucepan and then stir in the flour. Slowly whisk in the milk, ½ cup at a time. Continue to cook, stirring often, until the sauce thickens a bit; this béchamel with not be very thick. Add the nutmeg, mustard, and salt and pepper to taste. Remove from the heat and set aside.

In a heavy or preferably nonstick skillet on medium heat, warm the olive oil. Add the garlic, leeks, and thyme and sauté for 2 to 3 minutes. Add the wine, carrots, and broccoli stalks, cover, and cook for about 5 minutes. Add the broccoli florets, cover, and simmer for 3 or 4 minutes, until all of the vegetables are tender but still firm. Add a dash of salt and pepper and set aside.

Pour the canned tomatoes and juice into a bowl and crush the tomatoes by hand. Add the fresh basil, stir well, and set aside.

Preheat the oven to 350°.

Prepare a deep 8 × 12-inch baking dish with cooking spray or a light coating of oil.

Assemble the lasagne. Layer half of the tomato-basil mixture in the bottom of the dish, top with a single layer of noodles, half of the vegetables, a cup of the béchamel sauce, ¼ cup of the Parmesan, and 2 tablespoons of the grated mozzarella. Top with a second layer of noodles, the rest of the vegetables, the remaining béchamel sauce, a third layer of noodles, the rest of the tomato-basil mixture, and sprinkle the top with the remaining cheeses.

Cover and bake for 50 minutes. Uncover and bake for an additional 10 minutes. Allow the lasagne to rest for 10 minutes before serving.

PER 10-OZ SERVING: 347 CALORIES, 16.0 G PROTEIN, 8.6 G FAT, 48.2 G CARBOHYDRATES, 3.2 G SATURATED FATTY ACIDS, 1.8 G POLYUNSATURATED FATTY ACIDS, 2.6 G MONOUNSATURATED FATTY ACIDS, 52 MG CHOLESTEROL, 392 MG SODIUM, 3.5 G TOTAL DIETARY FIBER

MENU SUGGESTIONS Serve with a crisp green salad with **Orange Tarragon Dressing** (page 348) and a luscious dessert, such as **Fruit-filled Meringue Shells** (page 388).

LIGHTER LASAGNE

This lasagne is so rich with vegetables, herbs, and wine that you'll never miss the extra cheese and fat that we're accustomed to finding in standard recipes.

Serves 6 to 8

Preparation time: 40 minutes

Baking time: 60 to 70 minutes

2 cups cubed zucchini
1 cup cubed bell peppers
1 cup chopped tomatoes
4 cups sliced mushrooms (about 12 ounces)
¼ teaspoon salt
⅓ cup dry red wine
3 tablespoons chopped fresh basil
10 ounces fresh spinach, rinsed
2 cups low-fat cottage cheese
1 cup grated low-fat mozzarella cheese
¼ cup grated Parmesan cheese
1 recipe Tomato Wine Sauce (page 350) or
   3½ cups prepared tomato sauce
1 pound uncooked lasagna noodles (see Note, page 216)

Preheat the oven to 350°.

Combine the zucchini, peppers, tomatoes, mushrooms, salt, and wine in a saucepan, bring to a boil, cover, and then simmer on low heat for about 10 minutes, until all of the vegetables are tender and juicy. Stir in the basil and set aside.

Cover and cook the spinach on high heat in just the water clinging to the leaves for 3 minutes, until wilted but still bright green. Drain and chop coarsely. Combine with the cottage cheese, mozzarella, and Parmesan and set aside.

Spread 1 cup of the tomato sauce evenly on the bottom of a 3-inch-deep nonreactive 8 × 12-inch baking dish. Layer with 5 or 6 noodles, 1 generous cup of undrained vegetables, and 1 cup of the spinach-cheese mixture. Cover with a second layer of noodles, 1 cup of sauce, 1 heaping cup of vegetables, 1 cup of the spinach-cheese mixture, and a third layer of noodles. Finally, add the rest of the vegetables, the remaining spinach-cheese mixture, a fourth layer of noodles, and the rest of the sauce. Cover tightly with foil and bake until the noodles are tender, about 60 minutes. Let sit at least 10 minutes before cutting.

PER 12-OZ SERVING: 218 CALORIES, 17.7 G PROTEIN, 5.8 G FAT, 22.9 G CARBOHYDRATES, 3.2 G SATURATED FATTY ACIDS, .5 G POLYUNSATURATED FATTY ACIDS, 1.6 G MONOUNSATURATED FATTY ACIDS, 35 MG CHOLESTEROL, 480 MG SODIUM, 2.9 G TOTAL DIETARY FIBER

MENU SUGGESTIONS Serve with **Citrus-dressed Asparagus** (page 313) or with tossed salad with **Caesar Salad Dressing** (page 131) and some good crusty bread.

STUFFED MANICOTTI VERDE

Leeks delicately season this creamy spinach dish. We offer two possible wrappers for the filling. The manicotti shells require some additional cooking time, but if time is not a consideration, you may be hard-pressed to choose which you prefer.

FILLING

1 tablespoon olive oil

2 large garlic cloves, minced or pressed

5½ cups chopped leeks (white bulbs and tender green parts)

3 tablespoons water

20 ounces fresh spinach, rinsed and coarsely chopped

1 teaspoon dried basil

½ cup grated reduced-fat mozzarella cheese

⅓ cup grated Parmesan cheese

1½ cups nonfat ricotta cheese

½ teaspoon nutmeg

salt and ground black pepper to taste

14 manicotti (1-pound box dried pasta shells) or eight 8-inch wheat tortillas

3½ cups Tomato Wine Sauce (page 350)

Serves 4 to 6 generously

Preparation time: 30 minutes

Cooking and filling time: 30 minutes

Baking time: 25 to 30 minutes

Heat the olive oil in a large soup pot. Stir in the garlic, leeks, and water. Cover and gently sauté, stirring occasionally until the leeks soften, about 10 minutes. Add the spinach and basil. Cook, covered, for about 5 minutes, until the spinach wilts, stirring once or twice. Uncover and cook a few minutes longer on medium-high heat to evaporate as much excess moisture as possible. Drain, if necessary. Combine the mozzarella, Parmesan, ricotta, and nutmeg with the vegetables. Add salt and pepper to taste.

If you're filling manicotti, cook the pasta shells until al dente, 8 to 10 minutes. Drain well. Fill each manicotti and place in a lightly oiled 9 × 12-inch baking dish. Pour half of the tomato sauce evenly over the manicotti and cover tightly with foil. Bake at 350° for 30 minutes. Serve hot and pass the remaining tomato sauce at the table.

If you're filling tortillas, place ⅛ of the filling on the lower half of each tortilla and roll it up. Place a lightly oiled 9 × 12-inch baking dish, cover with a damp towel, and wrap tightly with foil. Bake at 350° for 25 minutes. Serve topped with tomato sauce.

PER 16-OZ SERVING: 492 CALORIES, 26.1 G PROTEIN, 12.1 G FAT, 70.6 G CARBOHYDRATES, 4.0 G SATURATED FATTY ACIDS, 1.4 G POLYUNSATURATED FATTY ACIDS, 4.6 G MONOUNSATURATED FATTY ACIDS, 72 MG CHOLESTEROL, 817 MG SODIUM, 6.1 G TOTAL DIETARY FIBER

MENU SUGGESTIONS Serve with **Cucumbers Vinaigrette** (page 133), **Broiled Zucchini with Herbs** (page 333), or **Carrot Orange Salad** (page 134).

CURRIED RICE NOODLES

We have mixed Indian curry spices with Asian noodles and sauce ingredients to create a colorful, exotic noodle sauté that is quick to make. To give the rice stick noodles more time to soften, cover them with boiling water before you prepare the vegetables for the sauté. If rice stick noodles are unavailable, use linguine or any Asian flat wheat noodle as a substitute—but don't use rice vermicelli.

Serves 4 to 6

Total time: 45 minutes

PASTA
½ pound rice stick noodles (page 436)

DRIED SPICES
2 teaspoons curry powder
1 teaspoon ground cumin
½ teaspoon turmeric
½ teaspoon ground coriander

SAUCE
2 tablespoons dry sherry
3 tablespoons soy sauce
¼ cup water
1 teaspoon sugar

VEGETABLES
1 tablespoon minced or pressed garlic
1 tablespoon grated fresh ginger root
1 tablespoon canola or other vegetable oil
1 cup thinly sliced red onions
1 cup peeled and julienned carrots
1 cup sliced red or yellow bell peppers
    (or a combination of colors)
4 cups thinly sliced bok choy (page 424)
salt and ground black pepper to taste

lime wedges
minced fresh basil, cilantro, or scallions

Place the noodles in a heatproof bowl and cover them with boiling water. Cover the bowl and set it aside.

Mix together the curry powder, cumin, turmeric, and coriander in a small bowl. In a separate bowl, combine the sherry, soy sauce, water, and sugar and set aside.

In a large nonstick or well-seasoned cast-iron skillet, combine the garlic, ginger, and oil and sauté on medium heat for about 2 minutes, stirring constantly. Add the red onions and carrots and cook for 3 to 5 minutes, stirring often. Add the bell peppers and continue to cook, stirring, for about another 4 minutes. Add the bok choy and dried spice mixture and cook for 1 or 2 minutes. Pour in the sauce mixture, cover, and simmer for another 2 minutes, or until the bok choy is tender.

Drain the rice noodles, which should be softened, and add them to the sauté. Stir until hot, then season with salt and black pepper to taste. Serve with lime wedges and your choice of basil, cilantro, or scallions.

VARIATIONS For a spicy hot dish, add cayenne, chili paste, or Tabasco to taste, or replace the dried spices with 1 or 2 tablespoons of Thai Curry Paste (page 365). Add cayenne with the red onions and carrots; add chili paste, Tabasco, or Thai Curry Paste near the end of cooking.

PER 9-OZ SERVING: 207 CALORIES, 5.7 G PROTEIN, 3.2 G FAT, 40.4 G CARBOHYDRATES, .3 G SATURATED FATTY ACIDS, 1.5 G POLYUNSATURATED FATTY ACIDS, .6 G MONOUNSATURATED FATTY ACIDS, 0 MG CHOLESTEROL, 482 MG SODIUM, 2.8 G TOTAL DIETARY FIBER

MENU SUGGESTIONS Pair with **Southeast Asian Coconut Zucchini** (page 334), **Citrus-dressed Asparagus** (page 313), **Mango Coconut Cucumber Salad** (page 136), **Cabbage Salad** (page 132), or **Broiled Eggplant Thai Style** (page 34).

roasted vegetables three ways 226

luscious basil and feta pizza 228

CURRIED SWEET POTATO ROTI 230

seitan fajitas 232

vegetable-filled pancakes 233

MUSHROOM SPINACH CRÊPES 234

sun-dried tomato polenta cutlets 236

another shepherd's pie 238

MUSHROOM POLENTA PIE 240

eggplant parmesan 241

vegetable filo roll extravaganza 242

MEXICAN STUFFED PEPPERS AND TOMATOES 244

middle eastern tofu-stuffed peppers 246

mushroom- and spinach-stuffed zucchini 247

SAVORY INDIAN SWEET POTATOES 248

stuffed baked potatoes 249

potato cheese gnocchi 250

CURRIED POTATO CABBAGE ROLL-UPS 251

swiss chard rolls two ways 252

fresh spring rolls 254

CABBAGE ROLLS 256

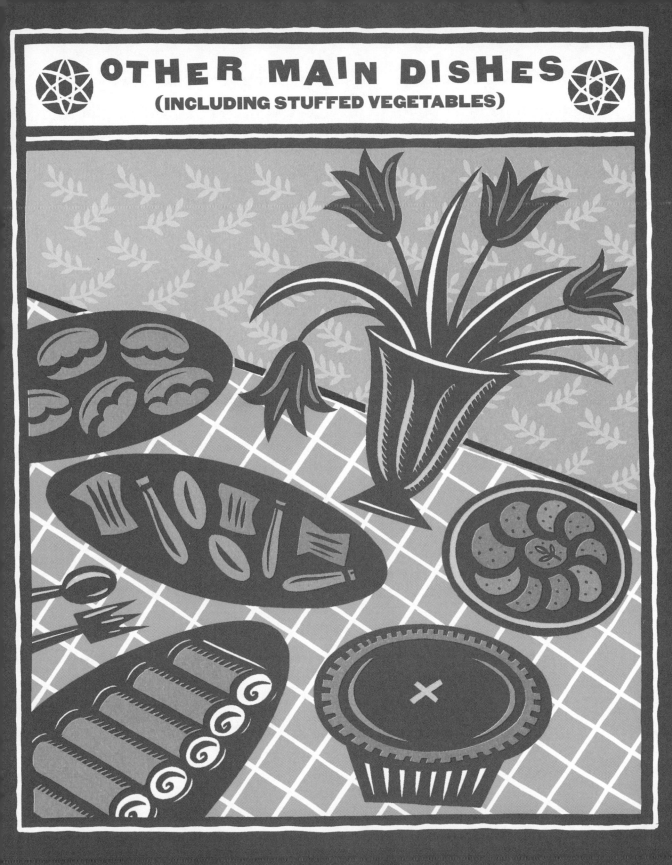

HOMESTYLE cooking from around the globe has always been a source of inspiration for us at Moosewood. The diverse collection of recipes in this chapter reflects both our interest in traditional cooking and our experimentation with cross-cultural "fusion cooking." This chapter includes stuffed vegetables, filled wrappers, and several other dishes that didn't slip easily into any other section.

The cuisines of the Mediterranean region are jumping-off points for our Vegetable Filo Roll Extravaganza, Eggplant Parmesan, polenta dishes, pizzas, and Potato Cheese Gnocchi. From cuisines farther north, we've adapted traditional shepherd's pie and cabbage rolls, giving them new twists with nontraditional ingredients such as soy sauce, tofu, and miso. Because we really like the distinctively crisp and juicy quality that roasting imparts, we've included both traditional and nontraditional roasted vegetables—Italian, Cantonese, and Caribbean.

Stuffing easily hollowed-out vegetables is an age-old technique and here we give you some of our favorites. The hearty low-fat stuffed potato recipes help to fill a void felt by many of us who are trying to eat lighter, and they come in Mexican-, Italian-, and Indian-inspired versions. We've taken tofu (originally Japanese) and mixed it with flavorings characteristic of the Middle East to create an unusual and satisfying stuffed pepper. And remember that you can stuff an eggplant, pepper, or zucchini with leftover grain pilafs, bean dishes, or seasoned mashed potatoes and then dress it up with a little sauce or salsa.

Besides stuffing vegetables, fillings are also good served inside wrappers of all kinds—pastry crusts, filo packages, tortillas, crêpes, and rice paper discs, to name a few. The simple corn or wheat tortilla of the Americas is an inexpensive, easily obtained food that is happily low in fat. Its mild, pleasing flavor and chewy, sturdy texture make it an excellent wrapper for vegetables of all sorts. We use tortillas in our Seitan Fajitas—a traditional fajita wrapper with an unexpected filling. We also substitute tortillas for some harder-to-find or trickier-to-use traditional wrappers, as in our Chinese-inspired Vegetable-filled Pancakes and Indian-style Curried Potato Cabbage Roll-Ups. Crêpes and rice paper discs, with lighter, more delicate textures, as well as Swiss chard and cabbage leaves are used to create packages and rolls in other recipes.

Browse through this chapter when you're in the mood to cook something out of the ordinary. You may find just the recipe to serve as a centerpiece for a special occasion.

ROASTED VEGETABLES THREE WAYS

Roasted vegetables have become a favorite menu item at Moosewood. We like to vary their seasonings, the "beds" we put them on, and the garnishes we put on top—depending on our moods and what's available. We serve roasted vegetables on rice, couscous, orzo, bulgur, and beds of steamed greens such as kale or Swiss chard. We top them with a little grated feta or Parmesan cheese, chopped toasted nuts, or baked tofu. Their versatility makes them a cook's delight.

All three of these recipes call for 10 to 12 cups of vegetables cut into chunks or slices, somewhat bigger than bite-sized. Choose at least four vegetables, keeping in mind color, texture, and flavor. Possibilities include potatoes, sweet potatoes, carrots, zucchini, yellow squash, mushrooms, eggplant, parsnips, turnips, bell peppers, asparagus, winter squash, and onions. We have suggested one of our favorite vegetable combinations in this recipe but by all means, feel free to experiment.

The fastest way to prepare this dish is to parboil the harder, longer-cooking vegetables briefly before roasting them, but it is also possible to bake everything without parboiling. We give directions for both methods.

Serves 4 to 6

Preparation time: 25 minutes

Baking time: 45 to 75 minutes, shorter time for parboiling method

2 potatoes, cut into 1-inch chunks or cut in half lengthwise and sliced crosswise into ½-inch-thick semicircles

2 sweet potatoes, peeled and cut into 1-inch chunks or sliced as above

2 carrots, peeled and cut into 1-inch chunks or cut on the diagonal into ½-inch-thick slices

1 large onion, cut into wedges

1 medium zucchini, cut into 1-inch chunks or cut on the diagonal into ½-inch-thick slices

2 bell peppers, cut into 1-inch chunks (two different colors is nice)

CHOOSE ONE OF THE FOLLOWING:

CANTONESE DRESSING

⅓ cup soy sauce

⅓ cup rice vinegar

1 tablespoon grated fresh ginger root

1 tablespoon honey

1 tablespoon dark sesame oil

3 garlic cloves, minced or pressed

½ teaspoon ground anise

ITALIAN DRESSING

4 teaspoons olive oil
¼ cup fresh lemon juice
6 garlic cloves, minced or pressed
3 tablespoons minced fresh rosemary
   (2 to 3 teaspoons dried and ground)
1 tablespoon minced fresh oregano
1 teaspoon salt

CARIBBEAN DRESSING

3 tablespoons soy sauce
1 tablespoon canola or other vegetable oil
2 tablespoons red wine vinegar
1 tablespoon packed brown sugar
1 small onion, coarsely chopped
½ teaspoon dried thyme
½ teaspoon ground cinnamon
½ teaspoon ground cloves
½ teaspoon ground black pepper
2 teaspoons grated fresh ginger root
1 large garlic clove, minced or pressed
1 fresh green chile, coarsely chopped, seeds
   removed for a milder "hot"

Preheat the oven to 425°.

Parboil the potatoes, sweet potatoes, and carrots in boiling water to cover for 2 minutes. Drain well. In a large bowl, combine the parboiled vegetables with the onions, zucchini, and bell peppers.

To make the dressing of your choice, either whisk together the ingredients in a bowl, or purée them until smooth in a blender or food processor.

Toss the vegetables well with the dressing. Place the vegetables in a single layer on a large unoiled baking tray and bake, stirring every 15 minutes, until all of the vegetables are tender, about 45 minutes.

To roast without parboiling, bake the vegetables in sequence. Prepare a large baking tray with cooking spray or a light coating of oil. Place the white potatoes and carrots on the tray and bake for 15 minutes. Add the sweet potatoes and bake for another 15 minutes. Remove the vegetables from the oven and transfer to a large bowl. Add the onions, zucchini, and bell peppers to the bowl and toss with the dressing of your choice. Spread the vegetables on the baking tray in a single layer and return to the oven. Bake until all of the vegetables are tender, about 45 minutes, stirring occasionally to prevent sticking.

PER 6.50-OZ SERVING (ALL 3 VARIATIONS ARE WITHIN 1 GRAM OF ONE ANOTHER IN FAT, PROTEIN, AND FIBER CONTENT): 169 CALORIES, 3.4 G PROTEIN, 2.8 G FAT, 34.1 G CARBOHYDRATES, .4 G SATURATED FATTY ACIDS, 1.2 G POLYUNSATURATED FATTY ACIDS, 1.0 G MONOUNSATURATED FATTY ACIDS, 0 MG CHOLESTEROL, 742 MG SODIUM, 4.1 G TOTAL DIETARY FIBER

MENU SUGGESTIONS Serve Cantonese Roasted Vegetables on rice, with tofu, and accompanied by **Japanese Sesame Spinach** (page 330) or a salad with **Creamy Ginger Miso Dressing** (page 343). Serve Caribbean Roasted Vegetables on steamed kale with **Jerk Tofu** (page 337) or toasted peanuts. Serve Italian Roasted Vegetables on couscous or **Orzo and Green Herbs** (page 183) with grated Parmesan.

Luscious Basil and Feta Pizza

Part of the fun of making your own pizza dough is the sensual pleasure of working with dough, the wonderful aroma, and the enjoyment of presenting a homemade pizza from your very own kitchen. This recipe is quite straightforward, but we slipped some rolled oats into the dough for texture. Topping choices are endless: we've given two possibilities, but we know you'll invent lots more of your own. See the variations for inspiration.

DOUGH

1 tablespoon baking yeast
1 teaspoon sugar
1 cup very warm water (105° to 115°)
½ cup rolled oats
½ cup whole wheat bread flour
1 teaspoon olive oil
1 teaspoon salt
1½ to 2 cups unbleached white bread flour

Makes one 12-inch
pizza; serves 4

Preparation time:
1½ hours

Baking time:
15 to 20 minutes

SIMPLE BASIL TOMATO TOPPING

2½ cups chopped tomatoes
1 large garlic clove, minced or pressed
¼ cup chopped fresh basil
¼ teaspoon salt

SAUTÉED BASIL LEEK TOPPING

1 teaspoon olive oil
2 cups finely chopped leeks
pinch of salt
2 cups chopped tomatoes
1 cup chopped roasted red peppers (page 436)
¼ cup chopped fresh basil

3 ounces grated feta cheese

Combine the yeast with the sugar and warm water in a large mixing bowl and set aside until bubbles rise to the surface, about 5 minutes.

Whirl the oats in a blender or food processor until they are the consistency of coarse flour. When the yeast is thoroughly dissolved and frothy, about 7 to 10 minutes, add the oat flour, whole wheat flour, oil, salt, and enough of the white flour to make a stiff dough. Turn out onto a lightly floured surface and knead for 5 to 7 minutes, until smooth and elastic, adding the remaining flour as needed.

Lightly oil or spray a large bowl. Place the dough in it, turn it once to coat, cover it with a damp towel, and allow to rise in a warm spot for about 30 minutes, or until doubled in size. While the dough is rising, prepare one of the toppings and grate the feta.

To prepare Simple Basil Tomato Topping, mix all of the ingredients in a bowl and set aside. Or, to prepare Sautéed Basil Leek Topping, heat the oil in a medium saucepan, add the leeks and salt, cover, and cook on medium-low heat for about 7 minutes, stirring now and then. Add the tomatoes and roasted red peppers, cover, and cook for 10 minutes, stirring a few times. Remove from the heat, stir in the basil, and set aside.

When the dough has doubled in size, preheat the oven to 450° and prepare a 12-inch pizza pan with cooking spray or oil.

Punch down the dough, turn it out onto a lightly floured work surface, and knead for about 1 minute. Using your hands or a rolling pin, stretch the dough into a large circle. Place the dough on the pizza pan and continue stretching it until it covers the pan. Using your fingers, make a slightly thicker edge of crust around the perimeter of the pan. Very lightly spray or oil the dough and allow it to rise in a warm place for 10 minutes. Evenly spread the topping of your choice on the dough, top with the grated feta, and bake for about 15 minutes, until the dough is golden brown and the cheese is melted.

VARIATIONS Other recipes in this book that make good pizza toppings are **Creamy Roasted Red Pepper Sauce** (page 355), **Savory Onion Marmalade** (page 363), **Smoky Eggplant and Pepper Spread** (page 122), **Susan's Pesto** (page 364), and the sauces from **Penne with Puttanesca Sauce** (page 214), **Pasta with Salsa Cruda** (page 212), and **Pasta with Eggplant** (page 205). Or combine **Tomato Wine Sauce** (page 350) or **Chunky Tomato Sauce** (page 351) with leftover **Broiled Portabella Mushrooms** (page 322), **Broiled Zucchini with Herbs** (page 333), **Zucchini with Cilantro Sauce** (page 335), or **Italian Roasted Vegetables** (page 226).

WITH SIMPLE BASIL TOPPING PER 10-OZ SERVING: 402 CALORIES, 15.0 G PROTEIN, 8.1 G FAT, 69.0 G CARBOHYDRATES, 3.7 G SATURATED FATTY ACIDS, 1.1 G POLYUNSATURATED FATTY ACIDS, 2.4 G MONOUNSATURATED FATTY ACIDS, 19 MG CHOLESTEROL, 995 MG SODIUM, 7.2 G TOTAL DIETARY FIBER

WITH SAUTÉED BASIL LEEK TOPPING PER 12.5-OZ SERVING: 449 CALORIES, 15.9 G PROTEIN, 9.4 G FAT, 77.5 G CARBO-HYDRATES, 3.9 G SATURATED FATTY ACIDS, 1.3 G POLYUNSATURATED FATTY ACIDS, 3.3 G MONOUNSATURATED FATTY ACIDS, 19 MG CHOLESTEROL, 899 MG SODIUM, 8.3 G TOTAL DIETARY FIBER

MENU SUGGESTIONS Pizza and soup is an excellent combination. We recommend **Orzo and Pea Soup** (page 93), **Spring Soup** (page 84), or **Minestrone Genoa** (page 86). Or serve with **Seasoned Steamed Artichokes** (page 311) or chilled **Cauliflower Agrodolce** (page 318). For dessert, we like **Our Best No-Butter Brownies** (page 387), **Ginger Peach Crumble** (page 386), or vanilla frozen yogurt with **Red Berry Kissel** (page 372) on top.

CURRIED SWEET POTATO ROTI

Roti is the name used in the Caribbean for rolled or folded dough turnovers that have a variety of fillings. Here we wrap flour tortillas around a smooth, curried sweet potato filling made more substantial and chewy by the addition of seitan, an increasingly popular wheat gluten product. For anyone who has never tried seitan, this dish is a great introduction.

Serves 4 to 6

Preparation time: 40 minutes

Baking time: 15 to 20 minutes

4 cups peeled and cubed sweet potatoes
1 tablespoon canola or other vegetable oil
2 teaspoons black mustard seeds
1 cup chopped onions
½ cup chopped bell peppers

SPICE MIXTURE
1 tablespoon grated fresh ginger root
1 teaspoon ground cumin
¼ teaspoon turmeric
¼ teaspoon cayenne, or to taste
¼ teaspoon ground cloves
¼ teaspoon ground cardamom
¼ teaspoon ground cinnamon

2 tablespoons fresh lime juice
1 tablespoon chopped fresh cilantro
8 ounces chopped seitan
salt to taste
6 eight-inch flour tortillas

nonfat sour cream or yogurt (optional)
chopped fresh parsley or cilantro

In a covered saucepan, bring the sweet potatoes and enough water to cover them to a boil. Reduce the heat, cover, and simmer for 10 minutes, or until soft.

Meanwhile, heat the oil in a saucepan and add the mustard seeds. Cook, stirring, for a minute or two, until they begin to pop. Add the onions and sauté for 5 minutes, until they begin to soften. Stir in the bell peppers and the spice mixture ingredients and cook for about 5 minutes, until the peppers are tender, adding about 3 tablespoons of the sweet potato water to prevent sticking.

Preheat the oven to 350°.

When the sweet potatoes are soft, drain them and mash them with the lime juice. Stir in the cilantro and seitan, then add the cooked onions and peppers and mix well. Sprinkle in salt to taste.

Prepare a baking dish with a light coating of oil or cooking spray. Place about ½ cup of filling on each tortilla, roll it up, and place it, seam side down, in the baking dish. Cover tightly with aluminum foil and bake for 15 to 20 minutes, until heated through.

Serve hot, topped with a dollop of nonfat sour cream or yogurt, if desired, and some chopped parsley or cilantro.

PER 9-OZ SERVING: 331 CALORIES, 9.0 G PROTEIN, 7.1 G FAT, 60.0 G CARBOHYDRATES, .7 G SATURATED FATTY ACIDS, 2.7 G POLYUNSATURATED FATTY ACIDS, 1.3 G MONOUNSATURATED FATTY ACIDS, 0 MG CHOLESTEROL, 104 MG SODIUM, 5.0 G TOTAL DIETARY FIBER

MENU SUGGESTIONS For a complete meal, begin with **Tropical Gazpacho** (page 78), and serve the roti on **Golden Basmati Rice** (page 185) topped with **Mango Peach Chutney** (page 362). Serve wedges of fresh melon for dessert with scoops of **Pineapple Buttermilk Sherbet** (page 394) or try a **Tapioca Fruit Parfaits** (page 375).

SEITAN FAJITAS

Former Moosewood collective member Bob Love introduced us to these tasty and quickly assembled fajitas, which make wonderful impromptu meals for family or guests.

6 eight-inch flour tortillas
1 fresh green chile, minced,
    seeds removed for a milder "hot"
1 garlic clove, minced or pressed
1½ cups sliced onions
1½ teaspoons ground cumin
1 teaspoon canola or other vegetable oil
2½ cups sliced red and green bell peppers
2 tablespoons prepared Mexican-style red salsa
1½ cups seasoned seitan (page 437),
    sliced into ¼ × 2-inch strips

shredded lettuce
chopped tomatoes
salsa (optional)

Serves 3 as a main dish, 6 as an appetizer

Total time: 15 minutes

> **NOTE:**
> To warm tortillas in the microwave, wrap the stacked tortillas in a paper towel and heat them until thoroughly warmed, about a minute. You can also heat each tortilla on a dry griddle or skillet for 1 to 2 minutes, flipping it over two or three times until hot.

Preheat a conventional or toaster oven to 300°.

Stack the tortillas together, then wrap and carefully seal them in aluminum foil and set aside.

In a nonreactive skillet, sauté the chiles, garlic, onions, and cumin in the oil for 5 minutes. Add the bell peppers and salsa, cover, and cook on medium heat for 5 minutes. While the vegetables cook, bake the tortillas for about 10 minutes, until soft and pliable and heated through (see Note).

Meanwhile, add the seitan to the skillet and cook, uncovered, until the vegetables are tender, about 3 to 4 minutes more.

Unwrap the foil package of tortillas carefully to avoid burning yourself. Place ⅙ of the filling on each warmed tortilla and roll it up. Serve immediately with lettuce and tomatoes and additional salsa, if desired.

PER 5.50-OZ SERVING: 164 CALORIES, 4.7 G PROTEIN, 3.5 G FAT, 29.6 G CARBOHYDRATES, .2 G SATURATED FATTY ACIDS, .8 G POLYUNSATURATED FATTY ACIDS, .3 G MONOUNSATURATED FATTY ACIDS, 0 MG CHOLESTEROL, 239 MG SODIUM, 1.3 G TOTAL DIETARY FIBER

MENU SUGGESTIONS Pair with **Spinach Avocado Grapefruit Salad** (page 135), **Spanish Potatoes** (page 324), or **Guacamole with Roasted Corn** (page 27). Frozen nonfat yogurt with fresh fruit is a perfect easy dessert.

VEGETABLE-FILLED PANCAKES

Warmed wheat tortillas serve as excellent wrappers for vegetables enlivened by a piquant Chinese black bean sauce. The sauce is simple, the tortillas are hot in minutes, and the broccoli and peppers are stir-fried, making this a snazzy but quickly executed dish. Be sure to have all of the ingredients prepared and easily accessible before you begin to cook.

¼ cup soy sauce
2 tablespoons rice vinegar
2 teaspoons brown sugar
2 teaspoons cornstarch, dissolved in ¼ cup cool water
4 eight-inch flour tortillas
2 teaspoons canola or other vegetable oil
2 teaspoons minced fresh green chiles,
   seeds removed for a milder "hot"
2 garlic cloves, minced or pressed
2 tablespoons Chinese black beans, rinsed (page 424)
2 tablespoons Chinese rice wine (page 424)
2 cups diced red or green bell peppers
½ cup peeled diced broccoli stems
4 cups loosely packed broccoli florets
1 cake tofu-kan, cut into small cubes (about 6 ounces) (page 439)

Serves 2

Total time: 30 minutes

Combine the soy sauce, rice vinegar, brown sugar, and dissolved cornstarch in a small bowl and set aside.

Stack the tortillas together, then wrap and carefully seal them in aluminum foil. Bake them in a 300° oven for about 10 minutes, until heated through (see Note, opposite).

Meanwhile, heat the oil in a wok or large skillet. Add the chiles, garlic, and black beans and stir-fry for 1 minute. Add the rice wine and when thoroughly hot, stir in the peppers and broccoli stems. Stir-fry for another minute and then add the broccoli florets, tofu kan, and ¼ cup of water. Cover and let steam for about 2 minutes, until the broccoli is just crisp-tender. Pour in the soy sauce mixture and stir-fry until the sauce begins to thicken and bubble. Remove from the heat.

To serve, place one warm tortilla at a time on a flat surface, put ¼ of the stir-fry filling on the half closest to you, and roll it up. Eat it like a burrito or an egg roll—very tidy folks could use a knife and fork.

PER 19-OZ SERVING: 493 CALORIES, 22.5 G PROTEIN, 14.4 G FAT, 73.0 G CARBOHYDRATES, 1.5 G SATURATED FATTY ACIDS, 6.0 G POLYUNSATURATED FATTY ACIDS, 2.3 G MONOUNSATURATED FATTY ACIDS, 0 MG CHOLESTEROL, 2351 MG SODIUM, 8.6 G TOTAL DIETARY FIBER

MENU SUGGESTIONS Serve with **Five-Spice Rice** (page 186) after **Vietnamese Hot and Sour Soup** (page 87) and serve **Ginger Peach Crumble** (page 386) to top off the meal.

MUSHROOM SPINACH CRÊPES

A savory vegetable and cheese filling rolled inside delicate crêpes is a tempting meal with a certain *esprit de France.* Crêpes can be a featured main-course item or be offered simply as appetizers. Many fillings are possible. Here we offer one of our favorites—rich, sautéed mushrooms and mellow spinach with sharp feta cheese. For a sweet filling, try Cinnamon Apple Crêpes (page 56).

The crêpes can be made ahead of time and frozen for a month or more, but remember to place a piece of wax paper between every crêpe so that you can easily separate them later.

Serves 5 or 6

Makes 14 to 16 seven-inch crêpes

Total time: 45 minutes

NOTE:
If you have two crêpe pans or skillets, using both pans simultaneously to cook the crêpes will significantly reduce preparation time.

CRÊPES
¾ **cup unbleached white flour**
½ **teaspoon salt**
½ **teaspoon baking powder**
1 **whole egg**
2 **egg whites**
1 **cup evaporated skimmed milk**

FILLING
10 **ounces fresh spinach**
3 **cups sliced mushrooms**
⅓ **cup dry sherry**
1 **garlic clove, minced or pressed**
1 **teaspoon dried basil**
¼ **cup grated feta cheese**
½ **cup low-fat cottage cheese**
salt to taste

Sift together the flour, salt, and baking powder. In a blender or food processor, whirl the dry ingredients with the egg, egg whites, and evaporated skimmed milk for about 30 seconds, until well blended. If necessary, stop once and scrape the sides of the blender or processor with a spatula.

Heat a nonstick 8-inch skillet or crêpe pan on medium-high heat (see Note). Ladle about ⅛ cup of batter into the skillet—use just enough to thinly coat the bottom of the pan. Tilt the pan in all directions to spread the batter evenly. Cook each crêpe until the underside is slightly browned and the top looks dry, ½ to 1 minute. Lift the edge of the crêpe with a spatula, take hold of it with the fingertips of both hands (being careful not to burn yourself), flip it over in one fluid motion, and cook the other side for 15 to 20 seconds, or until just light brown. Remove the crêpe to a platter.

Continue making crêpes and stacking them on the platter until no batter is left. The cooked crêpes won't stick together! If, however, the crêpe batter begins to stick to the cooking pan, try using a light coating of cooking spray.

Preheat the oven to 350°.

Wash the spinach, drain it, and place it in a large pot with whatever water clings to the leaves. Cover and cook on high heat just long enough to wilt the spinach, about 3 minutes, stirring occasionally to prevent sticking. Drain and set aside.

Combine the mushrooms, sherry, garlic, and basil in a saucepan and simmer on low heat for about 10 minutes. Remove from the heat. Coarsely chop the cooked spinach and add it to the mushroom mixture. Stir in the feta and cottage cheeses, mix well, and add salt to taste.

Place about 3 tablespoons of the filling on the lower half of each crêpe, roll it up, and lay it, seam side down, in a baking dish prepared with cooking spray. Cover and bake for about 15 minutes, until the cheeses are hot and bubbly.

PER 6-OZ SERVING: 157 CALORIES, 11.9 G PROTEIN, 2.9 G FAT, 19.1 G CARBOHYDRATES, 1.4 G SATURATED FATTY ACIDS, .3 G POLYUNSATURATED FATTY ACIDS, .8 G MONOUNSATURATED FATTY ACIDS, 51 MG CHOLESTEROL, 463 MG SODIUM, 2.0 G TOTAL DIETARY FIBER

MENU SUGGESTIONS Serve after **Spanish Potato Garlic Soup** (page 97) with a side dish of **Baked Beets and Shallots** (page 314) and follow with a crisp **Caesar Salad** (page 131). Nibble a few **Chocolate Hazelnut Biscotti** (page 392) between sips of dessert wine for a pleasant finish.

SUN-DRIED TOMATO POLENTA CUTLETS

We think that you'll be pleasantly surprised when you experience the crisp texture of these beautifully jeweled cutlets. You will never guess by tasting them how low-fat they are. We suggest topping each serving of cutlets with a ladle of Tomato Wine Sauce (page 350). Or try Savory Onion Marmalade (page 363) or a dollop of Susan's Pesto (page 364) for a change of pace. If there are leftovers, these cutlets are excellent cold and will travel well in a lunchbox or picnic basket.

Serves 6

Makes 12 cutlets

Preparation time: 40 minutes

Chilling time: 1 hour

Baking time: 30 minutes

½ **cup sun-dried tomatoes (about 10, not packed in oil)**
1 cup boiling water
1 teaspoon olive oil
½ **cup minced onion**
5 garlic cloves, pressed or minced
1¼ **teaspoons salt**
⅔ **cup chopped fresh basil (2 tablespoons dried)**
2 cups chopped mushrooms
3 cups water
1¼ **cups cornmeal**
2 cups bread crumbs
¼ **cup finely grated Parmesan cheese**
½ **cup loosely packed fresh parsley leaves**
3 to 4 egg whites (3 is enough if using extra-large or jumbo eggs)

Cover the sun-dried tomatoes with the boiling water in a non-reactive heatproof bowl and set aside.

In a small saucepan, warm the olive oil and sauté the onions, ⅓ of the garlic, and ¼ teaspoon salt for about 5 minutes, until the onions soften. Add ⅓ cup of the basil and the mushrooms, cover, and cook on low heat, stirring occasionally, until the mushrooms release their juices, about 10 minutes. Drain and mince the sun-dried tomatoes, add them to the mushroom mixture, and set aside.

In a medium saucepan, bring 3 cups of water, ¾ teaspoon salt, and another ⅓ of the garlic to a boil. Whisk in the cornmeal in a slow, steady stream, stirring rapidly to prevent lumps. Lower the heat and cook, uncovered, gently for about 10 minutes, stirring often, until the polenta is quite thick. Add the mushroom mixture to the polenta and mix well.

Prepare an 8 × 12-inch glass or porcelain baking dish with a light coating of cooking spray. Spread the polenta mixture evenly in the baking dish and chill in the freezer for ½ hour or in the refrigerator for at least 1 hour. When the polenta mixture has chilled enough to hold its shape when cut, it will be very easy to handle.

While the polenta is chilling, combine the bread crumbs, Parmesan, the parsley, and the remaining garlic and basil in a food processor or blender and whirl together until well mixed. Pour out into a large deep platter. In a separate large shallow bowl, lightly beat the egg whites and remaining ¼ teaspoon salt until slightly frothy.

Preheat the oven to 400°.

Cut the chilled polenta in half lengthwise, in thirds crosswise, and then cut each rectangular sixth in half on the diagonal. This mathematical wizardry makes 12 triangular cutlets (trust us). Using a spatula, remove each triangle from the baking dish, dip it in the egg whites, and then thoroughly coat it with the bread crumb mixture. Place the breaded cutlets on a large very lightly oiled or sprayed baking tray and bake for 20 minutes. With a metal spatula, carefully turn each cutlet over and bake for 10 minutes more, until golden brown.

PER 10-OZ SERVING: 362 CALORIES, 15.0 G PROTEIN, 5.7 G FAT, 63.9 G CARBOHYDRATES, 1.8 G SATURATED FATTY ACIDS, 1.2 G POLYUNSATURATED FATTY ACIDS, 2.1 G MONOUNSATURATED FATTY ACIDS, 4 MG CHOLESTEROL, 1316 MG SODIUM, 6.6 G TOTAL DIETARY FIBER

MENU SUGGESTIONS Serve with side dishes of **Citrus-dressed Asparagus** (page 313), **Carolina Kale** (page 321), or **Seasoned Steamed Artichokes** (page 311), or present with **Giambotta** (page 263) or **Tuscan Beans with Sage** (page 168). Luscious ripe pears or bunches of black grapes make a refreshing dessert.

ANOTHER SHEPHERD'S PIE

On damp or chilly nights, this hearty casserole is especially welcome. Although the recipe may seem complicated at first, it actually breaks down into three easy pieces: the mashed potatoes, the vegetable layer, and the mushroom gravy.

If you like, you can make the casserole ahead and bake it later. Once the mashed potatoes and vegetables are layered in the baking dish, it will keep fine, covered and refrigerated, for several days. Later, just make the mushroom gravy while the casserole bakes and you have a fancy dinner in no time.

When you cook the potatoes, cover them generously with water, since you will need about 3 cups of potato stock later in the recipe.

Serves 6

Preparation time: about 1 hour

Baking time: 15 minutes

MASHED POTATOES

5 cups peeled cubed potatoes
4 garlic cloves, peeled
½ to 1 teaspoon salt

VEGETABLE LAYER

1½ cups chopped onions
2 teaspoons canola or other vegetable oil
1 cup peeled and sliced carrots
    (about ½ inch thick)
3 cups cored and sliced cauliflower
1 cup diced red or green bell peppers
½ cup kasha (page 430)
¼ cup dry red wine or sherry
2 teaspoons dried dill
½ teaspoon dried marjoram
1 tablespoon soy sauce
salt and ground black pepper to taste

MUSHROOM GRAVY

5 cups sliced mushrooms (about 12 ounces)
⅓ cup dry sherry
1½ tablespoons soy sauce
¾ teaspoon dried marjoram
2½ tablespoons cornstarch dissolved in
    2 tablespoons cold water
ground black pepper to taste

fresh parsley sprigs or sliced scallions (optional)

In a saucepan, combine the potatoes, garlic, and salt in about 5 cups of water, cover, and bring to a boil. Simmer until the potatoes are tender, about 15 minutes.

While the potatoes cook, in a large nonstick saucepan or skillet (see Note), sauté the onions in the oil for 5 minutes, stirring frequently. Add the carrots and cauliflower, cover, and sauté for another 5 minutes. Stir in the bell peppers, kasha, wine or sherry, dill, marjoram, and soy sauce.

Drain and set aside the cooked potatoes, reserving the potato stock, which you will need for the kasha, for mashing the potatoes, and for making the gravy. Add 1½ cups of the potato stock to the vegetables and kasha, cover, and simmer for about 10 minutes, until tender. Add salt and pepper to taste.

Preheat the oven to 350°.

Meanwhile, mash the potatoes in a large bowl with about ½ cup of their stock. Evenly spread the mashed potatoes on the bottom of a lightly oiled or sprayed 8 × 12-inch baking dish. Layer the vegetable and kasha mixture on top. Bake, uncovered, for 15 minutes.

While the casserole bakes, combine the mushrooms, sherry, soy sauce, marjoram, and 1½ cups of the reserved potato stock in a saucepan and simmer until the mushrooms soften and release their juices, about 10 minutes. Whisk the dissolved cornstarch into the gravy and stir continuously for a few more minutes, until it thickens. Add pepper to taste.

To serve, cut the shepherd's pie into six pieces and ladle some gravy on top of each serving. Garnish with parsley or scallions, if desired.

VARIATION Kasha adds a subtle nutty flavor to the dish, but if you prefer, it can be omitted. Replace the kasha with another 1½ cups of chopped vegetables and reduce the amount of potato stock to about ½ cup—just enough to prevent the vegetables from sticking as they sauté.

PER 11-OZ SERVING: 227 CALORIES, 6.2 G PROTEIN, 2.6 G FAT, 44.4 G CARBOHYDRATES, .4 G SATURATED FATTY ACIDS, 1.3 G POLYUNSATURATED FATTY ACIDS, .5 G MONOUNSATURATED FATTY ACIDS, 0 MG CHOLESTEROL, 699 MG SODIUM, 6.7 G TOTAL DIETARY FIBER

MENU SUGGESTIONS Serve with a light, piquant side dish, such as **Cucumbers Vinaigrette** (page 133) or **Baked Beets and Shallots** (page 314). Try **Apple Cherry Crisp** (page 385) or **Maple Walnut Biscotti** (page 390) with fresh ripe pears and hot tea under a cozy.

MUSHROOM POLENTA PIE

Here's a soothing, warm golden dish that will please everybody. Spinach or other dark greens could replace the Swiss chard if you prefer. This casserole is especially good topped with Tomato Wine Sauce (page 350). To make this recipe most efficiently, prepare the polenta first and chop the other ingredients for the dish while it simmers.

3 cups water
1 cup cornmeal
½ teaspoon salt
3 teaspoons extra-virgin olive oil
1 large onion, chopped
1 large garlic clove, minced or pressed
3 cups thinly sliced mushrooms (about 10 ounces)
4 cups stemmed and chopped Swiss chard leaves, lightly packed
dashes of salt and ground black pepper
½ cup freshly grated Parmesan cheese

Serves 4 to 6

Preparation time: 35 minutes

Baking time: 25 minutes

Bring 2 cups of the water to a boil in a medium saucepan. While the water heats, stir the remaining cup of water into the cornmeal. When the water boils, whisk the wet cornmeal into it. Add the salt and 1 teaspoon of the oil, cover, and simmer on very low heat for 20 to 25 minutes, stirring often to prevent sticking. Remove from the heat. Prepare a 7 × 12-inch nonreactive baking dish with cooking spray or a very light coating of oil. Spread the polenta evenly over the bottom of the baking dish and set aside.

Preheat the oven to 400°.

Warm the remaining 2 teaspoons of oil in a large, preferably nonstick, skillet. Add the onions and garlic and sauté on medium heat until the onions are soft, about 10 minutes, stirring occasionally. Add the mushrooms and continue to cook until they are tender and have released their juices, about 5 minutes. Stir in the Swiss chard, sprinkle with salt and pepper, and cook, stirring often, for 2 to 3 minutes, until the chard has just wilted.

Spread the sautéed vegetables evenly over the polenta and top with the Parmesan. Bake for 20 to 25 minutes, or until sizzling hot. Cool for at least 10 minutes before cutting.

PER 7-OZ SERVING: 179 CALORIES, 7.7 G PROTEIN, 6.3 G FAT, 22.9 G CARBOHYDRATES, 2.6 G SATURATED FATTY ACIDS, .5 G POLYUNSATURATED FATTY ACIDS, 2.8 G MONOUNSATURATED FATTY ACIDS, 9 MG CHOLESTEROL, 462 MG SODIUM, 2.8 G TOTAL DIETARY FIBER

MENU SUGGESTIONS Serve after **Minestrone Genoa** (page 86) or **Basque White Bean Soup** (page 103) accompanied by **Cauliflower Agrodolce** (page 318), **Baked Beets and Shallots** (page 314), **Barbecue Beans** (page 156), **Tuscan Beans with Sage** (page 168), or a tossed salad with **Italian Tomato Basil Dressing** (page 347). A crisp dessert is in order—perhaps **Chocolate Hazelnut Biscotti** (page 392) with ripe autumn apples.

EGGPLANT PARMESAN

Once you've tasted this delectable dish, you will never again be tempted to fry eggplant slices. Here, the eggplant is baked with seasoned bread crumbs and just a hint of Parmesan cheese. You can make the Tomato Wine Sauce while the eggplant bakes. Don't forget that leftover Eggplant Parmesan tucked into Italian bread makes a great sandwich.

2 large eggplants, cut crosswise into ½-inch slices
   (about 2 pounds)
4 egg whites
¼ teaspoon salt
2 cups whole wheat bread crumbs
⅓ cup finely grated Parmesan cheese
1 large garlic clove, minced or pressed
2 teaspoons dried basil
3½ cups Tomato Wine Sauce (page 350)
1 cup nonfat ricotta cheese
2 cups grated low-fat mozzarella cheese (about 8 ounces)

Serves 6 to 8

Preparation time: 1 hour

Baking time: 25 to 30 minutes

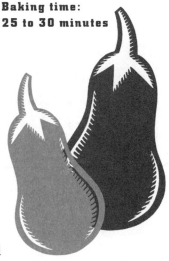

Preheat the oven to 350°.

Slice the eggplant and set aside. Find a bowl in which the eggplant rounds can lie flat and lightly beat the egg whites and salt in it. In another large bowl, combine the bread crumbs, Parmesan cheese, garlic, and basil.

Dip the eggplant slices in the egg whites, then dredge them in the bread crumb mixture to coat both sides evenly. Place the breaded slices on a baking sheet that has been prepared with cooking spray. Should you have any leftover bread crumb mixture, set it aside. Bake the eggplant for about 20 minutes on each side, until tender and easily pierced with a fork.

Spread about half of the sauce in the bottom of an 8 × 12-inch glass or nonreactive baking dish. Layer about half of the eggplant slices on top of the sauce. Spread all of the ricotta cheese evenly on the eggplant and top with about 1½ cups of the mozzarella. Use the rest of the eggplant slices for a second layer. Cover them with the remaining sauce and any extra bread crumb mixture. Sprinkle the top with the final ½ cup of mozzarella and bake, uncovered, for 25 to 30 minutes, until the cheese is melted and bubbly.

PER 9-OZ SERVING: 270 CALORIES, 19.8 G PROTEIN, 9.9 G FAT, 28.3 G CARBOHYDRATES, 4.7 G SATURATED FATTY ACIDS, .6 G POLYUNSATURATED FATTY ACIDS, 2.0 G MONOUNSATURATED FATTY ACIDS, 21 MG CHOLESTEROL, 760 MG SODIUM, 4.9 G TOTAL DIETARY FIBER

MENU SUGGESTIONS Pair with **Vegetables à la Grecque** (page 130), **Broccoli Rabe and Garlic** (page 315), **Orzo and Green Herbs** (page 183), or **Italian Roasted Vegetables** (page 226) drizzled with **Susan's Pesto** (page 364). Or, begin with **Broiled Portabella Mushrooms** (page 322) or **Savory Onion Marmalade** (page 363) on toast.

VEGETABLE FILO ROLL EXTRAVAGANZA

Garlic bread crumbs with a hint of Parmesan cheese adorn layers of crisp thin filo dough wrapped around savory vegetables into a long roll. When you slice the roll, the showy spiral-patterned servings look like the masterful work of a virtuoso. Take your bows and don't let on that it really wasn't a bit difficult.

Serves 6

Preparation time:
45 minutes

Baking time:
30 to 40 minutes

NOTE:
The filo rolls lose their delightful crispness if they sit too long. Make sure to serve them within ½ hour of removing them from the oven. It's best if you can serve them right away.

FILLING
1 cup chopped onions
1 cup peeled and julienned carrots
1 cup thinly sliced red bell peppers
1 cup julienned yellow squash or zucchini
2 cups sliced mushrooms (about 7 ounces)
¼ teaspoon dried tarragon
1 tablespoon chopped fresh basil (1 teaspoon dried)
salt and ground black pepper to taste

SEASONED BREAD CRUMBS
1 cup whole wheat bread crumbs
2 garlic cloves, pressed or minced
2 tablespoons finely grated Parmesan cheese

FILO
1 tablespoon olive oil
1 tablespoon butter
12 sheets of filo dough (⅓ package)
1 tablespoon fennel, poppy, or sesame seeds

In a covered nonstick saucepan prepared with cooking spray or 2 teaspoons of oil, sauté the onions on medium heat for 5 minutes. Add the carrots, cover, and cook for 5 minutes, stirring occasionally. Stir in the bell peppers and squash or zucchini, cover, and continue to cook for another minute. Add the mushrooms, tarragon, and basil and cook until the mushrooms release their juices and become tender, 5 to 10 minutes. Drain the vegetables and add salt and pepper to taste.

Combine the seasoned bread crumb ingredients in a bowl. Melt together the oil and butter on very low heat. Prepare a baking sheet with cooking spray or a light coating of oil.

Preheat the oven to 350°.

Place the bread crumbs and melted butter-oil mixture near the baking sheet and have a pastry brush or small clean paintbrush handy. Work quickly in a draft-free setting because the unoiled filo becomes brittle once exposed to the air. Unfold the stack of filo sheets next to the baking sheet.

To assemble the roll, take 3 sheets of filo from the stack and, in one smooth motion, lift all 3 together and lay the stack, unwrinkled, on the baking sheet. Lightly brush the top sheet with the melted butter-oil mixture. Sprinkle about ¼ of the seasoned bread crumbs over the filo sheet. Repeat the layers: 3 sheets of filo, melted butter mixture, bread crumbs, until the filo and bread crumbs are completely used.

Spread the vegetables evenly on the filo to within an inch of all four edges. Starting at one of the long sides, roll up the filo like a jelly roll, place the finished roll, seam side down, on the baking tray, and tuck in the ends. Brush with the remaining butter mixture and sprinkle with fennel, poppy, or sesame seeds. Bake for 30 to 40 minutes, until golden and puffed. Serve hot or warm (see Note).

PER 5-OZ SERVING: 183 CALORIES, 5.9 G PROTEIN, 7.2 G FAT, 25.3 G CARBOHYDRATES, 2.4 G SATURATED FATTY ACIDS, 1.1 G POLYUNSATURATED FATTY ACIDS, 3.0 G MONOUNSATURATED FATTY ACIDS, 7 MG CHOLESTEROL, 286 MG SODIUM, 4.1 G TOTAL DIETARY FIBER

MENU SUGGESTIONS Serve after **Chilled Beet and Buttermilk Soup** (page 79) or **Tomato Bulgur Soup** (page 101) and pair with **Seasoned Steamed Artichokes** (page 311), **Caesar Salad** (page 131), **Roasted Asparagus** (page 312), or lightly steamed slender green beans. End with **Dark Chocolate Pudding** (page 374) or **Lemon Pudding Cake** (page 377).

MEXICAN STUFFED PEPPERS AND TOMATOES

In an effort to think of more ways to use millet—a lovely grain—we developed this crowd-pleasing recipe. The traditional combination of black beans, corn, and chiles lends itself well to the nutty texture and taste of millet. You can stuff only peppers or only tomatoes, if you prefer, but we think that the combination is nicer. If you do stuff only peppers, add about ½ cup of water or tomato juice to the pan in place of the puréed tomatoes used here.

Serves 6

**Preparation time:
25 minutes**

**Baking time
45 to 50 minutes**

FILLING

1 cup millet

1¾ cups water

2 onions

2 large garlic cloves

1 large fresh green chile, seeds removed for a milder "hot"

2 teaspoons canola or other vegetable oil

2 teaspoons ground cumin

¾ teaspoon salt

1 medium tomato

2 cups fresh or frozen corn kernels

1½ cups cooked black beans (15-ounce can, drained)

3 to 4 tablespoons chopped fresh cilantro

salt to taste

3 large bell peppers, any color

6 large tomatoes

1 recipe Blender Hot Sauce (page 358), optional

Combine the millet and water in a medium saucepan, cover, and bring to a boil. Reduce the heat and gently simmer for 20 minutes.

While the millet cooks, chop the onions, mince or press the garlic, and seed and mince the chile. Warm the oil in a saucepan or skillet. Add the onions, garlic, chile, cumin, and ½ teaspoon of salt, cover, and cook for about 7 minutes, until the onions are soft. Chop and add the tomato, stir in the corn, cover, and cook for about 5 minutes, until all of the vegetables are tender. Add the black beans and cilantro. When the millet is ready, fluff it with a fork and stir it into the beans and vegetables. Add salt to taste and set aside.

Preheat the oven to 375°.

Cut the peppers in half lengthwise. Remove the seeds but leave the stem ends on so that the peppers will hold their shape during baking. Slice off and reserve the tops of the tomatoes, then remove and discard the cores. Being careful not to pierce the outer shell, scoop out the seeds and pulp with a small spoon. Combine the seeds and pulp, tomato tops, and ¼ teaspoon of salt in a blender or food processor and purée until smooth. Set aside.

Stuff each pepper half and each tomato with about ¾ cup of filling and place in a nonreactive baking pan. Pour the tomato purée around the stuffed vegetables, cover the pan tightly, and bake for about 45 minutes, until the peppers and tomatoes are tender and the filling is hot.

Serve the stuffed vegetables with some of the cooking juices spooned over them and top with Blender Hot Sauce, if you like.

PER 16-OZ SERVING: 330 CALORIES, 11.8 G PROTEIN, 4.8 G FAT, 64.4 G CARBOHYDRATES, .7 G SATURATED FATTY ACIDS, 2.4 G POLYUNSATURATED FATTY ACIDS, 1.0 G MONOUNSATURATED FATTY ACIDS, 0 MG CHOLESTEROL, 578 MG SODIUM, 7.5 G TOTAL DIETARY FIBER

MENU SUGGESTIONS Nibble on crudités dipped in **Guacamole with Cottage Cheese** (page 26) before the meal. Serve with **Sweet Potato Oven "Fries"** (page 326) and **Spinach Avocado Grapefruit Salad** (page 135). Try **Dark Chocolate Pudding** (page 374) or **Pumpkin Custard** (page 376) for dessert.

MIDDLE EASTERN TOFU-STUFFED PEPPERS

Stuffed vegetables in the Middle East would traditionally be filled with some kind of ground meat. At Moosewood, we use frozen tofu to create a chewy but light vegetarian main dish. These peppers are especially delicious served on a bed of rice and topped with Chunky Tomato Sauce (page 351) and a sprinkling of grated feta cheese.

Serves 4

Preparation time: 30 minutes, once the tofu is frozen and thawed

Baking time: 45 to 50 minutes

2 teaspoons canola or other vegetable oil
2 large garlic cloves, minced or pressed
1½ cups diced onions
pinch of cayenne
½ teaspoon ground cinnamon
1⅔ cups peeled and diced carrots
dash of salt
1 cup diced tomatoes
1½ cups grated frozen tofu (12-ounce cake) (page 419)
3 tablespoons soy sauce
1 tablespoon chopped fresh dill (1 teaspoon dried)
2 teaspoons fresh lemon juice
½ cup couscous
¼ cup hot water
3 tablespoons currants or raisins
4 large bell peppers
2 cups tomato juice

Warm the oil in a medium saucepan, add the garlic, onions, cayenne, and cinnamon, and sauté for 3 minutes. Add the carrots, sprinkle with salt, cover, and cook for 3 minutes. Add the tomatoes and cook for 2 minutes, until the carrots are just tender. Stir in the tofu, soy sauce, dill, lemon juice, couscous, and water and cook on low to medium heat for 2 minutes, stirring often. Cover tightly, remove from the heat, and set aside. After about 5 minutes, add the currants or raisins and adjust the seasonings if necessary.

Preheat the oven to 375°.

Cut the peppers in half lengthwise. Remove the seeds but leave the stem ends on so that the peppers will hold their shape during baking. Fill each pepper half with about ½ cup of filling and place it in a nonreactive baking dish. Pour the tomato juice into the bottom of the baking dish, cover tightly, and bake for 45 to 50 minutes, until the peppers are tender.

PER 14-OZ SERVING: 301 CALORIES, 14.2 G PROTEIN, 7.2 G FAT, 49.9 G CARBOHYDRATES, 1.0 G SATURATED FATTY ACIDS, 4.0 G POLYUNSATURATED FATTY ACIDS, 1.5 G MONOUNSATURATED FATTY ACIDS, 0 MG CHOLESTEROL, 1182 MG SODIUM, 6.8 G TOTAL DIETARY FIBER

MENU SUGGESTIONS Serve with cucumber slices topped with **Yogurt Tahini Dressing** (page 346) and **Seasoned Steamed Artichokes** (page 311). End with **Lemon Pudding Cake** (page 377).

MUSHROOM- AND SPINACH-STUFFED ZUCCHINI

Rich, savory portabella mushrooms and bright-tasting spinach combined with rice, sherry, extra-virgin olive oil, and dill make a dramatic filling for these zucchini boats.

3 medium zucchini
1 cup minced onions
2 large garlic cloves, pressed or minced
½ teaspoon salt
1 teaspoon extra-virgin olive oil
3 cups chopped portabella mushrooms, caps and tender stems
1 teaspoon dried dill
1 tablespoon dry sherry
2 teaspoons soy sauce
5 ounces spinach (5 cups, lightly packed)
1 cup cooked brown rice
salt and ground black pepper to taste
¾ cup tomato juice
½ cup grated fontina cheese

Serves 3

Preparation time: 30 minutes

Baking time: 30 minutes

Slice the zucchini in half lengthwise and, using a small spoon, scoop out the insides of the zucchini to leave a fillable shell.
Set aside.

In a skillet, sauté the onions, garlic, and salt in the oil on low heat, stirring often, until the onions soften. Add the mushrooms, dill, sherry, and soy sauce and cook for about 5 more minutes. When the mushrooms are just tender, remove from the heat and set aside.

Preheat the oven to 350°.

While the mushrooms are cooking, rinse and stem the spinach. In a saucepan, steam the spinach leaves in enough water to cover until wilted but still bright green. Drain and add it to the sautéed vegetables. Stir in the rice and add salt and pepper to taste.

Pour the tomato juice evenly around the bottom of an unoiled 8 × 12-inch glass or nonreactive baking dish. Press and mound ⅙ of the filling into each zucchini shell and arrange them in the baking dish. Sprinkle on the grated cheese, cover the pan tightly with foil, and bake for about 30 minutes, until the zucchini are tender and easily pierced with a fork. Uncover and bake for another 5 to 10 minutes, until the tops are browned.

PER 12-OZ SERVING: 236 CALORIES, 10.6 G PROTEIN, 8.5 G FAT, 31.8 G CARBOHYDRATES, 4.0 G SATURATED FATTY ACIDS, .8 G POLYUNSATURATED FATTY ACIDS, 3.0 G MONOUNSATURATED FATTY ACIDS, 22 MG CHOLESTEROL, 1030 MG SODIUM, 5.1 G TOTAL DIETARY FIBER

MENU SUGGESTIONS Serve with **Roasted Asparagus** (page 312), **Seasoned Steamed Artichokes** (page 311), or mixed salad greens with **Orange Tarragon Dressing** (page 348).

SAVORY INDIAN SWEET POTATOES

Creamy, sweet, and spicy, these stuffed potatoes are rich and satisfying. When you're baking sweet potatoes for another meal, put in a few extras so you'll have some prebaked for this dish. Serve on plain rice or Golden Basmati Rice (page 185) topped with Fresh Tomato Salsa (page 360) or Mango Peach Chutney (page 362) and, if desired, a dollop of nonfat yogurt.

2 large sweet potatoes
1 cup diced onions
⅓ cup water, unsweetened apple juice, or orange juice
3 garlic cloves, minced or pressed
1½ tablespoons grated fresh ginger root
2 teaspoons ground cumin
1 minced small fresh green chile,
    seeds removed for a milder "hot"
⅔ cup diced red and/or green bell peppers
3 tablespoons Neufchâtel (low-fat cream cheese)
1½ tablespoons fresh lemon juice
½ cup fresh or slightly thawed frozen green peas
salt and ground black pepper to taste

Serves 2 as a main dish, 4 as a side dish

Preparation time: 15 minutes

Baking time: 80 minutes

> **NOTE:**
> If you are stuffing previously baked, chilled potatoes, they may need to bake an extra 5 to 10 minutes in the oven to heat through.

Bake the sweet potatoes at 400° for about 1 hour, or until tender.

While the potatoes bake, combine the onions and water or juice in a medium saucepan. Cover, and simmer until the onions soften, about 5 minutes. Add the garlic, ginger, cumin, chile, and bell peppers, cover, and simmer until the peppers are tender, about 5 minutes. Remove from the heat. Cut the Neufchâtel into small pieces and stir it into the hot vegetable mixture to melt. Set aside.

When the sweet potatoes are baked, cut them in half lengthwise. Hold each potato half with a heavy towel or mitt in one hand and scoop out the central part of the flesh with a spoon. Leave about a ¼-inch shell so that the potatoes maintain their shape. Mix the potato flesh with the vegetable-cheese mixture. Add the lemon juice, peas, and salt and pepper.

Lower the oven temperature to 350°.

Stuff the potato shells with the filling. Place them in a lightly oiled baking dish. Cover and bake for 15 to 20 minutes (see Note), until thoroughly hot.

PER 7-OZ SERVING: 164 CALORIES, 4.3 G PROTEIN, 4.5 G FAT, 28.4 G CARBOHYDRATES, .1 G SATURATED FATTY ACIDS, .2 G POLYUNSATURATED FATTY ACIDS, 0 G MONOUNSATURATED FATTY ACIDS, 0 MG CHOLESTEROL, 118 MG SODIUM, 4.3 G TOTAL DIETARY FIBER

MENU SUGGESTIONS Serve to follow **Tropical Gazpacho** (page 78) or **Golden Split Pea Soup** (page 92) or accompany with **Lentil Salad** (page 151). For dessert, choose **Banana Bundt Cake** (page 382).

STUFFED BAKED POTATOES

Potatoes are high in complex carbohydrates and vitamin C and have no fat or cholesterol. Here are two fillings, one with bright Italian flair, the other with a Southwestern attitude.

4 baking potatoes (see Note)

Serves 4

Preparation time: 20 to 25 minutes

Baking time: 1¼ hours

NOTE:
Both stuffings work well in sweet potatoes, too.

SPICY BROCCOLI STUFFING

4 garlic cloves, pressed or minced

⅛ teaspoon hot pepper flakes

2 teaspoons olive oil

1 bunch broccoli or broccoli rabe, minced (about 4 cups)

1 cup water

CORN AND BEAN STUFFING

2 cups corn kernels

1 cup cooked pinto beans

2 cups prepared Mexican-style red salsa

½ cup chopped fresh cilantro (optional)

salt and ground black pepper to taste

8 pitted black olives, sliced

Preheat the oven to 400°. Slice the potatoes in half lengthwise and bake, cut side down, on a baking sheet for about 45 minutes, until soft. Remove from the oven.

For Spicy Broccoli Stuffing, sauté the garlic and pepper flakes in the oil for 1 minute. Add the broccoli and water, cover, and simmer for about 15 minutes. For Corn and Bean Stuffing, combine the corn, beans, salsa, and cilantro and mix well.

When the potato halves are cool, scoop out the centers, leaving ¼ inch of pulp on the skin. Mash the scooped-out potato pulp and stir it into the stuffing. Add salt and pepper. Refill the potato skins and bake for 30 minutes. Sprinkle with sliced olives and serve.

SPICY BROCCOLI STUFFED BAKED POTATOES PER 10-OZ SERVING: 228 CALORIES, 5.9 G PROTEIN, 5.7 G FAT, 41.4 G CARBOHYDRATES, .7 G SATURATED FATTY ACIDS, .4 G POLYUNSATURATED FATTY ACIDS, 1.8 G MONOUNSATURATED FATTY ACIDS, 0 MG CHOLESTEROL, 333 MG SODIUM, 5.9 G TOTAL DIETARY FIBER

CORN AND BEAN STUFFED BAKED POTATOES PER 15-OZ SERVING: 366 CALORIES, 11.8 G PROTEIN, 4.3 G FAT, 75.8 G CARBOHYDRATES, .6 G SATURATED FATTY ACIDS, .7 G POLYUNSATURATED FATTY ACIDS, .4 G MONOUNSATURATED FATTY ACIDS, 0 MG CHOLESTEROL, 778 MG SODIUM, 10.9 G TOTAL DIETARY FIBER

MENU SUGGESTIONS Serve Spicy Broccoli Stuffed Baked Potatoes beside **Tuscan Beans with Sage** (page 168) or **Broiled Portabella Mushrooms** (page 322).

For Corn and Bean Stuffed Baked Potatoes, try **Curried Carrot Parsnip Soup** (page 100) and tossed salad with **Cumin Yogurt Dressing** (page 132).

POTATO CHEESE GNOCCHI

These luscious "dumplings" are flecked with basil and seasoned with garlic. The actual hands-on time for making gnocchi is quite short, but since cooking and chilling times are required, you will need to plan ahead for this treat.

Serve Potato Cheese Gnocchi topped with our Tomato Wine Sauce (page 350) or Creamy Roasted Red Pepper Sauce (page 355). Or use them to enrich almost any brothy soup.

Serves 6 to 8

Makes about 60 balls

Baking the potatoes: 45 minutes

Preparation time: 10 minutes

Chilling time: 2 hours

Cooking time: 6 to 8 minutes per batch

NOTE:
Uncooked gnocchi dough balls will keep refrigerated in a covered, lightly oiled bowl for 2 or 3 days; frozen, the dough keeps for about a week. Allow the dough balls to return to room temperature before cooking.

Wrapped and refrigerated, cooked gnocchi keep for 2 or 3 days and can be frozen for 1 to 2 weeks or possibly longer. To serve, bring them to room temperature and then simmer in water or broth for a few minutes.

2 baked Idaho potatoes, peeled (about 1½ cups)
2 teaspoons chopped fresh basil (½ teaspoon dried)
2 garlic cloves, minced or pressed
½ teaspoon salt
1½ cups unbleached white flour
½ cup nonfat ricotta cheese or 1% cottage cheese
2 egg whites
½ cup grated Parmesan cheese

Place the potatoes, basil, garlic, salt, flour, ricotta or cottage cheese, egg whites, and Parmesan in a food processor bowl and blend for about 1 minute, until a sticky dough is formed. If necessary, stop and scrape the sides of the bowl with a spatula to help blend well. Transfer the dough to a lightly oiled bowl, cover, and refrigerate for 2 hours.

Turn out the chilled dough onto a well-floured surface. With floured hands, divide the dough into four sections and shape each section into a log about 1 inch in diameter. With a sharp knife, cut each log into 1-inch rounds. Using your palms, shape the rounds into balls and arrange them in a single layer on a floured platter.

Bring one or more large pots of salted water to a rapid boil and cook the gnocchi in small batches for 6 to 8 minutes per batch. Cook only as many gnocchi as can rise to the surface of the water without sticking together. Carefully remove the gnocchi with a slotted spoon to a warmed serving bowl. Keep the first batches warm in a 250° oven while you finish the final batches.

PER 3.20-OZ SERVING: 164 CALORIES, 9.2 G PROTEIN, 2.9 G FAT, 24.7 G CARBOHYDRATES, 1.8 G SATURATED FATTY ACIDS, .2 G POLYUNSATURATED FATTY ACIDS, .8 G MONOUNSATURATED FATTY ACIDS, 7 MG CHOLESTEROL, 384 MG SODIUM, .7 G TOTAL DIETARY FIBER

CURRIED POTATO CABBAGE ROLL-UPS

Samosas are an Indian favorite, deep-fried pastries with a spicy potato-vegetable filling. Our lighter version features a similar savory filling, but the tortillas provide a low-fat wrapper.

1 cup diced onions
½ teaspoon canola or other vegetable oil
1 garlic clove, minced or pressed
1 small fresh green chile, minced, seeds removed
   for a milder "hot"
½ teaspoon ground cinnamon
½ teaspoon ground dried mustard
½ teaspoon turmeric
¼ teaspoon ground cardamom
2 cups chopped cabbage
½ cup water
2 cups cubed potatoes (½-inch cubes)
1 cup cooked chickpeas (11-ounce can, drained)
salt to taste
4 eight-inch flour tortillas

**Serves 2 as a main dish,
4 as an appetizer**

**Preparation time:
25 to 30 minutes**

**Baking time:
10 to 20 minutes**

> **NOTE:**
> To save time, stack the tortillas, wrap tightly in foil, and heat for 10 minutes at 350° while the filling simmers. Then assemble and serve immediately.

Preheat the oven to 350°.

In a saucepan, sauté the onions in the oil on medium heat for 2 or 3 minutes. Add the garlic, chile, cinnamon, mustard, turmeric, cardamom, cabbage, and ¼ cup of the water. Cover and cook for 5 minutes, stirring occasionally. Add the rest of the water and the potatoes, cover, and simmer, stirring now and then, until the vegetables are tender, about 10 minutes (see Note). Stir in the chickpeas and salt to taste.

Place about ¼ of the filling on the lower half of each tortilla, roll it up, and lay it, seam side down, in a baking dish prepared with a very light coating of oil or cooking spray. Place a clean damp towel on top of the roll-ups, tightly cover the pan with aluminum foil, and bake for about 20 minutes, until thoroughly hot.

PER 10-OZ SERVING: 277 CALORIES, 8.1 G PROTEIN, 3.5 G FAT, 54.9 G CARBOHYDRATES, .2 G SATURATED FATTY ACIDS, .8 G POLYUNSATURATED FATTY ACIDS, .4 G MONOUNSATURATED FATTY ACIDS, 0 MG CHOLESTEROL, 281 MG SODIUM, 5.8 G TOTAL DIETARY FIBER

MENU SUGGESTIONS Serve on a bed of rice beside **Mango Peach Chutney** (page 362) or **Tomato Pineapple Salsa** (page 360) or top with chopped fresh tomatoes and a dollop of either plain nonfat yogurt or **Yogurt Tahini Dressing** (page 346). **Carrot Orange Salad** (page 134) is a colorful and refreshing accompaniment. Dessert might be **Mango-Banana Shake** (page 65).

Swiss Chard Rolls Two Ways

Here are not one but two versions of stuffed Swiss chard rolls, one with a hearty grain and mushroom filling, the other with a low-fat cheese filling. Once you have the knack for folding the chard leaves into little packages, the preparation is quite effortless.

Anytime you have leftover bulgur and/or rice, remember they're perfect for the mushroom filling. If you're cooking the rice and bulgur especially for this dish, prepare the Swiss chard leaves and the rest of the mushroom filling while the rice simmers and the bulgur soaks. You will need ⅓ cup of raw rice and ⅜ cup of raw bulgur.

For entertaining or festive occasions, serve both kinds of rolls; they complement one another nicely.

12 large Swiss chard leaves

Serves 4 to 6

**Preparation time
(with mushroom filling):
30 minutes**

**Preparation time
(with cheese filling):
40 minutes**

**Baking time:
30 to 40 minutes**

Mushroom Filling
1 cup finely chopped onions
4 garlic cloves, minced or pressed
1 teaspoon olive oil
1 celery stalk, chopped
½ teaspoon dried marjoram
1 cup sliced mushrooms (about 4 ounces)
1 tablespoon dry sherry
1 tablespoon soy sauce
½ teaspoon dried dill
pinch of thyme
1 cup cooked bulgur
1 cup cooked brown rice
2 tablespoons currants
1 tablespoon fresh lemon juice

Cheese Filling
2 leeks, well-rinsed and minced (about 1½ cups)
1 teaspoon olive oil
dash of salt
3 scallions, minced
1½ pounds 1% cottage cheese (about 3 cups)
2 tablespoons chopped fresh basil
salt and ground black pepper to taste

2 large tomatoes, sliced (optional)
1 cup tomato juice

nonfat sour cream or yogurt (optional)

Remove and discard the stems and any tough ribs of the Swiss chard. Blanch the leaves in boiling water for 3 or 4 minutes, until pliable. Set aside.

To prepare the mushroom filling, sauté the onions and garlic in the oil for 3 minutes. Add the celery and marjoram, cover, and cook on medium heat for 5 to 10 minutes, until the vegetables are softened. Stir in the mushrooms, sherry, soy sauce, dill, and thyme and simmer until the mushrooms are tender and juicy. Remove from the heat and stir in the bulgur, rice, currants, and lemon juice.

To prepare the cheese filling, sauté the leeks in oil for 2 minutes. Sprinkle with salt, cover, and continue to cook for 5 to 10 minutes, until tender and bright green, stirring often to prevent sticking. Remove from the heat. Add the scallions, cottage cheese, basil, and salt and pepper to taste and mix well.

Preheat the oven to 350°.

Prepare a 9 × 12-inch nonreactive baking dish with a very light coating of oil or cooking spray. Cover the bottom with the tomato slices, if using, and set aside.

Place about ¼ cup of the filling in the center of each Swiss chard leaf. Fold the sides of each leaf toward the center, and then roll it up from the stem end to the tip to form a neat little package. Place the rolls, seam side down, in the baking dish, pour the tomato juice over them, and cover tightly with aluminum foil. Bake for 30 to 40 minutes, until heated through. Serve the rolls with some pan juices spooned over the top and, if desired, garnish with a dollop of nonfat sour cream or yogurt.

SWISS CHARD ROLLS WITH MUSHROOM FILLING PER 7-OZ SERVING: 108 CALORIES, 3.7 G PROTEIN, 1.3 G FAT, 22.0 G CARBOHYDRATES, .2 G SATURATED FATTY ACIDS, .2 G POLYUNSATURATED FATTY ACIDS, .7 G MONOUNSATURATED FATTY ACIDS, 0 MG CHOLESTEROL, 362 MG SODIUM, 3.3 G TOTAL DIETARY FIBER

SWISS CHARD ROLLS WITH CHEESE FILLING PER 8-OZ SERVING: 125 CALORIES, 15.9 G PROTEIN, 2.1 G FAT, 11.3 G CARBOHYDRATES, .9 G SATURATED FATTY ACIDS, .2 G POLYUNSATURATED FATTY ACIDS, .9 G MONOUNSATURATED FATTY ACIDS, 5 MG CHOLESTEROL, 744 MG SODIUM, 1.9 G TOTAL DIETARY FIBER

MENU SUGGESTIONS Serve mushroom-filled Swiss Chard Rolls after **Cream of Cauliflower Soup** (page 90), **Chilled Beet and Buttermilk Soup** (page 79), or **Greek Lima Bean Dip** (page 23) with crudités. Serve **Carrot Orange Salad** (page 134) with the main dish.

Serve cheese-filled Swiss Chard Rolls with **Bulgur Rice Pilaf** (page 188), **Mediterranean Couscous Salad** (page 144), or **Mustard Carrots** (page 317). **Apple Apricot Strudel** (page 384) is a great dessert for either version of the rolls.

FRESH SPRING ROLLS

These little Vietnamese classics are crisp, coolly refreshing, and very pretty—the colors of the filling shine through the translucent wrappers. You can either present them finished on a platter or have the filling and wrappers ready and let everyone assemble their own.

We have given suggested amounts of filling for the rolls, but judging exactly the right amount comes only with practice. In general, it's better to err on the conservative side, as rolls that are stuffed too full are more difficult to roll and more likely to break open.

Having a few extra rice paper wrappers on hand is a good idea, since some may split while you are working with them.

Serves 6

Makes 12 rolls

Total time: 1 hour,
if the cook makes all
the rolls

> **NOTE:**
> To soften several discs before beginning to fill them, soften each one individually, and arrange on the towel side by side; don't stack them because they will stick together.

FILLING

3 ounces rice vermicelli *

2 to 3 cups shredded lettuce

1 cup minced scallions

1 cup peeled and shredded carrots

1 cup thinly sliced red bell peppers

24 medium-sized cooked shrimp (about 12 ounces),
   or 1¼ cups tofu-kan (page 439) strips (about 6 ounces),
   or 1½ cups shredded surimi or other seafood
   (about 8 ounces)

½ cup chopped fresh basil or cilantro, or a mixture

¼ cup chopped toasted peanuts (optional)

12 rice paper discs (see Note)
dipping sauce

Rice vermicelli may also be called rice "sticks" or noodles. Rice paper discs may also be called "spring roll wrappers." Both are available in Asian markets. We use discs that are 8 to 10 inches in diameter.

Place the rice vermicelli in a heatproof bowl, cover with boiling water, and set aside for 10 to 12 minutes, until soft. Drain well.

Assemble all of the filling ingredients, then dampen a clean dishcloth and lay it flat on a work surface.

Fill a large bowl with hot water. Holding a fragile rice paper disc by the edge, gently lower one side of it into the hot water—it will soften as it absorbs water. Slowly turn the disc in the water until it has completely softened, taking care not to force it or it may crack. Place the disc on the damp towel and flatten it out (see Note).

Using about 3 tablespoons of noodles, make a small bed of rice vermicelli just below the center of the disc (above the 6 o'clock position on a clock face). Top the noodles with 1 or 2 tablespoons of lettuce, a pinch of scallions, a sprinkling of carrots, 1 or 2 bell pepper strips, and finally either 2 shrimp, a few tofu-kan strips, or a spoonful of surimi or other seafood. Sprinkle on some basil and/or cilantro and chopped peanuts, if desired.

Fold the two side edges of the disc over the filling to form a rectangular shape with curved ends. Roll up from the bottom to make a neat little package. Place, seam side down, on a platter.

Soften and fill each of the remaining rice paper discs, cover with plastic wrap, and chill until ready to serve.

Serve with hoisin sauce thinned with a little water or with any simple dipping sauce of your choice. We make one by stirring 1½ tablespoons of brown sugar into ¼ cup of soy sauce and 2 tablespoons of rice vinegar or lime juice until dissolved.

PER 7.50-OZ SERVING: 234 CALORIES, 15.9 G PROTEIN, 1.0 G FAT, 39.8 G CARBOHYDRATES, .2 G SATURATED FATTY ACIDS, .4 G POLYUNSATURATED FATTY ACIDS, .1 G MONOUNSATURATED FATTY ACIDS, 111 MG CHOLESTEROL, 861 MG SODIUM, 2.0 G TOTAL DIETARY FIBER

MENU SUGGESTIONS Serve with **Vietnamese Hot and Sour Soup** (page 87), **Mango Coconut Cucumber Salad** (page 136), **Japanese Sesame Spinach** (page 330), or **Zucchini with Cilantro Sauce** (page 335). Or offer as an appetizer before **Southeast Asian Fish Rolls** (page 294) or **Watercress Omelet** (page 53). Complete this light, delicate meal with **Fruit-filled Meringue Shells** (page 388).

CABBAGE ROLLS

A luscious mushroom and tofu filling rolled in cabbage leaves: stuffed cabbage goes Moosewood. We almost always serve these on a bed of cooked brown rice.

Serves 6 to 8

**Preparation time:
35 minutes**

**Baking time:
20 minutes**

NOTE:

If you use Chinese cabbage, pull off 12 large leaves and blanch them for about 2 minutes.

1 large head green cabbage or Chinese cabbage (see Note)
2 medium onions
2 teaspoons olive oil
3½ cups chopped mushrooms
1 cup grated carrots
6 garlic cloves, minced or pressed
¼ teaspoon dried thyme
½ teaspoon dried dill
¼ cup minced fresh parsley
1 tablespoon fresh lemon juice
2 tablespoons soy sauce
1 tablespoon miso
12-ounce cake tofu, pressed and mashed (page 419)
1 cup tomato juice

Bring a large pot of water to a boil. Meanwhile, core the green cabbage and finely chop the onions. Carefully plunge the cabbage into the boiling water, cover, and cook for about 5 minutes or until the leaves pull away easily from the head. (Use two forks to test the readiness of the cabbage, one to steady the head in the water and the other to try to loosen a test leaf). Set aside 12 leaves to cool while you prepare the filling.

In a large skillet, sauté the onions in the oil for about 10 minutes, until translucent. Add the mushrooms, carrots, and garlic and cook, stirring often, for 3 minutes. Stir in the thyme, dill, and parsley and continue to cook until the mushrooms become soft and juicy. Add the lemon juice, soy sauce, miso, and mashed tofu and mix well. When the tofu is heated through, remove from the heat and set aside.

Preheat the oven to 350°.

Assemble the rolls. Put about ½ cup of filling at the broad end of each cabbage leaf, fold the side edges toward the center over the filling, and then roll up lengthwise. Place the rolls, seam side down, in an unoiled 9 × 12-inch baking pan and pour the tomato juice over them. Cover the pan tightly with foil and bake for 20 minutes, or until hot and steaming.

PER 8-OZ SERVING: 101 CALORIES, 6.1 G PROTEIN, 4.0 G FAT, 12.9 G CARBOHYDRATES, .6 G SATURATED FATTY ACIDS, 1.6 G POLYUNSATURATED FATTY ACIDS, 1.4 G MONOUNSATURATED FATTY ACIDS, 0 MG CHOLESTEROL, 394 MG SODIUM, 5.1 G TOTAL DIETARY FIBER

MENU SUGGESTIONS Serve on rice or noodles topped with either **Chunky Tomato Sauce** (page 351) or **Creamy Roasted Red Pepper Sauce** (page 355), and alongside **Mustard Carrots** (page 317) or **Baked Beets and Shallots** (page 314). Follow with a salad with **Honey Mustard Garlic Dressing** (page 342) and try **Tapioca Fruit Parfaits** (page 375) for dessert.

If you decide to make **Cabbage Rolls** with **Baked Beets and Shallots**, prepare the beets and put them in the oven. While they bake, you should have time to both prepare the cabbage rolls and put them in the oven with the beets for the final 20 minutes of baking—then both dishes will be ready to serve simultaneously.

giambotta 263

french vegetable bean stew 264

CARIBBEAN STEW 265

greek stew 266

mediterranean stew 267

THAI VEGETABLE CURRY 268

ukrainian beet and bean stew 269

armenian stew with pilaf 270

THREE SISTERS STEW 272

creole stew 273

persian split pea and barley stew 274

QUINOA VEGETABLE STEW 276

mushroom sesame tofu stew 277

wild mushroom stew trieste 278

SOUTHWESTERN HOMINY STEW 279

STEWS

Hearty **STEWS** are a great way to enjoy vegetables and legumes. Besides their nutritional value, stews offer a tempting assortment of textures, can be as plain or spicy as you like, and pair well with a wide variety of grains. The robust, unassuming meals in this chapter range from the rustic Greek Stew to the elegant Wild Mushroom Stew Trieste and feature fresh vegetables—best at the peak of the season.

Stews can be made frequently and with ease using whatever vegetables are available at any time of the year. As stew simmers, the different shapes, colors, and flavors of the vegetables and sauce slowly mingle into one collective dish, creating an interesting, colorful mélange with a dense, sometimes intense, flavor that is rich and filling.

Like soups, stews are a comforting, homey, and convenient one-dish meal that can be tasty and satisfying without adding much, if any, fat. At Moosewood, we cut stew vegetables into large-sized chunks—rather than the smaller bite-sized pieces used for soups or pilafs—to preserve the integrity of the vegetables. Slow cooking encourages the aromatic vegetables to release their juices, making a variety of sauces possible. The choice of the sauce and seasonings gives a stew its character, from the milder French Vegetable Bean Stew and Mediterranean Stew, to sparky Caribbean Stew and Creole Stew, to the more unusual flavors of Giambotta and Ukrainian Beet and Bean Stew.

For a basic stew, begin with a little oil and water and cook onions, garlic, herbs, and spices until soft and aromatic. Cut vegetables into large, uniform chunks and cook them just until tender. You don't want a delicate zucchini to dissolve into mush while the carrots are still crunchy, so add the carrots to the pot first and when they are at the crisp-tender stage, add the zucchini. In general, dense root vegetables such as carrots, parsnips, and beets need a longer time to cook than juicier ones such as tomatoes, zucchini, summer squash, and bell peppers.

As the vegetables simmer, a sweet and savory sauce begins to develop from their mingling juices. To create more sauce, add liquid to the stew. In most of our recipes, we use fresh or canned tomatoes or tomato juice, or occasionally stock or wine; and in one of our recipes, Thai Vegetable Curry, we use pineapple juice. As a thickener, we might add soft, creamy vegetables, such as potatoes, yams, squash, beans, or split peas. Tahini or peanut butter thickens Mushroom Sesame Tofu Stew, and cornmeal adds body to Three Sisters Stew. Hominy thickens Southwestern Hominy Stew, and yellow split peas add a natural density to Persian Split Pea and Barley Stew.

When the fat is all but eliminated, we need to look for other ways to heighten the flavor and richness of stews. All of our recipes suggest generous amounts of herbs and spices to intensify the character, aroma, and taste. Wild Mushroom Stew Trieste calls for the addition of sauerkraut, and Greek Stew features lemon and kasseri cheese. Many of our stews are made more substantial with whole grains: Armenian Stew is served with bulgur pilaf, and Quinoa Vegetable Stew goes naturally with the quick-cooking nutty, crunchy grain from Central and South America, quinoa.

Many stews taste even better the next day, so you can cook them ahead to reheat for dinner or make them in quantity for later in the week. Given a little extra time, the flavors of many stews become more complex, melded, and developed, which adds to their appeal. At Moosewood, we think stews are one of the most convenient, substantial, easy one-pot (and easy cleanup) meals around for busy people on the go.

GIAMBOTTA

This colorful, hearty Italian stew is a cousin of French ratatouille. We find that using less oil than is traditional allows the flavors of the vegetables and herbs to stand out more clearly. Although fresh fennel can be difficult to find sometimes, include it if you can for its mild, yet distinctive touch. Giambotta sits well and often tastes just as good or better the next day when the flavors have mingled. It can be served hot or cold.

2 garlic cloves, minced
2 medium onions, chopped
¼ teaspoon salt
2 teaspoons olive oil
1 small eggplant
3 small potatoes
1 fresh fennel bulb, thinly sliced
    (bulb part only, not the stems and fronds) (optional)
1 red bell pepper
1 medium zucchini
3 fresh tomatoes
¼ cup chopped fresh basil (1½ tablespoons dried)
salt and ground black pepper to taste

Serves 3 or 4

Preparation time: 25 minutes

Cooking time: 45 minutes

In a covered soup pot on low heat, sweat the garlic, onions, and salt in the oil for 5 to 7 minutes, stirring frequently, until the onions are translucent. Chop and add to the pot in the following order the eggplant, potatoes, the fennel, if using, the bell pepper, zucchini, and tomatoes. If using dried basil, sprinkle it into the pot now. Increase the heat slightly. Simmer for about 40 minutes or until the vegetables are tender. Stir in the fresh basil, if using, and add salt and pepper to taste.

PER 11-OZ SERVING: 180 CALORIES, 4.8 G PROTEIN, 3.4 G FAT, 36.5 G CARBO-HYDRATES, .5 G SATURATED FATTY ACIDS, .6 G POLYUNSATURATED FATTY ACIDS, 1.9 G MONOUNSATURATED FATTY ACIDS, 0 MG CHOLESTEROL, 219 MG SODIUM, 6.7 G TOTAL DIETARY FIBER

MENU SUGGESTIONS Serve with an Italian or sourdough bread with **Roasted Garlic** (page 43) or **Broiled Portabella Mushrooms** (page 322). Accompany with a tossed salad with **Italian Tomato Basil Dressing** (page 347) or **Apple Basil Dressing** (page 348). Try **Chocolate Hazelnut Biscotti** (page 392) with fresh fruit for dessert.

NOTE:
If you have the time and inclination, try baking the eggplant instead of stewing it. Baking gives it a rich, pronounced flavor and texture. To bake the eggplant, slice it in half lengthwise, score the flesh of each half, and place the halves, cut side down, on a lightly oiled baking sheet. Bake at 350° for 20 minutes, or until the eggplant is soft and the skin has shriveled. Remove it from the oven, cool slightly, and cut into cubes. Stir the eggplant into the simmering stew about 5 minutes before serving.

FRENCH VEGETABLE BEAN STEW

Tarragon is one of the few herbs that survives our winters here in Ithaca, so in the early spring when we spy its first soft leaves full of the promise of warm summer days and nights, we are inspired to create dishes in its honor. Tarragon should always be used fresh, and luckily this is more and more possible for those without gardens, since fresh tarragon has become widely available in supermarkets.

2 teaspoons olive oil
2½ cups chopped leeks, white and tender green parts
4 large garlic cloves, minced or pressed
2 teaspoons ground fennel
½ teaspoon salt
3 cups cubed potatoes
    (about 2 medium potatoes)
3 cups undrained canned tomatoes, chopped
    (28-ounce can)
½ cup dry white wine
1½ cups peeled carrot chunks
1½ to 2 cups cooked Great Northern or
    other white beans (15-ounce can, drained)
2 to 3 tablespoons minced fresh tarragon
3 tablespoons minced fresh parsley

Serves 4 to 6

Total time: 45 minutes

In a soup pot, warm the olive oil. Add the leeks, garlic, fennel, and salt, cover, and cook for 10 minutes on medium-low heat, stirring occasionally. Add the potatoes, tomatoes, and wine, cover the pot, and simmer for 10 minutes, stirring a few times. Add the carrots, cover, and gently simmer, until the vegetables are tender. (The cooking time will vary depending on how small you have cut your vegetables.) Add the beans, tarragon, and parsley and stir gently for 2 or 3 minutes until the stew is thoroughly hot.

PER 10-OZ SERVING: 240 CALORIES, 8.2 G PROTEIN, 2.4 G FAT, 45.6 G CARBOHYDRATES, .3 G SATURATED FATTY ACIDS, .4 G POLYUNSATURATED FATTY ACIDS, 1.2 G MONOUNSATURATED FATTY ACIDS, 0 MG CHOLESTEROL, 384 MG SODIUM, 6.3 G TOTAL DIETARY FIBER

MENU SUGGESTIONS Serve with **Buttermilk Rolls** (page 115) or French bread with **Roasted Garlic** (page 43), and with **Caesar Salad** (page 131) or **Seasoned Steamed Artichokes** (page 311) with **Green Mayonnaise** (page 344). For dessert, serve **Tapioca Plum Parfait** (page 375) or **Cinnamon Apple Crêpes** (page 56).

CARIBBEAN STEW

Caribbean Stew is especially good served on brown rice with Jerk Tofu (page 337). The three together will fill your kitchen with a heady, tropical aroma. To help preserve the bright colors of the vegetables, serve the stew soon after cooking.

Serves 4 to 6

Total time: 1 hour

1 large onion, chopped (about 2 cups)
½ teaspoon salt
2 teaspoons vegetable oil
½ teaspoon dried thyme
½ teaspoon ground allspice
1 minced fresh chile, seeds removed for a milder "hot"
1 large sweet potato, cut into medium chunks (about 2 cups)
2 cups water or vegetable stock
2 small zucchini, cut into 1-inch chunks (about 2 cups)
1½ cups undrained canned tomatoes, coarsely chopped
4 cups loosely packed shredded kale
1 tablespoon fresh lemon or lime juice
2 to 4 tablespoons finely chopped fresh cilantro
salt to taste

Sprinkle the onions with the salt. In a covered soup pot, sauté the onions in the oil for about 7 minutes, stirring occasionally. Add the thyme, allspice, and chile and continue to cook for another 1 or 2 minutes. Stir in the sweet potatoes and the water or stock and simmer, covered, for about 5 minutes. Add the zucchini and the tomatoes with their juice and simmer 10 to 15 minutes more, until all of the vegetables are barely tender. Add the kale and cook another 5 to 10 minutes. Stir in the lemon or lime juice, cilantro, and salt to taste.

PER 7.50-OZ SERVING: 147 CALORIES, 3.6 G PROTEIN, 2.2 G FAT, 30.4 G CARBOHY-DRATES, .3 G SATURATED FATTY ACIDS, 1.1 G POLYUNSATURATED FATTY ACIDS, .4 G MONOUNSATURATED FATTY ACIDS, 0 MG CHOLESTEROL, 331 MG SODIUM, 4.4 G TOTAL DIETARY FIBER

MENU SUGGESTIONS For a colorful tropical feast, start with Callaloo (page 105), serve the stew topped with roasted peanuts, and add Mango Coconut Cucumber Salad (page 136) or One Step Bean Guacamole (page 28) spread on flatbread. Dessert can be Tapioca Fruit Parfaits (page 375) or Coffee Angelfood Cake (page 378).

GREEK STEW

Kasseri cheese is a dry, crumbly sheep's milk cheese that melts readily. The small amount added here is just enough to coat the vegetables lightly, adding a smooth finish to this unpretentious, tangy stew.

Serves 4

Preparation time: 45 minutes

Simmering time: 20 minutes

1 teaspoon olive oil
2½ cups chopped onions
1 tablespoon minced garlic
1 teaspoon dried oregano
1 teaspoon salt
2 cups chopped fresh tomatoes
4 cups peeled and cubed potatoes (about 2 pounds)
1 pound green beans, stems removed (about 4 cups)
¼ cup chopped fresh parsley
½ cup grated kasseri or feta cheese (about 2 ounces) (pages 427–428)
juice of 2 lemons (about ¼ cup), or more to taste
ground black pepper to taste

Heat the oil in a nonreactive soup pot. Stir in the onions and garlic, cover, and sauté on low heat for 10 minutes, or until the onions are translucent, stirring often to prevent sticking. Add the oregano, salt, tomatoes, potatoes, and beans. Cover the pot and simmer for about 20 minutes, until the potatoes and beans are tender.

Just before serving, stir in the parsley, grated kasseri cheese, and lemon juice and pepper to taste. If you're using feta cheese rather than kasseri cheese, sprinkle it on top.

PER 15-OZ SERVING: 281 CALORIES, 9.1 G PROTEIN, 5.3 G FAT, 54.2 G CARBOHY-DRATES, 2.5 G SATURATED FATTY ACIDS, .7 G POLYUNSATURATED FATTY ACIDS, 1.6 G MONOUNSATURATED FATTY ACIDS, 13 MG CHOLESTEROL, 778 MG SODIUM, 8.5 G TOTAL DIETARY FIBER

MENU SUGGESTIONS With **Seasoned Steamed Artichokes** (page 311) or **Carrot Orange Salad** (page 134) and some crusty whole grain bread to sop up the juices, you have a lovely supper. For dessert, try **Creamy Dairyless Rice Pudding** (page 373) or fresh fruit and **Anise Lemon Biscotti** (page 391).

MEDITERRANEAN STEW

Simmering mild-tasting cannellini and garlicky sautéed vegetables in an herbed tomato-wine sauce makes for a dense and robust stew. Seafood lovers, try adding minced or whole clams—we think you'll be impressed with the results.

2 cups chopped onions
4 garlic cloves, minced or pressed
1 tablespoon olive oil
1 large red bell pepper, seeded and chopped
1 large green bell pepper, seeded and chopped
2 cups 1-inch asparagus pieces
1 cup dry red wine
3 cups diced yellow squash or zucchini
2 cups undrained whole tomatoes (16-ounce can)
⅓ to ½ cup chopped fresh basil
2 teaspoons chopped fresh oregano (1 teaspoon dried)
1½ cups cooked cannellini (15-ounce can, drained)
1 cup undrained whole or minced clams (two 6-ounce cans) (optional)

a few fresh basil sprigs

Serves 4 or 5

**Total time:
45 to 50 minutes**

Combine the onions, garlic, and oil in a saucepan. Cover and sauté on medium heat for 5 to 7 minutes, until the onions soften. Add the peppers, asparagus, and wine and simmer for 5 minutes. Stir in the squash or zucchini, tomatoes, basil, oregano, and beans. Cover and return to a simmer for 10 minutes. Add the clams, if using, cover, and continue to cook until all of the vegetables are tender, about 3 more minutes. Serve garnished with basil.

PER 10-OZ SERVING: 177 CALORIES, 6.5 G PROTEIN, 3.8 G FAT, 25.1 G CARBOHYDRATES, .5 G SATURATED FATTY ACIDS, .6 G POLYUNSATURATED FATTY ACIDS, 2.2 G MONOUNSATURATED FATTY ACIDS, 0 MG CHOLESTEROL, 300 MG SODIUM, 5.3 G TOTAL DIETARY FIBER

MENU SUGGESTIONS Serve on plain orzo, on **Orzo and Green Herbs** (page 183), or with a hearty bread to dunk into the stew. Good side dishes are **Broiled Portabella Mushrooms** (page 322) or **Mustard Carrots** (page 317). **Dark Chocolate Pudding** (page 374) is the perfect dessert.

THAI VEGETABLE CURRY

In this stew, pineapple juice replaces the coconut milk that would traditionally be used, a switch that lowers the fat content considerably. At Moosewood, we usually serve this dish on brown or basmati rice, but jasmine rice would be another excellent choice.

Serves 4 to 6

Preparation time: 30 minutes

Cooking time: 35 minutes

NOTE:
Our Thai Curry Paste (page 365) is perfect for this recipe. Commercial brands are often very spicy, so start with 1 or 2 tablespoons and add more to taste.

1 cup chopped onions
1 tablespoon canola or other vegetable oil
2 cups diced eggplant (1-inch cubes)
2 cups diced sweet potatoes (1-inch cubes)
3 tablespoons Thai curry paste (see Note)
1½ cups unsweetened pineapple juice
½ cup water
½ teaspoon salt
2 cups small cauliflower florets
1 cup cut green beans (1½-inch pieces)
1 cup chopped red bell peppers
1 tomato, diced
3 tablespoons fresh lime or lemon juice
2 tablespoons chopped fresh cilantro or basil

cooked rice
a few fresh basil or cilantro sprigs
chopped peanuts (optional)

In a covered soup pot, sauté the onions in the oil for about 5 minutes. Stir in the eggplant, sweet potatoes, and curry paste. Add the pineapple juice, water, and salt. Bring to a boil, and then reduce the heat and simmer for 5 minutes. Add the cauliflower and green beans and cook for another 5 minutes. Stir in the peppers, tomatoes, lime or lemon juice, and cilantro or basil. Simmer until the vegetables are tender, about 10 minutes.

Serve on rice with a few fresh herb sprigs and, if desired, some chopped peanuts.

PER 8-OZ SERVING: 136 CALORIES, 2.7 G PROTEIN, 2.3 G FAT, 28.0 G CARBOHYDRATES, .3 G SATURATED FATTY ACIDS, 1.3 G POLYUNSATURATED FATTY ACIDS, .5 G MONOUNSATURATED FATTY ACIDS, 0 MG CHOLESTEROL, 222 MG SODIUM, 3.7 G TOTAL DIETARY FIBER

MENU SUGGESTIONS Accompany with **Mango Peach Chutney** (page 362) and **Asian Cucumber Condiment** (page 367) or with **Mango Coconut Cucumber Salad** (page 136). End with **Tapioca Fruit Parfaits** (page 375), **Ginger Peach Crumble** (page 386), or **Pineapple Buttermilk Sherbet** (page 394).

Ukrainian Beet and Bean Stew

This stew will warm you on chill autumn evenings or when winter winds are howling. The red, burgundy, and orange stew topped with scallions and a drizzle of yogurt looks as brilliant as a Ukrainian babushka. With a loaf of rye bread, your meal is complete.

We like the effect of browning the onions and celery in a little oil, but you could make the stew with no oil at all by cooking the onions and celery in a cup of water on high heat for 4 or 5 minutes and proceeding with the recipe.

1 teaspoon vegetable oil
2 cups sliced onions
½ cup chopped celery
3 cups water
3 cups sliced cabbage
1 cup sliced carrots
3 cups chopped potatoes
4 cups peeled cubed raw beets (5 or 6 medium beets)
3 cups undrained whole tomatoes, chopped (28-ounce can)
2 teaspoons caraway seeds
2 tablespoons white or cider vinegar
½ teaspoon salt
2 cups cooked kidney beans (15-ounce can, drained)
1 tablespoon dried dill (¼ cup fresh)
ground black pepper to taste

chopped scallions
low-fat or nonfat yogurt

Serves 6 to 8

Preparation time: 15 minutes

Simmering time: 50 minutes

> **NOTE:**
> The sweetness of beets and carrots varies, so taste the stew for sweetness and tartness and add a little more vinegar and/or a pinch of sugar, if needed.

In a pot, heat the oil briefly, add the onions and celery, and sauté on medium heat, stirring continuously for 4 or 5 minutes, until browned. Add 1 cup of the water, cover, lower the heat, and simmer for 5 minutes. Add the cabbage and carrots, stir well, and simmer, covered, for 5 minutes. Add the remaining 2 cups of water, the potatoes, beets, tomatoes, caraway seeds, vinegar, and salt; bring to a boil, lower the heat, cover, and simmer for about 35 minutes, until the beets are tender. Add the beans and dill. When the stew is hot, add pepper to taste.

Serve topped with chopped scallions and a dollop of low-fat or nonfat yogurt.

PER 9-OZ SERVING: 191 CALORIES, 8.2 G PROTEIN, 1.4 G FAT, 39.3 G CARBOHYDRATES, .2 G SATURATED FATTY ACIDS, .6 G POLYUNSATURATED FATTY ACIDS, .2 G MONOUNSATURATED FATTY ACIDS, 0 MG CHOLESTEROL, 370 MG SODIUM, 4.6 G TOTAL DIETARY FIBER

MENU SUGGESTIONS For a Ukrainian feast, serve with **Garlic Basil Cheese Spread** (page 22) on **Herbed Cottage Cheese Bread** (page 113) or rye bread. Also offer **Cucumbers Vinaigrette** (page 133) or **Savory Stuffed Mushrooms** (page 42). **Red Berry Kissel** (page 372) is a great dessert choice.

ARMENIAN STEW WITH PILAF

Garlic, mint, basil, and lemon used in combination is a hallmark of Middle Eastern cooking. We recommend using fresh herbs when they are available; start with about a tablespoon of the fresh minced mint and basil and add more to taste.

This Armenian stew is a foolproof and filling dish. While the stew is fine served alone in bowls, bulgur pilaf makes a great companion. Bulgur is a wonderful grain; besides being nutritious, it has a pleasing, chewy texture and cooks faster than rice.

Serves 4

Total time: 1 hour

STEW

2 teaspoons canola or other vegetable oil

1 cup chopped onions

3 garlic cloves, minced or pressed

1 teaspoon dried mint

1 teaspoon dried basil

1 bay leaf

½ teaspoon salt

2 medium carrots, peeled and cut into 1-inch chunks (about 1 cup)

1 small zucchini, cut into 1-inch pieces (about 1 cup)

1 cup chopped fresh or canned tomatoes

½ cup tomato juice

1½ cups cooked fava beans (15-ounce can, drained)*

1 large bunch Swiss chard, torn into bite-sized pieces (about 8 cups loosely packed)

1 tablespoon fresh lemon juice

PILAF

2 teaspoons olive oil

⅓ cup finely chopped onion

1 garlic clove, minced or pressed

½ teaspoon salt

1 cup bulgur

2 cups water

¼ to ½ teaspoon chopped fresh rosemary

plain nonfat yogurt

Fava beans from the Middle East are usually smaller and tastier than other brands. They are sometimes called ful medamas.

Warm the oil in a heavy nonreactive soup pot or saucepan. Add the onions, garlic, mint, basil, bay leaf, and salt, cover, and cook for about 5 minutes, stirring occasionally, until the onions begin to soften. Add the carrots, zucchini, tomatoes, and tomato juice, cover, and simmer until all of the vegetables are tender, about 7 minutes. Add the fava beans and Swiss chard, cover again, and continue to cook about 2 minutes. Stir in the lemon juice, add more salt to taste, cover, and remove from the heat. Discard the bay leaf.

In a separate heavy saucepan, warm the olive oil for the pilaf. Add the onions, garlic, and salt, cover, and sauté for 5 minutes, stirring occasionally. Add the bulgur and stir continuously for about 2 minutes. Pour in the water, sprinkle in the rosemary, and bring to a boil. Then reduce the heat and simmer gently for 10 to 15 minutes, until the bulgur is tender but still a little chewy.

When the bulgur is almost ready, gently reheat the stew, if necessary. Ladle the stew on a bed of pilaf and garnish with a dollop of yogurt.

PER 10-OZ SERVING: 195 CALORIES, 10.6 G PROTEIN, 3.2 G FAT, 34.3 G CARBOHYDRATES, .4 G SATURATED FATTY ACIDS, 1.7 G POLYUNSATURATED FATTY ACIDS, .7 G MONOUNSATURATED FATTY ACIDS, 0 MG CHOLESTEROL, 569 MG SODIUM, 9.0 G TOTAL DIETARY FIBER

MENU SUGGESTIONS Serve **Seasoned Steamed Artichokes** (page 311) on the side with **Yogurt Tahini Dressing** (page 346). Fresh grapes and **Anise Lemon Biscotti** (page 391) will complete the meal.

THREE SISTERS STEW

Over 60 percent of the foods we eat today originated in the Americas. In Native American cosmology, corn, beans, and squash are called "the three sisters." They are often grown together, using an agricultural technique in which each crop supports and protects the others. Tasting this wonderfully hearty stew, we are reminded of their symbiotic relationship by the way the cooked corn, beans, and squash complement one another.

3 cups brown or cremini mushrooms
3 cups oyster mushrooms
2 cups coarsely chopped onions
2 to 4 garlic cloves, minced or pressed
2 teaspoons vegetable oil
2 teaspoons dried dill (1 tablespoon fresh)
1 teaspoon dried thyme
1 butternut or other winter squash, peeled, seeded, and
    cubed (2 pounds or about 6 cups, cubed)
1 red bell pepper, seeded and coarsely chopped
2 cups water or vegetable stock
2 cups fresh or frozen corn kernels
2 cups cooked kidney beans
2 tablespoons cider vinegar
salt and ground black pepper to taste
1 tablespoon cornmeal

Serves 4 to 6

**Total time:
45 to 50 minutes**

Wash the mushrooms with as little water as possible. Quarter the brown mushrooms. Trim the bottom(s) of the oyster mushroom clump(s) and gently pull them apart into smaller bite-sized clusters. Set aside.

In a covered soup pot on low heat, sauté the onions and garlic in the oil, stirring often, until the onions are translucent. Add the dill and thyme and cook for 2 minutes, stirring continuously. Add the squash, bell peppers, brown mushrooms, and water or stock and bring to a boil. Simmer until the squash is tender, about 3 to 5 minutes. Stir in the corn and beans. When the stew returns to a simmer, add the oyster mushrooms, vinegar, and salt and pepper to taste. Stir in the cornmeal and simmer, stirring often, until the broth is thickened.

PER 9-OZ SERVING: 257 CALORIES, 11.8 G PROTEIN, 2.8 G FAT, 52.3 G CARBOHYDRATES, .4 G SATURATED FATTY ACIDS, 1.4 G POLYUNSATURATED FATTY ACIDS, .6 G MONOUNSATURATED FATTY ACIDS, 0 MG CHOLESTEROL, 57 MG SODIUM, 3.6 G TOTAL DIETARY FIBER

MENU SUGGESTIONS Serve with **Wild Rice Waldorf Salad** (page 147) alongside **Almost Fat-Free Cornbread** (page 110), tortillas, or **Quinoa Pine Nut Pilaf** (page 184). End with **Apple Cherry Crisp** (page 385) or **Applesauce Spice Cake** (page 381).

CREOLE STEW

Frozen tofu when thawed is crumbly and chewy and adds texture to vegetable stews, but if you omit it you'll save 80 calories and 5 grams of fat per serving and the stew will still taste fine.

3 cups chopped onions
2 garlic cloves, minced or pressed
1 cup water
1 teaspoon salt
4 celery stalks
2 green bell peppers
2 medium zucchini or yellow squash
3 cups undrained canned tomatoes (28-ounce can)

CREOLE SAUCE

1 tablespoon vinegar
1 teaspoon prepared mustard
2 tablespoons tomato paste
½ teaspoon Tabasco or other hot pepper sauce (or to taste)
1 tablespoon molasses or brown sugar
½ teaspoon ground allspice
1 teaspoon dried basil
½ teaspoon dried thyme
½ teaspoon ground black pepper

1 cake tofu (12 ounces), frozen and thawed (page 419)
6 cups cooked rice
chopped scallions

Serves 6

Total time: 45 minutes

> **NOTE:**
> If you're making the stew ahead to reheat later, reserve about 2 tablespoons of the Creole Sauce to add just before serving.

In a covered soup pot on high heat, cook the onions and garlic in the water and salt, stirring frequently, for about 5 minutes. Slice and add in order the celery, bell peppers, and zucchini or squash. Stir well after each addition and add more water if the vegetables begin to stick. Add the tomatoes and lower the heat to a simmer.

Mix together the Creole Sauce ingredients and stir into the stew. Squeeze the water from the thawed tofu and crumble it into the stew. Simmer for at least 5 minutes more. Serve on rice topped with chopped scallions.

PER 15-OZ SERVING (INCLUDES TOFU): 381 CALORIES, 16.4 G PROTEIN, 6.1 G FAT, 68.4 G CARBOHYDRATES, .9 G SATURATED FATTY ACIDS, 3.1 G POLYUNSATURATED FATTY ACIDS, 1.3 G MONOUNSATURATED FATTY ACIDS, 0 MG CHOLESTEROL, 243 MG SODIUM, 5.1 G TOTAL DIETARY FIBER

MENU SUGGESTIONS Begin with **Smoky Eggplant and Pepper Spread** (page 122) on French bread.

PERSIAN SPLIT PEA AND BARLEY STEW

This combination of grains, legumes, and vegetables offers a pleasing mixture of textures. The barley adds chewiness and the yellow split peas help to thicken the flavorful vegetable stock. The currants and sweet spices nicely offset the tanginess of the lemon and yogurt.

Serves 4 to 6

Total time: 1 ½ hours

STEW

½ cup raw barley
1 bay leaf
1 large garlic clove
4 cups water
1 cup dried yellow split peas
1 teaspoon ground cardamom
½ teaspoon ground cinnamon
1 cup coarsely chopped onions
1 cup carrots, peeled and cut into 1-inch chunks
2 cups potatoes, cut into 1-inch chunks
1½ teaspoons salt
pinch of cayenne
2 cups Basic Vegetable Stock (page 73)
2 cups coarsely chopped fresh tomatoes
2 tablespoons currants
¼ cup minced fresh parsley
2 tablespoons fresh lemon juice (about 1 lemon)
salt and ground black pepper to taste

GARLIC YOGURT (OPTIONAL)

½ cup nonfat yogurt
2 minced small garlic cloves
pinch of salt

toasted pine nuts (optional*)
lemon wedges (optional)

To toast pine nuts, spread them in a single layer on an unoiled baking sheet and bake in a commercial or toaster oven at 350° for about 3 to 5 minutes, until just slightly deepened in color.

In a medium saucepan, bring the barley, bay leaf, garlic, and 2 cups of the water to a boil. Reduce the heat, cover, and simmer for 15 minutes. Add the split peas, cardamom, cinnamon, and the remaining 2 cups of water and simmer, covered, for another 45 minutes, or until the barley and split peas are soft and most of the liquid has been absorbed. Stir occasionally and, if necessary, add a small amount of additional water to prevent the mixture from sticking.

While the barley and split peas are cooking, place the onions, carrots, potatoes, salt, cayenne, and stock in a large saucepan. Bring the mixture to a boil, reduce the heat, and simmer, covered, for 10 minutes. Stir in the tomatoes and currants and continue to simmer, covered, for about 10 minutes, until the vegetables are tender. Add the cooked barley and split pea mixture. Stir in the parsley, lemon juice, and salt and pepper to taste. Discard the bay leaf.

If desired, combine the garlic yogurt ingredients in a small bowl. Sprinkle on a few toasted pine nuts and serve with several lemon wedges or a dollop of garlic yogurt.

PER 9-OZ SERVING WITHOUT GARNISHES: 252 CALORIES, 10.9 G PROTEIN, 1.0 G FAT, 53.0 G CARBOHYDRATES, .2 G SATURATED FATTY ACIDS, .4 G POLYUNSATURATED FATTY ACIDS, .2 G MONOUNSATURATED FATTY ACIDS, 0 MG CHOLESTEROL, 664 MG SODIUM, 12.9 G TOTAL DIETARY FIBER

PER 0.67-OZ SERVING: 11 CALORIES, 1.1 G PROTEIN, 0 G FAT, 1.5 G CARBOHYDRATES, 0 G SATURATED FATTY ACIDS, 0 G POLYUNSATURATED FATTY ACIDS, 0 G MONOUNSATURATED FATTY ACIDS, 0 MG CHOLESTEROL, 44 MG SODIUM, 0 G TOTAL DIETARY FIBER

MENU SUGGESTIONS Serve with **Smoky Eggplant and Pepper Spread** (page 122) or **Roasted Garlic** (page 43) with wedges of pita bread. A crunchy salad such as **Cabbage Salad** (page 132) or **Cucumbers Vinaigrette** (page 133) is welcome on the side. Finish with **Anise Lemon Biscotti** (page 391) and strong coffee or mint tea.

QUINOA VEGETABLE STEW

Quinoa, with its mild nutty flavor and somewhat crunchy texture, has the bonus of cooking in just 15 to 20 minutes. It's quickly becoming an American favorite and in the past few years has moved from relative obscurity to the shelves of most large supermarkets.

¾ cup quinoa
1½ cups water
1 cup fresh or frozen corn kernels
1 cup chopped onions
3 garlic cloves, minced or pressed
1 tablespoon olive oil
1 cup chopped bell peppers
2 cups chopped zucchini or yellow squash
5 cups chopped fresh or 3 cups undrained
    canned tomatoes (28-ounce can)
1 tablespoon chopped fresh cilantro
1 tablespoon chopped fresh basil
salt and ground black pepper to taste

a few cilantro or basil sprigs

Serves 4

Total time: 30 minutes

Thoroughly rinse the quinoa in a fine mesh strainer under cool running water and set aside to drain. Combine the quinoa and water in a saucepan, cover, and simmer for 15 to 20 minutes, until tender and fluffy. When the quinoa has cooked for about 10 minutes, stir in the corn, cover, and continue to cook.

Meanwhile, in a nonreactive or nonstick skillet, sauté the onions and garlic in the oil for 5 minutes, until the onions begin to soften. Add the bell peppers and zucchini or yellow squash and sauté for 5 more minutes. Stir in the tomatoes, cilantro, and basil, cover, and simmer for about 10 minutes, until the vegetables are tender. Add salt and pepper to taste.

Fluff the quinoa mixture, spoon it onto individual serving plates, ladle on the vegetable sauce, and top with cilantro or basil sprigs.

PER 13-0Z SERVING: 301 CALORIES, 9.2 G PROTEIN, 6.5 G FAT, 52.8 G CARBOHYDRATES, .6 G SATURATED FATTY ACIDS, .6 G POLYUNSATURATED FATTY ACIDS, 2.8 G MONOUNSATURATED FATTY ACIDS, 0 MG CHOLESTEROL, 271 MG SODIUM, 5.8 G TOTAL DIETARY FIBER

MENU SUGGESTIONS Dip into **One Step Bean Guacamole** (page 28) with fat-free tortilla chips before the meal. Serve the stew with **Spinach Avocado Grapefruit Salad** (page 135) or mixed greens with **Cumin Yogurt Dressing** (page 132). Dessert might be **Our Best No-Butter Brownies** (page 387) or **Pumpkin Custard** (page 376).

MUSHROOM SESAME TOFU STEW

Plain, simple, and satisfying, this stew is rich in both flavor and protein. It's one of those dishes that somehow becomes greater than the sum of its parts and is good served alone or on rice. Leftovers can be used to make a delicious soup—just add water or tomato juice.

4 cups chopped onions
½ cup water
3 cups sliced celery
4 cups sliced mushrooms (12-ounce package)
2 bay leaves
1 tablespoon grated fresh ginger root
2 cups undrained canned whole tomatoes, chopped
    (18-ounce can)
2 tablespoons tahini or peanut butter
1 cake tofu (12 ounces), pressed (page 419) and
    cut into bite-sized pieces
dash of salt or soy sauce to taste

Serves 4 to 6

Preparation time:
20 minutes

Cooking time:
25 minutes

In a covered soup pot on high heat, cook the onions in the water, stirring frequently, for 5 minutes. Add the celery and continue to cook, covered, stirring frequently for 5 minutes. Add more water if the vegetables begin to stick. Add the mushrooms, lower the heat, and cook until the mushrooms begin to release their juices, about 5 minutes. Stir in the bay leaves, ginger, and tomatoes and cook for 5 minutes. Stir in the tahini or peanut butter, add the tofu, and simmer on a heat diffuser or on very low heat for a few minutes more. Add salt or soy sauce to taste; discard the bay leaves and serve.

PER 9-OZ SERVING: 143 CALORIES, 8.7 G PROTEIN, 5.7 G FAT, 17.9 G CARBOHYDRATES, .9 G SATURATED FATTY ACIDS, 2.4 G POLYUNSATURATED FATTY ACIDS, 1.8 G MONOUNSATURATED FATTY ACIDS, 0 MG CHOLESTEROL, 232 MG SODIUM, 4.5 G TOTAL DIETARY FIBER

MENU SUGGESTIONS Serve with a crisp salad such as **Cucumbers Vinaigrette** (page 133) or **Cabbage Salad** (page 132). Finish with fresh fruit with **Maple Walnut Biscotti** (page 390).

Mushrooms are often considered to be just a decorative addition to a dish. We have seldom heard them applauded for their high nutritional value. Nevertheless, about 1½ cups of raw supermarket-variety mushrooms (the common Agaricus bisporus) supply 25 percent of the U.S. RDA for fiber and protein. Pair this with the fact that 1½ cups has only 25 calories, no sodium, and, of course, no fat, and it's caps off to the familiar fungi.

WILD MUSHROOM STEW TRIESTE

The cuisine of northeastern Italy reveals a fascinating intermingling of influences. This stew has a sweet-and-sour tang characteristic of many Eastern European dishes. Intense, woodsy wild mushrooms make it a dramatic dish.

½ ounce dried porcini mushrooms
½ cup dry red wine
¼ cup water
3 or 4 onions, chopped (about 3 cups)
3 garlic cloves, minced or pressed
1 teaspoon olive oil
1 large red bell pepper, chopped (about 1 cup)
4 cups assorted fresh mushrooms, such as cremini,
　　portabella, brown, chanterelle, oyster,
　　shiitake, and moonlight, cleaned and chopped if large
　　(about 1 pound)
1 teaspoon dried basil
1 teaspoon dried thyme
3 cups undrained canned tomatoes, chopped
　　(28-ounce can)
1 cup fresh or frozen green peas
¾ cup sauerkraut (or more, to taste)
salt and ground black pepper to taste

Serves 4

Total time: 45 minutes

Place the dried porcini, red wine, and water in a small saucepan. Bring to a boil on high heat. Immediately remove from the heat and set aside to soak for about 20 minutes.

In a nonreactive soup pot, sauté the onions and garlic in the olive oil for 2 minutes. Add the bell pepper, cover, and sweat on low heat for about 10 minutes, stirring occasionally to prevent sticking. Add the sturdier varieties of mushrooms, such as portabella, cremini, brown, and moonlight. Stir in the basil and thyme and cook for 5 minutes more.

Remove the porcini from the wine, squeeze dry, rinse with cold water, chop, and add to the stew. Strain the wine and stir it into the stew. Stir in the tomatoes, peas, and sauerkraut. Add the more delicate mushrooms, such as oyster, shiitake, or chanterelle. When the stew is hot, add salt and pepper to taste. Serve right away.

PER 12-OZ SERVING: 185 CALORIES, 7.9 G PROTEIN, 2.4 G FAT, 32.6 G CARBOHYDRATES, .3 G SATURATED FATTY ACIDS, .4 G POLYUNSATURATED FATTY ACIDS, .9 G MONOUNSATURATED FATTY ACIDS, 0 MG CHOLESTEROL, 559 MG SODIUM, 7.2 G TOTAL DIETARY FIBER

MENU SUGGESTIONS Polenta is our number one choice to accompany this stew. Or serve with **Potato Cakes** (page 327), **Baked Beets and Shallots** (page 314), and **Apple Apricot Strudel** (page 384).

SOUTHWESTERN HOMINY STEW

This hearty, smoky stew has the distinctive yet delicate flavor of hominy. Besides being easy and fun to roast, the peppers add a remarkably special flavor. Try serving it topped with some grated Cheddar or Monterey jack cheese.

1 cup chopped onions
3 large garlic cloves, minced or pressed
2 medium potatoes, cut into 1-inch chunks (about 2½ cups)
2 cups frozen lima beans
2 teaspoons ground cumin
1 teaspoon salt
3 cups Basic Vegetable Stock (page 73)
2 cups undrained canned tomatoes, chopped
1 roasted green bell pepper, seeded and coarsely chopped*
1 roasted red bell pepper, seeded and coarsely chopped*
1 roasted fresh green chile, seeded and minced*
1½ cups canned white hominy (15-ounce can, drained)
1 tablespoon finely chopped fresh cilantro

Serves 4

Total time: 45 minutes

To roast the bell peppers and chile, place them each directly on a stove burner and center them to maximize contact with the flames. Adjust the flames to medium-high heat and, using long tongs, turn the peppers and chile every 1 to 2 minutes to char the skin evenly, roasting for 5 to 10 minutes. Remove the blackened skin of the chile with a paring knife. Place the roasted peppers in a covered bowl or paper bag to cool before peeling and discarding the blistered skin. For another method, see page 418.

Combine the onions, garlic, potatoes, lima beans, cumin, salt, and vegetable stock in a 3-quart soup pot. Cover and bring to a boil, then lower the heat and simmer gently for about 5 minutes. Add the tomatoes with their juice. Stir in the roasted bell peppers, the roasted chile, and the hominy. Simmer the stew, covered, for about 15 minutes more, until the potatoes are tender. Add the cilantro and serve.

PER 13-OZ SERVING: 280 CALORIES, 10.8 G PROTEIN, 1.3 G FAT, 59.3 G CARBOHYDRATES, .1 G SATURATED FATTY ACIDS, .3 G POLYUNSATURATED FATTY ACIDS, .1 G MONOUNSATURATED FATTY ACIDS, 0 MG CHOLESTEROL, 839 MG SODIUM, 4.2 G TOTAL DIETARY FIBER

MENU SUGGESTIONS Serve with **Almost Fat-Free Cornbread** (page 110) or **Herb and Cheese Muffins** (page 112) along with **Guacamole with Cottage Cheese** (page 26). Either **Citrus-dressed Asparagus** (page 313) or **Spinach Avocado Grapefruit Salad** (page 135) work well as a light side dish. A good dessert is **Pineapple Buttermilk Sherbet** (page 394).

baltic fish 287

baked fish with mustard marinade 288

FISH WITH HERBS AND LIME 289

fish steaks with fennel 290

fish tagine with chermoulla 291

FISH WITH PINEAPPLE CHUTNEY 292

savory hoisin fish 293

southeast asian fish rolls 294

BAKED FLOUNDER ROLLS 295

herbed fish in a packet 296

breaded garlic dill fish 297

HONEY MUSTARD FISH 298

italian fish stew 299

poached fish with russian mushroom sauce 300

POACHED FISH WITH VEGETABLES 301

thai fish cakes 302

gingered shrimp and soba 303

SICILIAN SCALLOP SALAD 304

thai seafood yum 305

Nutritious, versatile, and widely available, **FISH** is at last coming into its own as an important staple in the North American diet. Native people living by bodies of water throughout the world have always valued the sustaining qualities of fish, but for many latter-twentieth-century American meat eaters, the enjoyment of fish has been a gradual and hesitant awakening. Fish can be an excellent transition food for people moving from a meat-focused diet toward a low-fat vegetable- and grain-based one. Because of its density and substance, fish satisfies the craving for meaty fare, yet conforms to health guidelines recommending a diet lower in fat and cholesterol.

Fish varies quite a bit in its oil content, ranging from higher levels in varieties that live deep in the ocean to leaner fish that live in lakes and rivers. The muscle tissue of deep-sea fish contains a high amount of polyunsaturated fatty acids known as omega-3, which researchers believe may lower blood cholesterol and triglycerides and may help prevent heart disease, arteriosclerosis, arthritis, and psoriasis by reducing the formation of blood clots and plaque buildup in blood vessels. Fish high in omega-3 are salmon, mackerel, herring, bluefish, tuna, swordfish, sardines, snapper, halibut, cod, haddock, and monkfish. Among the leaner seafood that contain significant amounts of omega-3 are trout, perch, bass, shad, carp, shrimp, crab, scallops, and lobster.

Modern storage, transportation, and aquaculture technologies have made a far wider variety of fish available in markets and super-markets. We hope you will try the varieties we have suggested and also be adventurous and try new kinds of fish when you see them in your market or when traveling to different areas of the country.

Shop for fish with the same discernment you use in selecting vegetables and fruit. Check the odor, firmness, and appearance. Select fish with either a sweet, mild, delicate odor or a fresh briny aroma, and avoid anything that smells strong, fishy, or offensive. The flesh should be moist, translucent, firm, and elastic, and the skin should be unblemished. In preparing our recipes, do not limit yourself to the recommended varieties of fish; very often the fish that is "on special" at the market is the freshest. The lower price is designed to move an abundant catch quickly, one instance in which you really do get the best for less. If fish has been previously frozen, use it immediately; refrozen fish will lose much of its flavor and moistness.

Don't shy away from "fresh frozen" fish, which means that the fish was frozen immediately at sea or onshore very soon after being caught. Fresh frozen fish may, in fact, be fresher than so-called fresh fish that may have spent several days on ice in the hold of a ship before being transported to the supermarket.

To thaw, transfer frozen fish from the freezer to the refrigerator for 24 hours, or remove the fish from the package and place it in a plastic bag in a sinkful of cold water for 1 to 2 hours. Pat the fish dry with absorbent paper and use it immediately. You can cook frozen fish without thawing by doubling the cooking time. The fish will release more water though, so if you're baking it with a sauce, thaw first.

It is important to cook fish just until the protein coagulates and the flavor is at its best. According to the Canadian Department of Fisheries, the rule of thumb is 10 minutes for every inch of thick-

The following chart describes some of the common varieties of fish found in U.S. supermarkets and restaurants. Use the chart to enrich your knowledge and to pique your curiosity about this very basic, yet versatile food.

LEAN SEA FISH

COD/SCROD *(young cod)*—smooth texture, tender, white flesh.

FLATFISH *(sole, plaice, flounder)*—Atlantic/Pacific coast; delicate, white or grey flesh.

HADDOCK—North Atlantic; white, lean flesh, slightly dry; available salted, smoked.

HALIBUT—North Atlantic and Pacific coasts; prime season: spring; white, firm, flat; good for poaching, steaming.

MAHIMAHI—Semitropical waters on both coasts; strong meaty flavor.

MONKFISH—firm, white, mild, versatile; "poor man's lobster."

OCEAN PERCH—Atlantic/Pacific coasts; pink flesh, mild flavor.

POLLOCK—North Atlantic/Pacific coasts; firm, white or grey, mild flavor.

RED SNAPPER—Atlantic/Pacific/Gulf coasts; firm, white flesh with red skin.

SEA BASS—Atlantic/Pacific coasts; firm flesh; may be baked, grilled, or broiled, if basted.

TURBOT—steaks; firm, white, mild.

WHITING *(Silver Hake)*—mid-Atlantic coast; spring/fall; soft flesh, delicate, versatile; available pickled, smoked, salted.

OIL-RICH SEA FISH

BLUEFISH—Atlantic/Gulf coasts; winter/summer; soft flesh, strong flavor.

HERRING—Atlantic/Pacific coasts; January/June; staple in Europe, in United States mostly available pickled, salted, smoked.

MACKEREL—Atlantic/Gulf of Mexico; soft flesh, savory flavor.

MAKO *(shark)*—North Atlantic; firm, ivory pink; lower fat; steaks may be baked, broiled.

POMPANO—Florida coast; October/May; firm, strong flavor; lower fat.

SALMON—wild Pacific salmon (chinook or king, chum, coho, pink, and sockeye) available seasonally; farm-raised salmon (Atlantic salmon, now endangered and not commercially fished) is often called "Norwegian" in the market; pale pink to orange to red flesh, unusual flavor not easily substituted for; good poached, broiled, baked, grilled, pan-grilled.

ness, measuring at the thickest part of the fish. When done, the flesh should be opaque, white, or pink. Any small traces of translucence will disappear as the fish continues to cook after it is removed from the oven. For grilled fish, allow 4 to 5 minutes on each side for 1-inch steaks, and for a subtle aromatic touch, throw thyme or rosemary on the glowing embers when you are ready to grill. Fish baked in a pack-

SMELT—Atlantic/Pacific coasts; firm, delicate.

SWORDFISH—Atlantic/Pacific coasts; fresh in warm weather, frozen in cold months; firm flesh, strong flavor; grilling, baking, broiling.

TUNA—temperate waters of both coasts; albacore has most delicate flavor; also bonito, bluefin, yellowfin; firm, pink to deep red flesh, steaklike texture; freezes well.

FRESHWATER FISH

CARP—Mississippi River; firm texture, sweet, white flesh.

CATFISH—farmed in Mississippi Valley; southern and midwestern tradition; firm, sweet, white flesh.

PERCH—eastern United States; firm, delicate, versatile.

STRIPED BASS—throughout United States; lean, firm, smooth texture.

STURGEON—farm-raised; meaty, mild; steaks and fillets.

TROUT—farm-raised in western United States; firm, delicate, pinkish-orange flesh; may be grilled, smoked, baked, broiled.

WHITEFISH—Northern lakes; mild, smooth, firm texture; grilled, baked, smoked.

SHELLFISH

CLAMS *(hard-shell)*—Atlantic/Pacific coasts; smaller are more tender, larger are tougher; rich in protein and minerals.

MUSSELS—lean, sweet, tender, farm-raised domestically or gathered wild on Atlantic/Pacific coasts and New Zealand.

SCALLOPS—**SEA**: year-round in North Atlantic; mild. **BAY**: Long Island/Massachusetts; rare and expensive. **CALICO**: Gulf waters; small; cook quickly; may have been soaked in phosphates, so ask if you wish to avoid. **PINK**: Washington/British Columbia; sold in shells; steam.

SHRIMP—75 percent imported from Asia/South America/Central America, most farm-raised, 25 percent domestic, wild from warm southern waters; almost all shrimp is frozen—if sold as fresh, it was previously frozen (only 2 percent is actually fresh and that 2 percent is consumed within fifty miles of where it was caught); degrades very rapidly—expect that it has been treated with sodium metabisulfite.

et or a sauce will require about 15 minutes for each inch of thickness.

We have tried to create recipes that are simple and straightforward in order to respect the delicate flavor and tender texture of most fish. Our goal is to enjoy the freshness of the fish as much as the added sauces, herbs, or flavorings. Our fish recipes are generally quick and easy to prepare, and provide a full ethnic range. Some are unusual, such as Sicilian Scallop Salad, Fish Tagine with Chermoulla, or Fish with Pineapple Chutney. Others are a variation on a familiar theme, such as Italian Fish Stew and Breaded Garlic Dill Fish. Recipes for special occasions could include Thai Seafood Yum or Herbed Fish in a Packet. Fish Steaks with Fennel and Savory Hoisin Fish can easily be adapted to grilling.

See the chart that follows for guidelines on selecting fish, and experiment with some unfamiliar offerings to broaden your fish and seafood horizons.

Fish can be a wonderful lean source of protein and essential oils (page 282). The following terms may be useful in selecting fish:

WHOLE FISH: The tail and head may be left on when poached, baked, or broiled, or the head and bones may be used in making stock.

FILLET: Sides of the fish are cut lengthwise, parallel to its backbone, and the bones are removed.

FRESH FROZEN: The fish is frozen on the ship or at shore immediately after being caught.

DRIED FISH: After being halved lengthwise or filleted, the fish is sun- or air-dried to reduce the moisture content for preservation.

FISH STEAKS: The fish is sliced into pieces 1 to 1½ inches thick, often through a section of backbone; this is a common form for larger varieties such as salmon, mako, halibut, or swordfish.

BALTIC FISH

We were excited when we perfected this lower-fat version of one of Moosewood's most popular, time-honored fish entrées. The original recipe, Fish Otis, has a lavish sour cream and dill topping that always wins raves from our customers. In our search for a way to preserve the richness while reducing the fat, we kept the dill and red onions, added potatoes for substance, and introduced horseradish and garlic for accents. With all of these creative additions, no one notices that nonfat sour cream has replaced the regular sour cream.

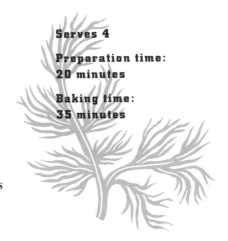

**4 five-ounce firm white fish fillets,
    such as scrod, haddock, or whiting**
2 large potatoes, peeled and sliced (about 4 cups)
3 garlic cloves, pressed or minced
salt and ground black pepper to taste
¼ cup fresh lemon juice
1 cup nonfat sour cream
2 tablespoons prepared horseradish
1 tablespoon chopped fresh dill (1 teaspoon dried)
1 small red onion, thinly sliced, or 1 cup chopped scallions

fresh dill sprigs
a few thin slices of pimiento or red bell pepper

Serves 4

**Preparation time:
20 minutes**

**Baking time:
35 minutes**

Rinse the fish, pat dry, and set aside.

Boil the potatoes and garlic in water to cover until the potatoes are tender, about 10 minutes. Drain and mash with a potato masher or heavy wooden spoon. Add salt and pepper to taste.

Preheat the oven to 350°.

Evenly spread the mashed potatoes on the bottom of a 5 × 8-inch baking dish prepared with cooking spray or a very light coating of oil. Lay the fillets on top of the potatoes and pour on the lemon juice. In a small bowl, combine the sour cream, horseradish, and dill and spoon it evenly over the fish. Top with the red onion slices or scallions. Cover and bake for about 35 minutes, until the fish flakes easily with a fork.

Use a few dill sprigs and slices of pimiento or bell pepper to garnish each serving.

PER 10-OZ SERVING: 269 CALORIES, 34.9 G PROTEIN, 1.3 G FAT, 26.6 G CARBOHYDRATES, .2 G SATURATED FATTY ACIDS, .4 G POLYUNSATURATED FATTY ACIDS, .2 G MONOUNSATURATED FATTY ACIDS, 70 MG CHOLESTEROL, 248 MG SODIUM, 2.1 G TOTAL DIETARY FIBER

MENU SUGGESTIONS Accompany with **Mustard Carrots** (page 317) or **Baked Beets and Shallots** (page 314). Finish with **Apple Apricot Strudel** (page 384) or **Red Berry Kissel** (page 372).

BAKED FISH WITH MUSTARD MARINADE

This quick and easy recipe can be served as an everyday kind of meal or as the main course of an elaborate and elegant dinner.

Serves 4 to 6

Preparation time:
10 minutes

Marinating time:
20 to 60 minutes

Baking time:
15 minutes

FISH
1½ pounds cod, scrod, haddock,
   or other firm white fish fillets

MARINADE
½ cup smooth or coarse Dijon mustard
⅓ cup fresh lemon juice
½ teaspoon dried thyme
1 to 2 teaspoons prepared horseradish
2 teaspoons grated lemon peel
¼ teaspoon ground black pepper

Rinse and dry the fish fillets and place them, skin side down, in a lightly oiled baking pan.

Whisk the marinade ingredients together in a mixing bowl or whirl them in a blender or small food processor. Pour the marinade over the fish, turning the fillets to coat both sides. Set aside in the refrigerator for 20 to 60 minutes.

Preheat the oven to 400°.

Place the baking dish, uncovered, in the oven and bake for 10 to 15 minutes, or until the fish is tender and flakes easily with a fork.

PER 5-OZ SERVING: 126 CALORIES, 24.3 G PROTEIN, 1.7 G FAT, 2.8 G CARBOHY-DRATES, .2 G SATURATED FATTY ACIDS, .3 G POLYUNSATURATED FATTY ACIDS, .1 G MONOUNSATURATED FATTY ACIDS, 56 MG CHOLESTEROL, 318 MG SODIUM, .3 G TOTAL DIETARY FIBER

MENU SUGGESTIONS Serve on rice with **Baked Beets and Shallots** (page 314) or with **Garlic Mashed Potatoes** (page 328) and **Gingered Fennel with Garlic** (page 320). For dessert, try **Apple Apricot Strudel** (page 384) or **Red Berry Kissel** (page 372). These fillets also make great sandwiches on rye bread or soft sourdough rolls.

FISH WITH HERBS AND LIME

This very simple fish dish features the assertive and yet compatible flavors of lime juice, garlic, scallions, rosemary, thyme, parsley, and paprika.

4 five- or six-ounce firm fish fillets,
    such as cod, red snapper, or turbot
¼ cup fresh lime juice
4 garlic cloves, pressed or minced
½ cup chopped fresh parsley
½ cup chopped scallions
1 teaspoon chopped fresh rosemary (½ teaspoon dried)
1 teaspoon fresh thyme leaves (½ teaspoon dried)
1 teaspoon sweet paprika
1 cup diced fresh tomatoes

Serves 4

**Preparation time:
20 to 25 minutes**

**Baking time:
25 minutes**

Preheat the oven to 375°.

Rinse the fish fillets, pat dry, and set aside. In a medium bowl, mix together the lime juice, garlic, parsley, scallions, rosemary, thyme, paprika, and tomatoes. Place the fillets in an unoiled, non-reactive baking dish and spread the topping evenly over the fish. Cover tightly with foil and bake for about 25 minutes, until the fish flakes easily with a fork.

PER 7.50-OZ SERVING: 160 CALORIES, 30.3 G PROTEIN, 1.5 G FAT, 6.0 G CARBOHYDRATES, .3 G SATURATED FATTY ACIDS, .5 G POLYUNSATURATED FATTY ACIDS, .2 G MONOUNSATURATED FATTY ACIDS, 70 MG CHOLESTEROL, 111 MG SODIUM, 1.4 G TOTAL DIETARY FIBER

MENU SUGGESTIONS Serve with **Caribbean Pigeon Pea Salad** (page 142), **Quinoa Black Bean Salad** (page 141), or **Baked Sweet Potato Salad** (page 137) alongside **Spinach Avocado Grapefruit Salad** (page 135) or tossed greens with **Cilantro Lime Yogurt Dressing** (page 345). Conclude with **Coffee Angelfood Cake** (page 378) or **Lemon Pudding Cake** (page 377).

FISH STEAKS WITH FENNEL

A Provençal-style sauce that combines the bright flavors of fennel, saffron, orange, and wine is a substantial accent for hearty fish steaks.

FISH

4 fish steaks, such as swordfish, monkfish, salmon,
    sea bass, mako shark, tuna (5 or 6 ounces each)
⅓ cup fresh lemon juice
¾ cup dry white wine
4 garlic cloves, minced or pressed

Serves 4

**Marinating time:
50 to 60 minutes**

**Preparation time:
20 minutes**

**Baking time:
25 to 30 minutes**

SAUCE

1 cup dry white wine
1 teaspoon ground fennel
1 teaspoon dried thyme
2 cups chopped leeks (white bulbs and tender greens)
generous sprinkling of salt and ground black pepper
3 cups thinly sliced fresh fennel bulb
generous pinch of saffron
¾ cup orange juice

2 oranges, sectioned, membranes and seeds removed (page 418)

Rinse the fish, pat it dry, and place it in a nonreactive baking dish.

Combine the lemon juice, wine, and garlic in a cup and pour over the fish. Cover and refrigerate for about an hour, turning once.

While the fish is marinating, prepare the sauce. Combine the wine with the ground fennel, thyme, leeks, and salt and pepper in a covered nonreactive saucepan. Bring to a boil, reduce the heat, and simmer for 5 minutes. Add the sliced fennel and continue to simmer for about 5 more minutes, until the vegetables are just tender. Crumble in the saffron. Add the orange juice and cook for another 2 minutes.

Preheat the oven to 350°.

Pour the sauce over the marinated fish steaks, cover, and bake for 25 to 30 minutes. Remove the dish from the oven and turn the oven to broil. Uncover the fish and decorate with the orange sections. Broil for 3 minutes, then serve immediately.

PER 10-OZ SERVING: 320 CALORIES, 30.0 G PROTEIN, 6.2 G FAT, 26.6 G CARBOHYDRATES, 1.6 G SATURATED FATTY ACIDS, 1.4 G POLYUNSATURATED FATTY ACIDS, 2.2 G MONOUNSATURATED FATTY ACIDS, 54 MG CHOLESTEROL, 216 MG SODIUM, 3.8 G TOTAL DIETARY FIBER

MENU SUGGESTIONS Serve at once on rice, couscous, or orzo accompanied by **Broccoli Rabe and Garlic** (page 315) or **Broiled Zucchini with Herbs** (page 333).

FISH TAGINE WITH CHERMOULLA

Here is a tantalizing blend of garlic, cilantro, and cumin sparked by fresh ginger and fresh chile. Fish baked in a lemony sauce is one of the all-time favorites at Moosewood. Served on bright yellow couscous, the dish looks quite luscious.

1½ pounds firm fish fillets or steaks,
    such as scrod, sea bass, or swordfish
1 onion, thinly sliced
1 carrot, thinly sliced
½ teaspoon salt
1 cup chopped fresh cilantro
10 garlic cloves, minced or pressed
2 tablespoons grated fresh ginger root
4 teaspoons ground cumin
1 cup fresh lemon juice (6 to 8 lemons)
1 fresh chile, minced, seeds removed for a milder "hot"
2 large tomatoes, chopped
salt to taste

cooked couscous

Serves 4

Preparation time: 35 minutes

Baking time: 20 to 25 minutes

Preheat the oven to 350°.

Rinse the fish fillets and set them aside. Prepare a nonreactive baking dish with cooking spray or oil very lightly. Arrange the onions and carrots in a layer to cover the bottom of the dish and place the fillets on top. Lightly sprinkle them with salt.

In a blender or food processor, combine the cilantro, garlic, ginger, cumin, lemon juice, chile, and half of the chopped tomatoes and purée to form a smooth sauce. Add salt to taste. Pour the sauce evenly over the fish and vegetables and top with the remaining chopped tomatoes. Cover tightly with foil and bake for 20 to 25 minutes, until the fish flakes easily with a fork. Serve immediately on couscous.

PER 10-OZ SERVING: 230 CALORIES, 37.3 G PROTEIN, 2.3 G FAT, 16.1 G CARBOHYDRATES, .3 G SATURATED FATTY ACIDS, .6 G POLYUNSATURATED FATTY ACIDS, .3 G MONOUNSATURATED FATTY ACIDS, 84 MG CHOLESTEROL, 494 MG SODIUM, 2.8 G TOTAL DIETARY FIBER

MENU SUGGESTIONS Serve accompanied by **Seasoned Steamed Artichokes** (page 311) or **Cucumbers Vinaigrette** (page 133). For dessert, try **Anise Lemon Biscotti** (page 391) with fresh fruit in season.

FISH WITH PINEAPPLE CHUTNEY

Refreshingly tart and sweet, our tropical fruit chutney is beautiful to behold too, with flecks of gold, red, and green adorning the tender fish fillets. The chutney is refreshing as a sauce on grilled fish or as a topping on bean and grain combos such as Festive Black Bean Chili (page 161), Sweet Potato and Black Bean Burrito (page 172), and Vegetable-filled Pancakes (page 233).

FISH

4 five- or six-ounce fish fillets or steaks, such as
    red snapper, pompano, tuna, or mahimahi

Serves 4

**Preparation time:
20 minutes**

**Baking time:
20 to 25 minutes**

CHUTNEY

1 cup fresh or undrained unsweetened canned
    pineapple chunks
1 teaspoon freshly grated lemon peel
1 lemon, peeled and seeded
1 fresh green chile, seeds removed for a milder flavor
1 cup chopped red bell peppers
¼ cup chopped scallions
2 teaspoons grated fresh ginger root
dash of Tabasco or other hot pepper sauce to taste
salt to taste

a few lemon wedges

Preheat the oven to 375°.

    Rinse the fish fillets, pat dry, and set aside. In a food processor or blender, briefly whirl the pineapple, lemon peel, lemon, chile, bell peppers, scallions, ginger, and Tabasco until the chutney has a confetti-like appearance. Add salt to taste.

    Arrange the fish in a lightly oiled nonreactive baking dish. Top with the chutney and bake, covered, for 20 to 25 minutes, until the fish flakes easily with a fork. Alternatively, grill the fish until tender and cooked through and serve it topped with the chutney. Garnish with lemon wedges.

PER 9-OZ SERVING: 188 CALORIES, 30.2 G PROTEIN, 1.3 G FAT, 14.6 G CARBOHYDRATES, .2 G SATURATED FATTY ACIDS, .5 G POLYUNSATURATED FATTY ACIDS, .2 G MONOUNSATURATED FATTY ACIDS, 70 MG CHOLESTEROL, 149 MG SODIUM, 1.3 G TOTAL DIETARY FIBER

MENU SUGGESTIONS Serve with **Golden Basmati Rice** (page 185) alongside **Citrus-dressed Asparagus** (page 313) or **Curried Squash** (page 332). For dessert, try **Banana Bundt Cake** (page 382) or **Tapioca Fruit Parfaits** (page 375).

SAVORY HOISIN FISH

This slightly piquant sauce works well on a variety of types of fish. We like it on scrod, catfish, perch, and mahimahi.

Savory Hoisin Sauce also makes an excellent marinade for grilled fish. Coat the fish with the sauce, marinate in the refrigerator for several hours, and grill. You might like to try the same marinating technique with slices of eggplant, zucchini, or tofu, baked or grilled.

FISH
1 pound fresh fish fillets or steaks

Serves 4

Preparation time:
5 to 10 minutes

Baking time:
25 to 30 minutes

SAVORY HOISIN SAUCE
2 tablespoons hoisin sauce (page 429)
2 tablespoons light miso
2 tablespoons sake or dry sherry
1½ teaspoons grated fresh ginger root
2 tablespoons fresh lime or lemon juice or rice vinegar

GARNISH
thinly sliced scallions
thinly sliced red bell pepper strips or pimientos
toasted sesame seeds*

*Toast a single layer of seeds on an unoiled baking tray
in a conventional or toaster oven at 350° for 2 to 3 minutes,
until fragrant and golden brown.*

Preheat the oven to 350°.

Rinse the fish, place it, skin side down, in a lightly oiled or sprayed baking dish, and set it aside. In a bowl, whisk together the hoisin sauce, miso, sake or sherry, ginger, and lime or lemon juice or rice vinegar. Pour the sauce evenly over the fish, cover, and bake for 25 to 30 minutes, until the fish flakes easily with a fork. Serve garnished with scallions, pepper strips, and toasted sesame seeds.

PER 5.75-OZ SERVING: 164 CALORIES, 25.5 G PROTEIN, 2.5 G FAT, 7.4 G CARBOHYDRATES, .4 G SATURATED FATTY ACIDS, 1.0 G POLYUNSATURATED FATTY ACIDS, .4 G MONOUNSATURATED FATTY ACIDS, 98 MG CHOLESTEROL, 464 MG SODIUM, .8 G TOTAL DIETARY FIBER

MENU SUGGESTIONS For a complete meal, serve the fish on rice with **Gingered Broccoli** (page 315) or **Japanese Sesame Spinach** (page 330), or with a simple tossed salad dressed with **Spicy Peanut Dressing** (page 349) or **Creamy Ginger Miso Dressing** (page 343).

SOUTHEAST ASIAN FISH ROLLS

The herb-based filling for these succulent fish rolls is a classic combination of Asian seasonings.

8 two- to four-ounce thin fish fillets, such as flounder or sole
¼ cup fresh lime juice (about 3 limes)
2 tablespoons soy sauce
4 garlic cloves, pressed or minced
¼ cup chopped fresh basil
1 teaspoon grated fresh ginger root
3 tablespoons chopped fresh cilantro
½ teaspoon freshly grated lime peel

Serves 4

Preparation time: 25 minutes

Baking time: 20 to 25 minutes

Preheat the oven to 375°.

Rinse the fish fillets, pat dry, and set them aside. In a medium bowl, mix together the lime juice, soy sauce, garlic, basil, ginger, cilantro, and lime peel. Lay the fillets, skin side up, on a cutting board or counter and spoon ⅛ of the filling onto one end of each fillet. Roll up each fillet and place the rolls close together in a nonreactive baking dish. Cover tightly with foil and bake for 20 to 25 minutes, until the fish flakes easily with a fork.

PER 5-OZ SERVING: 162 CALORIES, 31.9 G PROTEIN, 2.0 G FAT, 2.5 G CARBOHYDRATES, .5 G SATURATED FATTY ACIDS, .6 G POLYUNSATURATED FATTY ACIDS, .4 G MONOUNSATURATED FATTY ACIDS, 88 MG CHOLESTEROL, 542 MG SODIUM, .2 G TOTAL DIETARY FIBER

MENU SUGGESTIONS Serve with **Fragrant Jasmine Rice** (page 189) and **Southeast Asian Coconut Zucchini** (page 334). For a refreshing ending, serve **Pineapple Buttermilk Sherbet** (page 394).

BAKED FLOUNDER ROLLS

This dish is simple to make, yet elegant and flavorful. For variety, the flounder rolls may be baked on a layer of raw spinach, raw sliced mushrooms, or blanched French-cut green beans instead of on the zucchini we have suggested here.

Serves 4

**Preparation time:
15 minutes**

**Baking time:
20 to 30 minutes**

**2 medium zucchini, sliced into ½-inch rounds
(about 3 cups)**
4 flounder fillets (about 6 ounces each)
¼ to ½ cup Susan's Pesto (page 364)
¼ cup fresh lemon juice
ground black pepper to taste

Preheat the oven to 400°.

Spread the zucchini slices over the bottom of a lightly oiled 9 × 9-inch shallow baking dish.

Rinse and dry the flounder and lay each fillet, skin side up, flat on the counter. Place about a tablespoon of pesto on the center of each fillet and then roll it up. Arrange the flounder rolls on top of the zucchini, seam side down, sprinkle the rolls and zucchini with the lemon juice, and top each fillet with pepper.

Cover the pan with foil and bake for 20 to 30 minutes, until the fish is cooked through and the zucchini is tender.

PER 9-OZ SERVING: 143 CALORIES, 25.3 G PROTEIN, 3.0 G FAT, 7.3 G CARBOHY-
DRATES, .1 G SATURATED FATTY ACIDS, .4 G POLYUNSATURATED FATTY ACIDS,
1.3 G MONOUNSATURATED FATTY ACIDS, 38 MG CHOLESTEROL, 264 MG SODIUM,
1.9 G TOTAL DIETARY FIBER

MENU SUGGESTIONS Serve with rice, orzo, **Couscous with Peas and Onions** (page 179), **Millet Pilaf** (page 182), **Garlic Mashed Potatoes** (page 328), or parsleyed potatoes and accompany with **Caesar Salad** (page 131) or **Roasted Asparagus** (page 312). For dessert, try **Chocolate Hazelnut Biscotti** (page 392) and fresh fruit in season.

HERBED FISH IN A PACKET

These individually wrapped meals give each diner the pleasure of opening a package and deeply inhaling the aromas of fresh herbs before beginning to eat.

4 firm fish fillets, such as scrod, tuna, salmon, or haddock (5 to 6 ounces each)

2 tablespoons chopped fresh basil

2 teaspoons chopped fresh thyme, rosemary, tarragon, basil, or dill

dash of salt and ground black pepper

1½ to 3 tablespoons fresh lemon juice

1 tomato, thickly sliced

4 lemon slices or 8 lime slices

4 fresh thyme, rosemary, tarragon, basil, or dill sprigs

4 teaspoons capers (optional)

Serves 4

Preparation time: 25 minutes

Baking time: 15 to 20 minutes

Rinse the fish fillets and set aside.

Preheat the oven to 425°.

For each fillet, fold a 12 × 15-inch piece of parchment paper in half to form a 12 × 7½-inch rectangle and trim the corners to form a half heart shape, the way you would cut a large Valentine heart. Open the parchment on a flat working surface and place a fish fillet to one side of the center fold. Top the fillet with 1½ teaspoons of the chopped basil, ½ teaspoon of the chopped thyme or other herb of your choice, a sprinkling of salt and pepper, and 1 to 2 teaspoons of lemon juice.

Cover with a slice of tomato, 1 or 2 slices of lemon or lime, and a sprig of the fresh herb of your choice, and sprinkle on a teaspoon of capers, if desired. Fold the parchment over the fish and then, starting at one end and working your way around to the other end, carefully fold the cut edges twice (or three times if you prefer a crimped edge) to form a sealed packet.

Place the packets on an unoiled baking sheet and bake for 15 to 20 minutes—slightly longer for very thick fillets. The packets will become puffed and golden brown. Avoid the steam as you open a packet to check that the fish is cooked. When the fish flakes easily with a fork, open the packets and serve, or give each diner his own "present" to open at the table.

PER 7-OZ SERVING: 172 CALORIES, 33.6 G PROTEIN, 1.8 G FAT, 3.7 G CARBOHYDRATES, .3 G SATURATED FATTY ACIDS, .8 G POLYUNSATURATED FATTY ACIDS, .3 G MONOUNSATURATED FATTY ACIDS, 135 MG CHOLESTEROL, 211 MG SODIUM, .5 G TOTAL DIETARY FIBER

MENU SUGGESTIONS Serve each packet with couscous or rice and **Vegetables à la Grecque** (page 130), or with **Sweet Sweet Potatoes** (page 323) and a tossed salad with **Italian Tomato Basil Dressing** (page 347).

Breaded Garlic Dill Fish

Quick and easy to prepare, this bread crumb and wheat germ mixture forms a crisp, flavorful coating for baked fish. Double or triple the breading mixture to keep in the freezer for instant use.

Fish
1½ pounds firm white fish fillets, such as cod, scrod, haddock, or pollock

Breading Mixture
¾ cup fresh bread crumbs (see Note, page 298)
¾ cup toasted wheat germ
3 tablespoons chopped fresh dill
(1 tablespoon dried)
1½ teaspoons ground dried mustard
3 large garlic cloves, minced or pressed
salt and ground black pepper to taste

2 egg whites

Serves 4 to 6

**Preparation time:
20 minutes**

**Baking time:
20 minutes**

Preheat the oven to 350°.

Rinse the fish fillets, pat dry, and set aside. Toast the bread crumbs on an unoiled baking sheet in the oven for about 5 minutes, until lightly golden. Increase the oven temperature to 400°. In a large shallow bowl, combine the bread crumbs, wheat germ, dill, mustard, garlic, and salt and pepper. Lightly beat the egg whites in a separate shallow bowl. Dip the fillets in the egg whites and then dredge them in the bread crumb mixture to coat both sides evenly. Place the breaded fillets in a lightly oiled or sprayed 8 × 12-inch baking dish and bake, uncovered, for 20 minutes, or until the fish flakes easily with a fork. Offer several fresh lemon wedges with each serving and drizzle on the fresh juice to taste.

PER 7-OZ SERVING: 225 CALORIES, 30.9 G PROTEIN, 2.9 G FAT, 30.6 G CARBOHYDRATES, .5 G SATURATED FATTY ACIDS, 1.1 G POLYUNSATURATED FATTY ACIDS, .6 G MONOUNSATURATED FATTY ACIDS, 56 MG CHOLESTEROL, 209 MG SODIUM, 12.5 G TOTAL DIETARY FIBER

MENU SUGGESTIONS Serve with **Oven "Fries"** (page 326) and **Citrus-dressed Asparagus** (page 313) or with **Wild Rice Waldorf Salad** (page 147) and **Broiled Portabella Mushrooms** (page 322).

HONEY MUSTARD FISH

Sweet and tangy, with a crunchy coating, these fillets make a mouthwatering main dish that delights the senses with aroma, taste, and texture.

Serves 4

**Preparation time:
10 minutes**

**Baking time:
20 to 30 minutes**

4 catfish or salmon fillets (5 to 6 ounces each)
1½ tablespoons honey
1½ tablespoons Dijon mustard
1 to 2 tablespoons fresh lemon juice
¾ cup fresh bread crumbs (see Note) or
    ¼ cup cornmeal
½ teaspoon dried thyme
salt and ground black pepper to taste

NOTE:
To make your own bread crumbs, whirl any bread you have on hand in a blender or food processor for several seconds. At Moosewood we use whole wheat, rye, sourdough, and leftover cornbread, all of which make delicious crumbs. If you use an herbed bread, you may wish to eliminate or reduce the amount of thyme in this recipe.

Preheat the oven to 375°.

Rinse the fillets and pat dry; set aside. In a shallow bowl, whisk together the honey, mustard, and lemon juice. In a separate shallow bowl, combine the bread crumbs or cornmeal with the thyme and a few shakes of salt and pepper. Dip each fillet into the honey-mustard sauce and then dredge it in the bread crumb or cornmeal mixture to coat both sides evenly. Place the fillets in a sprayed or lightly oiled baking pan and bake, uncovered, for 20 to 30 minutes, or until thoroughly hot and tender.

PER 6-OZ SERVING: 253 CALORIES, 26.9 G PROTEIN, 5.5 G FAT, 23.0 G CARBOHYDRATES, 1.3 G SATURATED FATTY ACIDS, 1.6 G POLYUNSATURATED FATTY ACIDS, 1.7 G MONOUNSATURATED FATTY ACIDS, 85 MG CHOLESTEROL, 357 MG SODIUM, 1.0 G TOTAL DIETARY FIBER

MENU SUGGESTIONS The catfish fillets make a great Southern-style meal served with **Sweet Potato Oven "Fries"** (page 326) and **Zucchini with Cilantro Sauce** (page 335). Or try the salmon with **Bulgur Rice Pilaf** (page 188) beside either **Seasoned Steamed Artichokes** (page 311) or **Snap Peas with Mushrooms** (page 329).

ITALIAN FISH STEW

This stew combines some of the most aromatic herbs of the Mediterranean region—fennel, rosemary, and saffron—with the fragrance of olive oil and orange. If you have trouble finding fresh fennel bulb (sometimes mistakenly labeled "anise" in the supermarket), you can replace it with 2 cups of chopped celery and an additional teaspoon of ground fennel.

3 garlic cloves, minced or pressed
2 cups chopped onions
2 teaspoons olive oil
2 teaspoons ground fennel
½ cup white wine
4 cups coarsely chopped fresh fennel bulb, fronds reserved
4 cups cubed potatoes (about 1 pound)
2 cups clam juice (16-ounce bottle or can)
3½ cups undrained plum tomatoes, chopped (28-ounce can)
1 tablespoon freshly grated orange peel, preferably organic
1 tablespoon dried rosemary or 2 fresh rosemary sprigs
  (3 to 4 inches long)
generous pinch of saffron
1 pound firm fish fillets, such as black-tip shark,
  monkfish, cod, or halibut
salt and ground black pepper to taste

chiffonade of basil or chopped parsley

Serves 4 to 6

**Total time:
about 1 hour**

In a skillet, sauté the garlic and onions in the oil on medium heat, stirring frequently, for about 7 minutes, until the onions are translucent. Pour in a little water if needed to prevent sticking. Add the ground fennel and wine and cook for 2 minutes. Add the chopped fennel bulb, potatoes, clam juice, tomatoes, and orange peel. Wrap the rosemary in cheesecloth to make a bouquet garni or place it in a tea ball and add it to the stew. Bring the stew to a boil, lower the heat, cover, and simmer for 20 minutes.

Add the saffron and fish to the stew and simmer for about 10 minutes, until the fish flakes with a fork. Break the fish into bite-sized pieces. Add salt and pepper to taste. Serve immediately, topped with basil or parsley and decorated with the reserved fennel fronds.

PER 12-OZ SERVING: 238 CALORIES, 20.4 G PROTEIN, 3.1 G FAT, 30.2 G CARBOHYDRATES, .4 G SATURATED FATTY ACIDS, .6 G POLYUNSATURATED FATTY ACIDS, 1.4 G MONOUNSATURATED FATTY ACIDS, 68 MG CHOLESTEROL, 479 MG SODIUM, 2.0 G TOTAL DIETARY FIBER

MENU SUGGESTIONS Serve with **Mediterranean Couscous Salad** (page 144), a loaf of crusty sourdough bread, and a mixed green salad with **Italian Tomato Basil Dressing** (page 347). Finish with fresh fruit and **Anise Lemon Biscotti** (page 391) or with **Fruit-filled Meringue Shells** (page 388).

POACHED FISH WITH RUSSIAN MUSHROOM SAUCE

This delectable dish has such a delightful and heady aroma that you may find yourself danc-ing a korabushka in the kitchen. We've made it with and without the wine and have been pleased with the results both ways. Because the spring and fall fishing seasons for halibut are quite short, during most of the year you're likely to find it frozen. To defrost fish steaks, immerse them in a large pan of cold water and set it on the countertop for about an hour. Or place the pan in the refrigerator, where the fish will thaw in 6 to 8 hours.

Serve the fish in a shallow bowl covered with sauce and vegetables and offer some dark, crusty bread alongside for dipping, or serve it on rice accompanied by lemon wedges.

2 cups water or vegetable stock
½ cup dry white wine
⅔ cup finely chopped onions
1½ cups coarsely chopped red bell peppers
3 cups sliced mushrooms (about ⅔ pound)
2 teaspoons dried marjoram
2 teaspoons dried tarragon
salt and ground black pepper to taste
4 halibut steaks or other firm fish fillets such as cod,
    mako, or swordfish (about 6 to 8 ounces each)

Serves 4

**Preparation time:
10 minutes**

**Cooking time:
25 minutes**

Combine the water or stock and the wine in a heavy 9-inch skillet and bring to a boil. Add the onions, peppers, mushrooms, marjoram, and tarragon; return to a boil, then lower the heat and simmer for about 10 minutes, until the vegetables are tender and saucy. Add salt and pepper to taste.

Place 2 fish steaks in the simmering vegetable sauce, cover, and poach on medium-high heat for about 7 minutes. Remove the fish from the sauce and set aside. Poach the remaining 2 fish steaks in the same fashion, returning the first 2 fish steaks to the pan for the last 2 or 3 minutes of cooking to rewarm them.

PER 10-OZ SERVING: 233 CALORIES, 37.3 G PROTEIN, 1.8 G FAT, 12.1 G CARBOHYDRATES, .3 G SATURATED FATTY ACIDS, .6 G POLYUNSATURATED FATTY ACIDS, .2 G MONOUNSATURATED FATTY ACIDS, 84 MG CHOLESTEROL, 186 MG SODIUM, 2.7 G TOTAL DIETARY FIBER

MENU SUGGESTIONS Accompany with **Scalloped Potatoes and Carrots** (page 325) or **Orzo and Green Herbs** (page 183) and a tossed salad with **Honey Mustard Garlic Dressing** (page 342). For dessert, we suggest **Tapioca Plum Parfait** (page 375) or **Applesauce Spice Cake** (page 381).

POACHED FISH WITH VEGETABLES

This full-flavored, light, and visually appealing Asian-inspired dish combines the spicy warmth of ginger with the sparkle of citrus and the mellow simplicity of dashi.

1½ pounds cod, scrod, haddock, or other firm fish fillets
½ pound soba noodles (page 437) or whole wheat spaghetti
8 cups Konbu Dashi (page 75)
1 cup orange juice
½ cup soy sauce
¼ cup fresh lemon juice
¼ cup dry sherry
½ cup grated fresh ginger root
½ cup peeled and julienned carrots
½ red bell pepper, seeded and julienned
2 cups chopped bok choy

2 to 3 scallions, sliced on the diagonal
2 to 3 teaspoons dark sesame oil

Serves 4 to 6

**Total time:
40 minutes**

Bring a large pot of water to a rapid boil. Meanwhile, rinse the fish, pat dry, and refrigerate until ready to poach. When the water is boiling, stir in the noodles. Cook until al dente, drain, and set aside, covered.

In a large, nonreactive saucepan, combine the dashi, orange juice, soy sauce, lemon juice, and sherry. Bring to a boil and add the ginger, carrots, and bell pepper. Reduce the heat and simmer for 2 or 3 minutes, until the carrots are almost tender, then add the bok choy. When the bok choy is wilted, about 2 minutes, remove the vegetables from the broth with a slotted spoon and set them aside.

Return the broth to a boil and carefully ease the fish into the broth. Simmer for 3 to 5 minutes, just until the fish flakes easily with a fork.

Meanwhile, in individual bowls, make a bed of noodles and top the noodles with some of the vegetables. When the fish is ready, ladle on a fillet and some broth. Top each serving with scallions and a few drops of sesame oil.

PER 13-OZ SERVING: 358 CALORIES, 41.6 G PROTEIN, 6.3 G FAT, 32.7 G CARBOHYDRATES, 1.0 G SATURATED FATTY ACIDS, 2.4 G POLYUNSATURATED FATTY ACIDS, 2.0 G MONOUNSATURATED FATTY ACIDS, 84 MG CHOLESTEROL, 1764 MG SODIUM, 4.1 G TOTAL DIETARY FIBER

MENU SUGGESTIONS Serve with **Japanese Sesame Spinach** (page 330) and **Sushi Rice Salad** (page 146).

THAI FISH CAKES

These spicy little cakes are traditionally served as an appetizer, but you may decide to make a meal of them. The recipe can easily be doubled or tripled to feed more people (or to feed more to the same number of people). You can make the mixture a few hours ahead of time and refrigerate it until you're ready to cook.

We prefer the crisper outer coating that results from our stove-top method of cooking the fish cakes, but they can also be baked on a lightly oiled or sprayed baking pan at 350° for 15 to 20 minutes.

Serves 4 as an appetizer, 2 as a main course

Makes eight 2½-inch cakes

Total time: 25 to 35 minutes

½ **pound skinless white fish, such as scrod**
3 **tablespoons minced onions**
1 **egg white**
1 **tablespoon Thai Curry Paste (page 365)***
¼ **teaspoon salt**
2 **teaspoons cornstarch, plus some for dusting hands**
2 **tablespoons minced green beans (about 4 beans)**
2 **tablespoons minced red bell pepper**

Commercial curry pastes may be substituted for homemade, but you may wish to reduce the amount used, since many brands are extremely spicy. We suggest that you begin with 1 teaspoon and add more to taste.

Combine the raw fish, onions, egg white, curry paste, salt, and cornstarch in the bowl of a food processor and blend until well mixed but not totally smooth. Stir in the green beans and bell peppers.

Dust your hands with a little cornstarch to prevent sticking and form the mixture into eight patties. Lightly spray or oil a non-stick skillet and sauté the cakes in two batches on medium heat for about 4 minutes on each side, until golden and cooked through. Serve immediately.

PER 3-OZ SERVING: 79 CALORIES, 13.4 G PROTEIN, .6 G FAT, 4.1 G CARBOHYDRATES, .1 G SATURATED FATTY ACIDS, .3 G POLYUNSATURATED FATTY ACIDS, .1 G MONOUNSATURATED FATTY ACIDS, 49 MG CHOLESTEROL, 264 MG SODIUM, .4 G TOTAL DIETARY FIBER

MENU SUGGESTIONS Serve with **Asian Cucumber Condiment** (page 367), **Thai Curry Paste** (page 365), and/or **Pineapple Chutney** (page 292). As a main dish, serve with **Fragrant Jasmine Rice** (page 189) and **Zucchini with Cilantro Sauce** (page 335). Finish with one of the **Tapioca Fruit Parfaits** (page 375) or **Pineapple Buttermilk Sherbet** (page 394).

GINGERED SHRIMP AND SOBA

In this recipe, fresh plump shrimp are simmered in the familiar aromatic flavors of China and served on a bed of hearty and nutritious buckwheat noodles.

3 tablespoons soy sauce
2 tablespoons dry sherry
¼ cup unsweetened apple juice
2 tablespoons water
1 tablespoon grated fresh ginger root
1 large bunch broccoli, peeled and cut into
    bite-sized pieces and florets
8 ounces soba noodles (page 437)
1 tablespoon dark sesame oil
juice of 1 lemon
2 garlic cloves, minced or pressed
1 pound shrimp, peeled and deveined
½ cup chopped scallions

Serves 4

Total time: 45 minutes

NOTE:
Shrimp, crayfish, crab, lobster, and other shellfish are very low in fat, although pound for pound some do contain more cholesterol than meat or fish.

Bring a large covered pot of water to a boil.

Meanwhile, in a small saucepan, combine the soy sauce, sherry, apple juice, water, and ginger and simmer on medium heat for 5 minutes. Remove from the heat and set aside.

When the water boils, blanch the broccoli in the boiling water just until tender, 3 to 5 minutes. Using a large slotted spoon or a sieve, remove the broccoli and set aside to drain. Add the soba noodles to the boiling water and cook for 8 to 10 minutes, until tender but still firm.

While the noodles cook, combine the sesame oil, lemon juice, and garlic in a nonreactive skillet and warm on medium-high heat. Add the shrimp and sauté for 3 to 5 minutes, until just pink and tender. Set aside.

Drain the noodles and return them to the still warm pot. Add the broccoli, shrimp, scallions, and soy sauce mixture and, if necessary, toss briefly on medium heat until everything is hot. Serve immediately.

PER 15-OZ SERVING: 333 CALORIES, 32.5 G PROTEIN, 5.2 G FAT, 42.6 G CARBOHYDRATES, .9 G SATURATED FATTY ACIDS, 2.2 G POLYUNSATURATED FATTY ACIDS, 1.7 G MONOUNSATURATED FATTY ACIDS, 195 MG CHOLESTEROL, 951 MG SODIUM, 3.4 G TOTAL DIETARY FIBER

MENU SUGGESTIONS Serve with **Essential Miso Soup with Tofu** (page 80) and a tossed salad topped with **Spicy Peanut Dressing** (page 349). Finish with **Tapioca Plum Parfait** (page 375) for dessert.

SICILIAN SCALLOP SALAD

A Sicilian dish full of the specialties of the Mediterranean region, this colorful, refreshing salad combines sea scallops dressed with a light citrus and herb sauce and fresh greens.

SALAD

8 garlic cloves, minced or pressed
1 cup dry white wine
1 pound sea scallops, large ones cut in half crosswise
6 cups mesclun (page 431) and/or other mixed greens
1 red bell pepper, seeded and cut crosswise into rings
2 oranges, peeled, seeded, and sectioned (page 418)

Serves 4

Total time: 30 to 40 minutes

DRESSING

1 cup orange juice (strained, if fresh)
3 tablespoons fresh lemon juice
1 tablespoon olive oil
salt and ground black pepper to taste

chopped fresh basil (chiffonade is nice)

Combine the garlic and white wine in a saucepan and bring to a boil. Add the scallops and cook on medium-high heat for about 5 minutes, stirring often, until tender and opaque. With a slotted spoon, remove the scallops from the pan and set them aside in a bowl. Reduce the remaining garlic and wine to about ¼ cup by simmering for about 10 minutes and set aside to cool.

Spread the greens on a large platter and arrange the pepper rings and orange sections artfully around the edge. In a small bowl, mix together the orange juice, lemon juice, and olive oil. Add the reduced wine liquid and salt and pepper to taste. Toss the dressing with the scallops, then ladle them into the center of the serving platter and drizzle the rest of the dressing over the salad. Top with basil and serve immediately.

PER 14-OZ SERVING: 231 CALORIES, 16.1 G PROTEIN, 4.9 G FAT, 25.3 G CARBOHYDRATES, .5 G SATURATED FATTY ACIDS, .5 G POLYUNSATURATED FATTY ACIDS, 2.7 G MONOUNSATURATED FATTY ACIDS, 30 MG CHOLESTEROL, 216 MG SODIUM, 5.1 G TOTAL DIETARY FIBER

MENU SUGGESTIONS Serve with **Tabouli Salad** (page 145) or **Orzo and Green Herbs** (page 183) accompanied by **Curried Carrot Parsnip Soup** (page 100) and a loaf of crusty Italian bread.

THAI SEAFOOD YUM

This recipe was inspired by a dish we have eaten on numerous occasions at one of our local Thai restaurants. *Yum* in Thai means "salad," but the American colloquialism *yum* coincidentally describes this dish perfectly.

SAUCE

⅓ cup fresh lime juice
2 teaspoons sugar
2 tablespoons Asian fish sauce (page 420)
2 tablespoons chopped fresh cilantro

Serves 4

**Total time:
30 to 40 minutes**

FISH

1 fresh chile, seeded and minced
1 teaspoon canola or other vegetable oil
½ pound shelled and deveined medium shrimp
½ pound sea scallops, cut in half crosswise if large
¾ cup thinly sliced red onions

SALAD BED

4 cups mixed salad greens
2 tomatoes, cut into wedges

Whisk together the lime juice, sugar, fish sauce, and cilantro in a large bowl and set it aside. In a skillet, sauté the chile in the oil on medium heat for about 1 minute. Add the shrimp and sauté, stirring, until they begin to turn pink and curl and are heated through, about 4 minutes. Remove the shrimp to the bowl of sauce to marinate. Add the scallops to the skillet, sauté for 3 to 5 minutes, until cooked, and remove them to the bowl with the shrimp. Add the red onions to the seafood and toss to coat everything with the sauce.

Arrange the greens to cover a serving platter, mound the seafood in the center, and decorate the edge with the tomato wedges.

PER 10-OZ SERVING: 145 CALORIES, 19.6 G PROTEIN, 2.6 G FAT, 13.4 G CARBOHYDRATES, .4 G SATURATED FATTY ACIDS, 1.1 G POLYUNSATURATED FATTY ACIDS, .4 G MONOUNSATURATED FATTY ACIDS, 117 MG CHOLESTEROL, 778 MG SODIUM, 3.0 G TOTAL DIETARY FIBER

MENU SUGGESTIONS Serve with **Thai Fried Rice** (page 190) or **Curried Rice Noodles** (page 220) and offer a bowl of lime wedges at the table for squeezing on individual servings.

seasoned steamed artichokes 311

roasted asparagus 312

CITRUS-DRESSED ASPARAGUS 313

baked beets and shallots 314

gingered broccoli 315

BROCCOLI RABE AND GARLIC 315

morrocan carrots 316

mustard carrots 317

CAULIFLOWER AGRODOLCE 318

cauliflower with curry sauce 319

gingered fennel with garlic 320

CAROLINA KALE 321

broiled portabella mushrooms 322

sweet sweet potatoes 323

SPANISH POTATOES 324

scalloped potatoes and carrots 325

oven "fries" 326

POTATO CAKES 327

garlic mashed potatoes 328

snap peas with mushrooms 329

JAPANESE SESAME SPINACH 330

holiday cranberry squash 331

curried squash 332

BROILED ZUCCHINI WITH HERBS 333

southeast asian coconut zucchini 334

zucchini with cilantro sauce 335

THAI BAKED TOFU 336

jerk tofu 337

SIDE DISHES

One of the delights of dining out is the chance to sample an array of appetizers and **SIDE DISHES**, to try many little dishes instead of one main dish. This type of meal is a natural part of some cuisines. Middle Eastern *mezze*, Spanish *tapas,* and some Thai, Indian, and Japanese meals consist entirely of many colorful dishes eaten in small quantities. Other traditions favor a substantial entrée with one or two flattering side dishes that add eye-catching color and contrasting texture.

Either way, we've become devotees of side dishes. Browse through this section of our book with an open mind—you'll find side dishes to complement a main dish, but you may also find small dishes tempting enough to build a meal around. Try a meal composed of:

* Broiled Portabella Mushrooms, Garlic Mashed Potatoes, and Mustard Carrots
* Jerk Tofu, Carolina Kale, and Sweet Sweet Potatoes
* Scalloped Potatoes and Carrots, Holiday Cranberry Squash, and Seasoned Steamed Artichokes
* Roasted Asparagus, Baked Beets and Shallots, and Oven "Fries"

The most basic side dish—a plain steamed, boiled, or broiled vegetable—can be easily transformed into a memorable dish with the simple additions suggested below. Or drizzle on just a thread of good, fruity olive oil and add salt, freshly ground pepper, and a few chopped fresh herbs.

Steam vegetables in a little water or in a steamer basket above water. Cover the pan and cook until crisp-tender. Fragile snow peas and spinach cook in just a few minutes, while beets or whole artichokes may require 30 to 40 minutes. Greens, cauliflower, broccoli, zucchini, and summer squash steam in about 5 minutes. Denser, hardier vegetables such as carrots, green beans, winter squash, parsnips, and potatoes may need 10 minutes or more, depending upon how they are cut.

Broiling or grilling vegetables brings out their intrinsic sweetness. For zucchini, summer squash, sweet peppers, onions, fennel, tomatoes, eggplant, mushrooms, or asparagus, brush with a little olive oil, sprinkle with a little salt and pepper, and roast over or under a hot fire for a short time on both sides. Parboil carrots and potatoes first to speed their grilling time.

All of these nutritious and beautiful fruits of the harvest, picked and eaten at the peak of flavor and prepared when fresh, remind us again and again of the important relationship between the farmer and the cook, between the rich earth and our dependence on its gifts.

Here are suggestions for some delicious sauces, dressings, and other additions that can transform simple vegetables.

ASPARAGUS Steam and then dress with nonfat yogurt and snipped chives, Creamy Roasted Red Pepper Sauce (page 355), or grated fresh ginger and a splash of rice vinegar.

BEETS Dress cooked beets with vinegar, nonfat sour cream, fresh dill, and scallions. Or drizzle with Skordalia Thessalonike (page 354). Roast beets with new potatoes and pearl onions.

BROCCOLI Prepare as for Japanese Sesame Spinach (page 330). Steam broccoli and then drizzle with Skordalia Thessalonike (page 354) or dress with Japanese Carrot Dressing (page 346).

BRUSSELS SPROUTS Combine with rounds of carrots or parsnips for sweetness and color and dress with Honey Mustard Garlic Dressing (page 342) or Creamy Dill Dressing (page 342).

CABBAGE Dress shredded raw cabbage with Cumin Yogurt Dressing (page 132). Toss shredded steamed cabbage with Savory Onion Marmalade (page 363), raisins, and grated apple. Try cooked cabbage with Spicy Peanut Dressing (page 349), Thai Curry Paste (page 365), Hot Tamarind and Guava Sauce for Fish or Vegetables (page 356), or Asian Cucumber Condiment (page 367). Slow-cook shredded cabbage in a nonstick pan with a little apple juice or cider, and toward the end, add sugar and vinegar to taste for sweet-and-sour cabbage.

CARROTS Dress shredded raw carrots with Creamy Ginger Miso Dressing (page 343), Spicy Peanut Dressing (page 349), or Southeast Asian Pineapple Sesame Dressing (page 343). Dress steamed carrots with nonfat yogurt mixed with curry powder or chopped fresh mint, or with raspberry vinegar and snipped chives and/or tarragon. Top steamed carrots with Cilantro Pesto (page 364) or Salsa Verde Liguria (page 353). Cook carrots in marsala wine instead of water.

CAULIFLOWER Dress steamed cauliflower with Cilantro Pesto (page 364), Curried Mango Yogurt Dressing (page 151), Mango Peach Chutney (page 362) or commercial chutney, Tomato Pineapple Salsa (page 360), Tomato Corn Salsa (page 366), or your favorite commercial salsa, or nonfat sour cream or nonfat yogurt with dill and caraway seeds.

CORN Squeeze a wedge of lime over corn on the cob, brush with Cilantro Pesto (page 364), or sprinkle with Old Bay Seasoning. Stir Tomato Pineapple Salsa (page 360) or a commercial salsa into cooked frozen corn. Cook corn with curry powder and minced red bell pepper.

EGGPLANT Dress strips or rounds of steamed or baked eggplant with Yogurt Tahini Dressing (page 346), Cumin Yogurt Dressing (page 132), or Skordalia Thessalonike (page 354). Broil eggplant following the directions for Broiled Portabella Mushrooms (page 322).

GREEN BEANS Try steamed beans with Susan's Pesto (page 364) or Cilantro Pesto (page 364), the yogurt dressing from Cauliflower with Curry Sauce (page 319), or the sauce for Cauliflower Agrodolce (page 318). Or add a few steamed red pepper or carrot strips and top with chopped tomatoes and a splash of balsamic or herb vinegar.

GREENS Sauté greens in a nonstick pan with ginger, garlic, soy sauce, and mirin. Toss steamed greens with vinegar and Tabasco sauce, Spicy Peanut Dressing (page 349), or Japanese Carrot Dressing (page 346). Cook your favorite greens following the recipe for Gingered Broccoli (page 315) or Japanese Sesame Spinach (page 330).

PEAS Top steamed peas with Minted Dill Yogurt Dressing (page 345) or with homemade or commercial curry sauce or paste. Toss peas with orzo and Roasted Garlic (page 43).

POTATOES Dress with Italian Tomato Basil Dressing (page 347), nonfat sour cream with dill and chives, Susan's Pesto (page 364), Cilantro Pesto (page 364), Salsa Verde Liguria (page 353), Hungarian Lesco (page 357), Garlic Basil Cheese Spread (page 22), Caesar Salad Dressing (page 131), or Roasted Garlic (page 43).

WINTER SQUASH Cut in half, place a little Savory Onion Marmalade (page 363) in each cavity, and bake in apple juice. Dress steamed cubes of squash with Hot Tamarind and Guava Sauce for Fish or Vegetables (page 356), Hungarian Lesco (page 357), or hoisin sauce.

ZUCCHINI Dress steamed zucchini with Tomato Corn Salsa (page 366), Salsa Verde Liguria (page 353), or Chermoulla (page 291). Simmer zucchini in Chunky Tomato Sauce (page 351).

SEASONED STEAMED ARTICHOKES

Adding olive oil, vinegar, herbs, and spices to the cooking water makes these artichokes delicious enough to eat plain. Nevertheless, you may want to try dipping them into Orange Tarragon Dressing (page 348) or Skordalia Thessalonike (page 354).

We prefer regular artichokes with thorny tips, even though it takes a few minutes to trim them with a scissors. While the newer "thornless" varieties are slightly faster to prepare, we find they are just not as flavorful.

Serves 4

**Preparation time:
10 minutes**

**Cooking time:
20 to 35 minutes**

**4 artichokes
4 cups water
1 tablespoon olive oil
2 tablespoons wine vinegar
4 garlic cloves
4 bay leaves
1 teaspoon salt
12 black peppercorns
12 coriander seeds
½ teaspoon fennel seeds**

Slice off the stem and remove the tough outer leaves of each artichoke. Using kitchen scissors or a sharp knife, trim the thorny leaf tips and then rinse the artichoke thoroughly.

Place the artichokes, stem end down, in a saucepan. Add the water, oil, vinegar, garlic, bay leaves, salt, peppercorns, and coriander and fennel seeds. Cover and bring to a boil. Reduce the heat and simmer for 20 to 35 minutes, until tender.

Cooking time will vary depending upon the size and freshness of the artichokes. To test for doneness, using tongs, tug on an outer leaf or lift an artichoke from the pan and pierce the bottom with a knife. When a leaf can be removed with the slightest resistance or a knife easily pierces the bottom, the artichokes are done.

Serve hot, warm, or at room temperature.

PER 4.50-OZ SERVING: 94 CALORIES, 4.2 G PROTEIN, 3.8 G FAT, 14.3 G CARBOHYDRATES, .5 G SATURATED FATTY ACIDS, .4 G POLYUNSATURATED FATTY ACIDS, 2.7 G MONOUNSATURATED FATTY ACIDS, 0 MG CHOLESTEROL, 702 MG SODIUM, 6.5 G TOTAL DIETARY FIBER

MENU SUGGESTIONS These make good appetizers for any Mediterranean meal and work well on a variety of combination plates. Try them drizzled with **Yogurt Tahini Dressing** (page 346) before **Middle Eastern Chickpeas with Spinach** (page 169) and **Tabouli Salad** (page 145) on greens.

ROASTED ASPARAGUS

Roasting vegetables in an herbed vinaigrette is one of the tastiest methods for bringing out their bright natural flavors, and this recipe is proof. Look for asparagus that are uniformly green, firm, and with tightly budded tips. Discolored or shriveled tips or very dried woody stem ends may indicate that the asparagus are not as freshly picked and tender as they could be.

We think it's best to break off the tough white base of each stalk by hand rather than slicing the stem ends off with a knife. When you break the asparagus by hand, the spear will naturally snap at the juncture of the tough and tender parts, and then you can be sure that you are discarding the whole tough part and nothing but the tough part.

1 pound asparagus, cleaned, tough stem ends removed

Serves 4

**Preparation time:
10 minutes**

**Baking time:
20 to 25 minutes**

DRESSING

2 teaspoons olive oil

1 teaspoon balsamic vinegar

⅛ to ¼ teaspoon salt

1 garlic clove, minced or pressed

2 teaspoons minced fresh tarragon

Preheat the oven to 400°.

Toss together the asparagus and dressing in a bowl until the asparagus are well coated. Arrange the asparagus in a single layer on an unoiled baking tray. Bake for 20 to 25 minutes, until the asparagus spears are tender, stirring occasionally.

PER 4-OZ SERVING: 52 CALORIES, 3.2 G PROTEIN, 2.8 G FAT, 5.4 G CARBOHYDRATES, .4 G SATURATED FATTY ACIDS, .4 G POLYUNSATURATED FATTY ACIDS, 1.8 G MONOUNSATURATED FATTY ACIDS, 0 MG CHOLESTEROL, 79 MG SODIUM, 0 G TOTAL DIETARY FIBER

MENU SUGGESTIONS Make a bistro supper beginning with **Garlic Basil Cheese Spread** (page 22) on toast, followed by **Cassoulet** (page 160) and Roasted Asparagus; end with **Red Berry Kissel** (page 372) for dessert. Try along with **Orzo and Pea Soup** (page 93) and **Herb and Cheese Muffins** (page 112). Or serve as a side dish for **Mushroom Spinach Crêpes** (page 234), **Sun-Dried Tomato Polenta Cutlets** (page 236), or **Breaded Garlic Dill Fish** (page 297).

CITRUS-DRESSED ASPARAGUS

Citrus flavor enhances fresh asparagus without overpowering it, but this tangy and sparky marinade can add zip to almost any steamed vegetable—artichokes, carrots, zucchini, yellow squash, and sweet potatoes.

1 pound asparagus
2 teaspoons extra-virgin olive oil
4 teaspoons fresh lemon juice
4 teaspoons orange juice
generous pinch of cayenne
salt and ground black pepper to taste

Serves 4

Total time: 20 minutes

Snap off the tough stem ends of the asparagus spears. Rinse the spears and cut them into 2- or 3-inch pieces. Steam the asparagus in about an inch of water (or use a steamer basket) for about 7 to 10 minutes, or until just tender.

Meanwhile, whisk together the olive oil, lemon juice, orange juice, cayenne, and salt and pepper. As soon as the asparagus is ready, remove it to a serving bowl or plate, pour the dressing over it, and serve warm.

PER 4-OZ SERVING: 55 CALORIES, 3.3 G PROTEIN, 2.8 G FAT, 6.3 G CARBOHYDRATES, .4 G SATURATED FATTY ACIDS, .4 G POLYUNSATURATED FATTY ACIDS, 1.8 G MONOUNSATURATED FATTY ACIDS, 0 MG CHOLESTEROL, 49 MG SODIUM, .1 G TOTAL DIETARY FIBER

MENU SUGGESTIONS Offer with **Spanish Potato Pepper Frittata** (page 51), **Cassoulet** (page 160), **Breaded Garlic Dill Fish** (page 297), or with almost any meal in spring when fresh asparagus makes its fleeting appearance.

BAKED BEETS AND SHALLOTS

If you've never tasted baked beets, you're going to be pleasantly surprised when you try these. Baking concentrates the beets' flavor and sweetness.

If your beets have nice, tender greens, cut a couple of leaves crosswise into thin strips for an elegant and delicious garnish. A few lemon wedges are also nice for contrasting color and a touch of additional flavor.

2 pounds fresh beets (about 6 medium or 10 small beets)
½ pound shallots (about 8 large) or 3 medium onions,
    peeled and quartered
1 tablespoon vinegar
1 tablespoon olive oil
1 teaspoon salt
¼ teaspoon ground black pepper

shredded beet greens or chopped fresh parsley

Serves 6

Preparation time: 20 minutes

Baking time: 1 hour

Preheat the oven to 400°.

Wash the beets and trim the stems and tails. Peel the shallots. Place the beets and shallots or quartered onions on a large sheet of aluminum foil and fold the edges together to seal tightly. Bake for about 1 hour, or until the beets are tender and easily pierced with a knife.

Remove the packet from the oven and set it aside to cool. Meanwhile, in a cup or small bowl, stir together the vinegar, olive oil, salt, and pepper. When the beets are cool enough to handle, rub them to remove the skin, then cut them into chunks or wedges. Place the beets and shallots in a serving bowl. Drizzle the dressing over them and toss well. Serve warm or at room temperature, garnished with beet greens or parsley.

PER 6.50-OZ SERVING: 110 CALORIES, 3.3 G PROTEIN, 2.7 G FAT, 20.3 G CARBOHYDRATES, .4 G SATURATED FATTY ACIDS, .3 G POLYUNSATURATED FATTY ACIDS, 1.8 G MONOUNSATURATED FATTY ACIDS, 0 MG CHOLESTEROL, 507 MG SODIUM, 2.4 G TOTAL DIETARY FIBER

MENU SUGGESTIONS Serve with **Baltic Fish** (page 287), **Poached Fish with Russian Mushroom Sauce** (page 300), **Cassoulet** (page 160), or **Cabbage Rolls** (page 256).

GINGERED BROCCOLI

Here we've used basic Chinese sauce ingredients to make a simmering broth that infuses the broccoli with flavor as it steams.

1 head broccoli
1 tablespoon grated fresh ginger root
2 garlic cloves, sliced
¼ cup rice vinegar
1 tablespoon hoisin sauce (page 429) or sugar
2 tablespoons soy sauce

Serves 4 to 6

Total time: 15 minutes

Slice off and discard the tough base of the broccoli stems and cut the broccoli into spears.

Combine the ginger, garlic, vinegar, hoisin sauce or sugar, and soy sauce in a saucepan, bring it to a boil, and then ease in the broccoli. Steam the broccoli for 5 to 7 minutes, until tender but still brightly colored. Serve immediately with some of the sauce spooned over it.

PER 4-OZ SERVING: 41 CALORIES, 3.2 G PROTEIN, .4 G FAT, 8.3 G CARBOHYDRATES, .1 G SATURATED FATTY ACIDS, .2 G POLYUNSATURATED FATTY ACIDS, 0 G MONOUNSATURATED FATTY ACIDS, 0 MG CHOLESTEROL, 296 MG SODIUM, 2.9 G TOTAL DIETARY FIBER

MENU SUGGESTIONS Serve with **Five-Spice Rice** (page 186), **Vegetable Udon Sauté** (page 204), or **Cantonese Roasted Vegetables** (page 226). Or offer with **Mushroom Sesame Tofu Stew** (page 277).

BROCCOLI RABE AND GARLIC

Reminiscent of Mama's sautéed Italian greens but minus the olive oil, this simple preparation still enhances the distinctive bite of broccoli rabe.

1 bunch broccoli rabe
½ cup water
2 garlic cloves, minced or pressed
2 teaspoons soy sauce

Serves 4 to 6

Total time: 15 minutes

Wash the broccoli rabe and remove any tough stems. Chop it and set it aside.

Combine the water, garlic, and soy sauce in a saucepan, bring it to a boil, and then ease in the broccoli rabe. Cover and cook for 3 to 5 minutes, until crisp-tender.

PER 4-OZ SERVING: 34 CALORIES, 3.6 G PROTEIN, .4 G FAT, 6.1 G CARBOHYDRATES, .1 G SATURATED FATTY ACIDS, .2 G POLYUNSATURATED FATTY ACIDS, 0 G MONOUNSATURATED FATTY ACIDS, 0 MG CHOLESTEROL, 138 MG SODIUM, 3.4 G TOTAL DIETARY FIBER

MENU SUGGESTIONS Try an Italian meal with **Tuscan Beans with Sage** (page 168), **Penne with Puttanesca Sauce** (page 214), or **Mushroom Polenta Pie** (page 240). Or serve with **Vietnamese Hot and Sour Soup** (page 87), **Thai Fried Rice** (page 190), or **Sweet-and-Sour Lentils** (page 171).

MOROCCAN CARROTS

Sweet and flavored with aromatic spices, this side dish is good with tangy or bland foods. Traditionally, Moroccan-style carrots swim in butter, but we've found that a little extra citrus and a touch of cornstarch to help the spices coat the carrots transforms one of our favorite extravagant dishes into one of our favorite very-low-fat dishes.

⅓ cup currants
¼ cup hot water
3 cups peeled and thinly sliced or julienned carrots
1 cup orange juice
1 tablespoon fresh lemon juice
½ teaspoon cornstarch
½ teaspoon ground cinnamon
1 teaspoon ground cumin
pinch of cayenne
salt and ground black pepper to taste

chopped fresh parsley or mint (optional)

Serves 6

Total time: 20 minutes

Soak the currants in the hot water until plump, about 10 minutes.

Meanwhile, in a covered saucepan, blanch the carrots in boiling water until just tender, about 5 minutes. Combine the orange juice, lemon juice, and cornstarch, stirring well to dissolve the cornstarch. Drain the carrots and return them to the saucepan on medium heat. Add the juice mixture, cinnamon, cumin, cayenne, and the currants and their soaking liquid. Simmer, stirring often, for 5 minutes. Add salt and pepper to taste.

Serve warm or at room temperature, topped with chopped parsley or mint, if you like.

PER 4-OZ SERVING: 73 CALORIES, 1.4 G PROTEIN, .3 G FAT, 17.6 G CARBOHYDRATES, 0 G SATURATED FATTY ACIDS, .1 G POLYUNSATURATED FATTY ACIDS, 0 G MONOUNSATURATED FATTY ACIDS, 0 MG CHOLESTEROL, 75 MG SODIUM, 3.0 G TOTAL DIETARY FIBER

MENU SUGGESTIONS Begin with **Creamy Potato Kale Soup** (page 91), and serve with **Baked Flounder Rolls** (page 295) using **Cilantro Pesto** (page 364) in the recipe. Finish with **Chocolate Cocoa Cake** (page 380).

MUSTARD CARROTS

Bright orange carrots speckled with dark mustard seeds make for a very attractive, pickle-y side dish. Black mustard seeds are commonly used in Indian cooking. Less pungent than the yellow variety, they release their nutty flavor when heated in oil—with the unexpected bonus of a short musical burst of cheerful, rhythmic popping.

⅓ cup cider vinegar
1 tablespoon brown sugar
2 teaspoons Dijon mustard
½ teaspoon salt
1 teaspoon dried dill
2 teaspoons mustard seeds
1 pound carrots, peeled and cut into julienne sticks (about 3 cups)

Serves 4 to 6

**Total time·
30 to 35 minutes**

In a cup or bowl, stir together the vinegar, brown sugar, mustard, salt, and dill. Set aside.

In a saucepan, dry-roast the mustard seeds (page 419) for about 30 seconds, until they are browned and popping. Add the vinegar mixture and bring to a boil. Stir in the carrot sticks, cover, lower the heat, and cook until tender, about 15 to 20 minutes. Be vigilant for the last few minutes of cooking, stirring frequently when there is very little cooking liquid left. The finished carrots will be slightly caramelized. Serve hot or at room temperature.

PER 3-OZ SERVING: 49 CALORIES, 1.2 G PROTEIN, .6 G FAT, 10.9 G CARBOHYDRATES, 0 G SATURATED FATTY ACIDS, .1 G POLYUNSATURATED FATTY ACIDS, .3 G MONOUNSATURATED FATTY ACIDS, 0 MG CHOLESTEROL, 266 MG SODIUM, 2.4 G TOTAL DIETARY FIBER

MENU SUGGESTIONS Serve with **Orzo and Green Herbs** (page 183), or with **Baltic Fish** (page 287) and **Mushroom Wheatberry Pilaf** (page 195). Mustard Carrots are also a piquant side dish for **Cabbage Rolls** (page 256), **Macaroni and Cheese** (page 203), or **Garlicky Black-Eyed Peas 'n' Greens** (page 170).

CAULIFLOWER AGRODOLCE

Perhaps seafaring Venetians were inspired by Chinese sweet-and-sour dishes as they developed their own recipes. At any rate, Italian cuisine is now filled with many inventive *agrodolce*, or sweet-and-sour, vegetable dishes, which, in turn, inspired us to create an interesting new way to prepare cauliflower.

2 cups onions, thinly sliced
3 garlic cloves, sliced (1 tablespoon)
1 teaspoon olive oil
1 large cauliflower
3 cups undrained whole tomatoes (28-ounce can)
⅔ cup raisins
½ cup red wine vinegar
sugar, salt, and ground black pepper to taste

Serves 4 to 6

Preparation time: 15 minutes

Cooking time: 15 to 20 minutes

In a nonreactive saucepan, cook the onions and garlic in the oil for about 7 minutes on medium heat, stirring frequently. Meanwhile, core and cut the cauliflower into florets; there should be about 7 cups. Chop the tomatoes or squeeze them by hand and add them with their juice to the onions. Stir in the raisins and vinegar. When the onions are translucent, add the cauliflower florets and cook for 10 to 12 minutes, or until the florets can be pierced with a fork but are not falling apart. Add sugar, salt, and pepper to taste. Serve hot, at room temperature, or chilled.

PER 8-OZ SERVING: 125 CALORIES, 4.1 G PROTEIN, 1.6 G FAT, 27.5 G CARBOHYDRATES, .2 G SATURATED FATTY ACIDS, .3 G POLYUNSATURATED FATTY ACIDS, .6 G MONOUNSATURATED FATTY ACIDS, 0 MG CHOLESTEROL, 192 MG SODIUM, 3.9 G TOTAL DIETARY FIBER

MENU SUGGESTIONS Enjoy with **Oven "Fries"** (page 326) and **Broiled Portabella Mushrooms** (page 322). Geographically this dish is a natural ally of **Mediterranean Couscous Salad** (page 144), **Mushroom Polenta Pie** (page 240), and **Spanish Potato Pepper Frittata** (page 51), but it is also a flavor booster for blander dishes such as **Another Shepherd's Pie** (page 238), **Baltic Fish** (page 287), or **Garlicky Black-Eyed Peas 'n' Greens** (page 170). Serve leftovers as a chilled side salad for **Tuscan Sandwich** (page 124).

CAULIFLOWER WITH CURRY SAUCE

A snap to make, the curry sauce featured here can add spice and life to any steamed vegetable, but we think it's especially great on mild-flavored cauliflower.

Serves 2 to 4

Total time: 25 minutes

1 small cauliflower, cut into florets (about 3 cups)

CURRY SAUCE
1 cup chopped onions
1 teaspoon canola or other vegetable oil
1 teaspoon ground cumin
½ teaspoon ground coriander
½ teaspoon turmeric
pinch of cayenne, or more to taste
1 cup nonfat yogurt
salt and ground black pepper to taste

Steam the cauliflower for 15 to 20 minutes, or until tender.

While the cauliflower cooks, sauté the onions in the oil in a small skillet until golden, drizzling in a little water if necessary to prevent sticking. Add the cumin, coriander, turmeric, and cayenne and cook, stirring often, for another 2 minutes. Transfer to a blender or food processor, add the yogurt, and purée until smooth. Add salt and pepper to taste.

When the cauliflower is ready, remove it to a serving bowl, pour on the curried yogurt sauce, toss gently, and serve.

PER 5.5-OZ SERVING: 77 CALORIES, 5.2 G PROTEIN, 1.9 G FAT, 11.3 G CARBOHYDRATES, .3 G SATURATED FATTY ACIDS, .9 G POLYUNSATURATED FATTY ACIDS, .4 G MONOUNSATURATED FATTY ACIDS, 1 MG CHOLESTEROL, 101 MG SODIUM, 2.6 G TOTAL DIETARY FIBER

MENU SUGGESTIONS Serve with **Golden Split Pea Soup** (page 92), **Savory Indian Sweet Potatoes** (page 248), and **Mango Coconut Cucumber Salad** (page 136). Or try it with **Fish with Pineapple Chutney** (page 292), **Golden Basmati Rice** (page 185), and steamed green beans.

GINGERED FENNEL WITH GARLIC

The stimulating anise flavor of crisp fennel is infused with the sweet heat of ginger for a surprise wake-up call to the senses.

2 medium fennel bulbs (about 2 pounds)
2 garlic cloves, sliced
2 teaspoons vegetable oil
2 tablespoons grated fresh ginger root
½ cup orange juice (or sherry)
2 teaspoons sugar
salt and ground black pepper to taste

Serves 4 to 8

Total time: 20 minutes

Slice off the root end and trim the stalks and feathery fronds of the fennel bulbs, reserving a few fronds for garnish, if desired. Cut the bulbs into halves, remove and discard the tough inner cores, and slice thin.

In a large skillet, sauté the garlic and fennel in the oil on medium-high heat for about 7 minutes, stirring frequently and adding a splash or two of water if necessary to prevent sticking, until the fennel is golden brown. Add the ginger and the orange juice, cover, lower the heat, and simmer until the fennel is tender, about 5 minutes. Sprinkle on the sugar and salt and pepper to taste. Serve garnished with the reserved fennel fronds.

PER 4.50-OZ SERVING: 58 CALORIES, 1.5 G PROTEIN, 1.4 G FAT, 11.2 G CARBOHYDRATES, .2 G SATURATED FATTY ACIDS, .7 G POLYUNSATURATED FATTY ACIDS, .3 G MONOUNSATURATED FATTY ACIDS, 0 MG CHOLESTEROL, 82 MG SODIUM, .1 G TOTAL DIETARY FIBER

MENU SUGGESTIONS This side dish with a hint of licorice can fit into many ethnic cuisines. Try it with **Squash and Kale Risotto** (page 192), **Pasta and Sun-Dried Tomatoes** (page 208), **Tofu Vegetable Dumplings** (page 38), or **Bulgur with Savory Greens** (page 178).

CAROLINA KALE

Cooked until just tender, bright vitamin- and mineral-rich greens contrast beautifully with red tomatoes to make an appealing vegetable side dish or a topping for rice.

1½ pounds kale, collards, chard, beet greens,
   or mustard greens
2 cups chopped canned tomatoes and their juice or
   3 cups chopped fresh tomatoes
1 cup minced onions
1½ teaspoons ground cumin
2 garlic cloves, pressed or minced
1 teaspoon Tabasco or other hot pepper sauce or
   ¼ teaspoon crushed red pepper
½ teaspoon salt
ground black pepper to taste

Serves 4 to 6

Total time: 25 minutes

> **NOTE!**
> The cooking time will vary with the type and tenderness of the greens. If necessary, add a little water during cooking to maintain liquid in the bottom of the pan.

Wash the greens. Remove the large stems and any discolored leaves. Stack the leaves and slice them crosswise into ⅛-inch strips.

   Combine the tomatoes, onions, cumin, garlic, Tabasco, and salt in a saucepan, cover, and cook on medium heat for 5 minutes. Add the greens, cover, and gently simmer, stirring frequently, for 10 to 15 minutes, until the greens are tender (see Note). Add pepper to taste and serve.

PER 7-OZ SERVING: 65 CALORIES, 3.3 G PROTEIN, .8 G FAT, 12.3 G CARBOHYDRATES, .1 G SATURATED FATTY ACIDS, .2 G POLYUNSATURATED FATTY ACIDS, 0 G MONOUNSATURATED FATTY ACIDS, 0 MG CHOLESTEROL, 333 MG SODIUM, 2.7 G TOTAL DIETARY FIBER

MENU SUGGESTIONS Southern-style kale goes well with **Barbecue Beans** (page 156) or **Fat Tuesday's Skinny Red Beans** (page 165) with **Almost Fat-Free Cornbread** (page 110). Or try it beside **Honey Mustard Fish** (page 298) or **Mushroom Polenta Pie** (page 240).

BROILED PORTABELLA MUSHROOMS

With their earthy flavor and meaty succulence, giant portabella mushrooms presented on a bed of wilted spinach make an unusual and attractive side dish. Accompanied by a coarse, dark, whole grain bread to sop up the juices, this makes a satisfying meal for two.

Our dish was inspired by a recipe from Susan Jane Cheney, author of *Breadtime Stories* and a former Moosewood cook.

1 pound portabella mushrooms
1 tablespoon light miso
1 tablespoon balsamic vinegar
2 tablespoons water
2 teaspoons olive oil
10 ounces fresh spinach, stemmed and rinsed

**Serves 2 as a main dish
4 as a side dish**

Total time: 10 minutes

Preheat the broiler.

Carefully brush or wipe off any soil from the mushrooms. Trim the tough portions of the stems and cut the mushrooms into ½-inch-thick slices. Whisk together the miso, vinegar, water, and oil. Brush the mushroom slices with the marinade and place them on a baking sheet. Broil about 3 inches from the heat for about 5 minutes, until the mushrooms are browned and beginning to soften.

Meanwhile, steam the spinach in a covered pot on high heat, using only the water clinging to its leaves, for 1 or 2 minutes, or until just wilted but still bright green.

Spread the steamed spinach on a serving platter, arrange the broiled mushrooms on top, and serve right away.

PER 5-0Z SERVING: 62 CALORIES, 3.7 G PROTEIN, 3.1 G FAT, 7.0 G CARBOHYDRATES, .4 G SATURATED FATTY ACIDS, .5 G POLYUNSATURATED FATTY ACIDS, 1.8 G MONOUNSATURATED FATTY ACIDS, 0 MG CHOLESTEROL, 174 MG SODIUM, 3.4 G TOTAL DIETARY FIBER

MENU SUGGESTIONS Serve as a side dish with **Pasta with Salsa Cruda** (page 212) or **Greek Stew** (page 266). For a combo plate, combine with **Eggplant Strata** (page 32), **Mediterranean Couscous Salad** (page 144), or **Potato Beet Salad** (page 139). Or use as a main course with **Garlic Mashed Potatoes** (page 328) or **Millet Pilaf** (page 182) and a cucumber-tomato salad with **Apple Basil Dressing** (page 348).

SWEET SWEET POTATOES

Remember candied sweet potatoes and sweet potatoes with marshmallows? If you have fond memories of these dishes from Thanksgivings or Christmases gone by but find they just don't taste as good to you anymore, try this recipe.

2 pounds sweet potatoes, peeled and cubed (6 to 7 cups)
1 cup unsweetened apple, pear, or orange juice
¼ cup maple syrup or honey
1 teaspoon grated fresh ginger root
½ teaspoon ground cinnamon
¼ teaspoon ground cardamom
½ teaspoon salt

Serves 8

Preparation time: 20 minutes

Baking time: about 1 hour

Preheat the oven to 350°.

Carefully lower the sweet potatoes into about 8 cups of boiling water (enough to cover them) and simmer for 5 minutes.

Meanwhile, stir the juice, maple syrup or honey, ginger, cinnamon, cardamom, and salt together in a lightly oiled or sprayed 2-quart baking dish. Drain the sweet potatoes, add them to the baking dish, and stir well to coat with the juice mixture. Bake, uncovered, for about an hour, stirring every 15 minutes, until the sweet potatoes are tender and the juice mixture has thickened and coats the potatoes.

PER 5-OZ SERVING: 146 CALORIES, 1.8 G PROTEIN, .4 G FAT, 34.5 G CARBOHYDRATES, .1 G SATURATED FATTY ACIDS, .2 G POLYUNSATURATED FATTY ACIDS, 0 G MONOUNSATURATED FATTY ACIDS, 0 MG CHOLESTEROL, 165 MG SODIUM, 2.8 G TOTAL DIETARY FIBER

MENU SUGGESTIONS Serve alongside **Thai Fish Cakes** (page 302) with a green salad dressed with **Cilantro Lime Yogurt Dressing** (page 345). Or use as a sweet contrast with **Garlicky Black-Eyed Peas 'n' Greens** (page 170), or with **Kasha Pilaf** (page 181) paired with **Carolina Kale** (page 321).

SPANISH POTATOES

This spicy potato dish is a winter favorite, similar to those served in tapas bars.

2 pounds potatoes, cut into bite-sized wedges
2 cups chopped onions
2 to 4 garlic cloves, pressed or minced
2 teaspoons olive oil
2 teaspoons chili powder
1 cup undrained canned whole tomatoes (8-ounce can)
2 tablespoons chopped fresh parsley
salt and ground black pepper to taste

Serves 4 to 6

**Preparation time:
20 minutes**

**Cooking time:
25 minutes**

Place the potatoes in a soup pot with salted water to cover, bring to a boil, and then lower the heat to a rapid simmer and cook, partially covered, for 10 to 15 minutes, or until the potatoes just begin to soften.

Meanwhile, in a covered medium skillet, sauté the onions and garlic in the olive oil on low heat. Cover and continue to cook for about 10 minutes, until the onions are translucent. Add the chili powder and cook for 2 minutes more. Stir in the tomatoes and bring to a simmer.

Drain the barely tender potatoes and add them to the tomato mixture. Stir to combine and cook until the potatoes are tender, about 12 minutes. Sprinkle on the parsley, add salt and pepper to taste, and serve piping hot or cool to room temperature.

PER 7-OZ SERVING: 149 CALORIES, 3.2 G PROTEIN, 2.0 G FAT, 30.9 G CARBOHYDRATES, .3 G SATURATED FATTY ACIDS, .2 G POLYUNSATURATED FATTY ACIDS, 1.2 G MONOUNSATURATED FATTY ACIDS, 0 MG CHOLESTEROL, 93 MG SODIUM, 3.1 G TOTAL DIETARY FIBER

MENU SUGGESTIONS Serve with **Fish Steaks with Fennel** (page 290) followed by **Spinach Avocado Grapefruit Salad** (page 135) for a sunny Spanish meal. Or try beside **Spinach Mushroom Frittata** (page 52) or **Watercress Omelet** (page 53). For a glorious vegetable plate, combine with **Citrus-dressed Asparagus** (page 313), **Mustard Carrots** (page 317), and **Broiled Portabella Mushrooms** (page 322).

SCALLOPED POTATOES AND CARROTS

A classic favorite, disarmingly simple in its own right, is here greatly reduced in fat and brightened by thin slices of carrots. If you are a parsnip fan, try replacing some or all of the carrots with parsnip slices, which will add their singular, refreshing taste to this creamy, mild dish.

1 cup thinly sliced onions (1 medium onion)
¼ teaspoon dried thyme
1 tablespoon butter
1½ cups evaporated skimmed milk (12-ounce can)
1½ tablespoons unbleached white flour
⅛ teaspoon nutmeg
¾ teaspoon salt
¼ teaspoon ground black pepper
3 cups peeled and thinly sliced potatoes (about 4 potatoes)
1 cup peeled and thinly sliced carrots (about 2 carrots)

Serves 4

Preparation time: 20 minutes

Baking time: about 1 hour

Preheat the oven to 400°.

In a heavy skillet, sauté the onions and thyme in the butter on low heat for 5 to 7 minutes, until translucent, stirring regularly.

In a small bowl, whisk together the evaporated skimmed milk, flour, nutmeg, salt, and pepper.

Lightly oil a 1½- to 2-quart baking dish. Combine the potatoes, carrots, and sautéed onions in the dish and pour the milk mixture evenly on top. Cover tightly with foil and bake for 40 minutes. Lower the heat to 350°, uncover, and bake for about 30 minutes longer, or until the vegetables are tender and the top is golden hued. Serve piping hot.

PER 9-OZ SERVING: 215 CALORIES, 9.2 G PROTEIN, 3.3 G FAT, 38.0 G CARBOHYDRATES, 2.0 G SATURATED FATTY ACIDS, .2 G POLYUNSATURATED FATTY ACIDS, .9 G MONOUNSATURATED FATTY ACIDS, 11 MG CHOLESTEROL, 603 MG SODIUM, 3.4 G TOTAL DIETARY FIBER

MENU SUGGESTIONS Serve with **Honey Mustard Fish** (page 298) and either **Carolina Kale** (page 321) or **Broccoli Rabe and Garlic** (page 315), or try with **Barbecue Beans** (page 156) next to either **Snap Peas with Mushrooms** (page 329) or **Roasted Aparagus** (page 312).

OVEN "FRIES"

These potatoes really will satisfy the urge for good, old-fashioned greasy French fries, but they contain a lot less oil. They're good anytime, but are especially popular as an after-school snack.

2 pounds potatoes (3 large potatoes)
1 tablespoon olive oil
1 tablespoon paprika
1 teaspoon ground cumin
salt to taste

Serves 6

Preparation time: 10 to 15 minutes

Baking time: 45 to 60 minutes

Preheat the oven to 425°.

Wash the potatoes well and peel, if you wish. In a large bowl, stir together the olive oil, paprika, and cumin and set aside. Cut the potatoes lengthwise into slices no thicker than ½ inch. Then cut through the stacked slices to make ½-inch-wide strips. Toss the potatoes in the oil and spices until well coated. Arrange the potatoes in a single layer on a baking sheet prepared with cooking spray or lightly oiled. Bake for 45 to 60 minutes, stirring occasionally, until the fries are golden and crisp. Sprinkle with salt to taste and serve immediately.

VARIATIONS For Sweet Potato Oven "Fries," replace the white potatoes with 2 pounds of sweet potatoes (about 2 large sweet potatoes) and bake for 25 to 40 minutes.

For Spicy Oven "Fries" with an Indian flair, use either white potatoes or sweet potatoes, replace the cumin and paprika with 1 teaspoon of garam masala (page 428), 1 teaspoon of black mustard seeds (page 422), and ½ teaspoon of ground black pepper, and add 1 tablespoon of fresh lemon juice to the spice and oil mixture. Bake just until crisp.

PER 4.50-OZ SERVING OF ALL THREE VERSIONS: 131 CALORIES, 2.3 G PROTEIN, 2.7 G FAT, 25.3 G CARBOHYDRATES, .4 G SATURATED FATTY ACIDS, .3 G POLYUNSATURATED FATTY ACIDS, 1.8 G MONOUNSATURATED FATTY ACIDS, 0 MG CHOLESTEROL, 206 MG SODIUM, 2.5 G TOTAL DIETARY FIBER

MENU SUGGESTIONS You probably already have a favorite menu or two that includes fries. We like Oven "Fries" with **Watercress Omelet** (page 53) and sliced tomatoes or with **Fish Steaks with Fennel** (page 290).

POTATO CAKES

An alternative to traditional fried potato pancakes that is much lower in fat, these baked cakes with their crisp, tantalizing crusts are deceptively rich and very satisfying.

4 cups peeled cubed potatoes (about 2 large potatoes)
2 garlic cloves, minced or pressed
2 tablespoons low-fat sour cream or nonfat yogurt
1 egg white
1 tablespoon minced fresh parsley
1 scallion, minced
1 tablespoon chopped fresh dill
1 teaspoon fresh lemon juice
salt and ground black pepper to taste
1 cup fresh bread crumbs (page 422)
1 teaspoon olive oil

Serves 4

Makes 14 medium cakes

Preparation time: 20 minutes

Baking time: 25 minutes

In a medium soup pot, cover the potatoes and garlic with water, bring to a boil, and simmer for about 20 minutes, until tender. Drain the potatoes, reserving the stock for soup, and place them in a large bowl. Add the sour cream or yogurt, egg white, parsley, scallions, dill, and lemon juice and mash thoroughly. Add salt and pepper to taste.

Put the bread crumbs in a large shallow bowl and set aside.

Preheat the oven to 350°.

With your hands, spread the olive oil on a large baking sheet. (Having oiled hands will make it easier for you to work with the sticky batter.) Scoop ¼ cup of the potato mixture into your hands and shape it into a patty. Coat the patty evenly with bread crumbs on both sides, place it on the baking sheet, and continue until all of the potato mixture is used. You will have about 14 patties.

Bake, uncovered, for 15 minutes. Flip the potato cakes over and bake for 10 more minutes, or until browned and heated through.

PER 6-OZ SERVING: 245 CALORIES, 7.3 G PROTEIN, 2.9 G FAT, 47.6 G CARBOHYDRATES, .6 G SATURATED FATTY ACIDS, .6 G POLYUNSATURATED FATTY ACIDS, 1.5 G MONOUNSATURATED FATTY ACIDS, 0 MG CHOLESTEROL, 317 MG SODIUM, 3.6 G TOTAL DIETARY FIBER

MENU SUGGESTIONS Serve with **Barbecue Beans** (page 156) or **Baked Fish with Mustard Marinade** (page 288). Top with **Creamy Roasted Red Pepper Sauce** (page 355), **Corn Relish** (page 361), **Mango Peach Chutney** (page 362), or the usual favorites: hot homemade applesauce and sweet-and-sour red cabbage or beets vinaigrette. Try topped with nonfat sour cream or **Yogurt Cheese** (page 419).

GARLIC MASHED POTATOES

Several distinctive varieties of potatoes have made regular appearances in recent years, first in farmers' markets and now in most supermarkets. Our ideal choice for this dish is a yellow, buttery-flavored variety, such as Yukon Gold or Yellow Finn, but with the strong yet mellow flavor of garlic in this recipe, any potato will do. The buttermilk adds a mild tang, but if you prefer, replace it with potato cooking water for a dairyless dish.

These mashed potatoes stand on their own, not requiring a pool of melted butter to taste good; however, Mushroom Sauce (page 352) makes a wonderful gravy for them.

Serves 6

Total time: 40 minutes

3 pounds potatoes, peeled and cubed (about 6 cups)
10 garlic cloves, peeled
1 bay leaf
1 teaspoon salt
¾ to 1 cup buttermilk, heated
salt and ground black pepper to taste

In a large pot, combine the potatoes, garlic, bay leaf, and salt with just enough water to cover. Cover the pot, bring to a boil, and then lower the heat and simmer for 10 to 15 minutes, until the potatoes are tender. Drain. Remove and discard the bay leaf. Using a potato masher, mash the potatoes and garlic with enough buttermilk to achieve the consistency you like. Add salt and pepper to taste. Serve immediately.

PER 7-OZ SERVING: 171 CALORIES, 4.1 G PROTEIN, .4 G FAT, 38.5 G CARBOHYDRATES, .2 G SATURATED FATTY ACIDS, .1 G POLYUNSATURATED FATTY ACIDS, .1 G MONO-UNSATURATED FATTY ACIDS, 1 MG CHOLESTEROL, 167 MG SODIUM, 3.4 G TOTAL DIETARY FIBER

MENU SUGGESTIONS Serve with **Broiled Portabella Mushrooms** (page 322), **Jerk Tofu** (page 337), or **Middle Eastern Cannellini Patties** (page 119), or use as a starchy underpinning to **Wild Mushroom Stew Trieste** (page 278) or **Bean and Bean Gumbo** (page 157).

SNAP PEAS WITH MUSHROOMS

We look forward to the appearance of snap peas in home gardens and farmers' markets in the early summer months here in Ithaca. They are delicious added raw to salads or stir-fries, but even better if you blanch them for just a minute in boiling water. Here's a recipe for jazzing them up to make a special side dish.

2 cups snap peas
1 teaspoon olive oil
1 garlic clove, minced or pressed
2 cups sliced mushrooms
salt
1 tablespoon minced fresh mint
1 tablespoon minced fresh dill
1 teaspoon balsamic vinegar

Serves 4

**Preparation time:
10 minutes**

Total time: 15 minutes

Snap peas have a fibrous string should be removed before cooking. Hold the stem end, pinch off the top, and pull down the strings running along both sides. Set aside.

Warm the oil in a heavy skillet or saucepan, preferably nonstick or cast iron. Add the garlic, mushrooms, and a dash of salt, cover, and cook on medium-low heat, stirring occasionally, until the mushrooms release their juices and become tender, about 5 minutes. Add the snap peas, cover, and cook for another 2 to 3 minutes, until they are bright green and just tender. The liquid from the mushrooms should be enough to cook the peas, but add a tablespoon of water if necessary. Stir in the mint, dill, balsamic vinegar, and salt to taste and serve immediately.

PER 4-OZ SERVING: 51 CALORIES, 3.2 G PROTEIN, 1.5 G FAT, 7.0 G CARBOHYDRATES, .2 G SATURATED FATTY ACIDS, .2 G POLYUNSATURATED FATTY ACIDS, .9 G MONOUNSATURATED FATTY ACIDS, 0 MG CHOLESTEROL, 92 MG SODIUM, 2.7 G TOTAL DIETARY FIBER

MENU SUGGESTIONS We like Snap Peas with Mushrooms with **Potato Beet Salad** (page 139), **Baltic Fish** (page 287), **Swiss Chard Rolls Two Ways** (page 252), or **Macaroni and Cheese** (page 203).

Japanese Sesame Spinach

This slightly salty, slightly sweet, flavorful dish really engages the taste buds and encourages an enthusiastic consumption of healthful spinach, which is all to the good. Serve the sesame spinach warm as a side dish or chill for 30 minutes to serve as a salad. The sesame paste is also good on green beans and other lightly steamed greens, such as watercress, chard, or kale.

16 to 20 ounces fresh spinach
2 tablespoons sesame seeds
2 teaspoons sugar
1 tablespoon soy sauce

Serves 4

Total time: 15 minutes, if served hot

Chilling time: 30 minutes, if served cold

Clean and stem the spinach leaves. Shake off the excess water and place the spinach in a covered pot.

In a dry skillet on medium heat, roast the sesame seeds, stirring continuously, for a couple of minutes, until the seeds are fragrant and golden. With a mortar and pestle, grind together the sesame seeds and sugar, add the soy sauce, and stir to make a paste (see Note). Place the pot of spinach on high heat and steam for 2 or 3 minutes, until it is wilted but still bright green. Drain. Toss the spinach with sesame paste to coat the leaves evenly.

PER 4-OZ SERVING: 60 CALORIES, 4.1 G PROTEIN, 2.6 G FAT, 7.3 G CARBOHY-DRATES, .4 G SATURATED FATTY ACIDS, 1.2 G POLYUNSATURATED FATTY ACIDS, .9 G MONOUNSATURATED FATTY ACIDS, 0 MG CHOLESTEROL, 290 MG SODIUM, 3.5 G TOTAL DIETARY FIBER

NOTE:

If you don't have a mortar and pestle, crush the sesame seeds between two sheets of wax paper with a rolling pin. Stir the sugar and soy sauce until the sugar dissolves and then add the crushed sesame seeds.

MENU SUGGESTIONS Serve beside **Thai Fried Rice** (page 190), **Sushi Rice Salad** (page 146), **Savory Hoisin Fish** (page 293), **Thai Fish Cakes** (page 302), or **Vegetable Udon Sauté** (page 204). Many children really like this sesame spinach, so we have even served it with **Macaroni and Cheese** (page 203) or **Garlic Mashed Potatoes** (page 328)!

HOLIDAY CRANBERRY SQUASH

Moosewood collective member Nancy Lazarus invented this recipe as a colorful main course or side dish for autumn, winter, and holiday meals. The sweet-tart filling contrasts perfectly with the bland, smooth baked squash. If there is filling left over, serve it on the side with the squash or save it to serve with a later meal.

The filling can stand on its own as a good fresh cranberry sauce; this recipe makes about 4 cups. Allow it to sit for about 10 minutes before serving. Cover and refrigerate the sauce, which will keep for up to 2 weeks.

3 winter squash, such as acorn, buttercup,
    butternut, or delicata
2 cups minced onions
1 cup minced celery
1 teaspoon canola or other vegetable oil
3 cups fresh or 12 ounces frozen cranberries
½ teaspoon salt
1 cup unsweetened applesauce
2 teaspoons freshly grated orange peel
juice of 1 orange (about ½ cup)
½ cup pure maple syrup or ½ cup sugar, or to taste

Serves 6

**Preparation time:
30 to 35 minutes**

**Baking time:
30 to 45 minutes**

Preheat the oven to 400°.

Lightly spray or oil a large, flat-bottomed baking pan. Slice each squash in half lengthwise and remove the seeds. Place the squash, cut side down, in the baking pan, add water to about ½ inch, cover with aluminum foil, and bake for 30 minutes.

Meanwhile, in a covered nonreactive saucepan on medium heat, sauté the onions and celery in the oil, stirring often, for 10 minutes, until softened. Add the cranberries and salt, lower the heat, and simmer until the cranberries have popped, about 10 minutes. Remove from the heat and stir in the applesauce, orange peel, orange juice, and maple syrup. The filling should be tart—add just enough maple syrup to offset the sourness of the cranberries.

Remove the squash from the oven and turn the halves over in the pan. Fill each cavity with a rounded ½ cup of filling. Bake, uncovered, for 30 to 45 minutes, until well done.

PER 12-OZ SERVING: 195 CALORIES, 2.6 G PROTEIN, 1.2 G FAT, 48.0 G CARBOHYDRATES, .2 G SATURATED FATTY ACIDS, .6 G POLYUNSATURATED FATTY ACIDS, .2 G MONOUNSATURATED FATTY ACIDS, 0 MG CHOLESTEROL, 225 MG SODIUM, 4.2 G TOTAL DIETARY FIBER

MENU SUGGESTIONS Serve after **Dried Mushroom Soup with Barley** (page 94) or serve with **Barbecue Beans** (page 156) and **Brown Bread** (page 111) for an autumn harvest dinner, or with **Mushroom Wheatberry Pilaf** (page 195) or **Cabbage Rolls** (page 256) for a festive holiday meal.

CURRIED SQUASH

This good-looking dish is particularly welcome during the long winter months. When you finally trudge home through the snow or rain on one of those frigid, windy days that chill you to the marrow, it will warm you clear through.

SEASONED ONIONS
½ teaspoon black mustard seeds (page 422)
½ teaspoon fenugreek seeds (page 427)
2 teaspoons canola or other vegetable oil
1 cup chopped onions

CURRY BLEND
1 tablespoon grated fresh ginger root
½ teaspoon turmeric
½ teaspoon ground cumin
½ teaspoon ground coriander
½ teaspoon ground cardamom
pinch of cayenne

VEGETABLES
¾ cup water
2 cups chopped tomatoes
3 cups peeled, seeded, and cubed winter squash
1 red bell pepper, cut into 1-inch pieces
salt and ground black pepper to taste

Serves 4

**Total time:
30 to 40 minutes**

NOTE:
For a somewhat richer consistency, stir in ¼ cup of reduced-fat coconut milk at the end of cooking.
If you prefer or if winter squash is unavailable, use sweet potatoes instead of squash.

In a medium skillet, gently sauté the black mustard seeds and fenugreek seeds in the oil on low heat for several minutes, until they begin to pop. Add the onions, increase the heat to medium, and sauté for 5 minutes, until the onions begin to soften. Stir in the curry blend spices and sauté them for 1 minute, being careful not to let them burn. Add the water, a cup of the tomatoes, and the squash cubes and simmer for 10 to 15 minutes, until the squash is barely tender, stirring occasionally. Add the bell peppers and the rest of the tomatoes, cover, and cook until all of the vegetables are tender. Add salt and pepper to taste.

PER 12-OZ SERVING: 118 CALORIES, 4.2 G PROTEIN, 3.7 G FAT, 20.9 G CARBOHYDRATES, .5 G SATURATED FATTY ACIDS, 1.8 G POLYUNSATURATED FATTY ACIDS, .8 G MONOUNSATURATED FATTY ACIDS, 0 MG CHOLESTEROL, 64 MG SODIUM, 6.4 G TOTAL DIETARY FIBER

MENU SUGGESTIONS Serve as a bright complement to **Caribbean Pigeon Pea Salad** (page 142), **Fish with Pineapple Chutney** (page 292), **Garlicky Black-Eyed Peas 'n' Greens** (page 170), or **Thai Baked Tofu** (page 336) and **Golden Basmati Rice** (page 185).

BROILED ZUCCHINI WITH HERBS

In this easy, classically Mediterranean dish, zucchini emerges from the broiler with a still somewhat firm texture, coated with a lemony glaze and flavored with sweet herbs.

Although we have given broiling instructions here, this recipe is also excellent for outdoor grilling over coals in good weather. Simply marinate the zucchini in the olive oil, lemon, and herbs and baste it several times while grilling. We like to cut the zucchini on a severe diagonal to make elongated oval slices, good for both broiling and grilling techniques.

2 teaspoons olive oil
2 garlic cloves, minced or pressed
2 tablespoons fresh lemon juice
¼ cup finely chopped fresh parsley
½ cup finely chopped scallions
1 teaspoon minced fresh mint leaves
½ teaspoon dried thyme
dash of salt
¼ teaspoon ground black pepper
5 cups sliced zucchini (about 1½ pounds)
1 tomato, cut into wedges

Serves 2 to 4

**Preparation time:
15 minutes**

**Broiling time:
8 to 10 minutes**

Preheat the broiler.

In a large bowl, whisk together the olive oil, garlic, lemon juice, parsley, scallions, mint, thyme, salt, and pepper. Toss the zucchini and tomatoes with this mixture until evenly coated. Place the vegetables on a baking sheet and broil for 8 to 10 minutes, until the zucchini is just tender. Serve immediately.

PER 8-OZ SERVING: 64 CALORIES, 1.8 G PROTEIN, 2.6 G FAT, 10.3 G CARBOHYDRATES, .4 G SATURATED FATTY ACIDS, .3 G POLYUNSATURATED FATTY ACIDS, 1.8 G MONOUNSATURATED FATTY ACIDS, 0 MG CHOLESTEROL, 57 MG SODIUM, 3.3 G TOTAL DIETARY FIBER

MENU SUGGESTIONS We like this dish with **Swiss Chard and Tomato Frittata** (page 50), **Pasta with Salsa Cruda** (page 212), or **Mushroom Spinach Crêpes** (page 234). It is an agreeable addition to a combo plate with **Savory Stuffed Mushrooms** (page 42), **Greek Spinach Rice Balls** (page 35), and **Seasoned Steamed Artichokes** (page 311).

SOUTHEAST ASIAN COCONUT ZUCCHINI

Here's something to do with some of that seemingly endless crop of zucchini. Combining it with an Asian-inspired coconut-lime sauce creates a full-flavored side dish. The turmeric turns the zucchini a beautiful golden color, which looks particularly striking if served in a bright red bowl. This saucy dish is also nice served over rice, millet, or barley.

4 to 5 cups cubed zucchini
2 garlic cloves, minced or pressed
½ to 1 fresh chile, minced, seeds removed for a milder "hot"
½ teaspoon turmeric
1 teaspoon canola or other vegetable oil
2 scallions, chopped
2 tablespoons fresh lime juice
2 tablespoons chopped fresh basil
2 tablespoons chopped fresh mint
¼ cup reduced-fat coconut milk
salt to taste

Serves 4

Total time: 45 minutes

In a skillet, sauté the zucchini, garlic, chile, and turmeric in the oil for 5 minutes, stirring constantly. Add the scallions, lime juice, basil, mint, and coconut milk. Cover and cook on low heat for about 10 minutes, until the zucchini is tender. Stir occasionally and if necessary add a splash of water to prevent sticking. Add salt to taste. Serve hot.

PER 6.50-OZ SERVING: 56 CALORIES, 1.4 G PROTEIN, 2.6 G FAT, 8.2 G CARBOHYDRATES, .9 G SATURATED FATTY ACIDS, .7 G POLYUNSATURATED FATTY ACIDS, .3 G MONOUNSATURATED FATTY ACIDS, 0 MG CHOLESTEROL, 53 MG SODIUM, 2.4 G TOTAL DIETARY FIBER

MENU SUGGESTIONS Serve with **Southeast Asian Fish Rolls** (page 294), **Thai Fried Rice** (page 190), **Thai Fish Cakes** (page 302), or **Lentil Sambar** (page 166).

ZUCCHINI WITH CILANTRO SAUCE

Steamed zucchini is given a spark with this piquant sauce. When cut into sticks, zucchini holds its shape well during steaming.

Serves 4

Total time: 20 minutes

1½ pounds zucchini (2 large, 5 or 6 small)
2 tablespoons fresh lemon juice
¼ teaspoon Tabasco or other hot pepper sauce, or more to taste
2 tablespoons chopped fresh cilantro
⅛ teaspoon salt
⅛ teaspoon ground black pepper

Remove the ends of the zucchini and cut them lengthwise into halves. Slice each half lengthwise into 4 to 6 wedges. Cut the wedges crosswise into 3-inch-long pieces.

In a large, covered pot on high heat, bring a couple of inches of water to a boil. Fill a steamer basket or colander with the zucchini and lower it into the pot. Cover the pot and steam the zucchini for about 3 minutes, until crisp-tender.

Meanwhile, in a serving bowl, whisk together the lemon juice, Tabasco, cilantro, salt, and pepper. Toss the steamed zucchini in the sauce. Serve hot or at room temperature.

PER 6-OZ SERVING: 28 CALORIES, 1.1 G PROTEIN, .1 G FAT, 7.1 G CARBOHYDRATES, 0 G SATURATED FATTY ACIDS, 0 G POLYUNSATURATED FATTY ACIDS, 0 G MONOUNSATURATED FATTY ACIDS, 0 MG CHOLESTEROL, 84 MG SODIUM, 2.3 G TOTAL DIETARY FIBER

MENU SUGGESTIONS This fat-free side dish is appropriate with Mexican, Caribbean, West African, Southeast Asian, and Indian foods. Try it with **Black Bean Chilaquile** (page 164), **Seitan Fajitas** (page 232), **Thai Fish Cakes** (page 302), **Brazilian Rice** (page 187), **Black Bean and Hominy Frittata** (page 49), or **Curried Sweet Potato Roti** (page 230).

THAI BAKED TOFU

Tofu is an amazingly versatile food that absorbs the flavors of any sauce or broth almost like a sponge; thus, it can taste very different depending upon how it's prepared. Here it is sliced and baked with the hot curry paste and salty soy sauce characteristic of Thai cuisine to make 24 bite-sized triangles with crisp, savory outer coatings and creamy smooth centers.

2 cakes firm tofu (12 to 14 ounces)
¼ to ⅓ cup Thai Curry Paste (page 365)
2 to 4 tablespoons soy sauce

Serves 4 to 6

Pressing tofu time:
30 minutes

Press the tofu for at least 30 minutes (page 419).

Preheat the oven to 350°. Prepare a nonreactive 8 × 12-inch baking dish with cooking spray or a very light coating of oil.

Cut each tofu cake into three slices about ½ inch thick. Stack the slices and then cut through all three layers on the two diagonals, making an X. This will make 12 triangular pieces from each block of tofu. In the baking dish, gently toss them with the curry paste and soy sauce. Bake for 45 minutes, stirring gently twice during the baking.

Preparation time:
10 minutes

Baking time:
45 minutes

PER 4.50-OZ SERVING: 103 CALORIES, 9.9 G PROTEIN, 5.5 G FAT, 6.1 G CARBOHYDRATES, .8 G SATURATED FATTY ACIDS, 3.1 G POLYUNSATURATED FATTY ACIDS, 1.2 G MONOUNSATURATED FATTY ACIDS, 0 MG CHOLESTEROL, 381 MG SODIUM, 1.7 G TOTAL DIETARY FIBER

MENU SUGGESTIONS Serve with **Thai Fried Rice** (page 190) or **Curried Rice Noodles** (page 220). Other good accompaniments are **Asian Cucumber Condiment** (page 367), **Broiled Eggplant Thai Style** (page 34), and **Sweet Sweet Potatoes** (page 323).

JERK TOFU

At Moosewood we are always on the lookout for new dishes to add to our repertoire. Jay Solomon, an Ithaca chef and cookbook author famous for his tropical salsas and condiments, was our inspiration for this recipe. Jerk cooking is a Jamaican way to grill meat and seafood, and all food considered "jerk" has a characteristically sweet and spicy sauce.

Smelling this tofu as it bakes is almost as good as eating it. We guarantee it will bring eager guests and family members directly to the table. It is also delicious cold, packed into lunchboxes or snatched from the refrigerator for a snack.

2 cakes firm tofu (12 to 14 ounces)

JERK SAUCE
1 medium onion, coarsely chopped (about ½ cup)
3 fresh green chiles, seeds removed for a milder "hot"
3 tablespoons soy sauce
¼ cup red wine vinegar
2 tablespoons brown sugar
2 teaspoons grated fresh ginger root
2 garlic cloves, minced or pressed
1 teaspoon dried thyme
1 teaspoon ground cloves
1 teaspoon ground cinnamon
½ teaspoon ground black pepper

Serves 6

Pressing tofu time: 30 minutes

Preparation time: 10 minutes

Baking time: 1 hour

Place the cakes of tofu between two flat plates or baking pans. Weight the top with a heavy object, such as a book or a can, so that the sides of the tofu bulge slightly but don't split. Let stand for at least 30 minutes. While the tofu is pressing, combine the jerk sauce ingredients in a food processor or blender and purée until smooth. Set aside.

Preheat the oven to 400°.

Drain the pressed tofu. Cut each cake into three slices. Stack the slices and then cut through all three layers on the two diagonals, making an X. This will make 12 triangular pieces from each block of tofu. Gently toss the tofu triangles in the jerk marinade and place them in an unoiled 8 × 12-inch nonreactive baking dish. Bake for 1 hour, carefully turning the tofu about every 20 minutes.

PER 7-OZ SERVING: 151 CALORIES, 13.1 G PROTEIN, 7.4 G FAT, 11.7 G CARBOHYDRATES, 1.1 G SATURATED FATTY ACIDS, 4.1 G POLYUNSATURATED FATTY ACIDS, 1.6 G MONOUNSATURATED FATTY ACIDS, 0 MG CHOLESTEROL, 420 MG SODIUM, 2.6 G TOTAL DIETARY FIBER

MENU SUGGESTIONS Serve with **Caribbean Roasted Vegetables** (page 226) and try cooling **Pineapple Buttermilk Sherbet** (page 394) for dessert. Or serve on a plate alongside **Garlic Mashed Potatoes** (page 328) and **Carolina Kale** (page 321).

creamy dill dressing 342

honey mustard garlic dressing 342

CREAMY GINGER MISO DRESSING 343

southeast asian pineapple sesame dressing 343

green mayonnaise 344

MINTED DILL YOGURT DRESSING 345

cilantro lime yogurt dressing 345

yogurt tahini dressing 346

JAPANESE CARROT DRESSING 346

italian tomato basil dressing 347

orange tarragon dressing 348

SPICY PEANUT DRESSING 349

tomato wine sauce 350

chunky tomato sauce 351

MUSHROOM SAUCE 352

salsa verde liguria 353

skordalia thessalonike 354

CREAMY ROASTED RED PEPPER SAUCE 355

barbecue sauce 355

hot tamarind and guava sauce for fish or vegetables 356

HUNGARIAN LESCO 357

blender hot sauce 358

brazilian hot pepper and lemon sauce 359

FRESH TOMATO SALSA 360

corn relish 361

mango peach chutney 362

SAVORY ONION MARMALADE 363

susan's pesto 364

cilantro pesto 364

THAI CURRY PASTE 365

tomato corn salsa 366

asian cucumber condiment 367

DRESSINGS, SAUCES & SEASONINGS

People who are accustomed to meals rich in higher-fat foods frequently have the idea that low-fat meals will be less fully dimensioned. Our versatile, highly flavored **SAUCES** and seasonings may help to put that misconception to rest. We use fresh herbs, vegetables, condiments, fruits, and zesty chiles to produce saturated flavor that can transform simple fare.

Onions, bell peppers, and tomatoes are used throughout the world as the foundation for a multitude of recipes, and these simple ingredients need just a little back-up support to create inviting, naturally low-fat tomato sauces and salsas, onion relish, Hungarian Lesco, and Blender Hot Sauce. Roasted red peppers are prized for their lush smoothness and smoky flavor; they lend distinctive taste and texture to the Creamy Roasted Red Pepper Sauce. Tamarind, guava, and mango add their tropical appeal to an unusual sauce and a chutney sure to generate enthusiasm. We are excited to have created two pestos that are made without any oil and still convey the rich, herbed essence expected from that perennial favorite.

Most popular salad **DRESSINGS**, whether homemade or commercial, contain a substantial percentage of oil or other fats. We found it a challenge to create dressings with body and good taste that will coat salad greens or other foods and can be prepared without a laboratory and a degree in chemistry. There are plenty of low-fat salad dressings on the market, but many of them are high in sugar and use stabilizers and preservatives that we prefer to avoid. Our dressings rely on readily available foods, such as low-fat or nonfat yogurt, cottage cheese, or mayonnaise, as well as tomatoes, carrots, or miso to provide full body and texture. We urge you to look for a good-tasting nonfat yogurt made with active cultures and without a bevy of thickeners; Stonyfield Farm and Brown Cow are two excellent brands.

Even with reduced-fat dressings, it is important to monitor portion size. Tossing a salad with a moderate amount of dressing before serving rather than passing it at the table is the best way to control the fat content of each portion.

SEASONINGS give these dressings their distinctive personalities. Fresh and sun-dried tomatoes add tart-sweetness to Italian Tomato Basil Dressing. Roasted garlic provides a rich creamy quality and a deep, aromatic flavor to both the Honey Mustard Garlic and Orange Tarragon dressings. Pineapple imparts just the right touch of fruitiness to a Southeast Asian–style dressing, and a discreet amount of rich peanut butter or tahini is enough to enhance Spicy Peanut and Yogurt Tahini dressings.

Most of the recipes here are conveniently simple to prepare in a relatively short time. We give you storage life for those that can be made well in advance, as well as menu suggestions that we hope will jump-start your imagination for ways to enhance mealtimes and give flavor boosts to lower-fat dishes.

CREAMY DILL DRESSING

Nonfat cottage cheese gives this dressing its admirable full-bodied texture without adding even a gram of fat to your figure. This dressing is good paired with cooked potatoes, sliced cucumbers, or a simple tossed salad.

½ cup nonfat cottage cheese
½ cup buttermilk
¼ teaspoon salt
¼ teaspoon ground black pepper
¼ cup chopped scallions
1 tablespoon cider or white vinegar
1 tablespoon chopped fresh dill
½ to 1 teaspoon Dijon mustard, to taste

Makes 1 cup

Total time: 10 minutes

Combine all of the ingredients in a blender or food processor and purée until smooth. Covered and refrigerated, this dressing will keep for about a week.

PER 1-OZ SERVING: 14 CALORIES, 1.7 G PROTEIN, .1 G FAT, 1.0 G CARBOHYDRATES, .1 G SATURATED FATTY ACIDS, 0 G POLYUNSATURATED FATTY ACIDS, 0 G MONOUNSATURATED FATTY ACIDS, 1 MG CHOLESTEROL, 115 MG SODIUM, .1 G TOTAL DIETARY FIBER

HONEY MUSTARD GARLIC DRESSING

Here is a dressing that is thick, creamy, rich-flavored, and virtually fat-free—not to mention gorgeously colored. Why didn't we think of this sooner? Serve on tossed green salads, steamed green vegetables, or juicy tomato wedges, or use it on baked salmon.

Makes 1 cup

Total time: 10 minutes, with already roasted garlic

2 heads Roasted Garlic (page 43)
2 tablespoons Dijon mustard
1½ to 2 tablespoons mild honey
3 tablespoons cider vinegar
¼ cup unsweetened apple juice
¼ teaspoon salt
ground black pepper to taste

Squeeze the garlic paste from the roasted heads into a blender. Add the mustard, honey, vinegar, apple juice, salt, and pepper and purée until smooth and creamy. Tightly covered and refrigerated, it will keep for about 4 days.

PER 1-OZ SERVING: 30 CALORIES, .6 G PROTEIN, .2 G FAT, 7.3 G CARBOHYDRATES, 0 G SATURATED FATTY ACIDS, 0 G POLYUNSATURATED FATTY ACIDS, 0 G MONOUNSATURATED FATTY ACIDS, 0 MG CHOLESTEROL, 121 MG SODIUM, .2 G TOTAL DIETARY FIBER

CREAMY GINGER MISO DRESSING

Puréed silken tofu contributes a smooth and creamy texture to this spicy, gingery dressing. At Moosewood, we use a wonderful fresh tofu produced locally by Ithaca Soy, but silken tofu is also available in most supermarkets and health food stores.

Makes about ¾ cup

Total time: 5 minutes

4 ounces silken tofu (page 440)
2 tablespoons light miso
1 tablespoon rice vinegar
1 tablespoon chopped scallions
2 teaspoons grated ginger root
⅓ cup orange juice
1 teaspoon soy sauce
1 teaspoon brown sugar
1 teaspoon dark sesame oil

Combine all of the ingredients in a blender or food processor and purée until smooth. Covered and refrigerated, this dressing will keep for about a week.

PER 1-OZ SERVING: 31 CALORIES, 1.7 G PROTEIN, 1.5 G FAT, 3.1 G CARBOHYDRATES, .2 G SATURATED FATTY ACIDS, .8 G POLYUNSATURATED FATTY ACIDS, .4 G MONOUNSATURATED FATTY ACIDS, 0 MG CHOLESTEROL, 165 MG SODIUM, .4 G TOTAL DIETARY FIBER

SOUTHEAST ASIAN PINEAPPLE SESAME DRESSING

This slightly sweet dressing is brilliant on a crisp, well-chilled lettuce or cabbage salad. Use it to marinate cooked rice and finely diced vegetables. A refreshing change of pace, our pineapple sesame dressing is particularly inviting in hot weather.

¼ cup unsweetened crushed pineapple
1 tablespoon light miso
1 tablespoon soy sauce
1 tablespoon rice vinegar
¼ cup water
1 tablespoon dark sesame oil
1 garlic clove, minced or pressed

Makes ¾ cup

Total time: 5 minutes

Place all of the ingredients in a blender or food processor and purée until smooth. Covered and refrigerated, this dressing will keep for about a week.

PER 1-OZ SERVING: 33 CALORIES, .4 G PROTEIN, 2.5 G FAT, 2.4 G CARBOHYDRATES, .4 G SATURATED FATTY ACIDS, 1.1 G POLYUNSATURATED FATTY ACIDS, 1.0 G MONOUNSATURATED FATTY ACIDS, 0 MG CHOLESTEROL, 222 MG SODIUM, .2 G TOTAL DIETARY FIBER

GREEN MAYONNAISE

Not only a lovely shade of green, but also redolent with the scent of fresh herbs, this mayonnaise can be used as a sandwich spread, as a dip, in potato salads or other vegetable salads, in dressings, or on fish. This simple technique for "doctoring" prepared reduced-fat mayonnaise is endlessly adaptable, and we have given three variations: Mediterranean Mayo, Wasabi Mayo, and Salsa Mayo, all easy ways to perk up salads and sandwiches. If you're a fan of Japanese wasabi or of salsa, you're sure to love these spreads.

1 cup reduced-fat mayonnaise
¼ cup rinsed and stemmed fresh spinach, packed
¼ cup chopped scallions
¼ cup chopped fresh parsley
1 garlic clove, minced or pressed
1 tablespoon chopped fresh dill
1 tablespoon cider vinegar or fresh lemon juice
salt and ground black pepper to taste

Makes 1 generous cup

**Total time:
10 to 15 minutes**

Combine the mayonnaise, spinach, scallions, parsley, garlic, dill, and vinegar or lemon juice in a blender or food processor. Purée until smooth and evenly colored. Add salt and pepper to taste. Refrigerated and tightly covered, Green Mayonnaise will keep for about a week.

VARIATIONS For Mediterranean Mayo, combine 1 cup of reduced-fat mayonnaise with ¼ cup of roasted red peppers, 2 tablespoons of capers, and salt and pepper to taste. Purée until smooth and uniform in color—it will be a lovely orange-sunset color.

For Wasabi Mayo, combine 2 teaspoons of wasabi powder with 1 tablespoon of water and 2 teaspoons of lemon juice to form a paste. Cover and set aside for 5 minutes. Stir the wasabi paste into 1 cup of reduced-fat mayonnaise, add 4 teaspoons of minced scallion greens, and salt to taste. Try it on grilled tuna, in a potato salad, or with fresh ripe garden tomatoes.

For Salsa Mayo, combine 1 cup of reduced-fat mayonnaise with ½ cup of your favorite chunky salsa, about a tablespoon of lemon or lime juice, and 1 to 2 tablespoons of chopped cilantro, if you like. This is scrumptious on Chili Burgers (page 173).

PER 1.25-OZ SERVING: 42 CALORIES, .5 G PROTEIN, 3.6 G FAT, 2.1 G CARBOHYDRATES, .7 G SATURATED FATTY ACIDS, 0 G POLYUNSATURATED FATTY ACIDS, 0 G MONOUNSATURATED FATTY ACIDS, 14 MG CHOLESTEROL, 33 MG SODIUM, .2 G TOTAL DIETARY FIBER

MINTED DILL YOGURT DRESSING

Excellent as a sour cream substitute in cucumber or potato salads, this dressing can also make a tantalizing dip for stuffed grape leaves, Middle Eastern Cannellini Patties (page 119), falafels, and toasted pita. Its light, slightly tangy flavor goes well on fresh spinach greens with marinated mushrooms and a few pine nuts.

Makes 1 cup

Preparation time:
15 minutes

Sitting time:
30 minutes

1 cup nonfat or low-fat yogurt
2 teaspoons minced scallions or red onions
1 tablespoon minced fresh dill
1 teaspoon minced fresh mint
1 small garlic clove, pressed
2 teaspoons fresh lemon juice
pinch of sugar
salt to taste

Combine all the ingredients and set aside for at least 30 minutes to allow the flavors to marry. Covered and refrigerated, it will keep for about 10 days or for about a week past the expiration date on the yogurt container, whichever comes first.

PER 1-OZ SERVING: 17 CALORIES, 1.7 G PROTEIN, .1 G FAT, 2.4 G CARBOHYDRATES, 0 G SATURATED FATTY ACIDS, 0 G POLYUNSATURATED FATTY ACIDS, 0 G MONOUNSATURATED FATTY ACIDS, 1 MG CHOLESTEROL, 44 MG SODIUM, 0 G TOTAL DIETARY FIBER

CILANTRO LIME YOGURT DRESSING

This simple dressing is a good substitute when sour cream is called for in Mexican dishes. We recommend it for Baked Sweet Potato Salad (page 137), and it's also appealing on cucumber salad, green salads, and other potato and vegetable salads.

1 cup nonfat or low-fat yogurt
1 tablespoon minced fresh cilantro
1 tablespoon minced scallions or chives
2 teaspoons fresh lime juice
salt to taste

Makes 1 cup

Preparation time:
10 minutes

Sitting time: 1 hour

In a small bowl, combine the yogurt, cilantro, scallions or chives, and lime juice. Add salt to taste. Set aside for at least an hour to allow the flavors to meld. Stored refrigerated in a covered container, it will keep for 3 or 4 days.

PER 1-OZ SERVING: 17 CALORIES, 1.7 G PROTEIN, .1 G FAT, 2.4 G CARBOHYDRATES, 0 G SATURATED FATTY ACIDS, 0 G POLYUNSATURATED FATTY ACIDS, 0 G MONOUNSATURATED FATTY ACIDS, 1 MG CHOLESTEROL, 44 MG SODIUM, .1 G TOTAL DIETARY FIBER

YOGURT TAHINI DRESSING

A smidgen of tahini enriches this dressing and supplies a characteristic nut butter richness without adding lots of fat. It will dress up any green salad with a touch of the Middle East and is also the perfect topping for Middle Eastern Cannellini Patties (page 119) or Seasoned Steamed Artichokes (page 311).

1½ cups nonfat yogurt
1 tablespoon tahini
1 large garlic clove, minced or pressed
2 teaspoons fresh lemon juice
¼ teaspoon ground cumin
½ teaspoon salt
ground black pepper to taste

Makes 1 ½ cups

**Total time:
5 to 10 minutes**

Whisk together all of the ingredients in a mixing bowl. Refrigerated in a tightly covered container, it will keep for about a week.

PER 1-OZ SERVING: 27 CALORIES, 2.0 G PROTEIN, .9 G FAT, 2.8 G CARBOHYDRATES, .2 G SATURATED FATTY ACIDS, .4 G POLYUNSATURATED FATTY ACIDS, .3 G MONOUNSATURATED FATTY ACIDS, 1 MG CHOLESTEROL, 123 MG SODIUM, .2 G TOTAL DIETARY FIBER

JAPANESE CARROT DRESSING

Despite or perhaps because of its complex taste, everyone loves this dressing, the "secret sauce" served on salads at so many Japanese restaurants. We like to use this blend of traditional Japanese ingredients both on mixed green salads and as a marinade for cooked vegetable salads.

Makes ⅔ cup

Total time: 10 minutes

1 small carrot, peeled and shredded (about ½ cup)
2 tablespoons mirin (pages 431–432)
2 tablespoons rice vinegar or cider vinegar
1 tablespoon soy sauce
½ teaspoon dark sesame oil
2 tablespoons minced onions
1 tablespoon prepared mustard
1 tablespoon grated fresh ginger root (optional)

Whirl all of the ingredients in a blender until smooth. Well covered, it keeps in the refrigerator for about a week.

PER 1-OZ SERVING: 27 CALORIES, .4 G PROTEIN, .5 G FAT, 5.4 G CARBOHYDRATES, .1 G SATURATED FATTY ACIDS, .2 G POLYUNSATURATED FATTY ACIDS, .2 G MONOUNSATURATED FATTY ACIDS, 0 MG CHOLESTEROL, 174 MG SODIUM, .4 G TOTAL DIETARY FIBER

ITALIAN TOMATO BASIL DRESSING

The two major challenges that face the developer of a nonfat dressing are how to replace the flavor of the oil and how to replicate its coating ability. After attempting many unusual (and even bizarre) combinations of ingredients and techniques, we finally settled on this quite ordinary-looking recipe—which reminded us how difficult it can be at times to discover the essential and obvious.

Our efforts were rewarded, though. The first time we offered Italian Tomato Basil Dressing to top our mixed green salads at Moosewood, many of our customers immediately asked for the recipe, a sure sign of success.

6 sun-dried tomatoes (not packed in oil)
1 tomato, coarsely chopped (about 1 cup)
1 garlic clove, minced or pressed
¼ cup loosely packed, coarsely chopped fresh basil
¼ cup water
2 tablespoons balsamic vinegar
¼ teaspoon salt, or to taste

Makes about 1 cup

Total time: 5 to 10 minutes

Cover the sun-dried tomatoes with boiling water in a heatproof bowl and set aside. Combine the chopped fresh tomatoes, garlic, basil, ¼ cup of water, vinegar, and salt in a blender or food processor. When the sun-dried tomatoes have softened, drain and add them to the other ingredients and purée the mixture until smooth. Covered and refrigerated, this dressing will keep for about a week.

PER 1-OZ SERVING: 23 CALORIES, 1.2 G PROTEIN, .3 G FAT, 4.9 G CARBOHYDRATES, 0 G SATURATED FATTY ACIDS, .1 G POLYUNSATURATED FATTY ACIDS, 0 G MONOUNSATURATED FATTY ACIDS, 0 MG CHOLESTEROL, 209 MG SODIUM, 1.1 G TOTAL DIETARY FIBER

ORANGE TARRAGON DRESSING

Roasted garlic is a mellow counterpoint to the tang of orange juice and mustard in this creamy fat-free dressing. Both Orange Tarragon Dressing and our apple-basil variation owe much of their thick texture and body to roasted garlic. If you don't mind a dozen or so grams of monounsaturated fat sneaking into the recipe, both dressings are also good with about a tablespoon of olive oil. Drizzle it into the blender before adding the herbs.

Makes 1 cup

**Preparation time:
5 minutes, with
already roasted garlic**

**Sitting time:
30 minutes**

2 heads Roasted Garlic (page 43)
½ cup orange juice
2 teaspoons Dijon mustard
**2 tablespoons rice vinegar, white wine vinegar,
     or cider vinegar**
¼ teaspoon salt
⅛ teaspoon ground black pepper
1 teaspoon minced fresh tarragon (½ teaspoon dried)

Squeeze the garlic paste from the heads of roasted garlic into a blender. Add the orange juice, mustard, vinegar, salt, and pepper and purée until smooth and creamy. Add the tarragon and whirl briefly just to mix—there should be flecks of green throughout the golden dressing. Set aside for at least 30 minutes to allow the flavors to marry. Tightly sealed and refrigerated, the dressing will keep for about a week.

VARIATION For Apple Basil Dressing, use ½ cup of unsweetened apple juice instead of the orange juice and mince 8 large basil leaves in place of the tarragon. Add an additional tablespoon of vinegar, if you like. Purée the basil completely to make an attractive green dressing.

PER 1-OZ SERVING: 26 CALORIES, .9 G PROTEIN, .1 G FAT, 5.8 G CARBOHYDRATES, 0 G SATURATED FATTY ACIDS, 0 G POLYUNSATURATED FATTY ACIDS, 0 G MONOUNSATU-RATED FATTY ACIDS, 0 MG CHOLESTEROL, 92 MG SODIUM, .3 G TOTAL DIETARY FIBER

SPICY PEANUT DRESSING

Peanut sauces and dressings abound throughout most of Southeast Asia and Africa, where they are served on almost any vegetable and especially complement tender fresh greens.

Garlic, ginger, and chiles give this dressing brisk accents, and although the tomatoes and cilantro are unobtrusive, they lend body and depth. At Moosewood, we regularly enjoy Spicy Peanut Dressing on fresh young spinach with mung sprouts and grated carrots.

3 tablespoons peanut butter, at room temperature

¼ cup water

1 garlic clove, minced or pressed

½ to 1 fresh chile, minced, seeds removed for a milder "hot"

2 tablespoons cider or rice vinegar

1 tablespoon honey

1 tablespoon soy sauce

¼ cup diced tomatoes

2 teaspoons grated fresh ginger root

2 tablespoons chopped fresh cilantro

2 teaspoons fresh lemon juice

Makes about 1 cup

Total time: 20 minutes

In a blender, purée all of the ingredients until smooth and creamy. Serve chilled. This dressing will keep for 2 or 3 weeks tightly sealed and refrigerated. If it separates, shake it well until blended.

PER 1-OZ SERVING: 44 CALORIES, 1.6 G PROTEIN, 2.7 G FAT, 4.5 G CARBOHYDRATES, .5 G SATURATED FATTY ACIDS, .8 G POLYUNSATURATED FATTY ACIDS, 1.3 G MONOUNSATURATED FATTY ACIDS, 0 MG CHOLESTEROL, 137 MG SODIUM, .4 G TOTAL DIETARY FIBER

TOMATO WINE SAUCE

Our favorite simple tomato sauce—useful, highly flavorful, and velvety smooth. Fennel is the surprise touch here. We're not sure why, but something about its unexpected flavor often fools people into thinking that this is a meat-based sauce. Ladle over Stuffed Manicotti Verde (page 219), Mushroom Spinach Crêpes (page 234), or Mushroom- and Spinach-stuffed Zucchini (page 247).

2 teaspoons olive oil
1 cup finely chopped onions (about 1 medium onion)
2 medium garlic cloves, minced or pressed
¼ teaspoon salt
2 teaspoons ground fennel
1 teaspoon dried oregano
1 teaspoon dried basil
⅓ cup red wine
3 cups undrained canned tomatoes (28-ounce can)
salt and ground black pepper to taste

Makes about 3½ cups

Total time: 40 minutes

NOTE:
Because these are such useful all-purpose sauces, you may want to double the recipes—but no need to double the oil. The 2 teaspoons will be enough! Tightly sealed, they will keep refrigerated for at least a week and frozen for several months.

In a saucepan, warm the olive oil. Add the onions and garlic, sprinkle with the salt, cover, and sauté on very low heat for 5 to 7 minutes, or until the onions are beginning to soften. Add the fennel, oregano, and basil and cook for another minute. Pour in the wine and bring to a boil. Whirl the tomatoes in a blender until just puréed and add to the pan. Cover the sauce and simmer gently for about 20 minutes, stirring occasionally. Add salt and pepper to taste.

PER 2-OZ SERVING: 25 CALORIES, .7 G PROTEIN, .8 G FAT, 3.4 G CARBOHYDRATES, .1 G SATURATED FATTY ACIDS, .1 G POLYUNSATURATED FATTY ACIDS, .5 G MONOUNSATURATED FATTY ACIDS, 0 MG CHOLESTEROL, 118 MG SODIUM, .2 G TOTAL DIETARY FIBER

CHUNKY TOMATO SAUCE

A time-honored, standard tomato sauce that is easy to make and extremely versatile. Use it on pastas, stuffed vegetables, gnocchi, polenta, casseroles, or your favorite pizza.

1 medium onion, chopped (about 1 cup)
2 or 3 garlic cloves, minced or pressed
2 teaspoons olive oil
2½ cups undrained canned tomatoes (28-ounce can)
2 teaspoons dried basil (2½ tablespoons chopped fresh)
¼ teaspoon dried oregano (½ teaspoon chopped fresh)
1 tablespoon chopped fresh parsley
salt and ground black pepper to taste

Makes 3 cups

Total time: 25 minutes

In a heavy, nonreactive pan, sauté the onions and garlic in the oil for about 10 minutes on medium heat, until translucent. Stir often to prevent sticking. Drain the tomato juice into the sautéing onions. With a knife, chop the tomatoes right in the can and add them to the onions, or use your hands to squeeze them directly into the cooking pan. Stir in the basil, oregano, and parsley. Simmer, uncovered, for about 15 minutes, until the sauce has thickened. Add salt and pepper to taste.

PER 4-OZ SERVING: 43 CALORIES, 1.3 G PROTEIN, 1.8 G FAT, 6.2 G CARBOHYDRATES, .2 G SATURATED FATTY ACIDS, .2 G POLYUNSATURATED FATTY ACIDS, 1.2 G MONOUNSATURATED FATTY ACIDS, 0 MG CHOLESTEROL, 151 MG SODIUM, .4 G TOTAL DIETARY FIBER

MUSHROOM SAUCE

At Moosewood we really like this rich-tasting but very low-fat sauce. If you're unfamiliar with dried mushrooms, read our comments on page 418. Serve this sauce on pasta or fish, or use it as a gravy on steamed vegetables, mashed potatoes, or simple grains.

2 cups boiling water
½ ounce dried mushrooms, such as porcini,
    shiitake, chanterelle, or morel (about ⅔ cup)
2 cups finely chopped onions
1 teaspoon canola or other vegetable oil
4 cups cleaned, stemmed, and sliced
    fresh mushrooms (about 12 ounces)
1 bay leaf
1 teaspoon mixed dried marjoram, basil,
    rosemary, thyme, and sage
½ cup Madeira or dry sherry
1 teaspoon salt

Makes 3 cups

**Mushroom soaking time:
30 minutes**

**Preparation and cooking time:
35 minutes**

Total time: 1 hour

> **NOTE:**
> We don't add any thickening agent to this sauce, but if you prefer a gravy-like sauce, add some arrowroot or cornstarch dissolved in a little water and stir until the sauce becomes clear and has thickened to your liking.

Pour the boiling water over the dried mushrooms and set aside to soak for at least 30 minutes. Remove the mushrooms from the soaking liquid. Cut off and discard any tough stems and then slice or chop the mushrooms. Strain the liquid through a paper coffee filter. Reserve the mushrooms and liquid separately.

In a saucepan, combine the onions and oil. Cover and sauté the onions on medium-low heat for 10 minutes, stirring regularly. Add the fresh mushrooms, raise the heat, and stir until the mushrooms begin to release their juices, about 3 minutes. Add the bay leaf, herbs, Madeira or sherry, salt, and the reserved dried mushrooms and their soaking liquid.

Cover and simmer for about 15 minutes, until the mushrooms are tender. The rate at which the simmering liquid evaporates will vary depending upon the weight of the pan, tightness of the lid, and heat level, so stir the sauce occasionally and add a little water if needed. If at the end of simmering the sauce has not reduced enough, uncover and simmer for a few minutes. Discard the bay leaf before serving.

PER 1-OZ SERVING: 15 CALORIES, .4 G PROTEIN, .3 G FAT, 2.2 G CARBOHYDRATES, 0 G SATURATED FATTY ACIDS, .1 G POLYUNSATURATED FATTY ACIDS, .1 G MONOUNSATURATED FATTY ACIDS, 0 MG CHOLESTEROL, 100 MG SODIUM, .4 G TOTAL DIETARY FIBER

SALSA VERDE LIGURIA

Piquant green sauces made with parsley are a staple of northern and central Italian cooking. Usually they include a significant amount of oil. We experimented a lot to develop this recipe, which retains the essential character of traditional salsa verde but is greatly reduced in fat content. We call for fresh tomatoes (which are not traditional) and give the option of adding a little oil. If you add the oil, the sauce is smoother in texture and taste, but many of us prefer the no-oil version with its bit of extra bite.

We especially crave Salsa Verde, with its uplifting fresh scent, in the late winter and early spring when all outside is muddy and gray. Serve small amounts of this intensely flavored sauce on boiled potatoes, steamed cauliflower, or other vegetables. About 2 tablespoons of salsa per serving of baked or broiled fish should do nicely.

Salsa Verde keeps refrigerated in a tightly covered nonreactive container for 3 or 4 days.

Makes 1 cup

Total time: 10 minutes

> **NOTE:**
> A blender will produce a smoother-textured sauce than a food processor.

1 cup coarsely chopped fresh tomatoes
2 garlic cloves, minced or pressed
2 tablespoons chopped scallions or red onions
1 tablespoon coarsely chopped cornichons or
    other sour pickles
1 tablespoon rinsed capers
¼ teaspoon salt
1 tablespoon fresh lemon juice
pinch of sugar
1 cup firmly packed chopped parsley, preferably flat-leaf
1 tablespoon olive oil (optional)

In a food processor or blender (see Note), whirl the tomatoes, garlic, scallions or red onions, pickles, capers, salt, lemon juice, and sugar until smooth. Add the parsley and whirl until well blended. If adding olive oil, drizzle it in last and blend well. Serve at room temperature.

VARIATIONS For crunchiness and sweetness, stir ½ cup of minced red, yellow, or green bell peppers into the blended salsa.

Try adding ½ cup of fresh basil or a tablespoon of fresh tarragon, or both, for a more flavorful salsa.

Use only capers or only pickles.

PER 1-OZ SERVING: 8 CALORIES, .4 G PROTEIN, .1 G FAT, 1.7 G CARBOHYDRATES, 0 G SATURATED FATTY ACIDS, 0 G POLYUNSATURATED FATTY ACIDS, 0 G MONOUNSATURATED FATTY ACIDS, 0 MG CHOLESTEROL, 102 MG SODIUM, .4 G TOTAL DIETARY FIBER

SKORDALIA THESSALONIKE

Skorda, the Greek word for "garlic," is—for good reasons—the root of *skordalia*, the creamy, garlicky potato sauce popular throughout much of Greece and Macedonia. Our version is fat-free, tangy, and refreshing. Try it as a topping for steamed or raw vegetables and on broiled, poached, or baked fish. We especially like this sauce on steamed broccoli or asparagus spears with summer-ripe tomato slices.

This sauce keeps well for 3 to 4 days in the refrigerator, and the garlic flavor will intensify.

Makes 2 generous cups

Total time: 30 to 35 minutes

NOTE: Food processors will not work for this particular recipe. The texture of the potatoes becomes too gluey.

2 cups peeled diced potatoes
4 garlic cloves
1¼ cups plain nonfat yogurt
1 tablespoon chopped fresh dill
1 tablespoon chopped scallions
½ teaspoon salt, or more to taste
¼ teaspoon ground black pepper, or more to taste

Combine the potatoes and garlic in a saucepan with water to cover, bring to a boil, and then reduce the heat and simmer for about 20 minutes, until very soft. Drain and transfer to a medium mixing bowl. Mash together the potatoes and yogurt with a hand masher (see Note) until quite smooth. Stir in the dill, scallions, salt, and pepper. Serve immediately at room temperature or chill to serve later, allowing it to return to room temperature just before serving.

VARIATION If you prefer a stronger garlic kick, add a pressed raw garlic clove to the finished sauce.

PER 1-OZ SERVING: 24 CALORIES, 1.3 G PROTEIN, .1 G FAT, 4.7 G CARBOHYDRATES, 0 G SATURATED FATTY ACIDS, 0 G POLYUNSATURATED FATTY ACIDS, 0 G MONO-UNSATURATED FATTY ACIDS, 0 MG CHOLESTEROL, 89 MG SODIUM, .3 G TOTAL DIETARY FIBER

CREAMY ROASTED RED PEPPER SAUCE

Sometimes the simplest things in life are the most extraordinary, and this sauce is no exception to that truism. The sauce is quite versatile and can be served warm, at room temperature, or chilled, depending on the season and your whim. This would be equally nice made with roasted fresh bell peppers; see page 436.

⅔ cup drained canned roasted red peppers
⅓ cup buttermilk
salt and ground black pepper to taste

Makes 1 cup

Total time: 5 minutes

Purée the roasted peppers, buttermilk, and salt and black pepper in a blender or food processor until smooth.

PER 2-OZ SERVING: 18 CALORIES, 1.0 G PROTEIN, .2 G FAT, 3.4 G CARBOHYDRATES, .1 G SATURATED FATTY ACIDS, 0 G POLYUNSATURATED FATTY ACIDS, .1 G MONOUNSATURATED FATTY ACIDS, 1 MG CHOLESTEROL, 20 MG SODIUM, .5 G TOTAL DIETARY FIBER

MENU SUGGESTIONS Serve on any pasta topped with your favorite herb, or use it to dress up **Potato Cheese Gnocchi** (page 250), baked potatoes, stuffed vegetables, savory filled crêpes, or simple grain dishes, or as a marinade for steamed vegetables. Refrigerated this will keep for about a week.

BARBECUE SAUCE

Tangy and sweet, this sauce evokes summertime picnics in any season. Use it in Barbecue Beans (page 156), with Chili Burgers (page 173), or to add spark to simple bean dishes.

Makes about 1½ cups

Total time: 30 minutes

½ cup chopped onions
2 garlic cloves, minced or pressed
¼ cup soy sauce
¼ cup cider vinegar
¼ cup ketchup or tomato paste
½ cup unsweetened apple or orange juice
2 tablespoons prepared mustard
2 tablespoons molasses
½ teaspoon dried thyme
½ teaspoon ground black pepper

Combine all of the ingredients in a blender or food processor and purée until smooth. Simmer in a saucepan, uncovered, for 10 to 15 minutes, stirring often, until thickened. Tightly sealed and refrigerated, it will keep for at least 2 weeks.

PER 1-OZ SERVING: 22 CALORIES, .5 G PROTEIN, .1 G FAT, 5.3 G CARBOHYDRATES, 0 G SATURATED FATTY ACIDS, 0 G POLYUNSATURATED FATTY ACIDS, 0 G MONOUNSATURATED FATTY ACIDS, 0 MG CHOLESTEROL, 310 MG SODIUM, .2 G TOTAL DIETARY FIBER

Hot Tamarind and Guava Sauce for Fish or Vegetables

This hot, sweet, and tart sauce is delectable on steamed vegetables such as zucchini, cauliflower, green beans, and potatoes, or drizzle it over a vegetable platter of baked eggplant slices and roasted sweet potatoes, onions, and yellow squash. Our recipe will also dress 2 or 3 pounds of baked or broiled fish, which is enough for 6 to 8 individual servings.

Garnish with chopped scallions and thinly sliced or chopped red bell pepper, if you are in a decorating mood.

Makes 1 generous cup

**Preparation time:
25 minutes**

**Sitting time:
3 or 4 hours**

½ cup minced red onions
½ cup minced red bell peppers
1 fresh chile, seeded and minced, or
    Tabasco sauce or other hot pepper sauce to taste
2 garlic cloves, pressed or minced
½ cup hot water
¼ cup finely chopped fresh cilantro
1 teaspoon fresh lemon juice
1 teaspoon vegetable oil
2 tablespoons tamarind concentrate*
¼ cup guava paste*
½ teaspoon salt

Guava paste (pages 428–429) can be found in Latin American grocery stores and in the ethnic or condiment sections of many grocery stores. We developed this recipe using Goya brand guava paste, which we recommend. If you use some other brand of guava paste, you may need to add a little water to produce a smooth sauce. Tamarind concentrate (page 439) is available at Indian and Asian food markets.

In a blender or food processor, purée the red onions, bell peppers, chile, garlic, hot water, cilantro, lemon juice, oil, tamarind concentrate, guava paste, and salt until smooth. If the sauce is too thick, add water a little at a time until it is thick but pourable. Set aside for 3 to 4 hours for the flavors to meld.

Serve this sauce at room temperature or gently heated in a double boiler or on a heat diffuser to prevent scorching. When refrigerated, the sauce will keep for 4 or 5 days.

PER 2-OZ SERVING: 77 CALORIES, .9 G PROTEIN, 1.3 G FAT, 17.2 G CARBOHYDRATES, .2 G SATURATED FATTY ACIDS, .7 G POLYUNSATURATED FATTY ACIDS, .3 G MONOUNSATURATED FATTY ACIDS, 0 MG CHOLESTEROL, 309 MG SODIUM, 1.5 G TOTAL DIETARY FIBER

HUNGARIAN LESCO

Introduced to us by Anna Gardner, a great Hungarian cook and a friend of Moosewood's Nancy Lazarus, *lesco* (LEH-cho) is a simple but versatile sauce. Lesco's unique flavor is derived from the Hungarian hot peppers, which vary immensely in intensity of hotness, so use more or fewer peppers to match your taste.

Make big batches of lesco when the peppers and tomatoes are ripening fast and furious in your garden. It freezes beautifully and makes an excellent base for soups or stews—just add potatoes, zucchini, mushrooms, and whatever other appealing vegetables you have on hand. Lesco is delicious on firm white fish fillets (about ¼ cup per fillet), or try it on plain pasta or rice, with a dollop of low-fat or nonfat yogurt or low-fat sour cream, if desired.

2 large yellow or white onions, chopped (about 4 cups)
1 teaspoon canola or other vegetable oil
½ cup water
4 green bell peppers, stemmed, seeded, and chopped
2 to 4 Hungarian hot peppers, stemmed, seeded, and chopped (page 429)
4 fresh tomatoes, chopped (about 4 cups)
salt to taste

Makes 6 cups

Total time: 40 minutes

In a saucepan on medium heat, sauté the onions in the oil for a couple of minutes. Stir well, add the water, cover, and increase the heat to high. Cook for 5 minutes, stirring frequently. Add the bell peppers and the hot peppers, lower the heat to medium, and continue to cook, covered, stirring often, for 5 minutes. Add the tomatoes, mix well, and simmer for 15 minutes, until the onions and peppers are quite soft. Add salt to taste.

PER 2-OZ SERVING: 23 CALORIES, .7 G PROTEIN, .4 G FAT, 4.9 G CARBOHYDRATES, .1 G SATURATED FATTY ACIDS, .2 G POLYUNSATURATED FATTY ACIDS, .1 G MONOUNSATURATED FATTY ACIDS, 0 MG CHOLESTEROL, 11 MG SODIUM, .8 G TOTAL DIETARY FIBER

BLENDER HOT SAUCE

When you want a homemade hot sauce and you want it without a lot of fuss, try our quick blender method. The sauce takes almost no time to prepare, and then it dutifully simmers on your back burner while you move on to create the rest of your meal. Although there are a lot of commercial hot sauces available, we still haven't found one that competes with homemade.

Blender Hot Sauce will add a rich spiciness to bean dishes, chili, enchiladas, burritos, fajitas, frittatas, and casseroles.

1 cup chopped onions
1 cup chopped bell peppers
1 or 2 fresh green chiles, seeds removed
  for a milder "hot" (see Note)
5 garlic cloves, minced or pressed
4 cups chopped fresh or 3 cups chopped canned
  tomatoes with their juice (28-ounce can)
1 teaspoon ground cumin
1 teaspoon ground coriander
½ teaspoon dried oregano
2 tablespoons chopped fresh cilantro
salt to taste

Makes 3 cups

Preparation time: 20 minutes

Cooking time: 30 minutes

In a blender or food processor, combine the onions, peppers, chiles, garlic, tomatoes, cumin, coriander, oregano, and cilantro and purée until smooth. Transfer the sauce to a soup pot and simmer on low heat, uncovered, for about 30 minutes, or until the sauce has thickened and the flavors have mellowed. Stir often as it cooks and use a heat diffuser, if needed, to prevent sticking. Add salt to taste.

Hot sauce will keep for about 2 weeks, refrigerated and tightly covered.

PER 1-OZ SERVING: 11 CALORIES, .5 G PROTEIN, .1 G FAT, 2.4 G CARBOHYDRATES, 0 G SATURATED FATTY ACIDS, 0 G POLYUNSATURATED FATTY ACIDS, 0 G MONO-UNSATURATED FATTY ACIDS, 0 MG CHOLESTEROL, 44 MG SODIUM, .2 G TOTAL DIETARY FIBER

MENU SUGGESTIONS Serve in **Black Bean Chilaquile** (page 164) or on Caribbean-style black beans and annatto rice with or without that tempting dollop of low-fat sour cream or yogurt.

> **NOTE:**
> In place of fresh chiles, ½ teaspoon of cayenne can be used. After adding the cayenne, cook the sauce for 15 minutes, taste it for hotness, and sprinkle in a bit more cayenne, if desired. Be careful not to be heavy-handed when you adjust the cayenne, since the hotness of the sauce will increase somewhat as it cooks.
>
> If cayenne is not cooked sufficiently, it can be harsh tasting, so once the hot sauce has finished cooking, we do not recommend adding any more. Once you experiment and discover the perfect amount of cayenne for you, write it right on this page so you won't forget it. If you ever want to make a sauce hotter after it has cooked, add Tabasco or other hot pepper sauce to taste.

BRAZILIAN HOT PEPPER AND LEMON SAUCE

This is the hot, tart, oniony sauce that is traditionally served with feijoada (page 158), the Brazilian national dish. Black beans can't be feijoada without it.

2 or 3 fresh chiles (such as malagueta,
 tabasco, or habañero), seeded and chopped,
 or 4 or 5 preserved chiles
1 red onion, chopped (about 2 cups)
1 garlic clove, pressed and minced
½ cup fresh lemon or lime juice
½ teaspoon salt

Makes about 1 cup

**Preparation time:
10 minutes**

**Sitting time:
at least 1 hour**

In a blender or food processor, combine all the ingredients and purée just until a coarse sauce is produced. If using a blender, you may have to stop several times and scrape down the sides with a rubber spatula. To prepare by hand, mince the chiles, onions, and garlic and mix in the lemon juice and salt. Let the flavors meld for at least an hour at room temperature or for 3 hours refrigerated. Serve at room temperature.

This sauce can be kept covered in the refrigerator for 3 days.

PER 2-OZ SERVING: 24 CALORIES, .7 G PROTEIN, .1 G FAT, 6.4 G CARBOHYDRATES, 0 G SATURATED FATTY ACIDS, 0 G POLYUNSATURATED FATTY ACIDS, 0 G MONOUNSATURATED FATTY ACIDS, 0 MG CHOLESTEROL, 301 MG SODIUM, .9 G TOTAL DIETARY FIBER

FRESH TOMATO SALSA

This light, fresh salsa or its variation can be prepared in short order. Both make delicious toppings for Seitan Fajitas (page 232), Sweet Potato and Black Bean Burrito (page 172), or any beans and rice dish. Dip tortilla chips in the salsa, use it to spice up a pita sandwich, or add it to a bowl of plain rice with a few slices of fresh avocado.

Tortilla chips are certainly a part of the late-twentieth-century snack explosion. Low-fat and nonfat (baked) chips are now available or they can be made at home. Brush corn tortillas lightly (or not) with canola oil, salt lightly (or not), cut into eighths, and bake for 8 to 10 minutes at 350°. Excellent low-fat and nonfat chips can be found in most supermarkets and natural food stores.

Makes 3 cups

Total time: 15 minutes

3 cups diced tomatoes
1 small fresh green chile, minced, seeds
removed for a milder "hot"
1 tablespoon fresh lemon or lime juice
1 to 2 tablespoons minced fresh cilantro
salt and ground black pepper to taste

Combine all of the ingredients in a mixing bowl and serve at room temperature.

VARIATION For Tomato Pineapple Salsa, replace 1 cup of the diced tomatoes with ⅔ cup of fresh or unsweetened canned pineapple chunks. Also add 1 tablespoon of cider vinegar and 2 teaspoons of grated fresh ginger root.

PER 1-OZ SERVING: 6 CALORIES, .2 G PROTEIN, .1 G FAT, 1.3 G CARBOHYDRATES, 0 G SATURATED FATTY ACIDS, 0 G POLYUNSATURATED FATTY ACIDS, 0 G MONOUN-SATURATED FATTY ACIDS, 0 MG CHOLESTEROL, 10 MG SODIUM, .3 G TOTAL DIETARY FIBER

CORN RELISH

Intensely sweet-and-sour, this relish still retains a fresh taste and texture that is almost salad-like because it cooks for just 15 minutes. If you prefer a softer relish with a thicker sauce, simmer it longer—up to 45 minutes. It's important to chop the celery, bell peppers, and onions into pieces about the size of corn kernels for the best look and consistency.

We serve Corn Relish as an accent to other foods. It can make a bland dish more interesting for those at the table who want a little spark. Whether or not to add the fresh chile or hot sauce to it depends upon what else is being served. This versatile relish is good on simple grilled fish, potato salad, bean dishes, and sandwiches alike.

1½ cups fresh or frozen corn kernels
1 cup finely chopped celery
1 cup finely chopped red and/or green bell peppers
1 cup finely chopped red onions
⅓ cup brown sugar
1 cup white or cider vinegar
2 tablespoons prepared yellow or Dijon mustard
2 garlic cloves, pressed (about 1 teaspoon)
1 fresh chile, seeded and minced, or Tabasco or
    other hot pepper sauce to taste (optional)

Makes 4 cups

**Preparation time:
10 to 15 minutes**

**Cooking time:
15 minutes**

Combine the corn, celery, bell peppers, red onions, brown sugar, vinegar, mustard, garlic, and chile, if using, in an uncovered saucepan. Bring to a boil on high heat, then reduce the heat and simmer for 15 minutes, or longer if desired. Serve at room temperature. Stored covered in the refrigerator, Corn Relish will keep for 4 days.

PER 2-OZ SERVING: 43 CALORIES, .8 G PROTEIN, .3 G FAT, 10.6 G CARBOHYDRATES, 0 G SATURATED FATTY ACIDS, .1 G POLYUNSATURATED FATTY ACIDS, .1 G MONOUNSATURATED FATTY ACIDS, 0 MG CHOLESTEROL, 33 MG SODIUM, .8 G TOTAL DIETARY FIBER

MANGO PEACH CHUTNEY

A wonderful aroma will fill your house or apartment when you make this chutney. An elegant addition to any curry, it is an indispensable side dish for Lentil Sambar (page 166), Curried Potato Cabbage Roll-Ups (page 251), or Curried Sweet Potato Roti (page 230).

1 large mango, peeled and coarsely chopped
   (page 431)
2 cups fresh or frozen peaches, peeled and
   coarsely chopped
½ cup unsweetened apple juice
½ cup cider vinegar
½ cup packed brown sugar
1 medium onion, chopped
2 teaspoons grated fresh ginger root
1 small fresh green chile, seeded and minced
   (about 1 tablespoon)
¼ teaspoon ground cardamom
½ teaspoon ground cinnamon
¼ teaspoon salt

Serves 4 to 6

**Preparation time:
15 minutes**

**Cooking time:
45 to 60 minutes**

Combine all of the chutney ingredients in a nonreactive saucepan and bring to a boil. Reduce the heat and simmer gently, uncovered, for about 45 minutes, stirring occasionally, until thick and translucent. Cool or chill before serving.

This chutney will keep for several weeks stored in a tightly covered container in the refrigerator.

PER 3.50-OZ SERVING: 135 CALORIES, .9 G PROTEIN, .2 G FAT, 35.1 G CARBOHYDRATES, 0 G SATURATED FATTY ACIDS, .1 G POLYUNSATURATED FATTY ACIDS, .1 G MONOUNSATURATED FATTY ACIDS, 0 MG CHOLESTEROL, 109 MG SODIUM, 2.1 G TOTAL DIETARY FIBER

SAVORY ONION MARMALADE

As a condiment, this is top of the list. Long, slow cooking lends the onions succulence and depth, which, in turn, adds a wonderful rich flavor to almost any dish. Try this relish on bread, toast, biscuits, potatoes, pizza, in sandwiches, or in a soup or stew.

Although we like the bite that the balsamic vinegar and wine add, the marmalade is fine without them (sulfite-sensitive folks, rejoice!); so use neither, either, or both, as you like. Tightly sealed and refrigerated, Savory Onion Marmalade will keep for up to 3 weeks.

4 cups thinly sliced onions (about 3 large onions)
1 to 3 tablespoons water
6 garlic cloves, minced or pressed
½ teaspoon salt
dash of ground black pepper, or more to taste
½ teaspoon dried thyme
1 teaspoon balsamic vinegar (optional)
1 teaspoon dry red wine (optional)

Makes about 2 cups

**Total time:
30 to 45 minutes**

In a well-seasoned cast-iron or nonstick skillet, combine the onions, 1 tablespoon of the water, the garlic, salt, pepper, thyme, and vinegar and/or red wine, if using. Cover and cook on medium-low heat for 30 to 45 minutes, stirring often and adding water as needed, until the onions are dark brown, sweet, and richly flavored. Chill well before serving.

PER 1-OZ SERVING: 14 CALORIES, .5 G PROTEIN, .1 G FAT, 3.3 G CARBOHYDRATES, 0 G SATURATED FATTY ACIDS, 0 G POLYUNSATURATED FATTY ACIDS, 0 G MONOUNSATURATED FATTY ACIDS, 0 MG CHOLESTEROL, 76 MG SODIUM, .5 G TOTAL DIETARY FIBER

SUSAN'S PESTO

Susan Harville worked on a low-fat version of pesto until she scored with this one, which has a bright, fresh taste and almost no fat. We never tire of eating linguine with pesto, and this recipe makes exactly the right amount of pesto for one pound of pasta. Pesto is also good as a topping for baked potatoes or broiled fish, a dressing for steamed green beans or zucchini, a sandwich spread, and a flavoring for soups, stews, risottos, and omelets.

Susan's Pesto is best served immediately, but it will keep refrigerated for 3 or 4 days.

1 cup well-packed fresh basil leaves
1 cup chopped tomatoes
1 garlic clove, pressed or minced
1 tablespoon toasted pine nuts *
½ teaspoon salt

Makes 1 cup

Total time: 10 minutes

To toast pine nuts, spread them in a single layer on an unoiled baking sheet and bake in a conventional or toaster oven at 350° for about 3 to 5 minutes, until just slightly deepened in color.

Rinse and drain the basil leaves. In a blender or food processor, combine the basil, tomatoes, garlic, pine nuts, and salt and purée until smooth. You may need to stop several times to scrape the sides of the blender or processor bowl with a rubber spatula.

PER 1-OZ SERVING: 13 CALORIES, .7 G PROTEIN, .7 G FAT, 1.6 G CARBOHYDRATES, .1 G SATURATED FATTY ACIDS, .3 G POLYUNSATURATED FATTY ACIDS, .2 G MONOUNSATURATED FATTY ACIDS, 0 MG CHOLESTEROL, 135 MG SODIUM, .3 G TOTAL DIETARY FIBER

CILANTRO PESTO

This is every cilantro lover's dream. Try it spread on crusty Italian bread, in pasta or potato salad, or as a fresh cool salsa for spicy bean dishes, or use a dollop to enliven soup. This pesto is best when served immediately, but it will keep refrigerated for 3 or 4 days.

Makes 1 cup

Total time: 10 minutes

1 cup fresh well-packed cilantro leaves
1 tomato, chopped (about 1 cup)
1 garlic clove, pressed or minced
1 tablespoon toasted pine nuts (see instructions, above)
½ teaspoon salt

Rinse and drain the cilantro leaves. In a blender or food processor, purée the cilantro, tomato, garlic, pine nuts, and salt until smooth. You may need to stop several times to scrape the sides of the blender or processor bowl with a rubber spatula.

PER 1-OZ SERVING: 14 CALORIES, .7 G PROTEIN, .8 G FAT, 1.7 G CARBOHYDRATES, .1 G SATURATED FATTY ACIDS, .3 G POLYUNSATURATED FATTY ACIDS, .3 G MONOUNSATURATED FATTY ACIDS, 0 MG CHOLESTEROL, 155 MG SODIUM, .5 G TOTAL DIETARY FIBER

THAI CURRY PASTE

Here is an intensely flavored spice blend that can be used in a variety of dishes. Try it in Thai Vegetable Curry (page 268), in Thai Fish Cakes (page 302), or in any of the curry dishes in your regular repertoire. Toss some curry paste with steamed vegetables and serve them on Golden Basmati Rice (page 185), Fragrant Jasmine Rice (page 189), or plain brown rice. Tightly sealed and refrigerated, our curry paste will keep for at least a week, and it may also be frozen for extended storage.

If Thai basil and fresh lemongrass are available, they will give your curry paste the most authentic flavor.

¼ **cup chopped scallions**
¼ **cup chopped fresh cilantro, basil, or Thai basil**
2 tablespoons minced garlic cloves
2 tablespoons grated fresh ginger root
1 tablespoon freshly grated lemon or lime peel
   or minced tender inner stalk of fresh lemongrass
1 tablespoon brown sugar
1 or 2 fresh red or green chiles, minced
3 tablespoons fresh lemon or lime juice
1 tablespoon ground coriander
1 teaspoon turmeric
½ **teaspoon salt**

Makes a generous
½ cup

Total time:
10 to 15 minutes

Combine all of the curry paste ingredients in a blender or food processor and purée until quite smooth.

PER 1-OZ SERVING: 25 CALORIES, .8 G PROTEIN, .1 G FAT, 6.1 G CARBOHYDRATES, 0 G SATURATED FATTY ACIDS, 0 G POLYUNSATURATED FATTY ACIDS, 0 G MONOUNSATURATED FATTY ACIDS, 0 MG CHOLESTEROL, 176 MG SODIUM, .6 G TOTAL DIETARY FIBER

TOMATO CORN SALSA

This is a colorful salsa that is easy to make and brimming with sunny flavors. Serve on Chili Burgers (page 173), Seitan Fajitas (page 232), or beans and rice, or with chips or crudités. This will keep for 2 or 3 days but is best served the day it's made.

Makes 3½ cups

**Preparation time:
15 to 20 minutes**

**Sitting time:
15 to 20 minutes**

**1 cup fresh or frozen corn kernels
2 cups diced tomatoes
2 tablespoons diced red onions
¼ cup diced green bell peppers
1 tablespoon chopped fresh basil
½ to 1 fresh green chile, minced
1 tablespoon fresh lime juice
1 teaspoon cider vinegar**

Blanch the corn in boiling water to cover for 1 to 2 minutes, until just tender. Drain. In a large bowl, combine all of the ingredients and set aside for 15 to 20 minutes to allow the flavors to develop. Add salt, if desired, and serve at room temperature.

PER 3.25-OZ SERVING: 38 CALORIES, 1.3 G PROTEIN, .5 G FAT, 8.8 G CARBOHY-DRATES, .1 G SATURATED FATTY ACIDS, .2 G POLYUNSATURATED FATTY ACIDS, .1 G MONOUNSATURATED FATTY ACIDS, 0 MG CHOLESTEROL, 34 MG SODIUM, 1.4 G TOTAL DIETARY FIBER

Asian Cucumber Condiment

If you want to enliven a dish, this relish can do the job. It's sweet, sour, and spicy all at once. Try it as a side salad with Thai Fried Rice (page 190) or Southeast Asian Fish Rolls (page 294). If you prefer to omit the fish sauce, the flavor will be different but still delicious.

1 cucumber, peeled, halved lengthwise, and seeded
¼ cup peeled and shredded carrots
½ fresh chile, seeded and minced
¼ cup fresh lime juice or 3 tablespoons rice vinegar
1 tablespoon brown sugar
1 tablespoon Asian fish sauce (page 420) or salt to taste
1 tablespoon chopped fresh cilantro (optional)

Serves 4

**Preparation time:
10 minutes**

**Chilling time:
30 minutes**

Slice both halves of the cucumber crosswise on the diagonal to make thin crescents. In a large bowl, combine the cucumbers, carrots, and minced chile and set it aside. Whisk together the lime juice, brown sugar, and fish sauce or salt, and stir until the sugar completely dissolves. Pour the dressing over the vegetables and toss well. Add cilantro, if desired. Chill for 30 minutes to allow the flavors to meld.

PER 2.25-OZ SERVING: 27 CALORIES, .5 G PROTEIN, .1 G FAT, 7.0 G CARBOHYDRATES, 0 G SATURATED FATTY ACIDS, 0 G POLYUNSATURATED FATTY ACIDS, 0 G MONOUNSATURATED FATTY ACIDS, 0 MG CHOLESTEROL, 50 MG SODIUM, .6 G TOTAL DIETARY FIBER

red berry kissel 372

creamy dairyless rice pudding 373

DARK CHOCOLATE PUDDING 374

tapioca fruit parfaits 375

pumpkin custard 376

LEMON PUDDING CAKE 377

coffee angelfood cake 378

chocolate cocoa cake 380

APPLESAUCE SPICE CAKE 381

banana bundt cake 382

blueberry peach cobbler 383

APPLE APRICOT STRUDEL 384

apple cherry crisp 385

ginger peach crumble 386

OUR BEST NO-BUTTER BROWNIES 387

fruit-filled meringue shells 388

maple walnut biscotti 390

ANISE LEMON BISCOTTI 391

chocolate hazelnut biscotti 392

cardamom oatmeal cookies 393

PINEAPPLE BUTTERMILK SHERBET 394

vanilla cream 395

DESSERTS

DESSERTS may actually help some people stick to a lower-fat diet. One recent study found that eating a modest amount of sugar reduces cravings for fat. A little sweetness at the end of a meal—a diversion in more ways than one!

Nutritionists tell us it's a good idea to include more fruits in our daily diets. Fruits are filled with vitamins, minerals, and fiber. But even without this advice in mind, we think fresh seasonal fruit served at the end of a meal is an effortless, light, and appealing dessert. Imagine summer without watermelon or autumn without crisp apples? Tangerines truly brighten a cold-weather meal. We wait all winter for the first sweet strawberries of spring.

But sometimes a piece of fresh fruit just isn't enough to qualify as dessert for us, and we want a more elaborate grand finale, so, in addition to some naturally low-fat fruit preparations, we've included cakes, cookies, puddings, sherbet, and more, so that you need never feel a sense of "dessert deprivation." We've developed low-fat versions of traditional home favorites—brownies, banana cake, and chocolate pudding. Some classic desserts, such as angelfood cake, sherbet, and meringues, have always been low-fat; we have worked to heighten their flavor and to make them less like diet desserts. There are some elegant, company's-coming-to-dinner desserts, such as Apple Apricot Strudel, but most are simple, anyday fare, and nearly half boast a fat content of 10 percent or less!

The success of a low-fat dessert is very much dependent on its living up to our expectations. Is the brownie fudgy? the cake moist? the pudding creamy? We're happy to answer "yes" to all of these, thanks to a bit of trial and error. Low-fat baking calls for a sort of alchemy to produce moist, tender pastries with significantly reduced fat. The discovery in recent years that fruit purées can replace all or part of the fat in standard recipes has been a boon to low-fat bakers. The pectin in a fruit purée like applesauce behaves similarly to fats by forming a film around air pockets in baked goods. This helps to create loft, while the purée also provides natural sweetness and smooth texture.

When making desserts that don't rely on the richness of butter, cream, or eggs, it is especially important to use high-quality ingredients. Ensure good results by using ripe, flavorful fruit, real (not imitation) extracts and maple syrup, and fragrant, fresh spices. We favor unbleached white pastry flour because it makes a more tender and lightly textured low-fat pastry than all-purpose flour. The acidity present in yogurt and buttermilk tenderizes gluten, the component of flour that forms chewy-textured baked goods.

Lastly, certain recipes are best left alone. For example, a pound cake or shortbread without butter is certain to disappoint. Such desserts are best enjoyed only occasionally, when the balance of your diet can be streamlined to allow for a special treat.

RED BERRY KISSEL

Delicious, simple, healthful, easily prepared—this Scandinavian-style fruit pudding topped with Vanilla Cream is a great everyday family dessert, good for breakfast or brunch, or perfect company fare when served in clear glass dessert cups or stemware. The fruits are barely cooked, glistening jewel-like in the deep scarlet, translucent kissel.

We prefer a softly gelled kissel, so when we make it ahead, we reduce the potato starch or cornstarch to 2 tablespoons. Although it may seem too loose coming off the stove, it will become firmer overnight and be just right the next day.

Serves 6

**Preparation time:
15 to 20 minutes**

**Chilling time:
at least 20 minutes**

2 cups Concord grape or raspberry juice

**¼ cup sugar, or to taste—depending on the sweetness
of the juices**

**3 tablespoons potato starch or cornstarch dissolved in
½ cup grape or raspberry juice**

**1 pint fresh strawberries, hulled and sliced (about 1¼ pounds),
or 20 ounces frozen unsweetened whole strawberries**

3 cups fresh or 12 ounces frozen whole raspberries

1 teaspoon pure vanilla extract

2 cups Vanilla Cream (page 395)

In a nonreactive saucepan, combine the juice and sugar. Pour the dissolved potato starch mixture into the saucepan and slowly bring it to a simmer on medium-high heat, about 10 minutes. As soon as it begins to simmer, stir for about 5 minutes, until the cloudy juice becomes clear. Stir in the strawberries and raspberries and remove from the heat. Stir in the vanilla. Refrigerate for at least 20 minutes.

Serve chilled, either family-style in a bowl with the Vanilla Cream passed alongside in a pitcher, or in individual dessert cups or glasses topped with a dollop of Vanilla Cream.

PER 12-OZ SERVING: 291 CALORIES, 8.7 G PROTEIN, 1.1 G FAT, 63.4 G CARBOHY-DRATES, .5 G SATURATED FATTY ACIDS, .1 G POLYUNSATURATED FATTY ACIDS, .3 G MONOUNSATURATED FATTY ACIDS, 4 MG CHOLESTEROL, 189 MG SODIUM, 4.6 G TOTAL DIETARY FIBER

MENU SUGGESTIONS This kissel has particular appeal with foods of the north, such as **Cabbage Rolls** (page 256), **Cream of Cauliflower Soup** (page 90), **Baked Fish with Mustard Marinade** (page 288), **Baltic Fish** (page 287), **Another Shepherd's Pie** (page 238), or **Wild Mushroom Stew Trieste** (page 278).

CREAMY DAIRYLESS RICE PUDDING

This dairy-free rice pudding is perfect for vegans or those with lactose intolerance. But don't restrict yourself to making it just for those with special dietary needs or preferences—the whole family will love it for dessert, snacks, or breakfast.

4 cups water
¾ cup white rice (preferably basmati)
**1 quart reduced-fat or 1% soy milk,
    sometimes called soy drink (see Note)**
½ cup pure maple syrup
1 teaspoon ground cinnamon
1 teaspoon pure vanilla extract
¼ cup currants or raisins
1 teaspoon freshly grated lemon peel

sliced seasonal fruit (optional)

Serves 4 to 6

Total time: 55 minutes

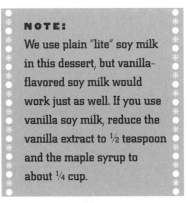

NOTE:
We use plain "lite" soy milk in this dessert, but vanilla-flavored soy milk would work just as well. If you use vanilla soy milk, reduce the vanilla extract to ½ teaspoon and the maple syrup to about ¼ cup.

Bring the water to a boil in a heavy saucepan. Add the rice and simmer, uncovered, for 5 minutes. Remove from the heat and allow to sit for 5 minutes. Drain the rice and return it to the pan with the soy milk, maple syrup, cinnamon, vanilla, currants or raisins, and lemon peel. Bring to a boil, then reduce the heat and simmer gently for 30 to 40 minutes, stirring often, until the pudding is thick and creamy. Serve warm or chill for at least 2 hours or overnight.

If you like, garnish the rice pudding with strawberry slices or other fresh fruit.

PER 6-OZ SERVING: 199 CALORIES, 6.0 G PROTEIN, 3.1 G FAT, 37.6 G CARBOHYDRATES, .4 G SATURATED FATTY ACIDS, 1.3 G POLYUNSATURATED FATTY ACIDS, .6 G MONOUNSATURATED FATTY ACIDS, 0 MG CHOLESTEROL, 23 MG SODIUM, 2.9 G TOTAL DIETARY FIBER

MENU SUGGESTION As a dessert, serve at the end of a light meal, perhaps one that features a vegetable stew or a combo of soup, salad, and bread.

DARK CHOCOLATE PUDDING

Most of the fat has been removed, but everything else you want in chocolate pudding is still here. It's thick, creamy, and satisfying—a comfort food. We know some people prefer to eat their chocolate as chocolate alone, but for the nonpurists we suggest garnishing with fresh seasonal fruit such as bananas, oranges, strawberries, or raspberries.

3 tablespoons cornstarch

3 tablespoons sugar

2 tablespoons unsweetened cocoa powder

2 cups skim milk

1 teaspoon pure vanilla extract

Serves 4

**Total time:
15 to 20 minutes**

In a saucepan, thoroughly combine the cornstarch, sugar, and cocoa. Add the milk and stir until very smooth. Cook on medium heat, stirring constantly, until the pudding comes to a boil. Then lower the heat and gently simmer, stirring continuously, for 3 or 4 minutes. Stir in the vanilla, pour the hot pudding into a decorative serving bowl or individual custard cups, and serve warm or chill for about 2 hours, until cold and set.

PER 4.50-OZ SERVING: 109 CALORIES, 4.4 G PROTEIN, .8 G FAT, 21.8 G CARBOHYDRATES, .4 G SATURATED FATTY ACIDS, 0 G POLYUNSATURATED FATTY ACIDS, .1 G MONOUNSATURATED FATTY ACIDS, 2 MG CHOLESTEROL, 59 MG SODIUM, .1 G TOTAL DIETARY FIBER

MENU SUGGESTION Dark Chocolate Pudding is good anytime, anyplace. And parents, remember, no matter how many fancy desserts are in your repertoire, this is most likely the one the kids will remember when they are grown and gone.

TAPIOCA FRUIT PARFAITS

You can let your artistic talents out of the closet for this dessert. Depending on which fruits you choose, Tapioca Fruit Parfaits can be a pastiche of colors and swirls. Strawberry-banana and orange-kiwi are two exceptional combinations out of many possibilities—use your imagination.

¼ cup granulated tapioca (not whole pearl)

2 to 4 tablespoons sugar

2 cups skim milk

2 egg whites, beaten until stiff (optional)

½ teaspoon pure vanilla extract

2 cups sliced fruit such as mangoes, papaya,
   oranges, bananas, strawberries, kiwi

toasted unsweetened dried shredded coconut (optional)

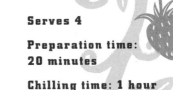

Serves 4

Preparation time: 20 minutes

Chilling time: 1 hour

Combine the tapioca, sugar, and ½ cup of the milk in a saucepan. On a medium flame, slowly add the rest of the milk in a steady stream and bring it to a boil, stirring constantly to prevent lumps. When the mixture boils, lower the heat and gently simmer for 5 to 7 minutes, or until the tapioca fully cooks and the pudding begins to thicken. If desired, fold in the beaten egg whites with a whisk and heat through. Remove from the heat, stir in the vanilla, and set aside to cool.

In four 8-ounce custard cups or parfait glasses, layer ¼ cup of the fruit, then ¼ cup of tapioca. Repeat with a second layer of fruit and tapioca. If desired, sprinkle with a little toasted coconut.

Chill for about an hour and serve.

PER 8-OZ SERVING: 173 CALORIES, 6.7 G PROTEIN, .6 G FAT, 36.7 G CARBOHYDRATES, .2 G SATURATED FATTY ACIDS, .1 G POLYUNSATURATED FATTY ACIDS, .1 G MONOUNSATURATED FATTY ACIDS, 2 MG CHOLESTEROL, 147 MG SODIUM, 1.7 G TOTAL DIETARY FIBER

MENU SUGGESTION This tapioca is a perfect finale to a Southeast Asian, Brazilian, Chilean, or Caribbean meal.

VARIATION To make the fruit layer for a Tapioca Plum Parfait, combine 2 cups of fresh pitted, chopped plums, 3 tablespoons of sugar, and ¼ teaspoon of ground ginger in a saucepan and cook on medium heat, stirring constantly, for about 10 minutes. Lower the heat and simmer until the plums are just tender and the sauce is thickened, about 5 minutes. Set aside. Prepare the tapioca and layer as described above.

PUMPKIN CUSTARD

Pumpkin is a great, cheap, underused source of beta-carotene. Forgo the high-fat crust of a pumpkin pie and enjoy this scrumptious, easily prepared dessert. If you're using canned pumpkin, be sure that it's an unsweetened purée, not pumpkin pie filling.

2 cups cooked pumpkin (16-ounce can)
1½ cups evaporated skimmed milk (12-ounce can)
2 eggs
3 egg whites
¾ cup pure maple syrup or brown sugar
1 teaspoon ground cinnamon
½ teaspoon ground nutmeg
½ teaspoon ground ginger

fresh apple slices (optional)

Serves 8

Preparation time: 10 minutes

Baking time: 45 to 60 minutes

Preheat the oven to 350°.

Prepare eight 6-ounce baking cups, such as custard cups or ramekins, with a light coating of cooking spray. Arrange the cups in a shallow, flat-bottomed baking pan.

Whirl all of the ingredients except the apple slices in a blender until smooth. Pour the custard into the baking cups. Pour boiling water into the baking pan to about a 2-inch depth. Bake for about 45 to 60 minutes, until a knife inserted in the center comes out clean. Remove the cups from the hot water and cool at room temperature, then refrigerate.

Serve chilled, garnished with fresh apple slices, if desired.

PER 6-OZ SERVING: 152 CALORIES, 7.4 G PROTEIN, 2.1 G FAT, 27.1 G CARBOHYDRATES, .7 G SATURATED FATTY ACIDS, .3 G POLYUNSATURATED FATTY ACIDS, .7 G MONOUNSATURATED FATTY ACIDS, 68 MG CHOLESTEROL, 231 MG SODIUM, .7 G TOTAL DIETARY FIBER

MENU SUGGESTION Pumpkin Custard is quite versatile—a perfect ending for a Caribbean or West African meal or for a New England harvest supper.

LEMON PUDDING CAKE

This favorite old-fashioned dessert separates into layers during baking—a tart-sweet pudding on the bottom and a light spongy cake on top. Serve it warm or chilled, plain or with fresh berries, for picnics, potlucks, family meals, or special dinners. Tightly sealed and refrigerated, Lemon Pudding Cake will keep for about 5 days.

Serves 6

**Preparation time:
20 minutes**

**Baking time:
45 to 50 minutes**

½ **cup unbleached white flour, preferably pastry flour**
½ **teaspoon baking powder**
1¼ **cups sugar, or more to taste**
1½ **cups buttermilk**
½ **cup fresh lemon juice (about 4 lemons)**
2 **egg yolks, lightly beaten**
2 **teaspoons freshly grated lemon peel (optional)**
4 **egg whites**
pinch of salt

Preheat the oven to 350°.

Prepare six 8-ounce ramekins or ovenproof dessert cups with a very light coating of cooking spray or oil. Place the cups in a 2-inch-deep baking pan. Begin to heat a kettle of water to a boil.

In a large bowl, combine the flour, baking powder, and ¾ cup of the sugar. (If you want a very sweet confection, use a whole cup of sugar.) Stir in the buttermilk, lemon juice, beaten egg yolks, and the grated lemon peel, if using, and set aside.

With an electric mixer, beat the egg whites and salt until the whites are stiff. Beat in the remaining ½ cup of sugar. Gently fold the egg whites into the batter. Spoon the batter evenly into the prepared cups. Pour boiling water into the baking pan until the water reaches halfway up the sides of the cups. Bake for 50 to 55 minutes, until puffy and golden.

PER 4.75-OZ SERVING: 229 CALORIES, 6.0 G PROTEIN, 2.6 G FAT, 46.6 G CARBOHY-DRATES, .9 G SATURATED FATTY ACIDS, .3 G POLYUNSATURATED FATTY ACIDS, .9 G MONOUNSATURATED FATTY ACIDS, 87 MG CHOLESTEROL, 139 MG SODIUM, .1 G TOTAL DIETARY FIBER

COFFEE ANGELFOOD CAKE

Angelfood cakes are intrinsically low in fat but can be rather insipid and uninteresting. This version, enhanced by the dark rich flavors of coffee and brown sugar and drizzled with a devilishly delicious mocha glaze, *is* quite heavenly. Serve it plain or with lightly sweetened fruit, such as raspberries, strawberries, peaches, oranges, or mangoes.

To maintain its delicate loft, the cake must be inverted and cooled for 2 hours before removing it from the pan. If your cake pan has little legs, it's fine to simply invert it. If not, then invert the pan on a long-necked bottle, such as a wine bottle, to cool.

We recommend that human beings vacate the premises while the cake is cooling to avoid the temptation to taste it before it is completely ready. Angels, we're told, can hover about without temptation, but we'll believe that when we see it.

Makes 1 cake

Serves 12

Preparation time: 30 minutes

Baking time: 40 to 45 minutes

Cooling time: 2 hours

NOTE:

Oil will ruin the light, airy texture of this cake, so be sure all bowls, utensils, and the cake pan are completely free of oil. A tube pan with a removable center and/or bottom is extremely helpful.

CAKE

1 cup unbleached white flour, preferably pastry flour

¾ cup sugar

¾ cup packed brown sugar

12 egg whites*

1 teaspoon cream of tartar

½ teaspoon salt

2 tablespoons instant coffee granules

1 tablespoon water

2 teaspoons pure vanilla extract

MOCHA GLAZE

2 ounces bittersweet chocolate

6 tablespoons freshly brewed strong coffee

2 tablespoons cocoa

¼ cup confectioners' sugar

For this cake, the egg whites must be completely free of yolk. Because egg whites separate more easily when cold, keep the eggs refrigerated until you're ready to separate them. Egg whites beat better at room temperature, however, so place the bowl of cold egg whites in a pan of hot water to bring them to room temperature.

Preheat the oven to 350°.

Sift the flour and sugar together three times and set aside.

Patiently sift the brown sugar into a separate bowl or, if necessary, press and gently crumble it with your fingers to urge it through a sieve. In a large bowl, beat the egg whites, cream of tartar, and salt with an electric mixer on medium speed (see Note). Increase to high speed and beat until soft peaks form. Sprinkle the brown sugar over the beaten egg whites. Continue to beat until stiff peaks form.

In a cup or small bowl, dissolve the coffee granules in the water and vanilla. Gently fold the coffee mixture into the egg whites with a rubber spatula, and then gradually fold in the flour mixture. Pour the batter into an unoiled 10-inch tube pan (see Note). Bake for 40 to 45 minutes, until the top of the cake quickly springs back when touched.

Invert the pan and cool the cake for 2 hours. Loosen the cake from the pan by carefully running a knife around the edges, then turn the cake onto a serving dish.

To make the glaze, combine the chocolate and coffee in a saucepan and gently heat for 5 to 10 minutes, stirring occasionally, until the chocolate melts. Ladle a small amount of the melted chocolate mixture into a bowl and combine with the cocoa to make a paste. Stir the cocoa paste into the saucepan until well blended. Beat in the confectioners' sugar until smooth and drizzle over the cake.

To serve, use a serrated knife to cut the spongy cake with a sawing motion.

> **NOTE:** Measure flour carefully and use level (not rounded) cups. If using all-purpose flour rather than pastry flour, you may need to reduce the flour by 1 to 2 tablespoons per cup to produce a moist, light dessert cake. If possible, always use pastry flour in low-fat baking.

VARIATION Here's another mocha glaze you can try: Combine 2 ounces of bittersweet chocolate, ¼ cup of Kahlúa, and 2 tablespoons of either hot water or milk in a saucepan. Gently heat just to the boiling point, stirring until the chocolate melts and the mixture is smooth. Beat in 2 tablespoons of confectioners' sugar and 2 tablespoons of cocoa and drizzle over the cake.

PER 3-OZ SERVING: 198 CALORIES, 5.5 G PROTEIN, 2.0 G FAT, 40.7 G CARBOHYDRATES, 1.1 G SATURATED FATTY ACIDS, 0 G POLYUNSATURATED FATTY ACIDS, 0 G MONOUNSATURATED FATTY ACIDS, 0 MG CHOLESTEROL, 170 MG SODIUM, .3 G TOTAL DIETARY FIBER

CHOCOLATE COCOA CAKE

Who can resist the aroma and flavor of chocolate? We certainly can't. So we were content to experiment until we made not just a good low-fat chocolate cake—but a *very* good low-fat chocolate cake. We lowered the fat in this recipe by reducing the amount of oil and using only one square of baking chocolate. Then we intensified the chocolate flavor with cocoa.

To "put the icing on the cake," brush it while still warm with a glaze made by stirring ¼ cup of amaretto into ¼ cup of unsweetened apricot preserves or jam. Alternatively, dust it with confectioners' sugar or drizzle with Mocha Glaze (page 378) after it has cooled.

Makes one 10-inch Bundt cake

Serves 16

Preparation time: 20 minutes

Baking time: 35 minutes

1 ounce unsweetened baking chocolate

¼ cup canola or other vegetable oil

1½ cups unbleached white flour, preferably pastry flour (See Note, page 379)

¼ cup unsweetened cocoa powder

¼ teaspoon salt

½ teaspoon baking soda

1 teaspoon baking powder

1 cup packed brown sugar

1 large egg

2 large egg whites

1 teaspoon pure vanilla extract

¾ cup buttermilk

Preheat the oven to 350°. Prepare a 10-inch Bundt pan with cooking spray or a light coating of oil and set aside.

In a saucepan, melt the chocolate in the oil on medium-low heat, stirring until thoroughly combined. Transfer to a mixing bowl and set aside. In a separate bowl, sift together the flour, cocoa, salt, baking soda, and baking powder and set aside. Beat the brown sugar into the melted chocolate until well blended. Add the egg and egg whites, one at a time, beating well after each addition. Stir in the vanilla. Alternate adding about ¼ cup of the buttermilk and ⅓ of the flour mixture, beating well after each addition.

Pour the batter into the prepared pan and bake for about 35 minutes, or until the cake pulls away from the sides of the pan and a knife inserted in the center comes out clean. Allow the cake to cool in the pan for 5 to 10 minutes, then invert it onto a plate. Serve warm or cool completely.

PER 3-OZ SERVING: 240 CALORIES, 4.5 G PROTEIN, 8.1 G FAT, 39.1 G CARBOHYDRATES, 1.9 G SATURATED FATTY ACIDS, 3.5 G POLYUNSATURATED FATTY ACIDS, 1.7 G MONOUNSATURATED FATTY ACIDS, 27 MG CHOLESTEROL, 162 MG SODIUM, .6 G TOTAL DIETARY FIBER

MENU SUGGESTIONS A chocolate cake on the table is a lovely surprise. Try it with a dollop of **Vanilla Cream** (page 395) or with plain yogurt slightly sweetened with maple syrup.

APPLESAUCE SPICE CAKE

Chock-full of goodies, Applesauce Spice Cake is moist and homey. Pure maple syrup adds a distinctive, sweet richness and flavor and warm spices perfume the cake throughout.

2¼ cups unbleached white flour, preferably pastry flour (see Note, page 379)

1 teaspoon salt

1½ teaspoons baking soda

2 teaspoons baking powder

1½ teaspoons ground cinnamon

½ teaspoon nutmeg

½ teaspoon ground cloves

1½ cups rolled oats

⅓ cup vegetable oil

1¾ cups pure maple syrup

5 egg whites

1½ cups unsweetened applesauce

confectioners' sugar (optional)

Makes one 10-inch Bundt cake

Serves 12

Preparation time: 40 minutes

Baking time: 45 to 55 minutes

Preheat the oven to 350°.

In a medium mixing bowl, sift together the flour, salt, baking soda, baking powder, cinnamon, nutmeg, and cloves. Stir in the oats and set aside. In a large mixing bowl, cream the oil and the maple syrup for at least 3 minutes, until well blended. Add the egg whites and beat on high speed for another 5 minutes, until light and fluffy. Thoroughly mix in the applesauce. Gradually add the flour mixture, beating well after each addition.

Lightly coat a 10-inch Bundt pan with cooking spray. Pour the batter into the pan. Bake for 45 to 55 minutes, until a knife inserted in the center comes out clean. Immediately invert the cake onto a serving plate and remove the pan. If desired, lightly dust the top of the cake with confectioners' sugar.

PER 4.25-OZ SERVING: 341 CALORIES, 6.9 G PROTEIN, 7.7 G FAT, 62.3 G CARBOHYDRATES, 1.1 G SATURATED FATTY ACIDS, 4.2 G POLYUNSATURATED FATTY ACIDS, 1.9 G MONOUNSATURATED FATTY ACIDS, 0 MG CHOLESTEROL, 340 MG SODIUM, 2.1 G TOTAL DIETARY FIBER

MENU SUGGESTIONS The ingredients for this light, fruity cake are available year-round, but we think it's most appreciated after a meal with autumn vegetables, such as **New England Squash Soup** (page 96), **Cabbage Rolls** (page 256), **Mushroom Polenta Pie** (page 240), or **Ukrainian Beet and Bean Stew** (page 269). Save a piece for breakfast with a cup of hot cider.

BANANA BUNDT CAKE

Here is a time-honored, homestyle recipe, best when made with very ripe or even overripe bananas. Overripe bananas can be frozen to use later. They become even sweeter and more flavorful.

The applesauce and bananas in this recipe combine to make a moist, tender cake with very little oil. For those who would like a sweeter cake, use 1 cup of brown sugar, use sweetened applesauce, or brush the cake with Mocha Glaze (page 378).

Makes one 10-inch Bundt cake

Serves 16

Preparation time: 20 to 30 minutes

Baking time: 50 to 60 minutes

Cooling time: 10 minutes

2½ cups unbleached white flour, preferably pastry flour (See Note, page 379)

2 teaspoons baking powder

1 teaspoon salt

½ teaspoon nutmeg

½ teaspoon ground cardamom (optional)

¾ cup brown sugar

2 eggs yolks

1 cup lightly mashed ripe bananas

¾ cup unsweetened applesauce

⅓ cup canola or other vegetable oil

1 teaspoon pure vanilla extract

4 egg whites

Preheat the oven to 350°.

Prepare a 10-inch Bundt pan with cooking spray or a light coating of oil.

Sift the flour with the baking powder, salt, nutmeg, and cardamom, if using, into a large mixing bowl. Add the brown sugar, mix well, and set aside.

Combine the egg yolks, bananas, applesauce, oil, and vanilla and mix well. Add the banana mixture to the dry ingredients and stir just until evenly blended.

Beat the egg whites until stiff but not dry. Gently fold the egg whites into the batter and pour it into the pan.

Bake for about 60 minutes, until the cake begins to pull away from the sides of the pan and a knife inserted in the center comes out clean. Cool on a rack for 10 minutes, and then invert onto a plate.

PER 2.25-OZ SERVING: 140 CALORIES, 3.5 G PROTEIN, 5.8 G FAT, 18.6 G CARBOHYDRATES, .9 G SATURATED FATTY ACIDS, 2.9 G POLYUNSATURATED FATTY ACIDS, 1.5 G MONOUNSATURATED FATTY ACIDS, 33 MG CHOLESTEROL, 207 MG SODIUM, 1.1 G TOTAL DIETARY FIBER

MENU SUGGESTIONS This is a wonderful dessert with foods from the southern United States, the Caribbean, West Africa, or Southeast Asia. It is a moist, sturdy snack cake for teatime or lunchboxes and the perfect birthday cake for anyone concerned about a healthful diet.

BLUEBERRY PEACH COBBLER

Everyone loves a cobbler. The juicy, fresh fruit with its pastry topping just begs to be admired —and then eaten. Lighter than pie because it has no bottom crust, our cobbler is a perfect choice to follow a rich meal. When we offer it at Moosewood, it is always one of the first desserts on the menu to sell out. Serve topped with Vanilla Cream (page 395), if you like.

FRUIT FILLING
4 cups peeled, pitted, and sliced peaches
2 cups blueberries
1 tablespoon unbleached white flour
¾ cup sugar
½ teaspoon ground cinnamon

TOPPING
1½ cups unbleached white flour
1 teaspoon baking powder
½ teaspoon salt
1 tablespoon sugar
2 tablespoons canola or other vegetable oil
¼ cup plain nonfat yogurt

Serves 6 to 8

**Makes one
10-inch round or
9-inch square cobbler**

**Preparation time:
30 to 35 minutes**

**Baking time:

40 to 50 minutes**

NOTE:
To make the dough in the food processor, pulse the flour, baking powder, salt, and sugar to mix. Pulse in the oil, followed by the yogurt.

Preheat the oven to 350°.

Prepare a glass, ceramic, or stainless steel 10-inch round or 9-inch square baking dish with a light coating of oil or cooking spray.

Combine all of the fruit filling ingredients and pour them into the baking dish.

Sift the flour, baking powder, salt, and sugar into a large mixing bowl (see Note). In a separate bowl, mix together the oil and yogurt. Fold the oil mixture into the dry ingredients with a fork. Using floured hands and working the dough as little as possible, form it into a ball. Turn the dough onto a floured surface. Cut the dough in half, place one half on top of the other, and press down. Repeat three times.

With a rolling pin or pressure from your hands, flatten the dough into a 10-inch circle or 9-inch square to fit your baking dish and place it over the filling. Bake for 40 to 50 minutes, until the crust is golden and a knife inserted in the topping comes out clean.

PER 6-OZ SERVING: 251 CALORIES, 3.5 G PROTEIN, 4.1 G FAT, 52.0 G CARBOHYDRATES, .5 G SATURATED FATTY ACIDS, 2.2 G POLYUNSATURATED FATTY ACIDS, .9 G MONOUNSATURATED FATTY ACIDS, 0 MG CHOLESTEROL, 196 MG SODIUM, 3.4 G TOTAL DIETARY FIBER

MENU SUGGESTIONS Serve with the fresh and flavorful meals of summer and early autumn, for brunch, dinner, or picnics.

APPLE APRICOT STRUDEL

Apples and apricots are an incredibly delicious combination. Here they are baked inside a flaky filo crust layered with almond cookie crumbs. Strudels always look impressive, but this filling takes only minutes to make, and once you develop a knack for working with the filo, the whole process is a snap. Serve with any Eastern European or Mediterranean meal.

FILLING

4 cups peeled chopped apples
¼ cup brown sugar
1 cup chopped dried apricots (about 4 ounces)
1 teaspoon ground cinnamon
¼ cup cornstarch

PASTRY

3 tablespoons butter, melted
3 tablespoons crushed amaretti*
6 sheets filo dough

*Amaretti are Italian almond meringue cookies. Many
brands are available in supermarkets and bakeries, or see
Sundays at Moosewood Restaurant (page 373) to make your own.
Two or three cookies, crushed, will be enough for this recipe.*

Serves 8 to 10

**Preparation time:
35 minutes**

Baking time: 30 minutes

Preheat the oven to 350°.

Combine all of the filling ingredients in a bowl, mix well, and set aside.

Lightly oil or spray a baking sheet, place the melted butter and crushed amaretti nearby, and have a pastry brush or small paintbrush handy. Work quickly in a draft-free setting because the unoiled filo becomes brittle once exposed to the air.

Unfold the stack of filo sheets next to the baking sheet. Take two sheets at once from the stack and, in one smooth motion, lift them and lay them flat on the baking tray. Lightly brush the top sheet with the melted butter and sprinkle it with 1 tablespoon of amaretti crumbs. Repeat this for two more layers, until all of the filo and amaretti crumbs are used.

Spoon the filling onto the filo, leaving about 2 inches uncovered on all four sides. Fold the shorter bottom and top edges toward the center, then starting at one of the long sides, roll up the filo like a jelly roll. Place the strudel, seam side down, on the baking tray and brush it with the remaining butter. Bake for about 30 minutes, until hot and golden.

Cool for 5 minutes, cut crosswise into 8 to 10 slices, and serve.

PER 3.50-OZ SERVING: 156 CALORIES, .9 G PROTEIN, 5.1 G FAT, 28.9 G CARBOHYDRATES, 2.2 G SATURATED FATTY ACIDS, .2 G POLYUNSATURATED FATTY ACIDS, 1.0 G MONOUNSATURATED FATTY ACIDS, 9 MG CHOLESTEROL, 60 MG SODIUM, 3.1 G TOTAL DIETARY FIBER

APPLE CHERRY CRISP

We're not sure just how old the idea of fruit crisp is, but it seems that it's been around at least as long as apple pie. There is something inherently gratifying about the combination of juicy fruit with a sweet crunchy topping. The textures complement one another to make a tantalizing dessert that doesn't require the additional time—and butter—of a piecrust.

Just as with pie making, however, once you have mastered the crisp topping, you can alter the fruit filling to reflect which fruits are in season and add at least half a dozen new desserts to your list. Pears, peaches, raspberries, blueberries, and strawberries are all good choices for crisp. Use a total of 6 cups of prepared fruit.

FRUIT LAYER

4 cups peeled and sliced apples
2 cups pitted fresh or frozen cherries, sweet or tart
½ cup brown sugar
1 teaspoon quick-cooking tapioca (not whole pearl)

Serves 6 to 8

Preparation time: 20 minutes

Baking time: 40 to 50 minutes

TOPPING

1½ cups rolled oats or Grape-Nuts cereal
¼ cup unbleached white flour
½ cup brown sugar
½ teaspoon ground cinnamon
1 egg white
1 tablespoon canola or other vegetable oil
1 teaspoon pure vanilla extract
2 tablespoons unsweetened apple or orange juice

Preheat the oven to 350°.

In a bowl, mix together the fruit layer ingredients. Pour the fruit evenly into a non-reactive 10-inch pie pan or a 9-inch square baking dish and set aside. In a large bowl, combine the oats, flour, brown sugar, and cinnamon. In a separate bowl, whisk together the egg white, oil, vanilla, and fruit juice and then stir into the dry ingredients until thoroughly combined. Carefully spread the topping over the fruit (be sure to cover the fruit entirely). Cover and bake for 20 minutes, then uncover and continue to bake for another 20 to 30 minutes, until the fruit is soft and bubbly and the topping is crisp and golden.

PER 7-OZ SERVING: 323 CALORIES, 5.8 G PROTEIN, 3.9 G FAT, 68.6 G CARBOHYDRATES, .6 G SATURATED FATTY ACIDS, 1.8 G POLYUNSATURATED FATTY ACIDS, 1.0 G MONOUNSATURATED FATTY ACIDS, 0 MG CHOLESTEROL, 21 MG SODIUM, 5.7 G TOTAL DIETARY FIBER

GINGER PEACH CRUMBLE

A spicy-sweet topping of crumbled gingersnaps turns peaches into a warm, homey dessert without the high fat content of traditional crisps and pies.

For much of the year, unsweetened peach slices, frozen at their peak, are preferable to the hard, flavorless fresh peaches in our markets that have been shipped from another hemisphere. But when they are in season, nothing can compare to the scent and succulence of a fresh, ripe peach.

1 pound frozen unsweetened sliced peaches
 or 3 cups peeled fresh peach slices
2 tablespoons packed brown sugar
½ teaspoon ground cinnamon
1 tablespoon fresh lemon juice
½ cup crumbled gingersnaps (about 8 gingersnaps)

frozen yogurt (optional)

Serves 4

**Preparation time:
10 minutes**

**Baking time:
20 minutes**

Preheat the oven to 425°.

Evenly distribute the peach slices in the bottom of an unoiled nonreactive 9-inch pie pan or 8-inch square baking dish. Sprinkle the peaches with the brown sugar, cinnamon, and lemon juice. Top with the crumbled gingersnaps. Bake for about 20 minutes, until the peaches are bubbling and tender when pierced with a fork.

Serve warm or at room temperature, plain or with frozen yogurt.

PER 5-OZ SERVING: 253 CALORIES, 2.3 G PROTEIN, 2.9 G FAT, 56.4 G CARBOHYDRATES, .5 G SATURATED FATTY ACIDS, .5 G POLYUNSATURATED FATTY ACIDS, 1.6 G MONOUNSATURATED FATTY ACIDS, 0 MG CHOLESTEROL, 195 MG SODIUM, 2.4 G TOTAL DIETARY FIBER

MENU SUGGESTION Appropriate with Southern foods and not out of place on an Asian menu, this crumble is so easy to make that it can be a last-minute addition to almost any meal. Try it for brunch topped with a dollop of nonfat yogurt.

OUR BEST NO-BUTTER BROWNIES

Adding applesauce, corn syrup, and cocoa to our favorite brownie recipe in place of the butter and some of the chocolate significantly reduces the fat content *and* produces fudgy brownies. These far surpassed our expectations of what's possible in a low-fat dessert and, just in case you need an excuse to taste one fresh from the oven, they really are best when eaten right away.

1 cup unbleached white flour

⅓ cup unsweetened cocoa powder

¼ teaspoon salt

½ teaspoon baking soda

1 teaspoon baking powder

1 ounce unsweetened baking chocolate

¼ cup canola or other vegetable oil

¼ cup light corn syrup

¼ cup unsweetened applesauce

1 cup packed brown sugar

1 teaspoon pure vanilla extract

1 large egg

1 large egg white

Makes 12 brownies

Preparation time: 15 to 20 minutes

Baking time: 30 to 35 minutes

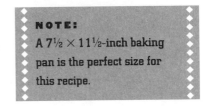

NOTE:
A 7½ × 11½-inch baking pan is the perfect size for this recipe.

Preheat the oven to 350°. Prepare a baking pan that is about 8 × 11 inches (see Note) with cooking spray or a light coating of oil.

Sift together the flour, cocoa, salt, baking soda, and baking powder and set aside. In a saucepan, melt the chocolate in the oil on medium-low heat and transfer to a mixing bowl. Stir in the corn syrup and applesauce. Add the brown sugar and vanilla and beat with a mixer or by hand for about 2 minutes, until creamy. Add the egg and egg white and beat for another minute or so, until smooth. Fold in the sifted dry ingredients until just mixed and pour the batter into the prepared pan. Bake for 30 to 35 minutes, or until a knife inserted in the center comes out clean.

PER 2-OZ SERVING: 200 CALORIES, 2.5 G PROTEIN, 6.7 G FAT, 34.5 G CARBOHYDRATES, 1.5 G SATURATED FATTY ACIDS, 2.9 G POLYUNSATURATED FATTY ACIDS, 1.4 G MONOUNSATURATED FATTY ACIDS, 22 MG CHOLESTEROL, 120 MG SODIUM, .4 G TOTAL DIETARY FIBER

MENU SUGGESTION Brownies are a treat any time, but they occupy a special place in the cuisines of the Tropics, whence cometh chocolate.

FRUIT-FILLED MERINGUE SHELLS

Meringue is a French term used to describe egg whites beaten with sugar, which is often used for pie toppings, icings on cakes, or in dessert soufflés. Here we add enough sugar to make a rather stiff meringue that can be formed into small bowl-like shapes and baked in a slow oven to form "hard meringue" shells. These can be used as the bases for a variety of very light, attractive, and elegant desserts.

We fill the meringues with fresh fruit and top them with a slightly thickened orange sauce. The combination is as intoxicating as ambrosia or nectar could ever be, and the meringue shells magically melt in your mouth. You really can't beat this fancy, yet fat-free dessert.

Parchment paper is the best choice for baking meringues, but if you don't have parchment paper on hand, don't despair—regular paper grocery bags will work. Do not, however, substitute wax paper; it won't work at all.

Serves 10

Makes ten 4½-inch fruit-filled shells and 1 cup of orange sauce

Preparation time: 20 minutes for meringue shells

Baking time: 1½ hours

Cooling time in oven: 1 to 2 hours

Total time for filling and sauce: 15 to 20 minutes

MERINGUE SHELLS
4 egg whites, at room temperature (see Note)
¼ teaspoon cream of tartar
¾ cup confectioners' sugar
1 teaspoon pure vanilla extract

ORANGE SAUCE
1 cup orange juice
1 tablespoon cornstarch
¼ teaspoon pure almond extract
1 tablespoon brandy or orange liqueur (optional)

FILLING
4 to 5 cups fresh fruit, such as sliced strawberries or peaches, blueberries, raspberries, or cherries

Preheat the oven to 250°.

Line a baking sheet with parchment paper and set aside.

Remove the bowl of egg whites from the water, add the cream of tartar, and beat with a mixer on medium speed until foamy. Increase the speed to high and beat until soft peaks begin to form. Gradually add the sugar ¼ cup at a time, continuing to beat until stiff and glossy. Beat in the vanilla.

Arrange the meringue on the baking sheet in ten equal mounds. Gently make a bowl-like depression in the center of each with a spoon. Bake the meringues for 90 minutes, until firm and lightly golden. Turn off the oven, but do not remove the baking sheet, and allow to sit for 1 to 2 hours. Remove the meringue shells from the baking sheet carefully, since they may be somewhat fragile. If you don't plan to serve immediately, transfer to an airtight container.

In a cup, mix together 2 tablespoons of the orange juice and the cornstarch to make a paste. Pour the rest of the orange juice into a small nonreactive saucepan and stir in the cornstarch mixture. Add the almond extract and the brandy or orange liqueur, if using, and cook on medium heat for 3 to 5 minutes, stirring until clear and thickened. Remove from the heat.

Fill each meringue shell with ⅓ to ½ cup of the fresh fruit. For a beautiful presentation on a platter, it's nice to use several different colors of fruit. Be whimsical. You can mix two kinds of fruit in one shell—make a melba meringue using peaches and raspberries together.

Drizzle about 1 to 1½ tablespoons of the orange sauce over each of the fruit-filled meringues—1 tablespoon is really plenty, but having just a little more sauce is awfully tempting. Serve immediately.

PER 4-OZ SERVING: 83 CALORIES, 2.2 G PROTEIN, .3 G FAT, 18.4 G CARBOHYDRATES, 0 G SATURATED FATTY ACIDS, .1 G POLYUNSATURATED FATTY ACIDS, 0 G MONO-UNSATURATED FATTY ACIDS, 0 MG CHOLESTEROL, 27 MG SODIUM, 1.6 G TOTAL DIETARY FIBER

MENU SUGGESTION Such a light and airy dessert is a perfect ending to a hearty Italian or French dinner. After just one bite, we're sure you'll hear satisfied *ooohs, mmms, ahhhs,* and other exclamations of delight.

NOTE:

To warm the egg whites, set the bowl of egg whites into a larger bowl of warm water until the egg whites reach room temperature.

The meringue shells work best when the humidity is low. On very humid days, they become slightly sticky as soon as you remove them from the oven and may not completely dry to a hard shell.

It is also best to fill and serve them right away. When they sit for more than an hour or so, they may become quite gooey and unappetizing. If you cannot use them right away, be sure to store them in an airtight container in a dry place such as your oven, a cupboard, or a breadbox.

MAPLE WALNUT BISCOTTI

At Moosewood, we regularly cross culinary boundaries and create hybrid recipes that combine two different ethnic food ideas in one dish. As with all hybrid experimentation, lots of the attempts are not worth repeating, but when you do produce a winner, there's just no doubt about it.

Here is a traditional Italian cookie with a New England twist. We took the basic dough and double-baking idea from the Italians, and the combination of maple syrup and walnuts from New England cuisine. The cornmeal adds just the right touch to the taste and texture. This is an exquisite biscotti, if we do say so ourselves.

1¾ cups unbleached white flour
½ cup cornmeal
1 teaspoon baking powder
¼ teaspoon salt
2 eggs
½ cup pure maple syrup
1 teaspoon pure vanilla extract
½ cup chopped walnuts

Makes about 36 biscotti

Preparation time: 10 to 15 minutes

Baking time: 40 to 45 minutes

Preheat the oven to 350°.

Prepare a baking sheet with cooking spray or a very light coating of oil.

In a large mixing bowl, sift together the flour, cornmeal, baking powder, and salt. Lightly beat the eggs and add them to the flour mixture. Stir in the maple syrup, vanilla, and walnuts, mixing just until the dough is smooth.

Using a rubber spatula and floured hands, scoop half of the dough out of the bowl and onto one side of the baking sheet. Shape the dough into a 15-inch log. Make a second log on the other side of the baking tray with the remaining dough. Space the logs at least 6 inches apart.

Bake for 25 to 30 minutes, until the top of each biscotti log is firm. Remove them with a long spatula to a wire rack and cool for 10 to 15 minutes. Cut each log on a severe diagonal into about twenty ½-inch-thick slices and place them, cut side down, on the baking sheet. Reduce the oven temperature to 325° and bake for 15 minutes.

Hot from the oven, the biscotti might be slightly soft in the center, but they will harden as they cool. Allow them to cool completely. Stored in a tin or other tightly closed container, they will keep for at least a couple of weeks.

PER 0.55-OZ SERVING: 52 CALORIES, 1.4 G PROTEIN, 1.4 G FAT, 8.3 G CARBOHYDRATES, .2 G SATURATED FATTY ACIDS, .7 G POLYUNSATURATED FATTY ACIDS, .4 G MONOUNSATURATED FATTY ACIDS, 15 MG CHOLESTEROL, 30 MG SODIUM, .4 G TOTAL DIETARY FIBER

MENU SUGGESTIONS Serve for breakfast, snacks, tea, or dessert with a cup of hot coffee or tea, a glass of dessert wine, or a side of fresh sliced fruit in season.

Anise Lemon Biscotti

Biscotti are the classic Italian dunking cookie. Because they are twice baked, these biscuits are hard, dry, and crunchy—made especially to be dipped in coffee, tea, or dessert wine. In this version, we have combined the traditional spicy flavor of anise with the tartness of fresh lemon peel. Stored in a tin or other tightly closed container, they will keep for at least a couple of weeks.

2 cups unbleached white flour
1 teaspoon baking powder
¼ teaspoon salt
1 cup sugar
2 whole eggs
1 egg white
2 tablespoons freshly grated lemon peel
1 tablespoon ground anise seeds

Makes about 36 biscotti

Preparation time: 10 minutes

Baking time: 40 to 45 minutes

Preheat the oven to 350°.

Prepare a baking sheet with cooking spray or a very light coating of oil.

Sift the flour, baking powder, salt, and sugar into a mixing bowl. In a separate bowl, lightly beat together the eggs and the egg white and add them to the flour mixture. Stir in the lemon peel and anise seeds, mixing just until the dough is smooth.

Using a rubber spatula and floured hands, scoop half of the dough out of the bowl and onto one side of the baking sheet. Shape it into a 15-inch log. Make a second log on the other side of the sheet with the remaining dough. Space the logs at least 6 inches apart.

Bake for 25 to 30 minutes, until the top of each biscotti log is firm.

Remove them with a long spatula to a wire rack and cool for 10 to 15 minutes. Cut each log on a severe diagonal into about twenty ½-inch-thick slices and place the slices, cut side down, on the baking sheet. Reduce the temperature to 325° and bake for 15 minutes.

Hot from the oven, the biscotti might be slightly soft in the center, but they will harden as they cool. Allow them to cool completely.

PER 0.62-OZ SERVING: 51 CALORIES, 1.2 G PROTEIN, .5 G FAT, 10.7 G CARBOHYDRATES, .1 G SATURATED FATTY ACIDS, .1 G POLYUNSATURATED FATTY ACIDS, .2 G MONOUNSATURATED FATTY ACIDS, 15 MG CHOLESTEROL, 32 MG SODIUM, .2 G TOTAL DIETARY FIBER

MENU SUGGESTIONS Serve with **Pineapple Buttermilk Sherbet** (page 394) or with **Tapioca Fruit Parfaits** (page 375).

CHOCOLATE HAZELNUT BISCOTTI

It's said that chocolate and hazelnuts are a match made in heaven. Luckily for us, Chocolate Hazelnut Biscotti and a strong, freshly brewed cup of coffee are a match made here on earth, where we can enjoy such pleasures as these.

Biscotti is Italian for *biscuits,* and most Italian households consider them a pantry staple. Serve with a hot drink or a chilled dessert wine.

2 cups unbleached white flour

¼ cup unsweetened cocoa powder

1 cup sugar

1 teaspoon baking powder

¼ teaspoon salt

½ teaspoon ground cinnamon

2 whole eggs

2 egg whites

1 tablespoon hot water

2 teaspoons instant coffee granules

⅓ cup chopped toasted hazelnuts (page 429)*

Makes about 40 biscotti

Preparation time: 15 minutes

Baking time: 45 to 50 minutes

*For a finer flavor, remove most of the toasted hazelnut skins by rubbing with a small towel. You'll be surprised how much flavor just ⅓ cup of hazelnuts adds.

Preheat the oven to 350°. Prepare a baking sheet with cooking spray or a little oil.

In a large mixing bowl, sift together the flour, cocoa, sugar, baking powder, salt, and cinnamon. Lightly beat the eggs and the egg whites and add them to the flour mixture. Stir in the hot water, coffee granules, and hazelnuts, mixing just until the wet dough is smooth.

Using a rubber spatula and floured hands, scoop half of the dough out of the bowl and onto one side of the baking sheet. Shape it into a 15-inch log. Make a second log on the other side of the sheet with the remaining dough. Space the logs at least 6 inches apart.

Bake for 25 to 30 minutes, until the top of each log is firm. Remove them with a long spatula to a wire rack and cool for 10 to 15 minutes. Cut each log on a severe diagonal into about twenty ½-inch-thick slices and place them, cut side down, on the baking sheet. Bake for 20 minutes at 325°. Remove the biscotti and allow them to cool. Stored in a tin, they will keep for a few weeks.

PER 0.65-OZ SERVING: 55 CALORIES, 1.4 G PROTEIN, 1.2 G FAT, 10.0 G CARBOHYDRATES, .2 G SATURATED FATTY ACIDS, .1 G POLYUNSATURATED FATTY ACIDS, .7 G MONOUNSATURATED FATTY ACIDS, 13 MG CHOLESTEROL, 30 MG SODIUM, .3 G TOTAL DIETARY FIBER

MENU SUGGESTIONS These biscotti go well with **Dark Chocolate Pudding** (page 374), **Red Berry Kissel** (page 372), **Pineapple Buttermilk Sherbet** (page 394) or ices, and fresh fruit.

CARDAMOM OATMEAL COOKIES

Here is an unusually tasty oatmeal cookie—a real delight for cardamom lovers. If you're not crazy about cardamom, reduce the amount in the recipe to ½ teaspoon or substitute ½ teaspoon of allspice.

Most low-fat cookies are not as crisp as their traditional higher-fat cousins. At first we tried various techniques to produce crisper low-fat cookies, but finally we saw the wisdom in accepting this cookie just as it is. It's moist with apple butter, delicious, and chewy—why try to make it into something else?

The best way to store low-fat cookies is in layers separated by wax paper or plastic wrap in an airtight container in the freezer. Defrost at room temperature for about 20 minutes before serving. If stored at room temperature in a closed container, the cookies stick together and become gooey, but if left in the open, they become stale. We recommend the freezing trick.

¾ cup apple butter

2 tablespoons canola or other vegetable oil

1 egg, lightly beaten

2 teaspoons pure vanilla extract

¾ cup packed brown sugar

¾ cup chopped raisins (optional)

1½ cups unbleached white flour

1 teaspoon baking soda

½ teaspoon salt

1 teaspoon ground cinnamon

1 teaspoon ground cardamom or ½ teaspoon ground allspice

2 cups rolled oats

Makes forty-eight 2½-inch cookies

Preparation time: 15 minutes

Baking time: 15 minutes

Preheat the oven to 350°.

Line a baking sheet with parchment paper or prepare it with a light coating of cooking spray or oil.

In a large bowl, mix together the apple butter, oil, egg, vanilla, and brown sugar until smooth. Stir in the raisins, if using. In a separate bowl mix together the flour, baking soda, salt, cinnamon, and cardamom or allspice. Stir in the oats. Add the dry ingredients to the wet ingredients and mix until well blended.

Drop the batter by the tablespoonful about 3 inches apart onto the baking sheet. Bake for about 15 minutes, until lightly browned. Transfer to a wire rack to cool.

PER 0.70-OZ SERVING: 65 CALORIES, 1.5 G PROTEIN, 1.2 G FAT, 12.3 G CARBOHYDRATES, .2 G SATURATED FATTY ACIDS, .5 G POLYUNSATURATED FATTY ACIDS, .3 G MONOUNSATURATED FATTY ACIDS, 6 MG CHOLESTEROL, 38 MG SODIUM, .8 G TOTAL DIETARY FIBER

PINEAPPLE BUTTERMILK SHERBET

This simple and delightful sherbet requires no special ice cream-making equipment—just a fork. It has a tangy flavor and gives the illusion of rich creaminess. Pineapple Buttermilk Sherbet will keep, stored in an airtight container in the freezer, for 1 to 2 weeks.

Makes 5 to 6 cups

Serves 8

Preparation time: 5 minutes

Freezing time: 3 to 5 hours

2 cups nonfat or regular buttermilk
2 cups undrained canned crushed pineapple (20-ounce can)
⅔ cup sugar

In a bowl, stir together the buttermilk, pineapple, and sugar until the sugar has dissolved.

Cover the bowl with plastic wrap and place it in the freezer. After about an hour, when the mixture has begun to harden, stir it with a fork until it becomes slushy. Cover and return to the freezer for another hour or two, until it is very stiff but not frozen solid. Stir it again with a fork and serve. If the sherbet has frozen hard, remove it from the freezer to soften for about 30 minutes before serving or whirl it in a food processor, scraping down the sides several times, for about 2 minutes, until well blended and smooth.

PER 4.50-OZ SERVING: 124 CALORIES, 2.1 G PROTEIN, .5 G FAT, 28.8 G CARBOHY-DRATES, .3 G SATURATED FATTY ACIDS, 0 G POLYUNSATURATED FATTY ACIDS, .2 G MONOUNSATURATED FATTY ACIDS, 2 MG CHOLESTEROL, 60 MG SODIUM, .4 G TOTAL DIETARY FIBER

MENU SUGGESTION The frosty, tart-sweetness of this sherbet is a cooling refreshment after any spicy meal, whether Caribbean, Creole, Mexican, Southeast Asian, North African, or West African.

VANILLA CREAM

This sauce is delectable . . . thick and creamy with a satisfying flavor, but it is best eaten immediately. So have everything else prepared, then purée the sauce just before serving. Offer it at the table in a small pitcher to pour over fruit, pudding, cake, or anything else that strikes your fancy. It's a fine low-fat substitute for whipped cream or crème fraîche.

Vanilla Cream will keep, well covered in the refrigerator, for up to 3 days.

1 cup low-fat cottage cheese
1 cup nonfat or low-fat yogurt
⅓ cup pure maple syrup
½ teaspoon pure vanilla extract

Makes about 2 cups

Serves 5 or 6

Total time: 5 minutes

Whirl all of the ingredients in a blender until smooth. Serve chilled.

PER 3-OZ SERVING: 89 CALORIES, 7.4 G PROTEIN, .8 G FAT, 12.8 G CARBOHYDRATES, .5 G SATURATED FATTY ACIDS, 0 G POLYUNSATURATED FATTY ACIDS, .2 G MONOUNSATURATED FATTY ACIDS, 4 MG CHOLESTEROL, 184 MG SODIUM, 0 G TOTAL DIETARY FIBER

NUTRITION FACTS

OUR DISCOVERIES ABOUT LOW-FAT COOKING AND EATING

At Moosewood, we believe the keys to healthy eating are variety, moderation, and knowing what is in the foods we buy. A little vigilance and label-reading can go a long way, and taking the extra time to eat better now could add years of healthy living to your life.

When we decided that it was high time to undertake the challenges of creating a low-fat cookbook, almost immediately we realized that, among other things, we had to plunge into the jungle of information about fat. Suddenly we were surrounded by conflicting reports and data, medical studies, current diets, U.S. government regulations, and the ongoing theories and debates on the subject by professionals in the health and nutrition fields.

At first, the prospect seemed a bit daunting, but as we tackled our task, dividing the various aspects of the overall project and sharing our findings with one another, we became really excited. We began to develop and learn new cooking techniques, sort through the research, and shape our vision of this cookbook. We've included this information on nutrition as a service to those who are curious or interested in learning about it. Those who are already knowledgeable may appreciate having a concise summary of the leading information easily at their disposal as they plan meals. There's nothing to stop you, however, from skipping this nutrition information and getting right to the food. Everything essential you need to know to prepare a delicious, low-fat dish is on the page with the recipe.

In this section, we offer you the fruits of our research labors. Our intention is to present the facts —distinguished from the theories—and to pass on to you the most widely agreed upon recommendations (as of 1996) regarding fat intake and your health. We hope that this information will make the technical terminology more accessible and help you better understand nutritional needs so you can make informed decisions about a healthful, balanced diet, one that you can enjoy and sustain over the long term.

There are a number of factors to consider when reviewing your diet and deciding how to improve it. You must take into account that our bodies need a certain amount of all dietary nutrients—fats, proteins, carbohydrates, and fiber. What has come to light is that the relationship and relative amounts of fat, protein, carbohydrate, and fiber in our bodies produce a complex set of interactions that affect both how our bodies use these nutrients and the quality of our functioning. Researchers agree it's an intricate process. It is nearly impossible to isolate a single factor and draw an unshakable conclusion, because interaction is the name of the game. As we search for healthy eating styles, however, we can recognize well-substantiated evidence that points us in the right direction.

Many experts, including Dr. Susan Calvert Finn of the American Dietetic Association, cite confusion, taste, and lack of time as major obstacles to nutritionally sound eating habits. Most Americans' average intake of saturated fat is at least 50 percent higher than the majority of experts believe it should be, while cholesterol and sodium levels are twice as high as they should be.

A typical American who eats a sufficient number of calories will almost certainly be getting enough protein. Although many of us worried about correctly combining vegetables and grains to create "perfect proteins" (ones that supply all eight of the essential amino acids we need from foods), we actually don't need all eight essential amino acids at every meal. We do need the full complement of amino acids every day or two, so, once again, a varied diet rich in plant-based foods will do the trick. Protein from meat and dairy products is inseparable from the high fat content of these foods and, if eaten, should be limited to very moderate portions. Doctors report that Americans suffer far more often from excessive protein consumption than from protein deficiency, which is rarely encountered.

Carbohydrates are the body's major energy providers and the American Heart Association recommends that 55 percent of one's total daily calories be from carbohydrate sources. Like protein, 1 gram of carbohydrates contains 4 calories, which is less than half the number of calories in a gram of fat.

The ratio of grams of carbohydrates to grams of fat in the diet should be at least 5 to 1.

So what about fat? Americans tend to consume a large percentage of their total calories from fat. (Each gram of fat contains 9 calories.) In 1960, 42 percent of the average American's dietary calories were derived from fat. In 1990, studies showed this percentage had dropped to about 34 percent, but present research puts the figure between 37 percent and 40 percent. And yet, according to the American Heart Association and the U.S. Food and Drug Administration (FDA), no more than 30 percent of our calories should come from fat.

Most experts agree that 30 percent is a realistic goal, but it is nevertheless a compromise, and there are many who say the figure should be lower. Marion Nestle, Ph.D, M.P.H., chair of the Department of Nutrition at New York University, believes that 30 percent is an arbitrary number with no scientific basis. Our own research of the available information leads us to believe that a *realistic* goal for the average healthy person could be between 20 percent and 25 percent of calories from fat. Twenty percent is the level commonly found in most Asian countries, where fish, grains, and vegetables comprise most of the diet. Respected nutritional advocates, such as Dr. Neal Barnard, president of the Physicians' Committee for Responsible Medicine, and T. Colin Campbell, Ph.D., of Cornell University, head of the Cornell-Oxford-China Diet and Health Project, recommend a very low-fat vegetarian diet based on the USDA's new four food groups of grains, legumes, vegetables, and fruits. Campbell's data suggests that reducing fat intake to 15 percent of total calories could prevent 80 percent or more of chronic degenerative diseases such as heart-related diseases, cancer, and diabetes before the age of sixty-five.

One thing all of the recent research on fat has shown is that all fat is not the same. The experts are still engaged in a debate, however, about whether the overall amount of fat or the type of fat in our diet is the most troubling. A diet high in monounsaturated fats will make LDLs (cholesterol-carrying lipids) more resistant to oxidation than a diet high in polyunsaturated fats. Because oxidized fat may be related to clogging of the arteries, many people are choosing monounsaturated oils for everyday use in cooking and we recommend canola and olive oil throughout this book. Please note that individual cholesterol levels are influenced by many factors and high cholesterol levels can't be detected except through periodic checkups.

Here are just a few more fat facts we think you should know. Fat calories are more readily converted to body fat than calories from carbohydrates. If, however, the body is deprived of dietary fat, it learns to store any kind of available calories as fat. So if weight loss is your goal, you need to incorporate low-fat foods, regular exercise, and moderate caloric intake into your planning. Even if it is mostly low-fat foods that you eat, overeating will still cause you to accumulate body fat.

Milk and cheese are both high in fat, and 60 percent to 70 percent of the calories in many cheeses are from saturated fat. Using low-fat or skim dairy products will certainly decrease the amount of fat you eat, but remember that even these lower-fat products are not really low in fat compared to grains, beans, or vegetables. Vegetables and fruits do need tiny amounts of fat in order to survive and function, but they are usually considered fat-free foods because the amount of fat they contain is negligible for all practical purposes. Six asparagus spears, for instance, contain about 0.3 grams of fat—very, very little. On the other hand, a tablespoon of any oil contains about 120 calories and 14 grams of fat, and gets 100 percent of its calories from fat. So before you slather on the butter or oil, remember it's going to cost you something—especially if you make a habit of it. See page 451 for a list of oils categorized by the type of fat that predominates in them. You will also find more detailed descriptions of monounsaturated, polyunsaturated, and saturated fats and how they relate to cholesterol levels in our bodies in the nutritional terms section that follows.

Once you develop a sensible diet, you won't need to monitor fat intake daily but will be able to maintain a balance over the long run. In the beginning, however, it's necessary to educate yourself about sources of fat and the relative amount you wish to consume.

FINDING YOUR PERSONAL FAT GOAL

Here are two ways to calculate the number of grams of fat you want as an upper limit or target each day. The first is a very rough measure that we like because of its simplicity; the second method is more precise but still not difficult to calculate.

TO HELP DETERMINE YOUR IDEAL DAILY LIMIT OF GRAMS OF FAT:

Decide your ideal body weight in pounds. For a 30 percent calories-from-fat diet, divide your ideal body weight by 2. The result is a ballpark figure for your fat limit in grams. For a 20 percent calories-from-fat diet, divide your ideal body weight by 3; for a 10 percent regimen, divide by 6.

FOR A MORE PRECISE CALCULATION OF YOUR IDEAL DAILY FAT INTAKE:

- Decide your ideal total calories per day.
- Decide how low-fat you want your diet to be (30%, 20%, or 10%).
- Multiply your ideal total calories by the percentage you chose (multiply by 0.3 for 30%, 0.2 for 20%, or 0.1 for 10%).
- Divide the result by 9 (1 gram of fat has 9 calories).

This will tell you how many grams of fat you want to consume at most when eating your chosen number of total calories per day.

AVERAGE DAILY DIETARY GUIDELINES FOR A MODERATELY ACTIVE ADULT

Each individual has somewhat different dietary needs based on body frame, weight, constitution, metabolism, overall health, and eating preferences. But as a starting point, this list shows the most widely accepted general guidelines as of the writing of this book.

Total Calories	2000
Total Fat	less than 65 grams
Saturated fat	less than 20 grams
Cholesterol	less than 300 milligrams
Carbohydrates	about 300 grams
Fiber	about 25 grams
Sodium	500 to 2400 milligrams
Protein	about 50 grams

After just a few weeks of watching what you eat, noticing the relative amounts of fat in your favorite foods, and paying attention to label information when you shop, you should develop a sense about fat intake without becoming a slave to your calculator. After all, it's the big picture that counts. Once you have developed regular everyday habits that keep your overall fat intake low, you can afford to enjoy that occasional splurge. Knowing the fat content of foods, staying aware of day-to-day eating patterns, and opting for lower-fat alternatives whenever possible may well bring about desirable changes.

NUTRITIONAL TERMS DEFINED

This section contains explanations of all the elements provided in the nutritional analyses of our recipes plus related terms commonly used in discussions of fats and cholesterol.

ANTIOXIDANT VITAMINS take their name from the term "antioxidant," which refers to the biological process of oxidation. Oxidation, which is essential to metabolism and energy availability, also produces by-products called *free radicals,* unstable molecules that can be damaging to our cells. Free radicals are unstable because they are missing an electron. They do their damage by borrowing electrons from our cells. Free radicals in our bodies can also be promoted by exposure to cigarette smoke, alcohol, the ozone and environmental pollutants, the ultraviolet rays in sunlight, and other forms of radiation. If cellular damage caused by free radicals is not prevented or repaired, illness can follow. There have been theories put forth that heart disease and certain cancers are the result of, or are assisted by, damage to arteries and genetic DNA by proliferating free radicals.

Antioxidants are molecules that circulate through our bloodstream looking for trouble. They are endowed with the capacity to freely give up extra electrons to correct the balance. Antioxidants are produced by our bodies and are in some of the foods we eat. With age, the body's ability to produce antioxidants declines, which can clearly be seen in the aging of skin, for example. Therefore, a dietary source of antioxidants becomes increasingly important. To date, the most helpful dietary sources of antioxidants have been identified as vitamins E, C, and A, or A's precursor, beta-carotene. Although there is widespread acceptance of the value of these vitamins, there is not absolute agreement on how they do what they do. As a result, opinions differ over whether vitamin supplements offer a protective effect or whether the other nutrients in antioxidant-rich fruits and vegetables enable the protective activity. Foods rich in vitamin C and beta-carotene are widely available; for a substantive list, see page 410. Vitamin E, which is plentiful in nuts and oils, may be more difficult to consume on a very low-fat diet. Those on strict low-fat regimens may need to conscientiously eat a sufficient amount of vitamin E-rich foods (page 410) or consult a knowledgeable person about supplements.

CAFFEINE The active ingredient in coffee, chocolate, black teas, some pharmaceuticals and colas and other soft drinks, it provides the lift that so many of us crave by mildly stimulating the nervous system. It increases respiration rate, heart rate, blood pressure, and adrenaline secretion. How much caffeine a person can tolerate is purely an individual matter. Too much caffeine can trigger agitation (to a degree that can be indistinguishable from an anxiety attack), heart palpitations, insomnia, stomach upset, and diarrhea. For some, caffeine increases appetite; for others, appetite is suppressed. In the realm of more significant health problems or bodily discomfort, studies have found an association between caffeine and high blood pressure, irregular heart beat, and fibrocystic change—a benign (noncancerous) breast condition. Caffeine also promotes excretion of calcium, which may be particularly significant for women, who suffer from calcium loss with aging to a greater degree than men.

CALORIES The term signifies the *potential* energy in a gram of food. This energy provides us with the wherewithal to move and think, and it enables our cells to carry on their metabolic and electrical activity. Different foods have different energy potential. For example, a gram of fat has 9 calories, whereas a gram of protein or carbohydrates has about 4 calories. There is, therefore, more energy potential in a gram of fat than in the other nutrients. The picture becomes more complicated, however, when energy *availability* is considered. Carbohydrate metabolism—especially of simple and refined carbohydrates—is easier, so energy is released quickly after one eats these foods. By the same token, one's hunger is not satisfied for long. On the other hand, foods containing fat, which is slow to metabolize, provide energy and give a feeling of satiety over a longer period of time .

CARBOHYDRATES Along with proteins and fats, these essential nutrients supply energy to our body, maintain proper functioning of the brain and nervous system, and provide the fiber so necessary to the health of our intestines and colon. At 4 calories per gram, carbohydrates are a quick source of energy. They metabolize easily and so are readily available for use by our bodies. Carbohydrates are divided into two classes—simple and complex.

Simple carbohydrates include the sweeteners: table sugar, brown sugar, honey, maple syrup, molasses, corn syrup, and fruit sweeteners. Jams, jellies, and fruit juices also fall into this category, as does any alcoholic beverage. Simple carbohydrates are our quickest source of energy, but because they lack bulk, they do not signal our brains when we've had enough, which can lead to overconsumption and weight gain.

Complex carbohydrates are vegetables, fruits, grains, and beans in their unaltered, unrefined form. Popular examples include potatoes, rice, whole wheat bread, split peas, and apples. Overall, complex carbohydrates appear to be more health promoting and satisfying. Because they are bulky and fibrous, complex carbohydrates are filling without being fattening and have proven to be important to proper digestion of fats and proteins as well as to elimination. They are also our best source of vitamins and minerals.

CHOLESTEROL Despite popular perception, cholesterol is not an enemy of the people. On the contrary, it is essential to our well-being. It helps to build and maintain cell walls, to sheathe nerve fibers, to synthesize vitamin D, and to provide the start-up material for certain hormones. It is also integral to the structure of the brain and, paradoxically, to the digestion of fats. Though not a fat, cholesterol is a pale, waxy, fatlike substance; chemically it is a solid alcohol.

The cholesterol in our bodies comes from two sources. It is manufactured by our bodies (mostly by the liver), and it enters our bloodstream from some of the foods we eat. If we ate no foods with cholesterol, the body would produce all of the cholesterol it needs. But if adequate or nearly adequate cholesterol is provided by our food intake, our body stops producing its own or cuts back. This is one way that cholesterol is regulated in the average healthy person.

Other animals also produce cholesterol for similar functions. Plants do not. So the cholesterol we take into our bodies always comes from animal foods and foods derived from animals. Examples include beef, poultry, pork, fish, shellfish, eggs, and milk and other dairy products. Since plants do not manufacture cholesterol, there is no cholesterol in vegetables, grains, beans, nuts and seeds, and products derived from these foods.

Lipoproteins transport fats and cholesterol through our bloodstream so they can be absorbed by our cells for metabolism, storage, recycling, and elimination. Because cholesterol and fats, also called *lipids,* are insoluble in water—the major component of our blood—they must be "repackaged" to allow for smooth travel and absorption. This transformation process occurs in the liver, where the fatty lipid molecules are wrapped in protein molecules. The result is lipoproteins in which these protein envelopes enable unimpeded passage and absorption of the fatty substances. Thus far, four lipoproteins have been identified. Chylomicrons and very low-density lipoproteins (VLDLs) provide transport for triglycerides (or fats), while low-density lipoproteins (LDLs) and high-density lipoproteins (HDLs) provide transport for cholesterol.

Low-density lipoproteins (LDLs) carry cholesterol to blood vessels. It is currently thought that LDLs can also deposit excess cholesterol in the walls of our arteries—the vessels that supply blood to the heart. Since clinical data has shown that 70 percent of the fat that blocks arteries in coronary artery disease (also called atherosclerosis) is cholesterol, it has been deduced that too high a level of LDLs may increase a person's risk for heart attack and stroke. To a degree, LDL level has been shown to be positively affected, or lowered, by a diet low in saturated fat.

High-density lipoproteins (HDLs) carry surplus cholesterol to the liver for recycling or elimination. HDLs appear to act as scavengers, actually cleaning up excess cholesterol from the bloodstream, cellular tissue, and arteries. High levels of HDLs have been associated with a reduced risk of coronary artery disease. HDL levels may be increased by losing weight, quitting smoking, and exercising. Although HDL levels are not directly affected by diet, a diet that reduces LDL levels improves the ratio between LDLs and HDLs, which may then lower one's risk for heart disease.

The total blood cholesterol level is calculated from the circulating lipoproteins that transport cholesterol in a person's bloodstream—high-density lipoproteins (HDLs), low-density lipoproteins (LDLs), and very low-density lipoproteins (VLDLs). VLDLs are large lipoproteins that primarily move triglycerides (fats) but also carry cholesterol. Once the triglycerides are transported to the cells for storage or metabolic activity, the smaller LDLs split off and continue on their way. These LDLs are calculated from the number of VLDLs in circulation.

Although there has been much emphasis placed on a person's total blood cholesterol level, the ratio between a person's LDL and HDL levels also appears to be quite important in a health assessment.

It was once thought that to lower a person's cholesterol level one could simply reduce his or her consumption of foods rich in cholesterol. The picture became more complicated when it was discovered that people who significantly reduced or eliminated their intake of high-cholesterol foods saw little difference in their total blood cholesterol levels.

What has come to light is that cholesterol is most effectively reduced in those persons who limit their cholesterol intake and eat a diet low in saturated fats. In fact, current evidence supports that saturated fats, more than dietary cholesterol itself, contribute to the elevation of cholesterol levels. Although cholesterol production, metabolism, and transport are not thoroughly understood, it has been suggested that the connection between saturated fats and elevated cholesterol may occur via an increase in LDL levels.

Some people with high cholesterol levels remain unaffected even by radical changes in diet or exercise. For these people, drug or intensive vitamin therapy has sometimes proven effective.

The interrelationships between LDLs, HDLs, and triglycerides are complex and need to be viewed as a whole for each individual. If you have personal concerns about your cholesterol, have your levels evaluated by someone knowledgeable.

FATS Along with proteins and carbohydrates, fats are one of the three primary energy-yielding nutrients and are essential to good health and body function. Eaten in moderation, fats are an efficient and concentrated source of energy, offering 9 calories for every gram of fat. They are vital to the structure and maintenance of our cells and hormones and provide a prolonged feeling of fullness and satisfaction. Fats, also called lipids, are necessary for healthy skin and hair and contain the important fat-soluble vitamins A, D, E, and K. If we consume enough calories, our bodies can synthesize fat from surplus proteins and carbohydrates. We do, however, have a need for essential fatty acids—fats we must get from dietary fats that the body cannot produce.

We use the word *fats* as an all-inclusive term for vegetable oils, margarine, butter, lard, shortening, tallow, and the fats that naturally occur in nuts, seeds, certain fruits and vegetables such as avocados and coconuts, meats, poultry, eggs, fish, shellfish, and milk and dairy products made from milk.

Though all are fats, these foods are put into different categories based on their relative percentages of saturated, monounsaturated, and polyunsaturated fats. Most fat-containing food is composed of all three types of fat. But if a food has a higher percentage of saturated fat than either monounsaturated or polyunsaturated fat, it is classified as a food high in saturated fat. Olive oil has a higher percentage of monounsaturates than either saturated or polyunsaturated fats so it is considered a monounsaturate.

There are also differences within each classification. Coconut oil and butter are both high in saturated fats but coconut oil is more highly saturated than butter. Degree of saturation or unsaturation is based on the chemical structure of each fat. Each type of fat will be discussed below, as will other terms and categories of fats, including hydrogenated and partially hydrogenated fats, transfatty acids, omega-3 fatty acids, and triglycerides.

A balanced diet, as we've learned, rarely consists of equal parts of fats, carbohydrates, and proteins. An individual's needs depend on geography, daily activity levels, and genetic background among other things. Perhaps because our economy today demands less physical activity and more desk work, or perhaps because oft-relied-upon convenience foods have such high fat contents, or maybe due to the interaction of environmental pollutants and other chemicals with the fat in our diet, our fat consumption is being linked to some of the gravest and most challenging illnesses of our times.

Hydrogenated oils are polyunsaturates chemically altered by high heat and the addition of hydrogen, which causes them to solidify at room temperature. Many food labels bear the terms "hydrogenated" or "partially hydrogenated vegetable oil." Margarine and shortening are good examples of hydrogenated fats.

Oils are hydrogenated for many reasons. They become spreadable, produce flakier crusts, have a lower rancidity point, and have a higher smoking point (which makes them better for deep-frying). Hydrogenated oils are less expensive than butter, and have a longer shelf life.

However, the process of hydrogenation saturates an unsaturated fat, nullifying its beneficial qualities. The hydrogenation process further changes the chemical structure of the unsaturated fat to produce a new kind of fat molecule called a *transfatty acid* or a *transfat.* Transfatty acids are not made by our bodies and occur naturally only very rarely in foods. There is some speculation that once the transfat is absorbed by our cells, it can impair cell function. Recent studies have shown that transfatty acids appear to raise cholesterol levels and to be directly implicated in coronary artery disease in women. As a result, current recommendations suggest limiting foods with hydrogenated fats. The food industry, too, has not turned a blind eye to these research findings, and has produced many margarines and spreads that are lower in hydrogenated oils. If you use these spreads on a daily basis, you may want to check that hydrogenated oil is not the first ingredient on the label.

Monounsaturated fats, according to growing clinical and cultural evidence, are becoming recognized as the healthiest choice among dietary fats. Especially in cases of coronary artery disease—which can induce heart attacks and strokes—these fats appear to lower the level of cholesterol-depositing LDL molecules, while allowing cholesterol-eliminating HDL molecules to remain stable. Because of the positive effects these fats can have on overall fat metabolism, the suggested level of monounsaturated fats is currently 10 to 15 percent of total calories. Monounsaturated fats are primarily found in foods from vegetable sources. Foods high in monounsaturated fats include olives, olive oil, almonds, almond oil, almond butter, canola oil (also called rapeseed oil), hazelnuts (also called filberts), and, to a lesser degree, peanuts, peanut oil, and peanut butter.

Omega-3 fatty acids are essential polyunsaturated fats found in plant and fish oils. They are recommended for inclusion in our diets because they may

lower cholesterol levels by positively affecting both HDL and LDL levels, normalize blood pressure, slow clotting time, slow progression of coronary artery disease, and reduce the inflammation that accompanies arthritis and asthma. Also called linolenic acids, these fats are found most abundantly in cold-water sea fish such as salmon, white albacore tuna, mackerel, and sardines. They are also present in canola oil, walnuts, and freshwater fish such as carp, lake whitefish, sweet smelt, and lake and brook trout.

Polyunsaturated fats, like monounsaturated fats, are found in the highest concentrations in foods of vegetable origin. Foods with high levels include sesame seeds, sesame butter, sesame oil, sunflower seeds, sunflower oil, safflower oil, corn oil, walnuts and walnut oil, and soybeans and soybean products such as soy oil, tofu, tempeh, and textured vegetable protein. Fats from this category are regarded as healthier fats than saturated fats since they appear to lower cholesterol-depositing LDL levels. Yet they are considered less beneficial than monounsaturated fats, since a diet very high in polyunsaturates appears to also lower cholesterol-eliminating HDL molecules. Nutritionists are also reluctant to recommend a diet strictly consisting of polyunsaturated fats because there is no evidence of any culture surviving solely on this type of fat. As a result, the recommended percentage of polyunsaturated fat is just 7 to 10 percent of one's total calories.

Saturated fats are those rich-tasting and creamy fats that are generally solid at room temperature. Saturated fats are most often found in foods of animal origin such as beef, pork, lamb, poultry, and eggs. They are also in whole and partially skimmed milk and related dairy products, such as cream, cheese, sour cream, and butter. The leaner the cut of meat or the lower the fat content of the dairy product, the lower the level of saturated fat. Fish and shellfish also contain saturates but at lower levels than lean meats. A small sampling of foods from the plant kingdom also contains saturated fats. These include coconuts, coconut

oil, palm oil, palm kernel oil, chocolate, and cocoa butter. Because a diet rich in saturated fats can raise blood cholesterol, the prevailing wisdom holds that a healthy person without cholesterol problems should consume an upper limit of 10 percent of total calories from saturated fats, though lower levels are encouraged.

Triglycerides are the chemical compounds that make up about 95 percent of the fat we consume and store as body fat. They are in foods derived from both animal and vegetable sources, so they can be saturated or unsaturated. Triglycerides are also produced by our bodies from the protein and carbohydrates we eat that are not immediately used for metabolism or energy needs. Once in our systems, triglycerides break down into fatty acids; they then become vehicles for fat-soluble vitamins and contribute to cell health, hormonal functioning, and energy storage and retrieval. There are two fatty acids that our bodies cannot synthesize, which we must get from foods —linoleic and linolenic acids. Peanut and corn oil are good sources of linoleic acid, and canola oil and cold-water sea fish are sources of linolenic fats. Without these fats, serious eczema-like skin conditions, growth retardation, and possible reduction of immune system functioning can result. Additionally, there has been growing evidence that essential fatty acids play a significant role in the structure and function of our eyes and central nervous system. Triglycerides, like cholesterol, are carried to our cells by lipoproteins. It is currently a subject of debate whether elevated triglyceride levels pose a risk to heart health, although they may signal a disturbance in other health areas.

FIBER The indigestible part of food. It is only found in foods from the vegetable kingdom, which, along with vegetables, include grains, beans, fruits, nuts, and seeds. Fiber acts as a cleanser, encouraging our intestines to move waste along, which can prevent constipation and intestinal bacterial infection. Fiber maintains the tone of the digestive tract, which can prevent or reduce conditions in which muscles have weakened, such as hemorrhoids and diverticulosis. Fiber may also help lower blood cholesterol and has been associated with a reduced risk of colon cancer. Nutritionists currently recommend an upper limit of 20 to 30 grams of fiber daily, because the prolonged feeling of fullness that fiber provides may keep some people from getting the calories they need for both nutrition and energy.

PROTEINS   Like fats and carbohydrates, proteins play a key role in our health. Proteins build and repair muscles, bones, skin, and blood; regulate hormones and enzymes; and help fight infection and heal wounds. Proteins are also integral to genes and chromosomes. Although this is an impressive list of responsibilities, getting sufficient protein is not a problem for most Americans. With the exception of pure fats, sugars, and fruits, protein is present in every food we eat. By consuming enough calories from a varied diet, there is little risk of protein deficiency. Only extreme diets with very low caloric intake may present cause for concern.

Just as fats are made of fatty acids, proteins are made of amino acids. Protein becomes usable when it is "complete," or when all twenty amino acids are present. Our bodies supply twelve of these amino acids, and the remaining eight, called essential amino acids, must be obtained from dietary sources. Some foods, like meat, fish, and dairy products, contain all eight essential amino acids. But all other foods have some, and many, such as soybeans, other legumes, and pasta, have six or seven of the eight. However, it is not necessary to combine all eight essential amino acids in each dish or meal; complete proteins can be created and consumed over the course of one or two days.

Today it is believed that consuming a broad variety of foods, including those in a purely vegetarian diet, will adequately meet the Recommended Daily Allowance for protein—50 grams per day for women over eighteen and 63 grams per day for men in the same age bracket. The average consumption of protein in the United States exceeds these recommendations by 15 percent for women and 40 percent for

men, a cause for concern, as researchers have associated high protein consumption with osteoporosis and kidney disease.

SALT   When used in proper proportions, this seasoning can bring food to life. If overdone, it can overwhelm all other flavors. In most cases, we suggest adding salt at the end of a cooking process or right at the table. Too much salt can put salt-sensitive individuals at risk for hypertension (high blood pressure)—another risk factor for heart disease. Since there is currently no way to test for salt sensitivity and because hypertension seems to increase with age, it is probably good to follow the National Academy of Sciences recommendation of 500 milligrams daily, which equals ¼ teaspoon of salt. The average American currently takes in 5000 to 7000 milligrams of sodium. A maximum standard of 2400 milligrams has currently been set for the healthy individual, although it is not a standard that is recommended.

For those who want to limit their salt intake for either culinary or health reasons, the key word to look for on the labels of processed foods is *sodium*, which is the salty ingredient in salt and other seasonings, additives, and preservatives. The American Heart Association compiled the following handy list of hidden sources of salt:

> *Monosodium glutamate* (MSG)–a flavor enhancer
> *Sodium bicarbonate* (baking soda)–a leavening agent
> *Sodium nitrate*–a meat-curing agent found in
>   hot dogs, sausages, fish, cold cuts, bacon, and other
>   smoked meats
> *Sodium benzoate*–a preservative
> *Sodium proprionate*–a mold inhibitor
> *Sodium citrate*–an acidity controller

Other ingredients with high sodium contents include soy sauce, miso, Worcestershire sauce, and hoisin sauce.

SUGARS   (See Carbohydrates.)

LABELS DEMYSTIFIED

UNDERSTANDING THE NUMBERS

Food labels let the buyer know exactly what is in foods that have been processed and packaged for consumption. The U.S. Department of Agriculture (USDA) regularly revises label regulations governing which information food producers and manufacturers must provide when

they package their products. The labels now required on nearly all food packages offer more useful, accurate, and complete information than ever before.

We can remember the times when almost no one bothered to read food labels. When most of us at Moosewood were growing up, convenient packaged or canned foods were synonymous with modernization. These foods, with their long shelf life and often high fat, salt, or sugar content changed the resulting American palate and created an overwhelming demand for snacks—quick hand-to-mouth food. Our taste buds lost some of their more refined abilities to savor fresh foods, and, regrettably, we became a population that depended on rich-tasting processed foods, which the ever growing and competitive food industry was glad to provide.

In those days, food labels seemed to be just so much arithmetic in tiny print. Most of us believed the labels were for the nutritional specialists in Washington, D.C., and people with special dietary needs. There was a naive belief—innocent or indifferent or both—that if the food passed USDA standards and was allowed on the market, then it was good food. For many, food was food, and perhaps in reaction to the days when sugar, butter, and meat were treasured commodities, the population binged on these readily available, affordable foodstuffs in all of their varied forms.

After several decades, however, we have had to pause and examine our eating habits and all of our packaged foods. We believe that everyone should learn what the numbers, nutrients, and ingredients on labels mean. Learning to read labels with wisdom means distinguishing natural preservatives from chemical additives, being able to spot unrealistic portion sizes, and knowing the USDA definitions of terms like "fat-free."

Food labels list ingredients by weight, with the largest amount first. Nutritional information must be provided if any health claims are made or if nutri-

ents have been added. The information is standardized to show serving size, servings per container, and then calories, total fat, saturated (and sometimes unsaturated) fat, cholesterol, sodium, carbohydrates, dietary fiber, protein, and vitamins A and C. Below this is a list that gives the percentage of the FDA's U.S. Recommended Daily Allowance for protein, vitamins, and minerals contained in one serving, based on a 2000-calorie diet.

When you begin to read the nutritional information on a label, remember it is given in weight by grams or milligrams per serving. To translate the raw label material into percentages can be helpful in determining whether the food is low-fat enough for your ideal standard.

Plenty of food without additives or preservatives and untreated with pesticides and fertilizers is available to us, and we suggest choosing these foods. The more natural our foods, the more nourishing they are, and the fewer toxins our bodies must eliminate. Some food preservatives and emulsifiers are not chemically produced. The following substances, which may not be familiar to you, are natural substances and additives and are considered safe: locust bean gum, carrageenan, guar gum, cellulose gum, ascorbic acid, arabic gum, calcium or sodium propionate, casein, citric acid, edta, gelatin, glycerin, lecithin, sodium benzoate, potassium sorbate, sorbitol, and starch.

We suggest refraining from eating anything that has chemical additives or preservatives. Because historically humans have not regularly ingested man-made chemical substances, we have no way to accurately predict the long-term effects. So we believe in the better-safe-than-sorry approach to eating. Additives to avoid include acesulfame K, artificial colorings, BHA, BHT, saccharin, MSG (monosodium glutamate), sodium nitrite, and sodium nitrate.

Since May 1994, food labels have been required to

list saturated fat content on food labels so consumers can know how much of an item's total fat is saturated. Listing unsaturated fat is voluntary, however, and when a label lists the amount of unsaturated fat, transfatty acids are included in this fat total, although technically transfats act more like saturated fats in terms of their negative effects on blood cholesterol (page 434). Until recently, the general public always equated unsaturated fat with "healthy" fat. Now, however, the story appears to be more complex, and the FDA did consider differentiating mono- and polyunsaturates from transfatty acids on labels. But despite much debate and discussion, no change has been instituted, since studies are not yet deemed conclusive enough.

In the world of fats, it seems safe to say that monounsaturated fats are the most potentially health-promoting, unhydrogenated polyunsaturates are the next most attractive, and the least desirable are the hydrogenated oils and saturated fats. So when you look at a label that gives the fat breakdown, it's worth noticing what kind of fat predominates.

We hope that the information we've presented on nutrition and labeling and these more than 300 recipes of truly tasty food will pique your interest in healthier lower-fat eating. And as you wend your way through the aisles of the grocery or supermarket, make use of those labels. They can be a meaningful tool in selecting what's right for you to eat.

Here are some suggestions for avoiding pitfalls and misunderstandings when buying packaged food products:

1. *Don't be fooled by buzzwords. Light, lite,* or *dietetic* may not mean low-fat, but may simply refer to less calories, sugar, or salt than the original version. They may even refer to the color or texture of a product. These terms do not necessarily ensure natural ingredients either; many so-called light products contain chemical additives and preservatives.

2. *Familiarize yourself with the official USDA definitions for "fat-free," "low-fat," and similar terms used in marketing and packaging* (see sidebar). They don't always mean what you might think.

3. *Notice the serving sizes.* Sometimes these are unrealistically small. If a bag of goodies lists a serving as $1/2$ ounce, but you eat an entire 8-ounce bag, you must multiply the amount of fat on the label by 16 to discover how many grams of fat you just consumed.

4. *Remember that "fat-free" means less than $1/2$ gram of fat per serving, not necessarily zero fat.* If the ingredient list includes butter or oils, nuts, or flour, there is definitely some fat involved. For instance, take a 6-ounce box of "fat-free" cookies. The serving size listed is $1/2$ ounce. If the box contains twelve cookies that means each cookie is one serving. But let's suppose each cookie contains 0.48 gram of fat, an amount that technically qualifies as "fat-free." Now suppose you're in a munching mood and devour all twelve cookies. Suddenly, you've chalked up ($12 \times 0.48 = 5.8$) nearly 6 grams of fat—not exactly a healthy fat-free snack. It's important to understand the truth of the matter and not be misled by tricky terminology.

5. *Understand the percentages.* "% fat-free" (which may be printed on a milk carton or pound cake label, for instance) indicates how much of the *weight* of the product can be attributed to its fat. Percentages can be misleading. If the other ingredients are very heavy, empty calories, or contain water, the fat-free percentage may be high. "90% fat-free" sounds good, but the

reality may be that the product is still loaded with actual grams of fat and may derive 80 percent or more of its calories from fat. The 2% on low-fat milk represents the fat content by weight; actually 38 percent of its calories come from fat. Low-fat milk is only considered low-fat in comparison to regular milk, which is high in fat. Read labels for actual grams of fat.

6. *Do be aware of calories as well.* Some nonfat or very low-fat commercial products are high in sugar or other sugary substances such as sucrose, fructose, honey, corn syrup, molasses, or maple syrup. These may be high in calories although low in fat. Remember that a diet too high in calories allows the body to produce fat even without dietary fat per se.

7. *Look for hidden fats.* Manufacturers can list certain ingredients such as oil with ambiguous statements such as "contains one or more of the following: soybean and/or palm kernel oil." Because palm kernel or coconut oils are highly saturated fats, you may want to avoid them, as we do in our cooking at Moosewood. In this case, because you cannot know if the product is made with unsaturated soybean oil or saturated palm kernel oil, you may want to pass it up.

8. *Scrutinize foods advertised as healthy, too.* Many "health food" snacks are made with coconut or palm kernel oil because these oils are inexpensive and store well, prolonging the shelf life of the product. Therefore, "health food" snacks may not really be much better (or in some cases, any better) than mainstream junk food. Read the small print—the labels are as close to the truth as you can get.

9. *Be a skeptic.* The FDA regularly checks the accuracy of food labels. Nationally distributed brands tend to have more precise labeling than some local or regionally produced foods. If the FDA discovers improper label information, the manufacturer is required to correct it immediately.

For even more detailed definitions see the pamphlet entitled Food Labeling Guide put out by the U.S. Department of Health and Human Services and F.D.A. in Washington, D.C.

"FAT FREE" must contain less than ½ gram of fat per serving.

"SATURATED FAT FREE" must contain less than ½ gram of saturated fat per serving and less than ½ gram of transfat per reference amount customarily consumed and per serving.

"LOW SATURATED FAT" must contain less than 1 gram of saturated fat per serving and not more than 15% of calories can derive from saturated fat.

"LOW FAT" must contain less than 3 grams of fat per serving (except milk).

"REDUCED SATURATED FAT" must contain 25% less saturated fat than the regular product.

"REDUCED FAT" (such as mayonnaise) must contain 25% less fat than the regular product.

"LIGHT" must contain 50% less fat than the regular product.

"NO CHOLESTEROL" means the product contains 2 milligrams or less of cholesterol per serving, but it may contain up to 2 grams of saturated fat—which can raise blood cholesterol.

"LOW CHOLESTEROL" must contain no more than 20 milligrams of cholesterol and no more than 2 grams of saturated fat per serving.

"REDUCED CHOLESTEROL" must contain 75% less cholesterol than the regular product.

2% OR LOW-FAT MILK contains 38% of calories from fat and 4.7 grams of fat per 8-ounce glass.

1% MILK contains 22% of calories from fat and 2.5 grams of fat per glass.

SKIM MILK contains 4% of calories from fat and 0.4 grams of fat per glass.

"LOW-CAL" means 40 calories or less per serving (or when the serving size is small, 40 calories or less per 50 grams of the food).

"REDUCED CALORIE" means 25% less calories per serving than the regular item.

"CALORIE FREE" means less than 5 calories per serving.

"SODIUM FREE" means less than 5 milligrams of sodium per serving (or per 50 grams of the food if the serving size is very small—i.e., when a serving is less than 30 grams or less than 2 tablespoons).

"LOW SODIUM" means 140 milligrams of sodium or less per serving (or when the serving size is small, per 50 grams of the food).

"VERY LOW SODIUM" means 35 milligrams of sodium or less per serving (or when the serving size is small, per 50 grams of the food).

"SUGARLESS" means contains no sucrose, but can contain other sugars such as corn syrup, dextrose, levulose, sorbitol, mannitol, maltitol, xylitol, or natural sweeteners at less than ½ gram per serving.

"NO ADDED SUGAR" means no sugars or ingredients containing sugars are added during processing. If the product is not also a low- or reduced-calorie food, then it must state that and direct consumers to read the nutritional label. The regular product it resembles and replaces may contain added sugars.

"REDUCED SUGAR" means at least 25% less sugar per serving than the regular item.

"HIGH FIBER" means 5 grams of fiber or more per serving, plus the food must either meet low-fat standards or indicate the total fat content next to the high-fiber claim.

"GOOD SOURCE OF FIBER" means 2.5 to 4.9 grams of fiber per serving.

VITAMINS AND MINERALS AT A GLANCE

In case we've whetted your appetite to know exactly what you're eating, here's a list of the vitamins and minerals often listed on labels and a little about them. Labels list the vitamins and minerals contained in the food and next to them a number that indicates the percentage of the U.S. Recommended Daily Allowances (U.S. RDA) met by eating one serving of the food. This percentage is based on a 2000-calorie diet, which is considered a reasonable number of daily calories for the average American adult.

THE VITAMINS

Learning the vitamin alphabet, like learning a language alphabet, takes some time at first but proves worthwhile in the end.

VITAMIN A is derived from carotene, a deep red or yellow organic compound responsible for the color in many yellow, orange, or rose-colored vegetables such as apricots, carrots, sweet potatoes, peaches, cantaloupes, and tomatoes. It is fat soluble, prevents night blindness, improves reaction time, and is essential to healthy skin and internal membranes. Other food sources are broccoli, kale, lettuce, watercress, dandelion greens, and fish liver oils, where it is especially abundant.

VITAMIN B COMPLEX refers to a group of twenty-four water soluble vitamins, widely distributed in plants and animals, that contribute to healthy heart activity, even energy, and strong nervous system reflexes. Below we list some of the most common B vitamins:

Vitamin B_1, known as thiamine, encourages appetite and guards the nervous system. Present in barley, millet, oats, beans, and yogurt.

Vitamin B_2 is the classification for riboflavin (also called vitamin G), niacin, and folic acid (also called vitamin B_c). B_2 promotes healthy skin, blood formation, and good eyesight. Folic acid is especially important for the prevention of neural tube birth defects in pregnant women. Found in leeks, eggs, cheese, milk, potatoes, tomatoes, turnips, and many fresh green vegetables.

Vitamin B_4, now called adenine, is found in milk, oatmeal, peanuts, yeast, and eggs.

Vitamin B_6, pyridoxine, is essential to the well-being of skin and nerves.

Vitamin B_{12} is a dark red, crystalline vitamin extracted from the liver and from certain mold fungi, which acts against pernicious anemia. It is also known as cobalamine.

VITAMIN C, or ascorbic acid, helps to guard against internal injuries such as muscle bruising. It promotes supple bones and healthy teeth and gums, and hinders the storage of fat in the body. There must be sufficient calcium available for the vitamin to be absorbed and utilized by the body. Present in broccoli, cabbage, cauliflower, kale, carrots, cantaloupe, citrus fruits, chiles, black currants, strawberries, and watercress.

VITAMIN D, found chiefly in fish liver oils, helps prevent rickets and other bone deficiencies, cooperates with phosphorus to burn sugar, and provides stability for our nervous system. Other sources include butter, cheese, mackerel, salmon, sardines, tuna, and—surprise—sunlight. Vitamin D_2 is known as calciferol.

VITAMIN E is a fat-soluble vitamin composed of three forms of organic alcohol known as tocopherol. It is a valuable energy source, aids circulation, tones muscles, inhibits premature aging, acts as an anticoagulant, and has been indicated in the prevention of sterility. Found in brown rice, wheat germ, sunflower seeds, lettuce, watercress, and eggs and in many oils including peanut, soybean, sunflower, and corn oils.

VITAMIN F is no longer commonly referred to as a vitamin at all, but is now known as unsaturated fatty acids!

VITAMIN H, called biotin, is actually another member of the B vitamin family.

VITAMIN K, found in green leafy vegetables, promotes blood clotting. Our bodies manufacture it, and foods that facilitate its internal production are soybeans, yogurt, peanuts, and milk.

VITAMIN L is the name given to two substances, one found in beef liver and the other contained in yeast. Both are water soluble and encourage normal milk formation and secretion in women.

VITAMIN P COMPLEX consists of a group of compounds that include the bioflavonoids. Found in most citrus fruits, its highest concentration resides in the pith and peel. Traces of vitamin P are also available in rose hips and grapes. It fosters healthy, permeable capillary walls—those outer surfaces of the tiny vessels that connect our arteries and veins—and helps prevent high blood pressure. Rutin is another name sometimes used to refer to vitamin P.

The Minerals

These vital substances are neither animal nor vegetable matter and are formed by inorganic processes. They have definite molecular and chemical compositions—often crystalline—that result in easily identifiable physical characteristics. Mineral salts are essential to health. They aid the body's process of buildup and repair, help prevent premature aging, and facilitate resistance to illness. Here is a quick checklist of some minerals our bodies use regularly.

CALCIUM This malleable, silver-white, metallic element is responsible for maintaining good muscle tone and resilient bones and teeth. It also enhances blood clotting, cell wall permeability, and proper enzyme functioning. As much as 98 percent of our bodies' calcium is stored in our bones. Because calcium is necessary for vital bodily functions, whenever our diets fail to provide sufficient calcium, our bodies must draw it from our bones. If this occurs repeatedly, our bones become depleted of their calcium store and we become susceptible to a host of problems including rickets, arthritis, rheumatism, poor vitamin C absorption, and weakened bone structure. Excessive consumption of fat, chocolate and cocoa, and foods such as spinach and rhubarb that contain oxalic acid all hinder the body's ability to absorb calcium. Foods rich in calcium are broccoli, cabbage,

kale, endive, watercress, lettuce, turnip greens, parsnips, carrots, onions, beans, bran, apricots, figs, lemons, limes, oranges, grapes, hazelnuts, almonds, tofu, eggs, buttermilk, milk, yogurt, unprocessed cheese, salmon, herring, sardines, maple sugar, blackstrap molasses, chives, and numerous herbs.

CHLORINE This greenish-yellow, readily liquefied gaseous element acts very closely with sodium in our foods. Deficiency—which is unusual—can lead to hair or tooth loss, indigestion, and weakened muscular strength. Consumed in excess (which is generally only a danger for those taking large supplemental doses), it increases fat accumulation, reduces iodine in the body, and diminishes stamina. Almost all plants are rich in chlorine. Other sources are radishes, kelp, olives, figs, milk, butter, and cheeses.

COPPER A reddish metallic element, copper aids the body in retaining iron long enough to make use of it. Prematurely greying hair often signifies a lack of sufficient copper in the diet. Copper is plentiful in wheat germ, blackstrap molasses, dried figs, and many nuts. Herbal sources include burdock root, parsley, stinging nettles, and yellow dock.

IODINE Essential to effective white blood cell activity, which rids our body of harmful bacteria, iodine is a greyish-black crystalline element. In the diet it enhances brain, thyroid, and nervous system functioning, promotes equanimity, increases muscular endurance, and prevents fat formation by promoting the process of oxidizing our food for energy. Foods with iodine are agar-agar, carrots, artichokes, asparagus, peas, onions, mushrooms, garlic, leeks, lettuce, spinach, watercress, bananas, strawberries, melons, beans, and mussels.

IRON A strongly magnetic metallic element that is silver-white in its pure form, iron must be accompanied by copper in order to function properly in our bodies. It helps produce rich, pure blood, transports oxygen throughout the body, strengthens nerves and muscles, aids circulation, sharpens vision, and plays a role in regulating heartbeat. Good sources of iron are oats, barley, rye, bran, wheat germ, lentils, all dried fruit, olives, prunes, apples, blackberries, raspberries, lettuce, spinach, cabbage, watercress, radishes, asparagus, blackstrap molasses, walnuts, eggs, and milk. One-half cup of parsley has more iron than $\frac{1}{4}$ pound of liver.

MAGNESIUM This light, malleable, silver metallic element is essential to proper adrenal gland functioning and tooth and bone formation. It catalyzes carbohydrate absorption and helps the body make good use of food. Deficiency is rare but can induce chronic constipation, sleeplessness, and exaggerated sensitivity to heat and cold. Large doses of magnesium should be avoided since it can have a depressant effect. The U.S. RDA is a "trace," or very small amount. Magnesium-rich vegetables and herbs are kale, cabbage, okra, kelp, parsley, and peppermint. Traces are also found in brown rice, oats, soybeans, spinach, watercress, legumes, turnips, citrus fruits, apples, cherries, prunes, almonds, figs, raisins, and egg yolks.

MANGANESE A brittle, easily oxidized, greyish-white metallic element that controls metabolism and is vital to the pituitary gland. It is a natural tonic to the nervous system and nourishes the linings of our bodily organs. Good sources are agar-agar, mint, nasturtium blooms, parsley, endive, liver, peanuts, walnuts, almonds, potatoes, and wheat germ.

PHOSPHORUS This soft, non-metallic element appears in several forms; white and yellow phosphorus are poisonous forms, while red phosphorus is not. Phosphorus is intimately linked with our bodies' cell structure and affects our bones, lungs, muscle stamina and coordination, gland secretion, and red blood cell count. A ratio of 1 part of calcium to $1\frac{1}{2}$ parts of phosphorus should be continually maintained in our systems. Our bodies are able to regulate this proportion as long as we eat enough foods that supply the two minerals and have a sufficient supply of vitamin D. Excellent sources of phosphorus include barley, brown rice, oats, lentils, garlic, caraway seeds, sorrel, cabbage, watercress, radishes, peas, cheese, eggs, most nuts and fruits, peanut butter, sesame, halibut, salmon, shrimp, and sardines.

POTASSIUM Also called kalium, this bluish-white highly reactive metallic element is always found in combined form in nature. It dispatches oxygen throughout our bodies, stimulating necessary oxygenation of our muscles and tissues, expanding lung capacity, and energizing the heart. Potassium helps destroy bacteria, speeds the healing of injuries, and may decrease a tendency to baldness. Too much salt in the diet robs our body cells of their potassium supply. Kelp and other seaweeds are wonderful suppliers of potassium. Many foods that are rich sources of potassium can lose as much as 75 percent of their potassium content during cooking, so it is important to eat at least some of these foods raw or lightly steamed on a regular basis. Carrots, cucumbers, asparagus, bananas, kohlrabi, onions, soybeans, turnips, parsnips, cabbage, cauliflower, corn, nuts, berries, oats, apples, plums, grapes, endive, lettuce, watercress, peppermint, potatoes, tomatoes, cod, paprika, and honey are all high in potassium.

SILICON This widely found nonmetallic element makes the bones and teeth hard, maintains an alkaline balance in the tissues, helps reaction time, and contributes to good eyesight. Silicon deficiency may result in lack of endurance, nervous debility, poor circulation to the hands and feet, and premature baldness. Its absence in the diet has also been correlated with rheumatism. Foods rich in silicon include cabbage, celery, artichokes, asparagus, cucumbers, onions, leeks, lettuce, spinach, tomatoes, turnips, barley, oats, nuts, sunflower seeds, and strawberries. Silica is the combination of silicon and oxygen in crystal form.

SODIUM Also known as natrium, this silver-white alkaline metallic element is naturally present in all of our bodily fluids and especially in the gastric juices of the stomach. Sodium's principal function is disposing of body acids and reducing excess mineral salts in the bloodstream. Sodium is lost through perspiration and to a much lesser degree through urination, so eating sodium-rich foods after strenuous exercise is often recommended. Deficiency can cause cramping and inhibit the quick healing of wounds. Care should be taken to avoid common table salt, or sodium chloride, as one's main source of sodium. Salt retains unnecessary liquid in the body, which may contribute to detrimental long-term effects such as overweight, heart disease, tumor formation, and even cancer. Sea salts have more mineral traces than regular table salt—some even have magnesium, potassium, and other minerals in the same proportions as they occur in our bodies. Nevertheless, we can readily obtain adequate quantities of sodium from foods without ever adding salt per se. Carrots, celery, beets, spinach, chives, sorrel, watercress, asparagus, cauliflower, apples, lentils, oats, nuts, and herring are all good sources.

SULFUR A pale yellow, nonmetallic element, sulfur aids the complexion, sound digestion, protein metabolization, the transportation of other mineral salts through the body, and the function of the brain and nervous system. It helps prevent constipation, stiffness, and bronchial disease. Sulfur occurs naturally in our bloodstreams, but we need supplementary amounts from our foods. Sources of sulfur are Brussels sprouts, cauliflower, cabbage, garlic, onions, radishes, potatoes, spinach, cucumbers, watercress, red currants, cranberries, figs, oranges, pineapple, coconut, chestnuts, egg yolks, cottage cheese, blackstrap molasses, horseradish, and fennel seeds.

ZINC This bluish-white metallic element helps the metabolism of carbohydrates and proteins, the respiration of our body tissues, and our voluntary muscle coordination. It also controls the storage of sugars and starches and has been found useful in the treatment of some diabetes cases. Beans, peas, vegetable greens (including carrot and beet tops), most nuts, wheat germ, and egg yolks all contain zinc.

GLOSSARY OF COOKING TECHNIQUES AND TERMS

AL DENTE A term applied to cooked pasta that is tender with a firm bite.

BEANS, COOKING DRIED There are many types of dried beans that offer endless opportunities for low-fat, carbohydrate- and protein-rich meals. Whenever possible, we cook dried beans from scratch to avoid the added salt and preservatives in many brands of canned beans. When the time just isn't there, we've discovered that Eden, Westbrae, Randall, Goya, and Sahadi brands process some of their canned beans without preservatives. Most do contain salt, but much of that can be removed by draining and rinsing the beans.

Most dried beans need to be softened by soaking before they are cooked. This is not necessary for smaller, softer beans, such as lentils or split peas, and even some larger, softer types, like black-eyed peas.

To prepare dried beans, spread them on a flat tray and sort through them, discarding stones and shriveled beans. Immerse the beans in cool water to rinse off any dust and to allow harvesting debris to float to the surface. Skim the debris and drain the beans.

Cover the beans with water—it should cover the beans by 3 to 4 inches—and soak by one of the following methods: a (1) place the beans in a cool spot to avoid fermentation and soak for 6 to 8 hours, or (2) bring the beans to a boil, immediately remove them from the heat, cover, and soak for 1 hour.

After soaking, drain the beans. Add fresh water, cover the pot, and bring the beans to a boil. Then lower the heat and simmer until the beans are thoroughly cooked. Check periodically that the beans are always covered with water and replenish as needed. (See the following chart for the best bean-to-water ratio.)

BLANCHING In our recipes, blanching is synonymous with parboiling—an ingredient is partially boiled for a short time. This simple technique extracts bitter flavors from vegetables and tones down strong ones, such as turnips, parsnips, and radishes. Blanching hard vegetables, such as potatoes and carrots, shortens subsequent roasting or grilling times. To blanch literally means "to whiten or lose color"; however, a quick scald actually intensifies the colors of vegetables, especially if you then quickly immerse them in cold water to halt the cooking process.

BRAISING To brown and then simmer in a covered pan either on the stove or in the oven. A heavy pan is best for braising. To braise without using fat or oil, arrange the prepared vegetables in a pan, cover them almost entirely with liquid, and boil until the liquid cooks away and the vegetables begin to brown. Add a

VARIETY	WATER-BEAN RATIO	COOKING TIME	COOKED QUANTITY OF 1 CUP DRIED AFTER SOAKING
Black (turtle) beans	3:1	1½ hours	3 cups
Black-eyed peas	3:1	30 minutes	2½ cups
Chickpeas (garbanzos)	4:1	1½ hours	3 cups
Kidney beans	3:1	1 to 1½ hours	2¾ cups
Lentils, brown	2:1	30 minutes	3 cups
Lentils, red	2:1	15 to 20 minutes	3 cups
Lima beans	3:1	1 hour	3 cups
Mung beans	3:1	45 minutes	3 cups
Navy (pea) beans	3:1	45 to 60 minutes	2¾ cups
Pinto beans	3:1	45 minutes	3¼ cups
Soybeans	4:1	2 hours	2¾ cups

small amount of additional liquid to dislodge any vegetables that have begun to stick to the bottom of the pan. Turn off the heat and proceed as the recipe directs. Good braising liquids include stock, wine, and juices; all will penetrate the ingredients to add flavor to the dish.

CARAMELIZING Cooking naturally sweet vegetables or fruits in a small amount of liquid on low heat for a long period of time, until the sugars in them are released and browned.

CHIFFONADING A decorative slicing technique for any broad, flat leaf—spinach, basil, leaf lettuce, and heartier greens like Swiss chard or beet greens are all good subjects. To chiffonade, roll the leaf lengthwise and then thinly slice it crosswise to produce ribbons of greens.

CHOPPING Cutting foods into uniformly sized pieces. In this book, chopping indicates pieces about ½ to 1 inch square or occasionally somewhat larger. The size of the pieces affects the length of the cooking time and the overall appearance of the dish. In general, we suggest onions be chopped into pieces ½ inch or smaller to ensure quick cooking to a soft texture. We chop vegetables intended for use in soups smaller than for those added to stews or sautés, in which larger pieces are both visually appealing and easier to eat.

DICING Cutting foods into small cubes ranging from ⅛ to ½ inch square. Cut vegetables into slices, stack the slices, and cut them into strips, then cut the strips crosswise into cubes.

EGG WHITES, SEPARATING Crack an egg and, holding it over a bowl, gently break it crosswise into halves, keeping the yolk in one half of the shell. Allow the egg white to drain into the bowl as you slip the yolk from one half of the shell to the other, being careful not to break the yolk.

EMULSIFYING To homogenize or make a uniform liquid mixture of a fat and a nonfat liquid. Mayonnaise is a good example of a food that has been emul-sified, as are salad dressings. There are different processes for emulsifying but the most relevant to the home cook is whirling in a blender or beating with a wire whisk. As a rule, emulsified saturated fats stay emulsified longer than unsaturated fats. If separation occurs, in a dressing for example, simply blend again.

FOLDING A technique for incorporating one ingredient into another by gently turning one part of the mixture over the other part with a spoon or rubber spatula. Folding, rather than stirring or beating, helps keep the air in whipped egg whites used to lighten a cake, pudding, or soufflé. It also prevents the gluten in flour from becoming overdeveloped when preparing quick breads or muffins.

GRAINS, COOKING

Barley Combine 1 cup of barley and about 5 cups of water in a soup pot and bring to a boil. Reduce the heat to a simmer and cook for about 1¼ hours, until tender. One cup of raw barley yields about 3¾ cups cooked.

Bulgur Combine 1 cup of bulgur, 1 cup of boiling water, and a dash of salt in a heatproof bowl. Cover and set aside for about 20 to 30 minutes. When all of the liquid has been absorbed, stir to fluff the grains. If still too chewy, add another ½ to 1 cup of boiling water. One cup of raw bulgur yields about 2½ cups cooked.

Couscous Traditionally, couscous is steamed over a simmering soup or stew. For convenience, combine equal amounts of raw couscous and boiling water or stock in a heatproof bowl. Cover tightly and let sit for about 5 minutes. Stir to fluff the grains, adding a small amount of hot water if the grains of couscous are still crunchy.

Kasha (buckwheat groats) Bring to a boil 2 cups of stock or water, a pinch of salt and pepper, and a teaspoon of oil. Meanwhile, in a skillet that has a tight-fitting lid, dry-roast 1 cup of kasha on medium heat, until fragrant. Add the boiling liquid, cover, and simmer on very low heat for 15 minutes. Fluff the grains with a fork before serving. For a breakfast cereal, use 3 cups of water or milk and ½ cup of grain.

Millet Combine 1 cup of millet, a pinch of salt, and 1¾ cups of water in a heavy saucepan. Cover and bring to a boil. Reduce the heat, stir, and gently simmer for about 20 minutes. Stir to fluff the grains—if it's still a little crunchy, add ¼ cup of boiling water, cover, and steam for 10 minutes more.

Polenta Bring 3 cups of salted water to a boil in a heavy saucepan. Add 1 cup of cornmeal in a thin, steady stream while whisking briskly. Reduce the heat to low and simmer for about 15 minutes, stirring occasionally. For a creamier consistency, cook longer on very low heat, stirring frequently to prevent sticking. One cup of cornmeal yields 3 cups of polenta.

Quinoa Thoroughly rinse 1 cup of quinoa in a fine strainer. Combine the quinoa and 2 cups of water in a saucepan, bring to a boil, then cover, lower the heat, and gently simmer for 15 to 20 minutes, until tender and transparent. One cup of raw quinoa yields about 4 cups cooked.

Rice Different varieties require different methods of cooking, so here's the scoop.

arborio rice To make risotto, see pages 191–194. Arborio rice can also be baked, using about 3 cups of liquid for every cup of rice.

basmati rice To cook brown basmati rice, follow the instructions for brown rice using 2¼ cups of water for each cup of rice. We recommend imported Italian white basmati rice. Rinse 1 cup of rice until the rinsing water is clear. Drain well, cover with 2 cups of cool water, and soak for 30 minutes. Drain the soaking water into a heavy saucepan and bring it to a boil. Then add the rinsed rice, lower the heat, cover, and simmer for about 15 minutes, until all of the liquid is absorbed. Fluff the grains with a fork and let sit for 5 minutes before serving.

brown rice Rinse 1 cup of rice well and let drain. Combine the rinsed rice and 2 cups of water in a heavy saucepan with a tight-fitting lid. (For greater quantities of rice, lower the proportion of water to rice: For example, for 3 cups of rice, use only about 4½ cups of water.) Cover and bring to a boil on high heat. When steam escapes from below the lid, lower the heat to very low and simmer for about 35 minutes, or until all of the water has been absorbed. Stir to fluff before serving. One cup of raw rice yields about 3 cups cooked.

jasmine rice Rinse 1 cup of rice well and let drain. Combine the rinsed rice and 1½ cups of boiling water in a saucepan. Cover and return to a boil, reduce the heat, and cook for about 15 minutes, until tender. Remove from the heat and allow to sit for 5 minutes before serving.

white rice Combine 1 cup of rice and 1¾ cups of water in a heavy saucepan with a snug lid. Bring to a boil and when steam escapes from beneath the lid, lower the heat and simmer gently for about 15 to 20 minutes, until all of the water is absorbed. Avoid using "instant" or "minute" types, since their flavor and texture are markedly inferior.

GRILLING A rapid, intense, dry heat method that gives foods crisp exteriors and moist, flavorful interiors. Foods are placed on a rack, stove-top grill, or ridged grill pan above a source of direct heat, usually gas, wood coals, charcoal, or an electric coil. Blanch harder vegetables such as carrots, potatoes, green beans, and cauliflower before grilling.

JULIENNING Slicing ingredients into 2- to 3-inch-long thin strips also called *matchsticks.* Their preparation is somewhat time-consuming, but julienned ingredients look beautiful in clear broths and festive in salads. A very sharp knife is helpful when hand cutting. A cutting device called a *mandoline* can be used to julienne ingredients.

MANGOES, CUTTING Mango pulp is very slippery, so care must be taken when peeling and slicing mangoes. Use a sharp knife. Mangoes have large pits and the pulp around the pits is often fibrous, so shallow slices from end to end along the broad, flat side work best. Don't try to cut a mango in half!

MASHING   Done to break down whole cooked beans, vegetables (most often, potatoes), miso, and tamarind. For beans and vegetables, cook them until very soft and place them in a large bowl with a small amount of liquid. Use a potato masher to press repeatedly and forcefully downward, crushing them into a soft, uniform mass that can become the basis for a filling for stuffed vegetables or savory pastries. To mash miso or tamarind, place a small amount in a sieve and push it through, using the back of a spoon. After mashing, the miso or tamarind can be more easily combined with water or stock and incorporated into soups, stews, or sauces.

MINCING   Mincing in this book refers to very finely dicing and is most often recommended for garlic, ginger root, chiles, and fresh herbs.

PASTA, COOKING   Bring about 4 quarts of water to a boil per pound of pasta—estimate about ¼ pound of dried pasta per person. Ease the pasta into the boiling water, stir with a wooden spoon to separate, and cover the pot. When it returns to a boil (the quicker, the better), remove the lid and stir again. Fresh pasta cooks in just a couple of minutes; dried pasta takes longer; test it every 1 or 2 minutes after the first few minutes to avoid overcooking it. When the pasta is al dente—tender with a firm bite—it's ready. Drain it in a colander, transfer to a warmed serving bowl while still wet, and toss with sauce, vegetables, and/or finely grated cheese.

PREHEATING THE OVEN   Preheating an oven can speed up cooking time by establishing an even heat from start to finish, but it is not essential unless cakes, pies, cookies, breads, or soufflés are being baked. We have attempted to place our reminder about 10 minutes before the baking will begin. If your oven preheats much faster or slower than this, you should adjust the point at which you turn it on accordingly.

PRESSING GARLIC   A technique that breaks up peeled garlic cloves into fine pieces so that its flavor and texture can be more thoroughly dispersed. Use a commercial garlic press (stainless steel or heavy-gauge steel presses with a jointed, movable pressing part are the most durable and effective) or mince fine by hand with a knife. Larger quantities of garlic can be pulverized in the bowl of a food processor for the same effect.

PURÉEING   Blending into a creamy, smooth sauce, paste, or pâté. Blenders, food processors, food mills, sieves, and strainers can all be used to purée ingredients.

ROASTING   This cooking method employs high, dry heat to sear in juices and develop the natural sugars of vegetables. Roasting can be done in an oven, over an open flame (as with bell peppers), in a hot dry skillet, or in smoldering ashes. To oven-roast mixed vegetables, see pages 226–227.

Roasting eggplant, stove-top method   With a fork, prick the eggplant in several places and wrap it in three thicknesses of aluminum foil. Place the wrapped eggplant directly on the stove burner and cook on medium heat. Using long tongs and an oven mitt to avoid burning yourself, turn the eggplant every 3 or 4 minutes, so that it chars evenly all around. After 15 to 20 minutes, when the eggplant is soft and collapsed, remove it from the heat. Taking care to avoid the escaping steam, peel back the foil, slice the eggplant in half lengthwise, and put it in a colander to cool and drain.

Roasting eggplant, oven method   Preheat the oven to 400°. Prick the eggplant in several places with a fork, set it on a baking pan, and bake for about 1 hour, or until the eggplant skin is crinkly and the pulp is very soft. When the eggplant cools, halve it and scoop out the pulp for use in dips, spreads, and purées.

Roasting garlic   Preheat the oven to 375°. Remove some of the outer papery skin from whole heads of garlic, but do not break the heads apart into separate cloves. Cut off the top ½ inch of each head. Place the heads of garlic in a small, unoiled baking dish or on a sheet of aluminum foil. Add a tablespoon of water and either cover the baking dish tightly with foil or fold the sheet of aluminum foil to form a sealed package.

Bake for 45 to 60 minutes, until the cloves are very soft to the touch. When cool enough to handle, squeeze out the garlic paste and discard the skins.

Roasting peppers, stove-top method Place a bell pepper directly on the stove burner and center it to maximize contact with the flame. Adjust the flame to medium-high and, using long tongs, turn the pepper every 1 to 2 minutes to char the skin evenly, roasting it for 8 to 10 minutes. When the skin is blackened and blistery and the flesh is soft, place the roasted pepper in a covered bowl or paper bag to cool. The steam created in these closed containers will loosen the pepper's skin. When the pepper is cool enough to handle, use a paring knife or your fingers to peel and discard the skin, then cut the pepper in half and remove the seeds.

Roasting peppers, oven method Preheat the oven to 550°. Arrange the peppers on a baking sheet and roast for 15 to 20 minutes. Turn several times, until the peppers are charred evenly on all sides. Transfer the peppers to a covered bowl or a closed paper bag. When the peppers are cool enough to handle, slice them in half lengthwise, remove the seeds and membranes, and peel away the bitter skins.

Roasting peppers, broiler method Cut the peppers in half and place them on a foil-lined broiler pan, cut side down. Broil for 5 to 10 minutes; if necessary, reposition them under the flame so that they will char evenly. Follow the steaming and peeling directions described in the stove-top and oven methods.

SAUTÉING A quick, high-heat cooking method that seals in the natural juices, sets colors, and preserves the integrity of each ingredient. Traditionally, a little oil is preheated in an open pan, but a small amount of broth, wine, or water can be used instead of oil. The process is a rapid one in which vegetables, for example, are added to a hot pan and stirred or shaken frequently to prevent sticking. The French verb *sauter* means "to jump," which is what the vegetables do when the frying pan is shaken. A well-sautéed vegetable is brightly colored and crisp-tender to the bite.

SECTIONING ORANGES Slice off the ends of an orange, place it, cut side down, on the working surface, and slice down the curved sides with broad strokes all the way around the outside, positioning the knife just deep enough to remove the peel and the white pith. Holding the peeled orange over a bowl to catch the dripping juices as you section it, slip a paring knife between the membrane and one of the sides of each orange section. Cut in toward the center of the orange and then cut back out the other side with a motion resembling a V; the orange section will fall into the bowl. Repeat this process around the entire orange and then squeeze the juice from the membrane into the bowl.

SEEDING We always remove the seeds of bell peppers and occasionally those of chiles and cucumbers. Seeding chiles decreases their hotness. Overly mature cucumbers have large seeds that can alter the texture and appearance of a dish—halve the cucumber lengthwise and scoop out the seeds with a spoon.

SIMMERING Cooking gently at a very low boil.

SLICING Cutting food into pieces, either crosswise or lengthwise depending on the intended use— sometimes to produce halves or quarters and sometimes to produce even slices usually from ⅛ to ¾ inch thick. Slices for any specific dish should be of uniform thickness to ensure uniform cooking.

SOAKING

Soaking dried mushrooms Immerse dried mushrooms in boiling water and set aside to soak for 20 to 30 minutes. Remove the mushrooms and discard any tough stems before slicing. Some mushrooms are gritty; you may need to strain the soaking liquid before using it in cooking.

Soaking sun-dried tomatoes Cover with boiling water and soak for 15 minutes. Drain and save the flavorful liquid for use in stocks and sauces.

SPICES, WHOLE

Grinding spices A regular practice at Moosewood. We grind whole spices just before using them to maximize their flavors and aromas. Small coffee grinders make perfect spice grinders and can also pulverize small quantities of grains, nuts, and seeds. If you have the time, patience, and muscular endurance, you can use the original spice grinder, a mortar and pestle. A mortar is a heavy ceramic, marble, or wooden bowl and a pestle is usually a small cigar-shaped mallet of equal durability. Whole spices are placed in the mortar and pounded to a fine powder with the pestle.

Roasting spices   Roasting whole dried spices strengthens and enhances the flavor and aroma. It is an especially good technique to use when a single spice is featured in a dish or when dried spices are used in uncooked dishes. Spices can also be spread on a dry tray and roasted in an oven or toaster oven. They usually brown quickly, so set your oven at 300° and check after 3 to 5 minutes, or when you notice their aroma. The most burnproof method is to toast spices in a dry, heavy skillet on medium heat. Shake the pan frequently for even browning.

SWEATING   A nonfat cooking method that utilizes and maximizes an ingredient's natural sugars and juices. Sweating involves cooking on low heat until the ingredient "sweats," or releases its own moisture. Cooking continues in these natural juices until a desired effect is achieved.

THICKENING, A LOW-FAT TECHNIQUE   To make a low-fat thickener that can sometimes substitute for the traditional butter-milk-and-flour roux, use a low-fat liquid such as stock, skim milk, or fruit juice and vigorously whisk in 2 tablespoons of flour per cup of liquid. With cornstarch, arrowroot, or potato starch, dissolve 1 tablespoon in an equal amount of cool water and then stir it into the liquid. Bring to a simmer on medium heat, stirring frequently. If using arrowroot and potato starch, the sauce will be finished and without a starchy flavor just before it comes to a boil; with cornstarch, the sauce is finished after it begins to boil and becomes clear; and with flour, the sauce will be opaque and require several minutes of simmering to avoid a raw flour flavor.

TOFU   See pages 439–440 for a description of tofu. This high-protein soy product has a high water content. We have found that after we extract water from tofu, it absorbs other flavors more fully. Extracting water also makes tofu denser and chewier so that it holds up better during cooking. Below are two methods for removing water from tofu:

Freezing tofu   Thawed frozen tofu has a very chewy texture. We use it in chili, cabbage rolls, and other dishes that traditionally use meat. To freeze, arrange the cakes of tofu on a plate or baking sheet and freeze for 4 to 6 hours. Transfer the frozen tofu to the refrigerator and thaw for 10 to 12 hours. If thawing is not complete when you are ready to cook, complete the process either by baking the tofu, covered, at 350° for 15 to 20 minutes or by zapping it for 5 minutes in a microwave. When the tofu is thawed, squeeze out as much water as possible, like you would a sponge. Don't worry about mangling it. Once squeezed, the tofu should be crumbled, shredded, or grated for use.

Pressing tofu   Sandwich cakes of firm or soft Chinese-style tofu between two plates or baking sheets. Rest a weight—a heavy can or book—on the top plate or baking sheet. Press for 30 minutes. Then remove the weight and the top cover and drain the water from the bottom plate. The tofu is now ready for use.

YOGURT CHEESE, MAKING   Naturally thick, creamy yogurt cheese can replace sour cream, heavy cream, or cream cheese in many savory and sweet recipes. Most nonfat yogurts work as well as the higher-fat yogurts.

For 1 quart of yogurt cheese, line a colander or large sieve with overlapping paper coffee filters or several layers of cheesecloth and set it in a large bowl. Spoon 1 quart of nonfat plain yogurt into the colander and cover with a plate or plastic wrap. Refrigerate for 3 to 4 hours, or overnight, and pour off the liquid whey that collects in the bottom of the bowl. Yogurt cheese has the consistency of soft cream cheese and will keep, well covered and refrigerated, for about 1 week.

GUIDE TO INGREDIENTS

ANISE The seeds of this herbaceous plant have been used for decades to lend a smoky, sweet, licorice flavor to cakes, cookies, curries, breads, cheeses, and liqueurs. Anise leaves, with their hint of licorice, can be minced into fruit salads and vinaigrettes or used whole as a garnish. (Fennel bulb, in the produce world, is often labeled anise, though the two plants are unrelated. The licorice flavor characteristic of both anise and fennel is most likely the root of this widespread confusion.) Anise seeds (aniseeds) are readily available in the spice section of most supermarkets. Fennel seeds—also licorice-flavored—are often interchangeable with anise seeds in ground spice combinations, although the seeds are not identical.

ANNATTO (*achiote seeds*) The rust-red seeds of an evergreen tree native to South America and the Caribbean. Though flavorless, annatto is prized in both the home kitchen and the commercial food world for its brilliant yellow-orange coloring property. At Moosewood, we gently heat the seeds in oil to extract their color. When we sauté raw rice or millet in a little of this annatto oil and then cook as usual, the finished grain has a bright yellow hue. To make ¼ cup of annatto oil, swirl 1 tablespoon of annatto seeds in ¼ cup of vegetable oil. Cook for about 5 minutes on medium-low heat, until the oil turns a deep red-orange. Strain the oil to remove the seeds and it's ready for use. Annatto oil, tightly capped and refrigerated, will keep for about a week. Annatto seeds can be purchased from Latin American and Caribbean food stores and specialty spice shops.

APRICOTS These rosy, delicate-looking fruits have dense flesh and a mild sweetness. Because of their firm texture, they hold up well as toppings on tarts and bottoms in upside-down cakes. Fresh and unsweetened canned apricots can be puréed and used as a replacement for oil in some baked goods recipes. Dried apricots, simmered in water and then puréed, can also replace oil, but because the dried fruit has such concentrated flavor, you will probably not use as much as you would of the fresh fruit purée.

Dried apricots are delicious and pair up well with almonds or hazelnuts. We prefer the unsulfured dried fruit for its purity and superior flavor. Although some imported varieties are plump and tender, many dried apricots need to be soaked before cooking. Look for different varieties of dried apricots at natural food stores, Middle Eastern groceries, and specialty fruit and nut shops.

ARTICHOKES This vegetable is exotic from the way it grows to the way it is eaten. Artichokes are the fruit of a low-growing, Dr. Seuss-like plant that has stems spiking in every direction and an artichoke globe dangling from each stem. Artichokes are fun to eat and can be a great vehicle for fresh herb vinaigrettes and light cream sauces. To prepare and cook fresh artichokes, see page 311. To eat an artichoke, pull off the leaves one at a time, dip the bottom edge of each leaf into the sauce, then scrape off the fleshy pulp with your teeth. Discard the rest of the leaf. After you've eaten the outer leaves, you'll come to small inner leaves, which are very tender and tasty. Beneath these leaves is a feathery, inedible choke. With a spoon, gently scrape out the choke to reveal the most delicious part of the artichoke, the heart. Cut the heart into bite-sized pieces, dip them into the sauce—or not—and swoon.

The peak season for fresh artichokes is spring, but they are available year-round in many supermarkets. Ready-to-use **artichoke hearts** are available frozen or packed in brine or in an oil marinade. We prefer the brine-packed variety; they have no added fat and, unlike the frozen hearts, they absorb flavor and piquancy from the salt and citric acid in their brine. Both canned and marinated artichoke hearts are usually located in the specialty or imported food section of the supermarket.

ASIAN FISH SAUCE (*nam pla*) A salty, Southeast Asian seasoning and condiment that adds depth and unique flavor to foods and is rich in protein and B vitamins. Fish sauce is an extract of fermented anchovies; don't be put off by its strong odor—it will quickly cook away. The best fish sauces are bottled and imported from Vietnam and Thailand. They are available at Asian food stores and many supermarkets.

ASPARAGUS Ah! One of spring's first offerings. Fresh, tender asparagus need very little help. Snap off their tough, white bottoms, hold them under gently running water to remove any sand, blanch them quickly until their color brightens, and serve with a lemon wedge and a splash of olive or walnut oil. When shopping for asparagus, choose stalks that are unblemished, uniform in size, and tightly budded.

AVOCADOS At Moosewood, we favor Hass avocados —a variety with a buttery taste, creamy texture, and lovely two-tone color. Hass are recognizable by their dark green pebbled skin. An avocado is ripe when it just yields to the pressure of your thumb; to speed ripening, place in a paper bag with a banana. Refrigerate once ripe. A squirt of lemon on the cut surface of an avocado will retard oxidation and keep the flesh from turning brown. Wrap cut avocados in plastic or place in an airtight container and store in the refrigerator.

Interestingly, avocados appear to vary in fat content. The October 1995 issue of *Health Magazine* reported that avocados harvested from April through October are three times fattier (6 grams versus 2 grams per ounce) than early season avocados available from November through March.

BAGUETTE Like its skinnier relative, the ficelle, this fat-free French bread is traditionally made with white flour, water, salt, and yeast. Because it contains no oil, French bread is best eaten the day it is made (if you can, wait till you get home). It can be used to good effect on days two and three, however, especially if stored in plastic. Day-old baguettes may be better toasted and stale baguettes make delicious French toast, bread puddings, croutons, and bread crumbs.

BARLEY A sweet, dense grain that adds substance and variety to soups, pilafs, and vegetable stuffings. Because of its density, it requires more water and longer cooking than most grains (page 415). We recommend using unrefined barley because it is a good source of protein, calcium, and iron. Pearled barley, which we never use, is little more than pure starch. Look for unrefined barley in natural food stores and in the bulk food section of large supermarkets.

BEETS This ruby root vegetable can be grated raw for use as a colorful salad garnish, cooked and pickled or marinated as a side dish, or added plain to soups and stews. When using raw beets, peel the skin with a paring knife or vegetable peeler before grating. If preparing cooked beets, boil or roast them in their jackets until tender. Drain and cool. When the beets can be handled, slip off the skins and proceed with your recipe.

BERBERE This luscious hot spice blend distinguishes many Ethiopian and Eritrean dishes, lending spark, depth, and flavor. Berbere is available where African provisions are sold and in specialty spice shops. It can be made at home by toasting and grinding dried red chiles, cumin seeds, cloves, and sweet paprika. To these spices, add smaller quantities of ground cardamom, black pepper, allspice, fenugreek, coriander seed, turmeric, cinnamon, dried ginger, and salt. Whether commercial or homemade, store berbere in a well-sealed jar or plastic bag and refrigerate.

BISCOTTI The generic term for a variety of Italian oblong cookies that have been twice-baked—to perfection. These delicious toasts, often flavored with anise or almond, are slightly sweet and crisp enough to dip in a favorite coffee, tea, or cocoa. Low-fat biscotti recipes appear in this book (pages 390–392), but commercial biscotti, which are available in many supermarkets, bakeries, and coffee shops, may be higher in fat, especially if they are nut-filled or frosted.

BLACK BEANS *(black turtle beans)* These dried legumes appear in many South American dishes. They should not be confused with Chinese black beans, which are a type of soybean that has been fermented and seasoned. For soaking and cooking instructions, see page 414. One cup of dried beans yields 3 cups of cooked. Canned (precooked) black beans are also widely available. Look for dried or canned black beans at natural food stores and Latin American markets and in the Latin American section of your supermarket.

BLACK-EYED PEAS A staple of Southern cooking, we also use black-eyed peas in Caribbean dishes in place of the more difficult to procure pigeon peas and field peas. Outside of the South, black-eyed peas are available dried, canned, or frozen—each tastes quite different, but all taste lighter than most other beans. Dried black-eyed peas do not need to be soaked before cooking, and 1 cup of raw, dried peas yields 2½ cups of cooked peas. Black-eyed peas are available in most supermarkets.

BLACK MUSTARD SEEDS Widely used as a spice in India, when heated, black mustard seeds have a nutty aroma and milder flavor than the more familiar yellow mustard seeds. For use in cooking, toast the seeds in a dry skillet and then grind them, or sauté the seeds in a small amount of oil until you hear them pop, and then drain and add them to your dish. Black mustard seeds can be found in Indian or Asian markets and in specialty spice stores.

BLACK PEPPERCORNS The dried berries of a tropical vine, peppercorns are a kitchen staple in their ground form. Black, green, and white peppercorns are all from the same plant. Green peppercorns are the unripened berry, black peppercorns turn from green to black after they've been dried, and white peppercorns are ripened, hulled, and processed. For the sharpest and freshest taste, we recommend freshly grinding peppercorns directly into a dish. For large quantities of ground pepper, use a spice grinder (pages 418–419).

BREAD CRUMBS Our recipes simply call for stale bread that has been pulverized in a blender or food processor. We generally use whole wheat bread, but for those on very low-fat diets, crumbs made from fat-free breads such as French, Italian, or nonfat pita breads can easily be substituted.

BROCCOLI RABE (rapini, broccoli rape, rappi, Italian broccoli, broccoli de rabe) This stalked vegetable resembles broccoli, except it has sparse florets and large, slightly bitter leaves, which are meant to be eaten. Chinese broccoli, though a different plant, looks similar and can be substituted for rabe. The Chinese variety is reputed to be extremely high

in calcium and also rich in vitamin A and iron. To prepare, sauté rabe quickly in olive or peanut oil with minced garlic and/or freshly grated ginger root. Toss with your favorite pasta or noodles. Look for broccoli rabe where you buy produce and in Asian markets.

BUCKWHEAT GROATS See **Kasha**.

BULGUR (cracked wheat) An unrefined, easily digestible whole grain popular in Armenia, Greece, Turkey, and the Middle East. Bulgur is most often used in side dishes or pilafs, or as a base for salads—tabouli salad being perhaps the most familiar. Wheat is parboiled to produce bulgur, so it is already partially cooked and therefore quick to prepare. Simply add an equal amount of boiling water to the bulgur, tightly cover the pot or bowl for 20 to 30 minutes, then stir to fluff. If the grains are too firm or chewy—they should be fluffy—add an additional ¼ cup of boiling water and cover for another 10 minutes. Bulgur is available in various grinds from coarse to fine at natural food stores and where Middle Eastern foods are sold.

BUTTERMILK It may sound like a high-fat product, but don't be misled; buttermilk is one of the original low-fat wonder foods. Buttermilk's thick and creamy texture is the result of fermenting skim or 1% milk with a bacterial culture. It has a slightly tangy taste—though much less so than plain yogurt—so it can be added to creamy soups, sauces, and baked goods without major sweetening adjustments.

CALLALOO A type of spinach native to the West Indies, callaloo also gives its name to a popular Caribbean stew in which it is the principal ingredient. In Ithaca, we've only been able to locate canned callaloo.

CANNELLINI These dried white kidney beans are present in the popular Italian minestrones and pasta e fagioli. In Ithaca, we have only found them canned, but perhaps an Italian market near you can supply the dried beans.

CAPERS The tiny, green buds of a flowering Mediterranean plant that come packed in brine or salt. We only use the brine-packed variety, which are less salty. They are used around the world as a sprightly ingredient in stews, sauces, and salads. The sharp, salty quality of capers makes them a good counterpoint to both acidic and creamy sauces and a particularly good complement to fish. The labor-intensive harvesting and importing of capers drives up their price; fortunately, they are an intense ingredient that should be used sparingly. Capers are available in the imported food section of many supermarkets and in gourmet shops.

CAROB *(St. John's bread)* The 4-inch-long carob bean grows on a Mediterranean evergreen tree in the locust family. It encases a seed that is processed into locust gum, a commercial food thickener. The pulp surrounding the seed is dried, roasted, and milled into carob powder. Carob powder has a pleasant, bittersweet taste that has gained a mixed reputation. Heralded by devotees as a guilt-free alternative to chocolate, carob sometimes provokes righteous indignation from those expecting chocolate, which it decidedly is not.

Carob, with its unique flavor, is a naturally sweet, low-fat, caffeine-free, and protein- and iron-rich food. With a little added sweetener, carob can be stirred into heated milk or soy milk for a soothing beverage, incorporated into bread doughs and cake batters, or made into a sauce for topping frozen yogurt. Carob powder can be found at natural food stores.

CASSAVA MEAL *(manioc flour)* This meal, ground from the tuber of the tropical cassava plant, is used as a starch and a condiment throughout much of South America and in other parts of the tropical world. (Our familiar tapioca is also derived from the cassava plant, but the 2 products cannot be substituted for each other.) Cassava meal can be found at African, Caribbean, and Latin American grocery stores and occasionally in large supermarkets with imported food sections.

CAYENNE A finely ground, dried hot red pepper. The name originally referred to peppers grown on the island of the same name in French Guyana, but today cayenne simply signifies ground red pepper and is made from peppers from many parts of the world. Cayenne is available in the spice section of the supermarket, or you can grind your own at home from either whole dried hot red peppers or crushed red pepper. See grinding spices, pages 418–419.

CELLOPHANE NOODLES *(bean threads)* Clear, cholesterol-free noodles made from mung bean starch. They add bulk and an enjoyable slippery texture to Asian soups and stews without being filling. They are also an option for people who are sensitive or allergic to wheat or gluten. To prepare cellophane noodles, soak them in hot tap water until soft before adding them to your dish. Cellophane noodles can be purchased in varying thicknesses at Asian food stores and often in the Asian section of large supermarkets.

CHANTERELLE MUSHROOMS A wild, edible, funnel-shaped mushroom found growing in dry, coniferous forests. Their pleasant taste is brought to life by grilling or lightly sautéing. Chanterelles are available fresh or dried. For preparation techniques for dried foods, see page 418. Wild mushrooms, especially dried, are intensely flavored, so a few go far. Chanterelles are available in the produce section of specialty markets or, if you're lucky, in the woods near your home (be sure you know your mushrooms or check with a mycologist).

CHICKPEAS *(garbanzo beans)* Popular in cuisines from Latin America to the Middle East, these versatile legumes find their way into spreads, salads, side dishes, and as major players in soups and stews. Chickpeas are prepared like other dried beans (page 414). One cup of raw chickpeas yields 3 cups of cooked. Canned chickpeas are readily available and dried chickpeas can be purchased at natural food stores and in the Latin American or ethnic section of many supermarkets.

CHILES *(chili peppers)* The hot members of the *Capsicum* family, which also includes sweet bell peppers. There is a staggering variety of chiles to choose from, with new ones appearing regularly thanks to hybridization. And there certainly is a market. Hot peppers are used the world over, from Eastern Europe's hot paprika to the fiery peppers in Szechuan cooking. At Moosewood, we always keep fresh serranos on hand and use them as our general-purpose chile. Our other favorites include habañeros, Scotch bonnets, jalapeños, and Thais.

Chiles are a favorite ingredient at Moosewood. Their piquancy not only lends heat and spice to certain traditional ethnic dishes, but it can wake up the flavors in many dishes or add just the right zing when needed. The hotness of chiles cannot be predicted. If you prefer milder food, remove the membranes and seeds. Bear in mind that some fresh chiles lose their heat during cooking. We suggest starting conservatively and tasting as you go.

When handling chiles, refrain from touching your eyes, lips, and other sensitive areas to avoid a nasty burning sensation, and wash with warm soapy water directly after touching chiles. If your skin is very sensitive, latex gloves can be worn during preparation. If you eat something too hot for your tolerance, don't reach for your water glass—water will only make the sensation worse. Instead, eat something starchy, like rice or a bit of bread. Fresh chiles are available at produce stands and supermarkets. Dried chili peppers, which will be hotter than the fresh, should be crushed, ground, or rehydrated before use. They can be found whole in some produce departments and in many ethnic grocery stores, or you can dry your own.

CHINESE BLACK BEANS *(fermented black beans, salted black beans, preserved black beans)* A pleasing blend of salty, spicy, and sweet, these fermented and seasoned black soybeans are salted and then treated with ginger and orange; no oil is used. We've found fermented beans to be especially good on fish and seafood, but the Chinese have also flavored meats, poultry, and vegetables with this seasoning for centuries. To use Chinese black beans, either mash the beans with a potato masher or chop them slightly. Their saltiness can be reduced by a quick rinse or else figured into the preparation of a dish. Chinese black beans can be found in plastic packages in Asian food stores and in the Asian section of some supermarkets.

Don't confuse or interchange them with dried black turtle beans—entirely different beans that are not processed as a flavoring agent.

CHINESE CABBAGE A generic name for a wide variety of greens in the cabbage family that are used most often in Asian cookery. Two that are widely available in produce markets are **bok choy** and **celery cabbage**. Bok choy has dark green leaves and a thick white stem. Both the leaves and the stem have a slightly bitter but not unpleasant taste. The stems should be cooked longer than the greens. Celery cabbage, named because it is shaped like a broad stalk of celery, is uniformly light green and sweet tasting. Again, the entire vegetable is usable. Chinese cabbages can be steamed or sautéed. They are often available in supermarkets and Asian markets, where you may also find other varieties that are well worth trying.

CHINESE CHILI PASTE This intensely flavored condiment lends a rich and spicy lift to Chinese and Southeast Asian dishes. If you're made of stern stuff, do as many Vietnamese do and spoon it on full strength. Supermarket shelves boast a huge variety of chili pastes. The most common are made of fermented and crushed chili peppers, salt, oil, and often garlic. Other pastes include preserved radish and fermented soybeans. We recommend Chinese chili pastes for their flavor and purity. Some Southeast Asian brands of chili paste contain preservatives and are simply not as good. Chinese chili pastes can be found in Asian food stores and in the Asian section of some supermarkets. Chili paste is generally bottled and will keep indefinitely if tightly capped and refrigerated.

CHINESE RICE WINE *(Shaoxing)* The cooking wine of China, this is a dry rice wine that, if necessary, can be replaced by a dry sherry. Sake and sweet cooking sherries are not substitutes. Chinese rice wine is available at Asian food stores and in the Asian section of some supermarkets.

CHOCOLATE Derived from the bean of the cocoa tree whose generic name *theobrama* means "food of the gods." Ripe cocoa beans are dried and then pressed to obtain cocoa butter; then the pressed pods are ground into cocoa powder. All chocolate is made from some combination of cocoa butter, cocoa powder, and sugar. Most of the fat in chocolate comes from the cocoa butter, which is why substituting cocoa powder for chocolate in a dish will lower its fat content.

COCOA See **Chocolate**.

COCONUT An excellent source of protein, vitamins, and minerals, coconut is also high in fat. Choose coconuts with unblemished shells without cracks. When you shake a coconut, you should hear the liquid in the center splash; otherwise it is old and the nutmeat is likely to be shrunken and less than tender. To add a bit of coconut flavor without as much fat, try some of the natural coconut flavorings available at natural food stores.

COCONUT MILK In Southeast Asia, Africa, and the Caribbean, this smooth, rich-flavored liquid is used in soups, sauces, curries, and desserts. We use unsweetened coconut milk without preservatives, such as Epicurean International brand, or we make our own by steeping fresh or dried coconut in an equal amount of hot water, then puréeing and straining. For extended storage, freeze leftover coconut milk in ice cube trays and then transfer the cubes to a closed container. Heavily sweetened cream of coconut intended for beverage mixers should not be used as a substitute. Reduced-fat coconut milk, however, is a welcome addition to the supermarket shelves and will work fine.

COCONUT RICE This golden-hued fragrant variation of plain cooked rice can add flair to many Indian, Asian, African, or Caribbean meals. Sauté 2 cups of brown rice in a little oil with ½ cup of unsweetened coconut flakes and 1½ teaspoons of turmeric for 1 or 2 minutes. Add 4 cups of water and ½ of a cinnamon stick, cover, and cook as usual (page 416). Remove the cinnamon stick before serving.

COLLARD GREENS A variety of cabbage that does not form a head. The pleasant taste of collards is milder than that of most of the cabbage family; collards are an excellent source of vitamins, minerals, and fiber. The stems are slender and tender and can be added to a dish along with the leaves. Collard greens readily absorb the flavors of vinegars, sauces, or spices and are often paired with beans in traditional Southern cuisine.

COOKING SPRAY Most supermarkets now offer oil in aerosol cans. Less oil can be more evenly distributed over a cooking surface when a spray is used—helpful for those who are trying to severely limit their fat intake. Look for cooking sprays that use canola or olive oils, since these monounsaturated oils are considered the healthiest choices by most present-day nutrition experts. Some of the cooking sprays advertise that they have a buttery flavor, which sounds appealing, but, alas, we didn't like any of the brands we tried and we recommend you avoid sprays bearing this enticing claim. For more information, see page 15.

CORNICHONS These small pickles are named for their shape, which resembles the horn (or *corne*) of an animal. Made from a special variety of cucumber that has a limited growing season, then cooked in vinegar or cured in brine, they can be a bit pricey, but their unique flavor is difficult to imitate. If you have difficulty finding them in the imported food section of the supermarket, fresh sour pickles are the closest substitute; dill pickles are not the same.

CORNMEAL A term for either yellow or white flour produced by stone-grinding or crushing corn. Stone-ground cornmeal retains the germ, while crushing removes both the hull and germ. Stone-ground cornmeal is often richer in flavor, with a somewhat higher moisture content than the crushed variety.

COTTAGE CHEESE Produced from skim milk and a starter—often rennet or buttermilk, cottage cheese has a creamy consistency, is high in protein and calcium, and comes in both large- and small-curd varieties. When drained and whipped, it makes a spread that is similar to cream cheese but much lower in fat. Even so, regular cottage cheese (4%) has 9.5 grams of fat per cup.

Nonfat offerings on the market boast no grams of fat and half the calories, but we are not impressed by the taste, texture, or performance of many of the nonfat brands. Knudsen has created a nonfat cottage cheese using cultured nonfat milk that is one of the few satisfactory ones we've found. In general, we recommend using 1% cottage cheese. Most 1% brands have about a quarter of the fat of regular cottage cheese, and they far surpass the flavor and texture of their nonfat counterparts.

COUSCOUS Finely pearled semolina is a durum wheat often used in pasta making. Originating in North African countries where grain was ground at home, couscous is now available ready to cook in boxes and in the bulk sections of many supermarkets. It is quick cooking, taking less than 10 minutes to become tender, and can be steamed in a sieve or covered with boiling water and fluffed before serving (page 415). Both whole wheat varieties with their light brown color and slightly nutty flavor and regular couscous with its yellow color and milder flavor are delicious and convenient.

CRANBERRIES, DRIED Sometimes called *craisins* due to their resemblance to raisins, dried cranberries are somewhat sweeter than fresh cranberries and add a tart-sweet, delicious flavor to desserts, rice dishes, and breads. Some varieties are sweetened. You can usually find them with the specialty items in supermarkets or at natural food stores or bakery shops.

CREAM OF TARTAR Technically potassium bitartrate, this sediment substance results from the winemaking process of grape fermentation. It is refined and used both alone and as a main ingredient of baking powder in pastries, cakes, quick breads, and other baked goods.

CROSTINI, or "toast" in Italian, is crisp sliced bread spread with a savory topping. The best bread for crostini is a coarse, firm whole grain loaf, but a thin Italian loaf or French baguette is acceptable.

CURRANTS A term used to describe both a dried variety of seedless grapes and the fresh berries from a bush of the genus *Ribes*. The berry bush variety can be red, white, or black and has a tart flavor; it is most often used in making jellies. The dried variety, whose quality depends on the type of grape and the soil conditions, is the one commonly used in cooking and is what we use at Moosewood. These currants are tiny, black, and sweet. Most come from the Vostizza region of Greece and are widely exported, although California, South Africa, and Australia also produce some currants for domestic use. Currants provide a raisinlike flavor without adding as much chewy texture to the dish. Their dark color also provides a visual accent when used as a garnish on curries, stews, or fruit salads.

CURRY The name originally given to those East Indian vegetable and meat dishes that use a pungent sauce made from curry spices mixed with a cooking liquid, yogurt, or coconut milk.

Curry paste is a Southeast Asian condiment that combines curry spices and vegetable oils. It is a highly concentrated flavoring, so adding a little can have a significant impact on a dish. We use curry pastes in soups, sauces, dressings, sautés, rice dishes, and, of course, in curries. Curry pastes, like curry powders, have a range of flavors and different levels of spiciness. To make one that we like at Moosewood, try Thai Curry Paste (page 365).

Curry powder is a combination of ground spices that almost always includes cumin, coriander, turmeric, cardamom, cayenne, and cinnamon and sometimes additional spices such as nutmeg, fenugreek, cloves, anise or fennel, and black pepper. When making your own, toast the seeds (page 419) just before grinding to produce a more robust flavor and to remove the harsher edge of uncooked spices. Most supermarket curry blends are uninteresting; we suggest you experiment at home to make a blend you like—and then write it down—or shop in Asian markets to discover a prepared curry powder that has the flavor and hotness you desire.

DASHI This Japanese stock is used for soups and sauces, for basting, and for cooking rice. The most common dashis are made by simmering konbu (a type of ocean seaweed or kelp), a combination of konbu and bonito flakes (a mackerel-like marine fish), or shiitake (dried mushrooms) in water and then straining. The strained cooking liquid is *dashi*. For our dashi recipes, see pages 75 and 76.

ESCAROLE Also known as batavia, this green vegetable grows in heads. It has broad, crisp, somewhat curly green leaves and a heart of paler yellowish-white leaves. It is pleasantly bitter, with a flavor similar to chicory or curly endive, and can be added raw to salads or steamed like spinach.

EVAPORATED SKIMMED MILK A thick, creamy, sweet, nonfat milk produced by evaporating 50 percent of the water from fresh skim milk. It can be used in puddings, pies, and sweet sauces. The heat required for canning evaporated milk caramelizes the milk sugar, giving it a light brown color and sweet taste. Evaporated skimmed milk is available in most supermarkets.

FARFALLE Butterfly or bow tie-shaped pasta.

FAVA BEANS A legume also known as broad beans, commonly used in Middle Eastern, Chinese, Italian, and North African cuisines. We use canned favas in our recipes—we have never found fresh ones available in our area but your farmer's market or Italian grocer may offer them. The bean is large, flat, and similar in color and shape to a lima bean. Although dried favas are higher in amino acids and vitamins B and E than canned or fresh, we don't recommend using them unless you find a reliable source. The dried beans we've tried have tough hulls and cook unevenly. Even with good-quality dried beans, it is best to remove the shells and tough outer skins of the beans before cooking.

FENNEL This member of the parsley family is native to the Mediterranean and is a widely cultivated aromatic perennial with umbelliferous, or umbrella-like, flowers. Both bitter

and sweet varieties are grown. The feathery fernlike leaves with their mild licorice flavor are delicious in soups or stews or for garnishing savory dishes. **Fennel seeds** are harvested from this plant and used whole in biscuits, marinades, and strudels or ground in soups, stews, curries, and sauces. The slightly sweet licorice flavor adds a depth and complexity to dishes—which sometimes makes them taste very much like meat-based versions. Fennel seeds are available in the spice section of supermarkets. We recommend grinding them (pages 418–419) just before use.

A different plant that also goes by the name of fennel is shorter and has a swollen leaf base that forms bulbs. **Fennel bulbs** have a crunchy texture like celery and can be sliced thinly and used raw in salads, cooked for a side dish, or incorporated into stews. Fennel bulbs, like common fennel, have a mild licorice taste and leaves that can be used as an herb or garnish. Fennel bulbs are popular in Italian cuisine and are sometimes referred to as Florence fennel. Produce markets often mistakenly label fennel bulbs as "anise."

Wild fennel—yet another type—is bitter and without the anise flavor. It is generally not used for culinary purposes.

FENUGREEK SEEDS The flat, oblong, brownish or yellowish seeds found in the pods of the fenugreek plant, a member of the pea family. Their bitter flavor adds a distinctive touch to dishes and is most widely encountered in Indian cuisine. We use freshly toasted (page 419) and ground (pages 418–419) fenugreek seeds in curries and dahls.

FETA This sharp, pure white, soft cheese from the Balkans, Greece, and the Middle East is traditionally made from goat's or sheep's milk. Usually sold in blocks, feta has a characteristic salty flavor because it is stored in brine to preserve it. Feta can be sliced and served as an appetizer, grated for a topping, or added to casseroles, omelets, dressings, sauces, or pastas. Middle Eastern groceries and most supermarkets stock it.

Those with allergies to cow's milk should check the ingredients on the label, since some fetas are made from cow's milk as well as from goat's and sheep's milk. Most American-made feta is lower in fat than varieties of cheese such as Cheddar, provolone, Swiss, or Muenster.

FETTUCCINE More often called tagliatelle in Europe, this long flat pasta noodle comes in many widths. Most commonly boiled until al dente and served with a sauce, olive oil, vegetables, or grated cheese, it rolls well onto a fork. Whole wheat and spinach varieties, in addition to the well-known semolina, are popular. It is available fresh in many Italian markets and dried in most supermarkets.

FIGS Both fresh and dried figs are available, and either way they are sweet and chewy. Fresh figs are high in fiber, especially the soluble fiber that can positively affect blood cholesterol levels—two fresh figs have more soluble fiber than ½ cup of Great Northern beans. Look for soft, plump figs with rich color. Dried figs are delicious as snacks and in desserts. Our favorite type is the Turkish Smyrna or its California relative, the Calimyrna. Black Mission figs are widely available, but they are generally smaller, drier, and not as sweet as the Smyrna variety.

FILBERTS See **Hazelnuts**.

FILO DOUGH *(phyllo)* Dough pressed into paper-thin sheets and used for making flaky, crisp strudels and pastries. Packaged filo dough is available in the refrigerated or frozen sections of many supermarkets and in Greek or Middle Eastern groceries.

FIVE-SPICE POWDER A fragrant, spicy Chinese seasoning made of ground Szechuan peppercorns, star anise, fennel, cumin, and cloves. Available in most Asian markets.

FLOUR Any ground cereal, such as wheat, oats, barley, rye, rice, and corn, is technically called *flour*, but most often the term applies to ground or milled wheat. At Moosewood, we use unbleached white all-purpose and pastry flours as well as whole wheat bread and pastry flours. Bleaching merely removes the slightly yellow color of the endosperm, that part of the wheat grain from which all flour is made. We think this is an unnecessary process and prefer unbleached varieties. While white flour produces the flakiest pastries, many tender pastries are possible with whole wheat flour or a combination of white and whole wheat flours. The whole wheat varieties are higher in fiber, vitamins, and minerals.

GARAM MASALA This North Indian roasted and ground spice mixture includes a combination of cardamom, cinnamon, cloves, coriander, cumin, and black peppercorns. Other spices that are occasionally added are fennel, nutmeg, mace, and saffron. Like curry powders, the exact blend of spices used in garam masala varies widely. Experiment with the ones in your local Asian markets or see almost any Indian cookbook for ideas. To make one that we like, see *Sundays at Moosewood Restaurant*, pages 293–294.

GARLIC This familiar aromatic herb is a perennial bulb that grows in round heads that harbor about 12 individual cloves. Select heads that are firm, look plump, are unshriveled, and have unbroken skin. Heads with large cloves are easier to peel. Elephant garlic, closely related to leeks, is about twice as large as regular garlic and is far milder in flavor. We never use dried garlic powder or garlic salt in our recipes. For peeling and roasting instructions, see pages 417–418.

GINGER ROOT Native to South Asia, India, China, and the West Indies, ginger is a firm light brown tuber with golden or amber flesh known for its spicy, pungent flavor. We most often use it finely grated. Ginger root is available in the produce section of most supermarkets and can be stored in a plastic bag and refrigerated for several weeks or frozen even longer. Dried crystallized ginger, often used in confections, has quite a different flavor and should not be substituted for fresh ginger root in our recipes.

GUAVA PASTE Made from the guava pulp collected during jelly making. Native to Central America and now grown in many tropical countries, guavas are greenish-yellow or pale pink in color and have thick rinds, a round shape, and a firm, soft, pulpy interior. The fruit can be sweet or somewhat sour, but it has the same distinctive, refreshing flavor that you must taste to know. Guavas are rich in phosphorus and vitamins A and C.

HAZELNUTS The fruit of the hazel tree is a hard-shelled nut with an oval kernel. It contains calcium, phosphorus, potassium, and sulfur—but is also high in calories and fat. Hazelnuts are usually sold dried, although it is possible to find some fresh nuts. Filberts are one variety of large, cultivated hazelnuts. For the best flavor and texture, we toast the nuts for about 10 minutes in a 325° oven, then rub them briskly with a towel to remove the skins.

HERBS Any of a variety of plants whose green leafy parts are used for seasoning, medicinal purposes, or for their fragrance. Herbs add flavor and fragrance to dishes but must be used with discretion. Certain combinations work better than others, and certain herbs are most associated with particular cuisines. Much herb expertise comes only with experience, and there is always the matter of personal preference as well.

Herbs we commonly use in cooking include basil, bay, chervil, cilantro, dill, marjoram, mint, oregano, parsley, rosemary, sage, tarragon, and thyme. We like to use fresh herbs for much of our cooking and never use dried parsley at all. Dried herbs have a concentrated, assertive flavor and should be added to dishes earlier in the cooking process, whereas fresh herbs should be stirred in near the end. When replacing dried herbs with fresh, use about three to four times the amount of fresh to dried.

HOISIN SAUCE This sweet Chinese condiment is traditionally used in *moo-shu* dishes, where it is spread on thin pancakes that are filled with stir-fried vegetables and rolled. Hoisin sauce is a deep chocolate-colored brown, has a smooth, thick texture, and contains soybeans, sugar, vinegar, and spices.

HOMINY Kernels of hulled, white maize that have a firm texture and a distinctive flavor. Grits are made of coarsely ground dried hominy. Whole hominy is available in the canned vegetable section of most supermarkets. Look for brands without preservatives or other additives.

HONEY The delectable, gooey, sweet substance manufactured by bees. Different honeys vary quite a bit in flavor. We recommend cooking with the milder, more neutrally flavored honeys, such as orange blossom or wildflower, which won't complicate the final taste of a dish or pastry. Stronger-flavored ones, such as buckwheat, conifer, and heather, should be used only when you wish to add that particular flavor to a dish or spread.

HORSERADISH An Eastern European perennial, horseradish is a traditional condiment in Russian, German, and Scandinavian cuisines. The grated flesh of the peeled root has a sharp, hot, cleansing bite. Jars of prepared horseradish packed in vinegar (and sometimes tinted bright fuchsia with beet juice) are found in the dairy section of supermarkets. Fresh horseradish can be grated directly onto dishes as an aromatic topping, much like freshly ground black peppercorns. Buy fresh roots that are very hard, have no soft spots, and have not begun to sprout.

HUNGARIAN HOT PEPPERS Small tapered peppers, longer than the average Mexican chiles and yellow or sometimes orange-tinted in color. Their appearance is similar to the Hungarian sweet banana pepper, which is perfectly mild, so most of us must depend on shopkeepers to label them correctly. The hot variety is often labeled Hungarian wax pepper or hot Hungarian wax pepper and is delicious minced into goulashes, sauces, dips, or relishes.

JERK A type of Caribbean seasoning that usually combines onions, chiles, nutmeg, allspice, cinnamon, and sugar for a piquant sauce or marinating blend.

KALE One of the best finds in the world of leafy greens, kale is a rich source of iron, fiber, and the vitamins A, C, and thiamine. As a late fall and early winter crop, it is a welcome source of fresh nutrients long after the abundance of summer has passed. Kale is one of recorded history's oldest vegetables—dating back to Anglo-Saxon times, when it was called peasant cabbage or winter greens. To keep kale (and most other leafy greens) crisp and fresh tasting, separate the leaves, rinse quickly, shake off the excess water, wrap in a dish towel, and then enclose in a plastic bag and refrigerate.

KASHA *(buckwheat groats)* Though botanically a fruit, in the world of food kasha is thought of as a cereal or grain. Kasha's seeds are protein- and vitamin-packed complex carbohydrates that cook up fluffy and flavorful. Kasha is most often used in pilafs, as part of vegetable and pastry fillings, and perhaps most notably in kasha varnishkas, an Eastern European kasha and bow tie noodle dish. Because it is not a true wheat, kasha—like other buckwheat products—is a good starch alternative for those who are wheat sensitive. People with nut allergies, however, may also have a reaction to buckwheat. For subtlety in cooking, choose among kasha's coarse, medium, and fine grades. The medium and fine grades serve as good hot cereals or fluffy bases for grain-based salads or vegetable fillings. Kasha can be purchased at natural food stores and in the kosher section of many supermarkets.

KASSERI CHEESE A mild, white, firm Greek cheese that is moderately low in fat and is available fresh for the table or dried for grating. Look for it where imported cheeses are sold.

KIDNEY BEANS These large, red, kidney-shaped dried beans are best known as the beans in chili con carne and three-bean salad. We use kidney beans in many Mexican, Creole, and Southwestern dishes. They are hearty, tasty, and colorful. Dried or canned beans are available at natural food stores and in the Latin American section of many supermarkets. If you are interested in beans canned without additives or preservatives, numerous brands line the shelves of natural food stores. For guidelines on cooking dried beans, see page 414. One cup of dried kidney beans yields 2¾ cups of cooked beans.

KONBU *(kombu; kelp)* Japanese people depend on this seaweed to enhance the flavor of their cooking. In an indirect way, so have cooks the world over, since the flavor enhancer MSG is extracted from it. In Japanese cuisine, konbu is used to flavor the traditional broth called dashi, which in turn becomes the foundation for many soups, stews, and dipping sauces. Konbu is available packaged and in bulk at many natural food stores and where Japanese foods are sold.

LEEKS This member of the onion family has a sweeter and less pungent taste than regular onions. With their narrow white bulbs and long-bladed green leaves, they closely resemble giant scallions and are good for soups, marinated vegetable plates, and delicate sauces. Sand and dirt often collect in the leaves of leeks. To clean and prepare them for use, slice off the tip of the root end and the tough part of the green leaves. Then slice the bulb in half lengthwise and separate the layers. Soak in cool water. Gently rub to remove the more stubborn grit. If the leeks will not be used whole in your recipe, chop them first, place in a strainer, and rinse well under running water.

LEMONGRASS An herb that distinguishes Southeast Asian cuisines and imparts a lemony aroma but not a strong citrus taste. Fresh lemongrass is a grey-green, 2-foot-long root stem. The usable portion is 6 to 8 inches of its bulblike base. Peel the tough external leaves. Then shred or slice the bulb. Dried shredded lemongrass is also available; soak in hot water for 30 minutes before using. When lemongrass is not available, lemon peel can substitute for—but will not replace the flavor of

—this ineffable herb. Lemongrass can often be found at Asian markets or in the Asian section of some diversified supermarket produce departments.

LENTILS These high-protein, quick-cooking legumes are the basis for many delicious soups, stews, side dishes, and salads. Lentils need not be soaked before cooking. The more familiar brown lentils cook in 30 to 40 minutes. Red lentils, which cook into a golden purée, need only 15 to 20 minutes. Try to find small French lentils, which remain firm and nutty after cooking. One cup of raw lentils yields 3 cups cooked. Lentils are available at natural food stores and many supermarkets.

MADEIRA A Portuguese wine fortified by the addition of brandy, Madeira is used in cooking, particularly French cuisine. Dry and sweet Madeiras are available at liquor stores.

MANGOES A staple fruit throughout much of the tropical world but perplexingly one that is only slowly gaining entry into our fruit repertoire in the United States. A ripe mango tastes heavenly. To determine ripeness, disregard its color and size and smell the stem end for a sweet scent. Mangoes that are odorless or winy are respectively underripe or overripe. A ripe mango should have the resilience of a ripe avocado, yielding to gentle thumb pressure. Store in the refrigerator when ripe. For instructions on peeling and slicing mangoes, see page 416.

MAPLE SYRUP One hundred percent pure maple syrup is golden bliss—which is why we insist on the real McCoy. It tends to be expensive, but our recipes rarely call for very much. While there are maple-flavored syrups available, they truly cannot be used as substitutes. Treat yourself if you haven't already. Your pancakes will taste better than ever. Pure maple syrup is available at many supermarkets, farm stands, and natural food stores.

MAYONNAISE Currently available at any major supermarket in low-fat, fat-free, and cholesterol-free versions. Some of these, like full-fat mayonnaise, contain hydrogenated oils (page 403). Spectrum Naturals, a manufacturer that specializes in oils, produces both a regular and a low-fat mayo that are additive-free and nonhydrogenated. Spectrum Naturals products are available at many natural food stores.

MESCLUN The original mesclun—a name derived from the French *mesclumo*, meaning "a mixture" —was composed of bitter greens such as chicory, dandelion, arugula, chervil, and salsify. Today mesclun refers to a mixture of bitter and sweet tender lettuces and the shoots and leaves of both wild and cultivated salad greens. It is often available at specialty markets, green-grocers, and some supermarkets.

MILK carton labels can be misleading. So the most relevant thing we can do is pass on a few facts. Per 8-ounce portion: whole milk contains 8.5 grams of fat, or 51 percent of calories from fat; 2 percent low-fat milk contains 4.7 grams of fat, or 35 percent fat; 1 percent low-fat milk contains 2.5 grams of fat, or 22 percent fat; skim milk or non-fat milk contains 0.4 grams of fat, or 4 percent fat. All milk fat is saturated fat.

MILLET This name applies to a number of grains, not all of which even belong to the same genus. The type of millet produced in the United States has tiny, round, yellow grains—familiar to many of us as a component of birdseed. Millet is not, however, strictly for the birds. Hulled, it is a quickly prepared, nutritious, and buttery grain that cooks in 20 minutes. It is a warming breakfast cereal and a good companion for strongly flavored stews. Millet is rich in iron, magnesium, and vitamins A and B. It is available at natural food stores and in the bulk section of many supermarkets.

MIRIN A Japanese sweet rice cooking wine used in stocks, dipping sauces, and marinades. Currently two mirins are on the market: hon-Mirin, a naturally brewed product of sake, sweet rice, and rice malt, and aji-Mirin, a wine that is seasoned with salt, fructose, and corn syrup. Serious Japanese cooks choose the hon-Mirin for its mild sweetness and subtle taste. If neither mirin is available, substitute ⅔ cup of dry sherry and ⅓ cup of sugar for 1 cup of mirin. Mirin is available where Japanese foods are sold.

MISO The salty, fermented soybean-grain paste used in Japanese cuisine to flavor broths, dipping sauces, marinades, and spreads. A variety of misos are available, ranging from the hearty red to the delicate yellow, depending on both the amount and type of salt and grain that are mixed with the beans and how long the mixture is fermented. Add miso at the end of cooking and, once added, do not allow your broth or stew to boil or the miso's highly useful digestive and antibacterial enzymes will be destroyed. Miso is available in Asian food stores, where Japanese foods are sold, and at natural food stores.

MORELS This variety of wild mushrooms has been described as sweet, nutty, and spicy. They can be used fresh or dried, but the dried mushrooms must be soaked in warm water for about 15 minutes before cooking. Both the fresh and dried mushrooms often have tough stems that must be discarded before using.

MUNG SPROUTS These slender, pearl-white sprouts are most crisp and best tasting when fresh— before they begin to yellow. They can be grown indoors and require nothing more than mung beans, a vessel, water, and a perforated lid. The result is a rich and available source of protein and vitamin C in the dead of winter. We use them to top salads, to stuff into pita sandwiches, and to garnish Asian dishes. Mung sprouts are available at Asian markets. They can be stored for 1 or 2 days in a sealed plastic bag in the refrigerator.

MUSTARD GREENS These beautiful ruffled leaves have an appealingly sharp bitter quality. Their hotness differs from that of dried mustard or chiles, and those who usually spurn hot spicy ingredients might want to give these a try. They are a mega-nutritious vegetable rich in beta-carotene, vitamin C, calcium, and potassium. Mustard greens bring zest to a salad

of milder, sweeter greens and add color and piquancy to blander foods like potatoes, polenta, pasta, or beans. Since they are often sandy, mustard greens should be cleaned thoroughly. Float the greens in cool water, so that the sand will sink to the bottom. Remove the greens, refill the sink, and repeat. Mustard greens are available in the produce section of many markets. A stronger-tasting variety can be found at Asian markets.

NAVY BEANS *(pea beans)* These small, white, dried beans are perhaps best known as the beans in Boston baked beans and navy bean soup. We think they are delicious in chilled bean salads, puréed and seasoned as a dip or spread, and as flavor magnets in a variety of bean and vegetable soups. Navy beans are available both dried and canned in supermarkets and natural food stores. A cup of dried navy beans yields 2¾ cups of cooked beans. For cooking instructions, see page 414.

NEUFCHÂTEL CHEESE A white, creamy cheese that, in many cases, can substitute for cream cheese, Neufchâtel is lower in fat than cream cheese—about 45 percent fat versus 85 percent fat. The name Neufchâtel derives from its home in France, where it has been produced since the Middle Ages. Neufchâtel is often foil wrapped like cream cheese and can usually be found near the cream cheese in supermarket dairy cases.

NORI *(laver)* A variety of seaweed that is sold dried in green-black sheets and perhaps is best known as the wrapper for sushi rolls. Before nori is used for sushi rolls, it should be toasted by waving it briefly over a candle or a medium flame on a gas stove. Toasted, nori has a deeper color and brighter sheen. Packaged toasted nori is also available. Both can be found where Japanese foods are sold and in natural food stores.

OILS A form of liquid fat used to prevent sticking and to add body, flavor, and a rich smoothness to foods, oil is a major ingredient in many dressings and sauces and a necessary component of many baked goods. For a discussion of oils and the types of fat they contain, see pages 402–404. Because olive oil and canola oil are high in monounsaturated fat and low in saturated fat, these are our first choices for home use. Because olive oil has a distinctive flavor, other oils cannot readily replace it in a recipe. Canola oil, on the other hand, can be replaced by another vegetable oil of your choice, but we recommend it for its potential health benefits despite its somewhat higher price.

OKRA This vegetable is popular throughout the world, but in the United States it has barely budged from the South since its arrival from Africa in the seventeenth century. At Moosewood, we've been including okra in more dishes over the last few years. It is tasty and nutritious and we love its splendid thickening quality. Because of okra's perishability, we rely on frozen okra for cooking and use fresh okra only for salads. Fresh okra is most often available in the summer. Choose the most tender, firm, and moist bright green pods. Avoid spotted, moldy, limp, or dry ones. Okra keeps for 1 or 2 days, refrigerated—but not in the crisper. Frozen okra is available whole or sliced in many supermarkets.

OLIVES Although relatively high in fat, olives add richness, color, tang, and saltiness to a dish; a little can go a long way. There are hundreds of varieties from many regions of the world, each with distinctive characteristics determined by the soil and climate in which it grows.

Calamata olives Dark blackish-brown olives with a glossy veneer and salty-sweet meaty taste, imported unpitted from Greece. We sometimes slice them away from the pits for use in very special traditional North African and Mediterranean dishes.

California ripe olives The black, pitted variety found in cans in the condiment aisle of almost any supermarket. Although they have less flavor than their imported counterparts, they add succulence, salt, and a mild olive flavor to salads, salsas, fillings, burritos, and tostadas.

Niçoise olives Small oval green or purplish-black olives with a milder flavor than calamatas, but with more depth and meatiness than the pitted California olives. Produced in Nice, in Southern France, they are available in gourmet and specialty food stores and are worth the splurge.

Spanish olives Unripened green olives stuffed with a pimiento or pickled sweet red pepper. We use these olives in enchilada fillings, in gazpacho, and sometimes in egg salads.

ORECCHIETTE "Little ears" in Italian, these small, flat, round shapes are a good choice for a pasta salad or a hearty sauce. Orecchiette can be found in Italian food stores and where imported pastas are sold.

ORZO Orzo is a small, rice-shaped pasta that adds great texture but is unobtrusive. Orzo cooks quickly, so it can be added raw to simmering soups and stews. It also provides a good bed for highly seasoned stews, fish, or seafood platters. Look for orzo in Italian or Greek groceries, gourmet food stores, and the ethnic section of your supermarket. Kids love it!

PARSNIPS Sweet root vegetables that look like ivory carrots, these are lovely puréed in soups or sliced in winter stews. Because parsnips can be strongly flavored and very sweet, be sure to taste them first. Mix them with milder-flavored carrots if more bulk is needed without added intensity. To prepare, peel parsnips as you would carrots and discard the woody core of the very large ones. They are available in the produce section of most supermarkets.

PASTA Perhaps dating back to pre-Roman Etruscan times in Italy, pasta has been produced commercially since 1400. Fresh pasta—which can be made at home—is always an egg and all-purpose flour pasta, whereas dry pasta is made in factories with semolina flour and water. Because Italy enforces rigid national standards for all pasta-making companies, the product quality is quite high and superior to most of our domestic pastas. Pasta is low in sodium and fat and high in iron, protein, and vitamin B. For a low-calorie pasta, try Buitoni brand.

Many shapes abound. Ones we use most often at Moosewood include farfalle (butterflies or bow ties), fettuccine ("small ribbons"), gemelli (with a loop at one end and curled around itself, like a twisted bobby pin), linguine ("small tongues"—long, thin, flat strands), manicotti ("small muffs"—large, ribbed, rectangular tubes), orecchiette ("little ears"), orzo (small rice-shaped pieces), penne (tubes with tapered ends, longer and thinner than ziti), rotini and spirali (twists and spirals), spaghetti ("strings"), vermicelli ("little worms"—small, fine, thin, squiggly pieces), and ziti (short fat tubes).

PEANUT BUTTER That luscious, addictive spread, which is packed with protein, carbohydrates, vitamins, minerals, and, alas, fat. There are reduced-fat peanut butters on the market but, like their full-fat predecessors, they contain hydrogenated fat (page 403) and often sugars, preservatives, and additives.

Natural peanut butters contain just peanuts and (sometimes) salt. Because the natural butters contain no stabilizers, the oil is unhomogenized, which means that it separates from the ground peanut purée. Part of this oil (but not all of it) can be poured off, thereby naturally reducing the fat content.

PENNE A short, tube-shaped pasta with tapered ends. Similar to ziti, but more slender, it accommodates rich, chunky sauces and works well in casseroles. It is available in the pasta section of many supermarkets and in Italian food stores.

PIGEON PEAS These field peas, also called Congo peas, gunga peas, or gandules, originated in Africa and are very popular in the Caribbean. Green or brownish-green in color, they are about the size of sweet green peas, but somewhat flattened in shape. Pigeon peas are available fresh, frozen, canned, or dried in stores that carry Caribbean, Asian, or African products. A 15-ounce can of pigeon peas, drained, yields about 1½ cups.

PIMIENTOS Most people use this term to refer to jarred or canned sweet red peppers—which is what we

mean in our recipes—although it can actually refer to green, yellow, *or* red bell peppers. Because of their sharp, sweet flavor (and high price), we use them sparingly in main dishes and as garnishes for salads or sandwiches. Pimientos are available plain or pickled, but we use plain. They are available in Italian and Greek groceries and in supermarkets.

PINE NUTS *(pignola nuts; pignoli)* The seeds of a Mediterranean pine tree, pine nuts have a rich, piney taste, made famous as a key ingredient in pesto Genovese. The cuisines of Spain, Eastern Europe, and North Africa also use pine nuts extensively; they appear in pilafs, cakes, cookies, and tortes. Before adding pine nuts to a preparation, lightly roast them in a dry skillet or toaster oven for the best results. Spread the pine nuts in a single layer on an unoiled tray and bake at 350° for 3 to 5 minutes, until just slightly deepened in color. Look for pine nuts in the imported food section of your supermarket, in Italian food stores, and where specialty foods are sold.

PINTO BEANS These medium-sized, brown-speckled dried beans are most often seen in Latin and South American cuisines. We use pinto beans for frijoles refritos (refried beans) and as a filling for enchiladas and burritos. Dried and canned precooked pintos are available at supermarkets and natural food stores. One cup of dried beans yields about 3¼ cups cooked. See page 414 for cooking instructions.

POLENTA The Italian word for corn, *polenta* has become the moniker for a soothing cornmeal pudding. The most basic version—yellow cornmeal, water, and salt—is also the lowest in fat. We serve it under saucy Italian or Spanish stews, or topped with maple syrup as a good hot breakfast cereal.

For polenta "cutlets," pour and spread the polenta onto a flat tray where it will stiffen as it cools. Cut the cooled polenta into triangles, dip them into seasoned bread crumbs, and bake until crisp outside and creamy within. Ladle on your favorite tomato sauce to complete the dish. To cook polenta, see page 416.

PORCINI An imported, dried, Italian wild mushroom with a deep, almost woodsy flavor. Although expensive, just a few porcini will add a lot of punch to a soup, stock, stew, or sauce. They are available, often packaged, in the Italian section of supermarkets. Look for mushrooms that are fleshy, whole, and fully opened.

PORTABELLA A cultivated domestic mushroom that is becoming increasingly popular in the United States, portabellas are very large with lightly speckled pale brown skins, thick stems, and a dense, chewy texture. Many supermarkets carry them fresh in their produce section year-round. Italian brown mushrooms are one particular type.

POTATOES First grown by the Incas, these easily digestible, starchy vegetable tubers are rich in carbohydrates, fiber, and vitamins B and C. Many varieties abound, but all of them can be categorized either as new (early) potatoes or as main-crop (mid- to late-season) potatoes, which store longer. We like to boil new potatoes and red-skinned Rosevals for purées, soups, salads, and sautés because we prefer their slightly sweeter, less starchy, bright flavor. Main-crop potatoes with waxy, yellowish flesh that becomes crisp quite readily are most often used for frying. For baking, we recommend Idaho potatoes with their softer, white interiors.

PUMPKIN This member of the gourd or squash family is most often associated in this country with the traditional Thanksgiving pumpkin pie. Fresh pumpkin is low in calories—only 31 per 100 grams—and is a good source of potassium. The soft orange or yellow flesh can be easily cubed, boiled, and puréed, and then added to baked goods in place of part of the oil called for in a recipe

—a nice trick for reducing the fat in some of those tempting homemade treats. Canned pumpkin purée is available in supermarkets, but be sure to check the labels because many contain sweeteners or additives.

QUINOA *(KEEN-wah)* Quinoa is no twentieth-century hybrid; its recorded history of cultivation and use date back to the Incan empire. Indigenous to South America, this wheat-free grain has been rediscovered in the last five years and is suddenly widely available. Quinoa contains all eight of the amino acids the body cannot produce, is rich in vitamins and minerals, cooks in about 15 minutes, is easily digestible, expands almost five times in cooking, and can be eaten plain or used to thicken soups and stews. It has a mild, nutty aroma and slight crunch. Pastas made of quinoa flour are also available. Quinoa and quinoa products can be found in natural food stores and in many supermarkets.

RAMEN NOODLES These precooked wheat noodles can be heated and ready to serve in just minutes. Made with either wheat flour and water or with wheat flour and oil, they are lower in fat than noodles made with eggs.

RICE Historians speculate it may have originated in India, but rice was definitely grown in China more than 3,000 years ago and is now one of the most cultivated grains in the world. Today many varieties grow in tropical, equatorial, and temperate zones across several continents. It is always eaten cooked, either hot or cold.

Arborio rice An Italian short-grain rice especially used in making risottos, this high-starch rice can absorb large quantities of liquid rapidly to make a creamy, velvety-textured dish, yet the centers of the rice kernels remain firm and chewy.

Basmati rice A fragrant Indian or Pakistani rice with small but long slender grains and a distinctive flavor reminiscent of roasted herbs. This rice has a rather smooth glossy texture and is less chewy than other types of rice. Both brown and white basmati rice are light and fluffy when cooked.

Brown rice Also known as husked or whole rice, brown rice retains more B vitamins,

phosphorus, and starch than white rice, which has been further processed. Brown rice, as the name suggests, has a characteristic light beige hue and is by far the most widely used grain at Moosewood. Short-, medium-, and long-grain varieties are all available. Short-grain rice—our rice of choice—is small, oval-shaped, and somewhat sticky or gummy. Most Japanese prefer *shinmai*, a short-grain newly harvested rice, which is available in the United States in October and November. Medium-grain brown rice has slightly longer grains, and while it is not as glutinous as short-grain rice, it is hearty and sticks together enough to be eaten easily with chopsticks. Long-grain brown rice, which is fluffy and dry with grains that remain separate, is used most often in Indian, Southeast Asian, and Middle Eastern cuisines. We also enjoy using long-grain rice during our warmest months, when its light quality is most welcome.

Jasmine rice A white rice with a full, aromatic—almost perfumed—bouquet and a slightly creamy texture, used most extensively in Indian and Caribbean cooking. It is absolutely delicious.

White rice Brown rice that has had the germ and the outer layers of its pericarp removed by rasping machines. Also known as polished rice, it cooks in a relatively short amount of time (about half that of brown rice). White rices, whether domestic, basmati, or jasmine, can be quite tasty, although nutritionally they are markedly inferior to brown rice. We think "instant" or "minute" types are not worth the savings in time because they have an insubstantial, grainy texture and flat flavor.

Wild rice Not actually rice, but the seed of an aquatic grass related to the rice plant. The seeds grow along the tall stalks of the plant and resemble tiny black sticks. Because harvesting is labor-intensive and availability is limited, wild rice is comparatively expensive, although delicious and quite beautiful.

RICE NOODLES *(rice stick noodles, rice vermicelli)* Available in varying widths, these make a good bed for sauces or a fine addition to soups and vegetable dishes. They need no cooking; simply soak rice noo-

dles in hot water before adding them to a broth or bringing them to the table. (Thicker noodles may need to be soaked in boiling water.) Rice noodles are a pasta option for those with wheat sensitivity. Find them in Asian markets and in the Asian section of many supermarkets.

RICE VINEGAR *(rice wine vinegar)* This mild, sweet Chinese vinegar is fermented from rice wine in three graduated strengths—white, red, and black. Our recipes refer to the white or mildest vinegar. Small amounts of distilled white vinegar or cider vinegar can be substituted. Rice vinegar is available in Asian food stores and where Asian foods are sold.

ROASTED RED PEPPERS These brilliantly colored, silky-textured, and smoky-flavored delights are made by cooking sweet red peppers over a flame and then removing the skin. We like them thinly sliced as eye-catching garnishes or added in modest amounts to certain mildly flavored sauces and casseroles for color and pizzazz. It is a simple matter to roast peppers at home but they also come canned or in glass jars. We've found that the peppers packed in glass taste better. Roasted red peppers are available where Italian foods are sold and sometimes in the canned vegetable section of the supermarket.

SALSA For eons this term has denoted a Mexican-style spicy tomato-chile sauce, usually cooked but sometimes *cruda*, or uncooked. In this decade, the salsa crudas appear to be ever expanding, encompassing a wide variety of fresh vegetables as well as tropical and temperate fruits, often intermixed and usually bathed in a spicy citrus dressing. The addition of fresh chiles, garlic,

and fresh herbs provides enough flavor to significantly reduce or eliminate the need for oil. Prepared tomato-chile salsas are available at the supermarket and natural food stores, often without additives or preservatives.

SEITAN Wheat gluten, seitan's other name, aptly describes this food, which is produced by removing the starch from the wheat, leaving behind the elastic, chewy, protein-concentrated gluten. It has been used in China and Japan for centuries as a high-protein meat substitute. Gluten is relatively flavorless but it absorbs flavors well. Added to stews, soups, and fillings, it provides nutrition and texture without being intrusive. Seitan is usually available canned at Asian food stores, and often fresh at natural food stores. Many seasoned varieties of seitan are also available.

SESAME OIL Available in two forms: a light oil pressed from unroasted sesame seeds and an amber, aromatic variety extracted from roasted seeds. We use the dark oil for flavoring or as a final touch to soups, stir-fries, and dipping sauces. The light oil cannot substitute in our recipes. Store sesame oil in a cool place or refrigerate it to prevent rancidity.

SHALLOTS In shape and structure, these members of the onion family most closely resemble an oversized clove of garlic, with a thin papery brown (or sometimes blue) skin. The similarity ends there, for the taste of shallots is delicate and sweet. They are a good choice in light sauces. Store shallots as you would onions, in a well-ventilated, cool enclosure. Shallots are often available in the produce section of the supermarket.

SHERRY This well-known wine of the Andalusia region of Spain is naturally dry and is fortified by the addition of brandy. Blends and sweetening come later as determined by the demands of the marketplace. At Moosewood, we always use a dry sherry for cooking and do not recommend substituting the products labeled "cooking sherry" for the sherry in our recipes.

SHIITAKE These meaty Japanese mushrooms are named for a type of beech tree called *shii* on which the fungus grows. The dried mushrooms, when reconstituted in water (page 418) and thinly sliced, have a silky, firm, chewy texture, an intense earthy flavor, and natural elegance. Fresh shiitake have become increasingly available in American markets. Choose firm, fleshy, aromatic mushrooms that are dry but not leathery. Shiitake are never eaten raw but otherwise can be used like common mushrooms. They do, however, contain less liquid than common varieties, so be careful not to burn them when sautéing or stir-frying. Simmering develops their satiny texture and woodsy flavor to the fullest.

SOBA These Japanese noodles contain a blend of buckwheat and wheat flours. The buckwheat gives the noodles a nutty, rich taste and makes soba a high-protein food. Certain varieties of soba may contain additional ingredients such as green tea or wild yam. Soba is available in Asian food stores and where Japanese foods are sold.

SOUR CREAM Both low-fat and nonfat versions are acceptable replacements for the full-fat original and provide significant savings in calories, fat, and cholesterol. While 1 tablespoon of full-fat sour cream contains 30 calories, 3 grams of fat, and 5 milligrams of cholesterol, the nonfat substitutes weigh in at 9 calories, no fat, and no cholesterol per tablespoon. Thickeners and additives are regularly used in nonfat sour cream substitutes. If you want to avoid these additives, we recommend Yogurt Cheese (page 419) as a good alternative. Low-fat and nonfat sour cream substitutes are available in the dairy case of most supermarkets.

SOY MILK This thick, dairy-free beverage is a decent alternative for those who are lactose intolerant or for anyone who wants to reduce their milk consumption. It is made primarily from soybeans, water, and salt, although it is often sweetened with barley malt or rice syrup and thickened with carageenan. Soy milk can be used in many of the ways dairy milk is used—in sauces, soups, and desserts or on cereal. The fat in all soy milks is polyunsaturated. An 8-ounce glass of whole soy milk contains 4 grams of fat, or 45 percent fat. Low-fat soy milks are also available, containing 2 grams of fat, or 25 percent fat. Additionally, the light or low-fat soy milks have a less pronounced soy taste. Soy milk also comes flavored for easier use in desserts and to enhance its appeal as a beverage. It is available at natural food stores and often at supermarkets.

SOY SAUCE At its best, soy sauce is made from soybeans, water, wheat, and salt—period. Some manufacturers offer more diluted and less good-tasting sauces with added caramel coloring, sweetening, and preservatives. Because soy sauces can vary in strength, we suggest tasting yours before adding it to a dish. Experiment with it— we've come to rely on soy sauce for depth and flavor in bean dishes and soups not even remotely connected to Asia, its continent of origin. Pure soy sauces are available in Asian markets, natural food stores, and in the Asian section of many supermarkets.

SULFITES This class of preservatives prevents bacterial growth, discoloration, and fermentation in foods. For centuries, sulfites or sulfur dioxide gas was thought to be safe. Then in the 1980s, a number of scientific studies found that it provoked allergic reactions, including some fatalities in asthma sufferers. Thereafter, the Food and Drug Administration prohibited its use on fresh fruits and vegetables in stores and restaurants, where consumers might unknowingly ingest it. Legally, sulfites must be listed on any canned or packaged product, though its use on seafood, particularly shrimp, often goes unpublicized. Dried fruits and wine are not covered under the sulfite ban on produce.

Nor is everyone sulfite sensitive. Thus far, no injurious effects have been discovered for those without respiratory or digestive reactions to the additive. Some discerning palates do claim that dried fruits without sulfites taste better. Fortunately, sulfite-free dried fruits are available at natural food stores and some liquor stores carry wine without added sulfites.

SUN-DRIED TOMATOES With their tart-sweet, salty flavor, sun-dried tomatoes enliven savory dishes and add a pleasant chewy texture. Available packed dry or in oil, they are usually found with the Italian specialties in supermarkets. Dry-packed tomatoes require soaking in hot water before using; oil-packed tomatoes are ready to use but are more expensive and higher in fat, of course.

SURIMI A processed white fish product, developed to simulate high-priced lobster and crabmeat, surimi is often used in sushi rolls. It is available at some fish markets and supermarket fish departments.

SWEET POTATOES The so-called "yams" found in most produce markets can be used interchangeably with sweet potatoes in our recipes. Botanically, the pale yellow sweet potatoes and the deep orange "yams" are both varieties of sweet potatoes. When the sweeter, dark orange potato was developed, it was marketed in the United States with the exotic, African-derived name: yam. A true yam, sold most frequently in Latin American markets, has a hairy, woody, brown exterior with a smooth yellow or white flesh and cannot be used for sweet potatoes in our recipes.

SWISS CHARD You may be surprised to learn this is actually a beet (!), *Beta vulgaris cicla*, with deep forest-green leaves and red ribs and without the bulbous root end. Some varieties actually have yellow or red leaves, but they are not common in the markets or gardens in this country. High in vitamins A, B, and C, chard is delicious steamed or added to soups, stews, vegetable side dishes, and casseroles.

Most commercially grown chard comes from New England.

TAHINI A smooth, beige, pourable paste made from unroasted, hulled sesame seeds, tahini is a favorite ingredient in Middle Eastern and North African cuisines—key in hummus, baba ghanouj, and falafel. Serious Middle Eastern diners dip wedges of pita bread into pure tahini spiked with a dash of cayenne.

There are other sesame pastes on the market that are not tahini and are not substitutes. Sesame paste or sesame butter, made of roasted and unhulled seeds, is much thicker, darker, and drier than tahini, with a consistency closer to peanut butter. Asian stores also carry a dark, thick paste that has a different taste. Tahini will be labeled as such and is available in Middle Eastern food stores, natural food stores, and where Greek and Middle Eastern foods are sold.

TAMARI A word that originally described the rich, salty liquid residue of the miso-making process, tamari is now often used interchangeably with soy sauce. A variety of tamari sauces are on the market. Most are intense, often wheat-free, soy sauces, unrelated to the original tamari.

TAMARIND CONCENTRATE A brown, glossy paste used as a flavoring in the cooking of India and East Africa where the tropical tree that yields tamarind seeds flourishes, tamarind adds a distinctive tartness and a lovely sienna glaze to the foods it flavors. It can be added directly to a simmering dish or dissolved first in water. Tamarind concentrate is available in small jars at Indian and Asian food stores.

TAPIOCA It may surprise many to learn that tapioca comes from the roasted and ground root of the tropical cassava plant (page 423). This root is processed to yield three grades of tapioca: large pearl, small pearl, and granulated. The granulated grade can be used as a transparent thickener, much like cornstarch or arrowroot, in sauces, broths, puddings, and pie fillings. The larger pearled tapiocas are familiar to most of us as the pudding we either loved or left. Instant tapioca is also available, but it is often

presweetened. Tapioca can usually be found in the pudding section of your supermarket.

TEMPEH This cultured soybean product, imported to the West from Indonesia, is a popular source of protein. Tempeh absorbs flavors well and has a chewy, meaty texture. We most often marinate it in soy sauce and spices, and then sauté or crisp-fry it. It can be eaten as a side dish or added to stews or pita sandwiches. Tempeh usually comes frozen and is most easily handled for food preparation semi-thawed and then cut into cubes. Tempeh can be found at most natural food stores.

THAI CURRY PASTES These exotic and aromatic spice blends are used to flavor sauces, stews, and noodle and rice dishes. The green pastes, which use fresh green chile as their base, are the hottest. Red pastes get their color from dried hot red peppers and the yellow pastes include a good amount of fresh or dried turmeric. Other ingredients in curry paste include a spice blend, peanut oil, and a fish or shrimp sauce (page 420) or paste. If desired, a good paste can be made without fish (page 365). Curry pastes are available at Asian food stores where Southeast Asian condiments are sold.

TOFU Also known as bean curd, regular tofu is a soybean product available in white cakes of varying weights and degrees of firmness. It has little taste of its own; its culinary value lies in its ability to absorb seasonings readily while contributing protein and substance to a dish. Tofu is a popular source of protein in Asian cultures, but we've found that it can also be incorporated into other ethnicities since it is such a flavor sponge. Tofu is available in supermarkets, natural food stores, and Asian markets.

Seasoned tofu Tofu-kan is a brand name that is sold in our community and in many cities along the East Coast. Look for it or for a kin—other tofu makers are distributing their own versions. In the wider world, tofu-kan most closely resembles Chinese five-spice tofu, which can often be found in Asian markets. Because of processing, seasoned tofu is extra-firm and can be tossed into salads, won't crumble in sautés, and makes a tasty textural protein source in sandwiches. Seasoned tofu can also be shredded for use in fillings.

Silken tofu Made with a higher ratio of soybeans to water than regular tofu and processed under water, silken tofu is rich tasting, with a somewhat higher fat content. The soybean taste is milder due to the water content and it has a silky, delicate mouthfeel. Unlike regular tofu, silken tofu purées smoothly with no trace of chalkiness. Silken tofu is ideal in richly flavored broths and purées and in dressings and dairyless fruit smoothies. Silken tofu is available in vacuum-packed boxes in the produce or Asian section of many supermarkets, in Asian food stores, and in natural food stores. Lite or low-fat silken tofu is also available.

TORTILLAS These unleavened flatbreads are the staff of life to most Mexicans. Corn and wheat tortillas are available in varying sizes. Corn tortillas tend to range from 4½ to 6 inches in diameter and wheat tortillas from 6 to 10 inches or larger. Traditionally, tortillas are made simply of corn or wheat flour and water, and some commercial brands are just as basic. However, if added fat and additives are a concern, read the labels because there are also numerous brands that include fats and preservatives in their products. Tortillas can usually be found in the dairy case or frozen food section of the supermarket. Additive-free tortillas can also be found at many natural food stores.

VINEGAR A sour liquid made from a diluted, naturally fermented substance such as wine, cider, or another alcoholic solution, the quality of the vinegar is determined by the quality of the liquid used to make it. You may develop preferences, using one type for certain kinds of dishes and another type for other dishes.

Apple cider vinegar Perhaps the most versatile vinegar we use, with an unobtrusive mild flavor and golden color.

Balsamic vinegar Aged Italian vinegar made from grapes, it has a russet color and sweet-sour flavor.

Distilled white vinegar Especially useful for pickling, Asian-style dressings, and Eastern European dishes. It is made from potatoes and is perfectly clear.

Herbed vinegars can be made by covering fresh, clean, dry herbs with vinegar, steeping them in a covered glass container on your sunniest windowsill for 4 to 6 weeks, straining the vinegar into a nonreactive pot, bringing it to a very gentle simmer, and then storing it in a sterilized jar in a cool place. These vinegars, which are also available in some supermarkets and gourmet food shops, add rich flavor to dressings, marinades, and sauces.

Malt vinegar Made from malted barley, it is extremely mild tasting and is especially popular in Britain.

Rice vinegar A mild, clear vinegar with a somewhat less acidic bite than either cider or wine vinegars. Excellent in Asian-style dishes.

Umeboshi vinegar A fuschia-colored vinegar made from the umeboshi plum with a complex sweet-sour-salty flavor that is so good it could become addictive.

Wine vinegars Made from either white or red wines, these vinegars add spark with their hearty, bright, assertive flavors. Red wine vinegars are usually stronger tasting than other varieties and are excellent in marinated vegetable salads and stews.

WASABI In Japanese cooking, this light green powder derived from a specific variety of radish root is mixed with water into a paste and used as a condiment or as a spicy addition to broths and dipping sauces. Wasabi is available in powder or paste where Japanese foods are sold and in natural food stores. Although premade paste is convenient, we don't recommend it; manys brands contain additives and the powder yields a more robust quality and flavor. To prepare fresh wasabi paste, combine equal amounts of powdered wasabi and tepid water and let sit for 10 minutes to fully develop its flavor. Like all ground spices, wasabi's flavor fades with time and exposure. To extend its life, wrap the opened container in plastic and refrigerate.

WATERCRESS One of the most nutritious greens around, watercress has a mild flavor with a peppery edge that adds bite to green salads and mild purées. Watercress grows wild near brooks and streams and is cultivated on farms. To store watercress, immerse the stems in a jar of water, loosely cover the leaves with a plastic bag, and refrigerate. Watercress is available in supermarkets and where specialty produce is sold.

WHEATBERRIES These seeds of cereal grass are most commonly milled into flour or processed in different ways for bread, noodles, hot and cold cereals, and cracked wheat (see **Bulgur**, page 422). Like rice or barley, wheatberries can also be cooked in their natural state. Because they are so hearty, we generally mix them with a lighter grain, such as rice or millet, for pilafs, grain salads, or vegetable fillings. You'll probably have the best luck locating wheatberries at natural food stores.

WINTER SQUASH Green- and orange-colored winter squash make delicious soups, shells for stuffed vegetables, and fillings for pies. They are a sweet and filling alternative to rice or potatoes. Some of the most user-friendly varieties of squash include acorn, buttercup, and delicata—all good for stuffing—butternut, turban, and small pumpkins. The large jack-o'-lanterns tend to be bland and pulpy. Winter squash are at their best in the fall, soon after harvest, and are available at supermarkets and produce stands.

WRAPPERS Either paper-thin, rectangular sheets of wheat dough or discs made with rice flour, wrappers are used for Asian spring and summer rolls. The wheat wrappers are usually in the freezer case in Asian markets and sometimes in the frozen food section of supermarkets. The wrappers from Asian stores tend to be thinner and more supple. Before using these wrappers, thaw for 3 to 4 hours. The rice flour wrappers, also available at Asian markets, need no refrigeration.

YOGURT The vast popularity of this tart, creamy dairy product seems directly related to its suggested health benefits. For starters, it is a low-fat food, made primarily from skim and nonfat dried milk and thickened with the addition of beneficial bacterial cultures. Low-fat yogurt contains about 4 grams of fat per 8-ounce serving and nonfat yogurt has no fat at all. Active bacterial cultures predigest the protein in yogurt, making it a more digestible milk product for many people. A body of evidence also suggests that these cultures may have a natural antibiotic effect against harmful bacteria that invade the digestive tract. And women have found yogurt effective against yeast infections for years. Some yogurt manufacturers heat-treat their yogurts to achieve a sweeter, less acidic taste. This treatment, however, renders the active cultures inactive, thereby nullifying their benefits. When yogurt is heat-treated, it must say so on the carton.

In cooked dishes, yogurt may curdle if overheated. To avoid this, either stir continuously on low heat or stabilize the yogurt by first dissolving 1 teaspoon of cornstarch in each cup of cool yogurt used. Yogurt is available in the dairy case of most food stores.

To make **Yogurt Cheese**, see page 419.

ZEST This refers to citrus peel, usually lemon or orange. You can make zest at home by grating the rind of the fruit or it can often be found in the spice section of the supermarket. We prefer it freshly grated just before use.

SPECIAL RECIPE LISTS AND MENUS

10 PERCENT OR LESS FAT

The following recipes derive 10 percent or less of their calories from fat. We were thrilled to discover that more than 100 of our recipes—about a third of the cookbook—were this low in fat, especially since we never compromised our insistence on excellent flavor and texture in favor of a lower fat content. We hope this list will be helpful to those on very restricted fat intake and to anyone else who wants to eat light for a while.

APPETIZERS

Greek Lima Bean Dip
Nori Vegetable Rolls
Roasted Garlic
Spinach Artichoke Heart Dip

BEANS

Barbecue Beans
Cassoulet
Festive Black Bean Chili
Sweet Potato and Black Bean
    Burrito
Vegetarian Feijoada

BREADS AND SANDWICHES

Almost Fat-Free Cornbread
Brown Bread
White Bean and Red Pepper
    Spread

BREAKFAST OR BRUNCH

Aafke's Spicy Quick Bread
Indian Potato Pancakes
Mango-Banana Shake
Peach-Berry Shake

DESSERTS

Anise Lemon Biscotti
Coffee Angelfood Cake
Dark Chocolate Pudding
Fruit-filled Meringue Shells
Ginger Peach Crumble
Lemon Pudding Cake
Pineapple Buttermilk Sherbet
Red Berry Kissel
Tapioca Fruit Parfaits
Vanilla Cream

DRESSINGS

Cilantro Lime Yogurt Dressing
Creamy Dill Dressing
Honey Mustard Garlic
    Dressing
Minted Dill Yogurt Dressing
Orange Tarragon Dressing

FISH

Baltic Fish
Fish with Herbs and Lime
Fish with Pineapple Chutney
Fish Tagine with Chermoulla
Herbed Fish in a Packet
Poached Fish with Russian
    Mushroom Sauce
Thai Fish Cakes

GRAINS

Brazilian Rice
Bulgur Rice Pilaf
Bulgur with Savory Greens
Curried Couscous Pilaf
Fragrant Jasmine Rice

OTHER MAIN DISHES

Another Shepherd's Pie
Fresh Spring Rolls

PASTA

Pasta with Beans and Greens
Pasta and Broccoli
Pasta with Eggplant
Pasta, Lentils, and Artichoke
    Hearts
Pasta with Salsa Cruda
Pasta and Sun-Dried
    Tomatoes

SALADS

Baked Sweet Potato Salad
Cabbage Salad
Carrot Orange Salad
Cucumbers Vinaigrette
Lentil Salad
Mediterranean Couscous
    Salad
Potato Bean Salad
Potato Beet Salad
Sushi Rice Salad
Tabouli Salad
Vegetables à la Grecque

SAUCES AND CONDIMENTS

Asian Cucumber Condiment
Barbecue Sauce
Blender Hot Sauce
Brazilian Hot Pepper and
    Lemon Sauce
Corn Relish
Mango Peach Chutney
Savory Onion Marmalade
Skordalia Thessalonike
Thai Curry Paste

SIDE DISHES

Garlic Mashed Potatoes
Gingered Broccoli
Holiday Cranberry Squash
Moroccan Carrots
Mustard Carrots
Sweet Sweet Potatoes
Zucchini with Cilantro Sauce

SOUPS

Basic Vegetable Stock
Shiitake Dashi
Southeast Asian Vegetable
    Stock
Catalan Potato Lima Soup
Chilled Beet and Buttermilk
    Soup
Cream of Cauliflower Soup
Cream of Green Vegetable
    Soup (all three variations)
Curried Carrot Parsnip Soup
Essential Miso Soup with Tofu
Golden Split Pea Soup
Harira
Japanese Soba and Vegetable
    Soup
Minestrone Genoa
New England Squash Soup
Orzo and Pea Soup
Savannah Beans and Greens
    Soup
Southwestern Corn and Potato
    Soup
Spring Soup
Tomato Bulgur Soup
Tropical Gazpacho

STEWS

Creole Stew
French Vegetable Bean Stew
Persian Split Pea and Barley
    Stew
Southwestern Hominy Stew
Three Sisters Stew
Ukrainian Beet and Bean Stew

QUICK AND EASY MEALS

This list will be helpful when time is at a premium. The average cook should be able to complete any of the following recipes in 30 minutes or less.

APPETIZERS

Broiled Eggplant Thai Style
Greek Lima Bean Dip
Guacamole with Asparagus
Guacamole with Cottage
    Cheese
Guacamole with Roasted Corn
Herbed Cottage Cheese Chèvre
    Spread
Indian Chickpea Spread
One Step Bean Guacamole
Spinach Artichoke Heart Dip

BEANS

Middle Eastern Chickpeas
    with Spinach
Tuscan Beans with Sage

BREADS AND
SANDWICHES

Asian Tofu Salad
Egg Salad
Ira's Lunch
Mexican Seitan Pita
Tempeh Salad Sandwich
Tuscan Sandwich

BREAKFAST
OR BRUNCH

Indian Potato Pancakes
Mango-Banana Shake
Peach-Berry Shake
Sesame Citrus Delight
Watercress Omelet

DESSERTS

Cardamom Oatmeal Cookies
Dark Chocolate Pudding
Ginger Peach Crumble
Vanilla Cream

DRESSINGS

Cilantro Lime Yogurt Dressing
Creamy Dill Dressing
Creamy Ginger Miso Dressing
Italian Tomato Basil Dressing
Japanese Carrot Dressing
Minted Dill Yogurt Dressing
Southeast Asian Pineapple
    Sesame Dressing
Spicy Peanut Dressing
Yogurt Tahini Dressing

FISH

Thai Fish Cakes

GRAINS

Couscous with Peas and
    Onions
Midsummer Risotto
Orzo and Green Herbs

OTHER MAIN DISHES

Vegetable-filled Pancakes

PASTA

Pasta with Beans and Greens
Pasta with Broccoli
Pasta with Chickpeas
Pasta with Salsa Cruda
Pasta and Sun-Dried
    Tomatoes
Penne with Creamy Walnut
    Sauce

SALADS

Cabbage Salad
Caesar Salad
Carrot Orange Salad
Chinese Orzo Vegetable Salad
Cucumbers Vinaigrette
Mango Coconut Cucumber
    Salad
Mexican Pasta Salad
Quinoa Black Bean Salad
Spinach Avocado Grapefruit
    Salad
Tabouli Salad

SAUCES AND
CONDIMENTS

Barbecue Sauce
Brazilian Hot Pepper and
    Lemon Sauce
Chunky Tomato Sauce
Cilantro Pesto
Corn Relish
Creamy Roasted Red Pepper
    Sauce
Fresh Tomato Salsa
Salsa Verde Liguria
Skordalia Thessaloniki
Susan's Pesto
Thai Curry Paste
Tomato Corn Salsa

SIDE DISHES

Broccoli Rabe and Garlic
Broiled Portabella
    Mushrooms
Broiled Zucchini with Herbs
Carolina Kale
Cauliflower Agrodolce
Cauliflower with Curry Sauce
Citrus-dressed Asparagus
Gingered Broccoli
Gingered Fennel with Garlic
Japanese Sesame Spinach
Moroccan Carrots
Mustard Carrots
Roasted Asparagus
Snap Peas with Mushrooms
Zucchini with Cilantro Sauce

SOUPS

Catalan Potato Lima Soup
Essential Miso Soup with Tofu
    (with Konbu Dashi)
Japanese Soba and Vegetable
    Soup
Korean Vegetable Noodle
    Soup
Tomato Bulgur Soup

VEGAN RECIPES

A vegan diet consists exclusively of food from the plant world. Even honey, which is made in part by bee secretions, is avoided by some vegans. All of the recipes in the list below are vegan.

APPETIZERS

Asian Eggplant Spread
Broiled Eggplant Thai Style
Greek Lima Bean Dip
Greek Spinach Rice Balls
Guacamole with Asparagus
Guacamole with Roasted Corn
Indian Chickpea Spread
Nori Vegetable Rolls
One Step Bean Guacamole
Roasted Garlic
Savory Stuffed Mushrooms
Spinach Artichoke Heart Dip
Tofu Vegetable Dumplings
Tunisian Potato Turnovers

BEANS

Barbecue Beans
Bean and Bean Gumbo
Cassoulet
Chili Burgers
Fat Tuesday's Skinny Red
    Beans
Festive Black Bean Chili
Garlicky Black-Eyed Peas 'n'
    Greens
Lentil Sambar
Sweet-and-Sour Lentils
Sweet Potato and Black Bean
    Burrito
Tuscan Beans with Sage
Vegetarian Feijoada

BREADS AND SANDWICHES

Asian Tofu Salad
Middle Eastern Cannellini
    Patties
Smoky Eggplant and Pepper
    Spread
Tuscan Sandwich
White Bean and Red Pepper
    Spread

BREAKFAST OR BRUNCH

Ful

DESSERTS

Apple Cherry Crisp
Creamy Dairyless Rice
    Pudding
Ginger Peach Crumble

DRESSINGS

Creamy Ginger Miso Dressing
Italian Tomato Basil Dressing
Japanese Carrot Dressing
Orange Tarragon Dressing
Southeast Asian Pineapple
    Sesame Dressing

GRAINS

Brazilian Rice
Bulgur Rice Pilaf
Bulgur with Savory Greens
Couscous with Peas and
    Onions
Curried Couscous Pilaf
Five-Spice Rice
Fragrant Jasmine Rice
Golden Basmati Rice
Kasha Pilaf
Midsummer Risotto
Millet Pilaf
Mushroom Wheatberry Pilaf
Orzo and Green Herbs
Quinoa Pine Nut Pilaf
Spring Vegetable Paella
Thai Fried Rice

OTHER MAIN DISHES

Another Shepherd's Pie
Cabbage Rolls
Curried Potato Cabbage Roll-
    Ups
Curried Sweet Potato Roti
Fresh Spring Rolls
Mexican Stuffed Peppers and
    Tomatoes
Middle Eastern Tofu-stuffed
    Peppers
Roasted Vegetables Three
    Ways
Seitan Fajitas
Stuffed Baked Potatoes
Vegetable-filled Pancakes

PASTA

Curried Rice Noodles
Pasta with Beans and Greens
Pasta, Lentils, and Artichoke
    Hearts
Pasta with Salsa Cruda
Pasta and Sun-Dried
    Tomatoes
Penne with Puttanesca Sauce
Vegetable Udon Sauté

SALADS

Caribbean Pigeon Pea Salad
Carrot Orange Salad
Chinese Orzo Vegetable Salad
Cucumbers Vinaigrette
Mango Coconut Cucumber
    Salad
Mediterranean Couscous
    Salad
Mexican Pasta Salad
Quinoa Black Bean Salad
Sesame Beets
Spinach Avocado Grapefruit
    Salad
Sushi Rice Salad
Tabouli Salad
Vegetables à la Grecque
Wild Rice Waldorf Salad

SAUCES AND CONDIMENTS

Barbecue Sauce
Blender Hot Sauce
Brazilian Hot Pepper and
    Lemon Sauce
Chunky Tomato Sauce
Cilantro Pesto
Corn Relish
Fresh Tomato Salsa
Hot Tamarind and Guava
    Sauce for Fish or
    Vegetables
Hungarian Lesco
Mango Peach Chutney
Mushroom Sauce
Salsa Verde Liguria
Savory Onion Marmalade
Susan's Pesto
Thai Curry Paste
Tomato Corn Salsa
Tomato Wine Sauce

SIDE DISHES

Baked Beets and Shallots
Broccoli Rabe and Garlic
Broiled Portabella
    Mushrooms
Broiled Zucchini with Herbs
Carolina Kale
Cauliflower Agrodolce
Citrus-dressed Asparagus
Curried Squash
Gingered Broccoli
Gingered Fennel with Garlic
Holiday Cranberry Squash
Japanese Sesame Spinach
Jerk Tofu
Moroccan Carrots
Mustard Carrots
Oven "Fries"
Roasted Asparagus
Seasoned Steamed Artichokes
Snap Peas with Mushrooms
Southeast Asian Coconut
    Zucchini
Spanish Potatoes
Sweet Sweet Potatoes
    (optional honey)
Thai Baked Tofu
Zucchini with Cilantro Sauce

CHILDREN'S FAVORITES

We have consulted with Moosewood parents and authors to compile this list of recipes, which are sure to be favorites with the children in your life.

SOUPS

Basic Vegetable Stock
Garlic Broth
Konbu Dashi
Shiitake Dashi
Southeast Asian Vegetable Stock
Asian Noodle Soup
Basque White Bean Soup
Callaloo
Carbonada
Catalan Potato Lime Soup
Curried Carrot Parsnip Soup
Dried Mushroom Soup with Barley
Essential Miso Soup with Tofu
Golden Split Pea Soup
Harira
Japanese Soba and Vegetable Soup
Korean Vegetable Noodle Soup
Minestrone Genoa
Orzo and Pea Soup
Savannah Beans and Greens Soup
Southwestern Corn and Potato Soup
Spanish Potato Garlic Soup
Spring Soup
Tomato Bulgur Soup
Tropical Gazpacho
Vietnamese Hot and Sour Soup

STEWS

Armenian Stew with Pilaf
Caribbean Stew
Creole Stew
French Vegetable Bean Stew
Giambotta
Mediterranean Stew
Mushroom Sesame Tofu Stew
Persian Split Pea and Barley Stew
Quinoa Vegetable Stew
Southwestern Hominy Stew
Thai Vegetable Curry
Three Sisters Stew
Ukrainian Beet and Bean Stew
Wild Mushroom Stew Trieste

APPETIZERS

Greek Spinach Rice Balls
Herbed Cottage Cheese Chèvre Spread
Tofu Vegetable Dumplings

BEANS

Barbecue Beans
Black Bean Chilaquile
Chili Burgers
Tamale Pie

BREADS AND SANDWICHES

Almost Fat-Free Cornbread
Buttermilk Rolls
Homemade Biscuits
Egg Salad
Ira's Lunch
Mexican Seitan Pita
Middle Eastern Cannellini Patties

BREAKFAST OR BRUNCH

Applesauce Cranberry Muffins
Banana Muffins
Cinnamon Apple Crêpes
Mango-Banana Shake
Peach-Berry Shake
Sticky Buns

DESSERTS

Apple Cherry Crisp
Banana Bundt Cake
Creamy Dairyless Rice Pudding
Dark Chocolate Pudding
Our Best No-Butter Brownies
Pumpkin Custard

FISH

Baltic Fish
Breaded Garlic Dill Fish
Herbed Fish in a Packet
Honey Mustard Fish

GRAINS

Bulgur Rice Pilaf
Couscous with Peas and Onions
Orzo and Green Herbs

OTHER MAIN DISHES

Another Shepherd's Pie
Luscious Basil and Feta Pizza
Potato Cheese Gnocchi
Stuffed Baked Potatoes
Sun-Dried Tomato Polenta Cutlets

PASTA

Lighter Lasagne
Macaroni and Cheese
Pasta with Chickpeas
Vegetable Lasagne Béchamel

SALADS

Chinese Orzo Vegetable Salad
Creamy Macaroni Salad
Mexican Pasta Salad
Wild Rice Waldorf Salad

SAUCES AND CONDIMENTS

Barbecue Sauce

SIDE DISHES

Garlic Mashed Potatoes
Gingered Broccoli
Jerk Tofu
Oven "Fries"
Potato Cakes
Sweet Sweet Potatoes

SOUPS

Cream of Cauliflower Soup
Dried Mushroom Soup with Barley
Golden Split Pea Soup
Japanese Soba and Vegetable Soup
Minestrone Genoa
Orzo and Pea Soup
Tomato Bulgur Soup

STEWS

Greek Stew
Persian Split Pea and Barley Stew

Six Festive Menus with a Theme

Here are some sample menus for special occasions. We have frequently given several options and each cook will of course vary the selections to accommodate time constraints and taste preferences.

Southeast Asian Menu

APPETIZER
Asian Eggplant Spread
OR
Asian Tofu Salad

SOUP
Vietnamese Hot and Sour Soup

MAIN DISH
Thai Vegetable Curry with Thai Baked Tofu
OR
Curried Rice Noodles
OR
Fresh Spring Rolls
OR
Southeast Asian Fish Rolls

GRAIN
Fragrant Jasmine Rice

DESSERT
Pineapple Buttermilk Sherbert

Summer Picnic

These foods travel well and do not need to be served hot. Choose several items for a delightful picnic.

Peach-Berry Shake
OR
Mango-Banana Shake

✳

Herbed Cottage Cheese Bread
OR
Tuscan Sandwich

✳

Creamy Macaroni Salad
OR
Baked Sweet Potato Salad
OR
Potato Beet Salad
OR
Caribbean Pigeon Pea Salad

✳

Citrus-dressed Asparagus
OR
Vegetables à la Grecque

✳

Jerk Tofu
OR
Barbecue Beans

✳

Cardamom Oatmeal Cookies
OR
Our Best No-Butter Brownies

Mediterranean Menu

APPETIZER
Tunisian Potato Turnovers
OR
Greek Lima Bean Dip

SOUP
Basque White Bean Soup
OR
Catalan Potato Lima Soup

MAIN DISH
Sun-Dried Tomato Polenta Cutlets with Tomato Wine Sauce
OR
Zucchini Saffron Pasta
OR
Herbed Fish in a Packet

SIDE DISH
Broiled Portabella Mushrooms
OR
Roasted Asparagus
OR
Seasoned Steamed Artichokes

DESSERT
Fruit-filled Meringue Shells
OR
Anise Lemon Biscotti

TEX-MEX MENU

APPETIZER
Guacamole with Roasted Corn
OR
Tomato Corn Salsa
with baked tortilla chips

SOUP
Southwestern Corn and
Potato Soup

BREAD
Almost Fat-Free Cornbread

MAIN DISH
Sweet Potato and Black Bean
Burrito
OR
Black Bean Chilaquile
OR
Mexican Stuffed Peppers
and Tomatoes
OR
Mexican Pasta Salad

DESSERT
Dark Chocolate Pudding
OR
Pumpkin Custard

NEW YEAR'S BUFFET

Here are suggestions for a
beautiful and delicious buffet.
What a great way to start
the New Year. Make as many of
these dishes as you dare!

Eggplant Strata

Thai Fish Cakes

Greek Spinach Rice Balls

Potato Cakes

Savory Stuffed Mushrooms

Smoky Eggplant and Pepper
Spread

Mushroom Pâté Almondine

Spinach Artichoke Heart Dip

Brown Bread

Herb and Cheese Muffins

Caesar Salad

Stuffed Manicotti Verde

Eggplant Parmesan

Vegetable Lasagne Béchamel

Baked Flounder Rolls

Apple Apricot Strudel

Maple Walnut Biscotti

Banana Bundt Cake

THANKSGIVING MENU

We often receive calls at
Moosewood asking for
suggestions for a vegetarian
Thanksgiving. Here
are some low-fat options.

SOUP
New England Squash Soup
OR
Cream of Green Vegetable Soup

BREAD
Buttermilk Rolls

MAIN DISH
Vegetable Filo Roll
Extravaganza
OR
Swiss Chard Rolls Two Ways
OR
Honey Mustard Fish

SIDE DISH
Holiday Cranberry Squash
OR
Sweet Sweet Potatoes
OR
Scalloped Potatoes and Carrots

SALAD
Cucumbers Vinaigrette

DESSERT
Coffee Angelfood Cake
OR
Lemon Pudding Cake

COMMON FOODS ANALYZED

Here is a list of relatively common foodstuffs—ones we use a lot at Moosewood—and a nutritional analysis of them that focuses mainly on their fat content. CBORD Group, Inc., has provided us with the information for this chart from their database, and although the information is accurate, it is still an approximation, since there are always variations in the quality and composition of foods. Each item is analyzed per designated portion for calories, total fat in grams, saturated fat in grams, and cholesterol in milligrams.

We have not listed most fruits and vegetables, because they all have no cholesterol and most have so little fat that it is considered negligible. We did list three exceptions to this rule: avocado, coconut, and mango.

We also have omitted breads, pastas, and tortillas from the list because they can vary tremendously, so we recommend reading the package labels for accurate information.

	CAL.	TOT. FAT	SAT. FAT	CHOL.
BEANS AND LEGUMES Portion: 1 cup canned or cooked				
black beans	218	0.7	0.2	0
black-eyed peas	185	1.3	0.3	0
cannellini	207	0.8	0.1	0
chickpeas	286	2.7	0.3	0
favas	187	0.7	0.1	0
kidneys	218	0.9	0.1	0
lentils	230	0.8	0.1	0
limas	234	0.2	0.0	0
navy beans	258	1.0	0.3	0
pigeon peas	203	0.6	0.1	0
pintos	233	0.9	0.2	0
split peas	231	0.8	0.1	0
soybeans	254	11.5	1.3	0
wheat berries	419	2.0	0.3	0
CHEESES Portion: ½ cup (grated or crumbled, if hard cheese)				
bleu	198	16.1	10.5	42
Brie	187	15.5	9.7	56
Cheddar	225	18.6	11.8	59
cottage cheese, regular	117	5.1	3.2	17
2%	102	2.2	1.4	9
1%	82	1.2	0.7	5
cream cheese	391	39.1	24.6	123
feta	197	15.9	11.2	66
fontina	218	17.4	10.7	65
gouda	239	18.4	11.8	76
gruyère	231	18.1	10.6	62
Monterey jack	209	17.0	10.7	50
mozzarella, regular	158	12.1	7.4	44
reduced fat	158	9.6	6.1	30
part skim	142	8.9	5.7	32
muenster	206	16.8	10.7	54
Neufchâtel	146	13.1	8.3	43
Parmesan	182	12.0	7.6	31
pecorina (Romano)	157	11.0	7.0	42
provolone	197	14.9	9.6	39
ricotta, regular	216	16.1	10.3	63
part skim	171	9.8	6.1	38

	CAL.	TOT. FAT	SAT. FAT	CHOL.
Swiss	225	16.5	10.7	55

EGGS AND DAIRY Portions: 1 medium raw egg, 1 cup dairy product

	CAL.	TOT. FAT	SAT. FAT	CHOL.
egg	75	5.0	1.5	213
egg yolk	59	5.1	1.6	213
egg white	16	0.0	0.0	0
buttermilk, regular	99	2.2	1.3	9
low-fat	78	1.1	0.0	0
coconut milk, regular	473	51.2	45.4	0
low-fat	209	19.8	11.9	0
condensed milk (sweetened)	980	26.6	16.8	104
evaporated milk, regular	339	19.1	11.6	74
skim	199	0.5	0.3	9
frozen yogurt				
low-fat	229	8.1	4.9	3
nonfat	207	0.1	0.0	0.0
half & half	313	27.6	17.2	89
ice cream	370	22.4	12.9	157
mayonnaise, regular	916	78.5	11.5	61
low-fat	232	13.2	6.7	103
milk, regular	150	8.1	5.1	33
2%	121	4.7	2.9	18
skim	86	0.4	0.3	4
sherbet	270	3.8	2.4	14
sorbet	259	0.2	0.0	0.0
sour cream, regular	411	40.2	25.1	85
low-fat	184	0.0	0.0	0
whipped cream	307	27.1	17.1	92
yogurt, regular	139	7.3	4.7	29
low-fat	149	3.5	2.3	14
nonfat	126	0.4	0.3	4

FISH AND SEAFOOD Portion: 6 ounces

	CAL.	TOT. FAT	SAT. FAT	CHOL.
catfish	259	13.6	3.0	109
clams	167	4.3	0.0	107
cod	179	1.4	0.2	80
flounder	344	13.9	3.4	153
halibut	407	30.2	5.3	100
haddock	191	1.6	0.3	126
herring	425	30.3	7.1	168
mackerel	228	4.4	0.8	116
mahi mahi	185	1.5	0.4	160
mako shark	221	7.7	1.6	87
monkfish	165	3.3	0.5	54
mussels	293	7.6	1.4	95
ocean perch	206	3.6	0.5	92
red snapper	218	2.9	0.6	80
salmon	350	21.0	4.3	107
scallops	191	2.4	0.0	90
scrod	179	1.5	0.3	94

	CAL.	TOT. FAT	SAT. FAT	CHOL.
sea bass	211	4.4	1.1	90
striped bass	211	5.1	1.1	175
shrimp	168	1.8	0.5	332
trout	323	14.4	2.5	126

FRUITS Portion: 1 medium

	CAL.	TOT. FAT	SAT. FAT	CHOL.
avocado	324	30.8	4.9	0
coconut, 1 ounce unsweetened dried flakes	188	18.4	15.8	0
mango	135	0.6	0.1	0

GRAINS Portion: 1 cup, cooked—unless specified raw

	CAL.	TOT. FAT	SAT. FAT	CHOL.
barley	194	0.7	0.1	0
bulghur	151	0.4	0.1	0
cornmeal (raw)	498	2.2	0.3	0
couscous	202	0.3	0.1	0
flour (raw)				
white	451	1.2	0.2	0
whole wheat	407	2.2	0.4	0
kasha	182	1.2	0.3	0
millet	286	2.4	0.4	0
oats, rolled	139	2.2	0.4	0
quinoa	636	9.9	1.0	0
rice				
basmati	201	0.5	0.1	0
jasmine	272	0.0	0.0	0
brown	218	1.8	0.4	0
white	263	0.6	0.2	0

NUTS, NUT BUTTERS & SEEDS Portions: ¼ cup shelled, raw nuts; 1 tbsp. nut butters and raw seeds

	CAL.	TOT. FAT	SAT. FAT	CHOL.
almonds	167	15.2	1.2	0
cashews	196	16.0	2.7	0
hazelnuts	214	21.1	1.1	0
peanuts	260	22.1	3.1	0
pecans	203	21.0	1.5	0
pinenuts	155	13.3	0.6	0
walnuts	163	16.0	1.1	0
peanut butter	94	8.0	1.5	0
sesame seeds	45	3.8	0.5	0
sunflower seeds	52	4.5	0.5	0
tahini	45	3.8	0.5	0

OILS Portion: 1 tablespoon

	CAL.	TOT. FAT	SAT. FAT	CHOL.
almond	120	13.6	1.1	0
butter	100	11.4	7.1	31
canola	120	13.6	1.0	0
coconut	124	14.0	12.1	0
corn	124	14.0	1.8	0
cottonseed	120	13.6	3.5	0
lard	16	12.8	5.0	12

	CAL.	TOT. FAT	SAT. FAT	CHOL.
margarine (stick)	102	11.4	2.0	0
olive	119	13.5	1.8	0
palm	124	14.0	6.9	0
palm kernel	124	14.0	11.4	0
peanut	119	13.5	2.3	0
safflower	124	14.0	1.3	0
sesame	120	13.6	1.9	0
soybean	120	13.6	2.0	0
sunflower	120	13.6	1.4	0
walnut	120	13.6	1.2	0

OTHER DAIRYLESS PRODUCTS Portion: 4 ounces

	CAL.	TOT. FAT	SAT. FAT	CHOL.
seitan	70	1	-	0
tempeh	226	8.7	1.3	0
tofu, regular	164	9.9	1.4	0
silken	86	5.4	0.8	0
tofu-kan	92	4.1	1.2	0
5-spice	89.6	5.2	.9	0

Portion: 1 ounce

	CAL.	TOT. FAT	SAT. FAT	CHOL.
miso	58	1.7	0.2	0
nori (seaweed)	113	0.0	0.0	0
olives				
California, black pitted	33	3.0	0.4	0
Calamata	96	10.1	1.1	0
Spanish green	33	3.6	0.4	0

COMPARING OILS

Vegetable oils vary in the amounts of saturated and unsaturated fats they contain. Here's a list of commonly used oils with their fat breakdowns for a 1 tablespoon portion.

	UNSATURATED		SATURATED
	MONO (G)	POLY (G)	(G)
BEST			
almond	10	2	1
canola (rapeseed)	8	4	1
olive	10	1	2
peanut	6	5	2
GOOD			
Corn	3	8	2
Safflower	2	10	1
WORST			
coconut	1	-	12
palm	5	1	7
butter	3	1	7
margarine	5	4	2
lard	6	2	5

SELECTED BIBLIOGRAPHY AND FURTHER READING

We culled much of our nutritional information from studying some of the sources listed below. So if you want to know more or would like to receive health newsletters, here are some suggested readings and places to investigate.

BAGGETT, NANCY. *Dream Desserts: Luscious, Low-fat Recipes.* New York: Stewart, Tabori and Chang, 1993.

BARNARD, NEAL, with recipes by Jennifer Raymond. *Food for Life.* New York: Harmony, 1993.

BRODY, JANE. *Jane Brody's Good Food Gourmet.* New York: Bantam Books, 1992.

DELLA CROCE, JULIA. *Italy: The Vegetarian Table.* San Francisco: Chronicle Books, 1994.

DEVI, YAMUNA. *Lord Krishna's Cuisine: The Art of Indian Vegetarian Cooking.* New York: E. P. Dutton/Bala Books, 1987.

DUONG, BINH, and MARCIA KIESEL. *The Simple Art of Vietnamese Cooking.* New York: Simon and Schuster, 1991.

GIOBBI, EDWARD, and RICHARD WOLFF, M.D. *Eat Right, Eat Well: The Italian Way.* New York: Alfred A. Knopf, 1985.

HIRSCH, DAVID. *The Moosewood Restaurant Kitchen Garden.* New York: Simon and Schuster/Fireside, 1992.

HOM, KEN. *Asian Vegetarian Feasts.* New York: William Morrow and Co., Inc., 1988.

JAFFREY, MADHUR. *Madhur Jaffrey's Far Eastern Cookery.* New York: Harper and Row, 1989.

JENKINS, NANCY HARMON. *The Mediterranean Diet Cookbook.* New York: Bantam Books, 1994.

LA PLACE, VIANA. *Verdura: Vegetables Italian Style.* New York: William Morrow and Co., Inc., 1991.

MADISON, DEBORAH. *The Savory Way.* New York: Bantam, 1990.

MATELJAN, GEORGE. *Baking without Fat.* Irwindale, California: Health Valley Foods, 1994.

MOOSEWOOD COLLECTIVE. *Moosewood Restaurant Cooks at Home.* New York: Simon and Schuster/Fireside, 1990.

O'CONNOR, JILL. *Sweet Nothings.* San Francisco: Chronicle Books, 1993.

ORNISH, DEAN. *Eat More, Weigh Less.* New York: HarperCollins, 1993.

PURDY, SUSAN G. *Have Your Cake and Eat It ,Too.* New York: William Morrow and Co., Inc., 1993.

RAICHLEN, STEVEN. *Steve Raichlen's High-Flavor, Low-Fat Vegetarian Cooking.* New York: Viking, 1995.

SHULMAN, MARTHA ROSE. *Mediterranean Light.* New York: Bantam Books, 1989.

———. *Provençal Light.* New York: Bantam Books, 1994.

SHURTLEFF, WILLIAM, and AKIKO AOYAGI. *The Book of Miso.* New York: Ballantine Books, 1982.

SIMMONS, MARIE. *The Light Touch Cookbook.* Shelburne, Vermont: Chapters, 1992.

SPILLER, GENE, with recipes by Deborah Madison. *The Super Pyramid Eating Program.* New York: Times Books/Random House, 1993.

YONEDA, SOEÏ. *The Heart of Zen Cuisine.* Tokyo: Kodansha International, 1982.

NEWSLETTERS

Nutrition Action Newsletter, Center for Science in the Public Interest, 1875 Connecticut Avenue, NW, Suite 300, Washington, DC 20009-5728, (202) 332-9110

Nutrition Advocate with News of the Cornell China Project, Advocacy Communications, Inc., 95 Brown Road, Post Office Box 4716, Ithaca, New York 14852, (800) 841-0444

Tufts University Diet and Nutrition Letter, 53 Park Place, New York, New York 10007, (800) 274-7581; in Colorado (303) 447-9330

University of California at Berkeley Wellness Letter, Health Letter Associates, 5 Water Oak, Fernandina Beach, Florida 32034, (904) 445-6414

MAGAZINES

Eating Well, Scott Mowbray, Publisher, Ferry Road, Post Office Box 1001, Charlotte, Vermont 05445-1001, (800) 678-0541

Natural Health, Christopher Kimball, Publisher, 17 Station Street, Post Office Box 1200, Brookline, Massachusetts 02147, (617) 232-1000

Vegetarian Times, Marianne Harkness, Publisher, 4 High Ridge Park, Stamford, Connecticut 06905, (800) 435-9610

ABOUT THE AUTHORS

This cookbook involved the enthusiastic labors of fourteen of Moosewood's twenty collective owners. The mathematically inclined could quite precisely describe the author then to be seven-tenths of the Moosewood Collective. But while accurate, the description doesn't quite capture the spirit of this multiheaded author. Besides, how could a fraction describe a whole group?

The Moosewood Collective changes slowly as time goes by, but the essence of who we are remains largely the same. We have recently grown from eighteen members to twenty. Our internal organization has shifted from large group meetings that discuss everything to smaller groups with more specific concerns and targeted goals. Our individual lifestyles vary and we are a diverse group, but we share many common values. Many of us have worked harmoniously together for fifteen years or more. Three threads run continuously through the tapestry of our workplace: a joyful exploration of good, healthful food; an enjoyment of and fairness to our fellow workers; and ongoing community involvement.

People often remark that we have not been spoiled by success, which we consider a compliment of the highest order. Restaurant work is hard, but perhaps this intensity is one of the essential ingredients that grounds us. We strive to demonstrate our appreciation for the diverse influences of the world's cuisines by integrating them into our own creations and culture. We value inclusiveness both in our cooking and in our way of working together. It has a peculiar kind of beauty.

Those who contributed directly to this book are Joan Adler, Ned Asta, Penny Condon, Tony Del Plato, Linda Dickinson, Susan Harville, David Hirsch, Nancy Lazarus, Eliana Parra, Maggie Pitkin, Sara Wade Robbins, Maureen Vivino, Lisa Wichman, and Kip Wilcox.

INDEX

additives and preservatives, 406; chemical, 408; natural, 406
Almost Fat-Free Cornbread, 110; variation, 110
American Dietetic Association, 397
American Heart Association, 397–98
amino acids, 405
Angelfood Cake, Coffee, 378; variation, 379
Anise (anise seeds, licorice), 420
   Lemon Biscotti, 391
annatto (achiote seeds), 142, 420
antioxidant(s), 400; vitamins, 400
Appetizer, 20–43. *See also* Salad; Sandwich Filling
   Asian Eggplant Spread, 24
   Chickpea Spread, Indian, 29
   Cottage Cheese Chèvre Spread, Herbed, 31
   Eggplant Strata, 32
   Eggplant Thai Style, Broiled, 34
   Garlic Basil Cheese Spread, 22
   Garlic, Roasted, 43
   Greek Lima Bean Dip, 23
   Guacamole with Asparagus, 25
   Guacamole with Cottage Cheese, 26
   Guacamole with Roasted Corn, 27
   Mushrooms, Savory Stuffed, 42; variations, 42
   Nori Vegetable Rolls, 36; variations, 37
   One Step Bean Guacamole, 28
   Potato Turnovers, Tunisian, 40
   Spinach Artichoke Heart Dip, 30
   Spinach Rice Balls, Greek, 35
   Tofu Vegetable Dumplings, 38
Apple
   Apricot Strudel, 384
   Crêpes, Cinnamon, 56
   Cherry Crisp, 385
   cider vinegar, 440
Applesauce
   and Cranberry Muffins, 61
   Spice Cake, 381

Apricot(s), 420; dried, 420
   Apple Strudel, 384
arborio rice, 435; cooking, 416
Armenian Stew with Pilaf, 270
Artichoke(s), 420; hearts, 420
   Heart Spinach Dip, 30
   Hearts, Pasta, and Lentils, 209
   Seasoned Steamed, 311
Asian. *See also* Chinese; Japanese; Southeast Asian
   Cucumber Condiment, 367
   Eggplant Spread, 24
   fish sauce (*nam pla*), 420
   Noodle Soup, 81
   Tofu Salad, 116
Asparagus, 421
   Citrus-Dressed, 313
   Guacamole with, 25
   Roasted, 312
   sauces for, 309
atherosclerosis, 402
average daily dietary guidelines, 399
Avocado, 421. *See also* Guacamole
   amount of fat in, 17
   Spinach Grapefruit Salad, 135

baguette (French bread), 421
Baked
   Beets and Shallots, 314
   Fish with Mustard Marinade, 288
   Flounder Rolls, 295
   Stuffed Potatoes, 249
   Sweet Potato Salad, 137
balanced diet, 403
balsamic vinegar, 440
Baltic Fish, 287
Banana
   Bundt Cake, 382
   -Mango Shake, 65
   Muffins, 62; variation, 62
Barbecue
   Beans, 156
   Sauce, 355
Barley, 415, 421
   and Split Pea Stew, Persian, 274

Basic Vegetable Stock, 73
Basil and Feta Pizza, Luscious, 228; variations (other pizza toppings), 229
Basmati Rice, 416, 435
   Golden, 185
Basque White Bean Soup, 103
Bean(s), 154–73. *See also* Black Beans; Black-Eyed Peas; Cannellini Beans; Chickpeas; Ful; Lentils; Lima Beans; Red Beans; Savannah Beans; Split Peas; White Beans
   Barbecue, 156
   and Bean Gumbo, 157
   and Beet Stew, Ukrainian, 269
   Cassoulet, 160
   Chili Burgers, 173
   dried, about cooking, 414; bean to water ratio, chart, 414
   (green), Potato Salad, 138
   and Greens, Pasta with, 210
   Guacamole, One Step, 28
   helping digestion of, 155
   Tamale Pie, 162
   Tuscan, with Sage, 168
   Vegetable Stew, French, 264
Beet(s), 421; peeling, 139
   and Bean Stew, Ukrainian, 269
   and Buttermilk Soup, Chilled, 79
   greens, 140
   Potato Salad, 139
   sauces for, 309
   Sesame, 140
   and Shallots, Baked, 314
berbere (hot spice blend), 421
Berry Kissel, Red, 372
Berry-Peach Shake, 66
beta-carotene, 400
Beverages
   Mango-Banana Shake, 65
   Peach-Berry Shake, 66
Biscotti, 421
   Anise Lemon, 391
   Chocolate Hazelnut, 392
   Maple Walnut, 390

Biscuits, Homemade, 114;
    shortbread variation, 114
Black Bean(s) (turtle beans), 421.
    See also Beans
    Chilaquile, 164
    Chili, Festive, 161
    and Hominy Frittata, 49
    Quinoa Salad, 141
    and Sweet Potato Burrito, 172
    Vegetarian Feijoada, 158
Black-Eyed Peas, 421–22
    'n' Greens, Garlicky, 170
black mustard seeds, 422
black peppercorns, 422
blanching (technique), 414
blood cholesterol level, total, 402
Blueberry Peach Cobbler, 383
braising (technique), 414–15
Brazilian
    Hot Pepper and Lemon Sauce, 359
    Rice, 187
    Vegetarian Feijoada, 158
Bread, 108–15. *See also* Muffins
    Biscuits, Homemade, 114;
        shortbread variation, 114
    Brown, 111
    Cornbread, Almost Fat-Free, 110
    Herb and Cheese Muffins, 112
    Herbed Cottage Cheese, 113
    Irish Soda, 59
    Rolls, Buttermilk, 115
    Spicy Quick, Aafke's, 60
bread crumbs, 422; making, 298
Breaded Garlic Dill Fish, 297
Breakfast (Brunch), 46–67
Broccoli
    Gingered, 315
    sauces for, 309
Broccoli Rabe (rapini, broccoli rape),
    422
    and Garlic, 315
Broiled
    Eggplant, Thai Style, 34
    Portabella Mushroom(s), 322
    Zucchini with Herbs, 333
Broth
    color of, 74
    Garlic, 74
    Konbu Dashi, 75; Konbu-Bonito
        Dashi variation, 75

Brown Bread, 111
brown rice, 435–36; cooking, 416
Brownies, No-Butter, Our Best, 387
Brunch (Breakfast), 46–67
Brussels Sprouts, sauces for, 310
buckwheat groats (kasha), cooking,
    415
Bulgur (cracked wheat), 415, 422
    Rice Pilaf, 188
    with Savory Greens, 178
    Tomato Soup, 101
Buns, Sticky, 58
Burrito, Sweet Potato and Black
    Bean, 172
"butter bean," 23
butter (high in saturated fat), 403
Buttermilk, 422
    and Beet Soup, Chilled, 79
    Pineapple Sherbet, 394
    Rolls, 115

Cabbage
    Chinese, blanching, 256
    Potato Roll-Ups, Curried, 251
    Rolls, 256
    Salad, 132
    sauces for, 309
Caesar Salad, 131
caffeine, 400
Cake
    Applesauce Spice, 381
    Banana Bundt, 382
    Chocolate Cocoa, 380
    Coffee Angelfood, 378;
        variation, 379
    Lemon Pudding, 377
calcium, in the diet, 411;
    foods rich in, 411
Callaloo (Caribbean), 105;
    spinach, 422
calories, 400

Cannellini (Beans), 422.
    See also Beans
    Patties, Middle Eastern, 119
    Tuscan, with Sage, 168
capers, 422–23
caramelizing (technique), 415
carbohydrates, 401; complex, 401;
    simple, 401
    as energy source, 397–98
    metabolism, 400
Carbonada (Chilean vegetable
    soup), 98
Cardamom Oatmeal Cookies, 393
Caribbean
    Pigeon Pea Salad, 142
    Stew, 265
carob (St. John's bread), 423
Carolina Kale, 321
Carrot(s)
    Dressing, Japanese, 346
    Moroccan, 316
    Mustard, 317
    Orange Salad, 134
    Parsnip Soup, Curried, 100
    and Potatoes, Scalloped, 325
    sauces for, 309
cassava meal (manioc flour), 423
Cassoulet, 160
Catalan Potato Lima Soup, 99
Cauliflower
    Agrodolce, 318
    with Curry Sauce, 319
    sauces for, 309
    Soup, Cream of, 90
cayenne (hot red pepper), 423
    replacing chiles, 358
cellophane noodles (bean threads),
    423
    about storing, 89
    Noodle Vegetable Soup, Korean, 89
chanterelle mushrooms, 423
Cheese
    amount of fat in, 17
    and Herb Muffins, 112
    and Macaroni, 203
    Potato Gnocchi, 250
    Spread, Garlic Basil, 22
chemical additives, 408

Cherry Apple Crisp, 385
Chèvre Herbed Cottage Cheese Dip,
    31
Chickpea(s) (garbanzo beans), 423
    Pasta with, 211
    Potato Bean Salad, 138
    with Spinach, Middle Eastern, 169;
        cannellini or butter bean
        variations, 169
    Spread, Indian, 29
chiffonading (technique), 415
Chilaquile, Black Bean, 164
children's favorite recipes, 445
Chilean vegetable soup
    (Carbonada), 98
chiles (chili peppers), 423–24
    and cayenne pepper, 358
Chili
    Black Bean, Festive, 161
    Burgers, 173
    paste, Chinese, 424
Chinese
    black beans (fermented), 424
    cabbage (bok choy and celery
        cabbage), 424; blanching, 256
    chili paste, 424
    Orzo Vegetable Salad, 149
    rice wine (Shaoxing), 424
chlorine, in the diet, 411;
    foods rich in, 411
Chocolate, 424–5
    Cocoa Cake, 380
    Hazelnut Biscotti, 392
    Pudding, Dark, 374
cholesterol, 401; functions of, 401–2
    derived from animal foods, 401
chopping (technique), 415
Chutney. See also Relish
    Mango Peach, 362
    Pineapple, Fish with, 292
chylomicrons, 401
Cilantro
    Lime Yogurt Dressing, 345
    Pesto, 364
    Sauce, Zucchini with, 335

Cinnamon Apple Crêpes, 56
Citrus
    -Dressed Asparagus, 313
    Sesame Delight (yogurt), 67
Cobbler, Blueberry Peach, 383
Coconut, 425
    Mango Cucumber Salad, 136
    milk, 425
    oil, 403
    rice, 425
Coffee Angelfood Cake, 378;
    variation, 379
collard greens, 425
Condiment. See Seasoning
Cookies, Cardamom Oatmeal, 393
cooking
    spray, 15, 425
    terms and techniques (glossary),
        414–41. See also individual
        term or technique
cookware, nonstick, 13–15
copper, in the diet, 411;
    foods rich in, 411
Corn
    and Potato Soup, Southwestern, 102
    Relish, 361
    Roasted, Guacamole with, 27
    sauces for, 309
    Tomato Salsa, 366
Cornbread, Almost Fat-Free, 110;
    variation, 110
Cornell-Oxford-China Diet and
    Health Project, 398
cornichons, 425
Cornmeal, 425
    Spice Muffins, 63
coronary artery disease, 402
Cottage Cheese, 425–26
    Guacamole with, 26
    Herbed Bread, 113
Couscous, 415, 426
    with Peas and Onions, 179
    Pilaf, Curried, 180
    Salad, Mediterranean, 144
cranberries, dried, 426
Cranberry
    and Applesauce Muffins, 61
    Squash, Holiday, 331

Cream
    of Cauliflower Soup, 90
    of Green Vegetable, 82;
        variations, 83
    of tartar 426
    Vanilla, 395
Creole Stew (tofu-vegetable), 273
Crêpes, 57
    Cinnamon Apple, 57
    Mushroom Spinach, 234
Crisp, Apple Cherry, 385
crostini, Italian "toast, " 426
Crumble, Ginger Peach, 386
Cucumber(s)
    about peeling, 133
    Condiment, Asian, 367
    Mango Coconut Salad, 136
    Vinaigrette, 133
currants, 426
Curried
    Carrot Parsnip Soup, 100
    Couscous Pilaf, 180
    Potato Cabbage Roll-Ups, 251
    Rice Noodles, 220; variations, 221
    Squash, 332
    Sweet Potato Roti, 230
Curry, 426; paste(s), 426; Thai, 439
    Paste, Thai, 365
    powder, 426
    Sauce, Cauliflower with, 319
    Thai Vegetable, 268
Custard, Pumpkin, 376

dairy products, substitutes for, 10–11
Dashi, 427
    Konbu, 75; Bonito variation, 75
definitions for food labels, USDA, 409
al dente, 414
Dessert, 370–93
    Anise Lemon Biscotti, 391
    Apple Apricot Strudel, 384

Apple Cherry Crisp, 385
Applesauce Spice Cake, 381
Banana Bundt Cake, 382
Blueberry Peach Cobbler, 383
Cardamom Oatmeal Cookies, 393
Chocolate Cocoa Cake 380
Chocolate Hazelnut Biscotti, 392
Chocolate Pudding, Dark, 374
Coffee Angelfood Cake, 378;
  variation, 379
Fruit-Filled Meringue Shells, 388
Ginger Peach Crumble, 386
Lemon Pudding Cake, 377
Maple Walnut Biscotti, 390
No-Butter Brownies, Our Best, 387
Pineapple Buttermilk Sherbet, 394
Pumpkin Custard, 376
Red Berry Kissel, 372
Rice Pudding, Creamy Dairyless,
  373
Tapioca Fruit Parfaits, 375
Vanilla Cream, 395
dicing (technique), 415
dietary
  fat, 398
  guidelines, average daily, 399
Dill Dressing, Creamy, 342
Dips and Spreads. See Appetizer;
  Sandwich Filling
dough, pizza, 228
Dressing, 340–41, 342–49.
  See also Relish; Sauce
  Apple Basil, 348
  Caesar Salad, 131
  Carrot, Japanese, 346
  Cilantro Lime Yogurt, 345
  Curried Mango Yogurt, 151
  Dill, Creamy, 342
  Ginger Miso, Creamy, 343
  Green Mayonnaise, 344
  Honey Mustard Garlic, 342
  Italian Tomato Basil, 347
  Japanese Carrot, 346
  Minted Dill Yogurt, 345
  Orange Tarragon, 348
  Southeast Asian Pineapple
    Sesame, 343
  Spicy Peanut, 349
  Yogurt Tahini, 346

Dried Mushroom(s)
  soaking, 418
  Soup with Barley, 94
Dumplings, Tofu Vegetable, 38

eating out, 13
Egg(s). See also Frittata
  American Dietetic Association
    guidelines for, 47
  Omelet, Watercress, 53
  peeling, 117
  Salad, 117
  using less, 10
  whites, separating (technique), 415
  whites, warming, 389
Eggplant
  baking, 263
  Parmesan, 241
  Pasta with, 205
  and Pepper Spread, Smoky, 122
  roasting, oven method, 417;
    stove-top method, 417
  sauces for, 309
  Spread, Asian, 24
  Strata, 32
  Thai Style, Broiled, 34
emulsifying (technique), 415
energy and carbohydrates, 401
escarole, 427
essential amino acids, 405
Essential Miso Soup with Tofu, 80
evaporated skimmed milk, 427

Fajitas, Seitan, 232
farfalle (pasta), 427
fat
  calories, 398
  goal, personal, 399

"fat-free," 407
fats (triglycerides), 401–2
  in food (energy-yielding
    nutrients), 402–3
fatty acids (linoleric and linolenic),
    404. See also transfatty acid
fava beans (Ful), 55, 427
Feijoada, Vegetarian, 158
Fennel, 427; bulbs, 427; seeds, 427
  Fish Steaks with, 290
  Gingered, with Garlic, 320
fenugreek seeds, 427
Feta cheese, 427–28
  and Basil Pizza, Luscious, 228;
    variations (other pizza top-
    pings), 229
fettuccine (pasta), 428
fiber in the diet, 404–5
figs, 428
filo dough, 428; using, 242
Filo Roll Vegetable Extravaganza, 242
Fish, 282–305. See also Shellfish
  about cooking (freshwater, lean,
    oil-rich, shellfish), 284–85;
    selecting, 286
  Baked, with Mustard Marinade, 288
  Baltic, 287
  Breaded Garlic Dill, 297
  Cakes, Thai, 302
  Flounder Rolls, Baked, 295
  frozen, 283
  Herbed, in a Packet, 296
  with Herbs and Lime, 289
  Hoisin, Savory, 293
  Honey Mustard, 298
  with Pineapple Chutney, 292
  Poached, with Russian Mush-
    room Sauce, 300
  Poached, with Vegetables, 301
  Rolls, Southeast Asian, 294
  Steaks with Fennel, 290
  Stew, Italian, 299
  Tagine with Chermoulla, 291
  and Vegetables, Guava and Hot
    Tamarind Sauce for, 356
Five-Spice
  powder, 428
  Rice, 186
Flounder Rolls, Baked, 295

flour, 428
folding (technique), 415
food additives and preservatives, 406
food labels, 406; understanding, 407; USDA definitions for, 409
free radicals, 400
French Vegetable Bean Stew, 264
Frittata. *See also* Eggs; Omelet
　　Black Bean and Hominy, 49
　　Spanish Potato Pepper, 51
　　Spinach Mushroom, 52
　　Swiss Chard and Tomato, 50
Fruit
　　-Filled Meringue Shells, 388
　　purées, using, 10
　　Tapioca Parfaits, 375
Ful (fava beans), 55

garam masala, 428
Garlic, 428
　　Basil Cheese Spread, 22
　　Broccoli Rabe and, 315
　　Broth, 74
　　Dill Fish, Breaded, 297
　　Gingered Fennel with, 320
　　Honey Mustard Dressing, 342
　　Mashed Potatoes, 328
　　Potato Soup, Spanish, 97
　　pressing, 417
　　Roasted, 43
　　roasting, 417
Garlicky
　　Black-Eyed Peas 'n' Greens, 170
　　potato sauce, Skordalia Thessa-lonike, 354
Gazpacho, Tropical, 78
Giambotta (Italian ratatouille), 263

Ginger
　　Miso Dressing, Creamy, 343
　　Peach Crumble, 386
　　root, 428
Gingered
　　Broccoli, 315
　　Fennel with Garlic, 320
　　Shrimp and Soba, 303
glossary (cooking terms and techniques), 414–41
Gnocchi
　　dough, uncooked, 250
　　Potato Cheese, 250
Grains, 176–96. *See also* Bulgur; Couscous; Kasha; Millet; Quinoa; Rice; Wheatberry
　　about cooking, 415–16
Grapefruit Spinach Avocado Salad, 135
Greek
　　Lima Bean Dip, 23
　　Spinach Rice Balls, 35
　　Stew, 266
Green Beans
　　Greek Stew, 266
　　Potato Salad, 138
　　sauces for, 309
Green Mayonnaise, 344
Green Sauce (Salsa Verde Liguria), 353
Greens. *See also* Kale
　　and Beans, Pasta with, 210
　　'n' Black-Eyed Peas, Garlicky, 170
　　collard, 425
　　Savory, Bulgur with, 178
　　sauces for, 309
grilling (technique), 416
Guacamole
　　with Asparagus, 25
　　Bean, One Step, 28
　　with Cottage Cheese, 26
　　darkening (surface), 25
　　with Roasted Corn, 27
Guava
　　and Hot Tamarind Sauce for Fish and Vegetables, 356
　　paste, 428–29
guidelines for healthy eating, 3–4
Gumbo, Bean and Bean, 157

Harira (North African soup), 85
Hazelnut(s) (filberts), 429
　　Chocolate Biscotti, 392
healthy styles of preparation, 9
heart attack and stroke, 402
Herb(s), 429
　　and Cheese Muffins, 112
　　Green, and Orzo, 183
Herbed
　　Cottage Cheese Bread, 113
　　Cottage Cheese Chèvre Spread, 31
　　Fish in a Packet, 296
　　vinegar, 440
high-density lipoproteins (HDLs), 401–2
high-fat liquids, 10
Hoisin
　　Fish, Savory, 293
　　sauce, 429
Homemade Biscuits, 114; shortbread variation, 114
Hominy, 429
　　and Black Bean Frittata, 49
　　Stew, Southwestern, 279
Honey, 429
　　Mustard Fish, 298
　　Mustard Garlic Dressing, 342
horseradish, 429
Hot
　　Pepper and Lemon Sauce, Brazilian, 359
　　peppers, Hungarian, 429
　　Sauce, Blender, 358
　　and Sour Soup, Vietnamese, 87; seafood variation, 87
　　Tamarind and Guava Sauce for Fish and Vegetables, 356
hummus. *See* Chickpea
Hungarian
　　hot peppers, 429
　　Lesco (sauce), 357
hydrogenated oils (fats), 403

Indian
    Chickpea Spread, 29
    Potato Pancakes, 54;
        sweet potato variation, 54
    Sweet Potatoes, Savory, 248
iodine, in the diet, 411–12;
    foods rich in, 412
Ira's Lunch (tofu-kan), 118
Irish Soda Bread, 59
iron, in the diet, 412; foods rich in,
    412
Italian. *See also* Minestrone; Pasta;
    Sicilian
    Fish Stew, 299
    Giambotta (stew), 263
    Tomato Basil Dressing, 347

Japanese
    Carrot Dressing, 346
    Sesame Spinach, 330
    Soba and Vegetable Soup, 88
    Soup, Essential Miso with Tofu, 80
    Stock, Konbu Dashi, 75; Konbu-
        Bonito Dashi variation, 75
    Stock, Shiitake Dashi, 76
Jasmine Rice, 436
    cooking, 416
    Fragrant, 189
jerk (Caribbean seasoning), 430
Jerk Tofu, 337
julienning (technique), 416

Kale, 430
    Carolina, 321
    Potato Soup, Creamy, 91
    and Squash Risotto, 192;
        vegetable variations, 193

Kasha (buckwheat groats), 430
    cooking, 415
    Pilaf, 181
kasseri cheese, 430
kidney beans, 430. *See also* Beans
    Chili Burgers, 173
Konbu Dashi (stock or broth), 75;
    Konbu-Bonito Dashi
    variation, 75
konsu (kombu, kelp), 430
Korean Vegetable Noodle Soup, 89

labels, food, 406
    understanding, 407
    USDA definitions for, 409
Lasagne
    Béchamel, Vegetable, 216
    Lighter, 218
leeks, 430
Lemon
    Anise Biscotti, 391
    and Hot Pepper Sauce, Brazilian,
        359
    Pudding Cake, 377
lemongrass, 189, 430–31
Lentil(s), 431
    Pasta, and Artichoke Hearts, 209
    Salad, 151
    Sambar, 166
    Sweet and Sour, 171
Lima (Bean(s)
    canned, 23
    Dip, Greek, 23
    Potato Soup, Catalan, 99
lipids, 401
lipoproteins, role of, 401
low-density lipoproteins (LDLS),
    401–2
low-fat, 407
    cooking, tips for, 9–13
    dairy products, using, 10–11
    recipes (10 percent or less), 442
    snacks, 12–13
    staples, using, 12

substitutions, 5–7
vegetarian diet, 398
lower-fat cooking techniques, 5–7

Macaroni
    and Cheese, 203
    Salad, Creamy, 150
Madeira wine, 431
magnesium, in the diet, 412;
    foods rich in, 412
Main Dishes, 224–56. *See also*
        Names of Main Ingredient
        (Fish, Pasta, Stews, etc.)
malt vinegar, 440
manganese, in the diet, 412;
    foods rich in, 412
Mango(es), 431
    -Banana Shake, 65
    Coconut Cucumber Salad, 136
    cutting technique, 416
    Peach Chutney, 362
Manicotti Verdi, Stuffed, 219
maple syrup, 431
Maple Walnut Biscotti, 390
Marmalade, Onion, Savory, 363
mashing (technique), 417
Mayonnaise, 431
    Green, 344
Mediterranean
    Couscous Salad, 144
    Menu, 446
    Stew, 267
menus, special, 442–47
Meringue Shells, Fruit-Filled, 388
meringues, egg whites for, 389
mesclun, 431
Mexican
    Pasta Salad, 148
    Seitan Pita, 120
    Stuffed Peppers and Tomatoes, 244

Middle Eastern
  Cannellini Patties, 119
  Chickpeas with Spinach, 169;
    cannellini or butter bean
    variations, 169
  Tofu-stuffed Peppers, 246
Midsummer Risotto, 191
milk, 431; substitutes for, 11
Millet 416, 431
  Mexican Stuffed Peppers and
    Tomatoes, 244
  Pilaf, 182
mincing (technique), 417
minerals and vitamins,
    Recommended Daily
    Allowance (RDA), 410–13
Minestrone
  Genoa, 86; riballita variation, 86
  Spring Soup, 84
Minted Dill Yogurt Dressing, 345
mirin (Japanese cooking wine), 431–32
misinformation (nutritional
    "breakthroughs"), 2–3
Miso (fermented soybean-grain
    paste), 432; for broth, 74
  Ginger Dressing, Creamy, 343
  Soup with Tofu, Essential, 80
monounsaturated fats, 403; and
    LDLS (cholesterol-carrying
    lipids), 398
Moosewood Restaurant
  ethnic grain-based cuisines, 5
  special menus at, 446–47
  special recipe lists at, 442–45
morels (wild mushrooms), 432
Moroccan Carrots, 316
Muffins
  Applesauce and Cranberry, 61
  Cornmeal Spice, 63
  Herb and Cheese, 112
  Pumpkin Oat, 64
mung sprouts, 432
Mushroom(s).
    See also Wild Mushroom
  Broiled Portabella, 322
  Dried, soaking, 418
  Dried, Soup with Barley, 94
  nutritional content of, 277
  Pâté Almondine, 121

Polenta Pie, 240
  Sauce, 352
  Sauce, Russian, Poached Fish
    with, 300
  Savory Stuffed, 42; variations, 42
  Sesame Tofu Stew, 277
  Snap Peas with, 329
  Spinach Crêpes, 234
  Spinach Frittata, 52
  -and Spinach-stuffed Zucchini, 247
  Three Sisters Stew, 272
  Wheatberry Pilaf, 195
Mustard
  Carrots, 317
  Honey Fish, 298
  Honey Garlic Dressing, 342
  Marinade, Baked Fish with, 288
  seeds, black, 422

nam pla (Asian fish sauce), 420
natural additives, 406
navy beans (pea beans), 432
neufchâtel cheese, 432
New England Squash Soup, 96
New Year's Buffet, 447
No-Butter Brownies, Our Best, 387
nonstick cookware, using, 13–15
Noodle(s)
  cellophane, 423; storing, 89
  not precooking, 216
  rice, 436
  Soup, Asian, 81
  Vegetable Soup, Korean, 89
Nori (seaweed), 432
  rolls, 37; sudore for making, 37
  Vegetable Rolls, 36; variations, 37
nutritional
  advocates, 398
  information on food labels, 406
  studies, 2–3
nuts and seeds, fat in, 17

Oatmeal Cardamom Cookies, 393
oil-based products (using less), 11–12
oils, 432–33
okra, 433
olive oil, 403, 433
olives, (calamata, California ripe,
    Niçoise, Spanish), 433
omega–3 fatty acids, 403; in plant
    and fish oils, 403
Omelet. See also Eggs; Frittata
    Watercress, 53
One Step Bean Guacamole, 28
Onion(s)
  and Feta Risotto, 194;
    variations, 194
  Marmalade, Savory, 363
  and Peas, Couscous with, 179
  Spaghetti with, 215
Orange(s)
  Carrot Salad, 134
  sectioning (technique), 418
  Tarragon Dressing, 348
orrecchiette (pasta), 433
Orzo (pasta), 433
  and Green Herbs, 183
  and Pea Soup, 93
  Vegetable Salad, Chinese, 149
  Oven "Fries, " 326

Paella, Spring Vegetable, 196;
    seafood variations, 197
Pancakes, Vegetable-Filled, 233
parboiling (technique), 414
Parfaits, Tapioca Fruit, 375
Parsnip(s), 433
  Carrot Soup, Curried, 100
Pasta, 200–20; various shapes,
    433–34. See also Noodles
  about not precooking noodles, 216
  with Beans and Greens, 210
  with Chickpeas, 211
  cooking (technique), 417
  with Eggplant, 205

farfalle, 427
fettuccine, 428
Lasagne Béchamel, Vegetable, 216
Lasagne, Lighter, 218
Lentils, and Artichoke Hearts, 209
Macaroni and Cheese, 203
Manicotti Verdi, Stuffed, 219
Penne with Creamy Walnut
    Sauce, 213
Penne with Puttanesca Sauce, 214
Primavera, 206
Rice Noodles, Curried, 220;
    variations, 221
Salad, Mexican, 148
with Salsa Cruda, 212; variations,
    212
Spaghetti with Onions, 215
and Sun-Dried Tomatoes, 208
toppings for, 202
Udon Vegetable Sauté, 204
Zucchini Saffron, 207
Pea and Orzo Soup, 93
Peach
    -Berry Shake, 66
    Blueberry Cobbler, 383
    Ginger Crumble, 386
    Mango Chutney, 362
Peanut
    butter, 434
    Dressing, Spicy, 349
Peas. See also Black-Eyed Peas;
        Chickpeas; Snap Peas;
        Split Peas
    and Onions, Couscous with, 179
    sauces for, 309
Penne (pasta), 434
    with Creamy Walnut Sauce, 213
    with Puttanesca Sauce, 214
Pepper(s)
    and Eggplant Spread, Smoky, 122
    Hot, and Lemon Sauce, Brazilian,
        359
    Hungarian hot, 429
    Potato Frittata, Spanish, 51
    red, roasted, 436
    Red, and White Bean Spread, 125;
        roasted garlic variations, 125
        roasting (broiler, oven, stove-
        top method), 418

Tofu-stuffed Middle Eastern, 246
and Tomatoes, Stuffed, Mexican,
    244
peppercorns, black, 422
Persian Split Pea and Barley Stew, 274
personal fat goal, 399
Pesto
    Cilantro, 364
    Susan's, 364
phosphorus, in the diet, 412;
        foods rich in, 412
Picnic, Summer, 446
Pie
    Mushroom Polenta, 240
    Shepherd's, Another, 238
Pigeon Pea(s), 434
    Salad, Caribbean, 142
Pilaf
    Armenian Stew with, 270
    Bulgur Rice, 188
    Curried Couscous, 180
    Kasha, 181
    Millet, 182
    Mushroom Wheatberry, 195
    Quinoa Pine Nut, 184
    stuffing for vegetables, 195
pimientos, 434
pine nuts, 434
Pineapple
    Buttermilk Sherbet, 394
    Chutney, Fish with, 292
    Sesame Dressing, Southeast
        Asian, 343
pinto beans, 434
    Chili Burgers, 173
Pita(s)
    Mexican Seitan (salsa), 120
    toasting, 120
Pizza, Basil and Feta, Luscious, 228;
    variations (other pizza top-
    pings), 229
Poached Fish
    with Russian Mushroom Sauce,
        300
    with Vegetables, 301
Polenta, 434
    cooking, 416
    Cutlets, Sun-Dried Tomato, 236
    Mushroom Pie, 240
polyunsaturated fats, 403

polyunsaturates, 403–4
porcini (wild mushrooms), 435
portabella (wild) mushroom(s), 435
    Broiled, 322
potassium, role of, 412;
        foods rich in, 412
Potato(es), 435.
        See also Sweet Potatoes
    Baked, Stuffed, 249
    Bean Salad, 138
    Beet Salad, 139
    Cabbage Roll-Ups, Curried, 251
    Cakes, 327
    and Carrots, Scalloped, 325
    Cheese Gnocchi, 250
    and Corn Soup, Southwestern, 102
    Garlic Soup, Spanish, 97
    Greek Stew, 266
    Kale Soup, Creamy, 91
    Lima Soup, Catalan, 99
    Mashed Garlic, 328
    Oven "Fries," 326
    Pancakes, Indian, 54; sweet
        potato variation, 54
    Pepper Frittata, Spanish, 51
    sauces for, 309
    Skordalia Thessalonike (garlicky
        potato sauce), 354
    Spanish, 324
    Turnovers, Tunisian, 40
preheating the oven, 417
preservatives and additives (food),
    406
pressing garlic (technique), 417
Primavera, Pasta, 206
proteins, 397; perfect, 397
    role of, 405
Pudding
    Chocolate, Dark, 374
    Cake, Lemon, 377
    Red Berry Kissel, 372
    Rice, Creamy Dairyless, 373
Pumpkin, 435
    Custard, 376
    Oat Muffins, 63
puréeing (technique), 417
Puttanesca Sauce, Penne with, 214

quick and easy meals, 443
Quinoa (grain), 435
　about cooking, 416
　Black Bean Salad, 141
　Pine Nut Pilaf, 184
　Vegetable Stew, 276

ramen noodles, 435
ratatouille. *See* Giambotta
recipe lists, special, 442–47
recipes, about using, 16–17
Red
　Beans, Fat Tuesday's Skinny, 165
　Berry Kissel, 372
　Pepper and White Bean Spread, 125;
　　roasted garlic variations, 125
　peppers, roasted, 436
Relish. *See also* Dressing; Pesto;
　　Salsa; Sauce
　Corn, 361
　Mango Peach Chutney, 362
　Onion Marmalade, Savory, 363
　Pineapple Chutney, Fish with, 292
Rice (arborio, basmati, brown,
　　jasmine, white), 435–36.
　　See also Risotto
　about cooking, 416
　Brazilian, 187
　Bulgur Pilaf, 188
　Five-Spice, 186
　Fragrant Jasmine, 189
　Golden Basmati, 185
　Noodles, Curried, 220;
　　variations, 221
　Pudding, Creamy Dairyless, 373
　Spinach Balls, Greek, 35
　Sushi Salad, 146
　Thai Fried, 190
rice noodles, 436
rice paper discs, softening, 254
rice vinegar (rice wine vinegar),
　　436, 440
Risotto
　Midsummer, 191
　Onion and Feta, 194

Squash and Kale, 192;
　　vegetable variations, 193
Roasted
　Asparagus, 312
　Garlic, 43
　Red Pepper Sauce, Creamy, 355
　red peppers, 436
　Vegetables Three Ways, 226
roasting vegetables (technique),
　　417–18; spices, 419
Rolls, Buttermilk, 115
Russian Mushroom Sauce, Poached
　　Fish with, 300

Salad, 128–51. *See also* Appetizer;
　　Sandwich Filling
　Asian Tofu, 116
　Cabbage, 132
　Caesar, 131
　Caribbean Pigeon Pea, 142
　Carrot Orange, 134
　Chinese Orzo Vegetable, 149
　Cucumbers Vinaigrette, 133
　Egg, 117
　Lentil, 151
　Macaroni, Creamy, 150
　Mango Coconut Cucumber, 136
　Mediterranean Couscous, 144
　Pasta, Mexican, 148
　Potato Bean (green), 138
　Potato Beet, 139
　Quinoa Black Bean, 141
　Sesame Beets, 140
　Sicilian Scallop, 304
　Spinach Avocado Grapefruit, 135
　Sushi Rice, 146
　Sweet Potato, Baked, 137
　Tabouli, 145
　Tempeh, Sandwich Filling, 123
　Vegetables à la Grecque, 130
　Wild Rice Waldorf, 147
Salad Dressing. *See* Dressing

Salsa, 436–37
　Cruda, Pasta with, 212;
　　variations, 212
　Mexican Seitan Pita, 120
　Tomato Corn, 366
　Tomato, Fresh, 360
　Verde Liguria, 353
salt in the diet, 405;
　　hidden sources of, 405
Sandwich Filling, 116–25.
　　See also Appetizer; Salad
　Asian Tofu Salad, 116
　Egg Salad, 117
　Eggplant and Pepper Spread,
　　Smoky, 122
　Ira's Lunch (tofu-kan), 118
　Mexican Seitan (salsa) Pita, 120
　Middle Eastern Cannellini
　　Patties, 119
　Mushroom Pâté Almondine, 121
　Tempeh Salad, 123
　Tuscan (tomatoes, greens, etc.), 124
　White Bean and Red Pepper
　　Spread, 125; roasted garlic
　　variations, 125
saturated fats, 403;
　　in foods of animal origin, 404
Sauce, 340, 350–60.
　　See also Dressing; Relish
　Barbecue, 355
　Hot, Blender, 358
　Hot Pepper and Lemon,
　　Brazilian, 359
　Hot Tamarind and Guava,
　　for Fish and Vegetables, 356
　Hungarian Lesco, 357
　Mushroom, 352
　Pesto, Cilantro, 364
　Pesto, Susan's, 364
　Roasted Red Pepper, Creamy, 355
　Salsa. *See* Salsa
　Skordalia Thessalonike (garlicky
　　potato), 354
　Tomato, Chunky, 351
　Tomato Wine, 350
sauté (with less oil), 9–10
sautéing (technique), 418
Savannah Beans and Greens Soup, 104
Savory
　Hoisin Fish, 293

Stuffed Mushrooms, 42; variations, 42
Scallop Salad, Sicilian, 304
Scalloped Potatoes and Carrots, 325
Scandinavian-style fruit pudding, Red Berry Kissel, 372
Seafood (mussels, scallops, shrimp, etc.)
    Paella, Spring (variation), 197
    Vietnamese Hot and Sour Soup (variation), 87
    Yum, Thai, 305
Seasoned Steamed Artichokes, 311
Seasoning, 341
    Asian Cucumber Condiment, 367
    Thai Curry Paste, 365
sectioning oranges (technique), 418
seeding (technique), 418
seeds and nuts, fat in, 17
Seitan (wheat gluten), 437
    Fajitas, 232
    Pita, Mexican, 120
Sesame
    Beets, 140
    Citrus Delight (yogurt), 67
    Mushroom Tofu Stew, 277
    oil, 437
    Pineapple Dressing, Southeast Asian, 343
    seeds, toasting, 88
    Spinach, Japanese, 330
Shake
    Mango-Banana, 65
    Peach-Berry, 66
Shallots, 437
    and Beets, Baked, 314
Shellfish
    about cooking, 285
    Scallop Salad, Sicilian, 304
    Shrimp, Gingered, and Soba, 303
    Thai Seafood Yum (scallops and shrimp), 305
Shepherd's Pie, Another, 238; variation, 239
Sherbet, Pineapple Buttermilk, 394
sherry, 437
Shiitake (wild mushrooms), 437
    Dashi, 76
    freezing and microwaving, 39
Shortbread, Homemade Biscuits, 114

Shrimp and Soba, Gingered, 303
Sicilian. See also Italian
    Scallop Salad, 304
Side Dishes, 308–37. See also Name of Vegetable; Tofu
silicon, in the diet, 413; foods rich in, 413
simmering (technique), 418
Skordalia Thessalonike (garlicky potato sauce), 354
slicing (technique), 418
snacks, low-fat, 12–13
Snap Peas with Mushroom(s), 329
soaking
    dried mushrooms (technique), 418
    sun-dried tomatoes, 418
Soba (Japanese noodles), 437
    Gingered Shrimp and, 303
    and Vegetable Soup, Japanese, 88
Soda Bread, Irish, 59
sodium (natrium), in the diet, 413; foods rich in, 413
Soup, 70–105
    Asian Noodle, 81
    Basque White Bean, 103
    Beans and Greens, Savannah, 104
    Callaloo (Caribbean), 105
    Carbonada (Chilean vegetable), 98
    Catalan Potato Lima, 99
    Chilled Beet and Buttermilk Soup, 79
    Cream of Cauliflower, 90
    Cream of Green Vegetable, 82; variations, 83
    Curried Carrot Parsnip, 100
    Dried Mushroom, with Barley, 94
    Essential Miso, with Tofu, 80
    Garlic Broth, 74
    Gazpacho, Tropical, 78
    Harira (North African), 85
    Japanese Soba and Vegetable, 88
    Konbu Dashi (stock or broth), 75; Konbu-Bonito Dashi variation, 75
    Korean Vegetable Noodle, 89
    Minestrone Genoa, 86; riballita variation, 86
    Orzo and Pea, 93

Potato Kale, Creamy, 91
Shiitake Dashi, 76
sour cream, amount of fat in, 17
Southeast Asian Vegetable Stock, 77
Southwestern Corn and Potato, 102
Spanish Potato Garlic, 97
Split Pea, Golden, 93
Spring (minestrone), 84
Squash, New England, 96
Stock, Basic Vegetable, 73
Tomato Bulgur, 101
Vietnamese Hot and Sour, 87; seafood variation, 87
sour cream, 437; fat in, 17
Southeast Asian. See also Asian
    Coconut Zucchini, 334
    Fish Rolls, 294
    Menu, 446
    Pineapple Sesame Dressing, 343
    Vegetable Stock, 77
Southwestern
    Corn and Potato Soup, 102
    Hominy Stew, 279
soy milk, 437–38
    sauce, 438
Spaghetti with Onions, 215
Spanish
    Basque White Bean Soup, 103
    Potato Garlic Soup, 97
    Potato Pepper Frittata, 51
    Potatoes, 324
Spice(s)
    Blend, Thai Curry Paste, 365
    Cornmeal Muffins, 63
    whole, grinding, 418–19; roasting, 419
Spicy Quick Bread, Aafke's, 60
Spinach
    Artichoke Heart Dip, 30
    Avocado Grapefruit Salad, 135
    Chickpeas with, Middle Eastern, 169
    Japanese Sesame, 330
    Mushroom Crêpes, 234
    Mushroom Frittata, 52
    and Mushroom-stuffed Zucchini, 247
    Rice Balls, Greek, 35

Split Pea
    and Barley Stew, Persian, 274
    Soup, Golden, 92
Spreads and Dips. *See* Appetizer;
    Sandwich Filling
Spring Rolls
    Fresh, 254
    rice paper discs for, 254
Spring Soup (minestrone), 84
Squash
    Curried, 332
    and Kale Risotto, 192;
       vegetable variations, 193
    Soup, New England, 96
    winter, 441
    Winter, Holiday Cranberry, 331
Stew, 260–79
    about seasoning, 261–62
    Armenian, with Pilaf, 270
    Caribbean, 265
    Creole (tofu-vegetable), 273
    Fish, Italian, 299
    Giambotta (Italian ratatouille), 263
    Greek, 266
    Hominy, Southwestern, 279
    Mediterranean, 267
    Mushroom Sesame Tofu, 277
    Quinoa Vegetable, 276
    Split Pea and Barley, Persian, 274
    Thai Vegetable Curry, 268
    Three Sisters (mushroom-
       vegetable), 272
    Ukrainian Beet and Bean, 269
    Vegetable Bean, French, 264
    Wild Mushroom, Trieste, 278
Sticky Buns, 58
Stock. *See also* Broth
    Basic Vegetable, 73
    or broth, Konbu Dashi, 75;
       Konbu-Bonito Dashi
       variation, 75
    Shiitake Dashi, 76
    Vegetable, Southeast Asian, 77
stroke and heart attack, 402
Strudel, Apple Apricot, 384

Stuffed
    Baked Potatoes, 249
    Mushrooms, Savory, 42;
       variations, 42
    Vegetables. *See* Peppers; Potatoes;
       Tomatoes; Zucchini
sudore, for nori wrappers, 37
sugars. *See* carbohydrates
sulfites (preservatives), 438
sulphur, in the diet, 413;
    foods rich in, 413
Summer Picnic, 446
Sun-Dried Tomato(es), 438
    about soaking, 418
    Pasta and, 208
    Polenta Cutlets, 236
surimi (processed white fish), 438
Sushi Rice Salad, 146
sweating (technique), 419
Sweet Potato(es), 438
    and Black Bean Burrito, 172
    Indian Potato Pancakes variation,
       54
    Indian, Savory, 248
    Roti, Curried, 230
    Salad, Baked, 137
    Sweet, 323
Sweet-and-Sour Lentils, 171
Swiss Chard, 438
    Rolls Two Ways (mushroom
       filling, cheese filling), 252
    and Tomato Frittata, 50

Tabouli Salad, 145
Tahini, 439
    Yogurt Dressing, 346
Tamale Pie, 162
tamari, 439
Tamarind
    concentrate, 439
    Hot, and Guava Sauce, for Fish
       and Vegetables, 356
Tapioca, 439
    Fruit Parfaits, 375

Tempeh (soybean), 439
    Salad Sandwich Filling, 123
Tex-Mex Menu, 447
Thai
    Baked Tofu, 336
    Curry Paste, 365
    curry pastes, 439
    Fish Cakes, 302
    Fried Rice, 190
    Seafood Yum, 305
    Style Eggplant, Broiled, 34
    Vegetable Curry, 268
Thanksgiving Menu, 447
thickening foods, a low-fat
    technique, 419
Three Sisters Stew (mushroom-
    vegetable), 272
Tofu (bean curd), 439
    freezing, 419; pressing, 409
    Jerk, 337
    -kan, Ira's Lunch, 118
    Mushroom Sesame Stew, 277
    Salad, Asian, 116
    seasoned, 439
    silken, 440
    for soup, 80
    -stuffed Peppers, Middle Eastern,
       246
    Thai Baked, 336
    -vegetable Creole Stew, 273
    Vegetable Dumplings, 38
Tomato(es)
    Basil Dressing, Italian, 347
    Bulgur Soup, 101
    Corn Salsa, 366
    and Peppers, Mexican Stuffed, 244
    ripening, 148
    Salsa, Fresh, 360
    Sauce, Chunky, 351
    Sun-Dried, Pasta and, 208
    Sun-Dried Polenta Cutlets, 236
    and Swiss Chard Frittata, 50
    Wine Sauce, 350
tortillas, 440
    Seitan Fajitas, 232
    Vegetable-Filled Pancakes, 233
    warming, 232, 251

total blood cholesterol level, 402
transfatty acid (transfat), 403
triglycerides (fats), 401–3, 404
Tropical Gazpacho, 78
Tunisian Potato Turnovers, 40
Tuscan
    Beans with Sage, 168
    Sandwich (tomatoes, greens, etc.), 124

Udon Vegetable Sauté, 204
Ukrainian Beet and Bean Stew, 269
umeboshi vinegar, 440
U.S. Department of Agriculture (USDA), 406; definitions for labels, chart, 409
U.S. Food and Drug Administration (FDA), 4, 398

Vanilla Cream, 395
vegan recipes, 444
Vegetable(s)
    Bean Stew, French, 264
    Carbonada (Chilean Soup), 98
    Caribbean Stew, 265
    Curry, Thai, 268
    -Filled Pancakes, 233
    Filo Roll Extravaganza, 242
    and Fish, Guava and Hot Tamarind Sauce for, 356
    à la Grecque, 130
    Italian stew, Giambotta, 263
    and Japanese Soba Soup, 88
    Lasagne Béchamel, 216
    Mediterranean Couscous Salad, 144
    Mediterranean Stew, 267
    and monounsaturated fats, 403
    -Mushroom Stew, Three Sisters, 272

Noodle Soup, Korean, 89
Nori Rolls, 36; variations, 37
Orzo Salad, Chinese, 149
Paella, Spring, 196
Pasta Primavera, 206
Poached Fish with, 301
Quinoa Stew, 276
Roasted, Three Ways, 226
Sauces for, 309
Soup, Green, Cream of, 82; variations, 83
Stew with Pilaf, Armenian, 270
Stock, Basic, 73
Stock, Southeast Asian, 77
-tofu, Creole Stew, 273
Tofu Dumplings, 38
Udon Sauté, 204
Vegetarian
    diet, very low-fat, 398
    Feijoada, 158
very low-density lipoproteins (VLDLS), 401–2
Vietnamese Hot and Sour Soup, 87; seafood variation, 87
vinegar (apple cider, balsamic, distilled white, herbed, malt, rice, umeboshi, wine), 440
vitamins, 400; and minerals, Recommended Daily Allowance (RDA), 410–13

Waldorf Salad, Wild Rice, 147
Walnut
    Maple Biscotti, 390
    Sauce, Creamy, Penne with, 213
wasabi (Japanese condiment), 440–41
Watercress, 441
    Omelet, 53
wheatberry(ies), 441.
    See also bulgur
    Mushroom Pilaf, 195
White Bean(s). See also Beans
    and Red Pepper Spread, 125; roasted garlic variations, 125
    Soup, Basque, 103

white rice, 436; cooking, 416
white vinegar, distilled, 440
Wild Mushroom. See also name of wild mushroom (chanterelle; Shiitake, etc.)
    Stew Trieste, 278
Wild Rice, 436
    Waldorf Salad, 147
wine vinegar, 440
Winter Squash, 441
    Holiday Cranberry, 331
    sauces for, 309
wrappers (rice flour, wheat), 441

Yogurt, 441
    amount of fat in, 17
    cheese, making, 419
    Cilantro Lime Dressing, 345
    Minted Dill Dressing, 345
    Sesame Citrus Delight, 67
    Tahini Dressing, 346

zest (citrus), 441
zinc, in the diet, 413; foods rich in, 413
Zucchini
    Broiled, with Herbs, 333
    with Cilantro Sauce, 335
    Mushroom-and-Spinach-stuffed, 247
    Saffron Pasta, 207
    sauces for, 309
    Southeast Asian Coconut, 334

Conversion Chart
Equivalent Imperial and Metric Measurements

American cooks use standard containers, the 8-ounce cup and a tablespoon that takes exactly 16 level fillings to fill that cup level. Measuring by cup makes it very difficult to give weight equivalents, as a cup of densely packed butter will weigh considerably more than a cup of flour. The easiest way therefore to deal with cup measurements in recipes is to take the amount by volume rather than by weight. Thus the equation reads:

1 cup = 240 ml = 8 fl. oz.   ½ cup = 120 ml = 4 fl. oz.

It is possible to buy a set of American cup measures in major stores around the world.

In the States, butter is often measured in sticks. One stick is the equivalent of 8 tablespoons. One tablespoon of butter is therefore the equivalent to ½ ounce/15 grams.

Oven Temperature Equivalents

FAHRENHEIT	CELSIUS	GAS MARK	DESCRIPTION
225	110	¼	Cool
250	130	½	
275	140	1	Very Slow
300	150	2	
325	170	3	Slow
350	180	4	Moderate
375	190	5	
400	200	6	Moderately Hot
425	220	7	Fairly Hot
450	230	8	Hot
475	240	9	Very Hot
500	250	10	Extremely Hot

Solid Measures

U.S. AND IMPERIAL MEASURES		METRIC MEASURES	
Ounces	Pounds	Grams	Kilos
1		28	
2		56	
3½		100	
4	¼	112	
5		140	
6		168	
8	½	225	
9		250	¼
12	¾	340	
16	1	450	
18		500	½
20	1¼	560	
24	1½	675	
27		750	¾
32	2	900	
36	2¼	1000	1

Liquid Measures

FLUID OUNCES	U.S.	IMPERIAL	MILLI-LITERS
	1 teasp.	1 teasp.	5
¼	2 teasp.	1 dessertsp.	10
½	1 tablesp.	1 tablesp.	14
1	2 tablesp.	2 tablesp.	28
2	¼ cup	4 tablesp.	56
4	½ cup		110
5		¼ pint/1 gill	140
6	¾ cup		170
8	1 cup		225
9			250, ¼ liter
10	1¼ cups	½ pint	280
15		¾ pint	420
16	2 cups		450
18	2¼ cups		500, ½ liter
20	2½ cups	1 pint	560
24	3 cups		675
25		1¼ pints	700
27	3½ cups		750
30	3¾ cups	1½ pints	840
32	4 cups		900
36	4½ cups		1000, 1 liter
40	5 cups	2 pints	1120

Ingredient Equivalents

all-purpose flour—plain flour
coarse salt—kitchen salt
eggplant—aubergine

half and half—12% fat milk
light cream—single cream
scallion—spring onion

unbleached flour—strong, white flour
zest—rind
zucchini—courgettes or marrow